SAMUEL MARSDEN V PHILO FREE:
AUSTRALIA'S FIRST LIBEL CASE

Edited by
Peter G. Bolt and Malcolm Falloon

Studies in Australian Colonial History, № 6

Freedom to Libel? Samuel Marsden v. Philo Free: Australia's First Libel Case
Studies in Australian Colonial History (ISSN 1834-6936) No. 6
© Peter G. Bolt 2017

Bolt Publishing Services Pty.Ltd.
ACN 123024920
www.boltpublishing.com.au

Email:
Information: info@boltpublishing.com.au
Orders: orders@boltpublishing.com.au

Cover picture:
Edward Charles Close. Sketch of the Philo Free trial, c. 1817. Edward Charles Close. Sketchbook of New South Wales views. Mitchell Library, State Library of New South Wales, SAFE/PXA 1187.

The essays in this volume have been peer reviewed.

ISBN   Paperback   978-0-9946349-2-4
       e-version   978-0-9946349-3-1

 A catalogue record for this book is available from the National Library of Australia

Cover design and layout by Lankshear Design.
Printed by Ingram Spark Lightning Source.

PUBLISHER'S PREFACE

Human history advances through countless ordinary events. Operating within a web of human relationships and from a variety of influences—strongly at work even if unseen and often unacknowledged by the persons themselves—human beings make decisions and act, thus making a mark on their world. Many actions pass by without much notice, simply becoming part of the day to day events that make up the fabric of ordinary human existence. However, sometimes the larger issues that are current, and the grander forces that are at work in human society, cause an ordinary event to stand out as somehow special, noteworthy, or significant, heralding or even bringing a turning-point in human experience.

Whereas many are content to live life as it is, others are inspired by a grander vision of what life ought to be. Rev. Samuel Marsden was one such visionary. The Parramatta parson was thoroughly committed to ordinary life, as shown by his relentless commitment to building the fledgling Australasian societies on productive industry operating within deeply humanitarian concerns. But the enormous energy he devoted to building a better world for all was inspired by his vision of the kingdom of God, and motivated by his grasp of the grace of God as revealed in Jesus Christ.

In January 1817, Marsden's ordinary life took a turn for the worse when Philo Free libelled Marsden and the South Seas missions under his care. The unseen forces that shaped him, and the Christian vision that motivated him, provoked him to legal action. This libel action would not be Australia's last, but as Australia's first it stands out as a key event that helped to build the free society that Marsden hoped for, and which Australia and New Zealand subsequently became.

In the year that marks the bicentenary of the Philo Free trials, those who hold to the Christianity of Marsden's vision are amongst the most persecuted people in the world, and the values of Western Civilization that defined Marsden's better world are undergoing serious revision. A society that allows its citizens both the privilege to speak freely to persuade others, alongside the protection against libellous speech which causes personal harm, is a society that champions freedom.

This recollection of the Philo Free event is timely. Marsden v Philo Free is part of the rich heritage of freedom that has already brought Australasians great benefit, and which the present generation needs to once again appropriate, so that the ordinary life of future generations might also be lived in freedom.

Peter Bolt
December 2017

STUDIES IN AUSTRALIAN COLONIAL HISTORY
ISSN 1834-6936

1. Peter G. Bolt, *Thomas Moore of Liverpool (1762–1840): One of Our Oldest Colonists. Essays & Addresses to Celebrate 150 Years of Moore College* (2007).

2. Peter G. Bolt, *William Cowper (1778–1858). The Indispensable Parson. The Life and Influence of Australia's First Parish Clergyman* (2009).
   – Full-text Edition
   – Commemorative Pictorial Edition produced for Cowper200.

3. Peter G. Bolt, *A Portrait in his Actions. Thomas Moore of Liverpool (1762–1840). Part 1: Lesbury to Liverpool* (2010)

4. Peter G. Bolt, *A Portrait in his Actions. Thomas Moore of Liverpool (1762–1840). Part 2: Liverpool to Legacy* (forthcoming)

5. David B. Pettett, *Samuel Marsden. Preacher, Pastor, Magistrate and Missionary* (2016)

6. Peter G. Bolt & Malcolm Falloon (Eds.), *Freedom to Libel? Samuel Marsden v Philo Free: Australia's First Libel Case* (2017)

7. David B. Pettett, *The Sermons Of Samuel Marsden. A Critical Edition* (forthcoming).

8. Craig Schwarze, *The Bishop of Botany Bay. The Remarkable Story of Richard Johnson, Australia's First Preacher* (forthcoming)

CONTENTS

1.	Peter G. Bolt	The Letter signed Philo Free.	1
2.	David B. Pettett	Marsden in the Hands of Australasian Historians.	36
3.	Joel Atwood	'So important in its nature, so difficult in its execution, and so doubtful in its result'. The Mission to the South Seas from 1786 to 1830.	47
4.	Greg Anderson	The early colonial mission context of *Philo Free*.	79
5.	Craig Schwarze	A Secret Enemy. The turbulent relationship between Marsden and Macquarie.	93
6.	Malcolm Falloon	Mission Trading In The South Pacific By The *Active* (1814-1822) and The Accusations Of Philo Free.	107
7.	Peter G. Bolt	The failure of the Philanthropic Society.	130
8.	Jane M. Tooher	A Friendship Revealed. The Marsden & Stokes Family Correspondence.	195
9.	David B. Pettett	Marsden's Supportive Circle. Friendship in Controversy.	218
10.	Elizabeth G. Moll	Unmasking A Shielded Secret Enemy. John Thomas Campbell and the Philo Free Trials.	229

11.	Michael Gladwin	The Bigge Picture: Colonial Manners, Mission, and the Imperial Context of Australia's First Libel Case.	265
12.	Caitlin Hurley	Freedom of Speech and of the Press in Colonial NSW.	290
13.	Alexander C. Bolt, Paul R, Cerotti, & Konrad Peszynski	Normative Ethics In Early Colonial Australia And The Country's First Libel Case.	311
14.	Malcolm Falloon	The Breaking of the Storm: Marsden and the Missionary Cause.	341
15.		Bibliography	357

CONTRIBUTORS

Greg Anderson was installed as the Anglican Bishop of the Northern Territory in November 2014. Prior to this he was the head of the Department of Mission at Moore Theological College Sydney. He has a particular interest in mission with Aboriginal Australians, arising from his experiences while researching traditional clan songs in Arnhem Land in the mid-1980s.

Joel Atwood and his family work with the Church Missionary Society in Vanuatu, training local leaders in university student ministry and theological education. He also assists in the training of preachers in the South Pacific with Langham Partnership. He holds degrees in nanotechnology and divinity, and is completing an MTh in the relationship of the human spirit and the divine.

Alexander C. Bolt is a late career academic having spent twenty-five years in senior leadership roles in the private sector. His experience spans successful start-ups, international corporate roles and on-going business consulting services. In addition to seven years as an executive board member he was the founding editor of two national magazines. Earning both his MBA (Executive) and Master of Commerce with Distinction, Alex is a current post-graduate lecturer at both RMIT and Laureate Universities. He is a fellow of the Australian Institute of Management (FAIM). A Critical Social theorist, Alex is currently completing Doctoral studies in the areas of Ethics, Leadership Ethics, and Corporate Social Responsibility (CSR). His article is co-authored by his supervisors Dr Paul Cerotti and Dr. Konrad Peszinski, Senior Lecturers, RMIT University, College of Business.

Peter G. Bolt is the Academic Director of the Sydney College of Divinity. He has published *William Cowper (1778–1858). The Indispensable Parson. The Life and Influence of Australia's First Parish Clergyman* (2009), and *A Portrait in his Actions. Thomas Moore of Liverpool (1762–1840). Part 1: Lesbury to Liverpool* (2010), and co-edited (with David Pettett), *Launching Marsden's Mission. The Beginnings of the Church Missionary Society in New Zealand, viewed from NSW* (2015).

Malcolm Falloon is a New Zealand Anglican minister currently undertaking doctoral studies through the University of Otago on the encounter between Māori and the CMS missionaries in pre-colonial New Zealand. Malcolm is the author of *To Plough or to Preach: Mission Strategies in New Zealand during the 1820s* (2010).

Michael Gladwin is Lecturer in History at St Mark's National Theological Centre in the School of Theology, Charles Sturt University, Canberra. A graduate of the Australian National University and the University of Cambridge, his research interests include the religious and cultural history of Australia and the British Empire, with a particular interest in the relationship between religion and war in Australian history. Michael is the author of *Captains Of The Soul: A History Of Australian Army Chaplains* (2013) and *Anglican Clergy In Australia, 1788–1850: Building A British World* (2015). He is also editor of *St Mark's Review*, one of Australia's longest-running theological journals.

Caitlin Hurley is an assistant minister at a local church in Sydney and works for GAFCON (Global Anglican Futures Conference). She studied history and politics at university and is passionate about Evangelical Christians writing church history.

Elizabeth Moll is a graduate of Moore Theological College and the University of Technology, Sydney. Like Samuel Marsden's wife Elizabeth, she is also married to an ordained Anglican clergyman — though with only three daughters. She serves on the Governing Board of Scripture Union NSW, and is currently undertaking further legal studies.

David Pettett has completed doctoral studies at Macquarie University, Sydney, examining the sermons of Samuel Marsden. David is a minister in the Anglican Church of Australia, Diocese of Sydney. He continues to teach pastoral care at Moore Theological College, Sydney and moderates pastoral care and parish focused ministry subjects for the Australian College of Theology. David has recently retired from managing prison and hospital chaplains in the Diocese of Sydney. He was himself a Hospital Chaplain and a Prison Chaplain as well as a Chaplain in the Royal Australian Navy. He has held various Parish positions in the Diocese and has been a Missionary, church planting in Japan. He has published a book on the sermons of Samuel Marsden, *Samuel Marsden, Preacher, Pastor, Magistrate and Missionary* as well as chapters in books on preaching in Australia, Marsden's mission to New Zealand and on Marsden's sermon in New Zealand on Christmas Day 1814 in *Te Rongopai 1814 'Takoto te pai!' Bicentenary reflections on Christian beginnings and developments in Aotearoa New Zealand*.

Craig Schwarze is an independent researcher living in Sydney. He has published several articles on Australia's colonial church history. He is currently preparing for publication *The Bishop of Botany Bay. The Remarkable Story of Richard Johnson, Australia's First Preacher*.

Jane Tooher is a member of the faculty of Moore Theological College, lecturing in Ministry, New Testament, and Church History. She is the Director of the Priscilla & Aquila Centre, which stimulates research and discussion about women serving in ministry in partnership with men. Before joining the faculty of Moore she served in parish ministry in Sydney and London.

Table of Figures and Illustrations

Figure	Title	Page
Cover	Edward Charles Close, Sketch of the Philo Free Trial, 1817. (Edward Charles Close—sketchbook of New South Wales views, c. 1817 Mitchell Library, State Library of New South Wales, Call No: PXA 1187)	Cover
1	Key to Edward Close's Sketch of the Philo Free Trial, 1817.	xi
2	Map of the South Pacific. (Tiff Atwood)	54
3	Map of Society Islands and Tahiti. (Tiff Atwood)	59
4	Magistrates Under Macquarie	94
5	Governors of NSW 1788–1821	101
6	Europeans at Rangihoua mission station during the voyages of the *Active*, 1814–1817	113
7	Voyages of the *Active*	128
8	Subscribers to the Philanthropic Society, January 1814.	157
9	Estimate of Duties Collected by the Naval Officer 1/7 to 30/9/1813.	168
10	Map of Rarotonga, 2017. (shutterstock.com)	174
11	Rarotongan 'Royalty'—a partial genealogy	175
12	Sketch of Tapaeru. (Maretu, *Cannibals & Converts*, 47).	178
13	The Marsden-Stokes Correspondence	217
14	Judge-Advocates of NSW	237

Figure 1: Key to Edward Close's Sketch of the Philo Free Trial, 1817[1]

The characters in the portrait have been identified as follows:
1. Crown Solicitor Frederick Garling[2]
2. The Defendant, John Thomas Campbell, aka 'Philo Free'[3]
3. Judge-Advocate John Wylde[4]
4. The youthful David Allen, articled to Solicitor Garland[5]
5. Ex-convict and solicitor George Crossley[6]
6. Solicitor William H. Moore, for the prosecution[7]
7. The prosecutor, Rev. Samuel Marsden[8]
8. A cameo of Sophia Campbell[9]

1   Although previously attributed to Sophia Campbell (Kerr & Falkus, *From Sydney Cove to Duntroon*, 44–49), since 2009 the portrait has been reattributed to Edward Close (SLNSW Catalogue, 'Edward Close Sketchbook').
2   Despite SLNSW Catalogue, 'Edward Close Sketchbook' suggesting this is 'possibly' Judge-Advocate John Wylde', Kerr & Falkus, *From Sydney Cove to Duntroon*, 46, correctly identify Crown Solicitor, Frederick Garling, as confirmed by comparison with another portrait (SLNSW: GPO 1 - 12061).
3   This is a probable guess, given that he is in the dock. There are no other portraits of J.T. Campbell for comparison; Kerr & Falkus, *From Sydney Cove to Duntroon*, 46.
4   Kerr & Falkus, *From Sydney Cove to Duntroon*, 46. A guess from knowledge of Wylde's role at the trial.
5   He is one of two figures explicitly labelled on the portrait, 'G. Allen'. Kerr & Falkus, *From Sydney Cove to Duntroon*, 44: 'assisting the lawyer for the defence [...] the young George Allen, articled to Frederick Garling, the Crown solicitor, early in 1817 when only 16 years old and fresh from England. His portrait epitomizes the "new chum" of tender years and is a far cry from the eminent and affluent citizen he was later to become, founder of a legal firm which still continues in Sydney'. There is a similarity between this youthful figure and the portrait of the elderly George Allen (SLNSW: ML 1241).
6   He is one of two figures explicitly labelled on the portrait, 'G. Crossley'. Kerr & Falkus, *From Sydney Cove to Duntroon*, 44, point out that by the time of the trial 'the rather villainous white-haired clerk to the right of the scene', George Crossley, 'had been disbarred from practice on his own account, but his unrivalled knowledge of court-room procedure kept him employed as a solicitor's clerk'.
7   Kerr & Falkus, *From Sydney Cove to Duntroon*, 46. A guess from proximity to Marsden, whom he represented.
8   Kerr & Falkus, *From Sydney Cove to Duntroon*, 46. This figure bears most resemblance to the portrait of Marsden in R. Jones' collection (SLNSW: PXA 972_5).
9   Kerr & Falkus, *From Sydney Cove to Duntroon*, 46.

CHAPTER 1

THE LETTER SIGNED PHILO FREE

Peter G. Bolt

To THE EDITOR OF THE SYDNEY GAZETTE.
MR. EDITOR,

Early in the last century the famous South Sea scheme was projected, and ran through its short-lived but disastrous career, all its dreams of golden showers having proved a mere illusion, by the bursting of that never-to-be-forgotten-bubble, which involved in its explosion a great mass of the English Nation, and induced much public distress; leaving all, but the few artful and designing projectors themselves, to deplore too late their credulity and national gullabillity [sic]. In our days, a "New South Wales Philanthropic Society" has been formed, and liberal subscriptions entered into for the laudable purpose of extending "protection and civilization to such of the Natives of the South Sea Islands as may arrive at Port Jackson." Now, Sir, although the circumstances will not perhaps warrant its being *also termed a bubble*, yet there are some features in the two schemes so much alike that I think an able hand could make no bad parallel between them—"*si jus est magnis componere parva*".[1] Thus, the South Sea scheme held out the bait or lure of such extravagant profits in the way of trade, that the sordid and mercenary were dazzled at the prospect, and shares originally purchased at £100, were frequently transferred at eight times that amount.—The illusion however lasted but a few months, and all the fabrick went to ruin, leaving not a wreck behind. The South Sea Islands Philanthrophists in 1813, without the temptation of the gilded pill of wealth uncountable having been held out to them, cheerfully subscribed their money under the assurance that they should have the spiritual consolation at least of having performed charitable acts, and rendered humane services to the Natives of the South Sea islands!—These were the profits that the subscribers in general had in view:— how they have been realized we now in 1817, all know too well; for, to this day, we have never been favoured even with a single report of the application of the funds; and thus, like the bubbletonians of 1720, after having come *down with our dumps*, we have had no return, either to our purse or to the stock of our benevolence; and "for aught that I can learn or read," we are not likely to be gratified with such a result.

In former times the active and enterprizing spirit of the Jesuits led them, for religion's sake ostensibly, to visit the most remote regions of the known world; their zeal for the Church of Rome never slumbered. But they soon superadded thereto the lust of wealth, power, and dominion; and that fraternity commencing in holy and religious zeal, degenerated into temporal factions, which at length wrought their own downfall, and relieved Europe from their domineering and tyrannical usurpation of the exclusive trade of those Settlements where they had established themselves.—*Now*, a missionary spirit of a somewhat more humble cast has pervaded the Islands in the South Seas, introducing with it the art of distillation, and that tiny race of animals, which on being boiled, do not prove to be lobsters!—An ardent thirst for the influence *of this spirit* at this time pervades the inhabitants of all the Islands of the Pacific, with which we have any intercourse; and pigs, and pine trees, New-Zeal-and flax, &c. are the returns made in full tale for the comforts of the spirit instilled into them, and by which they are inspired. The active exertions of him who is the worthy head of these sectarian visionaries or missionaries (whichever you please, Mr. Editor), in propagating the Gospel by such means, and the transmission from time to time of muskets and cutlasses, will, no doubt, redound much and highly to the honour of the Christian Mahomet, and of the church so planted, whilst the pecuniary advantage of the chosen-few will not be altogether overlooked. But what availeth all this, Mr. Editor, to you and me, in the common class of the subscribers? Those who bolt the pork and the profits, should, in my opinion un-bolt their coffers, and bear also the expences of their gospel venders and bacon curers; and, for myself, I shall be well content to see them possessed equally of the exclusive honour of evangelizing, by such means, the New Zealanders, the Otaheitans, the Eimeoaans, &c, &c. But to be very candid with you, I do not wish to see men in any garb, or under any mask or pretence whatever, arrogate to themselves such consequential airs of importance, for acts of public beneficence, which they have never exhibited in their private lives; and still less, if possible, in their public characters towards the abject Natives of New South Wales. True it is, that these people are not yet qualified or enabled to make other returns than those of humble gratitude and peaceful demeanour; and these, perhaps, are not worthy of being recorded in the faithful pages of an *Eclectic Review*, with the exalted deeds of the evangelizing heroes, whose never dying fames are there trumpeted forth.

Although this may be the case, I am notwithstanding one of those who wish to introduce civilization, and the pure doctrines of the Christian religion among the sable sons of Australia, maugre[2] all the objections started by vulgar prejudice, or sordid views of personal aggrandizement; and I do not hesitate to say, that I feel it an imperious duty owing to those among whom I live and have my subsistence, to make the effort to reclaim these children of Nature, even if that effort were to be rendered nugatory by any circumstances whatever. This leads me to inform you, and by that means the Public also, that in a conversation lately with some other members of the New South Wales Bubble (the trading concerns thereof being duly excepted from that appellation), it appeared to be the general wish that the subscriptions should be restored and appropriated to the establishment of schools for the children of the poor within the Colony, and the diffusion of Christian knowledge among the heathen natives. A Bible and general Book Society is I understand in contemplation, to be connected with the school institutions; and by these means (if even the advantage of the library originally destined for the poor, by its humane donors, should continue unavailable), the great and glorious object of dispelling the dark and gloomy clouds of ignorance under which it has pleased Providence to permit the Aborigines of this Colony to remain unto the present time, the nineteenth century of the Christian era, and the twentieth-ninth year of the British settlement on its shore, may be happily effected.

I can assure you, Mr. Editor, that many of the wisest and best men among us are most zealously anxious, for such establishments being commenced upon; and I have the vanity to think, that even the desultory remarks made in this hastily drawn up letter, written in my cabin, without the aid of books (for my little collection went a pilgrimage, I have been told, to the Friendly and Society Islands), will tend to remove some ill-founded prejudices, to confirm liberal and generous dispositions, and to open the eyes of all, to a sense of duty and Christian charity towards our adopted country, and its harmless, though uncivilized natives.

PHILO FREE
A SETTLER AT BRADLEY'S HEAD   4th January 1817[3]

Although dated 4 January, the first *Sydney Gazette* for 1817 was not printed until the following day.[4] Typesetting the issue, compositor George Williams had been excited.[5] After running as a two-page broadsheet

---

1   ['If the law is forced to settle small'. This is probably an allusion to Virgil, Georgics IV.176-8, where Virgil almost apologizes for comparing the work of the Cyclopses and that of bees: 'if it be allowable to compare small things with great' (si parvi licet componere magnis).]
2   [Archaic: notwithstanding.]
3   *SG* 4/1/1817. The letter is reprinted in several places, including: *HRA* 1.9.891 note 175; as part of Judge-Advocate Wylde's Report on the Criminal Trial (with interspersed comment), *HRA* 1.10, 448-450; as part of Judge Field's Report of the Civil Trial, *HRA* 1.10, 444-445; in the Macquarie University Governor Macquarie Collection, http://www.mq.edu.au/macquarie-archive/lema/1817/philofree4jan1817.html.
4   Examination of G. Howe, 21/10/1817, 459.
5   Compositor George Williams typeset Philo Free on 2 and 3 January 1817. He knew that the letter was given to George Howe by Campbell, and had seen his handwriting frequently enough to be thoroughly familiar with it. Philo Free was in Campbell's handwriting. Examination of G. Williams, 1/12/1817, 445.

basically since mid 1805, this was 'the first of the new form of four pages'.[6] However, it was not the new form that created a 'general sensation'[7] on the streets of Sydney, but a brief portion of its contents. Across one and a half columns, a four-paragraph letter sparked the first Libel Action in Australia[8]—or at least in the reconstituted Sydney Courts. According to solicitor W.H. Moore, such a response was to be expected, because 'anonymous publications [are] always infamous'.[9]

To be more technically correct, the letter was not anonymous (without name), but pseudonymous (with a false name), to deliberately mask the author's true identity. After becoming notorious in 1817, the pseudonym 'Philo Free' signed here, would later be attached to other public letters expressing similar outrage.[10]

As well as protecting the real author, a cleverly chosen *nom-de-plume* also provides the opportunity to summarize, or sloganize, in order to firmly thereafter embed the point being made in the readers'

6   Examination of G. Williams, 21/10/1817, 455. The *Gazette* had been four pages in the first two and a half years of production (Mar 1803 – mid June 1805), before switching to a usual two pages. Following the change, despite the official two pages, a four page issue occasionally appeared (1807: once; 1810: eight times; 1811 & 1812: ten; 1813: twelve; 1815: once; 1816: thirteen). To further complicate the picture, the *Gazette* erratically appeared with one or two page supplements, and occasionally issued extraordinary editions alongside the normal weekly offering. The earlier plan to move to four pages, 'when the press of information shall require it' (*SG* 2/1/1813), resulted in twelve four page issues in 1813, but things reverted to the usual two pages the year after. After almost monthly supplements in 1816, presumably the news of the colony had become sufficient to establish the change to an official four pages in 1817.
7   Opening Remarks of solicitor W.H. Moore, 21/10/1817, reported by Wylde, Minutes [Criminal Trial], 452.
8   It was the *Sydney Gazette* who declared the Criminal proceedings (21-23/10/1817) 'the first Trial for a libel in this country' (*SG* 1/11/1817). No doubt fueled by the *Gazette* report, this was also how it was discussed elsewhere at the time, see e.g. *Asiatic Journal and Monthly Miscellany*, Volume 6. It was also remembered as the first by later reports, e.g. *Truth* 27/2/1898. Several other cases have been claimed as earlier. Ratcliffe, '"Pens Dipped in Gall"', 7, notes that Marsden v. Mason (1806) is reputed as the first. The difference here seems to be that Mason defamed Marsden through spoken word, rather than libeling him through a public written document. See further the discussion in , 'Unmasking A Shielded Secret Enemy', in this volume.
9   Opening Remarks of solicitor W.H. Moore, 21/10/1817, reported by Wylde, Minutes [Criminal Trial], 452.
10 'Philo Free' wrote at the expense of the new Bank of Australia (*SG* 9 and 21/11, 7, 10/12, 17/1827), once (21/11) with explicit mention of Campbell (who retired as a director of the Old Bank) and several allusions to the libel case. He also suggested (no doubt sarcastically) that selections of the Bigge Report should be published as biographical sketches of some in the colony. The editor responded that he was afraid of 'the semblance of libel' and 'rip[ping] up old sores' (30/11/1827). Philo Free's 'ridiculous letters' were attacked by 'Q' in the *Australian* 12/12/1827. The *Gazette*, however, argued that 'this ancient Correspondent is apt to put us in mind of a comet, which, as it rushes with excentric [sic] velocity through space, shows that it possesses fire in its tail' (*SG* 17/12/1827). In that same issue, 'Philo Free, the Younger' emerged as another correspondent.

minds. In this case, the combination of a transliteration of the Greek word for 'Love' (Philo) adding solemnity through classical pretensions, and the English word 'Free' makes the meaning clear: the author was concerned about something love-less.[11]

And, indeed, this was not the first time a *nom-de-plume* had been adopted by a correspondent to the *Sydney Gazette* making a similar charge. By 1817 another pseudonymous author had become the champion of indigenous Australians, pressing for someone to take the Christian gospel to them, along with its requisite accompanying love. Across at least a decade, this concern for the original inhabitants of NSW was relentlessly pursued by the self-styled 'Philanthropus', 'the lover of humanity'.

In July 1810, he had burst into the consciousness of the readers of the *Gazette* to ask of them a simple question:[12]

> The Great Creator having made of One Blood all Nations of the Earth, and taking for granted that the Natives of New South Wales are capable of instruction and civilization, I should be extremely obliged by the favor of an Answer to the following Query, either publicly through your Paper, or privately to be left at the *Gazette* Office:
>
> Query.—What plan can be adopted, what means used, or what steps taken, whereby we may most speedily and effectualy [sic] civilize and evangelize the Natives of New South Wales, local circumstances considered?

The question is reminiscent of several asked previously in London by the Eclectic Society, resulting in the formation of the Society for

---

11 Long after J.T. Campbell had been proven to be the author and an apology wrested from him through the intervention of His Majesty's ministers, he offered, not as a justification, but an 'extenuation', that his actions were 'altogether dictated by a feeling' that Marsden had shown 'marked disrespect' for Macquarie by not attending his meeting of the Native Institution 'some days before', 'altho' I knew him to be sitting in a house within a few yards of where the Meeting was held'. This 'did not fail to make an impression on my mind by no means favourable to Mr Marsden's Philanthropy'. Campbell to Macquarie, 31/3/1819.
  Campbell and the others who felt Marsden lacking in love were not apprised of the full situation. Marsden was also offended by the meeting's close proximity, but for different reasons: '[…] the meeting of the natives took Place on the 28th of Decr 1816. This Institution is established close to my Church at Parramatta and within a few yards of my own House. I believe it hath now been established above two years. The Governor has never invited me to see it, nor mentioned that there was such an Institution to me, nor expressed a wish that I should assist in instructing the Children. […] I shall be exceeding happy to see any thing done for the poor natives, and should readily lend any Assistance in my Power. Was I permitted to do so. I only mention this Circumstance to shew the Spirit of the times'. He points out that his two colleagues were invited to the Committee, although living at Windsor and Sydney! Marsden to Pratt, 22 January 1817.
12 *SG* 7/7/1810.

Missions in Africa and the East (1799), which later became the Church Missionary Society (1812).[13] When the British Government made plans to found a penal settlement in NSW, this sparked the initial discussion 'What is the best method of planting and propagating the Gospel in Botany Bay?' (1786), and this became a strong impetus behind the appointment of Richard Johnson as the first Chaplain, hailed by his supporters as the first 'missionary to the South Seas', with Samuel Marsden being the second.[14] With NSW covered, they turned elsewhere, asking 'What is the best method of propagating the Gospel in the East Indies?' in 1789, and then, in 1791, 'in Africa', before casting the net more generally in 1796 and 1799 to 'the Heathen'.

Because of the similarity between his query with these landmark discussions in evangelical mission history, Philanthropus emerges as someone who shared the missionary vision that brought Johnson and Marsden to NSW in the first place.[15] He received an initial answer in the next *Gazette*, from 'A Friend to Civilization'.[16] With mission being closely associated with 'civilization', this correspondent gave further flesh to the suggestion inherent in their pseudonym, noting that Philanthropus 'suggested the idea of rescuing the Natives of New South Wales from their deplorable state of barbarism'. After surveying the obstacles inherent with the race that need to be overcome, this 'Friend' recommended persuading aboriginal parents to part with their children so that they might be reared in white families, learn English and be educated—an early plan that will appall contemporary Australians coming to terms with the national trauma that is the 'Stolen Generation(s)'.

Since the 'Friend to Civilization' had observed that the whites had often provided an example of Christian morality or kindness to the Natives of NSW, a further pseudonymous correspondent, Tiro (= 'recruit,

---

13 See, further, Atwood, 'The Mission to the South Seas', Chapter 3 in this volume.
14 See Schwarze, 'Richard Johnson and Samuel Marsden'.
15 The author may have been the Rev Robert Cartwright. This can be pieced together from scraps of evidence: in 1819 Philanthropus stated that he had deplored the lack of mission to the aboriginal people for 'near ten years' (*SG* 24/7/1819), and in May 1820, he stated that he 'is now closing his eleventh year's residence in New South Wales' (*Monitor* 20/5/1820). Recruited by Marsden, Cartwright arrived with him on the *Ann* on 27/2/1809 (SG 3/10/1810). He worked with this vision all his days, firstly at Windsor, then Liverpool, then Sydney, before eventually at his own initiative becoming an itinerant evangelist and missionary to the aboriginal people in the Southern districts; Cable, 'Cartwright, Robert'.
16 However, due to its late arrival and length, it was inserted across three issues, *SG* 14 & 28/7, and 11/8/1810.

novice') called for 'a Plan that might be adopted in this Country for the most effectually removing those evils of which we complain, viz. suppressing vice and establishing amongst us that Christian morality which a people honoured with revelation ought to practice', as well as to educate and bring up the children of the poor.[17]

After this brief flurry of correspondence Philanthropus went silent for almost a decade. But he had left his mark, and the issue of bringing Christian 'civilization' to the natives of New Holland continued to be discussed with great concern for years to come. The true 'lover of humanity' would be concerned for the Australian Aborigine.

Emerging again in July 1819 and adopting the genre of a dialogue with a friend, Philanthropus rejoiced that there were then some efforts amongst the children, since the founding of the Native Institution at Parramatta in 1814, but what of the 'many hundreds of adults, and the children who continue in a state of barbarism on the sea shores and through the woods?', he asked. What can be done? What plan can be adopted, 'that they may know the benefits of Christianity, become an honour to our nation, and a future blessing to this land?' As a solution he suggested that 'a pious and steady man' be found who would 'devote himself to their best interests, and to this end would embrace every suitable opportunity to go out and discourse with them freely on religion and civilization'. The dialogue partner apparently rejoindered:

> and surely these people have as strong a claim on European charity and missionary exertions as any other natives in all the South Seas? Nay, are they not justly entitled to the first regards of old England? And, to a reflecting mind, must it not appear very strange that no Society of Christians has yet commiserated their case? Ought we not to shew piety at home, in the first place? And, then, if after a fair and reasonable trial they should reject every entreaty, and despise all the grace of the Gospel, turn to the Islanders at a distance?[18]

By 1819, Philanthropus was not content to simply point out a group of people representing a potential mission field and to ask 'how?'. Now the natives local to Australia were played off against those of the more distant islands and declared to be the first priority. As a query becomes a critique,

---

17   *SG* 3/11/1810.
18   *SG* 24/7/1819.

it is difficult not to hear the influence of Philo Free, two years after it appeared in the new four-page *Gazette* to create a 'general sensation'. Not only is the 'lover of humanity' directed towards Australia's 'sable sons', but they must do so before turning to the islands. Or, to reverse the same thought in the direction set by Philo Free: to go to the distant islands rather than beginning at home, is actually an act of the love-less.

The letter

Philo Free is upset at the failure of the Philanthropic Society, which was set up late 1813/ early 1814 to care for the natives of the South Seas. Despite money being taken, no report of its application to this worthy cause has been given and nor, he suspects, will it ever be given (ll. 23–36). The missionary spirit that purportedly lay behind this 'love of humanity' had degenerated into a zeal for the temporal rewards from trade and, because the Australian Aborigines had nothing deemed worthwhile to trade, no missionary effort was expended on them (ll. 75–78). This is the love-lessness epitomised by the Philanthropic Society taking subscribers' money in the name of missionary zeal to the South Seas, and giving no spiritual return at all.

The letter begins by drawing an analogy between the Philanthropic Society and the 'famous South Sea scheme' (ll.1–8). The South Seas Company was founded in 1711 and, as with the East India Company before it, it was granted a monopoly to trade—this time in South America. Since Philo Free complains several times about the missionaries' exclusive rights to trade in the South Seas, perhaps lying in the background is the Governor's recent rejection of the request of a Sydney consortium calling themselves the 'New Zealand Trading Company' to be granted a monopoly.[19] This effectively left the missionaries sitting

---

19 In 1810, Simeon Lord, Francis Williams, and Andrew Thompson made an unsuccessful attempt to establish a factory in New Zealand. Due to Lord's enormous losses (he claimed more than £12000) incurred through the destruction of his uninsured cargo on the *Boyd*, the plan lay dormant until May 1814, when he learned other merchants were interested. Lord and Garnham Blaxcell then formed a public company, which was announced in June over their signatures, along with those of William Campbell, Richard Brooks, W.H. Broughton, and John Dickson (*SG* 18/6/1814). This was followed up with a Memorial to Macquarie in October; Memorial of Merchants, Traders, and Others, to L. Macquarie, 3/10/1814. Although Macquarie had no objection to the idea of a factory, he refused to give Government money to the scheme or to grant rights to exclusive trade; Macquarie to Bathurst, 24/6/1815 (*HRA* 1.8, 561). Hainsworth, *The Sydney Traders*, 183.

pretty in terms of trade.

When the South Seas Company was formed, Britain was at war with Spain, who controlled South America, thus rendering any prospect of trade mere fantasy. The Company never returned any profits and after rising enormously in value its stock peaked and crashed in 1720 in the famous 'South Seas Bubble' (see l.33).[20] For the purposes of his analogy, Philo Free points to the 'mere illusion' of success, which, when the bubble burst, led to 'much public distress' in an 'explosion of the great mass of the English Nation', who were left deploring their credulity and gullibility, notwithstanding clear profits for 'the few artful and designing projectors themselves' (ll.5–8).

With this known disaster introduced, the point of contemporary comparison is drawn (ll.8–12) with the recently formed 'New South Wales Philanthropic Society' which has taken 'liberal subscriptions' for the 'laudable purpose' of protecting South Seas Natives as they visit Port Jackson. Some may object that this Society be termed a bubble, but there are several features that make the parallel apt (ll.12–17). Firstly, the South Sea scheme promised extravagant profits in terms of trade, but the illusion lasted mere months. In 1813, the NSW Philanthropists promised not wealth, but spiritual profits of humane and charitable acts in the South Seas Islands, but nothing is known of these profits because by 1817 'all know too well' that there has been no report of how the subscriptions were applied, nor is this likely to occur (ll.17–36).

The author then expands rather sarcastically on the results that *are* known. In what is meant as an odious comparison, the contemporary 'missionary spirit' is compared with the zeal of the Jesuits of a previous age, which started religious, but became temporal—and even treasonous[21]—and was tyrannically expressed in 'exclusive trade [in] those Settlements

---

20 The Harvard Business School website has a South Sea Bubble collection with a short history: Harvard Business School, 'History'.
21 Sharp, *The World, the Flesh & the Devil*, 337 and notes: The Jesuits were a hot topic at the time. The anonymous *A Brief Account of the Jesuits* published in 1815 and Poynder's more substantial *History of the Jesuits* in 1816, retold the already well-known story. After being suppressed for '[stealing] the empires of France and Spain in Latin America', the Pope had restored the order in 1814, provoking concern in the House of Commons. In 1810, Joseph Fox, *An Appeal*, had sympathetically compared the LMS Directors to the Jesuits, because they were 'great traders'. In 1817, Philo Free picked up the analogy, but combined it with the feared negative reputation of the order and extended the comparison to the missionaries themselves, and to their agent in Sydney. Sharp takes pains to demonstrate just how mistaken the analogy was (see pp. 338–339, 342, 348, 360–362, 462).

where they had established themselves' (ll.44–46). The mention of 'spirit' allows for a mingling with the recent scandal of some of the missionaries introducing 'the art of distillation',[22] along with 'that tiny race of animals, which on being boiled, do not prove to be lobsters!' (ll.48–50)—an allusion that eluded even readers at the time. Other items of trade (pigs, pine trees, the punned 'New-Zeal-and flax'), suggest that the supposed spiritual profits are, in fact, as temporal as that of the Jesuit missions, and that the returns of trade show the true spirit of these 'visionaries' and 'missionaries' (ll.46–56). What the New Zealand Company hoped for, the missionaries were now receiving.[23]

The argument then narrows its focus to 'the worthy head' of this missionary group, who seeks to propagate the gospel by such means, including the occasional running of 'muskets and cutlasses'—alluding to yet another rumour of suspect practice amongst the missionaries.[24] By raising such scandals, the sarcasm drips from the page as the author attributes this as the 'honour' that 'redound[s]' for 'the Christian Mahomet' and 'the church so planted', and, for which, once again, only 'the chosen-few' will receive their 'pecuniary advantage' (ll.55–62).

Drawing the editor towards him, the author complains that the profits of the few 'availeth' not to 'you and me, the common class of subscribers'. Once again, it is the exclusivity that seems to annoy Philo Free, that is, of evangelizing in this temporal profit-earning fashion. He claims that he would not mind if they were given 'the exclusive honour of evangelizing by such means' in New Zealand, Tahiti, Eimoa (ll.63–69). But what annoys him is the hypocrisy of 'arrogat[ing] to themselves such consequential airs of importance, for acts of public beneficence, which they have never exhibited in their private lives', nor towards the

---

22 This was recent news. On 22 October 1817, under cross-examination at the Criminal trial, Marsden noted that he had heard from the Society in London that the missionaries on Tahiti had been accused of 'distilling Spiritous liquors' and denied the charge, 'a year and a half or two years ago', ie. about the beginning of 1816; Cross Examination of Samuel Marsden, 22/10/1817, Wylde, Minutes [Criminal Trial], 465.
 LMS had reported the problem much earlier: Burder to S. Marsden, 21/12/1813, Postscript: 'We are concerned to find that Mr Bicknell has been making & selling Rum. The Directors totally disapprove of this'.
23 Philo Free appears to have wanted the same situation as had prevailed with the East India Company (see Metaxis, *Amazing Grace*, Chapter 20), but found the reverse instead: The Company took the profits, but (until 1813) permitted no missionaries. But in New Zealand, the missionary was permitted, but not a monopoly of trade.
24 The essays by Atwood (Chapter 3) and Falloon (Chapter 6) touch on this further.

indigenous population of NSW (ll.69–75). The reason given is that the local natives are not able to make 'other returns than those of humble gratitude and peaceful demeanour', that is, they have no pecuniary advantage to the missionary. The sarcasm continues with the suggestion that to evangelise aboriginal Australians would not lead to an article in *the Eclectic Review*, where 'the exalted deeds of the evangelizing heroes, [and their] never dying fames are [...] trumpeted forth' (ll.78–80).

Philo Free then identifies himself as one who wishes 'to introduce civilization, and the pure doctrines of the Christian religion' among 'the sable sons of Australia' (ll.81–89). This then leads him to report the general wish amongst 'some other members of the New South Wales Bubble'—who are not interested in 'the trading concerns' that the subscriptions be 'restored and appropriated' to educating the children of the poor and to dissemination of Christian Knowledge amongst indigenous Australians (ll.89–97).

Tying this in with the 'Bible and general Book Society' under contemplation in connection to school institutions, he is unable to resist a reference to the Lending Library, which 'continue[s] unavailable', as he hopes for better things for the Aborigines of this Colony (ll.97–106). In 1810 NSW Chaplain, Rev. Samuel Marsden, returned to NSW with a collection of books for the purpose for lending out to the needy, but no books had ever been put out on loan. A series of letters in the *Gazette* in 1814 had asked some hard questions which caused the parson public grief.[25] But even now they 'continue unavailable'.

The final paragraph sustains the focus on the 'uncivilized natives' of NSW, with one final allusion to Marsden's controversial Lending Library in the mythical reference to the author sitting in a ship's cabin off Bradley's Head, writing this letter 'without the aid of books (for my little collection went a pilgrimage, I have been told, to the Friendly and

---

25 The library was reported in [Evangelical Magazine], 'New South Wales', 343. The 'Free Settler' letters appeared in *SG* 4/3/1814; 12/3/1814; 19/3/1814 and 2/4/1814, with Marsden's reply in 26/3/1814. According to [Evangelical Magazine], 'Account of the Rev. Samuel Marsden's Exertions', 539, one of Marsden's last acts before leaving England was the securing of a Lending Library worth £3-400 value, 'to consist of the most valuable and useful publications in religion, morals, mechanics, agriculture, commerce, general history, and geography; to be lent out under his own control, and that of his clerical colleagues, to soldiers, free settlers, convicts, and all others who may have time to read, so as to prevent idleness, and occupy the mind in the best and most rational manner'. That it was 'to be lent out under his own control' endorses Marsden's claim that this was never intended to be a public lending library.

Society Islands' (ll.107–117). In favour of schools, but frustrated at the slow pace at which general education was emerging, especially given the lending library issue, he notes, sarcastically, that as he sits in his ship's cabin off Bradley's head, his own library had gone on a journey to the Friendly and Society islands. The only kind of education that is happening, and into which his own resources have been drained, is (supposedly) out there in the South Seas and not at home in NSW! Like Marsden's lending library, his library has also gone astray. And that is not a good situation for a literary man to find himself in.

The Genre

The allusion to the *Eclectic Review* is probably almost sufficient to show that the author was a literary person. But the letter also contains a great many clues that its author was not only well-read, but probably fancied himself for being so. How many *Gazette* readers would understand his often superior and occasionally archaic (l.84, maugre; compare 'availeth', l.62) vocabulary, or the Latin by which he justifies his opening analogy (ll.16–17), let alone its reference to Vergil's comparison between bees and giants?

But the letter's pretentious airs were all part of its chosen genre. The piece was clearly meant to be a political satire,[26] which was an extremely popular genre in eighteenth century England—even if perhaps on the decline by 1817.

By its comparison with the South Seas Bubble, the opening paragraph already hinted towards these satirical intentions. Although it was not the only speculation that went wrong in 1720, £100 shares in the South Seas speculation blew out to £1000 before dramatically collapsing.[27] Even though the occasionally retold stories of Bubble success may have inspired many a speculator, even in NSW,[28] since the economic troubles at home were caused by speculations in lands far away, there were clear warnings in it for schemes attached to such new and expanding

---

26 Cf. Sharp, *The World, the Flesh & the Devil*, 335: 'Campbell's satire'.
27 *SG* 25/11/1824, noting, by comparison, that shares in the York Buildings Company rose thirty fold.
28 Such as the 'curious anecdote' published in *SG* 17/10/1818, about the anonymous gentleman who never returned for a parcel left with a banking house. When opened, the £30,000 gained from the South Seas speculation was invested and the interest given to the poor.

economies.[29] When the Australian Agricultural Company was floated in 1824, for example, the *Australian* accused it of being nothing but 'a fraudulent bubble'.[30] Across the press corridor on the same day, after explicitly drawing attention to 'the mania for new projects which existed in 1720', in which 'no less than 200 schemes of various kinds were set on foot, of which no trace remains at the present day', the *Gazette* moralized from the past, that 'The fate of all those splendid undertakings afford a salutary lesson to the speculators of the present period'.[31] In the mid-eighteen-twenties the glut of English goods being sold in the new republics of South America provoked a 'fall in the price of public securities' in England that was declared to be 'unprecedented since the South Sea Bubble of 1720', and—with schemes such as the Agricultural Company emerging— antipodean economic types were alarmed about potential ripple effects.[32]

If the South Seas Bubble was so firmly embedded in the cultural memory that it inspired fear in the hearts of humorless financiers for over a century, it is no surprise that it also frequently emerged as the butt of witty sarcasm, especially as the exalted wisdom of hindsight gave the lampoonist the secure superiority necessary for their mockery.[33] Such sarcasm was perhaps even more poignant in the British Colony now located in the very South Seas that promised overblown profits to their great, great grandfather's generation. As the only public literary organ of NSW, the *Gazette* was familiar with Bubble humour. In fact, just six months after the first issue (5/3/1803), readers were amused by 'the Repulse':

> A Rake to an Uncle apply'd for a SUM,
> Convinc'd that the Old One would lend it;
> But deaf to intreaty, the answer was Mum,

---

29 NSW was not the only concern in the early nineteenth century. The *Colonial Times & Tasmanian Advertiser* 9/6/1826, reported a meeting of 14 Dec 1825 chaired by the Lord Mayor of London in the Mansion House, in response to the grave financial situation brought on Britain by new republics in South America, so overstocked with British goods, that they could be bought there cheaper than in England. The paper drew explicit connections with the 1720 speculations.
30 *Australian* 25/11/1824.
31 *SG* 25/11/1824.
32 *Colonial Times & Tasmanian Advertiser* 9/6/1826, concluded the report on the meeting chaired by the Lord Mayor of London held on 14 Dec 1825: 'we have little doubt but the New Companies of these Colonies will suffer with the rest'.
33 The usual 'black humour' was part of the response, with, for example, a set of playing cards each card with a satirical comment on the fiasco, enabling it to be mocked during every card game for years to come; see Harvard Business School, 'Humour'.

"I'll KEEP it--- perhaps you might spend it."

"Good Sir", urged the Nephew, "when last you reliev'd me,
With honour I paid off the score."
"You did," answered Testy, and then so DECEIV'D me,

That Zooks I'll be BUBBLED no more."[34]

If Philo Free had waited until the mid-twenties to put pen to paper, amidst the fears of economic crisis his attempt at humor may have been declared to be in bad taste. But in January 1817 Philo Free could safely pursue his own purposes by drawing upon the heritage of ridicule attached to the Bubble. His opening comparison set the mocking tone of political satire. With this hint towards his genre, no doubt Philo Free expected his more astute readers to recognize the game he was about to play at the expense of this new project in NSW— the Philanthropic Society and the broader missionary movement that lay behind it. Little did he know how much it would misfire. With satire, the fun is only shared amongst those in the superior circle of the mocker. Those it mocks are generally not amused. If the victim is a Bible reader, such mockery is a mark of wicked men, working in league with the devil.[35]

One literary allusion in particular—obscure as it is—served to set the letter explicitly within the genre of political satire or even lampoon, so popular in England across the eighteenth century. As he parodied the dis-virtues of his particular Bible-reading victims[36]—the South Sea missionaries and especially their 'worthy head'—Philo Free noted that, alongside the art of distillation, the missionary spirit introduced 'that tiny race of animals, which on being boiled, do not prove to be lobsters!' (ll. 48–50).

Alongside the social problems it caused, the introduction of the

---

34 SG 7/8/1803.
35 Cf. Psalm 1. For Marsden's link between the wicked and the devil, see, e.g. Sermon 18:14–15 (Moore College): 'Nor will their enemies fail to take advantage of any unwatchfulness on their part as they are always alive to embrace every opportunity that may occur to distress and annoy the believing soul. Satan & his agents whether they consist of the powers of darkness who are under his immediate authority or wicked men who are under his influence know the most convenient time to make their attacks upon believers, the place where they are most open to assault, nor have they any security against their enemies, but by guarding every pass and standing continually in their watch tower'.
36 Following in the footsteps of Robert Southey's 1809 attack on the mission ('Transactions'), so 'full of skeptical jibes'; Sharp, *The World, the Flesh & the Devil*, 338.

European presence in the South Seas led to a great deal of collateral environmental damage. Sometimes this was intentional, as part of the drive to bring European civilization to parts of the world they had newly 'discovered' and now wished to tame for their own advantage. At the same time, it must be said that many of the local inhabitants of the islands welcomed the white men, with the perceived advantages of their tools, their knowledge, or the status accruing to those they befriended.[37] And so European goods were traded, European plants and foodstuffs were grown, and European domestic livestock introduced.[38] Even if imposed with little thought about the cultures, civilizations, or environments already in existence, this kind of damage can perhaps be regarded as positively motivated but with unintended and unforeseen consequences. But at the same time, the human visitors brought by passing ships accidentally introduced their animal counterparts. Upon disembarking, European dogs, cats, and rats began an irreversible devastation of the local fauna. They in turn brought their own 'tiny race of animals', namely, the flea.[39]

Like his use of Latin, Philo Free's strange expression is a literary allusion, intended to be recognised by the high-brow and so to enhance the prestige of author as one of their own. However, in colonial New South Wales it was obviously lost on most of his contemporaries. This became evident when J.T. Campbell, accused of being 'Philo Free', faced the criminal court (21-23/10/1817), where the vague explanation was given that the expression referred to 'a certain loathsome and uncleanly species of vermin'.[40] Even Cambridge-educated Judge Advocate Wylde evidently missed the allusion to the flea. Or perhaps, like the Bible-reading types, the legal types were equally immune to such exalted literary wit.

For if there were any high-brow readers of the *Gazette* who were insiders to Philo Free's literary circle, at this point they would have

---

37 See, for example, the approach of Vincent O'Malley, *The Meeting Place*, who discusses the encounter between the European and the Māori as one of cultural encounter and exchange.
38 See the discussions of 'botanical imperialism', e.g. Brockway, 'Plant Imperialism'.
39 Sometimes the fleas came via New South Wales. Oral tradition blames the *Cumberland* for first introducing fleas on Rarotonga during her 1814 visit; Maude & Crocombe, 'Rarotongan Sandalwood', 51 n.76, with Gosset, 'Notes', 14. For the significance of the *Cumberland*'s visit for the series of events associated with the Philo Free letter, see Bolt, 'The Failure of the Philanthropic Society', Chapter 7 in this volume.
40 See Wylde, Report [Criminal Trial], 447 and 448.

chuckled at his cleverness.[41] The 'tiny race of animals, which on being boiled, do not prove to be lobsters!' was a double allusion. For those with the eyes to see, the expression invoked both the humble flea and the mighty figure of Sir Joseph Banks, the botanist who travelled with Captain Cook in the *Endeavour* to be part of the English 'discovery' of Australia (1770), and who originally suggested his 'Botany Bay' as a fitting place for an English Penal colony (1779).[42] After collecting about 7000 specimens on his voyage with Cook, Banks continued to be closely connected with sea captains and others who collected on his behalf for years to come. He was in touch with Thomas Haweis, the man instrumental in the founding of the London Missionary Society. He was Haweis' source of information about Tahiti, and, once the LMS missionaries were scattered through the islands, he corresponded with them in their various stations.[43] Haweis was not the only prominent English evangelical that Banks knew. He mingled with the likes of William Wilberforce and the Clapham Sect and, like them, he kept a close interest in the emergent Colony of NSW, corresponding with NSW Governors and other prominent settlers.[44] Although his reputation waxes and wanes in subsequent historical discussion, without doubt Banks was an influential figure in the infant-and-child colony of NSW and rightly hailed in Australia as at least some kind of hero.[45]

But that is not the reception he always received during his lifetime. By 1817, Banks had already become part of the common stock of the

---

41 No doubt there would have been some. Parramatta resident George Suttor, for example, a protégé of Banks, later wrote some memoirs of his mentor, which reveals he was familiar with Peter Pindar's attacks, noting that Banks 'laughed at the witty though virulent poet', *Memoirs*, 45; Smith, *Life of Banks*, 328; for Suttor, see Parsons, 'Suttor, George (1774–1859)'.

42 See Smith, *Life of Banks*, Ch. 13; Gascoigne, 'The Scientist as Patron', 253. This is largely the reason for the attempt to accord him the title 'Father of Australia', wresting it from Macquarie. This title was used to toast Macquarie at the Anniversary Dinner in January 1827 (*Monitor* 27/1/1827). Later that year, Governor Phillip received the same title (*SG* 10/10/1827: 'Governor PHILLIP, the Father of Australia, inasmuch as he was the Founder of this infant though rising empire'), but by November the Turf Club toasted Macquarie with it again (*Monitor* 12/11/1827). By the anniversary dinner of 1830, the argument seems to have been judiciously settled in favour of Phillip, with toasts taken to: 'The Memory of Governor Phillip, the founder of the Colony.--(In silence)' and 'The Memory of Governor MACQUARIE, father of Australia.--(In silence.)'; (*SG* 28/1/1830).

After George Suttor, *Memoirs* (1855), noted that in London he had heard Banks called the father of the infant colony of NSW, the idea was promoted firstly by Barton (1889) and then by Maiden (1909), and others beyond; see Gascoigne, 'The Scientist as Patron', 254–259.

43 Garrett, *A Way in the Sea*, 3.
44 Gilbert, 'Banks, Sir Joseph'.
45 His changing reputation is surveyed by Gascoigne, 'The Scientist as Patron'.

political satirist. Even before he was appointed President of the Royal Society (1778–1820), Banks was mocked in the role. How could a Natural Historian be a worthy successor to a mathematician of the likes of Sir Isaac Newton?[46] In the context of a century given to witticism and political satire, the earlier raised eyebrows soon devolved into open mockery and lampoon, and, 'standing in the fiercest glare of publicity', Banks became a frequent victim:

> The Scoffer was abroad, everywhere. No one, in any stage of life, could escape him. Notoriety of any sort was exposed to his wiles. Lampooning was the rage; and clever lampooners could make money of it. [...]
>
> In point of fact, Banks proved an excellent target for the shafts of caricature. He was well-born, and hobnobbed with sailors. He was a man of fortune, and recklessly defied the conventions in the disposal of his income. He was a personal friend of the King, a circumstance fatal in its relation to the discontented spirits of the day.[47]

Although a great specimen collector, even in his lifetime Banks was mocked because he wrote very little.[48] One detractor famously attempted to fill the gap in Banks' publication record by putting a theory in his mouth that left him the object of ridicule well beyond his lifetime:

> Some discontents arising among the more enlightened members of the R--- Society, on account of Sir Joseph's non-communication of wisdom to the Royal Journals, spurred the knight on at last to open his mouth.
>   He told an intimate friend that he had made a discovery that would astonish the world, enrich the journals, and render himself immortal—with the most important confidence and philosophic solemnity, he affirmed that he was upon the very eve of proving what had never entered into the soul of man; viz. that fleas were lobsters.[49]

---

46 Later historians would agree. According to Gascoigne, 'The Scientist as Patron', 243, 244, Banks 'published very little and left no indelible mark on any scientific discipline', and, after he died in 1820, he sunk quickly into 'oblivion'.

47 Smith, *Life of Banks*, 175. When Smith initially had difficulty finding a publisher for his work, he was advised to include some of the caricatures of Banks to increase its popular appeal; Gascoigne, 'The Scientist as Patron', 249.

48 This received comment in the funeral oration delivered by Baron Georges Cuvier at the Academy of Sciences, Paris (2 Apr 1821): 'The works which this man leaves behind him occupy a few pages only; their importance is not greatly superior to their extent; and yet his name will shine out with lustre in the history of the sciences', as quoted by Cameron, *Sir Joseph Banks*, 209. See also Gascoigne, 'The Scientist as Patron', 243.

49 Wolcot, *Works*, 10.

With little from Banks' own pen, it is difficult to say what he would have thought of this theory, said to be his. Although regularly repeated amongst satirists ever since, even at the time, others suspected the attribution was completely fabricated.[50]

Of course, the art of the lampoonist is to exaggerate the barest grain of truth for its ridiculous and humorous potential. If there is anything behind this particular mockery, it may go back to one of Banks' early observations. When voyaging with Cook off the coast of Patagonia in January 1769, Banks had identified the shrimps that previous ships' captains had reported were in sufficient quantity to colour the sea red. These were the 'lobster krill', or, more exactly, 'the pelagic *Grimothea* stage of *M. gregaria*'.[51] Sailing over sixty years before Charles Darwin sailed the same waters and almost a century before the data collected on that cruise led to Darwin's theory of evolution being published in *On the Origin of Species by Means of Natural Selection* (London, 1859) and *The Descent of Man* (London, 1871),[52] Banks' observations may have led

---

50   One contemporary reviewer clearly took it as fictional, 'the president is supposed to have suspected fleas to be lobsters, from their shape, and to have brought his hypothesis to the test of experiment by boiling, expecting them to turn red'; [Critical Review], 'Review of *A Benevolent Epistle*', 429. A later writer reflected back some forty years with the same doubt as to the facts: 'Dr Walcot represented Sir Joseph Banks as boiling fleas in order to ascertain whether they turned red like lobsters; and the traveller Bruce as cutting his beefsteaks from a living animal and then sending the bullock to graze. Who now doubts at this time of day that Sir Joseph Banks and Bruce were benefactors of society', [Westminster Review], '[Review of] *Crotchet Castle*', 208.
     In 1810, Samuel Butler, *Letter to the Rev C.J. Blomfield*, 73 note, mentioned Lucian's description of fleas, each the size of twelve elephants, before referring the reader to Banks, 'whose elaborate researches into the history of fleas are already recorded to his immortal honour, and whose dignified letter to the National Institute at Paris, I frequently read with great edification and delight'. However, Butler is clearly writing satirically, so his statement cannot be taken as merely factual, and this statement is probably already influenced by Pindar. Even within the same satirical stream the theory was sometimes explicitly registered as a fabrication. In 1873, despite assuming that Banks really conducted the boiling experiment, Butler's friend Dudgeon, *Columbia*, 200, had his philosopher Schnüffelpilz declare that 'it is highly improbable that [Banks] indulged in any such illogical exclamation, which, though it is recorded in the writings of the celebrated contemporary poet, Peter Pindar, must be held to be merely a poetical version of some expression of annoyance he may really have given utterance to'.
51   Matthews, 'Lobster-Krill', 481: 'Sir Joseph Banks during Cook's first voyage found *Grimothea* off the coast of Patagonia. He says, "2nd January 1769. Met with some small shoals of red lobsters, which have been seen by almost everyone passing through these seas; they were, however, so far from colouring the sea red, as Dampier and Cowley say they do, that I may affirm that we never saw more than a few hundreds of them at a time. We called them *dancer gregarius*". On his return he sent his specimens to Fabricius who first described the species scientifically and named it "*Galatheagregaria*". For the original, see Banks, *The Endeavour Journal*.
52   Townley, 'Darwin, Charles Robert'.

to his own speculations about biological inter-relationships. Perhaps to the eye of the natural historian, the tiny crustaceans off the coast of South America bore a resemblance to the common flea.

But if they were related, how could this connection be established? Whatever the truth of the matter—and we can suspect the amount is very little—, Banks was said to have proposed an experiment: if the flea was boiled, would it, like the lobster, turn red?

The man who fostered this rumour for his own profit was the Scottish doctor and failed clergyman, John Wolcot, who made his mark as a political satirist writing under another classically-alluding pseudonym, Peter Pindar.[53] Writing from the time he moved to London in 1781 until his death in 1819, he managed to avoid being charged with libel, despite satirizing members of the esteemed Royal Academy (1785–86), and then moving on to the King and the Royal Family and members of the King's ministry. As president of the Royal Society (1778–1820), Sir Joseph Banks frequently suffered under Pindar's wit, whether in brief allusion or entire poems at his expense.[54] When he turned his ridicule on Banks, he frequently did so by metonymy, epitomizing Banks by the flea.[55]

Peter Pindar was fond of utilizing 'loathsome vermin' to serve his satirical purposes. According to the anonymous writer of his obituary (1819), after 'incidentally assail[ing]' His Majesty in his earlier works, in 1786:

> the next step of the poet was to assign an entire work to the loyal and laudable project of rendering his Sovereign ridiculous. The *Lousiad*, a clever mock-heroic, in four cantos, was the result: it requires no comment, since no ability can excuse a production which only proved that he who disregarded his God did not honour his King.[56]

---

53 See Carr, 'Wolcot, J.'; Maylon, 'Peter Pindar and his World'. For a contemporary account see his own autobiography introducing, *Odes, Epistles &c*, or that on his death, see [Literary Gazette], 'Dr John Wolcott'. His adopted pseudonym was taken from the Ancient Greek lyric poet, Pindar (c. 522 – c. 443).
54 Smith, *Life of Banks*, 177–179.
55 Perhaps due to Pindar's influence, in the later repetitions of the odious comparison with Newton at his expense, Banks, in fact, *became* the flea. E.g. Smith, *Life of Banks*, p.175 n.1 reports the lines of astronomer Rev. Thomas John Hussey sent to Charles Babbage in January 1830:
> "I think I've seen these things look very small,
> I've seen a mouse in honest Cluny's stall,
> I've seen a flea upon a lion's hide,
> And Banks's bust with Newton's side by side."
56 [Literary Gazette], 'Dr John Wolcott'.

With the classical allusion apparently requisite to this kind of satire—this time to Virgil's *Aeneid*—, the *Lous-iad* arose from the legendary tale of a louse being found on the king's plate. It sold so well that it went to a seventh edition by the following year. In Canto III, all these avid readers were introduced to Banks, the newly installed President of the Royal Society, and his theory about fleas:[57]

> There curs'd, SIR JOSEPH BANKS, in quest of fame
> At finding fleas and lobsters not the same.

After Banks had served as President for several more years, Pindar deemed the great man's theory worthy of more sustained attention, publishing 'Sir Joseph Banks and the boiled fleas, an ode'. The poem appeared in 1790 as part of the volume *A benevolent epistle to Sylvanus Urban, alias Master John Nichols, printer*,[58] at the same being extracted by several prominent journals, including *The Analytical Review*, *The Critical Review*, and *The Edinburgh Magazine*.[59]

Despite *The Edinburgh Magazine* reprinting the poem in its Poetry section under the title 'Sir Joseph's Breakfast', elsewhere in the same issue the reviewer of *Sylvanus Urban* tutt-tutted over Pindar's treatment of Banks:

> He attacks without reserve or compassion all characters in which any opening can be discovered for detraction or ridicule. Unfortunately, it must often happen, that such characters are not among the unworthy or the censurable, but such only where some trifling foibles, or imperfections, give room for the thoughtless to laugh, or the envious to rejoice at their exposure. Serious vice admits not of this mortifying ridicule; were Sir Joseph Banks a Murderer of men, instead of an Impaler of butterflies, a few indignant *juvenalian* lines were all that party or wit could bring against him.[60]

---

57 Wolcot, *The Lousiad: an Heroi-comic Poem*. The poem was republished in *Works* 1.273. See also the line in *Sylvanus Urban*, 6: 'more blest on this earth a frog to see,/ to find a cockleshell, and boil a flea,/ than dwell in yonder skies with glory crown'd,/ where frogs, nor fleas, nor cockleshells abound'.

58 John Nichols, satirised as Sylvanus Urban, took over the editorship of *The Gentleman's Magazine* from Samuel Johnson in 1778; Aitken, 'Nichols, John'.

59 [Analytical Review], 'Art. XIII. *A Benevolent Epistle*', 437–440; [Critical Review], 'Review of *A Benevolent Epistle*', 426–429; [Edinburgh Magazine], 'Sir Joseph's Breakfast', 360.

60 [Edinburgh Magazine], 'Review of *A Benevolent Epistle*', 349. For the poem: p.360.

The poem had its own introduction, in which Sir Joseph Banks revealed his theory and the experiment to test it:[61]

> Jonas Dryander was ordered to collect fifteen hundred fleas, and boil them; which, if they changed to the fine crimson of the lobster, would put the identity of the species beyond the possibility of doubt—at length the beds of the president were ransacked by his flea-crimp, honest Jonas—fifteen hundred of the hopping inhabitants were caught, and passed the dreadful ordeal of boiling water; with what success, O gentle reader, the ode will inform thee.

The ode itself opens with Sir Joseph at the breakfast table being joined by Swedish fellow-botanist, and librarian both for Banks and for the Royal Society, Jonas Dryander, pictured as his servant:

> In Jonas Dryander, the fav'rite came,
> Who manufactures all Sir Joseph's fame—
> "What luck?" Sir Joseph bawl'd— "say, Jonas, say"—
> "I've boil'd just fifteen hundred"—Jonas whin'd—
> "the dev'l a one change colour cou'd I find" —
> Intelligence creating dire dismay!
> Then Jonas curs'd, with many a wicked wish,
> Then show'd the stubborn fleas upon a dish.
> "How!" ror'd the president, and backward fell—
> "there goes, then, my hypothesis to hell!"—
> And now his head in deep despair he shook;
> Now clos'd his eyes, and now upon his breast,
> He mutt'ring dropp'd his sable beard unblest'
> Now twirl'd his thumbs, and groan'd with piteous look.

The next stanza pictures Aubert, Blagden, Planta, and Woide sitting awe-struck,[62] followed by the crowd, clamouring for Banks to explain:

---

61 [Analytical Review], 'Art. XIII. *A Benevolent Epistle*', 439–440; [Edinburgh Magazine], 'Sir Joseph's Breakfast', 360.
62 Alexander Aubert, merchant and astronomer; Sir Charles Blagden, doctor and natural historian; Joseph Planta, librarian of the British Museum, were all members of the Royal Society and supporters of Banks' Presidency. Follow the index in Smith, *Life of Banks*. Karl Gottfried Woide, or, in England, Charles Godfrey Woide, was a Reformed pastor, an orientalist and librarian at the British Museum; see Courtney, 'Woide, Charles Godfrey'. He was struck by apoplexy while conversing in Banks' house on 6 May 1790 before dying on the 9th. Although post-dating the publication of Pindar's poem by some six months, as the circumstances of his death became known, his demise may have added extra spice to readers who delighted in the ridicule of Banks.

> Dumb to their questions the GREAT MAN remain'd:
> the knight, deep pond'ring, nought vouchsaf'd to say;
> Again the *gentlemen* their voices strain'd;
> Sudden the PRESIDENT OF FLEAS, so sad,
> Strides round the room with disappointment mad,
> Whilst ev'ry eye enlarg'd with wonder rolls;
> And now his head against the wainscot leaning,
> "Since you *must* know, *must* know (he sigh'd) the meaning,
> Fleas are not lobsters, d—mn their souls".[63]

With all his literary posturing, by publishing in the *Gazette*—the only literary vehicle available in NSW—Philo Free may have been dreaming of being the antipodean Peter Pindar. Eighteenth century England had bred 'a small tribe of men, who either distrusted or despised the public recognition of virtue and worth, [who] earned their living by reckless defamation, and the best men suffered with the worst'.[64] But if John Wolcot managed to attack the great ones of the land for thirty years and survive without being charged with libel, surely there was no danger in Philo Free becoming the political satirist of NSW!

His literary pretensions were immediately seized upon in the next issue of the *Gazette* and ridiculed by yet another pseudonymous satirist, 'A Poor Scholar'.[65] Because of its central requirement to appeal to a group of insiders at the expense of a set of outsiders, satire always risks being misunderstood and failing badly. 'A Poor Scholar' adopted the same genre, but shifted the imaginary players. Now it is 'Philo Free' who is the victim, and the general audience of the *Gazette* is amused at his expense. For, in the cruel and fame-envious circles of the satirist, whatever he thought he was trying to do, he had failed miserably, and so his public exercise now warranted the public mockery he had attempted to mete out to others.

For those standing outside with 'A Poor Scholar' the letter was nonsense, just as patent as it was obscure. He dramatically pictured the letter baffling not only Sydneysiders, but also 'a body of occult

---

63 With pretended innocence, the poem was published with the note: 'The author would not have so frequently taken the liberty of putting vulgarisms into the worthy president's mouth, had he not previously known that Sir Joseph was the most accomplished swearer of the Royal Society'.
64 Smith, *Life of Banks*, 173.
65 *SG* 11/1/1817.

philosophers, distinguished by the titles of opaquati, illuminati, ignorati, literati, obscurati, and glitterati', before pretending to reveal its inner mysteries with his own further obfuscations. He concluded his gleeful demolition by suggesting that 'unless [Philo Free] will condescend to give us some explanation of his object, or a guide to lead us to it, [he] may retire from public notice much in the same way as a blind man begs to be excused giving his opinion of colours'. If Philo Free made his meaning clear, then it could only be clear to some secret society, not to the public at large.

But for those it left stinging, the letter was a clear-as-crystal public attack which left their reputation in the eyes of that same public—no matter how unsuspecting—in need of a public redemption.

The Libelled

On reading the letter in the *Gazette*, Rev. Samuel Marsden, immediately recognized himself as its victim. Within two days of its printing, Marsden began legal proceedings, informing Judge-Advocate John Wylde that he had been grossly libeled as the Chaplain of the Colony, calling particular attention to the paragraph: 'In former times the Active and enterprising Spirit of the Jesuits' and ending with 'whose never dying Names are there trumpeted forth' (ll.37–80), but noting that 'there are other Paragraphs in this Letter of which I have just Cause to complain'.[66] Because Marsden was not explicitly named anywhere in the letter, if he was to establish the charge of libel, he had to prove that the attack was directed against him.

Fairly new to the Colony, Wylde was not sufficiently aware of the facts to feel the letter's sting. For irony, sarcasm, satire, or lampoon to have their desired effect, readers must share with the author a certain knowledge of the facts to which he aims to give his particular slant.[67] Wylde later admitted that those who knew the facts may have come to a different conclusion, but from the time Marsden first approached him through to when he was called to give account of the Criminal trial, he maintained that the letter was not clearly directed against Marsden. Rather surprisingly, given the

---

66 Marsden to Wylde, 7/1/1817. This is clearly 'the paragraph that most infuriated Marsden'; Sharp, *The World, the Flesh & the Devil*, 334, and 446–447. See also Marsden, *An Answer to Certain Calumnies*, 77–78.
67 See Booth, *A Rhetoric of Irony*.

obscurity of some of the expressions noted at the time and ever since, he also maintained that its metaphorical references had sufficient clarity to be interpreted simply within the confines of the letter itself.[68]

After pondering for a week, he responded to the first flush of Marsden's outrage by denying that there was a problem. He certainly regretted the publication of an article 'which could possibly be considered or construed as reflecting upon you or the respectable Societies connected with you in Missionary purposes and Exertions', and so he had asked 'Mr Secretary Campbell as Censor of the press' to explain, which he had done. But Wylde still didn't see the problem:

> I could not trace sufficient of allusion or remark or circumstance to perceive that yourself or any other Individual was particularly pointed out and designated, [...].
>
> I have had the Letter much in consideration; because if I could satisfied [sic] myself, that in the plain obvious and natural construction of it the Writer of the Letter must be understood to designate and therefore have in purpose maliciously to defame any particular person or Individuals (as to constitute a Libel, the writing you are aware, must descend to Particulars and refer to Individuals and not be of general observation only or against a particular order of Men) I should have felt it my duty and would have performed that Duty of filing and Exhibiting as Judge Advocate of the Colony a public charge against the printer, unless the Author had been given up. But I really have been and am unable to fix upon any passage from any knowledge that I have, which by Inuendo in any Indictment I could shew as reflecting upon yourself or any particular Individual. All the observations and remarks in terms and construction are limited and pointed to the islands and Inhabitants of the islands in the Pacific, [...][69]

Wylde nevertheless agreed to proceed if Marsden could supply affidavits 'that any part or the whole of it in their Judgment plainly and obviously

---

68 See Wylde, Minutes [Criminal Trial], 20/3/1821, 475: 'There are other cases, in which the meaning may be intelligible only to persons where, pointing at some real or supposing peculiarity in the object libelled, the meaning is on that account capable of being understood and the application of it known only by persons, who have a degree of knowledge of the party libelled, which is not possessed by the public at large'. But, even at this distance, he nevertheless claimed that the letter was 'perfectly intelligible *per se*' and its meaning 'so perspicuous and clear in the expression and tense of the libellous Matter' that it only needed to be proven that it referred to Marsden.

69 Wylde to Marsden, 14/1/1817.

is directed against and intended to designate yourself'.

In principal, this should have been an easy task, for Marsden felt that 'the whole Colony knew that the writer meant me, by the words Christian Mahomet, as well as in many other Parts that Insinuations were levelled at me'.[70] Although Marsden could have supplied many more, the witnesses who were prepared to put themselves on oath 'duly sworn on the Holy Evangelists' before Wylde in January 1817 were clearly not so confused about the object of Philo Free's attentions. Typical of others, Gregory Blaxland strongly asserted that in 'every part thereof' he:

> verily Believes and has no Doubt, that the Rev.d Sam.l Marsden Principal Chaplain of this Colony is meant and intended to be described and alluded to.[71]

Although Marsden saw himself as clearly in Philo Free's crosshairs, he took action in order to defend the reputation, and so the cause, of the two missionary societies.[72] Although by 1817 the Church Missionary Society's mission in New Zealand was still in its infancy, the London Missionary Society had been in Tahiti since 1797. The regular traffic between Port Jackson and Tahiti enabled the *Gazette* to report regularly on the state of the mission, and, after the conversion of Pomare II in 1812, especially on its success. In this period of its history, readers who opposed the mission would be increasingly annoyed as reports became increasingly positive. When the *Governor Macquarie* returned in March 1815, for example, it brought particularly glowing news of the good progress of the gospel on Eimeo.[73] This was just five months after

---

70 Marsden, Notes on J. Wylde's letter of 23/1/1817, 28/1/1817 [unsent]. He stated there were 'five hundred others were ready to do the same if necessary, and men of the first Rank and Respectability in the Colony'.
71 Testimony of Gregory Blaxland, [January 1817]. Marsden adds that Blaxland's testimony was 'similar to the others that have been taken upon the same Subject before Mr Judge Advocate Wylde. In January last'.
72 Marsden to Bathurst, 8/12/1817: 'But as it was sent into the world, under such an apparent public sanction, and likely in its operation to affect the character of many innocent individuals I felt myself compelled to appeal to the Courts of Justice, in order to justify my own public reputation, and to defend that of those who are associated with me in promoting the Civilization of the Natives in the South Sea islands—I am informed, My Lord, that the Libel hath already found its way to the *Asiatic Mirror*, and probably before this period may also have been noticed in other public papers in different parts of the world—There can be no doubt but that it was the Author's intention that it should be as publicly and universally known, as the light of the Sun, and that it should injure the general Interest of the Societies in the public opinion, and expose them and their Missionaries to unmerited odium and Contempt'.
73 SG 4/3/1815.

Marsden had unsuccessfully urged the Philanthropic Society to investigate the conduct of the crew of her partner vessel, the *Cumberland*. Perhaps the opportunity to act as a messenger of good news about the mission gave ship's captains a ready means of distracting any potential inquiry into their crew's questionable conduct? But rather than being distracted, Philo Free explained any missionary success in terms of the rumors of their own questionable conduct. In the very pages, which so often attempted to warm the heart of the Colony with the civilization of the Tahitian or the New Zealander, Philo Free went for the missionary jugular.

However, despite some items clearly attacking the missionary societies, Marsden was in no doubt that he was the chief victim of the libel.[74] In his opinion, the writer 'meant to ruin my private character, on account of my public conduct as Agent to the Missionary Society'.[75]

But could it be clearly proven that the Chaplain was the libel victim? No doubt there were others on the outside like 'A Poor Scholar' and, later, Judge-Advocate Wylde, who were not clear it was about the parson or that this could be imputed from what was said. However, at the October 1817 Criminal trial several witnesses easily made that imputation, testifying that the letter clearly alluded to Marsden, whether in general, according to Michael Robinson, or in particular matters of detail. Marsden was clearly the 'worthy head' (l.55) of the group in view and the 'Christian Mahomet' (l.60; so Edward Eagar; Greg Blaxland; Richard Jones).[76] Other phrases depicting aspects of Marsden's persona made the reference even clearer, such as 'mask and garb' (l.70), referring to his clerical profession; 'bolt the pork and profits', to the New Zealand trade in flax and timber, and the Tahitian trade in pork (l.64; Eagar). But not only did the allusion to him taking the lead as one of the 'evangelising heroes' further clarify Marsden as the object of the libel (l.79; Blaxland), but the reference to the *Eclectic Review* (l.78) 'can point to no-one else' (Jones). For, 'the Plaintiff's exertions as Agent to the Missionaries have been recorded in the *Eclectic Review*' (Eagar).

Philo Free's letter was the first occasion for the *Eclectic Review* ever

---

74 He demonstrated this to the court through referring to the details of the letter; see, Cross Examination of Samuel Marsden, 22/10/1817, 463–466.
75 Cross Examination of Samuel Marsden, 22/10/1817, 465.
76 For their testimony, see Wylde, Minutes [Criminal Trial], 446 (Eagar; Robinson; Blaxland), 447 (Jones).

to be mentioned in the *Sydney Gazette*, although the English journal had been published monthly since 1805. Founded by dissenters, the editor at the time and for almost twenty years more (1813–1836) was the hymn-writer and abolitionist, Josiah Conder.[77] It was closely associated with the evangelical cause, for all profits were donated to the British and Foreign Bible Society. This magazine was read in NSW, and at the criminal trial Edward Eagar reported that he knew the issue in which Marsden was referred,[78] and a member of the Criminal Court noted that they had 'seen the name of Mr Marsden mentioned once in the *Eclectic Review* at very considerable length'.[79] Marsden himself was not a regular reader of this journal, but at the Criminal trial, he admitted to having seen his name in it 'six or seven years ago'.[80]

In November 1809, while Marsden was still on passage back to NSW from a two year visit to England, the *Eclectic Review* had published an article recounting his achievements with high praise: 'unborn empires are dependent on his exertions; and his name will be the theme of the new world, as long as there is a heart to feel reverence, or a tongue to utter praise' (p.995). The Marsden eulogy rather oddly interrupts a review of M. François Péron's account of the French scientific expedition to *Terra Australis* commanded by Nicholas Baudin (1800–1804).[81]

Having received official news of the end of hostilities between England and France, at the end of June 1802 Baudin's expedition sailed into Port Jackson as two vessels, the sloops *Geographe* and *Naturaliste*, and left in November as three, having also purchased the locally-built Schooner, *Casuarina*.[82] M. François Péron was the onboard naturalist who eventually recorded their discoveries in the interest of nation and science. The first volume of his account of the voyage was published in French in 1807 and an incomplete English translation in 1809. Both were reviewed

---

77 See, Boase, 'Josiah Conder'.
78 Examination of Edward Eagar, 23/10/1817, Wylde, Minutes [Criminal Trial], 468.
79 Remark by unidentified Member of Criminal Court, 23/10/1817, Wylde, Minutes [Criminal Trial], 468.
80 Cross Examination of Samuel Marsden, 22/10/1817, Wylde, Minutes [Criminal Trial], 466.
81 Marchant & Reynolds, 'Péron, François'. See also Marchant & Reynolds, 'Baudin, Nicolas Thomas'.
82 The reviewer reported that the *Geographe* arrived on the 20th and the *Naturaliste* on the 28th; [Eclectic Review], 'Art. I. *Voyage de Découvertes aux Terres Australes*', 980. In fact, the *Naturaliste* had arrived 24 April, departed, and, after being forced back by bad weather, returned. After buying the *Casuarina* from Governor King, the three vessels departed on 18 November; Péron, *A Voyage of Discovery*, 270, 271, 311.

together in the November 1809 issue of the *Eclectic Review*.[83]

Coincidentally, the English version of Péron's account was published in London just as Marsden was returning from his two year visit[84] to speak with Government and others about NSW affairs and to recruit more clergy to work alongside him, as well as some brave souls prepared to live amongst the Māori for the sake of bringing them the gospel. His visit was well-received by Government officials, who subsequently acted on some of his suggestions for the betterment of NSW, and especially by the evangelical circles who had kept a keen eye on NSW from before its inception. During his visit Marsden enjoyed the company of Dr John Mason Good and struck up a friendship with a London Barrister, Mr Daniel Parken, who happened to also be the 'conductor' of the *Eclectic Review*. Olinthus Gregory later explained the sequence of events:

> not long after Mr Marsden quitted his native shores, in 1809, Mr Parken noticed a warm eulogium upon him in M. Péron's "Voyage of Discovery to the Southern Hemisphere", performed by order of Buonaparte. Regarding this as a favourable opportunity of doing justice to the character, motives, and undertakings of his reverend friend, he immediately solicited the assistance of Dr Good, whose friendship he also enjoyed. The aid which he thus entreated was supplied with such cheerfulness and promptitude, that within twenty-four hours he received the following spirited and characteristic sketch.[85]

What Parken had noticed was a footnote in the French version (not brought over into the English publication),[86] in which Péron briefly paraded Marsden's achievements for the colony in the short eight years he had been there and expressed his appreciation of Marsden's hospitality: 'this respectable pastor [who] conducted me himself with the most affectionate kindness! Who could have believed it!'.[87]

---

83 [Eclectic Review], 'Art. I. *Voyage de Découvertes aux Terres Australes*', 977–996.
84 After leaving NSW on the *Buffalo* on 10 February 1807 (*SG* 4,11/1 and 15/2/1807), fellow-passenger to Governor King, he arrived in England 8 November 1807 (*The Morning Chronicle* 11/11/1807) and sailed on the Transport *Anne* on 25 August 1809, via Rio de Janeiro, to arrive at Sydney Cove on 27 February 1810 (Willetts, 'Convict Ship Anne 1810'; *SG* 3/10/1810).
85 Gregory, *Memoirs of the Life, Writings and Character of the Late John Mason Good*, 387. After explaining its origin, Gregory then repeats Good's account (pp.387–395) before updating the account of Marsden's achievements (pp.395–400).
86 This is one example of the 1809 English version being 'an incomplete translation'; Brown, *Ill-Starred Captains*, 506
87 [Eclectic Review], 'Art. I. *Voyage de Découvertes aux Terres Australes*', 988; [Evangelical Magazine], 'Account of the Rev. Samuel Marsden's Exertions', 499.

Dr Good's account began by quoting the whole of Péron's footnote about Marsden, before declaring the compliment apt and recounting Marsden's achievements to date. Evidently Parken simply inserted Good's account into an independently written piece, which left the supposed review of Péron's journal looking rather odd. After nine pages describing the French expedition prior to its arrival in Port Jackson, the Marsden footnote was added, allowing Péron to kiss Marsden on both cheeks as a launch-pad for Good's eight page digression, further praising Marsden's achievements in NSW, before returning to one final page on Péron's—which complained that there was no space left for a more detailed account. However significant the achievements of this scientific expedition to *Terra Australis* sponsored by the Emperor and King of England's oldest enemy, they were thus eclipsed by those of the Parramatta pastor!

Marsden's story was assured of an even wider readership amongst already sympathetic circles, when the December issue of the *Evangelical Magazine* immediately also published Good's account, under the heading: 'An Account of the Rev. Samuel Marsden's exertions for the benefit of the British settlement in New South Wales'—noting it as an extract from the *Eclectic Review*.[88] With Marsden already having made a positive impression in well-connected evangelical circles, these publications now sealed his position in those circles as 'a renowned religious hero'.[89]

Taking comfort that Marsden was already on the *Ann*, on his way back to NSW (departed 25/8/1809; arrived 27/2/1810), his self-styled eulogiser felt safe to further polish the glow from Péron:

> This compliment is due to one of the most excellent characters of the day.—a character that seems expressly formed by Providence to produce a most beneficial change throughout not only the limited tract of New South Wales, but the vast extent of Australasia; to Christianize

---

88 [Evangelical Magazine], 'Account of the Rev. Samuel Marsden's Exertions'.
89 Sivasundaram, *Nature and the Godly Empire*, 150. He continued to be highly esteemed in English evangelical circles. For example, the *Evangelical Magazine 1811*, while reporting on 'the present state of evangelical religion in the islands of the Pacific', praised Johnson and Marsden; [Evangelical Magazine], 'A Concise View', 498–499. What was published reflected the esteem in which he was held by supporters; see the 'Report of the Leicester and Lancashire Association', *Missionary Register* 1815 [Jan], 10, which after lamenting the loss of Schwartz, Gericke, Martyn Brown, adds: 'but how base would be our pinings [?], when we have a Kolhoff, a Corrie, a Marsden, a Thomason, a Carey, and a Marshman still remaining …'.

and civilize the barbarians that constitute its original inhabitants and to re-Christianize and re-civilize the hordes of wretched culprits that are vomited by our prison-ships upon its shores. Our readers, we trust, will be pleased to become a little more acquainted with a man, who promises to flourish so fairly in future history; and, if the feelings of friendship should give somewhat too high a colouring to the sketch, they will at least admit, when they have perused it, that there is some apology for the excess. As for the subject of it he is now at too great a distance to be affected by any eulogy we can offer, or we should be compelled to silence.[90]

But it would only be a matter of time before this article would follow him for the consumption of others in the Colony. Obviously when it arrived, it rankled those less-disposed towards the Chaplain—those in the circles of Philo Free.[91]

The author

With the deliberate choice of pseudonymity, the author was not about to give himself away easily. Despite his self-description as 'a settler at Bradley's Head', nobody lived on that promontory on the northern side of Port Jackson.[92] It was where ships sat awaiting unlading or departure. By picturing himself as a 'settler' sitting in a ship's cabin, whether arriving or departing, Philo Free postures as one not really in the colony, able to report on its events with some detachment.

He identifies himself as both well-apprised of the Philanthropic Society at its foundation in 1813, and, by his 'we' and 'our', as a member of the 1817 group wondering where the money went (ll.8–9, 23–25; 30–36)—recognising that Mr Editor is a fellow subscriber with himself (ll. 63–64). He claims to be entirely happy with the work of mission in the South Seas, but not with the missionaries' trading activities, nor

---

90 [Eclectic Review], 'Art. I. *Voyage de Découvertes aux Terres Australes*', 988; [Evangelical Magazine], 'Account of the Rev. Samuel Marsden's Exertions', 498–499.
91 Other editions of the *Eclectic Review* may have also informed Philo Free. The *Eclectic Review* Jan to June 1812, for example, had an article, 'Despotism, or the Fall of the Jesuits', pp.584ff, as well as 'The Present State of the Moravian Missions', pp.621ff. This was not the last time that the *Eclectic Review* article would be used as a weapon against Marsden; see the rants of *The Monitor* 27/9/1827, 11 & 13/10/1828.
92 As noted by 'A Poor Scholar', *SG* 11/1/1817: 'The mysterious signature of Philo Free I pretend not to develop any more than the possibility of his living at Bradley's Head, where I am told there is neither house, hut, or cabin'.

with what he sees as the hypocrisy of their enterprise (ll.66–74) and finds this especially focused on their neglect of indigenous Australians (ll.74–77), of whose civilization he is a supporter (ll.81–89). Apparently along with other members of the Philanthropic Society, he wishes their subscription money to be put to this purpose instead (ll.91–106, 115–117).

However, despite the claimed support for the missionary cause, Philo Free seems impatient with the evangelical movement and especially with its 'worthy head' in the South Seas. The expressed support of this literary man may have been more for the work of 'civilization', especially to be wrought through schooling (see ll.82–117), but he was clearly impatient with the movement's prepossessing 'zeal'. In the same way that the zeal of Australia's early Chaplains opened them up to be criticized for being 'Methodists' (a label they wore with distinction),[93] it became usual for those critical of evangelical zeal to be impatient with both the Church Missionary Society and the Bible Society—[94] let alone the London Missionary Society because of its association with Dissenters. Philo Free mocked and misattributed the missionary zeal of his moving targets—a zeal for which Samuel Marsden was renowned.[95] To sting the evangelicals more sharply, he labelled their leader a 'Christian Mahomet', an arch-rival to Christian mission, and likened

---

[93] F. Grose wrote that Richard Johnson was 'one of the people called Methodists, a very troublesome, discontented character'; Grose to Dundas, 4/9/1793—Dundas was himself unimpressed with Methodists; see Metaxis, *Amazing Grace*, 200. T.F. Palmer applied the term to praise Johnson as 'a most dutiful son of the Church of England. [...] A Moravian Methodist. I believe him to be a very good, pious, inoffensive man'; T.F. Palmer to Lindsay, 15/9/1797. Similarly, Johnson praised his own dear Mary, as 'about ½ a Baptist and 1/2 a Methodist'; R. Johnson to Fricker, 30/5/1787, but, on the other hand, he wryly remarked that Chaplain James Bain, 'seems to be greatly caressed by our great ones, & I fancy is not suspected as being a Methodist'; R. Johnson to Fricker, 4/10/1791. After hearing just five Sundays of sermons, Major Edward Abbott expressed of William Cowper: 'I fear he is a Methodist'; Abbott to Piper, 18/9/1809. Macquarie's later invective against Marsden included a slur at his 'Methodistical Principles'; Macquarie to Bathurst, 7/10/1814. Yarwood, *Samuel Marsden: Survivor*, 37, 161. This long-standing prejudice was so strong that during his long campaign against slave-trading, even though someone like Hannah More retained the respect of her social class despite becoming known as 'the Queen of the Methodists', Wilberforce was cautious that his political moves should not be seen as 'Methodist'; see Metaxis, *Amazing Grace*, 82, 84.

[94] See, for example, Bishop Broughton's view that Rev. William Cowper would show 'a grain or two of warmer preference for Church principles over those of the Bible Society', W.G. Broughton to E. Coleridge, 14/2/1842; and the famous Protest to the formation of a branch of CMS in Bath made by the Archdeacon of Bath, Josiah Thomas, on 1st December 1817, but re-published in the *Sydney Gazette* in the following May, 'without any comment' (*SG* 23/5/1818).

[95] Josiah Thomas particularly disliked the 'zeal' apparent amongst the evangelicals, for it was used to separate 'serious Christians and Evangelical ministers' from others; *SG* 23/5/1818.

their zeal to that of the Jesuits, the arch-opponents of Reformation Protestantism.[96]

However, it was not a good time to launch such criticism in Sydney. Founded in 1804, the success of the British and Foreign Bible Society was applauded by the *Gazette* in September 1815:[97]

> Much exertion has been used in providing for the information of countries that were before unknown, except upon the general map, in those sacred works, which will remain for ever, and in those precious tenets which distinguish the Christian from the Savage, whose ferocity can alone be conquered by a just mode of thinking, and by a due appreciation of these precious truths which are communicated by the Gospel. It is strange as it is gratifying to observe, that in the short space of eleven years, the Holy Scriptures have been translated into almost the whole of the known languages of the Earth; and still more pleasing to reflect, that whensoever they obtain an introduction they are sought after with an avidity which is of itself sufficient to stamp their value with mankind.

The success of the British and Foreign Bible Society was updated in the *Missionary Register* in March 1816, which had probably arrived in NSW just before Philo Free put pen to paper, reporting (to 31/12/1815) 8 Auxiliaries in the United Kingdom, 38 in 'Foreign Parts', with printing in 63 different languages, and that year 114,000 Bibles and 139,600 Testaments being distributed, bringing the total distributions of the Society since its foundation to 1,787,879 Bibles and Testaments. In addition, in the eleven years of its existence, it had also given away an additional £108,247-8-5 and spent £348,593-13-6 ¾.[98] The British and Foreign School Society had also been recently formed (noted by Philo Free, ll.97–99).[99]

With this precedent, it is no surprise that the evangelicals of NSW were also moving towards setting up their own chapter to continue this work of God. Two issues after Philo Free, the *Gazette* reported that a shipment of Bibles and Testaments from the English Committee

---

96 Marsden's zeal for the missionary cause was patent to all. See, for example, the comment by LMS Missionaries to Directors, 21/10/1812, that Marsden 'manifested an ardent zeal for the success of the Mission, and a hearty readiness to serve its interests'.
97 *SG* 30/9/1815.
98 'British & Foreign Bible Society', *Missionary Register 1816*, 92–95.
99 'British & Foreign School Society', *Missionary Register 1816*, 99–100.

had already arrived, consigned to the Governor who entrusted them to clergymen Marsden, Cowper, and Cartwright for distribution to anyone in the Colony who wished to avail themselves of the gift, in order to gain 'the inestimable Benefits of a full Knowledge of the Holy Scriptures'.[100] Was it the projected formation of a Bible and Book Society that, at least in part, galled Philo Free? Another evangelical society to take his money? Another collection of books which, like the Lending Library, may simply go astray?

Although he clearly missed the satirical intents of this author with literary pretensions, it didn't take long for Samuel Marsden to see himself as victim and to suspect that this Philanthropic Society member, who hated the hypocrisy of missionary trade and fame, and loved the local natives, was the Governor's Secretary, J.T. Campbell. He quickly set the legal machinery in motion.

At the Criminal trial in October, Frederick Garling defended Campbell by arguing that the letter, not proven to be written by his client, was a 'free discussion serviceable to religious and moral subjects' and that its 'animadversion is not upon persons but upon Acts, not necessarily charged upon any Individual'. Even though he admits that 'the author treats the matter with raillery and sarcasm, and perhaps the work is felt the more by the prosecutor', 'the author seems desirous of doing some good'.[101]

Despite Garling's defence, however, J.T. Campbell's adventure in political satire was beginning to be wrecked on the rocks of legalities:

> The Court determined and adjudged That the Defendant was Guilty of having permitted a public Letter to be printed in the *Sydney Gazette*, which tends to vilify the public Conduct of Mr Marsden, the Prosecutor, as the Agent of the Missionary Society for propagating the Gospel to the South Seas, and which it was in the power of the Defendant in his official Capacity, as Secretary to His Excellency The Governor of this Territory, to have prevented the publication of.[102]

---

100 General and Government Order, *SG* 18/1/1817.
101 F. Garling for the Defendant, 23/10/1817, Wylde, Minutes [Criminal Trial], 470, 471.
102 Decision of Criminal Trial, 23/10/1817, Wylde, Minutes [Criminal Trial], 472. Wylde also notes that on 29/10/1817 W.H. Moore chose 'not to move the Court for Judgement on the Defendant', due to Marsden's plan to 'bring an Action for Damages in the Civil Court', and so the Defendant was given leave to be discharged.

Once tried again in the Civil court in December, its stronger judgement found J.T. Campbell to be the author of the letter signed 'Philo Free'. By March 1819 Government intervention had wrested from him an almost apology.[103] His pseudonymous literary exercise had earned him fame, but perhaps not the kind of fame he had longed for. He went down in history as the perpetrator of Australia's first legally proven libel.

---

103 J.T. Campbell to Macquarie, 31/3/1819.

CHAPTER 2

MARSDEN IN THE HANDS OF AUSTRALASIAN HISTORIANS

David B. Pettett

For over two centuries, those who have written about the Rev Samuel Marsden can generally be divided into two very different camps. There are those who want to emphasise the 'Flogging Parson' and see a vengeful cleric, neglecting his duties and being more concerned about his own wealth and reputation than the souls of convicts and Aboriginals. Then there are those who see his evangelical faith and his mission to the New Zealand Māori, and believe the man could do no wrong as he struggled in the darkest corner of the Lord's vineyard to bring the gospel of Jesus Christ to an evil and adulterous generation. Not all these authors have addressed the issues surrounding the Philo Free case and some, notably those who are Marsden supporters, have passed over the case with scant attention. For example, Marsden biographer of the early twentieth century, the Rev S. M. Johnstone, devoted just seven pages of his 242-page volume to the issue.[1]

Among modern authors who are negative towards Marsden is the Australian historian Robert Hughes, author of *The Fatal Shore*.[2] Hughes' focus is larger than Marsden but when he writes of him Hughes reveals much of his own prejudices against evangelical Christians. Hughes describes Marsden as, 'a grasping Evangelical missionary with heavy shoulders and the face of a petulant ox'. He declares that Marsden's

---

1 Johnstone, *Samuel Marsden*. See pp. 143–149 for Johnstone's comments on the Philo Free case.
2 Hughes, *The Fatal Shore*.

'hatred for the Irish Catholic convicts knew no bounds. It spilled into his sermons'.[3] However, a close examination of all the extant copies of Marsden's sermons reveals that he makes no direct reference at all to the Irish or to Catholics in any sermon.[4]

Marsden's critics, almost without exception, fall into the camp of those who do not understand, or who oppose, the evangelical agenda of Christian mission. These opponents include Bill Wannan who has a somewhat questionable definition of a 'religious man'.[5] Quinn in *Altar Ego* clearly and vehemently opposes an evangelical agenda and, it would seem, anyone who opposes Irish Catholics.[6] There are also those authors who have accepted, unquestioningly, a negative reputation of Marsden. In her book on early Sydney, Grace Karskens shows herself to be such a scholar.[7] For example, when speaking about women and farmers, while not referencing Marsden, Karskens is in remarkable agreement with a number of things he has said. But when she does refer to Marsden directly her comments are invariably negative. For example, she describes Marsden as 'uncompromising' in his dealings with the Aboriginal people and writes that Governor King and Marsden 'exploited' 'probable' tribal hostilities.[8] Karskens does not mention the Philo Free case in her book.

Quinn seems intent on destroying Marsden's reputation in New Zealand as the Apostle to the Māori. In his book *Samuel Marsden: Altar Ego*, he tries to paint Marsden as 'evil and corrupt' in his dealings with both the Māori and the missionaries he supervised there.[9] Quinn is

3   Hughes, *Fatal Shore*, 187.
4   In various collections around the world there are 135 sermons. There are 98 in the Moore Theological College collection in Sydney. There 25 in the Family Collection, held by the Rev Samuel Marsden who has retired with his wife Mary to Cornwall, U.K. The remainder are scattered in ones and twos in various libraries and archives in Australia and New Zealand. Mitchell Library in Sydney holds five sermons in all. However, the Library's record: Call Number: MAV / FM4 / 10844 a little misleadingly refers to this record as 'sermons of Samuel Marsden and others'. Rather than being Marsden's actual sermons, they are notes written by others as they have listened to the sermons delivered by Marsden.
5   Wannan's original book published in 1962 had the title: *Very Strange Tales: The Turbulent Times of Samuel Marsden*. This was republished in 1972 as: *Early Colonial Scandals: The Turbulent Times of Samuel Marsden*. In this later edition Wannan declares that, 'In the final analysis, Marsden was not a deeply religious man', 178.
6   For example, in speaking of Marsden Quinn says, 'His relentless pursuit of Irish conspiracies was atavistic: blind, unreasoning hatred', *Samuel Marsden*, 25.
7   Karskens, *The Colony*.
8   Karskens, *The Colony*, 488–489.
9   Quinn, *Samuel Marsden*, 184.

described in his book as 'New Zealand's foremost expert in Crown Lynn pottery'. Quinn is apparently no historian and interprets Marsden with a historiography informed by his own clear prejudices, constantly applying twenty-first century values and understanding to early nineteenth century incidents. In the Epilogue to this book Quinn again turns from the area of his own expertise and becomes a psychologist, diagnosing Marsden as a psychopath.[10] It is hard to take this work seriously but it highlights the fact that there are still those today who fixate on one side or the other when it comes to Samuel Marsden. It further highlights that in the tradition of Marsden interpretation some scholars have accepted a negative evaluation of Marsden without any further investigation.

Quinn shows his lack of scholarship when he says, 'SM won two libel cases for the *Philo Free* letter'[11] misunderstanding that the first trial, which found against Campbell, was not a civil case of libel but a criminal case. On almost every page of his book Quinn spits bile, happy to show his contempt and hatred of Marsden and his work. He points out that Campbell's lawyer, Garling, wanted to call some of the New Zealand missionaries as witnesses to the civil trial. Because of the inevitable delays this would cause, Garling's motion was denied but Quinn declares, 'Had Garling cross examined the missionaries—and he should have—the whole rotten Pacific mission edifice would have collapsed'.[12]

In the historiography of research on Marsden, Quinn sits at the end

---

10   Quinn, *Samuel Marsden*, 171–174. Despite protesting that, 'I am no psychologist and may not label SM a psychopath. I have not.' (p. 174), over these four pages Quinn tells us how he has consulted psychologists and learned from them the traits of the psychopathic personality. Donald W. Black in *Bad Boys, Bad Men: Confronting Antisocial Personality Disorder (Sociopathy)* confirms this understanding of psychopathy when he says, 'Self-interest is a natural component of the human makeup, but it is especially strong in antisocials and leaves many of them unable to develop full compassion, conscience, and other attributes that make for successful social relations' (p. 144). Quinn uses this to show that Marsden fits the definition. For example, 'Full-blown psychopaths lack empathy'. But Quinn goes too far in applying this understanding to Marsden by adding, 'This lack [of empathy] was one of the most obvious features of SM's life' (p. 172). On the contrary, there are many instances in Marsden's sermons that show compassion for his people. In speaking of the sins he condemns, Marsden's language is often inclusive, an indication of his pastoral concern. His heartfelt compassion for those in the Colony, who had entered bigamous marriages, having left a spouse in England, is palpable in his evidence at the Bigge Enquiry. See Marsden's evidence to the Bigge Enquiry, 27/12/1820.
11   Quinn, *Samuel Marsden*, 92.
12   Quinn, *Samuel Marsden*, 93.

of a line of secular writers whose tendency is to minimise the place and influence of people of Christian faith. Added to this there are those who hold some prejudice against Marsden where he has taken a stand opposite to one they may hold.

Refreshingly, one of the latest books to be published on Marsden is by an author who, while not sharing Marsden's Christian faith, has written a well-balanced biography. A New Zealander living in London, Andrew Sharp, spent eight years researching his new biography on Marsden, *The World, the Flesh & the Devil*. He deals extensively with the Philo Free case, concluding that, 'The first Philo Free trial revealed as much about New South Wales society as about Marsden'.[13] Sharp argues that the case highlighted the issue of men (for it was only men who featured in this whole episode) vying for power and status according to their position in society. In the end, Sharp concludes that all of Marsden's and Macquarie's letter writing and publishing in defence of their own character and conduct has done justice to neither of them.

There are those among Marsden's biographers who have written hagiography and can see no wrong in the man. Without exception, these biographers are writers who hold the same evangelical faith as Marsden and have written in the late nineteenth and early twentieth centuries. J.B. Marsden, not a relative, was an Anglican cleric of the late nineteenth century who has written on Marsden as well as on the Puritans, and on the Rev. Hugh Stowell (1799–1865), another Anglican cleric who was Rector of Christ Church, Salford in the U.K. in the mid-1800s. While J.B. Marsden describes Marsden as a man 'who, in the simplicity of his faith as well as in zeal and self-denying labours, was truly an apostolic man',[14] he is also conscious of the danger of eulogising his subject too far.[15]

Later historians and scholars who might share Marsden's evangelical position seem to approach the balance Marsden's biographer A. T. Yarwood hoped for. In the preface to *Samuel Marsden: The Great Survivor*, Yarwood says that he 'became sharply aware of the dichotomy' of 'two separate and conflicting traditions' around Marsden:

---

13 Sharp, *The World, the Flesh and the Devil*, 446.
14 S. Marsden & J.B. Marsden, *Life and Labours*, 1. See also the version edited by James Drummond, *Life and Work of Samuel Marsden*.
15 Marsden, *Memoirs*, 280.

one based on his image as the "Apostle to the Māori", the other drawn from contemporary writers in New South Wales such as Campbell, Macquarie, Wentworth and Lang, who execrated him as the opponent of a humane and liberal governor, a cruel magistrate, and a self-seeking materialist who neglected the Australian Aborigines and who concentrated on Polynesian evangelism because this was supposed to offer him rich prospects of trade "cloaked under a surplice".

While declaring that he, 'At no stage [...] regarded myself as an apologist for Marsden', Yarwood then says:

> It will be a sufficient reward if my book succeeds in linking this colonial churchman to his English origins and confronting the upholders of the two simplistic traditions with the flawed but satisfying reality of what I take to be the true Samuel Marsden.[16]

Here Yarwood is not trying to rescue Marsden's reputation, but is holding to a hope that there will be less polarisation and more balance in studies and comments on Marsden. Unfortunately, this balance is still not seen in many who do not side with or understand evangelical Christianity. For the most part they continue to write negatively about Marsden and fail to understand his background and motivations.[17]

Yarwood also published an article in which he speaks of Marsden in mostly positive terms.[18] He does, however, state in this article that he thinks Marsden made a 'disastrous' decision in becoming a magistrate. Certainly, had Marsden not taken on this role he would not be known today as the 'Flogging Parson'.

In his biography of Marsden, Yarwood devotes a whole chapter to Philo Free. He believes that Macquarie and Campbell continued to obstruct Marsden for which he had, 'good cause for complaining to private friends in England about secret obstructions and persecution from senior members of the administration'. He describes Macquarie as being, 'Obsessed with self-justification' and as having lost all sense of

---

16 Yarwood, *Samuel Marsden: Survivor*, xi-xii. For a good summary of his longer biography, see 'Marsden, Samuel (1765–1838)'.
17 These writers include: Belich, *Making Peoples*; Ellis, *Lachlan Macquarie*; Hughes, *The Fatal Shore*; Jones & Jenkins, *Words between Us*; Karskens, *The Colony*; McDonald, *The Ballard of Desmond Kale* (While this book is a work of fiction the lead character is an undisguised portrayal of Marsden who returns to the colony as a convict); Quinn, *Samuel Marsden*; Salt, *These Outcast Women*; Smith, *Australia's Birthstain*.
18 Yarwood, 'The Missionary Marsden'.

objectivity, 'being incapable of rational judgement or fairness towards the parson'.[19] Yarwood further surmises that Macquarie and Campbell must have privately discussed Marsden's opposition and strategized against him. He believes Macquarie must have been fully aware from the outset that Campbell was the author of the Philo Free letter.

The larger issue, however, was not Marsden's reputation as he instigated legal proceedings of libel against Campbell. The cause and reputation of the missionary efforts in the South Pacific were issues of far more serious import than one man's reputation. Yarwood notes that following the court cases, Marsden considered leaving the colony, but was sustained, 'by faith in the rectitude of his cause'. Yet sustenance came not only from his own faith but also from a group of LMS supporters who expressed the hope that the legal victories, 'would help in overcoming the "dreadful spirit of hostility against the Missionaries"'. They also praised Marsden for, 'saving their cause from "serious and lasting Injury"'.[20] While Marsden may have suffered personal stress, the LMS supporters believed the victory was more significant for the ongoing mission to the South Seas.

There are many published works supportive of Marsden. The earlier examples tend to be hagiographies which can be unhelpful. Cyril Davey, a man of evangelical persuasion has written many short books on prominent Christian figures, including Martin Luther, John Wesley, Gladys Aylward (a missionary to China), Florence Nightingale, Mother Teresa and another English missionary to China, Hudson Taylor, who founded the China Inland Mission. Another book by Davey is about the Japanese Christian social reformer, author, and leader of labour and democratic movements, Toyohiko Kagawa. Davey has written of Marsden in *Chief of Chiefs*.[21] It is short at only 32 pages and as the title indicates is a book that speaks highly of Marsden. It falls into the category of hagiography along with J.B. Marsden's work mentioned earlier, as well as several books by A. H. Reed,[22] T.R. Seddon's book on several *Saints and Heroes of our own Day*[23] and Alexander Williamson's

---

19 Yarwood, *Samuel Marsden: Survivor*, 199.
20 Yarwood, *Samuel Marsden: Survivor*, 200.
21 Davey, *Chief of Chiefs*.
22 Reed, *First New Zealand Christmases*; *Samuel Marsden, Pioneer and Peacemaker*; and, *Samuel Marsden: Greatheart of Maoriland*.
23 Seddon, *Saints and Heroes of Our Own Days*.

Samuel Marsden, the Apostle of New Zealand.[24] Pekenham Walsh in *Modern Heroes of the Mission Field* is typical of these hagiographers with statements like, 'We can well imagine with what earnestness the vigorous and devoted man of God pleaded the cause of his *protégés* with the committee of the Church Missionary Society' and 'such was the first entrance of the Gospel into New Zealand, and such the heroic man who gained that entrance for it, no less by his kindness than by his courage'.[25] These words of high praise have more to do with promoting a certain style of Christian piety than any real historical research and therefore give us little insight into the difficult issues surrounding Philo Free.

A continuing interest in Marsden is evidenced in an increasing number of journal articles and theses. Most of these try to promote a more positive, but balanced image. It seems that those who are interested in Marsden today are mostly from an evangelical background. Meredith Lake is a modern scholar whose research interests include the history of student evangelicalism and faith-based charity in the twentieth century. Her writing on Marsden is balanced. She does however argue that he gained personal satisfaction more from his agricultural activities than those of a more spiritual nature.[26] Her writings include a chapter in a book on colonial missionaries which makes a small contribution on Marsden and another chapter in a book dealing with Marsden's mission to New Zealand in which she speaks of Marsden's benevolence to the 'poor heathen'.[27] Lake's PhD dissertation on colonisation discusses Marsden in two chapters.[28] She understands the Protestant piety of not driving a great wedge between the sacred and the secular but applies this concept too completely to Marsden when she says 'he found affirmation of his calling [to ministry …] in the material rewards of his worldly toil'.[29] Certainly Marsden believed that his material prosperity was God's blessing, but to say that he regarded this as affirmation of his ministry is a step beyond which Marsden himself would go.

Equally unpersuasive is the view expressed by Grace Karskens that,

---

24 Williamson, *Samuel Marsden*, 125, 134.
25 Walsh, *Modern Heroes of the Mission Field*, 124, 134.
26 Lake, 'Samuel Marsden, Work and the Limits of Evangelical Humanitarianism'.
27 Lake, 'Salvation and Conciliation'; '"Promoting the welfare of these poor heathens"'.
28 Lake, 'Such Spiritual Acres'. See Chapter Four: 'An Agricultural Imagination, Samuel Marsden's cultivation of soils and souls' (pp. 121–156); and Chapter Five: 'Inducing Industrious Habits, Samuel Marsden's attitudes to convicts and Aborigines' (pp. 157–190).
29 Lake, 'Such Spiritual Acres', 155.

with little apparent success in his preaching, Marsden 'threw himself instead into farming, stock raising and the study of the nature and soil of the colony'. Karskens concludes that 'Marsden found farming more interesting than preaching'.[30] A reading of Marsden's sermons, however, shows that Marsden regarded preaching as his most important work and that the results were not up to him but to God.

Surprisingly, Marsden has some unwitting support from Karskens on two significant issues. Marsden suffers today for his criticism of 'wayward' women and his attitude towards them. Karskens shares this wariness of convict women, and their ability to lure men to their ruin. She writes approvingly of the concerns held by the authorities over the behaviour of these women. She says, 'Men in authority were wary of convict women too, because of their power to seduce soldiers away from their duty and sailors from their ships'.[31]

Karskens also gives unconscious support to Marsden regarding the indolence of farmers. In notes he wrote about the soil of the Hawkesbury region Marsden complained about the lack of industry amongst the farmers. And yet Marsden was not alone in his negative evaluation. Karskens does not attack the parson for his derogatory comments about these indolent farmers. She does not seem to be aware that Marsden recorded this assessment. Rather, Karskens notes that the image of early farmers in the colony as 'hopeless, inept, lazy, sinfully wasteful' came from observations of visitors to the colony.[32] These issues highlight the practice among some authors who have accepted a negative evaluation of Marsden without further investigation. In Karskens' case, she has said the same things Marsden said (and got into trouble for saying) but she seems to be unaware of her agreement with Marsden. When she speaks of him directly, she speaks of him, his attitudes and his activities, negatively.

Lorraine Ratcliffe's M.A. thesis on Philo Free also tends to be negative towards Marsden and critical of Yarwood's treatment of the Philo Free case. She sees Marsden as the aggressor and Macquarie as somewhat the victim. 'Marsden imposed his protestations on a variety

---

30 Karskens, *The Colony*, 140.
31 Karskens, *The Colony*, 318.
32 Karskens, *The Colony*, 115.

of influential friends, while Macquarie remained relatively taciturn'.[33] Ratcliffe believes Marsden was simply concerned for power. '[H]e wanted to appear to be at the helm of decision-making, on an equal footing with the governor'.[34] Her interpretation of his motivations is very different to that of Yarwood. 'What Yarwood admires as Marsden's "remarkable capacity for evoking and maintaining warm, devoted affection and admiration from a wide circle of friends" was, in fact, a form of manipulation over correspondents'.[35] She brings the dispute down to a power struggle between Marsden and Macquarie seeing it as a 'public contest of personal authority' where 'Macquarie found himself in the eye of the storm over privileges he extended to emancipists, while Marsden strove for the public respect he regarded as his entitlement'.[36] She believes neither man 'emerged socially unscathed' from this dispute but that the ultimate winners were the emancipists who 'benefited mostly from the transferral of the Philo Free conflict to England, as it provided them with opportunities of asserting their claims for political power and equal status'.[37]

Two other significant theses are worthy of note. In her M.Litt. thesis Jan White argues for a more nuanced understanding of the colonial clergy. She argues that they were not simply men out of touch with their flocks. They were not men who simply administered a rule of law and church but were unable to meaningfully engage the attention of their people.[38] In an M.A. thesis from 1939 William Menzies Robb argued that Marsden was just the right man for the chaplaincy to which he was appointed.[39] Whether or not Marsden was the right man for the Colony of New South Wales, he fulfilled the purposes of his evangelical backers in having a vision for taking the gospel to the people of the South Seas.

The origins of the epithet, 'Flogging Parson', are obscure. White, after noting that 'the Evangelical clergy of early New South Wales have not fared well at the hands of posterity', goes on to say that Australian

---

33 Ratcliffe, '"Pens Dipped in Gall"', 10.
34 Ratcliffe, '"Pens Dipped in Gall"', 11.
35 Ratcliffe, '"Pens Dipped in Gall"', 14.
36 Ratcliffe, '"Pens Dipped in Gall"', 66.
37 Ratcliffe, '"Pens Dipped in Gall"', 69.
38 White, 'A Master and his Men'.
39 Robb, 'The Reverend Samuel Marsden, pioneer'.

historians, 'led by Ellis, Ward, and Manning Clark, have tended to accept criticisms of Marsden from his contemporaries at face value, and to ignore the more positive assessments that are also extant'.[40] In particular, White notes that the appellation 'the flogging parson' was first coined by Ward as late as 1958, although it was said of Marsden by his contemporaries that, 'He sentences the prisoner on Saturday, admonishes him from the pulpit on Sunday, and flogs him on Monday'.[41]

It seems that almost any modern scholar writing about colonial times cannot help but have a swipe at Marsden even where his deeds do not have a prominent place in their work. One such recent work is *Girt: The Unauthorised History of Australia* by David Hunt. Hunt takes all the stereotypes of Marsden and replays them, even tipping his hat to Robert Hughes' description when he paints Marsden as a man, 'With a ruddy face, piggy snout, melon-shaped head and the strength of an ox on steroids'. Hunt also mistakenly believes that in his role as a magistrate Marsden was, 'rapidly earning himself the nickname of the Flogging Parson'.[42]

One recent work that generally manages to avoid the stereotypes and present Marsden with a refreshingly balanced depiction, while acknowledging his very different reputations on both sides of the Tasman, is Rachel Standfield's *Race and Identity in the Tasman World, 1769-1840*. In discussing Philo Free, however, Standfield does play to the stereotype of Marsden as being implacably opposed to Aboriginal people. With regard to the evangelical imperative of evangelising native peoples, Standfield asks the question, 'why Marsden did not feel he could satisfy what evangelicals considered an imperative, rather than an impulse, amongst the indigenous population of New South Wales'.[43] Standfield refers to Bishop Thomas Wilson's essay prepared for the evangelisation of North American natives, copies of which were brought to New South Wales on the First Fleet, in the hope of making sense of Marsden's lack of imperative amongst the Eora people. Based on the ideas in Wilson's essay Standfield concludes, 'Marsden

---

40 White, 'A Master and his Men', vi, 13.
41 This saying is anecdotally attributed to the early 1800s and probably follows the flogging of Paddy Galvin, an Irish convict sentenced by Marsden and Richard Atkins to daily flogging until he gave up the hiding place of weapons he was alleged to have hidden.
42 Hunt, *Girt*, 161.
43 Standfield, *Race and Identity*, 103.

saw one people who he thought tractable and ready for civilization and Christianity, and another population who he felt would be incorporated into the lowest roles in British society, and where religion might help resign them to their fate'.[44] She also believes that Marsden, even after the reprimand of the Philo Free letter and its subsequent court cases, maintained a 'disgust at Aboriginal people'.[45] And yet, if she had read Marsden's sermons, Standfield would not have seen 'disgust' but, rather, a high regard for Aboriginal people being expressed by Marsden. In Sermon 81 of the Moore College collection of Marsden's sermons, Marsden declares that the 'natives of this colony' are morally superior to the convicts whom he described in the same sentence as 'men of wicked and abandoned character'.[46] Marsden's sermons also give a more specific understanding of his strategic thinking on the issue of evangelisation of the local Aboriginal people and why he turned more evangelistic effort towards New Zealand.

This review of Marsden in the hands of Australasian historians and authors highlights the fact that Marsden remains a controversial figure. Many writers still, uncritically accept a negative assessment of Marsden and write unthinkingly, perpetuating the stereotypes. These authors tend to be those who do not share Marsden's evangelical faith. The older writers who do share this faith have tended to write in terms far too glowing and have glossed over the more difficult issues. In more recent times, with some exceptions, both those who share and those who do not share Marsden's Christian convictions and imperatives of mission, are presenting a more balanced picture of the man and his times.

---

44 Standfield, *Race and Identity*, 105.
45 Standfield, *Race and Identity*, 134.
46 Sermon 81, Moore College Collection. This sermon is based on the Bible text Hebrews 11:19. In it Marsden uses some very direct address to his congregation about their lives and the negative impact their 'vices' have on their own children.

CHAPTER 3

'...SO IMPORTANT IN ITS NATURE, SO DIFFICULT IN ITS EXECUTION, AND SO DOUBTFUL IN ITS RESULT...'[1]

The Mission to the South Seas from 1786 to 1830

Joel Atwood

Although Marsden has received his due in most things, his biographers have not always acknowledged that it was his direction and policies which most influenced the Church, London, and Wesleyan Missionary Societies in the South Seas until 1826.[2]

While the Philo Free case is of great legal importance in and of itself, it is remarkable to notice the context in which the court decided the libel was committed: 'The verdict in this instance pronounced the defendant guilty of having permitted the printing of a letter in the *Sydney Gazette*, tending to vilify the public conduct of the Prosecutor, not in his clerical or magisterial capacities, *but as the Agent for the Missionary Societies for propagating the Gospel in the South Sees*' [sic.].[3] Given the significance attributed to Marsden's involvement in global mission, this chapter will paint the backdrop to the Philo Free

---

1 Joseph Hardcastle (the Treasurer) on behalf of the Directors of the London Missionary Society to Samuel Marsden; LMS to S. Marsden, 15/9/1802.
2 Gunson, *Messengers of Grace*, 12.
3 SG 1/11/1817, emphasis added. All spelling within quotations is reproduced verbatim, including non-standard capitalisation.

case by sketching the history of the South Sea missions from the foundation of the Australian colony through the establishment of Marsden's outreach in New Zealand.[4]

1. The Explorers—Quiros to Cook

The story of missionary involvement in the South Pacific begins a great deal further back than Port Jackson, and, oddly enough, in Spain. Pedro Fernandez de Quiros, having encountered the Solomon Islands in a previous Spanish exploration of the South Pacific, petitioned Pope Clement VIII and Philip III of Spain for three years before being commissioned to return and continue the explorations in 1603.[5] He embarked in 1606 along with one hundred and thirty men and six Catholic priests. In his travels, he would likely sight Tahiti for the first time, and also stumble upon the northern tip of Vanuatu's largest island. Thinking it to be the long-sought great south continent, they named it *Terra Australis del Espiritu Santo*.[6] Quiros rather optimistically built a wooden settlement and declared it, 'Nuova Jerusalema'. This new Jerusalem was not as peaceful as its biblical namesake, as the sailors ended up in frequent and violent conflict with the communities of Big Bay. Despite this, Quiros insisted upon the spiritual significance of the land, conducted Mass, and even appointed knights and administrators for this outpost of Spain. The crew grew weary of the danger, and while Quiros slept in his cabin, his men sailed the ship out of port. Before Quiros could recover his pride and begin again, Spain was supplanted in their explorations of the South Pacific by the Dutch, British, and French fleets. The archipelago would wait 162 years before their next contact with these pale strangers and their strange religion as Louis Antoine de Bougainville began to map the islands for the French, followed closely by Captain James Cook on behalf of the British Empire.[7]

---

4   Given the focus of our volume, primacy of space will be given to the missions in Tahiti and New Zealand rather than in Tonga, the Cook Islands, or eventually, Melanesia.
5   Garrett seems a little too confident of the missionary nature of this enterprise, Garrett, *To Live Among the Stars*, 1. Quiros' own motives are difficult to ascertain, although in the royal commission the king cites the following as the grounds for his successful petition: 'the service of God and my [the king's] service, and the conversion of these people [of the Pacific] to our holy faith, and the good that might accrue from the discoveries', Quiros, *The Voyages*, 168. See further extracts from the various orders surrounding his mission in Quiros, *The Voyages*, 168–172.
6   Four centuries on it is still known as 'Espiritu Santo', or more commonly, 'Santo'.
7   MacClancy, *To Kill A Bird with Two Stones*, 36–37.

2. The Chaplain—Richard Johnson
2.1 First Minister of the New Continent

Cook's journey covered much of what we would now consider the South Pacific, arriving at Tahiti on April 13, 1769, and spending some months prior to sailing south-west in search of *Terra Australis*, and made it as far south as to chart the coast of New Zealand before reaching south-east Australia in mid-April the next year. During his 1769 trip, Cook expressed doubt about Western involvement in the South Pacific islands, noting that,

> it is very unlikely, that any measure of this kind should ever be seriously thought of, as it can neither serve the purposes of public ambition, nor of private avarice; and, without such inducements, I may pronounce, that it will never be undertaken.[8]

Cook was mistaken. Tahiti became an early point of contact for Europeans with Polynesia, including a five-month stay by William Bligh and his ill-fated breadfruit expedition on the *Bounty* in 1789.[9] The information he gathered would later prove further incitement for the London Missionary Society founder, Thomas Haweis, to pursue the South Pacific as the Society's first destination.[10] The British Empire would also pursue the idea of a far-southern colony, making preparations for the First Fleet to sail for Botany Bay. To accompany them for spiritual guidance and counsel was to be the first Antipodean clergyman—Richard Johnson. For a time the story spread of Johnson being a last-minute (or even night-before) appointment when the Eclectic Society realised their oversight. However, Johnson was approached by John Newton and later William Wilberforce in mid-1786, and after much anxiety appointed as 'Chaplain of the settlement' of New South Wales as early as October 24, 1786.[11]

---

8   Cook, *Voyage to the Pacific Ocean*, 2:77.
9   Shaw, 'Bligh, William (1754–1817)'.
10 Bligh's wife, Betsy, is said to have been a fervent Evangelical of Lady Huntingdon's circle, Garrett, *A Way in the Sea*, 3. For the sake of consistency, and despite their several changes of name that will be listed in time, 'The Missionary Society' will be referred to purely as the LMS or 'the Society' throughout; the *Church* Missionary Society will be referred to by its full name or as the CMS.
11 Cable lists the date as 1784, which seems odd given that Johnson was not ordained until 1786, Cable, 'Johnson, Richard (1753–1827)'. See the excerpts from Newton and Wilberforce's correspondence in Schwarze, 'Richard Johnson and Samuel Marsden', 7, and a brief but helpful glimpse of the background British politics in Mason, *The Moravian Church*, 78–79.

Departing with the First Fleet of convicts and soldiers, Johnson brought with him literature to aid in his task, a 'large number of religious books and tracts' from the Society for the Propagation of the Gospel in Foreign Parts (SPG) and the Society for the Promotion of Christian Knowledge (SPCK).[12] After a chaotic first Sunday, the first official church service on Australian soil was conducted on February 3, 1788, with the full complement of officers and convicts present.[13] Beset with erratic health, Johnson struggled to make inroads with the spiritual lives of the convicts. He is often contrasted with the much more robust and vigorous Marsden who would be sent as second chaplain, and rarely in a positive light.[14] While few would count a fleet of convicts forced to the other side of the planet an easy congregation, Johnson must be credited with thinking beyond the colony and developing an early tenderness towards the indigenous Australian communities near to him, even exploring with 'our great ones' in England the possibility of sending out missionaries specifically to begin work in reaching them.[15]

One of Johnson's last acts before returning to England was the reception of the missionaries fleeing Tahiti. However close he would later become to Marsden, Rowland Hassall fondly remembered his year with Johnson, and mourned the departure of his 'mother and father [...] and] good friend'.[16]

---

12 Cable, 'Johnson, Richard (1753–1827)'. Mackaness gives some sense of what Johnson (or the SPCK/SPG) saw as the primary needs of his flock, enumerating these resources as 4,200 books including 200 copies of *Exercises Against Lying*; 50 *Caution to Swearer*, 100 *Exhortations to Chastity*, and 10 *Dissuasions from Stealing* as well as Bibles, portions of Scripture, Prayerbooks, and Catechisms; Johnson, *Some Letters of Rev. Richard Johnson*, chap .1.
13 We are told by Lt. Ralph Clark that the teaching was on Ps 116:12, 'What shall I render unto the Lord for all his benefits towards me?' and it was a 'very good sermon', Clark, 'Journal Kept on the *Friendship*'.
14 Take, for example, one CMS history which gives no mention of Johnson's many years of service prior to and alongside Marsden, his battles with ill-health, and what he did manage to achieve in a difficult context, but rather simply states that he 'proved unequal to the post, and returned home', Hole, *The Early History of the CMS*, 6–7.
15 Johnson to Fricker, 18/3/1791. While tempting to compare this with the emotions of the first Philo Free letter and its plea for introducing 'civilisation; and the pure doctrines of the Christian religion among the sable sons of Australia', that would be to ignore the polemics of the 1817 letter. While hardly provable, there is also something charming in Yarwood's estimation that the emotion of Philo Free may simply reflect the heatwave Sydney was experiencing until 7th Jan, 1817; Yarwood, *Samuel Marsden: Survivor*, 195.
16 Bonwick, *Australia's First Preacher*, 138.

2.2 Chaplain or Missionary?

While Johnson has received his fair share of criticism for his ill-health and striking contrast with the vivacity and boldness of his successor, it must be remembered in a history of South Sea missions that he was himself commissioned *as a missionary*. Prior to the Eclectic Society's discussion of 'the best method of Planting and Propagating the Gospel in Botany Bay', Newton had already asked Johnson if he possessed 'the spirit of a missionary', which, it seemed, he did, for after a bout of insomnia over the invitation to be chaplain of this fledgling colony, Johnson accepted due to the 'propriety, nay, the necessity of some person going out in that capacity'.[17] This seems a fairly novel development in an era when 'chaplain' and 'missionary' were treated as distinct categories. The SPG (founded in 1701) and the SPCK (founded in 1698) were the main Church of England organisations for overseas work, and while not in ideal shape to capitalise on the new lands opened up by British explorers, had already confined its work to providing clergy for the colonies and dependencies of Great Britain, literature, and education to aid in their care of settlers.[18] It was only a number of decades after Johnson's departure that Thomas Scott of the Eclectic Society (and later the Church Missionary Society) would articulate this unspoken division by describing the work of the chaplain being the care of a converted colony, whereas a missionary was primarily concerned with going 'where Christ has not been named'.[19] Perhaps due to the pioneer nature of the geography, or the generally-agreed upon degenerate state of those accompanying him, or even perhaps with ultimate aims to use the colony as a spearhead into work amongst the indigenous peoples of this new continent, Johnson was sent and self-identified as a kind of missionary-chaplain, combining Newton's 'missionary spirit' with the expectations of establishment church ministry placed upon him by the

---

17 See the memoirs dated 16/4/1794, in Moore, Marsden, and Johnson, 'Papers of Richard Johnson and Samuel Marsden [M677]', cited in Schwarze, 'Richard Johnson and Samuel Marsden', 7–8.
18 Stock, *One Hundred Years*, 3. One notable exception to this was the lay missionary in Bengal, J. L. Kiernander, supported by SPCK, who began work in 1758, see Hole, *The Early History of the CMS*, 2.
19 Scott, 'Address to Missionaries', 125. Johnson is reported as having asked the Moravian Brethren to 'pray for him that he may be a blessing both to convicts and savages', Mason, *The Moravian Church*, 80.

British government.[20]

2.3 The Moravian Influence

The shape of Johnson's work can likely be traced to the influence of one of the only contemporary models of mission work available to him—the *Unitas Fratrum*, or Moravian Church.[21] Not only was the Wesleyan strand of the evangelical revival strongly shaped by this group—and so the ecclesiastical milieu of many of the key figures in this account—Johnson himself and his immediate circle appear to have been directly influenced by them.[22] Both Johnson and Marsden were subscribers to the Moravian magazine, 'Periodical Accounts', as were many of the luminaries of the Eclectic Society involved in the foundation of the LMS and CMS such as Newton, Pratt, Thornton, and Wilberforce.[23] Beyond this was a great network of 'personal contact' throughout the 1770s and 1780s.[24] In 1797, the Unitarian activist Thomas Palmer would even describe Johnson, not unkindly, as 'A Moravian Methodist'.[25] Indeed, Johnson seems to have maintained contact with the British Brethren at least until 1792.[26] This suggests that to understand Johnson, and indeed, the wider evangelical movements of the time, we must briefly outline the nature of Moravian missionary thinking as part of the theological and practical backdrop to what would come.

Johnson is said to have first made contact with this famously missionary church while in London, seeking advice on 'preaching the

---

20 In his reflections upon the Eclectic Society, Josiah Pratt notes the oddness of this combination: 'this appointment of a Chaplain was, from the first, regarded in connection with the heathen', Pratt & Pratt, *Memoir of the Rev. Josiah Pratt*, 463.
21 The Moravian Church traces its heritage back to the proto-Reformer, Jan Hus (1372–1415), but was revived in 1727 by Count Nicholas von Zinzendorf. On the wider influence of the Moravians upon the English Revival and its heirs, see Mason, *The Moravian Church*; Podmore, *The Moravian Church in England*. My thanks to Felicity Jensz and Malcolm Falloon for suggesting Mason to me.
22 Thomas Haweis and John Newtown were directly influenced, for they appear to have been quite familiar, even close, with the leader of the British Moravians from 1768–1786, Benjamin La Trobe; Mason, *The Moravian Church*, 63.
23 Note that the data is only extant for 1797–1801 and so it is uncertain when they began receiving such direct information and influence. See the Appendix in, Mason, *The Moravian Church*, 202–203.
24 Mason, *The Moravian Church*, 89.
25 Palmer to Lindsay, 15/9/1797.
26 Mason, *The Moravian Church*, 80.

Gospel to the heathen'.[27] This is unsurprising, given that the Reformed churches dominant in Europe at the time were distinctly inexperienced with cross-cultural ministry and work amongst entirely unengaged people-groups. By contrast, the Moravian Church perceived itself as 'a Missionary Church',[28] different from the other Protestant churches, not by organisation or theology, but 'by sphere and method'.[29]

Some of this method may be glimpsed in the 1784 manual, *Instructions for the Members of the Unitas Fratrum Who Minister in the Gospel among the Heathen*.[30] Their doctrine of conversion emphasised, 'the necessity of a change of heart [...] and then to show that true faith [it] must manifest itself as the power of God in the life by the fruits of the Spirit'.[31] This facet of their missiology was to have a profound impact upon John Wesley, shape the Methodist movement that would arise from his ministry, and eventually exert an incredible influence in Fiji, Tonga, and Samoa in the South Pacific.[32] After 'one or more persons, in whom a good beginning appears to be made', they are to be taken aside and instructed more fully on sin, salvation, the resurrection of all and judgement to come.[33] They valued unity amongst missionaries as a prime witness to those to whom they sought to proclaim the gospel, as well as to ensure long-term

---

27 It is also reported that Newton had used the promise of Moravian brethren on the mission field of Australia to convince Johnson—a promise that came as a surprise to the Moravians. A formal request would later come from Captain Sir Charles Middleton (a key naval figure in Pitt's plans for the penal colony and later founding member of the CMS) and Wilberforce himself.

28 Jensz, 'Imperial Critics', 188. This is not only expressed as part of their 'calling' in their instructional handbook, it was also evidenced in the raw statistics of their denomination: 'a large minority of their membership became missionaries, and almost everyone within the Church contributed in some form to the missionary movement. The proportion of missionaries within the Church was extraordinarily high, at one in sixty (for the rest of the Protestant world the proportion was around one in five thousand)', Jensz, 'Imperial Critics', 189. This self-identity apparently extended far beyond the Moravians themselves, with even the Archbishop of Dublin and the Governor of Victoria, Australia, claiming that '*only* the Moravian Church could be successful amongst the degraded Aborigines', Jensz, 'Three Peculiarities of the Southern Australian Moravian Mission Field', 11.

29 Thompson, *Moravian Missions*, 462. For a broader investigation of Moravian thought, polity, and activity, see Mason, *The Moravian Church*, chap. 1.

30 Spangenberg, *Instructions for the Brethren*, published first in German in 1782 and then in English in 1784. Two other pamphlets published by La Trobe in the 1770s were key in rehabilitating the image of the Moravian church in England: La Trobe, *A Succinct View*; Spangenberg and La Trobe, *A Concise Historical Account*; see Mason, *The Moravian Church*, 65.

31 Spangenberg, *Instructions for the Brethren*, 19; Thompson, *Moravian Missions*, 467.

32 Jensz, 'Imperial Critics' 189.

33 Spangenberg, *Instructions for the Brethren*, 21–22. One aspect of their ethos that certainly was not adopted by the LMS was their hesitancy towards catechism and any delay in baptising converts.

sustainability of the mission.³⁴ This also likely guided their broad ethos of 'non-extension' of the denomination in favour of evangelistic opportunity, and a desire to operate from a set of core theological beliefs, largely concerned with soteriology.³⁵ The Moravians also placed a high priority upon linguistic scholarship as a prelude to effective missionary work in another culture, and upon the place of singing and of prayer in the life of the missionary and their supporting churches.³⁶

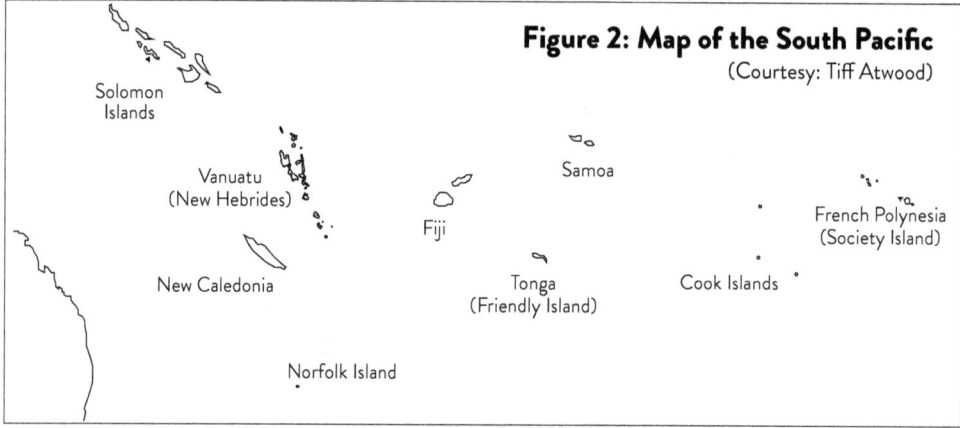

Figure 2: Map of the South Pacific
(Courtesy: Tiff Atwood)

In common with the discussions to occur in the mission Societies, and around Marsden's missiology, the Moravians also compared the relative importance of practical work in a community set alongside direct gospel preaching to that community, concluding that those engaged in each are of equal value to the Lord, but that all involved 'ought also to take a hearty share in the chief points, the preaching of the gospel and

---

34 Spangenberg, *Instructions for the Brethren*, 13.
35 Their 'purpose [was] to give the glorious gospel to the largest number of those who had never heard it', Thompson, *Moravian Missions*, 463. Their core theological commitments are expressed in Spangenberg, *Instructions for the Brethren*, 2. There is very little here that an evangelical Anglican such as Johnson or much of the Eclectic Society would have issue, despite the tension with Moravians entwined with the Whitefield/Wesley split of the 1740s and following. This was expressed in the pre-LMS *Evangelical Magazine* article (likely written by Thomas Haweis) that argued, 'that the Moravians should not be ignored on account of past excesses of enthusiasm or differences in doctrine over inessentials'; Mason, *The Moravian Church*, 75. Given the status of pneumatology in Reformed circles in the 18th century, their concern for adequate communication of the doctrine of the Holy Spirit after the prime message of salvation in Jesus Christ is proclaimed is also noteworthy; Spangenberg, *Instructions for the Brethren*, 18. On the matter of their 'non-extension', note that they do not hesitate to impress the Brethren polity and community life upon new converts, along with the necessary history to understand what is, and what is not, suitable to their context; Spangenberg, *Instructions for the Brethren*, 48.
36 Spangenberg, *Instructions for the Brethren*, 10; Thompson, *Moravian Missions*, 467, 477–78.

the care of souls'.[37] Many of these emphases in missionary work can be seen in Carey's Baptist Missionary Society; the Eclectic Society; and its heirs, the LMS and CMS; though perhaps less explicitly in the individual ministry of their missionaries and agents.[38] At the very least:

> as the pace of the missionary awakening accelerated the example of the Moravian Church added a real and practical force to that sense of guilt felt by evangelicals and inner compulsion that they ought to do something for the conversion of heathens to Christianity.[39]

In Johnson, we see the South Sea missions begin as they would initially continue—with tentative workers prepared to follow their deepest convictions of the deep spiritual need of others, whatever difficulties they foresaw.

3. The Societies—the LMS, the CMS, and the South Seas

3.1 The Birth of the London Missionary Society

While Johnson was labouring in the early days of the colony, and Carey authoring, 'An Enquiry into the Obligations of Christians, to use means for the Conversion of the Heathen', the effects of the evangelical revivals were still being felt in the United Kingdom.[40] Whitefield had reinvigorated the spiritual life of the Church of England, and the Wesleys had ushered in the new and curious force of the Methodist Societies.[41] The 'Eclectic Society' was formed in 1783 as a hub of evangelicalism within the Anglican Church in Britain, and is remembered for its luminaries, such as John Newtown, John Venn, and Josiah Pratt, who brought a

---

37 Spangenberg, *Instructions for the Brethren*, 42–43.
38 Regarding the BMS, see the argument for Moravian influence in Stanley, *The History of the Baptist Missionary Society, 1792-1992*; Mason, *The Moravian Church*. It is also interesting to note that the missionary work Johnson wished for amongst indigenous Australians would be undertaken, in part, by the Moravian Church in Victoria from 1848 to 1908 (with mixed success); see Jensz, *German Moravian Missionaries*; Thompson, *Moravian Missions*, 415–51.
39 Mason, *The Moravian Church*, 89.
40 Interestingly, while Carey is often credited with being the first in English-speaking circles to use the Great Commission of Matthew 28:18-20 for the incitement of mission, it appears the Moravians were almost a decade ahead of him; Spangenberg, *Instructions for the Brethren*, 2.
41 Ellis, *The History of the LMS*, 1:4–5.

global dimension to the evangelical scheming of the revivalists.[42] It would seem that '[t]he coincidence of geographical discovery and evangelical revival was too striking to be anything less than a divine summons to convert the latest-known corner of the earth'.[43]

From this intersection of evangelical revival and the ever-increasing awareness of the world through Cook's explorations grew a fierce desire for the spread of the gospel in new fields ideal and idyllic for this to happen, and in this *The Missionary Society* (later, the London Missionary Society or LMS to distinguish it from the many others appearing in its wake) would flourish. Few individuals typify the exploratory spirit and evangelistic fervour more than Thomas Haweis, then rector of Aldwinkle, Northamptonshire, chaplain to the Countess of Huntingdon, and a key founder of the LMS.[44] As early as 1787, Haweis shared his desire for a mission to Tahiti with Lady Huntingdon, who sought out two young students to train under Haweis and who were to accompany Bligh on his second trip to the islands. While this does not appear to have eventuated, Haweis is credited with being the driving force behind the Society actually sending out missionaries itself eight years later.[45] It was not until November, 1794, that another key figure, Dr. David Bogue, was called to London on business, and while there was part of a meeting, 'with a view to the ultimate formation of a society on a comprehensive scale for sending missions to the heathen'.[46]

---

[42] Piggin, *Spirit of A Nation*, 1; Ellis, *The History of the LMS*, 1:4; Lovett, *The History of the London Missionary Society, 1795–1895*, 1:3. See too the 'Eclectics' role in the formation of the Church Missionary Society within the Church of England; Cole, *A History of the Church Missionary Society of Australia*, 4; '[T]he same impulse, and to a remarkable extent the same men, helped to create other Societies', *The Church Missionary Society*, 2. It is also worth noting the flurry of other Societies formed in this period, the Baptist Missionary Society (1792); the Edinburgh or Scottish Missionary Society (1796); the Glasgow Missionary Society (1796); and eventually the Wesleyan Missionary Society (1817); Ellis, *The History of the LMS*, 1:3.

[43] Davies, *The History of the Tahitian Mission 1799-1830*, xxvii.

[44] Haweis was another evangelical figure deeply fond of and influenced by the Moravian church from as early as 1760, and even when facing a long illness drafted (but never finalised) a will leaving his estate to La Trobe for the 'benefit of the Heathen Missions', Mason, *The Moravian Church*, 75.

[45] Ellis, *The History of the LMS*, 1:20. As the cause of the failure, Horne cites the decision of the Archbishop not to ordain the two men as they had not studied at university; Horne, *Story of the L.M.S.*, 4.

[46] Ellis, *The History of the LMS*, 1:16. Present at this first of many meetings at Baker's Coffee House (and later, with more present at the Castle and Falcon Inn) were Bogue, Brooksbank, Eyre, Love, Reynolds, Steven, Wilks, and Townsend. See the account in Horne, *Story of the L.M.S.*, 9–10.

3.2 The Shape of Mission in the early LMS

Prior to focussing on Marsden and his role in the South Sea missions, it is worth noting the founding characteristics and strategy of the LMS in its infancy. Regarding the characteristics of the LMS, a glimpse of their initial flavour is found in the use of time in the many meetings held prior to the formal founding of the Society Bogue alludes to above. Ellis makes much of how they were largely devoted to prayer ('a large portion of the time, one hour at least'), solemnly undertaken in the spirit of the evangelical revivals to which they owed their faith.[47] To this was added study of 'those parts of the Holy Scriptures which relate to the extension of the Redeemer's kingdom on earth'.[48] Such focus on prayer and missionary texts in these meetings reached a climax on February 17, 1795, with 34 ministers committing to 'exert ourselves for promoting the great work of introducing the Gospel and its ordinances to heathen and other unenlightened countries'.[49] In true British style, this in itself was not yet formal enough, and led to yet more plans and proposed meetings, letters seeking and offering support, until September 21, 1795, when the Reverends Boden, Bogue, Brooksbank, Burder, Eyre, Greathead, Hill, Haweis, Hey, Lambert, Platt, Parsons, Ray, Reynolds, Saltern, Steven, Waugh, Wilks, and 'many others in town and from the country' met again in the Castle and Falcon Inn, followed by a formal ceremony in the Countess of Huntingdon's chapel the next day.[50] The Missionary Society was born with, '[t]he sole object [...] to spread the knowledge of Christ among heathen and other unenlightened nations'.[51]

Regarding the strategy of the LMS, some insights may be gained from the two directors of the first 25 most often credited with shaping the direction of the Society, Haweis and Bogue. During the earliest days of the LMS, they strongly disagreed about the aim and approach of the missionary task.[52] Bogue's thinking was marked by two emphases which led him to prefer sending missionaries to 'already civilised' countries: (1) a preference for missionaries to be more rather than less educated;

---

47 Ellis, *The History of the LMS*, 1:17.
48 Ellis, *The History of the LMS*, 1:18.
49 Quoted in Ellis, *The History of the LMS*, 1:18–19.
50 Ellis, *The History of the LMS*, 1:23–25.
51 Ellis, *The History of the LMS*, 1:26.
52 A transcript of Bogue's address appears in the opening pages of Lovett, *The History of the London Missionary Society, 1795-1895*, 1:6–9.

and (2) a belief that it is not the responsibility of missionaries to 'civilise' people. Thomas Haweis, however, was convinced that the South Pacific was the correct locus of the Society's work:

> Peculiarly favourable circumstances will engage attention to these countries. The fertility of the soil—the beauty and healthiness of the climate—the uncivilised state of the natives, which gives Europeans so great an advantage over them—the facility wherewith settlements may be formed—and the easiness with which they can be maintained—besides the probability, that the spirit of commerce and adventure will make some essay to secure the first advantages, and forward civilisation, if the gospel which we have sent them should not by its own divine power produce all the happy effects upon the natives, which we hope and expect to hear.[53]

Bogue's vision seems to have been partly representative of the earliest missionaries. While many of them were of lower British class, and less educated, their leaders for the first three decades were largely those of higher standing and education—particularly in linguistics aiding their Biblical translations.[54] Bogue appears to have been in the minority in his opinion that 'already civilised' countries were a better choice for missionary activity, as they were more 'rational' and so more easily won over to the Christian religion.[55]

Haweis proved more persuasive, and succeeded in his proposal

---

53 Haweis, *An Impartial and Succinct History*, 3:379–80. These words strongly echo those in *The Evangelical Magazine* from 1795 where he again lists the climate, abundance of food, temper of the people, and 'early collection of a number together for instruction'; Haweis, 'The Very Probable Success of a Proper Mission to the South Sea Islands'. Some of his passion for the region appears to have been due to the influence and guidance of Joseph Banks; Sivasundaram, *Nature and the Godly Empire*, 3. Sivasundaram and many others provide no source for this, but Ellis points to a letter from Haweis to Ambrose Serle Esq. wherein 'the accounts of Cook's voyages [...] excited in his mind a strong desire that efforts might be made to send missionaries to Tahiti', as well as to contact Haweis had with Bligh and Banks in pursuit of passage for Waugh and Price; Ellis, *The History of the LMS*, 1:6. It should be noted that according to Ellis, Matthew Wilks, minister of the London Tabernacle, first mentioned the South Sea Islands once the Society had actually formed, to which Haweis added his voice; Ellis, *The History of the LMS*, 1:28. The idyllic description of the South Pacific islands by Haweis stands in remarkable contrast to Marsden's 1818 message through Pratt to a clergyman bound for New Zealand from England, 'it will be well for him to remember that when he leaves England for a Savage nation, he leaves the goodly Land of Canaan, the Land flowing with milk and Honey', Marsden to Pratt, 26/9/1818, 6.
54 *Pace* Gunson who places an inordinate amount of confidence in the class-aspirations of the early missionaries; Gunson, *Messengers of Grace*, chap. 1; Gunson, 'Evangelical Missionaries in the South Seas, 1797–1860', 11–34.
55 Falloon, *To Plough or to Preach*, 14. See also Gunson, *Messengers of Grace*, 96.

of the South Pacific, and Tahiti in particular, to be the first field for the Society's work. By this time it had been 25 years since Cook's first journey to Tahiti, 10 years since Bligh's visit to Tahiti, 10 years since Haweis first pursued Tahiti as a missionary destination, and nearly two decades since Ma'I, the Huahine 'Noble Savage', was brought to Britain to delight the upper classes.[56] At last missionary volunteers were selected, and the first exclusively 'missionary ship' was purchased, the *Duff*, and stocked largely by the goodwill and generosity of 'the Society's friends'—apothecaries, shipwrights, and cartographers.[57]

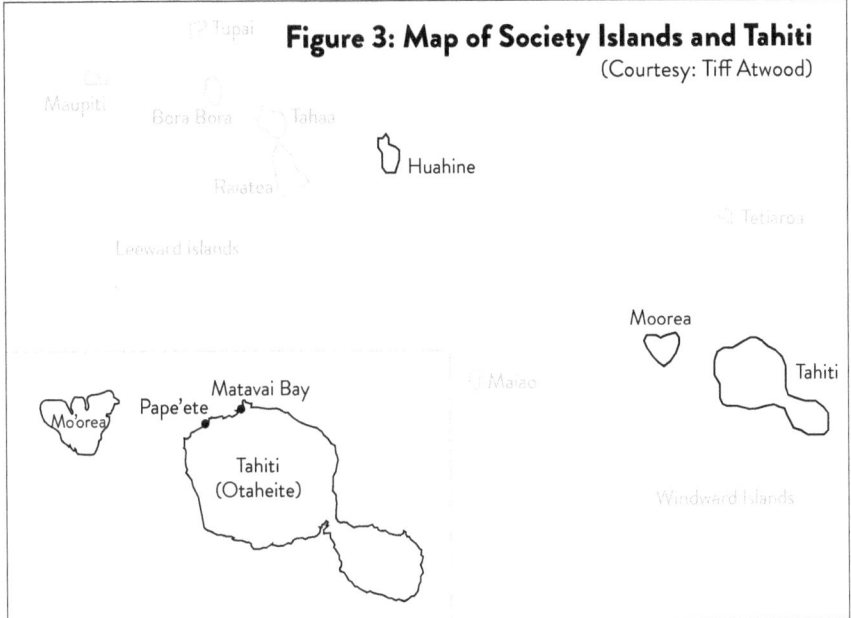

Figure 3: Map of Society Islands and Tahiti
(Courtesy: Tiff Atwood)

The Tahitian mission and its 'messengers of peace'—39 in all, including four ordained clergy, one surgeon, five missionary wives, and three children—were commissioned on July 27 in the full ecumenical spirit the Society was founded upon.[58] They embarked on the morning of August 10, 1796, and—after a delay in Spithead as they awaited military

---

56 Davies, *The History of the Tahitian Mission 1799–1830*, xxvii. Haweis was to live a further two decades past this first missionary outing for the LMS. He saw the LMS mission to Tahiti through its glorious outset, swift abandonment, return over many years, and final traction in the conversion of Pomare II.
57 Horne, *Story of the L.M.S.*, 20–21.
58 Ten ministers from ten different denominations were engaged in the service; Ellis, *The History of the LMS*, 1:42.

escort—at last left British waters on September 23.[59] By March 1797, the *Duff* landed on Otaheite (now 'Tahiti').[60] The men on board were: the Reverends James Cover, John Eyre, John Jefferson, and Thomas Lewis; along with Henry Bicknell, Daniel Bowell, Benjamin Broomhall, John Buchanan, James Cooper, John Cock, William Crook, Samuel Clode, John A. Gillham (the surgeon), Peter Hodges, William Henry, John Harris, Samuel Harper, Rowland Hassall, Seth Kelso, Edward Main, Isaac Nobbs, Henry Nott, James and William Puckey, Francis Oakes, William Smith, William Shelley, George Vason, and James Wilkinson.[61] The women and children on-board were Mary Cover; Elizabeth Eyre; Elizabeth Hassell; Sarah Henry; and Mary Hodges. The three children were James Cover (12 years old), Thomas Hassall (2 years old), and Samuel Otoo Hassall (16 weeks old).[62] Many of these would, for good

---

59 Ellis, *The History of the LMS*, 1:43. The *Duff* had intended to convoy with the East-India fleet, but missed them by a few days. The delay awaited the arrival of the HMS *Adamant*, escorting some ships bound for Gibraltar; Smith, *Journal of a Voyage in the Missionary Ship Duff*, 4.

60 There is a slight discrepancy in the numbers cited. Ellis notes 'thirty in number, six of whom were married', Ellis, *The History of the LMS*, 1:42; whereas Horne lists 'thirty missionaries [...] four trained and ordained ministers; twenty-five were artisans, and one was a surgeon'; Horne, *Story of the L.M.S.*, 23. Horne's numbers are corroborated with the list of names in LMS, *A Missionary Voyage to the Southern Pacific Ocean*, 5–6 and repeated in Garrett, *To Live Among the Stars: Christian Origins in Oceania*, 12. The raw number of unmarried missionaries in this earliest effort casts into doubt Middleton's idea that 'the role of domesticity was of central importance' and 'men were encouraged, and expected, to marry before moving into the mission field in order to demonstrate the model of ideal European gender roles and to save themselves from the perils of indigenous women'; Middleton, 'Missionization in New Zealand and Australia: A Comparison', 173. The list of ages in LMS, *A Missionary Voyage* suggests many of them were between 20–25 years old, and so less likely to be married in the 1700s when the average age of marriage in England was 30 as demonstrated by Allan Kulikoff, *From British Peasants to Colonial American Farmers*, 227–229. Garrett similarly oversimplifies things to speculate that Haweis intended the unmarried to marry local women who would be easily converted and make good wives for them; Garrett, *To Live Among the Stars*, 11.

61 A full list including occupations can be found in LMS, *A Missionary Voyage to the South Pacific Ocean*, 5–6. Mr & Mrs J. Hudden embarked the voyage, but after a rough first leg, Mrs Hudden was not up to it and they disembarked at Portsmouth seven days later (p.13; see also Smith, *Journal of a Voyage*, 4–5). Bowell, Buchanan, Cooper, Harper, Kelso, Nobbs, Shelly, Vason, Wilkinson, and Gaulton were to be stationed on Tongatapu in the Friendly Islands (now Tonga), where Harper, Bowell, and Gaulton lost their lives in a civil war. Vason married into a chiefly family before repenting and returning to Britain in 1801, and the remaining missionaries ended up in Sydney within two years. Harris and Crook were based on the Marquesas Islands—Harris left almost immediately, and Crook remained for some time before returning to NSW and then spent 1815-1830 on Tahiti.

62 James Cover Jnr. was in the final stages of consumption upon departure, and died only a few days into the journey on September 25. He was buried at Portsmouth, see LMS, *A Missionary Voyage to the Southern Pacific Ocean*, 14, and Smith, *Journal of a Voyage in the Missionary Ship Duff*, 5. The naming of Samuel Hassall as 'Otoo' appears to have been intended to honour Tu (Pomare I), the paramount chief of Tahiti. This would prove to be a faux pas as it was later be revealed to the missionaries that only members of royal family were entitled to this name.

or ill, find their way fairly swiftly to Sydney.

3.3 The Prelude to the Church Missionary Society

While in many ways less historically significant than the formation of the LMS, the Church Missionary Society (unnamed in its first meeting, and then known as 'The Society for Missions to Africa and the East' until 1812 when the colloquial attribution 'Church' was formally adopted into 'The Church Missionary Society for Africa and the East', and eventually, the CMS) was of such significance in the history of the South Sea missions that a brief narrative of its inception is warranted before returning to the Tahitian mission.

The Eclectic Society had long occupied itself with missionary topics since its fateful 1786 discussion of 'bringing the Gospel to Botany Bay'.[63] A key figure in these discussions appears to have been the Rev. Charles Simeon of Cambridge. He raised the question of 'What is the best method of propagating the Gospel in the East Indies?' in 1789, and then, in 1796, 'With what propriety, and in what mode, can a Mission be attempted to the Heathen from the Established Church?'.[64] As the centenary history indicates, 'the form of the question marks a step in advance. It is no longer Botany Bay, or the East Indies, or Africa. It is "the Heathen" that are thought of'.[65] Significant too, is the introduction of the role of the Church of England in mission.[66] While not lost in the intervening years,[67] this refining of 'the question' continued with the discussion on March 18, 1799, prompted by John Venn, 'What methods can we use more effectually to promote the knowledge of the Gospel among the Heathen?'. This discussion moved the question from 'What

---

63 Missionary discussions appeared amongst many more broadly theological or uniquely British ones, see Pratt, *Eclectic Notes*.
64 Stock, *One Hundred Years*, 4, 10.
65 Stock, *One Hundred Years*, 10. The reference to 'Africa' arises from an identical question put forward on the 24th October, 1791 by Rev. Melville Horne, Chaplain at Sierra Leone, but with regards to 'propagating the Gospel in Africa'; Pratt & Pratt, *Memoir of the Rev. Josiah Pratt*, 464. On the significance of the anti-slavery movement and Sierra Leone for the Eclectics and ultimately the CMS, see the stimulating discussion in Hole, *The Early History of the CMS*, chap. 1.
66 Hole, *The Early History of the CMS*, 25–26.
67 The topic of mission was even forcefully raised by Wilberforce in the 1792 Parliament in an attempt to require the East India Company to cease obstructing missionary efforts in the subcontinent and fund chaplaincy on land and by sea as a requirement for the renewal of their license; Hole, *The Early History of the CMS*, 19–20.

ought the church to do?' to 'What can we do?'.[68] Now made rather more personal, this regular meeting took on a more significant tone. Simeon would brook no further delay, exclaiming, 'we have been dreaming these four years, while all Europe is awake!'.[69] By the end of the night, it was resolved that a new Society be formed immediately to promote salvation in the world from within the Church of England.[70]

On Friday, April 12, 1799, once again in the first floor rooms of the Castle and Falcon in Aldersgate Street, 16 clergy (nine of whom were of the Eclectic Society) and nine laymen met to form this new Society. None of the Eclectic luminaries appear to have been present, though Wilberforce was put forward as President (a position he would later refuse) and Henry Thornton, another MP involved in the anti-slavery movement, was appointed Treasurer.[71] John Venn took the chair. A prospectus was drawn up, but no further action was considered possible until a 'respectful letter' was sent to the Archbishop of Canterbury, John Moore, the Bishop of London, Beilby Porteus, as well as the SPCK mission committee.[72] While the evangelicals involved in the new Society were not popular with the churchmen in authority, and at least Venn and Simeon had been explicitly excluded from involvement in the existing 'mission' arms of the SPG and SPCK, they were unwilling to proceed without some form of approval from the establishment they were seeking to bring to bear on a waiting world. In a politically astute move, Wilberforce delivered the letter, but had to wait for a full year before seeking a response in person.[73] Whether due to the personage attending him, or out of genuine support, the Archbishop assented to

---

68 Stock, *One Hundred Years*, 10.
69 This is likely a reference to the excitement generated by the Napoleonic Wars; Stock, *One Hundred Years*, 11.
70 Oddly, the *Eclectic Notes* mention the discussion of 'the important subject of A MISSION CONNECTED WITH THE EVANGELICAL PART OF THE CHURCH OF ENGLAND', occurring on February 18, 1799, but gives none of the details of the discussion as it does for all the other meetings, merely noting that it occurred; Pratt, *Eclectic Notes*, 95. This may have been an unminuted discussion that prompted the formal proposal of Venn on March 18, as hinted at in Pratt and Pratt, *Memoir of the Rev. Josiah Pratt*, 468. Pratt's notes from the March 18 meeting are themselves quite limited, providing only the barest outline of Venn's reasoning for why Anglican clergy were prevented from joining the LMS (later supplemented by Rev. William Goode's notes), *Memoir of the Rev. Josiah Pratt*, 470–71. Perhaps the discussion was simply too absorbing, as Pratt himself is credited with providing its conclusion, 'Let us regard ourselves as forming the Society'; *Memoir of the Rev. Josiah Pratt*, 471.
71 He was appointed apparently *in absentia*, Stock, *One Hundred Years*, 11.
72 Stock, *One Hundred Years*, 12.
73 A copy of the letter may be seen in Hole, *The Early History of the CMS*, 45–46.

this new work, and on August 4, 1800, the CMS committee began their work in earnest.[74]

The biggest struggle of these early years was to identify suitable candidates for missionary service—no young evangelical clergyman appeared fit for cross-cultural service in the first two full years of CMS operations.[75] In 1802, two key events occurred. The first was the replacement of Thomas Scott as secretary of the CMS by Josiah Pratt, who would hold the post for 21 years, and prove to be one of the most vital figures in the Society's growth, and be the primary interlocutor with Marsden throughout his work as CMS agent in the South Seas.[76] The second was the recruitment of three missionary candidates—two ordained Lutherans from Germany, Renner and Hartwig, and one Englishman, Henry Martyn.[77] Martyn was bound for India, but could not be appointed as a 'missionary' under the rule of the East India Company who allowed no such thing. However, one of their British directors, Charles Grant, happened to have been a member of the Eclectic Society, and so arranged his appointment as chaplain beginning in 1805.[78] The next Englishmen to be appointed were sent to the remotest part of the globe—New Zealand—as part of Samuel Marsden's efforts to begin a work amongst the Māori. Hall and King, a joiner and shoemaker, were exactly what Marsden was hoping for—practical men who could serve as 'lay settlers' teaching useful skills to the indigenous peoples while laying the foundation of gospel proclamation.[79] Exactly how Marsden managed to convince this Society, so orientated towards 'Africa and the East', to send some of their earliest workers to the South Pacific may become clear as his story, personality, and dogged pursuit of the New Zealand mission is continued below.

---

74 Stock, *One Hundred Years*, 12.
75 Stock, *One Hundred Years*, 19.
76 Pratt and Pratt, *Memoir of the Rev. Josiah Pratt*, 32–47.
77 For a Society concerned with the established church in England it may seem odd to have recruited clergy from an entirely different denomination and country, but this was apparently an accepted practice in the SPCK that appears to have been acceptable to the CMS committee too. Renner and Hartwig were to work primarily in West Africa amongst the Susoo; Stock, *One Hundred Years*, 20; Hole, *The Early History of the CMS*, chap. 2.
78 Stock, *One Hundred Years*, 20. Martyn is another remarkable figure of the period. He worked for six years in India, moved to Persia in ill health where he faced strong and violent opposition from Islamic clerics, before dying in Armenia in 1812 at the age of only 32 years.
79 Stock, *One Hundred Years*, 22.

3.4 The Shape of Mission in the early CMS

The shape of mission in the earliest days of CMS are even easier to discern than that of the LMS. John Venn provided the core missionary principles he would inculcate into the CMS in his address to the Eclectic Society in 1799, and the anti-slavery efforts of many of the founding members leant a natural bias towards West Africa for their initial work.

Venn's principles were five: (1) 'Follow God's leading', (2) 'Begin on a small scale', (3) 'Put the money in the second place, not the first', (4) 'Under God, all will depend on the type of men sent forth', and (5) 'look for success only from the Spirit of God'.[80]

Even their initial direction was not exclusive. While they had natural connections with Africa, and in particular, Sierra Leone, the CMS explored the opportunities in Ceylon (now Sri Lanka), China, Caucasus, Persia (now Iran), and the Middle East in their earliest days. They even directed funds towards Bible translation projects in Arabic, Persian, and the West African Susoo language, showing both a remarkable prescience for the key locations of today, and a prime emphasis on access to Scripture in local languages.[81] This would stand in contrast to later Church of England missions, such as the more establishment 'Melanesian Mission' launched under the inimitable Bishop Selwyn of New Zealand and flourishing under the first Bishop of Melanesia, John Patteson. Patteson chose the Mota language of northern Vanuatu (from the 23 that he purportedly spoke) to use as the ecclesiastical language, and translated a handful of biblical books into it alone.[82]

---

80 Stock, *One Hundred Years*, 15; cf. the two reconstructions of Pratt and Goode in Pratt & Pratt, *Memoir of the Rev. Josiah Pratt*, Appendix 1.
81 Stock, *One Hundred Years*, 16–17.
82 The Melanesian Mission's approach to evangelism was to recruit young men from the islands, bring them to Auckland (and later Norfolk Island) for catechetical training, and then return them as evangelists to their home islands. While brilliant in its focus upon evangelism 'from within', many of the catechists found the cultural distance between their schooling and their communities too great and forsook their training to completely re-enter their society. For more on the Melanesian Mission, see Rutledge, 'Patteson, John Coleridge (1827–1871)'; Hilliard, *God's Gentlemen*.

4. The 'Cowards'—The Tahitian Mission

The Tahitian mission itself is as significant as it is difficult to pin down with accuracy. Amidst the hagiography of the Society's commemorative writings and the scathing revisions of recent decades, the motivations and impacts are somewhat opaque. Only the barest narrative of the early days of the mission will be given, with some attention given to the cause of the earliest missionaries to flee to Sydney and so into Johnson and Marsden's sphere.

By most accounts the missionaries were initially well received in Tahiti. Forty priests of Oro, the main deity and war-god of Tahiti, along with their high priest, Hamancmane (Mannemanne), even came aboard the *Duff* for their inaugural Sabbath day service.[83] While they shared no common language, it appears the Arioi (the religious order of Oro) understood that some liturgy was involved.[84] This honour and acceptance was followed within a few days with an introduction to Pomare I and his son (later to be known as Pomare II; both were also called 'Tu'). Pomare I was the paramount chief of Mo'orea, and his son of Porionu'u, although the missionaries appear to have understood them to be sovereigns of all Tahiti. This attribution of rule was supported by the 'cession' of Matavai to the visitors.[85] Bligh had developed good relationships with the senior Pomare years before, and the bamboo house built for him was made available for 17 of the 30 missionaries to settle.[86] This was not the freehold grant it was perceived to be, but rather a gesture of hospitality and provision for these newcomers which they would be expected to reciprocate with access to their goods and support in tribal conflicts, of

---

83 Ellis, *The History of the LMS*, 1:46; Garrett, *To Live Among the Stars*, 14–15. Hamancmane is now more commonly transliterated as Mannemanne.
84 The Arioi were especially known for their ritual dancers associated with fertility in service of the god Oro of Raiatea; Garrett, *A Way in the Sea*, 2.
85 Davies, *The History of the Tahitian Mission 1799-1830*, xxxviii; Ellis, *The History of the LMS*, 1:49. Cook and Bligh apparently had been told that Pomare was ruler and accepted and propagated it as fact, or at least as resonant with their idea of monarchical rule.
86 Horne, *Story of the L.M.S.*, 26–27. It seems that the Tahitians had a fondness of sea captains, with Tu and Mannemanne, another priest, exchanging gifts and seeking friendship with Captain James Wilson of the *Duff*. He was also the one to seek and obtain permission for the missionaries to use the Bligh house, and appears a remarkable evangelical character in his own right, worthy of some historical attention; Murray, 'In the Shadow of the Missionary Captain', 75. See Wilson, *The Life and Dreadful Sufferings of Captain James Wilson*; Murray, 'In the Shadow of the Missionary Captain', 73–77.

which Tu was still involved with rival chiefs.[87]

As Gunson delights to labour, the earliest LMS missionaries appear to have been 'godly mechanics'—drawn from the more practical castes of British society.[88] The majority of them had experience in field preaching (again linked to their roots in the evangelical revival) and seem to have been apt in their trades but little educated in theology, biblical studies, or linguistics; and few, if any, had any experience outside their own country.[89] This eventually gave them advantages in operating a printing press, developing viable trade, and even shipbuilding, yet did not entirely prepare them for making early contact with an entirely different collection of cultures, languages, religions, and the rugged life of dependency on new lands and peoples.[90]

Precisely what occurred in the subsequent months as these missionaries sought to connect with the Tahitians, learn their language, and preach the gospel, is unclear. What is clear is that, within months, the mission was in trouble. The Christian God was not as sought after as Western goods. Mannemanne, high priest of Oro, said of their patron-chief: 'You give him much *paraow* (talk) and much prayers … but very few axes, knives, scissors, or cloth'.[91] One year into the LMS mission, the brig *Nautilus* arrived from America, short on supplies, and eager to trade their muskets and powder for local produce. The missionaries interrupted this transaction to offer pork and fruit for free rather than see the weapons introduced into Tahitian society. This appears to have

---

87 Garrett particularly notes how Peter Hagerstein, a Swede, had previously shown Pomare I how effective cannon and muskets were in warfare, and Pomare II certainly appears to have understood their strategic importance; Garrett, *To Live Among the Stars*, 6–7.
88 'Godly men who understand Mechanic Arts', to be precise; London Missionary Society, 'Board Minutes, 28 September 1795'. This seems to place more emphasis on character than later historians have suggested, whatever moral failings the small minority of early LMS missionaries may have fallen into. It is interesting to note a similar bias towards the practical strata of European society in their Moravian predecessors and contemporaries; Thompson, *Moravian Missions*, 475. Gunson's argument that missionary work presented an opportunity for societal advancement underplays the missiologically-driven preference for practically-skilled workers in the Moravian, CMS, and Methodist missions of this era.
89 Gunson, *Messengers of Grace*, 36, 88, 90.
90 Not that the four ordained (and slightly more schooled) missionaries fared much better in the early years. It does not appear that the entire Evangelical movement in England was unaware of the cross-cultural challenge. Thomas Scott of the Eclectic Society impresses the difficulty of such a lifestyle and pleads 'to accommodate yourselves to them, with patience and meekness'; Scott, 'Address to Missionaries', 134. The mismatch of character and preparation is called a 'widespread opinion' in Bonwick, *First Twenty Years of Australia: A History Founded on Official Documents*, 231.
91 Garrett, *To Live Among the Stars*, 16.

annoyed the locals involved, and when combined with the subsequent shakedown of four of the missionaries travelling to see Pomare I, it appears that the missionaries were well aware they were not universally welcomed any longer.[92] Eleven missionaries took passage on the *Nautilus* for Sydney, leaving seven of the original number on Tahiti.[93]

What caused this abandonment of their station? Breward suggests that it was missionary failure, rooted particularly in a lack of preparation for the 'culture shock that awaited them'.[94] Others have suggested that persecution by the priests of Oro led to a wise and necessary retreat.[95] Still others that it was their perception of the imminent civil unrest between local leaders that forced the missionaries' hands.[96] Or was it simple friction from 'the meeting of two dissimilar societies', the relaxed and sensual Tahitians neither understanding nor tolerating the British 'moral obsession'?[97] Samuel Clode, himself one of those who fled to Sydney (only to meet a grisly end soon after), claims 'there was nothing that would satisfy them [the Tahitians] but our property'.[98] While the preceding events may well have generated a broad anxiety as to their relationship with the islanders, raw fear alone does not quite account for the motivations of all of those who fled. Richard Johnson wrote to the LMS after receiving the Tahitian missionaries to note how anxious Henry was to return to Otaheite and how apt he appeared to be for the work there.[99] Perhaps each of the 11 bore their own reasons for departing, and should not suffer the predilections of later historians.

---

92 The shakedown seems likely to have little to do with the missionaries directly, but rather was due to their association with Pomare I, and perpetrated by islanders loyal to Pomare II, whose relationship was tense with his father at this time.
93 John Eyre, John Jefferson, Benjamin Broomhall, John Harris, Thomas Lewis, Henry Bicknell, and Henry Nott remained. William Henry and his wife returned in early 1800. Of these, Lewis would cohabit with a Tahitian woman, be cut off from his brethren, and die under curious circumstances in November, 1799; Harris would leave for Port Jackson in January, 1800; and after denying the immortality of the soul, Broomhall was excommunicated and married a Polynesian in June, 1800.
94 Breward, *A History of the Churches in Australasia*, 24.
95 Or the incredibly vague, 'fear for their lives'; Cox, *The British Missionary Enterprise Since 1700*, 84.
96 Lovett, *The History of the London Missionary Society, 1795-1895*, 1:15; Bonwick, *Australia's First Preacher*, 120; Morrell, 'The Transition to Christianity in the South Pacific', 102. This is perhaps supported by Marsden's allusion to 'a single battle between two contending chiefs' in his letter to the LMS Directors regarding the Tahitian mission; Marsden to LMS, 30/1/1801, fol. 3.
97 Garrett, *A Way in the Sea*, 2.
98 Quoted in Bonwick, *Australia's First Preacher*, 122. Clode was murdered in early July, 1799.
99 Bonwick, *Australia's First Preacher*, 135.

Regardless, the fleeing missionaries arrived in Sydney in April, 1798.[100]

In Sydney, they met and were sheltered by Johnson, and soon after entered the much longer care of Samuel Marsden. Both chaplains were very supportive of the missionaries in heart and practice, even though both expressed to the Society that at least some of those who remained in Sydney were ill-suited to the work they had embarked upon.

Tahiti would remain a frustrating field for the Society for many years, with the Napoleonic Wars interfering with naval traffic throughout Europe and restricting the number of vessels available for trade and contact with the South Pacific. This prevented much in the way of communication from London. Despite this, it remained of sufficient interest to those in Australia that the death of Pomare I in late October, 1803 was reported 'with sorrow' in the *Sydney Gazette*.[101] The missionary remnant found their fate tied to Pomare II, whom they taught to read and did all they could to instruct in the ways of the Christian faith. Some hope was glimpsed when Pomare II wrote to the LMS directors in 1807 to promise to 'cast off all evil customs' and the worship of Oro, even as he asked for firearms, property, and clothing. Within a year, he, and those surviving missionaries, would be driven from his island by civil war and unable to return for some years.[102]

The years of investment on the part of the missionaries were not in vain. In 1812, Pomare II professed faith in the Christian God, and once he retook power on his home island constructed a chapel 760 feet long in 1818.[103] This occupied an old ritual site for Oro, and proved a key symbol in the conversion that culminated in his baptism on May

---

100 'The despatch from Governor Hunter, dated April 14, 1798, notes the arrival of the men by the *Nautilus* brig from Tahiti', Bonwick, *First Twenty Years of Australia: A History Founded on Official Documents*, 232.

101 'An event to the consequences of which Mr. Jefferson looks with doubt and uncertainty, although the island is now in a state of tranquillity', SG 2/10/1803. Note the familiarity assumed with the Tahitian missionaries.

102 Nott and Pomare II appeared to have formed a very strong bond, and it seems Nott did not waste the opportunities afforded by this exile to argue for the weakness of Oro; Garrett, *To Live Among the Stars*, 20–21.

103 Marsden to Stokes, 14/6/1819. Pomare II's conversion and construction of the chapel was considered of sufficient import to be reported in the *Sydney Gazette*: 'The King Pomarree has been at length admitted a member of the Christian Church, having received baptism, after a long attentive observer of its advantages, and harmony of its dictates. His zeal is manifested to a surprising extent, assembling his people, inviting and encouraging them by his own example to devout exercises; and he has lately erected a large and very long building at Papaoa, as a place of worship [...] it is called the Royal Mission Chapel, and is 712 feet long by 54 wide', SG 6/11/1819.

16, 1819.[104] While never a prime example of Christian monarchy—dying in 1821 from alcohol related illness and never really forsaking his *mahu* (effeminate male courtesans)—Pomare II's conversion marked a turning point in the fortunes of the Society in the South Pacific, and turned Tahiti into their dream: a launching pad for other mission stations throughout Polynesia.[105] As Marsden would relate to the LMS in the wake of this change of heart:

> Nothing like this, as I have had occasion before to remark, has occurred since the days of the Apostles. The work is all of God. The Missionaries, humanly speaking, had no strength for such a work; although, in the discharge of their duty, they have endured hardship and privations which will never be known in Europe. Indeed, it is probable, men of more refined education and habits could not have borne them [...] Satan has lost so much of his dominion in the Islands, that he will never regain his former hold.[106]

5. The Parson—Samuel Marsden in the South Seas
5.1 Marsden and the Missions

Having seen the foundational role of Richard Johnson in Port Jackson, and the hopeful start to Protestant mission in the South Seas at Tahiti, we now see the two come together in the story of Samuel Marsden. Marsden arrived as assistant chaplain to the colony of NSW in 1794.[107] The ministry was, as Johnson had discovered, difficult, and not helped by the frequent clashes with military and civil leadership. In 1800, Marsden was petitioning the government to return to England, intent on doing so by mid-1801.[108] By that time, Marsden had a very different view of the opportunities of his location.[109]

Three events appear crucial to his involvement in the South Sea

---

104 Davies, *The History of the Tahitian Mission 1799-1830*, 220ff.
105 While the focus on Pomare II is purely maintained given the early missionary efforts with his father, in truth more 'grass-roots' conversions were widespread from 1811 onwards. In 1816 the missionaries ceased to keep a record of those who converted for it was 'no longer a distinguishing mark'; Davies, *The History of the Tahitian Mission 1799-1830*, 196. In defence of the authenticity of Pomare II's faith, he did not retaliate in traditional fashion when ambushed celebrating the Sabbath on 12 November, 1815.
106 Marsden to Pratt, 8/6/1819.
107 Elder, *The Letters and Journals of Samuel Marsden, 1765–1838*, 27.
108 Marsden to Stokes, 22/2/1800.
109 Marsden to Stokes, 22/8/1801.

missions: his visit to Norfolk Island in 1795; the arrival of the Tahitian missionaries; and his subsequent appointment as agent for the LMS and CMS for the South Pacific.

The first of these was under duress from the newly-appointed Lieutenant-Governor Paterson. However, the visit to Captain King on Norfolk Island was Marsden's first encounter with the New Zealand Māori, if indirectly. In an ill-fated attempt to develop their flax industry, King had employed two kidnapped Islanders, Tuke and Huru, and had been impressed—not by their ignorance of flax-production, a predominantly female affair—but their 'keenness of intellect and manliness of character'.[110] He regaled Marsden with tales of their acuity, and this seed, once planted, would grow over the coming ten years.

The second key event provided welcome evangelical company to the chaplains.[111] Marsden grew close to several of the Tahitian missionaries, none moreso than Rowland Hassall who became a close business associate, fellow preacher, and whose son, Thomas, would marry Marsden's own daughter.[112] It would prove not only an encouragement to receive these missionaries, but mark a redirection of Marsden's work for the next four decades of his life.

The precise circumstances which led to Marsden being made the local agent of the Society has also been difficult to discover. His assistance to the Tahitian missionaries in Port Jackson from 1798 onwards was appreciatively received as a 'peculiar providence' by both Joseph Hardcastle and Thomas Haweis on behalf of the LMS directors throughout 1802.[113] Just prior to the sending of these letters, the directors had received a letter written by Marsden in January, 1801, to provide 'a few General observations' on 'the Mission to those Islands in

---

110 Elder, *The Letters and Journals of Samuel Marsden, 1765-1838*, 28.
111 Though not all of the missionaries impressed them. In his analysis to the LMS Directors of the Tahitian mission in 1801, Marsden describes 'some who have come to the Colony' as 'profane in their lives', Marsden to LMS, 30/1/1801. This may refer to John Cock, whom Marsden apparently clashed with; William Smith who prior to writing *Journal of a Voyage on the Missionary Ship Duff* was imprisoned in Sydney for debt; or Francis Oakes who accepted a land grant and apparently ceased all religious involvement until much later in his life.
112 Piggin, *Spirit of A Nation*, 17.
113 LMS to Marsden, 15/9/1802. This letter also cites copies of the anniversary sermons and 'reports of the Directors' sent to Marsden on the *Cato* so as to 'make you acquainted with the different objects which occupy their attention' (pp. 2–3). While circumspect, it is possible this refers to additional administrative information provided to their newly-appointed agent.

the South Seas'.[114] These observations range from fairly direct critiques of the Society's selection of a missionary—who should 'not be a Novice', 'a good man in the strictest sense of the word, but also well informed', and of 'a lively turn of mind [rather] than gloomy and heavy', for 'the more easy and affable the missionary [...] the more easily will he gain the confidence and good opinion of the Heathen'; to recommendations such as the provision for self-defence and a clear and older team leader ('a Guardian or Parent') in a location to guide the mission, rein in the 'sensuous natures' of the young single men, and promote unity amongst the missionaries; emphasise agricultural skill for self-sustenance; and, with some forcefulness, the great need for regular communication with the Society. As would become a recurrent theme through the rest of his involvement in the South Seas, Marsden also notes that:

> Should the Missionaries be active and industrious not only in instructing the Native in the principles of Religion and Morality, but in Agriculture and following the different Branches of the Arts and Sciences as far as their knowledge may extend, they would easily convince the Natives by real facts of the Superiority of their wisdom.[115]

Marsden wrote again twice in 1801, once in August and once in November, to update the LMS on the state of their missionaries in the colony.[116] In the August letter, Marsden expressed his intention to have visited Tahiti on the *Porpoise* but was prevented by Governor King. He did, however, send 'a few Articles' to the handful remaining in Tahiti, offering to act as the LMS' agent in receiving any supplies from them to

---

114   Marsden to LMS, 30/1/1801. The handwritten note in the corner notes 'Read 19 April, 1802, DL', noting the reading of it more than a year later before the LMS committee. The full copy of the letter is available in the SOAS archive, and several brief extracts are published in J.B. Marsden, *Life of Rev. Samuel Marsden*, 39ff. J.B. Marsden is no relation. The letter also notes that these observations are offered in response to some request of the LMS, but does not reflect any official role as indicated by the quite general wishes for the success of the Society in the final paragraph.
115   Marsden to LMS, 30/1/1801, fol. 11. For further examples of Marsden's preference for 'civilising' (e.g. agriculture) as a prelude and complement for evangelism, see, e.g. the Western farming practices taught alongside catechesis at Marsden's Parramatta 'seminary' for Māori; Marsden to Stokes, 16/12/1817; Prentis, 'Rangatire and Tohunga of Parramatta'. For a more thorough background and analysis of Marsden's approach to mission, see especially Falloon, *To Plough or to Preach*; and more briefly Davidson, 'Culture and Ecclesiology'.
116   Although there is no explicit record of when the August letter was received and read, the November letter was read in July, 1802, as per the marginalia on the first page of Marsden to LMS, 5/11/1801.

forward onto Tahiti.[117] It has been difficult to find the actual documentation formalising Marsden's relationship with the LMS, but it seems likely that in response to his interest in the mission shown in the letter from January 1801—and his extant care for and further work on the behalf of the mission in Tahiti as well as its refugee missionaries in Port Jackson—that the LMS extended the offer to function as their agent in the South Seas sometime in early 1802.[118] Marsden acknowledges a letter from the LMS in this time period in a letter dated March, 1804, although he makes no reference to any new arrangement.[119]

Given the reputation LMS had developed, and would continue to have for much of the next 40 years, of being thoroughly out of touch with the realities faced by their workers—and a tendency to hand down definitive decisions with minimal information and from great distance—the presence of a (mostly) respected but *local* figure to act as a form of immediate director was vital to the recovery of the fragile South Sea efforts.[120] While Marsden came from the same evangelical circles as the founders of the CMS, his involvement with the CMS appears to have been solidified during his visit to England in 1808, when he wrote to the Committee to suggest a 'missionary settlement' in New Zealand. This led to a special meeting of the CMS Committee being convened with Marsden present on April 4, 1808.[121]

Marsden proved more than adequate in the role, capable of a vast volume of correspondence with the LMS, and eventually CMS, boards, providing invaluable support for the remaining workers in Polynesia, maintenance of his ministerial and legal duties, his thriving agricultural work, and pursuing his ultimate passion of establishing a mission in New Zealand.

5.2 The 'Christian Mahomet' and the Missions

While a great deal could be explored of Marsden's direct involvement in

---

117 Marsden to LMS, 15/8/1801.
118 This is supported by the oblique references to Marsden's work and his January, 1801 letter in Haweis to Hardcastle, 24/3/1802.
119 My thanks go to Malcolm Falloon once again for pointing me to these early letters between the LMS and Marsden, and for providing the most plausible timeline for how the relationship evolved between 1801–1804 when Marsden's agency is unambiguous.
120 Breward, *A History of the Churches in Australasia*, 24.
121 Hole, *The Early History of the CMS*, 141.

the South Sea missions from 1801 to his death, two events provide the key backdrop to the Philo Free case. These are the instigation of Marsden's trading with missionaries in Tahiti and the establishment of the New South Wales Society for affording Protection to the Natives of the South Sea Islands and promoting their Civilisation.

Very early in Marsden's relationship with the LMS missionaries, Shelley returned to Tahiti. Through this connection, Marsden and a number of other Sydney merchants and captains sought to establish a salted pork trade.[122] The missionaries would collect and salt down the pork, and trade it for provisions and goods with ships from Sydney, who were in dire need of food in the colony at that time. Sadly, part of the payment for these shipments turned out to be muskets, which horrified Marsden, and would continue to do so for many years, as evidenced by his treatment of one of his pioneer NZ missionaries, Thomas Kendall, removed in 1823 for trading in weapons with the Māori.[123]

Secondly, on December 20, 1813, Marsden oversaw the creation of The New South Wales Society for affording Protection to the Natives of the South Sea Islands and promoting their Civilisation.[124] Their aim was to provide some measure of protection for those islanders who arrived in Port Jackson as crew on ships, and to instruct them in both Christianity and agriculture. This included explicit permission being required for 'Natives of the South Sea Islands' to reside with any person in the settlement, as well as a subcommittee to hear the grievances of islanders and act as their legal representatives. The idea lay entirely with Marsden rooted in his experience of mistreatment of Māori at the hands of ship-masters, and drew the sympathy of Macquarie.[125] Over £200 were collected in initial contributions.[126]

As well as the eventual accusations of financial mismanagement by Campbell, the pursuit of justice was not especially successful. In 1814 W. C. Wentworth, the son of one of the founding members of this Philanthropic Society, was engaged in a violent incursion into

---

122 Garrett, *A Way in the Sea*, 6–7. The prime partner appears to have been Robert Campbell. For more on the pork trade, see Maude, 'The Tahitian Pork Trade'.
123 Elder, *The Letters and Journals of Samuel Marsden, 1765-1838*, 45.
124 [Missionary Register], 'New South Wales Society for affording Protection', 459. Following common practice, the meeting was chaired by the Provost Marshall, William Gore.
125 See Marsden to Pratt, 15/3/1814, which was quoted in [Missionary Register], 'New South Wales Society for affording Protection', 460–62.
126 [Missionary Register], 'New South Wales Society for affording Protection', 462.

Rarotonga (Cook Islands), during a misguided visit in quest of sandalwood. Marsden called for an inquiry into the trip, but the special meeting called ended in a cover-up of the entire event.[127] The aim of the Philanthropic Society to instruct islanders in both agriculture and the faith is typical of Marsden, with his well-worn adage of 'civilising' and 'evangelising' going hand in hand. The prime example of this was in Marsden's work in New Zealand, which brings this narrative to a close.

6. The 'Plundering' Preacher—Marsden in New Zealand

> By contrast with the evangelical mission to the convicts, the mission to the Pacific Islanders enjoyed remarkable success. Early evangelicals believed that New South Wales would be the base from which the islands of the sea would receive the Gospel. From Sydney would radiate the missionary advance of the church into New Zealand, Tahiti, Tonga and Fiji, Samoa and New Caledonia, New Hebrides and New Guinea, eventually into the countless millions of Asia.[128]

While Marsden's influence was felt throughout the South Pacific due to his role in the missionary societies, he was most personally and passionately involved in founding the first substantial missionary effort on New Zealand soil.[129] On top of his Norfolk Island visit a decade before, his interest in the Māori appears to have been stimulated by the visit to Port Jackson of Te Pahi in 1805. Marsden met and befriended the chief at Governor King's residence, and soon afterwards departed for his tour of England, in which he lobbied for the funds to establish a mission in New Zealand.[130] He reiterated his plea before the CMS council in 1807, and in writing to their secretary in March, 1808.[131] While a further six years would pass before he actually travelled to the

---

127 Garrett, *A Way in the Sea*, 6. See further, Bolt, 'The Failure of the Philanthropic Society', in this volume.
128 Piggin, *Spirit of A Nation*, 14. For a well-rounded series of papers on Marsden's missionary efforts in New Zealand, see the sister volume of this collection, Bolt & Pettett, *Launching Marsden's Mission*.
129 For some of the differing evaluations of Marsden's work from both Australian and New Zealander perspectives, see David Pettett's survey in Chapter 2 of this volume, as well as Lange, 'Admiring, Disdainful, or Somewhere in the Middle'.
130 Middleton, 'Missionization in New Zealand and Australia: A Comparison', 174.
131 Marsden to Pratt, 24/3/1808, 1; Yarwood, 'Marsden, Samuel (1765–1838)'.

islands himself, Marsden's course is plain from very early in the nineteenth century. Throughout his initial passion and planning, Marsden was fixed on the idea that commerce with natives was key to the success of any mission.[132] On the one hand, this went a long way to solving the problems of provision that the Tahitian mission struggled with (the natives not being quite as forthcoming with supplies as the LMS founders thought they would), but on the other increased the likelihood of the same issue arising as it did in Tahiti: the trade of muskets in return for food.[133] The long-term sustainability of the mission was not quite as readily achieved as Marsden would have liked, but he repeatedly and strongly cited the potential economic advantages as giving them priority. Foremost amongst his evidences for New Zealand's suitability was the lack of familiarity amongst the 'civilized world' with the country's goods; secondly, its proximity to Port Jackson and Norfolk Island for ease of communication and care of missionaries; and thirdly, the clergy in these colonies were 'of the established Church', and so of influence in their settlements, and entitled to aid and protection by the secular leaders rather than their resistance.[134]

This led Marsden to return to Sydney aboard the *Ann* with two missionaries he had identified for the work in New Zealand, John King, and William Hall. With typical credit to divine providence, they shared the journey with Duaterra (Ruatara), a New Zealander and nephew of Te Pahi, Marsden's old acquaintance. Word arrived soon after their return of the burning of the *Boyd* by New Zealanders and the cannibalism of almost all of those on board. Blame was laid squarely at the feet of Te Pahi.[135] Time would prove that rather than leading the attacked, Te Pahi in fact happened upon the aftermath and was attempting to save some survivors.[136] In the meantime, the planned mission to New Zealand was delayed, and Marsden left to care for the Māori in Sydney, with King and Hall waiting for 'a more favourable account from New Zealand

---

132 Note the intermingling of desires for both a 'Christian Church' and 'a little settlement' to be established amongst 'that Noble Race of People', Marsden to Stokes, 15/6/1815.
133 See Maude, 'The Tahitian Pork Trade', 73–76.
134 Marsden to Pratt, 24/3/1808, 1–3.
135 For details, see, Bolt, 'The *Boyd* Set-Back'.
136 *SG* 1/9/1810.

before we proceed to go there'.[137]

This four year gap saw Marsden purchase the *Active*, a brig, for £1,400.[138] Despite the accusations to come about his benefiting from a missionary vessel, this amount came entirely out of his own pocket, without any initial investment by the CMS or LMS.[139] While a pecuniary drain upon him for many years to come, having access to his own ship allowed Marsden to not only pursue the trade he saw as beneficial for civilisation in Polynesia, but also enable his own seven trips to the New Zealand between 1814-1837.[140]

Of these, Marsden's first is rightly remembered as the first formal Christian service held on New Zealand on December 25, 1814.[141] Te Pahi's nephew, Ruatara, provided the local support and protection for the initial establishment of the mission station. Such was the contrast Marsden felt between the opportunities in this new field to the difficulties and moral failings of those in his own colony that he returned from his first visit speaking to Mrs Marsden of leaving Australia. She responded, 'What will New Zealand do? What will the Missionaries at Olaketa do?'.[142] He did not, in the end, flee to New Zealand, nor, as

---

137 William Hall to Pratt, 25/4/ 1810, cited in Bolt, 'The *Boyd* Set-Back', 66. This is most likely due to the incorrect retaliatory killing of Te Pahi by British seaman, which may have rendered the situation in New Zealand unsafe for a time for Europeans, see Middleton, 'Missionization in New Zealand and Australia: A Comparison', 175. Given his strong will and entrepreneurial attitude exhibited elsewhere, it seems out of character for Marsden to be delayed for four years by fear alone. It may be that Macquarie restricted Marsden's travel in this period.
138 This may well have been the outworking of his earlier conviction that of paramount importance in the work of CMS was the ongoing communication with, and support (in the form of 'Supplies, Protection, and Encouragement') from the nearby colonies; Marsden to Pratt, 24/3/1808, 3–4. For the voyages of the *Active*, see further, Falloon, 'Mission Trading', in this volume.
139 And, in his own words, with 'more money than I could well command', being forced to borrow for the purchase in expectation of her 'fly[ing] over these seas like the Dove with the Olive branch to carry the glad tidings of Salvation to all who have never seen anything of Civil life or known anything of the Gospel', Marsden to Stokes, 15/6/1815.
140 Yarwood, 'Marsden, Samuel (1765–1838)'. The *Active* initially bore Thomas Kendall and William Hall, lay CMS missionaries, on a scouting mission in 1814. They met with Ruatara who had gone ahead to ensure smoother relations with Marsden's agents; Garrett, *To Live Among the Stars*, 62. In the aftermath of the Philo Free case, Marsden testified in court, with support eventually from the Societies in London, that the *Active* was only intended to pursue trade to defray the costs of it supporting the missionaries on location; Johnstone, *Samuel Marsden*, 144–45.
141 Cole, *A History of the Church Missionary Society of Australia*, 6. Marsden preached from Luke 2:10. For a discussion and reconstruction of the sermon, see Pettett, 'Samuel Marsden: Christmas Day 1814'.
142 Marsden to Stokes, 15/6/1815.

MISSION TO THE SOUTH SEAS   77

some have accused him, did he feel this temptation only as a 'greener pasture' after failures with indigenous Australians, but rather, and characteristically, because he saw an opportunity provided by God in his providence:[143]

> The local situation of the Islands of New Zealand, the Climate, Soil, Natural Productions, and Inhabitants, are all favourable for Missionary Labours; and I firmly believe that the time is come for the Gospel to be preached to them.[144]

While the New Zealand mission would not be an entirely rosy affair, the 1820s and 30s saw a building of momentum which those on board the *Duff* could only have dreamed of. Tahiti and Raiatea began sending local and European workers to the Cook Islands, Tonga began to respond remarkably (especially to the Wesleyan work Marsden came to coordinate from Sydney as well), Samoa and Niue were reached, and these Polynesian bases provided the 'local teachers' who formed the frontline of evangelism for Tuvalu, Solomon Islands, and Vanuatu—where our story began with Quiros three hundred years before.

7. Philo Free and the South Sea Missions

Even the barest sketch of the South Sea missions gives some idea of how complex a period the late 18th and early 19th centuries were for the missionary enterprise. Whatever else one may want to say about his character, methods, and achievements, Marsden must be credited with the enormous work of managing the logistics for three separate Societies, handling the often tense political situation in his colony, the upkeep of his ministry and magisterial roles in Parramatta, the care of his wife, and his own passion-project in New Zealand. This combination of responsibilities provided more than enough opportunities to collect enemies, as this very commemoration demonstrates.

It is hoped that this account of the missionary background, however brief, may at the very least give some idea of the stage on which the Philo Free drama played out, as well as aid the understanding of some

---

143 'N.S. Wales would not have detained me had it not been the post which the Great Captain of Salvation assigned me *for the good of the Heathen*'; Marsden to Stokes, 14/6/1819. See also Falloon, 'The Openings of Providence'.
144 [Missionary Register], 'Mr Marsden's Second Visit', 306.

of the direct issues raised in the Philo Free letter, such as the sale of muskets in New Zealand, the accusation of alcoholic distillation, the direction of attention and finance to the South Pacific rather than indigenous Australia, and the 'profiteering' of an inactive Philanthropic Society. What seems clear is that Marsden's involvement logistically, ideologically, and practically, in the missionary outreach to the South Pacific provided the openings that Campbell used in his satirical attack. While it seems unlikely that personal defence had no part in it at all, Marsden repeatedly insisted that he only pursued the libel case, despite the legal and 'Christian Principles' involved, because of his defence of the movements he was involved in: 'I did not feel for myself, so much as I did for the important Cause of the mission—I was fearful from opposition, it might be crushed in its Infancy'.[145]

---

145   Marsden to Pratt, 26/9/1818, 1.

CHAPTER 4

THE EARLY COLONIAL MISSION CONTEXT OF *PHILO FREE*

Greg D. Anderson

Marsden's vindication in the charge of libel against Philo Free (John Thomas Campbell) does not foreclose on the possibility of investigating further the history of Christian mission among the Aboriginal people of New South Wales in the early colony. There are few happy stories in that history, but providing some context around the particularities of the Philo Free matter can give further depth to our understanding of some of the dynamics in play. The purpose of this chapter is to present a brief account of the attitudes to Aboriginal people among Christians in the early colony and how this interacted with attempts to bring them to a saving knowledge of God through the gospel of Jesus Christ and to establish them in Christian discipleship. It shall be argued that although Marsden's defence against Philo Free's attacks was legally successful, Aboriginal mission in fact had taken a significantly second place in Marsden's evangelistic aspirations, largely because the cultural differences between somebody like him and the Aboriginal people of Sydney whom he encountered resulted in attitudes that made evangelistic mission highly problematic. Views similar to Marsden's were widely held in the colony, including among Christians.

Accounts of Marsden's own attitudes and practice in Aboriginal mission have been provided elsewhere,[1] but we may summarise them before turning to the broader context of Aboriginal mission in the early

---

1   See, for example, Standfield, *Race and Identity*; Yarwood, *Samuel Marsden: Survivor*; Quinn, *Samuel Marsden*; and Anderson, 'Culture and mission'.

colony, since Marsden's prominence in the colony meant that his views were significantly influential.

Philo Free's letter to the *Sydney Gazette* of January 4, 1817, made a number of claims with regard to the conduct of Christians and philanthropic donors to mission in Australia and the Pacific, and these claims certainly included Marsden, as Marsden himself appreciated. Philo Free wrote *inter alia* 'I do not wish to see men in any garb, or under any mask or pretence whatever, arrogate to themselves such consequential airs of importance, for acts of public beneficence, which they have never exhibited in their private lives; and still less, if possible, in their public characters towards the abject Natives of New South Wales'.[2] This charge was that those who had staked out the high moral ground of funding mission (particularly in the Pacific) had been hypocritically deficient in their favour towards Aboriginal people. In his letter, Philo Free asserted that he himself was 'one of those who wish to introduce civilization; and the pure doctrines of the Christian religion among the sable sons of Australia' and to 'reclaim these children of Nature' under 'the great and glorious object of dispelling the dark and gloomy clouds of ignorance under which it has pleased Providence to permit the Aborigines of this Colony to remain unto the present time'. We cannot test the sincerity of Philo Free's self-evaluation, although we may note that Marsden himself doubted that sincerity.[3] We may also note how he lumps together 'civilising' and Christian doctrine in a way that was widespread among English-speaking missionaries around the globe.[4] On the whole, as we shall see, the attitude of the colonists towards the Indigenous population was almost entirely negative.

There is no doubt that the Philo Free trial was surrounded by the tension between Marsden and Governor Lachlan Macquarie. A particular issue that arose subsequently, but which is relevant to the discussion here, is Marsden's defence against remarks made about him by Macquarie that impugned Marsden's commitment to Aboriginal

---

2   *SG* 4/1/1817.
3   'I should not notice these things but to put you on your Guard—as any stranger would think that the man who could express himself in this manner must be a friend to the pious Character; and would countenance what he professes to approve—you will from what judgment you may think proper of the enclosed, but believe me, it contains words without meaning', Marsden to LMS, 17/5/1817.
4   See Bolt, 'The Letter', pp.32–33, which exegetes strong hostility towards evangelicals in Philo Free's letter.

people. In 1826, nearly five years after Macquarie's resignation from the post of Governor, and two years after his death, Marsden published *An Answer to Certain Calumnies in the Late Governor Macquarie's Pamphlet*.[5] A particular focus was the Native Institution, which Macquarie had established in 1814 in Parramatta, in an attempt to care for, educate and 'civilise' Aboriginal children, as a perceived remedy to their continuing in a state of degradation and depredation as fringe-dwellers in the colony. In answer to Macquarie's assertion that Marsden had neglected the Native Institution, Marsden made three points. First, he had recommended the site, near Parramatta, and facilitated its acquisition for the Institution. Second, Macquarie had not appointed him to the committee overseeing the Institution, despite it being in his parish; and had in fact appointed to the committee two of the colony's assistant chaplains despite their living fifteen and twenty miles from Parramatta. This passing over clearly derived, in Marsden's opinion, from Macquarie's hostility to Marsden, because Marsden was appointed to the committee immediately on the arrival of Macquarie's successor, and remained on it until the committee was closed down. Third, Macquarie had never invited Marsden to visit or engage with the Institution, and Marsden writes that he would have happily done so if that invitation had come. It is clear, then, that Marsden was stung by this criticism, and believed it was unjustified. He wanted to be perceived as someone who was not prejudiced against the welfare of Aboriginal people or opposed to Aboriginal mission. That is not to say, however, that his own close interactions with Aboriginal people and missionaries to Aboriginal people did not have an effect on him.

Two such matters give some insight into Marsden's own attitude to Aboriginal people. First, the Marsdens took into their household two young Aboriginal children, who came to be known as Harry and Tristan. Marsden wrote of Harry, thirty years later, that he had lived with the Marsdens for a considerable time. 'He learned to speak our language, and while he was with me behaved well. [...] But at length he joined the natives in the woods, and from that time to the present, he only paid me occasional visits [...] he never seems to think that he lost anything by living in the woods'.[6] More is known about Tristan. He was

---

5 Marsden, *An answer to certain calumnies*.
6 Marsden to Archdeacon Thomas Scott 1826; cited in Harris, *One Blood*, 43.

taken 'from his mother's breast' at about the age of four, and stayed with the Marsdens from about 1794 until the time the Marsdens travelled to England in 1807.[7] It was clearly the Marsdens' intention to keep him away from his countrymen and to educate him, probably for domestic service. Elizabeth Marsden wrote in 1796 that he had 'no inclination to go among the natives and has quite forgotten their manners'.[8] The *Sydney Gazette* in an obituary in 1804 to James Bath, another Aboriginal child who had been taken into a colonial household, declared similarly that Tristan 'showed the same dislike to others of his own complexion as [had James]'.[9] En route to England, however, at about the age of sixteen or seventeen, he ran away from the Marsdens in Rio de Janeiro, and some years later returned to Australia with another colonist and rejoined his people. Marsden was never able to persuade him to return to the English way of life. Writing with hindsight, Thomas Hassall expressed his opinion that Tristan had been schooled in 'all that was bad' by convict servants in the Marsden household,[10] as was evidenced in Tristan succumbing to the temptation to get drunk while on the voyage to England. Marsden also in retrospect declared that Tristan had always 'wanted that attachment for me and my family that we had just reason to expect and he always seemed to want that fine feeling which is the bond of social life'.[11] There seems little doubt that these relationships weighed heavily in developing Marsden's view that Aboriginal people had inherently limited prospects for integrating with colonial life, which in his mind seemed closely bound up with being Christians.

The second matter, and perhaps deriving from the first in shaping Marsden's views, was Marsden's relationship with Lancelot Threlkeld, who founded a mission on the shores of Lake Macquarie, north of Sydney, among the Awabakal people. Threlkeld was a member of the London Missionary Society (LMS) who had served in Tahiti from 1817 until the death of his first wife in 1824. On coming to Sydney in 1824, he was persuaded by LMS inspectors to establish a mission to Aboriginal people, which began in 1827. It was clear from early in his time at Lake Macquarie that he did not believe his financial allowances

---

7   Standfield, 'The Parramatta Māori Seminary', 124.
8   Eliza Marsden to Mary Stokes, 1/5/1796 (Mackaness, *Some Private Correspondence*, No. 5).
9   James Bath obituary, SG 2/12/1804; cited in Standfield, 'Parramatta', 125.
10 T. Hassall, 'Account of Tristan's disappearance'; cited in Standfield, 'Parramatta', 125.
11 Marsden to Bigge, [1820]; cited in Fletcher, *Clean, Clad and Courteous*, 16.

were adequate to the task of establishing a station and engaging with local Aboriginal people. The LMS, on the other hand, believed he was profligate and finally insisted that all his expenses be approved by Marsden, who had been appointed as the LMS agent in New South Wales. Marsden and Threlkeld's relationship is documented in the letters between them, correspondence with the LMS, letters to the editor of the *Sydney Gazette*, and letters to and from the Sydney Presbyterian minister John Dunmore Lang, who seems to have had an antipathy towards Threlkeld from an early stage.[12] Although Marsden tended to write courteously to Threlkeld—courtesy which was rarely reciprocated—it is clear that he felt the whole project of the Lake Macquarie mission was misconceived, particularly with regard to finances. The problem of money seems to have revolved around what constituted 'necessities' for the establishment and maintenance of the mission. Threlkeld seems to have understood this much more liberally than Marsden and the LMS. Contributing towards the sour relationship was also Threlkeld's hostility, as a Congregationalist, to Marsden as a representative of the established Church of England, despite Marsden's evangelical convictions. In the end, it is difficult to determine whether Marsden's awkward relationship with Threlkeld contributed to his negative attitude to the Lake Macquarie mission, or whether his negative attitude to Aboriginal mission contributed to the breakdown of trust with Threlkeld. But to have the concrete issue of a mission which needed constant funding despite Marsden's scepticism concerning its usefulness or fruitfulness, must have had an effect on Marsden's attitude to the evangelisation of the Indigenous people. Threlkeld was eventually forced to change course when LMS closed the mission and Threlkeld transferred his enterprise to a different location, funded by the colonial government for some years from late 1829.

But these specific examples of Marsden's interaction with Aboriginal people and with missionaries to them must be set in the broader context of attempts to reach out with the gospel to the land's original inhabitants. To what extent were there more positive attitudes or positive efforts to evangelise them?

It is worth noting that the early years of the colony were more or

---

12 See, for example, Champion, 'Lancelot Edward Threlkeld'. Ironically, in the light of the Philo Free case, Threlkeld ended up suing Lang for libel.

less concurrent with the rise of the modern Protestant missionary movement. William Carey's seminal work *An enquiry into the Obligations of Christians, to use means for the conversion of the heathens* was not published until 1792, and became a stimulus for the establishment of numerous missionary societies, including his own Baptist Missionary Society in 1792, the non-denominational (although eventually dominated by Congregationalists) LMS in 1794 and the (Anglican) Church Missionary Society (CMS) in 1799.

The first chaplain to the colony, Reverend Richard Johnson, had taken an Aboriginal teenage girl into his home, as a survivor of the 1789 outbreak of smallpox.[13] His hopes for Aboriginal mission were expressed in a letter in 1790 in which he said of this girl, Abaroo, that he had 'taught her the Lord's Prayer &c—& as she comes better to understand me, endeavour to instruct her respecting a supreme Being &c.—Wish to see these poor heathen brought to the Knowlege of X'tianity, & hope in time to see or hear of the dawnings of that time when these shall be given for our Lord's inheritance, & the uttermost parts of the earth for his Possession [quoting Psalm 2:8]'.[14] A letter one year later, however, reports that Abaroo had not continued to be engaged so happily in Johnson's household, and that she had begun returning to 'the woods' for some time.[15] In the same letter, Johnson indicates that he has written to 'some of our great ones' urging that missionaries be sent out to the colony soon. Although he does not specify that he means for the Aboriginal context, we may assume this was the case since it follows immediately after his news about Abaroo.

Even at this very early stage of 'mission' in the colony, it is clear that the approach was strongly in the direction of associating promulgation of Christian faith with English cultural forms. We may assume that Johnson taught Abaroo the Lord's Prayer in English, and we may expect that he attempted to explain that meaning. But there is no indication of seeking to understand her world view, including what she may or may not have understood about a supreme being.

This same correlation of 'Christianising' and 'civilising' Aboriginal

---

13 There is ongoing controversy about whether it was in fact smallpox or chickenpox. See recent discussion in Warren, 'Smallpox at Sydney Cove', and Carmody on ABC Radio National's program *Ockham's Razor*, September 19, 2010.
14 Johnson to H. Fricker, 9/4/1790.
15 Johnson to H. Fricker, 18/3/1791.

people was expressed in the work of the Native Institution, mentioned above in connection with Marsden's self-defence against Macquarie. Although established in 1814 by the government, not as a missionary enterprise, its goals included religious education as well as the teaching of reading, writing and manual and domestic arts.[16] The first headmaster, William Shelley, had been an LMS missionary in Tonga before arriving in Sydney, and must surely have had evangelistic aspirations for those who would be educated there. It may have been Shelley who suggested the founding of the Native Institution,[17] but Macquarie consulted Marsden for his opinion also and Marsden endorsed the proposal.[18] Shelley died not long after the establishment of the Institution in July 1815, and the work was taken over by his wife, until 1823, when it was divided into separate girls and boys schools, before finally closing in 1825.[19] By 1823, 64 children had been pupils of the Institution,[20] that is, on average, seven new children each year.

It was not until 1821 that the first person appointed specifically for the task of Aboriginal mission arrived in Sydney. William Walker was recruited by the Wesleyan Methodist Missionary Society, which had decided in 1820 in London to seek such a person.[21] This was under the influence of Samuel Leigh, who had arrived in Sydney as a Methodist clergyman in 1815, although it seems Leigh himself had not engaged in Aboriginal contact. According to Woolmington, Walker 'began by wandering around the countryside talking to Aborigines',[22] and until 1822 visited the residents of the Native Institution, until stopped by Marsden who in that year was appointed to the Institution's committee. Walker concluded, however, that itinerating with Aboriginal people was ineffective. He wrote to the Wesley Methodist Missionary Society General Secretaries that 'Traversing the woods in their tribes and living in a kind of domesticated manner with them will never do the work nor will it prove conducive to their more quickly and readily receiving the blessed and saving truths of religion.'[23] Perhaps responding to his

16 W. Shelley to L. Macquarie, 8/4/1814 (*HRA* 1.8, 371).
17 Bridges, 'The Church of England and the Aborigines', 108.
18 Marsden, *Against Certain Calumnies*.
19 Reece, *Aborigines and Colonists*, 63 n.1.
20 Woolmington, 'Early Christian Missions to the Australian Aborigines', 18.
21 Bollen, 'English Missionary Societies and the Australian Aborigine', 268.
22 Woolmington, '"Writing on the Sand"', 78.
23 W. Walker to WAMS; cited in Harris, *One Blood*, 49.

ejection from the Native Institution, the Methodists allowed him to supervise their own small version of the institution, also in Parramatta, but it was short-lived. Around the same time, an assistant, John Harper, was appointed to serve with Walker. He was given the task of establishing a mission station in the Wellington Valley, west of the Blue Mountains on the fringe of colonisation, which included agricultural work and a school. Both proved unsuccessful, and an investigation in 1826 resulted in the station closing.[24] Harper claimed to have made progress in learning the language of the people, and whether the claim is true or not, it at least indicates that he valued, or believed others (although the number cannot have been large) would value, the attempt at engaging culturally in that way. He blamed the failure of the enterprise on the proximity of the immorality of the white colonists, although correspondence by Walker, the Attorney-General and Archdeacon Scott indicate that Harper was not held in high regard by those who were committed, at least in theory, to Aboriginal mission.[25] In 1824, after the Native Institution was reorganised along gender lines, Walker and his wife were assigned to the supervision of the girls' section. This, too, ended in ignominy, with Walker and his wife being removed from the Wesleyan Mission Society in 1826.

Threlkeld's mission at Lake Macquarie has already been mentioned with regard to Threlkeld's relationship with Marsden, but it is worth considering the methodology Threlkeld sought to employ. He wrote to Attorney-General Saxe Bannister in 1825 that he thought it right to 'first obtain the language, then preach the Gospel, then urge from gospel motives to be industrious, at the same time become a servant to them to win them to that which is right'.[26] Threlkeld's effort to learn the Awabakal language was significant, and resulted in four publications of linguistic description,[27] the Gospel of Luke in 1830,[28] and an incomplete and unpublished translation of the Gospel of Mark from about 1838.[29] When LMS dismissed Threlkeld and closed the mission, Threlkeld moved to

24 Woolmington, '"Writing"', 79.
25 Woolmington, '"Writing"', 79.
26 L. Threlkeld to Saxe Bannister, 27/9/1825, cited in Woolmington, '"Writing"', 80 and Harris, *One Blood*, 57.
27 Woolmington, '"Writing"', 80; Harris, *One Blood*, 56.
28 Harris, *One Blood*, 56.
29 Roberts, 'Language to save the innocent'.

a new site on the other side of the Lake, which he called Ebenezer, but he continued with his linguistic research and translation. The newly appointed Archdeacon Broughton (1829), later to become the first and only Bishop of Australia (1836) then Bishop of Sydney (1847), commended, although with reservation, the support of this work to Governor Darling, including advocating specific financial provision for the production of vernacular biblical and linguistic material, which resulted in the publication of Luke's Gospel.[30] Roberts argues that Threlkeld 'genuinely believed that codifying the Aboriginal language and teaching them, and Europeans, to read it, was fundamental to bringing Aborigines into the light of God, and to bringing the races together into a shared, civilised community'.[31] This was radically out of step with prevailing views, including Marsden's, although we may note Marsden's commitment across the Tasman to the learning and use of Māori language.[32] Apart from his work on language, Threlkeld showed eagerness in collecting information on Aboriginal culture that demonstrated their intelligence, ingenuity and capacity to use and relate to the environment, again counter to the dominant English society's attitude. In the end, however, despite all his efforts, and the finance provided by Government and private donors, Threlkeld's work was abandoned because the Aboriginal population of the area was diminishing rapidly under the impact of colonial expansion, and in 1841, fourteen years after beginning the mission, he moved back to Sydney.

The final mission that began in reasonable proximity to Sydney in Marsden's lifetime was the CMS mission in the Wellington Valley, in the vicinity of what had been the Wesleyan mission founded by John Harper. A New South Wales CMS Auxiliary had been formed by Marsden in 1821, comprising Marsden's under-chaplains, Cartwright and Hill, and Captain Francis Irvine, who had arrived from India in

---

30 Bollen, 'English Missionary Societies and the Australian Aborigine', 271 n.40. To know about a language, of course, does not indicate ability to use it. Roberts cites Broughton telling Darling that Threlkeld could not engage in lengthy conversation, even on ordinary topics, with Aboriginal people in Awabakal—although it is not clear that Broughton can have had much evidence of this as early as 1830, and his expectations as to what constituted a lengthy conversation, and what intellectual discourse sounded like, may have created a grid that misinterpreted the data in any case.
31 Roberts, 'Language to Save the Innocent', 120.
32 See Marsden to Pratt, 7/2/1825. Marsden was a pioneer in the learning of Māori and language learning was a key strategy of the Polynesian and Māori mission.

1820—it was quickly disbanded, but reformed in 1825.³³ Cartwright and Hill advocated for a stronger emphasis on the evangelisation of Aboriginal people, in the face of Marsden's increasing efforts in New Zealand, which had begun in 1814.³⁴ CMS in London authorised the establishment of a station, but made it clear that it would not provide money to build or run it. The colonial government committed itself to providing a land grant, and the allowances for two missionaries, but the amount proved inadequate. The local Auxiliary was urged by CMS not to solicit for private donations, in case these reduced the pressure on the government to provide the financial support, which CMS believed was the government's obligation. Marsden's own view of the mission was somewhat negative. Although he recognised the Christian duty to seek to improve the Aboriginal people's situation, he was pessimistic about the enterprise's success.³⁵ He wrote near the time of the commencement of the Wellington mission that 'I have from the first considered this Mission a Govt Establishment'.³⁶ The mission began with only three whites: William Watson and his wife, and J.C.S. Handt. Handt was subsequently replaced by another German, James Günther, and a farmer, William Porter, joined the team in 1838. The mission only lasted ten years. The negative influence of convicts who worked in the neighbourhood was regarded as unhelpful; drought conditions meant that the agricultural output was less than expected; but far worse was the deterioration of the relationships among the missionaries themselves. Porter was accused of sexual misconduct with the women who lived at the mission, and was sacked.

It is clear from these accounts that mission among Aboriginal people in the Sydney area had not met with the kind of success that Marsden and other church leaders in the colony might have hoped for. Three interwoven factors stand out as of continuing importance, not just at

---

33 The CMS Auxiliary Committee formed 2 Mar 1821 dissolved on 27 September the same year, due to conflict between Marsden and Irvine. After Irvine left NSW in 1824, it was re-established 7 Feb 1825. After London's approval arrived, a Corresponding Committee of CMS was formed on 29 Apr 1826 with the mandate of conducting the Australasian mission to Aboriginal Australians and Māori.
34 Yet Marsden was nevertheless involved in the initiation of the CMS mission to Aboriginal people; see Marsden to Pratt, 7 & 8/2/1825; Marsden to Coates, 17/3/1825.
35 Marsden to Coates 21/11/1825: 'Whether any thing can be done with these degraded Tribes, I have my doubts. It is our duty to try what we can do'.
36 Marsden to W.G. Broughton, 3/11/1832; cited in Bollen, 'English Missionary Societies and the Australian Aborigine', 275 n.69.

that time, but for many decades as the contact between the gospel and Aboriginal people spread across the continent.

First, the colonists had an almost universally low view of Aboriginal people. We have seen that Threlkeld was an exception, but he stands out in marked contrast with the majority view. Reece and Woolmington provide evidence of this from contemporary writing.[37] Marsden himself wrote that Aboriginal people were 'very low in the Scale of Human Beings'.[38] The Methodist Samuel Leigh similarly believed that 'the Aborigines [...] are by appearances little above the brute beast'.[39] Aboriginal abuse of alcohol and lack of clothing were frequently cited as indicators of their moral depravity. An article in the *Sydney Gazette* in 1837 reported on 'the largest mob we have ever witnessed [... who] exhibited their beastly antics, and brutal contests, in a state of semi-nudity, and complete drunkenness in that character of ferocity which savages only can assume'.[40] A commonly held view, based on a contemporary understanding of the biblical narrative, was that humans had started well and that therefore less 'civilized' peoples had declined into degradation.[41] The Presbyterian William Ridley said in a lecture in Macquarie Street in 1864 that 'The Australian race, on retiring from the presence of more energetic and intellectual nations, chose not to retain the knowledge of God, or the means of individual and social progress; and *as a necessary consequence* [my emphasis], declined from generation to generation, until even the use of housing and of clothing was forgotten'.[42] Thus, there was a collective moral culpability in Aboriginal culture. The observation that Aboriginal people, when confronted with what the colonists believed was their own superior culture, seemed to disdain it rather than aspiring to 'improvement', was seen as proof of this.[43] A particular case was that Aboriginal religion did not seem to know of a god or gods; and their apparent rejection of

---

37 Reece, *Aborigines and Colonists*. Woolmington, 'Early Christian Missions to the Australian Aborigines'.
38 Marsden to Coates, 17/3/1825, cited by Woolmington, 'Early Christian Missions to the Australian Aborigines', 103.
39 S. Leigh to A. Clark, 14/10/1817, cited by Woolmington, 'Early Christian Missions to the Australian Aborigines', 104.
40 *SG* 30/3/1837.
41 Woolmington, 'Early Christian Missions to the Australian Aborigines', 89; citing Murray, *Enquiries Historical and Moral*.
42 Ridley, *The Aborigines of Australia*.
43 Woolmington, 'Early Christian Missions to the Australian Aborigines', 169.

the proclamation of God by Christians cemented their degraded status. The occasional voice sought to point out that what the English saw of Aboriginal practice was in great part the result of the collision with a European culture that was no model of Christian morality. Governor Hunter himself wrote about the colonists in 1798 that 'a more wicked, abandoned and irreligious set of people have never been brought together in any part of the world'.[44] One response to this was to seek to establish missions as far as possible geographically from the colonists. Reverend Joseph Orton told the Wesleyan Missionary Society in 1836 that a mission would need to be 500 miles from Sydney to have any chance of success.[45]

Second, flowing from these negative perceptions, it did not take long before many Christians regarded the conversion of Aboriginal people as a hopeless case. The Quaker Daniel Wheeler, who arrived in Sydney in 1834, concluded that 'every attempt to assist them [is] fruitless'.[46] By 1842, the British Secretary of State for War and the Colonies, Lord Stanley 'questioned the wisdom or propriety of continuing the missions any longer in the face of the despondent reports he had received from the missionaries themselves', including the missions at Lake Macquarie, Wellington Valley, Moreton Bay (Brisbane) and Port Phillip (Melbourne).[47] Marsden himself had come to this opinion relatively early. In 1826, he wrote that 'I am convinced we cannot do more for them than to give them a Loaf of Bread when hungry and a Blanket when cold—more they will not let us do'.[48] With this attitude, it is hardly surprising that he turned his efforts to New Zealand.[49] Again, there was the occasional voice expressing a different view. A letter to the *Sydney Gazette* under the name Philanthropus (probably Robert Cartwright)[50] in January 1824 said, 'It is with no small regret, that I feel myself, even at this period of Missionary zeal, and progress of Christianity through the world, urged to complain, that the case of

---

44 Hunter to Portland, 1/11/1798 (*HRNSW* 3, 441).
45 Reece, *Aborigines and Colonists*, 65.
46 Wheeler, *Effects of the Introduction of Ardent Spirits and Implements of War*, 4; cited by Reece, *Aborigines and Colonists*, 8.
47 Woolmington, 'Early Christian Missions to the Australian Aborigines', 6.
48 Marsden to W.A. Hankey & G. Burder, 12/9/1826; cited by Bollen, 'English Missionary Societies and the Australian Aborigine', 284.
49 See further Anderson, 'Culture and Mission'.
50 Harris, *One Blood*, 33.

the New Hollanders obtains but little regard'.⁵¹

The third factor was a widespread view that again flowed from these first two factors. Because Aboriginal people were regarded as so degraded, and because they were perceived as unable to be reached in their natural state by the gospel, they needed to be 'civilised', or brought closer to English mores, before they would be capable of understanding and embracing Christian faith. At the very least, it was believed that 'civilisation' and Christianity were necessarily linked. Philanthropus himself in an earlier letter to the *Gazette* had challenged the colony to formulate a plan to 'speedily and effectualy [sic] civilize and evangelize' the original inhabitants.⁵² Marsden had been a strong advocate of the 'civilise first' approach from early in his ministry in Sydney. We have seen already how he took two Aboriginal children into his household and celebrated their gradual adoption of English values. As Marsden contemplated the establishment of a mission among Māori people in New Zealand, he suggested that artisans would be the best missionaries because they would introduce and model commercial skills, which would advance the Christian cause because 'civilisation opens a way for the gospel'.⁵³ The advice of LMS to the missionaries in 1810 was that they should, 'contribute to the civilisation of the heathen and thus prepare them for the reception of moral and religious instruction'.⁵⁴ The problem for Marsden and others was that few Aboriginal people, particularly adults, showed interest in assimilating into the colonial society. Part of the rationale for the founding of the Native Institution by Macquarie was that children could be shaped more readily into English ways of life. As was the case, however, with Abaroo, Harry and Tristan, mentioned above, once such children reached adolescence there was a strong pull to return to their own people. There was an alternative view held by a number of Christians in the colony, that the 'civilisation' project would never succeed until Aboriginal people were converted. Woolmington mentions a number of missionaries and churchmen in Sydney who took this position, including Bishop Broughton, Reverend William Cowper of St Philip's, Church Hill, Threlkeld, Günther, Tuckfield from Port

51 *SG* 8/1/1824.
52 *SG* 7/7/1810.
53 Marsden to Hardcastle, 25/10/1810. Note, however, that he noted this sequence was not always followed; see, Marsden to Burder, 7/10/1814.
54 LMS Secretaries to Marsden, 19/3/1810.

Phillip, and the Lutherans from Moreton Bay, Eipper and Schmidt.[55] She points out, however, that for all of them, it was a theoretical position—none claimed to have seen conversions which then translated into a 'civilised' life. Attempts at simply engaging with Aboriginal people and evangelising them without seeking to 'civilise' them seem to have vanished in New South Wales after Walker's early attempts at itinerating. Only one attempt at this seems to have been undertaken in the first half of the nineteenth century, on the other side of the continent. The Italian Catholic missionary, Don Angelo Confalonieri, arrived destitute at Victoria settlement at Port Essington on the Northern Territory coast in 1846, following a shipwreck and the drowning of his two missionary companions. He had prepared himself in his native Trento for the arduous existence he anticipated having in Australia, and was not to be deterred by disaster from persevering in his aim. For two years he joined the Iwaidja and Garig tribes, travelled around the Cobourg Peninsula with them, refrained from trying to teach them agriculture or manual arts, learnt and documented their language and taught the Christian faith, until his death from malaria in 1848.[56]

These three factors significantly shaped Aboriginal mission for the whole colonial period, and indeed set a mould that would have long-lasting effects. The practice of assimilating Aboriginal people into the dominant culture as part of the mission effort lasted well into the twentieth century, with little variation. Marsden's own attitude in early Sydney may have been a dominant force in reinforcing this approach—although as we have seen, there was always a minority counterpoint—and it may also have been that he was unable to see past his own cultural values to imagine another way forward. Despite his protestations in the light of Philo Free's letter that he was no less supportive of Aboriginal mission than others, it was his energetic efforts to establish the gospel among Māori people, rather than in New South Wales, that earn him a bright place in mission history.

---

55 Woolmington, 'The Civilisation/Christianisation Debate', 96–97.
56 Girola & Pizzini, *Nagoyo*.

CHAPTER 5

A SECRET ENEMY

The turbulent relationship between Marsden and Macquarie

Craig Schwarze

Lachlan Macquarie, fifth governor of New South Wales, and Samuel Marsden, senior chaplain of that same colony, first encountered one another not beneath the wild antipodean sun but rather within the dignified halls of privilege and power in 19th century London.

Marsden was in England at that time attempting to drum up support for his proposed mission to New Zealand. When he learned of Macquarie's appointment as governor, he organised a meeting with him in order to secure his support for the New Zealand venture. Marsden was encouraged by this meeting, and left it convinced that he had found an ally in Macquarie.[1]

Nine years later we find the men meeting together again, but this time under very different circumstances. Macquarie commenced the meeting with this extraordinary attack:

> I have long known, Mr Marsden, that you are a secret Enemy of mine—and as long as you continued only a secret one, I despised too much your malicious attempts to injure my character to take any notice of your treacherous conduct.[2]

How can we explain this transformation? In just a few short years the men have moved from a state of easy tranquility to the most naked aggression. This chapter will document the deterioration of the

---

1   Marsden to Pratt, 9/5/1809.
2   Macquarie to Marsden, 8/1/1818.

relationship between Marsden and Macquarie, and will consider how this provides context for the famous Philo Free case.

At first glance Marsden and Macquarie would appear to be natural allies. Macquarie was deeply concerned about the moral and religious state of the colony, and took steps to increase church-going and marriage amongst the colonists. More significantly, he was a great admirer of William Wilberforce, the famous abolitionist and MP—the same Wilberforce who was a regular correspondent with Marsden, and who was responsible for his appointment as chaplain in the first place.[3]

Figure 4: Magistrates Under Macquarie

Appointed Prior to Macquarie, continuing in office under Macquarie:

Name	Date Appointed	Location
Samuel Marsden	1795	Parramatta

Persons acting as Magistrates in 1809:

Capt. William Lawson	Col. George Johnston	Major Edward Abbott
Surgeon John Harris	Garnham Blaxcell (resigned in April)	Robert Fitz
Surgeon Charles Throsby (resigned in September)	Alexander Riley	William Broughton

Magistrates Appointed by Macquarie in 1810:

Name	Date Appointed	Location
Capt. John Murray (73rd)	January	Parramatta
William Broughton	January	Sydney
Robert Campbell	January	Sydney
John Palmer	January	Sydney
Andrew Thompson	January	Hawkesbury
Capt. William Kenny (73rd)	January	Port Dalrymple
Lieut. Tankerville A. Crane (73rd)	January	Norfolk Island
Lieut. John Purcell (73rd)	March	Newcastle
Alexander Riley	March, on resignation of Robert Campbell	Sydney
Simeon Lord	May	Sydney
D'Arcy Wentworth	May	Sydney
Thomas Moore	May	Georges River [Liverpool]
Capt. John Murray (73rd)	June	Hobart
Lieut. Robert Durie (73rd)	June	Parramatta
William Cox	October, on the death of A. Thompson	Hawkesbury

---

3   McLachlan, 'Macquarie, Lachlan (1762–1824)'.

Magistrates under Macquarie, 1813–1817, by station:

Station	1813	1814	1815	1816	1817
Magistrates of Territory & Dependencies				D'A. Wentworth J.T. Campbell	D'A. Wentworth J.T. Campbell
Sydney	Ellis Bent W. Broughton A. Riley D'A.Wentworth S. Lord	Ellis Bent W. Broughton A. Riley D'A.Wentworth S. Lord	Ellis Bent J.H. Bent W. Broughton A. Riley D'A.Wentworth S. Lord	W. Broughton A. Riley S. Lord	W. Broughton (absent in Tas) A. Riley S. Lord
Parramatta	Rev. S Marsden	Rev. S Marsden	Rev. S Marsden H. McArthur	Rev. S Marsden H. McArthur	Rev. S Marsden H. McArthur
Windsor	W. Cox	W. Cox	W. Cox	W. Cox	W. Cox
Wilberforce	Rev. R. Cartwright	Rev. R. Cartwright	Rev. R. Cartwright	Rev. R. Cartwright	Rev. R. Cartwright
Castlereagh	J. Mileham	J. Mileham	J. Mileham	J. Mileham Rev. H. Fulton	J. Mileham Rev. H. Fulton
Liverpool	T. Moore	T. Moore	T. Moore	T. Moore	T. Moore
Bringelly				R. Lowe	R. Lowe
Newcastle	Lieut. J. Skottowe (RN)	Lieut. J. Skottowe (RN)	Lieut. Thomas Thompson (46th)	Lieut. Thomas Thompson (46th)	
Hobart	Capt. J. Murray (73rd) Rev. R. Knopwood L. Fosbrook	Capt. J. Murray (73rd) Rev. R. Knopwood L. Fosbrook A.W.H. Humphrey	Rev. R. Knopwood A.W.H. Humphrey J. Gordon F. Williams	Rev. R. Knopwood A.W.H. Humphrey J. Gordon F. Williams A.F. Kemp	Rev. R. Knopwood A.W.H. Humphrey J. Gordon F. Williams A.F. Kemp
Port Dalrymple	Maj. A. Geils (73rd) Capt. J. Ritchie (73rd)	Maj. A. Geils (73rd) Capt. J. Ritchie (73rd)	Capt. J. McKenzie (46th) T. Archer	Brev. Maj. James Stewart (46th) T. Archer	Brev. Maj. James Stewart (46th) T. Archer

New Commission, 31 March 1820, in consequence of 'doubts in regard to jurisdiction of some':

Wm Broughton	Simeon Lord	Thomas Moore	William Cox
James Mileham	Hannibal McArthur	Robert Lowe	Henry Fulton
John Brabyn	William Lawson	William Howe	Archibald Bell

New Commission issued in consequence of the Demise of King George the Third, February 1821:

Wm Broughton	John Piper	D'Arcy Wentworth	John Harris
Thomas Moore	William Lawson	William Cox	Sir John Jamison
James Mileham	William Howe	Hannibal McArthur	Archibald Bell
John T. Campbell	William Minchin	Robert Lowe	Frederick Goulburn
Henry Fulton	Edward Riley	Richard Brooks	Thomas McVitie
John Brabyn			

Macquarie was perhaps mindful of Wilberforce when he gave the first orders that were fated to bring him into conflict with Marsden. Soon after the new governor arrived in the colony, he informed Marsden that he wished to appoint him commissioner of the toll road he was planning to build between Sydney and the Hawkesbury. Marsden agreed, but was surprised to subsequently read in the *Sydney Gazette* that two former convicts, Andrew Thompson and Simeon Lord, both recently appointed as magistrates, had also been selected as commissioners.

This decision upset Marsden greatly. He felt that asking him to serve with such men compromised the dignity of his office. In addition to their convict heritage, both Thompson and Lord were men of 'loose morals', living in open fornication. Even worse, Lord had been investigated over an improper relationship with two young girls at the female orphanage, of which Marsden was a patron.[4]

Marsden quietly approached Macquarie and asked permission to decline the commission. Macquarie was very displeased, and told Marsden he considered his refusal to be disrespectful, and even 'an act of hostility against his government'. Macquarie insisted that Marsden give his refusal in writing. Marsden did so, but Macquarie seemed to become even more upset, and stated that Marsden would be facing a court martial if he were a military officer.[5]

Marsden later suggested that all of his subsequent trouble with the Governor could be traced back to this incident. For the moment, however, things appeared amicable. For example, later that same year we find Macquarie on his first inspection of the interior of the colony. After several days in Sydney's south-west (much of it spent in the company of Thomas Moore), he and his party headed north to Parramatta.

There he spent several days with Marsden, and according to Macquarie's diary it was all very genial. On 10 November 1810, Marsden and Macquarie rode around the district together inspecting the farms, while their wives spent the day together at home. The next day Macquarie went to church and writes that Marsden gave 'a very good sermon'. The following day the Marsdens and Macquaries dined

---

4 Yarwood, *Samuel Marsden: Survivor*, 129–130.
5 Marsden, *Answer to Calumnies*, 5.

together in the evening.⁶ There is nothing in this admittedly brief account that suggests the two men were in open conflict at this time. They may well have been operating under a strained truce.

The next several years saw the Chaplain and Governor work together quite effectively. Macquarie instituted a regime of moral improvement, insisting that the settlers observe the Sabbath, and that couples marry rather than co-habit. By 1813, Marsden would write to a friend that a 'wonderful change' had come over the colony, which he attributed to his partnership with the Governor. His daughter Ann would go so far as to describe Macquarie as 'a great friend to the Gospel'.⁷

The regard appears to have been mutual. Macquarie re-appointed Marsden as a magistrate in 1812 and was so pleased with his work in that capacity that he published the following tribute in 1813:

> His excellency the Governor embraces this opportunity of returning his most sincere thanks to the Rev. Samuel Marsden [...] for his able, firm and unwearied Exertions as a Magistrate.⁸

This period of concord was not to last. A new struggle between Chaplain and Governor was ignited in early 1814 when Macquarie published a general order in the *Sydney Gazette*, essentially accusing the colonial grain farmers of 'price-gouging' the government. As a major agriculturalist himself, Marsden no doubt felt the sting of Macquarie's censure. What really upset him, however, was that he was required to read the notice in church—not just once, but twice.⁹

He complied the first time but refused to do so again, complaining that such notices were inappropriate from the pulpit. Any feeling of charity that Macquarie harboured for his chaplain appears to have completely evaporated by this time, as he severely criticized the Chaplain for his 'highly improper and disrespectful' conduct, and warned him of severe consequences if such disobedience were ever repeated.

Macquarie even wrote to the Colonial Secretary, Lord Bathurst, for a ruling on the matter, and accused Marsden of 'illiberal sentiments and bigoted principles'. For his part, Marsden sought help from his patrons in England. Although he was to lose the battle over the reading

---

6   Macquarie, *Journal*, Entries for 10–12/11/1810.
7   Yarwood, *Samuel Marsden: Survivor*, 139–140.
8   SG 3/4/1813.
9   Yarwood, *Samuel Marsden: Survivor*, 153.

of government notices in church (as this was already common in England), he scandalised both the Archbishop and William Wilberforce with his reports of the moral behaviour of the emancipist magistrates that Macquarie had appointed. Wilberforce had formerly been an ally of Macquarie, but would increasingly turn against him in the coming years. It seems very likely that Macquarie learned of the damage Marsden had done him.[10]

Further trouble soon followed, and in many respects this new affair foreshadowed the Philo Free incident. The catalyst, absurdly, was a library. Whilst in England in 1809, Marsden had placed the following advertisement in the *Evangelical Magazine*:

> Proposals have been circulated for instituting a Lending Library, for the general benefit of the inhabitants of New South Wales. In that colony, books of every kind are extremely scarce; it is therefore highly desirable that a public library should be formed, containing books suited to the poor settlers employed in agriculture, the soldiers, and the convicts. Those who have a disposition to improve their minds, have, at present, scarcely any opportunity on account of the want of books. Treatises on divinity and morals, history, voyages and travels, agriculture in all its branches, mineralogy, and practical mechanics, would be peculiarly acceptable. Donations for this purpose in money, books, or tracts will be thankfully received by the Rev. Samuel Marsden, chaplain to the colony.[11]

The public responded generously, and Marsden returned with a collection worth between £300 and £400. He built a small room on his property to house the books, but did nothing to formalise arrangements for lending or consulting them, and nor did he advertise their availability.

In early 1814, a series of pseudonymous letters appeared in the *Gazette*, asking about the lending library. Someone styling himself 'A Free Settler' declared that he doubted the existence of said library, because otherwise the Chaplain would surely have housed the collection at Sydney (where the population was greatest), and readily publicised the availability of the volumes. No, he concluded disingenuously, any books in the Chaplain's possession must be private property.[12]

---

10   Yarwood, *Samuel Marsden: Survivor*, 154.
11   [Evangelical Magazine], 'New South Wales' (1809), 343.
12   *SG* 19/3/1814.

Marsden wrote a rather stiff letter in response, stating that there was no public library—rather, he had been given a few volumes by some friends to lend out at his own discretion. This was inaccurate in at least two respects—he had been given more than 'a few' books, and the original advertisement specifically mentioned that the donations were for a 'public library'. Marsden's letter prompted a further response from 'A Free Settler', ostensibly thanking the Chaplain for clarifying the situation, but managing to deliver a few more veiled barbs.[13]

Marsden was incensed, surmising that he was virtually being accused of theft. He wrote to Macquarie, asking that the Governor order the Editor of the *Gazette* to reveal the identity of 'A Free Settler'. The allegations, he maintained, would severely damage his reputation both in England and in the Colony.[14]

Macquarie refused to co-operate, stating that the letters in question were not of an 'offensive personal nature'.[15] By this time Marsden was convinced that the letters were written by John Thomas Campbell, Macquarie's secretary and close friend. He later described Campbell as his 'secret enemy', and believed he was responsible for a long-running and clandestine campaign against the Chaplain.[16]

What was the source of this enmity? Marsden put it down to anti-Evangelical sentiment. He said that Campbell was 'bitter against all Methodists', and consequently strongly disapproved of Marsden's beliefs and conduct.[17] Marsden was further convinced that Macquarie was protecting Campbell. If so, it is very possible that Macquarie himself was a party to the attacks by 'A Free Settler'. In any event, Marsden was aggrieved but could do nothing, and so let the matter drop.[18]

A further arena for conflict opened soon after. The matter itself was once again quite minor, but it showed that Macquarie's opinion of Marsden had sunk very low, and that the Governor was willing and able to exert his influence over ecclesiastical affairs.

Marsden had received several copies of a new psalter composed by the Rev. William Goode, a leading evangelical in London. Marsden was

---

13 SG 2/4/1814.
14 Marsden to Macquarie, 9/4/1814; Sharp, *The World, The Flesh & The Devil*, 309–312.
15 Yarwood, *Samuel Marsden: Survivor*, 154.
16 Marsden to Macquarie, 11/8/1818; Marsden to LMS Directors, 14/3/1817.
17 Marsden to LMS Directors, 17/5/1817.
18 Yarwood, *Samuel Marsden: Survivor*, 154.

enthusiastic about this work, and began using the new psalms in place of those prescribed in the Book of Common Prayer.[19]

When Macquarie heard about this innovation, he wrote to Lord Bathurst and essentially asked permission to put a stop to it. His justification was that this small departure from the correct form of worship could lead to even larger deviations in the future—possibly even fomenting dissent. He noted that this risk was exacerbated by the fact that Marsden was born 'of low rank' and that he also possessed 'Methodistical' tendencies. Bathurst responded that, while he did not think Marsden guilty of any attempt at theological innovation, he did consider it would be 'inconvenient' to set a precedent for altering the worship service in the Book of Common Prayer. He therefore instructed Macquarie to 'suppress' such novelties.[20]

It's hard not to see this letter, written in late 1814, as an attempt to damage Marsden's reputation amongst the political élite of England. Governor and Chaplain were now engaged in a clandestine war. From this point onwards, their relationship would be marked by a series of minor slights, interspersed with bouts of outright hostility.[21]

An example of the latter came after the death of Ellis Bent, the Judge Advocate, in November 1815. Bent had initially supported Macquarie's policy on the appointment of emancipists as magistrates, but had gradually swung around to Marsden's position—and his relationship with Macquarie had suffered as a result. In a regular Sunday sermon after the funeral, Marsden included Bent's death amongst other 'calamities' falling upon the inhabitants of the Colony which gave 'reason to apprehend that God is angry with us for our sins'. Closely following one of Charles Simeon's outlines (as was his custom), he used this list to urge repentance, holding up the biblical example of the king of Nineveh, who repented in sackcloth and ashes. Perhaps because the relationship between the two men had already deteriorated badly, Macquarie misunderstood Marsden's sermon and, fixated on a detail while missing its main point, furiously declared it to be blasphemous.[22]

---

19 Sharp, *The World, The Flesh & The Devil*, 313–314.
20 Macquarie to Bathurst, 7/10/1814 (HRA 1.8, 336–337); Bathurst to Macquarie, 2/12/1815 (HRA 1.8, 637).
21 Yarwood, *Samuel Marsden: Survivor*, 181–200; Sharp, *The World, The Flesh & The Devil*, 326–333.
22 Pettett, *Samuel Marsden*, 58–69; Sharp, *The World, The Flesh & The Devil*, 330.

It would be time-consuming and tedious to review every subtle insult exchanged by the men in subsequent years. Enough has been written here to demonstrate the amount of hostility that existed between the Governor and Chaplain at the time of the Philo Free controversy in 1817. Other papers in this volume describe the incident itself in detail, but it is clear that Macquarie was no neutral arbiter in the conflict between his secretary and the colonial chaplain. Indeed, a case can be made that Macquarie himself was a party to the offending "Free Settler" letters.[23]

Figure 5: Governors of NSW 1788–1821

1.	1788 – Dec 1792	Captain Arthur Phillip, RN
	Dec 1792 – Dec 1794	Interregnum: Francis Grose
	Dec 1794 – Sept 1795	Interregnum: William Paterson
2.	Sept 1795 – Sept 1800	Captain John Hunter, RN
3.	Sept 1800 – Aug 1806	Captain Philip Gidley King, RN
4.	Aug 1806 – Jan 1808	Captain William Bligh, RN
	Jan – July 1808	Rebel government: George Johnston
	July 1808 – Jan 1809	Acting governor: Joseph Foveaux
	Jan 1809 – Jan 1810	Acting governor: William Paterson
5.	Jan 1810 – 1821	Lachlan Macquarie

By this time the Governor was facing pressure on all sides, and was losing the favour of Lord Bathurst. It seems likely that he felt the outcome of the Philo Free affair as another personal blow, for he tendered his resignation on the same day that the judgement was handed down. As it happened, Bathurst did not accept the resignation and asked him to reconsider.[24]

It seems possible that Marsden caught wind of Macquarie's resignation, for his next move was rather reckless. The catalyst, once more, seems trivial in hindsight.

The public space known as the Domain was protected on the south side by a 10 feet (3m) high wall, with the official entrance near the north. The Governor was frustrated that the populace often preferred scaling

---

23 Yarwood, *Samuel Marsden: Survivor*, 199.
24 Macquarie to Bathurst, 1/12/1817 (*HRA* 1.9, 495–502); Bathurst to Macquarie, 18/9/1818 (*HRA* 1.9, 838–840).

the wall to using the authorised entry, and so he devised increasingly severe sanctions for such offenders. Back in 1816 he ordered three men to be flogged for illegally entering the space, and promised more of the same if people kept climbing the wall.[25]

Had the 3 men been convicts, such action would scarcely have raised an eyebrow. But the men in question were free men, and so the colony (and even some back in England) were scandalized. The whole affair became an indelible stain on Macquarie's reputation.[26]

The matter had rather died down when, 18 months later and immediately following Macquarie's resignation, Marsden took a deposition on the incident from the public executioner, Thomas Hughes. Marsden later claimed that Hughes had begged him to hear the deposition, while Hughes claimed that he had been bullied into going by one of Marsden's employees.[27]

The Governor was utterly furious when he learned of this, guessing that Marsden intended to transmit the information back to Downing Street in order to damage him. The Chaplain was summoned to Government House on January 8, 1818, and found the Governor there sitting behind his great table, flanked by his private secretary Thomas Campbell, John Watts the regimental aide-de-camp, and the Reverend William Cowper, Assistant Chaplain in Sydney.[28]

A single chair sat before the table and Marsden was sharply ordered to sit down. At this point, as he later wryly noted, he knew he was in 'a pretty mess'. Forbidding interruptions, the Governor read from a long and angry prepared statement:

> I have long known, Mr Marsden, that you are a secret Enemy of mine - and as long as you continued only a secret one, I despised too much your malicious attempts to injure my character to take any notice of your treacherous conduct;—but now that you have thrown off the mask, and have openly and Publickly manifested your hostile and factious disposition towards me [...]
>
> I consider, Sir, that act of yours, not only as most insolent and impertinent as it respects myself Personally;—but also, as highly

---

25 Ellis, *Lachlan Macquarie*, 341.
26 Ellis, *Lachlan Macquarie*, 342.
27 Ellis, *Lachlan Macquarie*, 449.
28 Ellis, *Lachlan Macquarie*, 449; Sharp, *The World, The Flesh & The Devil*, 476–478.

> insubordinate and seditious; in as much as such conduct, on your part, tends to inflame the mind of the Inhabitants, excite a Clamour against my Government, bring my administration into disrepute, and disturb the General Tranquility of the Colony [...]
>
> Viewing you now, Sir, as the Head of a Seditious low Cabal—and consequently unworthy of mixing in Private Society or intercourse with me, I beg to inform you that I never wish to see you excepting on Public Duty;—and I cannot help deeply lamenting, that, any man of your Sacred Profession should be so much lost to every good feeling of Justice, generosity and gratitude, as to manifest such deep rooted malice, rancour, hostility and vindictive opposition towards one who has never injured you.[29]

Marsden agreed to obey the Governor's injunction, but later wrote that His Excellency 'might as well have beat an anvil as to excite fear in my mind where no fear was'.[30]

Macquarie had little time left in the colony. In 1819 John Thomas Bigge arrived in Sydney, appointed special commissioner to examine the government of the colony. The relationship between Bigge and Macquarie soon soured, and the Governor resigned before Bigge had completed his initial report. This time his resignation was accepted.[31]

Macquarie could not let go of his resentment towards Marsden, however. In 1821 he published a pamphlet defending his administration, and he took every opportunity he could to criticise the Chaplain. Consider this example:

> The Rev. Mr. Marsden, being himself accustomed to traffic in spirits, must necessarily feel displeased at having so many public-houses licensed in his neighbourhood.[32]

Or this one —

> Mr. Marsden's statement, on which this opinion is founded, appears to have been drawn up with the view of acquiring a great name for himself, by detracting from the claims or merits of other persons.[33]

---

29   Macquarie to Marsden, 8/1/1818.
30   Marsden to Alexander Riley, 19/5/1818 (Bennett, *A Letter*, 124). Ellis, *Lachlan Macquarie*, 451.
31   McLachlan, 'Macquarie, Lachlan (1762–1824)'.
32   Macquarie, *A letter to the Rt. Hon. Viscount Sidmouth*, 14.
33   Macquarie, *A letter to the Rt. Hon. Viscount Sidmouth*, 17.

And Macquarie made this ironic response to Marsden's purported great sorrow over the state of the [female convicts in the?] colony —

> As to Mr. Marsden's troubles of mind, and pathetic display of sensibility and humanity, they must be so deeply seated, and so far removed from the surface, as to escape all possible observation [...] his deportment is at all times that of a person the most gay and happy: when I was honoured with his society, he was by far the most cheerful person I met in the Colony. Where his hours of sorrow were spent, it is hard to divine; for the variety of his pursuits, both in his own concerns and in those of others, is so extensive, in farming, grazing, manufactories, public and private agencies, and bartering transactions, that, with his clerical duties, he seems, to use a common phrase, to have his hands full of work: and the particular subject to which he imputes this extreme depression of mind, is, besides, one for which few people here will give him much credit.[34]

Marsden was understandably upset by this publication. In 1826 he authorised the publication of a booklet called, 'An answer to certain calumnies in the late Governor Macquarie's pamphlet ...'. In this he responded in detail to each of the charges Macquarie laid at his door. The tone is measured and gracious, and he quotes extensively from relevant letters to establish his points. And so the final note was sounded and this sad relationship was brought to its close.[35]

There are several different ways to try and understand the enmity between the two men. It is tempting, for example, to see the feud as an embodiment of the emancipist vs exclusivist conflict that was a very real part of this period of colonial history. This view would see Macquarie as the great leveler, the champion of convicts, whilst Marsden fought to preserve privilege for the élite and the free.

There is certainly an edge of truth to this idea. Marsden himself stated that the grudge started due to a difference of opinion over the appointment of former convicts (living immorally) as magistrates. However, the men appeared to have a good working relationship in the years following this appointment, right up until 1814. Also, this view does not really explain the specifics of the conflicts themselves, and is actually contradicted by some of them. For example, two of the men flogged for

---

34 Macquarie, *A letter to the Rt. Hon. Viscount Sidmouth*, 18.
35 Marsden, *Answer to Calumnies*.

entering the Domain were actually emancipists, and would probably not have agreed that Macquarie was the champion of their kind!

Another angle suggests itself. Perhaps this was an example of church vs state, with Marsden the champion of a particularly conservative style of Christianity and Macquarie playing the role of free-thinking humanist. Once more, the facts themselves do not support this idea. Macquarie was not an Evangelical, but he certainly gave every indication of being a believing Christian. And in the one instance where the men did clash specifically over ecclesiastical matters (with regards to the singing of the Psalms), it was Macquarie who took the decidedly more conservative approach.

No, the reason behind the conflict is both more obvious—and perhaps more depressing to modern sensibilities. This was a clash of wills, a dispute between two powerful men who were both proud and even egotistical, who both felt their honour had been called into question, and who were unwilling to overlook a slight.

Macquarie seems most concerned about the preservation of his authority. As a military commander, he was used to being obeyed. He responded very aggressively whenever Marsden challenged or defied him. As the years passed Macquarie began to suspect (with some justification) that Marsden was undermining his authority both within the colony and also back in England. The relationship could not survive in such circumstances.

Marsden seems mostly concerned about preservation of his reputation. His first clash with the Governor occurred when he was asked to serve on the roads commission with two emancipists, and refused to do so because he felt it compromised his dignity and rank. But the real turning point in the relationship appears to have occurred in 1814, when Macquarie criticized the colonial grain growers for their pricing tactics. Marsden's agricultural concerns were always a sensitive topic for him, and interaction between Governor and Chaplain were troubled from this day onwards. The Chaplain was especially hurt by the letters published by both A Free Settler and Philo Free, and there is a case to be made that Macquarie secretly endorsed these documents.

This dispute shows both men in a poor light, considered by modern standards. Marsden may well have felt that he ultimately prevailed. Whilst Macquarie returned to England with a cloud over his head, the

Chaplain remained in the colony and prospered for a further twenty years.

But the broad strokes of popular history would paint a different story. By the turn of the century, Macquarie was being revered as the 'Father of Australia', and one of the great heroes of the period. Marsden, by contrast, was already being portrayed as the great colonial villain and is remembered in contemporary Australia chiefly as 'the flogging parson'. In this dispute, Marsden was the ultimate loser, and Macquarie proved to be a costly enemy indeed.

CHAPTER 6

MISSION TRADING IN THE SOUTH PACIFIC BY THE *ACTIVE* (1814–1822) AND THE ACCUSATIONS OF PHILO FREE

Malcolm Falloon

Introduction

In his pseudonymous 'Philo Free' letter, John Thomas Campbell, Private Secretary to Governor Macquarie, attacked the trading operations of the South Seas missions, insinuating that they were merely a scheme for Samuel Marsden's personal self-aggrandisement and financial gain.[1] Campbell compared the missionaries to the Jesuits of former times, who displayed a similar 'lust of wealth, power, and dominion'. As well as implying that the true items of exchange were alcohol and arms, Campbell asserted that the trade in pigs, timber and flax, was for the financial benefit of a few well-placed individuals such as Marsden, whom he styled the 'Christian Mahomet'. Therefore, Campbell maintained, if Marsden wished to claim the honour of evangelising the Pacific, he ought also to bear the full cost of maintaining his 'gospel vendors and bacon curers'. This chapter will explore the nature and extent of the missionary trade in the South Pacific, particularly focusing on the mission brig, *Active*, which over the course of fourteen voyages was the main vehicle for that trade in the years 1814–1822 (See Figure 7). Philo Free was published in January

---

1 SG 4/1/1817. Yarwood, *Samuel Marsden: Survivor*, 194–200; Sharp, *The World, the Flesh & the Devil*, 333–339.

1817 shortly after the *Active* returned from its fifth voyage to New Zealand and its first to the Society Islands of Tahiti.

The Purchase of the *Active*

For a number of years, Marsden had advocated for a ship to support both the London Missionary Society (LMS) in the Pacific and the forthcoming Church Missionary Society (CMS) mission to New Zealand.[2] The proposal was well received in London by a number of influential backers such as William Wilberforce and Thomas Haweis.[3] The CMS, having taken advice from the British Moravian, Christian Latrobe, recommended that Marsden form an Auxiliary Society in NSW for the purpose of maintaining a vessel and managing the New Zealand mission.[4] However, in a joint letter from himself and four other local clergymen, Marsden informed the CMS that 'under present existing circumstances' the formation of a public Auxiliary Society was not feasible.[5] The CMS, while sympathetic to Marsden's situation, responded with the suggestion that at least a Corresponding Committee be formed to handle the affairs of the Society.[6]

The urgency of purchasing a vessel for the mission became apparent when Marsden was quoted £600 to hire a ship for a single trip to New Zealand.[7] So when the 110 ton brig, *Active*, was put up for sale, he took the opportunity to purchase the vessel for £1400, having had it surveyed

---

2   Marsden to Pratt, 25/10/1810; Sharp, *The World, the Flesh & the Devil*, 379–387.
3   Wilberforce to Pratt, 23/1/1812; Pratt to Marsden, 18/3/1814.
4   Pratt to Marsden, 18/8/1814. For Latrobe's advice to the CMS and a general discussion of the benefits of operating a missionary ship see the 'Origin, History, and Manner of Conducting the Intercourse of the United Brethren'. 229–242. See also, Pratt to Marsden, 16/12/1814.
5   Marsden et al. to Pratt, 25/10/1815. The circumstances concerned the failure of the Philanthropic Society to investigate the actions of the *Cumberland* in Rarotonga. See Bolt, 'The Failure of the Philanthropic Society', Chapter 7 in this volume.
6   Pratt to Marsden, 5/9/1816.
7   Marsden to Pratt, 15/3/1814; Marsden to Pratt, 28/10/1815. The owners wanted £100 per month hire (plus £20 for victuals) for a minimum of six months. The vessel concerned was probably the 100 ton colonial schooner *Governor Bligh* (owners J. Grono & J. Benn; see *NSW Almanac 1813*, 24), recently returned from a sixteen-month voyage off the coast of New Zealand; SG 18/12/1813. In 1806, Marsden had personally hired the colonial sloop *Hawkesbury* to convey relief supplies to the LMS missionaries stationed in Tahiti; Sharp, *The World, the Flesh & the Devil*, 347. The vessel was really too small to make sure a dangerous passage. The missionaries on Tahiti were astounded: 'He [Captain Edwards] has narrowly escaped being lost. Indeed the bark is so small, that we are surprised she ever reached this place'; quoted in Maude, 'The Tahitian Pork Trade', 66.

by Captain Eber Bunker and then spending a further £500 on outfitting.[8] Marsden intended to personally contribute £1200 towards the cost and proposed that the CMS would make up the remaining £700, though he later took on the full sum himself.[9] At this initial stage, Marsden estimated that the annual operating costs of the *Active* would be £1500, of which, he hoped, £1000 might be offset by trade, leaving the LMS and CMS to cover the remaining £500.[10] The CMS, conscious of not creating ill-feeling between the two societies, recommended that the LMS be charged only for their actual costs and that the CMS would cover the remainder.[11]

The First Four Voyages (1814–1815)

The first voyage of the *Active* was an exploratory trip to the Bay of Islands, from 14 Mar–23 Aug 1814.[12] The captain was Peter Dillon, who was accompanied by the missionaries Thomas Kendall and William Hall—Marsden having had permission to go declined by Governor Macquarie. The cargo of timber obtained during this trip was listed by Marsden as having realised £144 12s 3d, which was used to offset future expenses.[13] During the return trip to NSW a violent argument occurred between Dillon and Kendall, which accounts for Dillon being quietly replaced as captain for subsequent voyages.[14]

The master of the *Active* for the next four trips was Thomas Hansen,

---

8   *Certificates Concerning the Active*, 22/9/1814; Marsden to Pratt, 30/9/1814. Bunker was a pioneer of whaling in the South Seas; Hodgkinson, *Eber Bunker of Liverpool*. Bunker was about to sail for England and Marsden commended him to the CMS as a reliable informant concerning the affairs of the colony and Marsden's plans; Marsden to Pratt, 30/9/1814.
9   Marsden to Pratt, 15/3/1814. Marsden informed Bigge that he funded the purchase by selling £900 worth of sheep and borrowing the rest on credit; Marsden to Bigge, 28/12/1819 (*HRNZ* 1.452). Also Yarwood, *Samuel Marsden: Survivor*, 164; and Wylde, Report of the Judge-Advocate [criminal trial] (*HRA* 1.10, 453, 467).
10 Marsden to Pratt, 22/9/1814; Marsden to Pratt, 10/6/1815.
11 Sharp, *The World, the Flesh & the Devil*, 382–385.
12 Arrival and departure dates for the *Active* have been drawn from the *Sydney Gazette* in conjunction with Cumpston, *Shipping Arrivals and Departures*. Additional dates, and occasional modifications, are sourced from the various archives of the CMS and LMS.
13 *An Account of Expenses of the Active and the Different Necessities for the Settlement of New Zealand*, 21/6/1815. Earlier Marsden had estimated the value of the timber at about £100; *CMS's Account with Marsden on Account of the brig Active*, 4/10/1814. Yarwood reports the return was £300 but does not provide a reference; Yarwood, *Samuel Marsden: Survivor*, 167. Sharp reports £200, but again with no reference; Sharp, *The World, the Flesh & the Devil*, 407.
14 Kendall reported being struck on the jaw by Dillon in the course of what appears to be a drunken argument. Kendall, Journal, 5/8/1814. He later recalled that Dillon attempted to shoot him; Kendall to the Chairman of the Missionary Committee, 28/9/1822. See also Binney, *The Legacy of Guilt*, 40.

the father of Hannah King, one of the three missionary wives about to settle in New Zealand. Hansen was known to Captain Bunker and had a reputation for honesty, though Marsden did not consider him a 'pious' man.[15] The second voyage of the *Active* (19 Nov 1814–22 Mar 1815) established the first mission station in New Zealand at Rangihoua in the Bay of Islands, and this time Marsden was allowed to accompany the party. The *Active* was able to return to NSW with a cargo of 4848 feet of timber, 1344 pounds of flax, and a small quantity of fish and pork.[16] Marsden estimated the cargo's value at £451 4s, which included an anticipated £242 cost to cover the duty levied on imported timber by the colonial government.[17] Although, as it turned out, Governor Macquarie would waive the duty for the voyage, Marsden continued to be concerned that future government duties would threaten the economic viability of his scheme. The regulations had stipulated duty at a rate of 1s per solid foot on all timber brought through the port, which would have amounted to a 40% tax on the gross profit.[18] If the duty was re-instated, which Marsden saw as a real possibility, he considered that it would be, effectively, a prohibition on New Zealand timber, and would allow the mission's opponents to 'greatly impede the work merely by depriving those who were carrying it on of the means, in laying on heavy duties'.[19]

Marsden's worst fears were realised during the *Active*'s third voyage to New Zealand (27 Apr–8 Aug 1815) when the Governor re-imposed the duty, albeit at a lesser rate. Marsden argued that, given its humanitarian nature, the government had an obligation not to lay such a heavy burden on the mission, especially when the amount collected was trivial in comparison to the government's overall revenue. Governor Macquarie for his part did not wish to set any precedent that others might exploit. In the end, the Governor agreed to halve the rate of duty to 6d per solid

---

15 Marsden to Pratt, 30/9/1814.
16 Cumpston, *Shipping Arrivals & Departures*, 96, reports 159 spars and ½ ton flax.
17 Nicholas, *Narrative of a Voyage to New Zealand*, 2.213. Marsden sold the timber to Captain Joseph Underwood at a rate of 2s 6d per solid foot; Marsden to Pratt, 26/10/1815; Marsden to Pratt, 30/6/1815. Underwood was a trader in the South Pacific and upon his return to England he was commended to the CMS by Marsden as a reliable informant; Marsden to Pratt, 30/6/1815.
18 Marsden to Pratt, 15/6/1815. A wide range of import duties had been announced by the Governor on 26 June 1813, with New Zealand timber levied at 1s 6d per solid foot. Timber sourced from the coast of NSW had a lower duty of 1s, and this lesser rate appears to be the amount Marsden expected to be applied in the *Active*'s case. Pork remained duty free. See 'Schedule of Duties', *SG* 26/6/1813; Sharp, *The World, the Flesh & the Devil*, 319.
19 Marsden to Pratt, 15/6/1815.

foot, which was publicly announced, 19 Aug 1815, eleven days after the return of the *Active* to port.[20]

Marsden had further concerns about what he considered to be unreasonable taxes. He estimated that the port duties alone were at least £20 every time the *Active* entered the harbour. For instance, although the *Active*, along with other small colonial vessels, had no need of a pilot, it was still charged the same £7 pilotage as larger foreign ships, which had amounted to £30 in the past year alone.[21] However, what irked Marsden the most was paying a duty of 2s 6d for each person leaving port, even when they were neither part of a ship's company, nor a paying passenger, as was the case with Māori who were visiting Marsden's native seminary at Parramatta.[22] Consequently, when the *Active* departed on its fourth voyage (9 Sep–28 Nov 1815), Marsden had to pay the clearance fee for seventeen Māori who were returning to New Zealand. In addition, Secretary Campbell insisted that the individuals appear before him in person to pay the tax, which Māori were generally reluctant to do as it offended their sense of mana (dignity).

The imposition of this tax brought Marsden into direct conflict with Campbell: 'I remonstrated with the Secretary, told him as they were not under any civil government, nor belonged to any vessel as sailors, that I thought they could not with any propriety be subject to the same regulations as British subjects'.[23] As far as Marsden was concerned, the

20 Government Public Notice, *SG* 19/8/1815. The *Active* paid duty of £19 1s on 130 logs and spars, and 1 ton of flax (*HRA* 1.9, 84).
21 Marsden to Pratt, 26/10/1815. Maude, 'The Tahitian Pork Trade', 64, reports that in 1805 there were twenty-one locally owned vessels in NSW with only two over 100 tons. The *NSW Almanack* for 1813/1814 listed thirty-seven colonial vessels with seven over 100 tons; quoted in Cumpston, *Shipping Arrivals & Departures*, 90. In May 1813 Lord Bathurst appointed former NSW army captain, John Piper, as Naval Officer and Collector of Duties. He began his duties in February 1814; *HRA* 1.7, 705. Piper was not paid a salary, but as Naval Officer, he was allocated 5% of the revenues collected; *HRA* 1.9, 244–7. There was also a duty charged on the size of departing vessels at a rate of 6d per ton payable to the Governor's Secretary, John Thomas Campbell. Although Campbell received a salary, it is likely that he was also entitled to a percentage of the revenue gathered. In the years 1812–1816, Campbell's salary was £282 10s, but for the year 1817, it was increased to £365 (see Sharp, *The World, the Flesh & the Devil*, 438). This increase probably represents the monetarising of Campbell's income from port duties and passenger clearances in response to Bathurst's request to Macquarie, 4/12/15, to eliminate colonial allowances and adjust salaries accordingly (*HRA* 1.8, 646–7; 1.9, 241, 244).
22 The official reason for the imposition was to prevent convicts or debtors absconding from the colony undetected. However, John Nicholas, Marsden's travelling companion to New Zealand, had a more cynical view: 'I cannot help thinking that all this preventive caution is used only to fill the purse of the Governor's secretary, who makes no inconsiderable sum by this species of exaction'; Nicholas, *Narrative of a Voyage to New Zealand*, 1.35.
23 Marsden to Pratt, 26/10/1815.

Governor's change in policy with regard to the duty on timber and the intransigence of his Secretary was part of a larger pattern of opposition: 'I hope these vexatious things will in time be removed', said Marsden, 'and that we shall have persons in certain situations that will not be so inimical to all true piety, and pious men. A man can scarcely commit a greater crime in N. S. Wales than to be righteous over much'.[24]

If the first two voyages of the *Active* were primarily for the establishment of the mission in New Zealand, the third and fourth were primarily concerned with trade. Marsden had left behind two sawyers and a blacksmith to help the missionaries build their houses and to prepare sawn timber ready for the *Active*'s return. As well as sending their wives and children to join them, Marsden had promised the sawyers a 5% share of the cargo's value as an incentive.[25] In addition, Marsden had found six runaway convicts in New Zealand. Three he returned to NSW, but three others he had left behind to assist the mission. In all, the Rangihoua mission station formed a European community of twenty-five men, women, and children.[26] (See Figure 6).

It appears that these two trading voyages to New Zealand were relatively successful, returning a full hold of timber and spars. The third voyage returned 130 logs and spars along with one ton of flax, while the fourth returned 120 spars and half a ton of flax.[27] By trading in timber, the *Active* had avoided direct competition with other shipping, which was more concerned with being resupplied with pork and potatoes. Already Māori were reserving those items for the general shipping where they could be exchanged for muskets, whereas the missionaries traded in agricultural tools.[28] Thomas Kendall reported that they had traded a hundred axes since the *Active*'s first voyage, with demand remaining as strong as ever.[29] To meet the demand, Marsden suggested that the CMS might split its £500 contribution to the running costs of the *Active* into £200 of naval supplies and £300 of iron and various other implements.[30]

---

24 Marsden to Pratt, 26/10/1815.
25 A common practise of a sailor's 'lay', or share, instead of wages.
26 Marsden to Pratt, 15/6/1815.
27 HRA 1.9, 84, 88. The *Active* was charged £19 1s duty for the cargo of the third voyage and £6 5s for the cargo of the fourth. The accounts of the New Zealand mission for the first year included payment to the sawyers for 22,208 foot of timber; Marsden to CMS, 8/3/1816.
28 Kendall to Marsden, 6/7/1815.
29 Kendall to Pratt, 19/10/1815.
30 Marsden to Pratt, 10/6/1815. It was advantageous to acquire Naval supplies in England as Marsden claimed there was a 2–300% premium in the colony.

MISSION TRADING IN THE SOUTH PACIFIC BY THE ACTIVE 113

Figure 6: Europeans at Rangihoua mission station during voyages of the Active, 1814–1822.

"First Settlement, 1814"	Kendall	Thomas	missionary, teacher	22 Dec 1814	31 Jan 1825
voyages 1-2	Kenall	Jane	missionary wife	22 Dec 1814	31 Jan 1825
	Kendall	Thomas Surfleet	child of missionary	22 Dec 1814	31 Jan 1825
	Kendall	Basil	child of missionary	22 Dec 1814	31 Jan 1825
	Kendall	Joseph	child of missionary	22 Dec 1814	31 Jan 1825
	Hall	William	missionary, carpenter	22 Dec 1814	9 Apr 1825
	Hall	Dinah	missionary wife	22 Dec 1814	9 Apr 1825
	Hall	William Carruthers	child of missionary	22 Dec 1814	9 Nov 1819
	King	John	missionary, shoe-maker & twine spinner	22 Dec 1814	permanent
	King	Hannah	missionary wife	22 Dec 1814	permanent
	King	Philip Hansen	child of missionary	22 Dec 1814	permanent
	Hansen	Hannah	mother of Hannah King, wife of master of Active, Thomas Hansen	22 Dec 1814	8 Nov 1815
	Hansen	Thomas (jnr)	settler, son of Thomas & Hannah Hansen	22 Dec 1814	permanent
	Hall	Walter	convict, blacksmith	22 Dec 1814	13 Nov 1816
	Campbell	William	convict, sawyer, weaver, flax dresser	22 Dec 1814	13 Nov 1816
	Conroy	Matthew	convict, sawyer	22 Dec 1814	13 Nov 1816
	Stockwell	Richard	convict, servant to Kendall family	22 Dec 1814	15 Jun 1817
1815-1816	King	Thomas Holloway	child of missionary	20 Feb 1815	12 Nov 1818 (death)
Voyages 3-5	Hall	Dinah Catherine	child of missionary	12 May 1815	9 Apr 1825
	Hall	Eleanor	convict wife	18 May 1815	13 Nov 1816
	Hall	child	child of convict	18 May 1815	13 Nov 1816
	Conroy	Ann	child of convict	18 May 1815	13 Nov 1816
	Thorn	William	convict, carpenter	28 Sep 1815	16 Mar 1816
	Rogers	Joseph	settler	28 Sep 1815	4 Oct 1815
	Rogers	Susannah	settler wife	28 Sep 1815	4 Oct 1815
	Shergold	John	convict, sawyer	28 Sep 1815	9 Dec 1816
	Shergold	Sarah	convict wife	28 Sep 1815	9 Dec 1816
	Hansen	Elizabeth	settler wife of Thomas Hansen (jnr)	23 Feb 1816	permanent
	Conroy	James	child of convict	23 Feb 1816	13 Nov 1816
	Matthews	Tully	convict, sawyer, brickmaker	23 Feb 1816	13 Nov 1816
	Carlisle	William	missionary settler, farmer	23 Feb 1816	9 Nov 1819
	Kendall	Samuel	child of missionary	5 Jun 1816	31 Jan 1825
	King	John Wheeler	child of missionary	29 Sep 1816	permanent

1817-1819	Hansen	Hannah King	child of settler	11 Jan 1817	permanent
Voyages 6-10	Carlisle	Elizabeth	missionary wife	22 May 1817	9 Nov 1819
	Carlisle	Mary Ann (Amelia)	child of missionary	22 May 1817	9 Nov 1819
	Gordon	Charles Moltson	missionary settler, agriculturalist	22 May 1817	9 Nov 1819
	Gordon	Maria	missionary wife	22 May 1817	9 Nov 1819
	Kendall	Susannah	adult child of missionary	22 May 1817	31 Jan 1825
	Kendall	Elizabeth	adult child of missionary	22 May 1817	31 Jan 1825
	Carlisle	James William	child of missionary	6 Oct 1817	9 Nov 1819
	Kendall	John	child of missionary	13 Jan 1818	31 Jan 1825
	Carlisle	John	child of missionary	16 May 1818	9 Nov 1819
	Boyle	James	convict, fish salter	19 Jun 1818	27 Nov 1821
	Hansen	Thomas	child of settler	20 Sep 1818	permanent
	King	Jane Holloway	child of missionary	10 Dec 1818	permanent
	Hall	Henry	child of missionary	8 Jan 1819	9 Apr 1825
	Gordon	Ann	child of missionary	19 Apr 1819	9 Nov 1819
	Bean	William	settler, carpenter	12 Aug 1819	5 May 1822
	Bean	Elizabeth	settler wife	12 Aug 1819	27 Nov 1821
	Fairburn	William	settler, carpenter	12 Aug 1819	5 May 1822
	Fairburn	Sarah	settler wife	12 Aug 1819	27 Nov 1821
	Butler	John	missionary, clergy	12 Aug 1819	14 Nov 1823
	Butler	Hannah	missionary wife	12 Aug 1819	14 Nov 1823
	Butler	Samuel	settler, adult son of missionary	12 Aug 1819	5 May 1822
	Butler	Hannah	child of missionary	12 Aug 1819	14 Nov 1823
	Hall	Francis	missionary, teacher	12 Aug 1819	5 Dec 1822
	Kemp	James	missionary, blacksmith	12 Aug 1819	permanent
	Kemp	Charlotte	missionary wife	12 Aug 1819	permanent
	Puckey	William	settler, carpenter	12 Aug 1819	16 Feb 1826
	Puckey	William Gilbert	missionary, adult son of William Puckey	12 Aug 1819	permanent
	Hansen	Jane Elizabeth	child of settler	[Sep] 1819	permanent
1820-1822	Shepherd	James	missionary, gardener	Feb 1820	permanent
Voyages 11-14	Kemp	Henry Tracy	child of missionary	18 Jan 1821	permanent
	Hall	John Silas	child of missionary	21 Jan 1821	9 Apr 1825
	Shepherd	Harriet	missionary wife	24 Mar 1821	permanent
	Lee	John	convict, stockman	24 Mar 1821	27 Nov 1821
	Forster	Thomas	Blacksmith	unknown	27 Nov 1821
	Hansen	William Brind	child of settler	[Jul-Dec] 1821	permanent
	Cowell	John	missionary, ropemaker	13 Feb 1822	14 Nov 1823
	Cowell	Mary	missionary wife	13 Feb 1822	14 Nov 1823

While Marsden complained about the rate of duty imposed, he also found it difficult to sell any timber that was brought back as logs rather than as sawn planks. Marsden suggested that Hall increase capacity by actively recruiting Māori to work as sawyers. He also considered the possibility of setting up a sawmill in New Zealand.[31] Marsden hoped that the *Active*'s fifth voyage, and her first to Tahiti, would prove to be more profitable.

First trading voyage to Tahiti (24 Jan - 29 Dec 1816)

That the *Active* had waited until 1816 before venturing to Tahiti was due to the political turmoil that overtook the Society Islands in the period following the conversion of Pomare II in July 1812, until the battle of Feipi in November 1815.[32] With Pomare back in control of Tahiti and the Windward Islands, the timing seemed more favourable for the *Active* to visit. Marsden expected the voyage to take about eight months and so invested £1000 of his own money in outfitting, including sixty tons of casks and twenty tons of salt.[33] The casks and salt were to enable the *Active* to trade in pork, which, being duty free in NSW, Marsden hoped would give a better return on investment.

The pork trade with the Society Islands had been established by Governor King in 1801, and was carried on for the next fifteen years by private traders whose main articles of exchange were firearms. During this time the LMS missionaries were drawn into acting as purchasing agents for the shipping, making their own salt with a boiler that Governor King had given them for the purpose. In his study of the pork trade, H. C. Maude calculated that over this period there were, on average, three shipments of pork per year imported into NSW. The profits were modest: Maude estimates that the gross profit on twenty tons of pork would have been a little over £1000, giving a margin of 20%.[34] Although the missionaries at times also bartered with muskets for their own needs, these were few in number compared to those

---

31 Marsden to Pratt, 10/3/1816.
32 Sharp, *The World, the Flesh & the Devil*, 358; Gunson, *Messengers of Grace*, 283.
33 Marsden to Pratt, 10/3/1816. In the end, the voyage took eleven months.
34 Maude, 'The Tahitian Pork Trade', 71. Maude based his calculation on a fifty-five ton ship making two trips a year and pork priced at 6d per lb. By comparison, the profit on sandalwood could be as high as 200%.

supplied by the colonial shipping.[35]

Supplies of pork however, became scarce during times of conflict, and even after Pomare's victory in 1815, it took some time for levels to rebuild. Consequently, the year 1816 turned out to be a difficult time for the *Active* to begin trading with the Islands. John Davies, a LMS missionary on Moorea (Eimeo) wrote to Marsden:

> We are sorry to observe that the vessel has happened to arrive at one of the worst of times that we have seen in these Islands as it respects procuring a cargo of pork, the late wars in the Islands together with the many vessels that have lately called here, having almost entirely stripped the Islands of hogs.[36]

He informed Marsden that when the *Active* arrived in Tahiti there had already been five ships in the previous six months, with three still at anchor.[37] Between these five vessels, upwards of one hundred tons of pork were exported back to NSW, with the lion's share of sixty tons secured by the brig, *Governor Macquarie*.[38] Another LMS missionary on Moorea, William Henry, was surprised that Hansen had managed to procure any pork at all, and he commended Hansen to Marsden for his diligence.[39] Hansen had obtained forty-six hogs in the Leeward Islands, though to do so he had had to trade one of the ship's cannon in exchange. On returning to Moorea in the Windward Islands, Henry assisted Hansen in persuading Puru, the Christian chief of Huahine, to part with another eighty hogs in exchange for the *Active*'s other great gun, making a total cargo of thirteen tons for the return to NSW.[40]

---

35 Sharp, *The World, the Flesh & the Devil*, 345–354. The LMS missionaries also caused controversy by distilling alcohol on the Islands, but they were adamant it was not for trading purposes or to supply the indigenous population (pp. 353–354).
36 John Davies to Marsden, 13/8/1816.
37 The three at anchor were the *King George*, *Queen Charlotte*, and the *Endeavour*. The two vessels that had already sailed were the *Governor Macquarie*, and the *Trial*.
38 Maude, 'The Tahitian Pork Trade', 88–89. Even William Campbell, commander of the *Governor Macquarie* found trading conditions difficult: 'The difficulty of procuring a cargo was extremely great […] the war that has almost desolated the main Island of Taheite (Otaheite) in the next place produced a universal lassitude with respect to a property that was always open to spoliation and destruction, and of course but little stock was cultivated; whilst the general state of poverty that prevailed scarely left the means of supporting themselves'; quoted in Maude, 'The Tahitian Pork Trade', 68.
39 Henry to Marsden, 12/8/1816.
40 Maude, 'The Tahitian Pork Trade', 88–89; Marsden to Pratt, 3/3/1817. Marsden reported the cargo returned to NSW as twelve tons.

Marsden's expectation was for an eight-month voyage, but the duration was greatly extended by the *Active* sustaining damage to its hull while trading off New Zealand's North Cape.[41] The damage caused the boat to leak badly with the result that she had to be hoved down in Tahiti for repairs, adding three months to the voyage. In addition, when the *Active* finally returned to the Bay of Islands on its way to NSW, it found that no timber had been prepared by the missionaries for export. Conflicts within the Rangihoua mission, at times violent, had led to a breakdown in any coordinated effort to retain wood for the *Active*. The mission's difficulties were further compounded by a lack of meat, exacerbated by the *Active*'s delay, that led to the sawyers striking work and returning to NSW by the next passing ship, the *King George*. Marsden, realising that the *Active* had been delayed, had sent supplies to the Bay of Islands by the *Queen Charlotte*, but the workmen had already abandoned the mission by the time the ship arrived.

The *Active* arrived back in NSW on 29 December 1816, just before the Philo Free letter appeared in the *Sydney Gazette* of 4 January 1817. It was a voyage of almost a year and yet one that had failed to cover expenses let alone yield a profit. Marsden wrote to Pratt:

> The last time the *Active* went the voyage proved very unfortunate [...] The *Active* returned again to Port Jackson with very little cargo, thro' the neglect and drunkenness of the Master and his wife. I had fitted her out at a very heavy expense and she was to have returned with a cargo of pork—but brought about 12 tons—From the injury she has sustained I am compelled to new sheath her bottom which will be a very heavy expense in this colony where labour is so high.[42]

As well as blaming Hansen's ill-considered actions and drunkenness, Marsden also singled out the actions of William Hall for building a house across the bay from Rangihoua at Waitangi without permission and using timber that could have been reserved for the *Active*.

> When the *Active* returned to N. Zealand, Mr Hall had left the Settlement, and had gone to Whytanghee [Waitangi]. Not a spar, nor a plank had been procured for the vessel to bring back—which was a very

---

41 Hansen, however, was able to rescue the survivors of the *Betsy* who had managed to land on the North Cape. McNabb, *From Tasman to Marsden*, 198–202.
42 Marsden to Pratt, 3/3/1817.

great disappointment, as well as a very heavy loss.[43]

With the combined pressure of the Philo Free accusations and the poor performance of the *Active*, Marsden's health began to suffer:

> All these things have been almost more than I could bear. I have none to assist me, either with advice or money. The cloud is at present so thick, that I cannot see my way thro' and what the end will be I cannot tell.[44]

One immediate consequence of the Philo Free libel was the establishment of an LMS Auxiliary Committee in New South Wales to manage its affairs.[45] The committee, however, almost immediately ran into difficulties. With the *Active* undergoing repairs, the committee looked to engage another ship to transport the Orsmond's to their missionary station in Tahiti. Unfortunately, due to their lack of experience, the committee felt obliged to accept what Marsden considered an exorbitant price of £100 for their passage. The LMS in London were equally horrified and requested that Marsden revert to the old manner of managing their affairs through a single agent rather than by a committee, and thus the auxiliary was dissolved.[46] Marsden had contemplated a similar auxiliary society for the CMS mission, but agreeing with his colleagues that it was still not politically viable, he proposed instead the formation of a corresponding committee.[47]

John Youl, one of Marsden's supporters and a fellow chaplain, wrote to the CMS in Marsden's defense. Far from profiting from the voyages of the *Active* as Philo Free alleged, Youl considered that Marsden was personally many hundreds, if not thousands of pounds out of pocket: 'If you were to see him [Marsden] and hear his daily conversation you would find he is a Missionary in soul and body and this is why they hate him'.[48] Perhaps Youl had in mind the capital cost of the *Active* when referring to Marsden's losses, for the CMS was always concerned that

---

43 Marsden to Pratt, 3/3/1817. The Naval Office reported 13 tons of pork, 19 logs pine, 1019sq ft; Cumpston, *Shipping Arrivals & Departures*, 102.
44 Marsden to Pratt, 3/3/1817.
45 Memorandum concerning the New South Wales Auxiliary Missionary Society, 3/2/1817; Rules for the New South Wales Auxiliary Missionary Society, 10/2/1817; Marsden to the NSW Auxiliary Committee of the LMS, 8/2/1817.
46 Marsden to LMS, 5/3/1817; LMS to Marsden, 28/4/1818.
47 Vale, Fulton, Cartwright, Cowper and Marsden to Pratt, 26/10/1815; Marsden to Pratt, 26/10/1815; Marsden to Pratt, 22/1/1817; Youl, Cartwright and Marsden to Pratt, 27/3/1817.
48 Youl to Pratt, 29/3/1817.

Marsden be fully reimbursed for his expenses, which Marsden himself estimated to be currently £250 per year.[49]

Mission trade and Muskets: Voyages 6–10 (1817–1819)

The sixth voyage, delayed by the need for repairs, was further delayed when the *Active* became the centre of Marsden's growing conflict with Secretary Campbell. Marsden had been unable to obtain a timely clearance for the *Active* due to Campbell's intransigence over bonds required for three Māori passengers.[50] In addition, Campbell had refused to supply Marsden with any goods from the Government stores for the use of the mission. Marsden saw this as the culmination of seven years of deliberate obstruction by the Governor's right-hand man, and it galvanised him into action. 'I have at last been compelled to open war', Marsden told a London friend. 'I had no alternative; but either to give up the Cause of the missions, and conform my conduct to the Laws of others; or to defend myself and the interests of Religion'.[51]

The *Active* eventually sailed 17 April 1817—and six days later Marsden filed his suit with Judge Advocate Wylde.[52] Not surprisingly, given the previous voyage, a new master had been appointed: Joseph Thompson, a captain with considerable experience whaling in the southern seas. Though there was generally a high turnover of crew between voyages, John Hunter (carpenter) and Thomas Hamilton (cook) had been members of the *Active*'s crew from the beginning and were retained by Thompson, with Hunter becoming First Mate.[53] Two new sailors, John Watson and Samuel Boborah (a Tahitian), joined the *Active* for this trip and were regular crewmembers for the remaining voyages. The purpose of the sixth voyage was a short trip to New Zealand to deliver the missionary settlers William Carlisle and Charles Gordon, and their families. The cargo returned was listed as an

---

49   Marsden to Pratt, 3/4/1817.
50   Bigge, Transcript of interview with Marsden, 27/12/1820 (*Evidence to the Bigge Reports*, II:113); Marsden to Pratt, 26/9/18.
51   Marsden to [John Mason Good], 17/5/1817.
52   Bigge, Transcript of interview with Marsden, 27/12/1820, (*Evidence to the Bigge Reports*, II:113); Marsden to Wylde, 23/4/17.
53   John Hunter went on to command the *Governor Macquarie* in 1822 for Pomare III of Tahiti; Maude, 'The Tahitian Pork Trade', 66. Both Thompson and Hunter were interviewed by Commissioner Bigge concerning the *Active*; *HRNZ* 1.499–506.

unspecified number of 'Spars'.[54]

The vessel arrived in the Bay of Islands on 22 May and it was probably at this point that Richard Stockwell joined the crew. Stockwell was a young convict recommended to the missionary Thomas Kendall as a family servant, and who had lived with them at Rangihoua since the beginning of the mission.[55] However, a violent dispute had erupted between Stockwell and Kendall in late December 1816 that made his position with the family untenable.[56] The arrival of the *Active* was his first opportunity to leave the mission, but he remained as a member of the *Active*'s crew for the next three voyages. Despite having previously held Stockwell in high regard, Kendall expressed the wish to have no further contact with him.[57] It was later alleged that the cause of the dispute between them was Kendall's discovery that Stockwell had been having a sexual affair with his wife, Jane, who had then become pregnant and borne a son.[58]

The next two voyages were more substantial trading ventures that also extended to Tahiti. The seventh voyage, 4 Sep 1817–24 Mar 1818, delivered six missionary families to Tahiti, including the missionary John Williams. Also accompanying them was Captain Nicholson, who was to take command of the missionary brig, *Haweis*, currently being built in Tahiti by the missionaries in collaboration with Pomare II. Plans for the construction of a missionary vessel dated back to 1812 but had to be put on hold for a time. Now, with the arrival of John Williams, the final iron-work was completed and the ship was launched in December 1817.[59]

The *Active* returned from Tahiti with sixteen tons of pork and obtained 8000 foot of sawn plank in New Zealand on the way.[60] As a

---

54 Cumpston, *Shipping Arrivals & Departures*, 104.
55 Kendall to Woodd, 13/2/1815.
56 William Hall, Journal, 30/12/1816, in *Son of Carlisle*, 25; Binney, *Legacy*, 18.
57 Kendall to Marsden, 6/3/1818.
58 William Hall to the Secretary, 6/4/1822; Marsden to Pratt, 10/2/1820. Note that Marsden's reference to the affair has been crossed out but is still legible in the original, see Binney's discussion; Binney, *Legacy*, 208 n.22. The dates of the *Active*'s visits to New Zealand confirms Binney's view that the child concerned was Samuel Kendall, born 5 Jun 1816; Binney, *Legacy*, 18.
59 Kent, *Company of Heaven*, 54; Gunson, *Messengers of Grace*, 116; Sharp, *The World, the Flesh & the Devil*, 351–353.
60 Kendall to Marsden, 20/4/1818; Maude, 'The Tahitian Pork Trade', 89. Cumpston, *Shipping Arrivals & Departures*, 111.

consequence, Marsden informed the CMS that he would be charging them the reduced amount of £120 to cover the *Active*'s costs.[61] In the following year, 1818, the *Active* made its eighth voyage, 30 May 1818– 29 Dec 1818, and its third and final trip to the Society Islands. This time the tonnage of pork was much reduced (4.5 tons), for by now the Haweis was making the first of its three voyages to Port Jackson delivering fifteen tons of pork.[62] Thompson, however, was able to secure an alternative cargo of six to seven tons of coconut oil, which was the first consignment to be imported into NSW: 'useful for lamps and soap-making', reported the *Sydney Gazette*.[63] The availability of the Haweis to maintain communications with the Islands and the unprofitable nature of the pork trade in general, were enough to prevent any further excursions by the *Active* beyond New Zealand waters.[64] In addition, the need for salted pork was beginning to wane in New South Wales as local production rose to meet consumer demand. The Tahitian demand for muskets also declined as peace became established among the Islands: money was rapidly replacing barter as the preferred medium of exchange.[65]

That was not the case in New Zealand, however, where during the year 1818 the missionaries became openly involved in the musket trade.[66] Muskets had always been traded by the shipping entering the Bay of Islands, though the NSW government limited the number of muskets carried by ships leaving Port Jackson to that required for defensive purposes only. The *Active*, for instance, on its first voyage carried twelve muskets, but on subsequent voyages the number was limited to three.[67] From the accounts kept by the mission during its first eighteen months,

---

61 Marsden to Pratt, 13/8/1818.
62 McNabb, *From Tasman to Marsden*, 210; Maude, 'The Tahitian Pork Trade', 89. The *Haweis* on its two subsequent voyages returned 17 and 22 tons, before the missionaries were forced by the Directors of the LMS to sell their shares in the *Haweis*; Rev. S. Marsden to Commissioner Bigge, 28/12/1819 (HRNZ 1.452–453); Gunson, *Messengers of Grace*, 116–117; Sharp, *The World, the Flesh & the Devil*, 598–599.
63 SG 9/1/1819. Cumpston, *Shipping Arrivals & Departures*, 114, lists the cargo as '81 logs pine 1479 ft, etc, 6 tons oil. Pork, spars, flax, etc'.
64 The 10th voyage of the *Active* did not include Tahiti, contrary to what Maude, 'The Tahitian Pork Trade', 89, assumes. Thompson told Bigge he had made only two voyages to Tahiti; HRNZ 1.499.
65 Maude, 'The Tahitian Pork Trade', 69; HRNZ, 1.503.
66 Sharp, *The World, the Flesh & the Devil*, 422–423.
67 Wylde, Report of the Judge Advocate [Criminal Trial], 21-23 Oct 1817, 454. See also Hunter's interview with Bigge, HRNZ 1.503, 505.

there was no indication that muskets were being bartered at that early stage.⁶⁸ Instead, the early trade with Māori relied heavily on the work of the blacksmith, Walter Hall. Hall was a convict whom Marsden had placed in New Zealand to assist the mission along with several others who worked as sawyers. The economic situation changed significantly, however, toward the end of 1816 when Hall and the sawyers left New Zealand and the mission was increasingly forced to rely on Māori workers who had a growing reluctance to accept the mission trade items.⁶⁹

At the beginning of 1818, Kendall informed Marsden that Māori were no longer prepared to exchange timber for axes but were demanding muskets from the mission.⁷⁰ This was mainly due to a commercial competitor, the *Harriet*, having arrived in the Bay of Islands mid-1817 and flooding the market with trade goods. The *Harriet*'s captain, James Jones, had previously been the First Mate on the *Jefferson* which had been in the Bay during the *Active*'s second voyage in 1815. Jones must have been impressed with the potential of the trade, for he had returned in the *Harriet* to obtain spars for the English market. Even so, he needed missionary assistance to obtain his cargo, not least because he also had to contain a mutiny from nine of his crew.⁷¹

Yet explicably, from the end of August 1818, the missionary William Hall recorded in his journal that Māori were fully engaged in sawing

---

68 Marsden's Account of Expenses, 25 Feb–1 Nov 1814; Marsden's Account of Expenses, 7/3/1816; Marsden's Account with the CMS, 8/3/1816; Walter Hall's Return, 6/7/1815; Walter Hall's Return, 2/10/1815. Hall submitted each of his returns via the *Active* to NSW after the third and fourth voyages. There was no return for 1816 as Hall had left New Zealand before the *Active* arrived in New Zealand from Tahiti.
69 William Hall, Journal, 14/11/1817, in *Son of Carlisle*, 38.
70 Kendall to Marsden, 3/3/1818.
71 William Hall, Journal, 7/7/1817 and 3/8/1817, in *Son of Carlisle*, 34–35. Toward the end of the *Harriet*'s stay, Jones had became increasingly fearful of Māori retaliation due to the misconduct of his crew with Māori women, and he abruptly left New Zealand claiming that Pomare, the local rangatira (who had taken the name of the Tahitian chief), had attempted to seize and plunder his vessel. When the *Harriet* arrived in Sydney the *Gazette* published an exaggerated account, claiming it presented 'a picture of the natives of that island as by no means flattering to the humane wish for their civilization'; *SG* 20/9/1817. According to the *Gazette*, 'The overbearing insolence of the chiefs of this inhuman race of people it is impossible to form an adequate idea of'. Marsden believed the article to be a direct falsehood designed by John Thomas Campbell to undermine the cause of the CMS mission; Marsden to Pratt, 4/2/1818. Given that the report was published a month before the first *Philo Free* libel trial, Marsden was probably right. Kendall reported a very different version of events the following year; Kendall to Marsden, 21/4/1819. See also Thompson's evidence to Commissioner Bigge, HRNZ 1.501.

large quantities of timber.[72] Thompson, however, still claimed that the timber from the eighth voyage in 1818 was purchased with 'articles of husbandry, for which they [Māori] show a strong desire'—though the volume obtained was not as great as the previous voyage.[73] And to do so, he had to source the timber from the Caville Islands to the north of the Bay of Islands, rather than from the Kawakawa, the usual area within the Bay.[74] While the *Active* herself may not have been directly involved, clearly the trading relationship between missionary and Māori had changed significantly, and by the end of 1818 (as it was later admitted) trading in muskets and powder had become commonplace among the missionaries.[75] The trade was never sanctioned by Marsden or the CMS, but arose from the missionaries trading privately as individuals rather than collectively as a mission, a practice that, though against the rules of the mission, was difficult to proscribe.[76] The missionaries argued that they were forced into the practice on the basis of necessity, claiming that Māori would no longer take their mission trade. It was a claim that neither Marsden nor the CMS were prepared to accept, who both rejected the 'nefarious' trade as incompatible with the missionary vocation. In addition, privately trading in muskets put each missionary in direct competition with his colleague, forcing those who relied solely on legitimate trade to go without.[77]

The return of the *Active* in December 1818 alerted Marsden to the trouble that now afflicted the mission. On its ninth voyage (22 Mar–30 Jul 1819), the *Active* carried Marsden's letter of reply along with one

---

72 William Hall, Journal, 26/8/1818, in *Son of Carlisle*, 46.
73 SG 9/1/1819.
74 Kendall to Marsden, 3/3/1818.
75 Kendall to Marsden, 27/9/1821. Contrary to the fanciful views of Quinn, *Samuel Marsden: Altar Ego*, 103–122, the missionary barter in muskets was neither systematic nor extensive. The limited nature of the missionary trade in muskets is supported by Wright, *New Zealand*, 89. The missionaries were at times paid in munitions by the sea captains for acting as their agents. However, although ships leaving Port Jackson were restricted by regulation in the number of muskets they could carry, there was evidence that muskets were cut down and concealed among personal affects in order to avoid detection. Some missionaries also used personal agents in England to supply them with arms. Marsden reported that John King's mother-in-law, Hannah Hansen (wife of Thomas Hansen, the *Active*'s second master) was convicted and transported for possession of muskets stolen from the 48th Regiment stationed in Sydney. Marsden to Pratt, 11/3/1822; Marsden to Pratt [No1], 7/9/1822; Marsden to Pratt [No2], 7/9/1822.
76 Marsden was ignorant of what was being sent privately to NZ; Marsden to the Settlers, 24/2/1819; Marsden to Pratt, 24/2/1819.
77 Sharp, *The World, the Flesh & the Devil*, 507–513.

from the CMS clearly ruling out the practice of bartering in muskets. In response, the missionaries met and signed an agreement to abstain from all private trading including muskets. But it was not long before the trade resumed: even Marsden's second visit to the mission in August 1819 only stopped the trade for a time. It wasn't until the following year, with the departure of Kendall on his unsanctioned visit to England, that Marsden was finally able to stem the flow.[78] The ninth voyage returned a cargo of salted fish (one ton) in addition to the usual pork and sawn timber.[79] Marsden had sent the convict James Boyle over to New Zealand on the Active's previous trip with the purpose of making salt and supplying fish to the Active.[80]

The tenth voyage of the Active (15 Oct 1819–30 Nov 1819) arrived in New Zealand while Marsden was still on his second visit to the Bay of Islands. He had arrived on the American ship, *General Gates*, which he hired for its larger capacity in order to carry the new missionaries and their families: John Butler, James Kemp and Francis Hall.[81] The new missionaries established a second mission station at Kerikeri under the patronage of Hongi Hika further around the bay from Rangihoua. The *Active* returned to NSW with Marsden and a number of others associated with the mission.[82] Perhaps due to the demands of building the new station, the *Active* carried no timber, though it did purchase in New Zealand the equipment needed for its new venture: whaling.[83]

Whaling: Voyages 11–14 (1820–1822)

Upon the return of the *Active* from its tenth voyage, Marsden set about

---

78 Minutes of Special Committee, Rangihoua, 12/4/1820; Marsden to Pratt, 22/9/1820.
79 Cumpston, *Shipping Arrivals & Departures*, 116.
80 Marsden on his third visit to New Zealand dismissed Boyle for 'improper conduct' (presumably cohabitating with Māori women), though he did not return to New South Wales until 27 Nov 1821; Hall, *Journal*, 29/6/1818; Marsden to Kendall, 17/1/1822.
81 Before the sailing of the *General Gates*, Marsden received a letter from the Judge Advocate's secretary, J. J. Moore, informing him that the south seas missions would no longer be charged port duties for passengers; J. J. Moore to Marsden, 21/7/1819.
82 Although Macquarie had been forced by the Colonial Office to grant Marsden leave to visit New Zealand, he limited the time for which Marsden could be absent from the colony to four months; SG 7/8/1819; Marsden to Pratt, 14/7/1819.
83 Marsden had become convinced that timber was never going to be profitable; Marsden, 22/3/1819. Marsden had sent a letter via three whaling captains authorising Kendall to buy their equipment before they left New Zealand for England; Kendall to Marsden, 21/4/1819; Marsden to Pratt, 9/6/1819.

making new arrangements for its management. He had the brig revalued at £1500, and handed it over to be managed fully by the CMS as part of the New Zealand mission, giving them the option to sell the *Active* should they so desire.[84] This signaled Marsden's intention of finally establishing an auxiliary or corresponding society in NSW. But any opportunity to do so was cut short by the arrival of the *HMS Dromedary* requesting Marsden's return to New Zealand to help procure spars for the Royal Navy. His third visit to New Zealand became the longest, lasting from 14 February to 20 December 1820: a total of ten months. So it was not until 2 March 1821 that a Corresponding Committee of the CMS was eventually formed.[85]

In the meantime, Thompson had sailed the *Active* on the first of its four whaling expeditions, departing 7 February 1820. From the first, Thompson had been an advocate of whaling, having previously had four to five years experience in the fisheries around the New Zealand coast.[86] Marsden had supported the idea at the time but it was not until the end of the eighth voyage that he formed concrete plans for the *Active*'s conversion, citing as reasons the continued high duty imposed on timber and the unprofitable nature of the Tahitian trade.[87] Contracts for the sale of the resulting whale oil were arranged by Marsden's agent, Robert Campbell, with the merchant, William Kermode, who then on-sold the oil in London and made payment to the CMS.[88]

The south seas whalers hunted two species of whale: the southern right whale and the sperm whale. The southern right whales migrated north during the winter (April to August) from Antarctic waters to their breeding grounds in Storm Bay, at the mouth of the Derwent River, Tasmania. The more valuable sperm whales were hunted during the

---

84 Valuation of the Brig *Active*, 8/12/1819; Marsden to Pratt, 7/2/1820 [No1]; Marsden to Pratt, 7/2/1820 [No2]. The hand-over of the *Active* was back-dated to 31 Aug 1819, when John Butler had became the superintendent of the New Zealand mission.
85 *Minutes of the Corresponding Committee*, 2/3/1821.
86 Thompson to Marsden, 22/3/1817. Thompson gave the example of his last voyage: he left NSW, 23 Nov 1815, in a three-boat ship and spent December to April on the NZ coast and obtained 96 tons of sperm oil. He estimated that if the *Active* was fitted as a two-boat ship then 60–70 tons of oil could be expected each season. Marsden supported the scheme; Marsden to Pratt, 27/3/1817.
87 Marsden to Pratt, 24/2/1819. Marsden consoled himself with the fact that the traders, Birnie and Co., also lost £1000 on two trips to the Pacific; Marsden to Pratt, 22/3/1819.
88 Robert Campbell to William Kermode, 11/2/1820; Robert Campbell to CMS, 10/8/1820; Robert Campbell to CMS, 2/9/1820. Black oil was priced at £18 per ton, and sperm oil at £35 per ton.

summer (October to April) off the coast of New Zealand (between the East and North Capes).[89] Consequently, the four whaling voyages of the Active alternated between the Derwent River (with Hobart as a base) and the Bay of Islands. Thompson reported that the oil from the first whaling expedition was sold to Kermode for £1764.2.2.[90] Using a rate of £18 per ton, this sum represented almost 100 tons of black (southern right whale) oil. The second whaling expedition (10 November 1820–4 March 1821) took the *Active* to New Zealand where thirty tons of sperm whale oil were obtained with an estimated value of £1,000.[91] The next two voyages (16 April–8 September 1821, and 31 December 1821–31 July 1822) brought a yield of seventy-five tons of black oil and thirty-five tons of sperm oil, respectively.[92] The income derived from these voyages meant that Marsden was able to cover the missionary salaries for the year 1821 without drawing on the Society in London.[93]

Dispute over the use of the *Active*

Yet, everything was not plain sailing. It turned out that the *Active* did not make for a good whaler due to its slow speed and small capacity.[94] Marsden proposed that the CMS purchase a larger vessel in England and have Captain Bunker sail it out to NSW. A joint meeting of the CMS, the LMS, and Wesleyan Societies was held in London, but the proposal was rejected.[95] The CMS were wary of being drawn into a purely commercial activity beyond that of offsetting expenses. In addition, a dispute had arisen over the first consignment of oil that had had to be settled in the courts.[96] These factors led the CMS to instruct Marsden to sell the *Active* as soon as other means became available to

---

89 Clayton, *An Alphabetical List of Ships*, 3–4, 269–270; Thompson's evidence to Commissioner Bigge, HRNZ 1.502.
90 Thompson to CMS, 8/8/1820.
91 *SG* 10/3/1821; Cumpston, *Shipping Arrivals & Departures*, 126.
92 Ship News, *SG* 10/3/1821; 2/8/1822. Cumpston, *Shipping Arrivals & Departures*, 128; SG 2/8/1822.
93 Marsden to Pratt, 19/9/1821.
94 Marsden to Pratt, 10/6/1821.
95 Pratt to Marsden, 16/4/1822.
96 Pratt to Marsden, 15/6/1821; Pratt to Marsden, 13/3/1821. Marsden to Pratt, 18/9/1821. For this reason Marsden decided to sell the oil from the third whaling expedition in Port Jackson rather than London so as to relieve the CMS of the risk.

maintain effective communications with New Zealand.[97]

By this stage, a Corresponding Committee of the CMS had finally been established in NSW on 2 March 1821.[98] The secretary, Captain Francis Irvine, had arrived in the colony the previous year from Calcutta where he had been involved with various mission groups. Unfortunately, Irvine and Marsden differed over a number of mission policies that forced the dissolution of the committee within the year, on 27 September 1821.[99] Irvine had opposed the use of the *Active* for whaling and wanted instead to develop the trade in New Zealand flax.[100] To do so, Irvine advocated that the mission should openly trade in muskets—a view in which he was encouraged by Thomas Kendall who had newly returned from England.[101] Kendall himself had no intention of abiding by Marsden's prohibition on muskets, and on returning to New Zealand obtained the support of his colleagues in attempting to overturn the ban.[102] In addition, Marsden faced angry accusations from John Butler, that he (Marsden) had been just as complicit in the trade by receiving the *Active*'s cargoes of timber in the full knowledge of how they were purchased.[103] It was a charge that Marsden strongly denied.[104]

On the *Active*'s return from its fourteenth and final voyage, Marsden advertised the brig for sale. The CMS had already confirmed their wish to divest themselves of the asset, and Marsden anticipated that the purchase of the *Queen Charlotte* by the late Pomare II would be

---

97 Pratt to Marsden, 16/4/1822. Marsden agreed with the instruction to sell, though he was aware that it also left the missionaries vulnerable to unscrupulous traders like Edward Eagar; Marsden to Pratt, 19/9/1821.
98 Minutes of the Corresponding Committee, 2/3/1821.
99 Sharp, *The World, the Flesh & the Devil*, 552–553.
100 Captain Irvine to the Assistant Secretary, 20/3/1821; Minute of Capt. Irvine relative to the *Active*, 22/3/1821.
101 Marsden to Pratt, 7/9/1822. Irvine was motivated in part by his post-millenial views of New Zealand as the beginning of the fifth monarchy; Irvine to Assistant Secretary, 20/3/1821.
102 Kendall to Marsden, 27/9/1821; Minutes of Quarterly Meeting of Missionaries and Settlers, 2/10/1821. Marsden replied to Kendall's letter, 17/1/1822. Kendall responded, 26/2/1822. The CMS then dismissed Kendall for musket trading, though Marsden had already suspended him for adultery; Pratt to the Missionaries and Settlers, 6/9/1822; Marsden to Kendall, 11/6/1822.
103 Butler, Journal, 23/8/1821; Butler to Marsden, 8/1/1822.
104 Marsden to Butler, 22/1/1822. Note that the copy of this letter in the Hocken library and available through the Marsden online archive has four of the twelve pages missing. This problem is compounded by Barton publishing a transcript of the incomplete letter; Barton, *Earliest New Zealand*, 196–201. Barton has been followed by Quinn and Sharp; Quinn, *Samuel Marsden: Altar Ego*, 127; Sharp, *The World, the Flesh & the Devil*, 565. For details see Falloon, 'Research Note', 9–10.

sufficient to maintain communications with New Zealand in addition to the Islands.[105] A sale was not made, however, until 1825 when Marsden accepted an offer of $2000.[106] The delay was caused by the changes made by Governor Brisbane in 1822 to the colonial currency, which by 1825 had reverted again to a sterling standard.[107]

Figure 7: Voyages of the Mission Brig, *Active*, 1814-1822

VOYAGE	PORT JACKSON, NSW DEPARTURE	BAY OF ISLANDS, NZ ARRIVAL	BAY OF ISLANDS, NZ DEPARTURE	SOCIETY ISLANDS (TAHITI) ARRIVAL	SOCIETY ISLANDS (TAHITI) DEPARTURE	PORT JACKSON, NSW RETURN	CARGO
	**First Five Voyages (1814-16)**						
1st	14 Mar 1814	10 Jun 181	25 Jul 1814			23 Aug 1814	spars and flax
2nd	19 Nov 1814	22 Dec 1814	26 Feb 1815			22 Mar 1815	4848 ft timber (159 spars), 1344 lb (½ ton) flax, small quantity fish & pork
3rd	27 Apr 1815	18 May 1815	11 Jul 1815			8 Aug 1815	130 logs and spars, 1 ton flax
4th	9 Sep 1815	28 Sep 1815	31 Oct 1815			28 Nov 1815	120 spars, ½ ton flax
5th	24 Jan 1816	23 Feb 1816	16 Mar 1816	8 May 1816	17 Oct 1816		
		28 Nov 1816	9 Dec 1816			29 Dec 1816	13 tons pork, 19 logs, 1019 ft timber.
	**South Seas Trading (1817-19)**						
6th	17 Apr 1817	22 May 1817	15 Jun 1817			25 Jul 1817	spars
7th	4 Sep 1817	22 Sep 1817	9 Oct 1817	Nov 1817	Jan 1818	24 Mar 1818	16 tons pork, 47 logs, 8984 ft plank timber.
		23 Feb 1818	7 Mar 1818				
8th	30 May 1818	19 Jun 1818	9 Jul 1818	Aug 1818	8 Oct 1818	29 Dec 1818	4.5 tons pork, 6000 ft plank timber, 6-7 tons of coconut oil.
		21 Nov 1818	8 Dec 1818				
9th	22 Mar 1819	5 May 1819	17 Jun 1819			30 Jul 1819	3 ton pork, 1 ton saltfish, 5246 ft plank timber.
10th	15 Oct 1819	28 Oct 1819	9 Nov 1819			30 Nov 1819	
	**Four Whaling Expeditions (1820-22)**						
11th	7 Feb 1820					25 Aug 1820	98 tons black oil
12th	10 Nov 1820	3 Jan 1821	22 Jan 1821			4 Mar 1821	30 tons sperm oil
13th	16 Apr 1821					8 Sep 1821	75 tons black oil
14th	31 Dec 1821	22 Jan 1822	8 Apr 1822			31 Jul 1822	35 tons sperm oil.

---

105 Marsden to Pratt, [25/9/1822].
106 Marsden to the Assistant Secretary, 30/6/1825. Elder estimates the sum in pounds to be about £400; *The Letters and Journals of Samuel Marsden*, 328.
107 Heydon, 'Brisbane, Sir Thomas Makdougall (1773-1860)'.

Summary

The fourteen voyages of the *Active* covered a period of nine years, 1814–1822. During that time, the brig was in regular communication with the mission stations in Tahiti and New Zealand, trading with the indigenous populations in order to offset expenses. The main forms of trade in the first five years were salted pork from Tahiti and timber from the Bay of Islands, in exchange for mission goods, consisting of ironwork and agricultural tools. The financial return, however, was not enough to cover the expenses of the *Active*, which had to rely on subsidies from London to balance the books. Samuel Marsden particularly lamented the imposition of government duties that he saw as making the whole enterprise unprofitable and as a sign of on-going opposition from the colonial Governor and his private Secretary.

The competitive nature of the pork trade, however, was also a contributing factor, as was the difficulty in obtaining adequate supplies of timber from New Zealand. In addition, the private trading of the missionaries in muskets and other munitions, particularly in the two-year period 1818–19, compromised the timber trade. For these reasons, the *Active* in its later voyages turned to whaling in search of greater profits. This gave the *Active*, despite being under-sized, its greatest level of profitability although it still did not clear its expenses. The CMS in London, however, were uncomfortable with being drawn into what appeared to them to be a purely commercial enterprise and so opted to have the *Active* sold.

With regard to the accusations of Philo Free, the above analysis confirms that Marsden correctly claimed that the trading operations of the *Active* were never on a commercial footing. Furthermore, although the CMS had underwritten the running-costs, Marsden had personally made a significant capital investment in purchasing the brig with no prospect of a realistic financial return. Consequently, at the time of writing his pseudonymous letter, John Thomas Campbell had no grounds for making his accusations based on the trading operations of the *Active* in the South Pacific.[108]

---

108 This conclusion is also supported by Sharp, *The World, the Flesh & the Devil*, 386–387.

CHAPTER 7

THE FAILURE OF THE PHILANTHROPIC SOCIETY

Peter G. Bolt

In January 1817, after Samuel Marsden commenced legal proceedings for being libeled by the letter signed 'Philo Free', Judge-Advocate Wylde asked J.T. Campbell why, as Government censor of the *Gazette*, he had permitted its printing. Although later events proved him disingenuous (he was proven to be its writer),[1] at that time Campbell explained that:

> I felt a degree of satisfaction by the revival in it, of the Philanthropic Society question, which in common with many other of its Members I had often lamented should have lain so very long in a dormant state. With the subject (which I do consider an interesting one) the letter commenced, and with it, it also ended, giving the first and last impression and bias of my mind exclusively to that favorite object. In my earnest desire to see something done in this business [...]'[2]

1. Origins
1.1 Marsden Calls a Meeting
On 20 December 1813, a group of prominent Sydney citizens met in the Long Room of the New Store, to discuss how to prevent Englishmen

---

1 Marsden pointed out that as a member of the committee resident in Sydney, if Campbell was really interested in the Philanthropic Society, 'his enquiries might have been fully satisfied at any time on the spot, without any reference to me whatever as Secretary to the Society residing at Parramatta'; Marsden to Wylde, 16/1/1817. Despite feigning ignorance of its purposes, J.T. Campbell was well aware of the atrocities that resulted in the Philanthropic Society, because he had the task of certifying the copies of the depositions sent to Bathurst were true to the original. See note to enclosures to Gov. Macquarie to Earl Bathurst, 17/1/1814, (*HRA* 1.8.111).
2 J.T. Campbell to Wylde, 14/1/1817.

mistreating the peoples indigenous to the South Pacific.³

Earlier that year (8 May), this same cause had been tacked onto the agenda of the first voluntary society to be formed in the colony, 'The New South Wales Society for Promoting Christian Knowledge and Benevolence in these Territories and Neighbouring Islands'.⁴ Unsurprisingly, given the title, two out of the three original objectives were related to South Sea missionary concerns: 1) relieving the distressed and enforcing the sacred duties of Religion and Virtue in NSW; 2) protecting the natives of the neighbouring islands; 3) assisting the missionaries at Otaheiti and the islands. Both Macquarie and Marsden considered the objectives too broad. When the Governor suggested the Society focus upon the first, the long-term assistance to the poor of NSW began, for which the society—after being rebadged (June 1818) as the much simpler 'Benevolent Society of New South Wales'—is still famous. It was left to the emergence of the second voluntary society in New South Wales 'to take into Consideration some measure for affording Support and Relief to the Natives of the South Sea Islands, who may come to Port Jackson, and to promote their Civilization'.

After the Chairman, William Gore, opened, the Rev Samuel Marsden took the floor. As the colony's Provost Marshall, Gore had summoned the meeting on December 11,⁵ being requisitioned to do so by several respectable inhabitants of Sydney: Samuel Marsden, David Allan, D'Arcy Wentworth, William Broughton, John Oxley, Garnham Blaxcell, Simeon Lord, and Alexander Riley.⁶ But this was always Marsden's meeting. After almost two decades in NSW he had become a champion for his fellow human beings in the South Seas, whose lives had been thrown in the balance by the arrival of European adventurers. The world would soon know it as Marsden's meeting. When the *Missionary Register 1814* reported the meeting, it added the note that: 'this Institution owes its existence to the deep interest which Mr Marsden has long felt in the civilization and conversion of the Islanders of the South Seas' and that its formation

---

3   *NSW Philanthropic Society, Minutes*. Comments below on the occurrence and outcomes of the meeting are drawn from these minutes, unless otherwise stated.
4   For this paragraph, see Scifleet, *Benevolent Society*, 3–4; Bolt, *William Cowper*, 118, 147–148.
5   *SG* 11/12/1813. In the next *Gazette* the petition and announcement were repeated, but the venue was changed from the Orphan school to 'the lower Room in the Government New Store, in George-street'; *SG* 18/12/1813.
6   According to 'A Spectator' (*SG* 11/1/1817), 'seven [sic] gentlemen, whose circumstances and character were such as to give due weight to the proposition'.

was part of 'the unwearied exertions which he is making in behalf of these numerous tribes'.[7] In the view of Marsden's evangelical network at home, Richard Johnson was the first Missionary to the South Seas, and Marsden was the second.[8] As he stood to address those present, Marsden had the people in his mission field at heart.

But the meeting did not arise solely out of this positive gospel vision. Four months later, Marsden explained to his friends in the Church Missionary Society:

> I have long wished for an opportunity to bring forward some of the Masters of Vessels, who visit the Islands in the South Seas, for their wanton cruelties, robberies, and murders of the Natives; in order to put a stop to these acts of violence in future as far as possible.[9]

Marsden had ready sources of information about happenings in the islands. A steady stream of islanders had lived with Marsden for many years at Parramatta,[10] since at least the visit of Te Pahi, a chief from the Bay of Islands.[11] As agent of the London Missionary Society, Marsden was well-connected to the missionaries working in Tahiti. In February 1810, as the first CMS missionaries, recruited during Marsden's visit to England (he left NSW in Feb 1807) and destined for New Zealand, waited in Sydney, delayed by the destruction of the *Boyd*,[12] a group of LMS missionaries arrived (17/2/1810), having fled troubles in Tahiti.[13] Everyone was aware of the difficulties the indigenous people of the South Seas were having at the hands of the Europeans, but, with his close information, Marsden was outraged.

The usual white man's narrative warned against the 'treachery' of the natives, but Marsden's investigations led him to reverse the usual story:

> I should recommend masters of vessels who may visit New Zealand to be very cautious unless they can depend upon the proper behaviour of their respective crews. The New Zealanders will not be insulted with impunity, nor be treated as men without understanding, but will

---

7 [Missionary Register], "New South Wales Society for affording Protection', 459–460.
8 Schwarze, 'Richard Johnson and Samuel Marsden'.
9 Marsden to Pratt, 15/3/1814 (Extract: *Missionary Register 1814*, 460).
10 For a later period, see Prentis, 'Rangatira'.
11 Te Pahi's first visit to Port Jackson was from 22/11/1805 to 26/2/1806, *SMH* 6/10/1857.
12 See Bolt, 'The *Boyd* Set-Back'.
13 Davies to LMS Directors, 24/2/1810.

THE FAILURE OF THE PHILANTHROPIC SOCIETY

assuredly resent and revenge an injury as soon as opportunity permits.[14]

By 1813, the time had come for some concerted action.

1.2 What the Ear Heard about what Eyes had seen

Like others inspired by the English evangelical revival and St Paul's letter to the Romans (chapter 13), Marsden believed in the Rule of Law. With his magistrate's head hearing his missionary heart, Marsden believed that British law ought to be able to protect those of the South Seas from the atrocities of British sailors. Prior to calling his meeting, he had busily gathered evidence:

> A few months ago, I received information that the master of a vessel from Port Jackson had treated a New Zealander very ill, by beating him cruelly, stripping him naked, and taking from him what little property he had acquired by acting as a sailor onboard. These acts took place in the Bay of Islands. I wrote an Official Letter to the Governor, (a copy of which I herewith transmit,) when the Master of the Vessel arrived, requesting that his Excellency would cause an inquiry to be made, which was done. I immediately brought forward another Master of a Vessel upon a similar charge.[15]

In the letter to which he alludes, written on November 1, 1813, Marsden provided a catena of atrocities for Governor Macquarie's benefit,[16] to spur him to use English law to protect these victims of the English people, for their sake and for the sake of European shipping. For without proper redress, the natives only have the law of retaliation to fall back on. Citing two recent examples, Marsden was convinced that:

> The fatal loss of the *Boyd* and the *Parramatta*, and the murders of their Captains and Crews, and of several Crews belonging to boats of different people Vessels, were occasioned by the unprovoked cruelties of the Europeans.

---

14 Marsden to Macquarie, 30/5/1815 (*HRNZ* 1.399). When justifying the purchase of the *Active* to CMS, he noted that 'the wanton acts of oppression, robberies, and murders committed on the persons and properties of the natives of New Zealand, have compleatly destroy'd all confidence in the Europeans. They manifest every wish to cultivate our friendship; but woeful experience has taught them not to trust us too much', Marsden to Pratt 22/9/1814 (*Missionary Register 1815*, 266).
15 Marsden to Pratt, 15/3/1814 (Extract: *Missionary Register 1814*, 460).
16 Marsden to Macquarie, 1/11/1813.

While openly motivated by his own missionary goals, Marsden argued more generally from utility. Preventing European cruelty would build a better future for everyone:

> Should the natives of New Zealand be treated with Justice and humanity by the Europeans and their persons and property protected from the hand of fraud and violence, I am persuaded that all Hostilities and Murder would cease on their part and a Friendly intercourse would soon be open between [them] and the settlement, which will greatly benefit this Colony. They are a noble race of Men and capable of every mental improvement. They would soon learn our simple Arts and form habits of Industry. This I am fully convinced of from the Knowledge I have of their Character and endowments.

It was rarely possible to call ships captains to account for atrocities committed, because they either died in native retaliation, or, having escaped that primal form of human justice in the islands, they escaped British justice by sailing away. But when the *King George* arrived in Port Jackson,[17] and Marsden heard of the onboard mistreatment of Mookiki, a New Zealander taken from Port Jackson to the Bay of Islands, he seized the opportunity and pressed Macquarie to investigate with a view to 'instituting some judicial enquiry'. On soil declared to be a British colony and before a properly appointed British governor, Marsden offered to lay out the evidence against the master, Mr Lasco Jones, and to provide the testimony of the biblical 'two or three witnesses' to establish European mistreatment more generally:

> When these informations, or Affidavits, are submitted to Your Excellency's consideration, Your Excellency will then Judge what restraints may be deemed necessary to lay upon such Masters of Vessels

---

17 On 16 February she arrived from a 14 whaling months voyage (*SG* 20/2/1813), during which the mistreatment occurred at the Bay of Islands. Marsden heard the reports after her arrival (Marsden to Macquarie, 1/11/1813). She left again for the Derwent on 19 May (*SG* 22/5/1813), where she sailed in company with the *Cumberland* and *Active* (*SG* 21/8/1813). When she returned on 9 October (*SG* 9/10/1813), since Mookiki had returned to Sydney on the *Active* on 21 August, Marsden seized the opportunity to press for prosecution and wrote his letter of 1 November to the Governor. The magistrates did not take the charges seriously (Marsden to Pratt, 15/6/1815). When Jones returned on 3 March 1815 after an unsuccessful voyage of 15 months (*SG* 4/3/1815), Marsden, having gained more information whilst in New Zealand, took the opportunity to press further charges before the Sydney bench on 12, 15, 19 April 1815; See Proceedings of Magistrates Court [Lasco Jones], 12/4/1815. Jones was replaced by R.S. Walker in March (*SG* 11/3/1815) before the *King George* sailed on 2/5/1815 (*SG* 6/5/1815). He announced his imminent departure in *SG* 10/6/1815.

as leave this Port for New Zealand, and what instructions to Give them in future.

Although incidents of European cruelty were widely-known in the early years, they only occasionally made the written record, and then usually suitably disguised by the standard narrative of South Seas' native treachery, aggression and savagery. No doubt many more incidents went unrecorded. Those who worked amongst them, like Marsden, inspired by Jesus' Great Commission to reach all nations, heard many similar reports from the native grass-roots across many years.[18]

One of the earliest was at the beginning of 1793, when HMS *Daedalus*, Lieut. Hanson, kidnapped two young New Zealanders, Hoodoo and Tokee, and took them to Port Jackson. The *Shah Hormuzear* then left them on Norfolk Island, where they were mystified to learn that the white men expected them to know about dressing flax—a job done by the women in New Zealand. When the *Britannia*, William Raven, returned them in November, Lt. Gov. King travelled on board 'in order to prevent any insult or injury being done to them'.[19]

It is true that many islanders showed an interest in joining European ships for the adventure of travelling to lands far away. There are several famous examples of those who were taken to England, some meeting English nobility or even royalty.[20] But many were simply kidnapped, men for the crew and women for their sexual exploitation. And once on board, whether of their own free will or not, they were often abused and unpaid, before being dropped at a destination far from their own home—as if, for an islander, any island would do.

Such occurrences were treated so casually, such as Lasco Jones warning about Otaheitian Jack, said to be deluding ships calling at the Bay of Islands, who 'was left there by the *Seringapatam*, upwards of four

---

18 See, e.g. Deposition of James Elder before Marsden, 12 November 1813; Henry to Macquarie, 16/11/1813; Davies to Macquarie, 11/9/1813. In Marsden to Macquarie, 30/5/1815, Marsden documents at least seven other vessels apart from the *Boyd*, involved in the mistreatment of New Zealanders. For Marsden's missionary vision, see Pettett, 'Strategy'.
19 Marsden to Macquarie, 30/5/1815 (*HRNZ* 1.333). Cf. Bolt, *Portrait*, 81, 237–238.
20 E.g., Moehanga (Moyhanger), 1806; Teina (Tyeena) and Maki, 1806; Te Pahi's son, Matara (Ma-Tara), 1807; Ruatara (Duaterra), 1809; Maui (Mowhee), 1816; Tuai (Tooi) and Titeri (Teeterree), 1818; Meiri (Mayree), 1819; Hongi Hika (Shunghee) and Waikato (Wycotto), 1820.

years since'.²¹ Even the ordinary person on the Sydney streets would be aware of the presence of these people wrenched from their homeland and never able to return, because some had become their neighbours. Take for example, Foo Foo, the young Tahitian woman brought to Port Jackson in 1813 by the *Mercury* who subsequently lived with the ship's owner, Mary Reiby. Unfortunately, she soon 'unaccountably disappeared' and a notice in the advertising columns of the *Gazette* warned that 'any who shall detain her against her inclination will be prosecuted with the utmost rigor'.²²

This was certainly Ruatara's story, found dumped in England by Marsden in 1809, and later dumped again at Norfolk Island.²³ When Marsden bundled the mistreated Ruatara onto the *Ann* to start his journey home, the two men were already acquainted from Ruatara's earlier visit to Sydney.²⁴ Marsden saw this re-acquaintance and the opportunity to spend so much time on the voyage, and then to have Ruatara to live with his family for some three years, as a good gift of God's Providence, for it allowed the Mission to New Zealand to begin, even before white missionaries arrived in the country. The friendship formed between these two men from very different cultures, went on to have enormous significance for the South Pacific.

As their friendship grew and Marsden learned more of Ruatara's story, he became amazed that Ruatara still had such a high regard for the whites:

> No man could ever be worse treated than Duaterra [Ruatara] has been very often by Europeans; but he has the strongest attachment to them.²⁵

---

21 SG 20/2/1813, suggesting that 'this villain' was a risk for getting more people eaten like the *Boyd*. To the contrary, it is likely that he was the Tahitian who helped Marsden in his inquiries into that incident.
22 SG 27/11/1813. For Reiby's ownership of the *Mercury*, see SG 30/5/1812.
23 After Ruatara lived with Marsden for 9 months, Feb to Nov 1810, he was abandoned by the *Frederick* on Norfolk Island, before being returned to Port Jackson to be with Marsden again, bringing his time with the Marsdens to about three years; Pettett, *Samuel Marsden*, 38–39.
24 In Marsden to Pratt, 28/10/1815, Marsden said he first met Ruatara 'nearly ten years ago'. In 1805, Ruatara and two other New Zealanders had joined the *Argo* in the Bay of Islands for a five month voyage on the New Zealand coast. They returned to the Bay on 18 March, before arriving in Sydney 8 April 1806 (SG 13/4/1806). This makes it impossible for Ruatara to have accompanied Te Pahi on his visit 27/11/1805 to 24/2/1806 (*pace* SMH 6/10/1857; Pettett, *Samuel Marsden*, 38–39), but provides two brief visits of his own in 1806, first in April and then between 20 September and 12 October 1806.
25 Marsden to Pratt, 20/9/1814 (*Missionary Register 1815*, 196).

But Ruatara's experience was by no means unique, and Marsden's list of atrocities grew longer the more he heard.

1.3 Documenting Atrocities

Oral accounts of native mistreatment had circulated long enough for many to think it normal practice. When presented with the possibility of prosecuting Lasco Jones, Marsden began to bring the oral accounts into the documentary record for the benefit of British law.[26] His concern to do so is echoed in Thomas Kendall's words home:

> The people of England, through a natural bias in favour of their own countrymen, can dwell on the cruelties and savage habits of the people of New Zealand. But the time is now arrived when they must hear of the cruelties of men, who bear the Christian Name, among these very savages; and this by official documents, supported and reported and established by respectable witnesses.[27]

After writing to the Governor on 1 November, Marsden began taking depositions from those with first-hand experience of abuses perpetrated in the Pacific. As he was engaged in doing so, in a month of an extraordinary number of 'openings of Providence', a second ship's captain sailed into Port Jackson, equally worthy of prosecution.[28]

On Tuesday 9 November 1813, Captain Theodore Walker brought in the brig *Endeavour*, having sailed from Tahiti in company with the *Daphne*, which arrived the next day. Walker had regained the *Daphne* after she was seized in a bloody mutiny on 29 August, in which the master, Michael Fodger, was one of those killed. Saturday's *Gazette* provided a dramatic account, written up as yet another example of the random violence of the natives of the South Seas—this time the twenty

---

26 In a sense, by so doing, Marsden anticipated the Cook Island land courts at the beginning of the 20th century and New Zealand's Waitangi Tribunal (1975–); see, for example, Campbell, 'History in Prehistory', and Williams, 'Reparations and the Waitangi Tribunal', and the Waitangi Tribunal website.

27 Kendall to CMS [1814], printed in the April issue of *Missionary Register 1815*, 188. Especially reflecting upon the *Boyd*, Kendall refers to documents in Marsden's possession intended to be 'made public in England' that will vindicate the South Sea Islanders.

28 'I see the footsteps of Divine Providence strongly marked in many circumstances, that have happened in these parts of the world: all tending to make way for the blessing of the Gospel', Marsden to Pratt, 15/3/1814 (Extract: *Missionary Register 1814*, 461). See further, Falloon, '"Openings of Providence"'.

five Tahitians shipped on board as divers.[29]

Owned by Isaac Nichols, the *Endeavour* was one of the eleven vessels over 50 tons on the colonial registry at that time, competing in 'Australia's infant trade with the Pacific islands', which, since 1812, 'was experiencing its first recession'.[30] Fijian sandalwood was in short supply, the Tahitian civil war [1808–1815] had decreased the supply of pork, and shipping was wary of visiting New Zealand after the burning of the *Boyd*. The race was on to find new cargoes from previously unexploited islands.

Because of his connections, Marsden could listen below the public report. As it happened, George Bicknell, the nephew of LMS Missionary, was on board the *Daphne* during its seizure and one of only six crewmen to survive. With the *Endeavour* came a letter from missionary and magistrate William Henry recounting Bicknell's report of events of the *Daphne*, and one from John Davies on behalf of all the missionaries.[31]

Magistrate D'Arcy Wentworth had already deposed Dillon about an affray in the Fiji islands involving the *Hunter* and the *Elizabeth*. When he arrived in Port Jackson with two native woman aboard, he was called to account before the magistrate on 6 November.[32]

Marsden started documenting eyewitness evidence of former atrocities on 10 November—coincidentally the same day that Thomas Kendall, the next missionary for New Zealand, disembarked from the *Earl Spencer*.[33] Marsden deposed John Besent in the Parramatta court, who had jumped ship in the Bay of Islands in March 1812 and lived with the Māori for six months.[34] When he arrived the wreck of the

---

29 *SG* 13/11/1813. Cf. Yarwood, *Samuel Marsden: Survivor*, 149: 'The *Gazette* rarely presented this aspect of the picture [i.e. white provocation], tending to see islanders' reprisals as examples of native treachery'. However, rather than letting all blame fall upon the *Gazette*, it should be remembered that it was reporting the account of the white men involved.

30 For this paragraph, Maude & Crocombe, 'Rarotongan Sandalwood', 33–34, who count eleven Colonial Vessels over 50 tons; cf. *Almanac* 1813, 24–25. For the significance of the sandalwood (and pork) trade see Hainsworth, *The Sydney Traders*, Ch. 11, and Sykes, 'Sandalwood'. Also Maude, 'The Tahitian Pork Trade: 1800–1830'.

31 *SG* 13/11/1813; Henry to Macquarie, 16/11/1813; Davies to Macquarie, 11/9/1813.

32 Deposition of Peter Dillon, 6/11/1813; Glenholme to Dillon, 5/11/1813; Dillon to Glenholme, 6/11/1813.

33 Kendall left England on 31 May (sailed 2 June, see *SG* 9/10/1813) and disembarked 10 October, *Missionary Register 1815*, 101.

34 Deposition of John Besent [Re *Parramatta*], 10/11/1813.

Parramatta[35] was between Cape Brett and Terra's [Tara's] district. He learned that the schooner had arrived from Port Jackson (1809) in need of provisions and the natives had supplied them with a plentiful supply of Pork, Fish, and Potatoes, but instead of paying for them, the ship weighed anchor and threw the natives overboard and fired upon them with small shot. Besent had himself met three of the natives who had been wounded in this event. When caught by a contrary wind, the vessel had been driven onshore and the natives had taken their revenge for being defrauded, cutting off the entire crew.

In a second deposition on 13 November, Besent also reported what he had learned about the *Boyd*, confirming what the New Zealanders had told Marsden soon after it had happened.[36] Captain Thompson had flogged a Chief's son, and, upon landing, his father, Tipphookee, organized revenge and Thompson and the rest of the crew were killed. Te Pahi, then chief at the Bay of Islands, had nothing to do with the destruction of the *Boyd*.

Between Besent's two depositions, on the 12th, Marsden heard from a former LMS Missionary at Parramatta in regard to the *Royal Admiral*, the *General Wellesley*, and the *Seringapatam*.[37] In 1800 James Elder was taken to Tahiti on the *Royal Admiral*, Willliam Wilson, which brought 300 convicts for NSW. During nine weeks in New Zealand at the River Thames, he saw several natives defrauded, which brought on quarrels likely to have serious consequences. There was also another vessel there at the time, which drove off the natives who supplied them with provisions and fired upon them. The natives were friendly and helpful and none from the *Royal Admiral* were injured by them. Two Europeans had been living with the natives two years, and one came with this ship when it left.

In 1807, after the *General Wellesley*, Capt. Dalrymple, touched at

---

35 Part-owned by J. Macarthur and G. Blaxcell, after an extremely successful voyage to the Society Islands (June-Dec 1807) bringing 75600 lbs of Pork to Sydney and probably causing the pork price to fall, the *Parramatta* was wrecked in 1809; Hainsworth, *The Sydney Traders*, 159 n.7, 163–164, 237. NZ writers understand that the district was that of Tara of Kororāreka in the Bay of Islands, rather than Te Ara (George) of Whangaroa. E.g. Salmond, *Between Worlds*, 368.
36 Deposition of John Besent [Re *Boyd*], 13/11/1813. Marsden to Pratt, 25/10/1810. For more of the story, see Bolt, 'The *Boyd* Set-Back'.
37 Deposition of James Elder, 12/11/1813. Elder arrived with the other missionaries in February 1810, but, on Marsden's advice, he did not return to Tahiti with the others in 1811; see Gunson, 'Elder'.

Tahiti, Elder travelled with her to see other islands and act as interpreter. On Prince of Wales Island, 4–500 men, women and children, came to the beach to watch the ship pass. 'The Captain wantonly and barbarously and without the least provocation whatever [...] fired 5 or 6 large guns with grape shot', despite Elder's remonstrances, in order to strike terror into native hearts and to demonstrate the power the English possessed. The only thing that stopped him was when a gun exploded and took a sailor's arm off at the shoulder, leading to his death. Some of the natives later visited Elder at Tahiti and informed him that several people had been killed and wounded.

In 1808, the *Seringapatam* touched at Tahiti in distress, bound for Port Jackson, and Elder took passage on her. She cruised about two months on the North Coast of New Zealand, with about 7 or 8 English ships, and then put in to the Bay of Islands for about a week. Here Elder saw the natives defrauded of potatoes, and other natives enticed below, stripped and robbed and beaten off the ship, despite the natives being 'friendly' and ready to supply refreshments. After such abuse, Elder was astounded that the Europeans hadn't been beaten or murdered. He was convinced that if the New Zealanders were treated with 'any degree of common justice, honest, and civility', Europeans might live safely amongst them.

During his time in Tahiti, Elder had heard often of Europeans out for their own gain, assisting one group of natives to destroy another, sowing the seed for civil war and endangerment of future European shipping.

When the *Endeavour* and *Daphne* arrived in the midst of his gathering evidence, and the story was reported in the *Gazette*, Marsden travelled to Sydney to depose *Daphne* crew members, Hendrike, French, Jones, and Randall.[38] He heard about 'some Cruelties, which were committed in the vessel'.[39]

Abraham Hendrike gave a detailed deposition, which the three others swore to be substantially correct.[40] In September 1812, Hendrike shipped with the *Daphne*, Michael Fodger, touching at New Zealand and

---

38 Deposition of Abraham Hendrike, 16/11/1813.
39 This is Wentworth's incidental remark, see W.C. Wentworth to T. Moore, 6/11/1815.
40 Deposition of Abraham Hendrike, 16/11/1813. French couldn't recall whether Amile was hanged on the *Endeavour* or the *Daphne*, but he knew it was one of them!; Deposition of Thomas French, 16/11/1813.

then to the Palmerstone Islands, where Fodger had left six Europeans the year before, four Englishmen and two Portuguese. On approaching the island, one of these men swam to the ship and informed Fodger that John Bearback [Burbeck], the principal of the gang, and another, Michael Cuff, had been murdered and another speared through the back. One of the Portuguese was the murderer. Fodger would not stay to get the rest of the gang off the island, despite the urgings of his crew. They proceeded to Ulitea, in the Society Islands, and procured a load of pork and then Bolabola for some more, where they learned that the Uliteans had intended to attack Fodger when he was on the island previously with the brig *Trial*. They picked up two Europeans left on Bolabola, then dropped on Eimeo the man they had picked up at Palmerstone so that he could inform William Henry, the LMS missionary appointed by Macquarie as magistrate, about the murders. They shipped six natives as pearl divers at Otaheite, and then five more from the island Anna, and a lascar named Amile, before proceeding to the pearl islands for a cargo of pearl and pearl shells. Running out of provisions, they sailed to Otaheite, where the six Tahitians left the ship, since Fodger had not paid them. When the Europeans complained of the provisions, Fodger ordered five of them (William Ralph, George Roberts, John Carr, James Welsh, and William Gerrard) set ashore without food or clothes, and ordered his Mate to shoot the first man who attempted to go below to get his belongings. Henry Williams was shot through both thighs by Fodger, and another wounded with the butt end of a pistol. He eventually allowed them their clothes, but told a native chief to send his men after them 'to strip them and beat their brains out with stones'. Hendrike deposed that he saw this detail written in the log of the *Queen Charlotte*, William Shelley Master, by the officer Mr Davey, as reported by the natives of Otaheite. Fodger shipped fifteen more natives as divers, thence to Tabooway, where he picked up five Europeans formerly of the brig *Trial*, then Roorootoo where he picked up three natives. At Reematerra eighteen natives and three small canoes brought fruit and produce to the ship. The captain invited them on board, and their canoes drifted off. When the captain ordered them off the ship, they were driven off into the water and fourteen of the eighteen were drowned as they were swimming for their canoes, Hendrike remonstrating with Fodger to tack towards their canoes before putting them off. At the island of Sebroovoi, the chief of the island came on board offering to sell sandalwood for some European cloth, but Fodger offered Tokeys which the chief refused, and so Fodger kept him prisoner on ship until the sandalwood was brought, and he fired at two other chiefs in the canoes, but they escaped. When the sandalwood was brought, Fodger let the chief go, and only gave for the ton and a half of sandalwood two puppies and some bad Tahitian cloth. Near the island of Arava, the Tahitians and other coloured men mutinied, killing Fodger, William Gill, and severely wounding Chief Mate Christian Kisaskyó Vanderkiste, who escaped with four other wounded and three others (John Mellon, Edward Collyer, John Queen, Robert Roways, Joseph Shell, Terry Thompson and John Riley). Leaving the eight on Arava, which is quite barren, despite pleas to bring them and not leaving them any means of procuring subsistence, the remaining seven of the crew (six Europeans and one Lascar) were compelled to sail the brig to Otaheite, arriving on 31 August.

When the *Endeavour*, Theodore Walker, came along side and learned of the mutiny, that night she was fired upon and returned fire, and the mutineers fled the ship. At about daybreak, Walker ordered the *Daphne* boarded, and upon discovering the lascar Amile to have been active in the mutiny, he took him to the *Endeavour*, hanged him and then shot him while hanging. After sailing to Eimeo for repairs, the crew begged Walker to go to Arava to rescue the eight, but he could not due to contrary winds, and so the vessel came to Port Jackson.

Although the *Gazette* cast Theodore Walker as the hero rescuing the mutinied *Daphne*, he had been previously involved in atrocities. Back in Parramatta court on 19 November, Marsden heard Jacob Williams depose that, while the *Boyd* was still in Sydney Cove, he proceeded for New Zealand with Captain Walker on the Schooner *Mercury* (17 Oct 1809).[41] Once in the Bay of Islands, Walker was involved with an attempt to steal potatoes from Te Pahi's island.

The November inquiries opened a Pandora's box! As a result, Theodore Walker was investigated for the murder of Amile, the lascar. Everyone agreed the lascar should have been put to death for taking a leading role in the mutiny on board the *Daphne* and the murder of her

---

41 Deposition of Jacob Williams, 19/11/1813. For the departure date, see *SG* 5/5/1810. After proceeding to Tahiti for pork, the *Mercury* returned on 3/5/1810.

Captain, Michael Fodger (whose cruelties led to the mutiny), but this should have been through due legal process. However, when Walker's case was heard on 4 and 11 December, Judge-Advocate Bent declared that no court in NSW had the jurisdiction to try the crime.[42] In a long delayed process, Macquarie's superiors advised him to send Walker to England for trial, along with the witnesses—although he never got there and died in NSW after this Damocles sword hung over his head for more than a decade.[43]

However, during the initial investigation of Walker, a discovery was made that set off yet another series of unfortunate events for the natives of the South Seas that became a test case for the newly formed Philanthropic Society.

1.4 Outlawing Atrocities: Governor Macquarie's Proclamation (1/12/1813)

Although Marsden's relationship with the Governor would soon turn sour,[44] in this period —hailed as 'the high point of collaboration' between the two men—,[45] Macquarie had been urged to support the mission[46] and Marsden enjoyed his support. With the evidence before him, Macquarie was spurred into action:

> The facts which I circumstantiated, induced his Excellency to issue a Proclamation for the Protection of the Natives of the South Sea Islands; and to require all Masters of Vessels, who clear out of this Port, to enter into a bond that they will not commit any of those acts of Fraud and Violence upon the natives. In this Case I obtained the utmost of my wishes.[47]

---

42 Depositions of French, Jones, Hendrick, and Randall, 4/12/1813. Also on the Bench: W. Broughton, D'A Wentworth, A. Riley, S. Lord; Theodore Walker declaration of Not Guilty, 11/12/1813.
43 After Bent's decision, Macquarie asked for advice (Macquarie to Bathurst, 17/1/1814) to receive Bathurst's recommendation (Bathurst to Macquarie, 12/7/1815), to which Macquarie agreed (Macquarie to Bathurst, 18/3/1816). Instead of going for trial, Walker continued voyaging on various vessels (presumably still on bail) and in May 1824, while Master of the *Newcastle*, died in an alcoholic stupor—for which the *Gazette* condemned him (*SG* 27/5/1824).
44 See Schwarze, 'A Secret Enemy', in this volume.
45 Yarwood, *Samuel Marsden: Survivor*, 148. Cf. Sharp, *The World, the Flesh & the Devil*, 308–309.
46 Gambier to Macquarie 22/3/1813, which presumably arrived with the *Earl Spencer* on 10 October.
47 Marsden to Pratt, 15/3/1814 (Extract: *Missionary Register 1814*, 460–461). Yarwood, *Samuel Marsden: Survivor*, 148, even states that 'Macquarie responded sympathetically to the problems outline by his senior chaplain'.

Such matters had been forced upon Macquarie from his first days as Governor. Just after he arrived, Sydney reeled at the news of the burning of the *Boyd* and the almost complete destruction of those on board.[48] The new Governor immediately took charge. His desires for the safety of British subjects kept Marsden's mission team in NSW until the end of 1814— to Marsden's immense frustration.

But in the interim, the two men worked together to bring some Law and Order to the Pacific peoples. As early as August 1811, Macquarie delegated authority to Ruatara and his companions Korra Korra [Korokoro] & Shungie [Hongi Hika] to be the ones to give permission for ship's captains to bring New Zealanders off the island,[49] and in September he made LMS missionary William Henry magistrate for the Society Islands.[50] Later, in November 1814 as the *Active* was about to depart with Marsden and his CMS missionaries onboard, Macquarie re-issued this authority for the three New Zealanders,[51] and, at Marsden's suggestion, appointed missionary Thomas Kendall as magistrate in the Bay of Islands.[52]

Although the November 1813 depositions ranged across disparate incidents from different vessels, their combined picture added detail to the extent of the problem and forceful leverage for Marsden with Macquarie. Marsden was hopeful:

> I think much has been done here in clearing away the difficulties. From the Depositions which I shall transmit for the information of the Society [CMS], you will see what just cause the Natives of different Islands have to redress their own wrongs upon the Europeans.[53]

---

48 See Bolt, 'The *Boyd* Set-Back'.
49 Ruatara, Korra Korra & Shungie, Authorised, 15/8/1811.
50 See W. Henry, Commission, 18/9/1811; W. Henry, Appointed Magistrate, 28/9/1811; Macquarie to Bathurst, 17/1/1814 (*HRA* 1.8.96–97). Yarwood, *Samuel Marsden: Survivor*, 150, gives the mistaken impression that Henry was appointed at the end of 1813.
51 Ruatara, Korra Korra, & Shungie, General Order, 9/11/1814.
52 Government and General Order 12/11/1814, announced Kendall's appointment as magistrate. See also Marsden to Pratt, 18/11/1814: 'At my request [...]'. These appointments had a tenuous basis in law, but although Yarwood, *Samuel Marsden: Survivor*, 150, correctly notes they required 'the back[ing] by indigenous chiefs', his declaration that they 'remained ineffective' requires closer definition. The appointments certainly proved effective in providing a British subject officially appointed to a role recognized by British law who could take depositions in cases of other British subjects perpetrating atrocities in the South Seas. Was this —and its potential deterrent value— what Marsden had in mind, or did he imagine more would be achieved?
53 Marsden to Pratt, 15/3/1814 (Extract: *Missionary Register 1814*, 461).

But Marsden believed that the law of retaliation could be prevented through the intervention of the rule of British law. English evangelicals knew what could be accomplished through their Parliament, with the English Reformation as their heritage and the recent success of their social causes, especially the hard-won victories of William Wilberforce against the slave trade. God had ordained the 'powers that be' (Romans 13:1 KJV) and England had already benefitted greatly from grass-roots agitation towards better—and more Christian— laws. Marsden's confidence in the rule of law was later displayed when in the Bay of Islands. Hearing about the fraud, cruelty and hostage-taking of the *Jefferson* and the *King George*, he assured the New Zealanders 'that both King George and Governor Macquarie would punish any act of fraud and cruelty committed by the Europeans, whenever they were informed of them'.[54]

On 1 December, in the interests of establishing 'some effectual measures [...] to prevent the continuance of a conduct and behaviour, at once repulsive to humanity and interest', Macquarie issued a Government and General Order which was his first proclamation attempting to bring Rule of British Law to the South Pacific.[55] The preamble made mention of 'the many, and it is to be feared just, complaints' about the conduct of masters and crews 'towards the natives of New Zealand, Otaheite, and other islands in the South Pacific'. The additional note that 'several ships their masters and crews, have lately fallen a sacrifice to the indiscriminate revenge of the natives of the said islands, exasperated by such conduct', makes Macquarie's position quite clear: the Europeans were the aggressors and ultimately to blame for these incidents. Drawing on the details of Marsden's depositions, the Order carefully specifies the kinds of crimes in view. A catalogue of the kind of dreadful treatment that had been previously inflicted upon the people of the South Seas by passing seamen was now officially written into the European public record. To prevent further loss of life, trouble,

---

54 Testimony of New Zealanders to Marsden (*HRNZ* 1.425-426). Believing in the power of Macquarie's decree, when he returned from his first trip to New Zealand, Marsden brought a Tahitian and a New Zealander with him with the intent of recovering payment or punishment for frauds committed against them by a ship's captain (Lasco Jones); see Marsden to Pratt, 15/6/1815.
55 Government and General Order, 1/12/1813, *SG* 4/12/1813. Marsden had the '17 or 18 year-old' Mowhee write this notice out as he was returning to New Zealand, taking pride in the young man's facility with English; Marsden, Notice to Natives of the South Sea Islands, 1/12/1813; cf. Marsden to Pratt, 12/10/1814, which mentions Mowhee again copying this GGO.

and threat to trade, his Order imposed a penal bond of £1,000 for any vessel cleared out of Sydney for the South Seas, which would be forfeit for such misbehaviour.

From now on the duly appointed British authority required that:

> the officers and Crew of the said Vessel, shall each and every of them peaceably and properly demean themselves, and be of their good Behaviour towards the Natives.

This was further specified in the negative, that:

> they shall not commit any Acts of Trespass upon the Plantations, Gardens, Lands, Habitations, Burial Grounds, Tombs, or Properties of the Natives

and they:

> shall not make War, or cause War to be made upon them, or in any Way interfere in the Disputes, Quarrels, and Controversies of the said Natives, or stir up, excite, or foment any Animosities among them.

They shall 'leave the Natives of the said Islands to the free uninterrupted, and undisturbed Enjoyment of their religious Ceremonies, rites, or Observances'. Ship's Captains were prohibited from taking any male from his island, 'whether as a Mariner, or Diver, or for any other Purpose whatsoever', without their free consent and, upon discharge, they were to pay lawful wages due before depositing him 'wheresoever he shall be requested by him or them so to do'. In addition, to take away a female from her island not only required her 'free Will and Consent' and the permission of her people, but also required the written consent of the Governor, or those bearing his authority.

Macquarie's aim to bring the Rule of Law to the Islands is clear in his final—presumably designed to be ominous—paragraph:

> And whereas the Natives of the said Islands are under the Protection of His Majesty, and entitled to the good Offices of his Subjects; all Persons whatsoever charged by the Oaths of credible Witnesses with any Act of Rapine, Plunder, Robbery, Piracy, Murder, or other Offences against the Law of Nature and of Nations, against the Persons and Properties of any of the Natives of any of the said Islands, will upon due Convictions, be further punished with the utmost rigour of the Law.

THE FAILURE OF THE PHILANTHROPIC SOCIETY

In late 1814, on the eve of the *Active* sailing, Macquarie would again back up his authorized representatives (Kendall, Ruatara, Korokoro, and Hongi) by issuing a second protective order.[56] With Macquarie's Orders, it looked as though the moral lessons had at last been learned from earlier massacres. However, the legal lessons were yet to be learned. For Macquarie's NSW was far from His Majesty's Home Territories, and the Islands further still.

But neither Marsden nor Macquarie were daunted, and neither did they lack broadness of vision. The proclamation of 1 December 1813 was meant to change the world:[57]

> I see the footsteps of Divine Providence strongly marked in many circumstances, that have happened in these parts of the world: all tending to make way for the blessing of the Gospel. The attention of those in authority would not have been awakened to the sufferings of the Natives of the South Sea Islands, unless some great crimes had been committed. Those crimes will produce the effect. His Excellency assured me, that he would write both to the Governor-General of India, and also to his Majesty's Ministers, to request that they will not allow any vessel to sail, either from England or India, to these Seas, till the Masters had entered into the necessary bonds for their good conduct toward the Natives. From this you will see that the Missionaries will be more secure from the hand of violence, than they could otherwise have been.[58]

When the *Earl Spencer* sailed for England on 26 January,[59] it carried a letter from Macquarie reporting his proclamation and respectfully

---

56 Government and General Order 9/11/1814, *SG* 12/11/1814. This was after over three years of no ship's captain being prepared to take the missionaries to New Zealand, 'for fear of his ship and crew falling a sacrifice to the natives'; Marsden, First Visit to New Zealand (*HRNZ* 1.337), necessitating Marsden's purchase of his own vessel, the *Active*. Macquarie had forbidden Marsden from going until after the *Active*'s successful return from her first voyage (7/3 to 21/8/1814). See Falloon, 'Mission Trading', in this volume.

57 It is unfair on both men—and more the mark of cynical history writing than impartial observation—, for Yarwood, *Samuel Marsden: Survivor*, 151, to charge both men, in forming the Philanthropic Society, with being motivated by 'a form of enlightened self-interest'. Neither Macquarie's desire to protect whites from retaliation, nor Marsden's to 'create a safe and receptive environment for his missionaries', can be labelled 'self-interest' at all, but rather a 'social interest' that displays these men acting to fulfil the responsibilities of their own particular office for the greater good —and not just for their own society, but for the world at large. Yarwood should have stopped with the observation that the formation of the Society was 'humane'. The immense personal and financial costs Marsden bore on behalf of the mission speaks strongly against his missionary concerns being motivated by self-interest; see, e.g., Sharp, *The World, the Flesh & the Devil*, 361–362, 387.

58 Marsden to Pratt, 15/3/1814 (Extract: *Missionary Register 1814*, 461–462).

59 *SG* 5/2/1814.

suggesting that Earl Bathurst consider 'whether it might not be expedient to follow it up by Subjecting the Masters of South Sea Whalers [ie ships of the East India Company] and of other Merchant Ships, frequenting those Islands from England and India, to Similar Regulations'. He included the evidence of atrocities by which he had been convinced, duly documented by his magistrates in November. He was cautious but hopeful:

> It is yet too soon to be enabled to say how far the desired Object of protecting the Persons and Property of those Natives may be effected by this Measure, but I have Sanguine Hopes that the Rapacity and Cruelty of our sailors will be in some Degree at least restrained, and that the Intercourse of Trade with those Islands will be rendered more secure than at present.[60]

But with Walker's case already stalled, whether British law could act in this way as the instrument of Divine Providence was still an open question.

1.5 Prosecuting Atrocities: The Philanthropic Society as A 'Proclamation Society'

Bolstered by the proclamation of 1 December 1813, Samuel Marsden then set about mobilizing the population of Sydney, expecting great things:

> My next step was to try if I could not get a society formed for the protection of the natives of the South Sea Islands who may come to Port Jackson. In this I also succeeded far better than I expected. I have no doubt but this society will greatly aid the missions to New Zealand, and to the other islands. I consider this institution to be of vast importance to the common cause. [...] The Church Missionary Society will see, from all these circumstances, that Divine Goodness is preparing a way for these poor Heathens to receive the glad tidings of the Gospel.[61]

---

60 Gov. Macquarie to Earl Bathurst, 17/1/1814, enclosing the decree (*HRA* 1.8.98–100), the letters from missionaries Henry (pp.100–10) and Davies (pp.102–103) and in regard to Dillon's case (pp.111–112), as well as depositions from Dillon (pp.103-107), Hendrick (pp. 107–110), Jones (p.110), French (pp.110-11), Randall (p.111) sworn before the individual magistrates, as well as their testimony before Ellis Bent and a Bench (pp.112-118), and the papers regarding Walker (see p.113, and note about Enclosures 6–8, not reproduced in *HRA*).
61 Marsden to Pratt, 15/3/1814 (Extract: *Missionary Register 1814*, 461).

THE FAILURE OF THE PHILANTHROPIC SOCIETY 149

Societies were small groups of people with a common cause. Their role was already well-established in English evangelicalism before the nineteenth century saw their proliferation, both in England[62] and Australia.[63] Together with seven prominent citizens, Marsden requested William Gore to summon a public meeting to form a society, and the Provost-Marshall's duly published an advertisement in the *Gazette* on 11 and 18 of December, calling people together on the 20th.[64]

On Christmas Day, the *Gazette* published a report of the meeting, informing its readers that subscriptions were now open for the 'New South Wales Philanthropic Society, for the Protection and Civilization of such of the Natives of the South Sea Islands who may arrive at Port Jackson'.[65] In his opening speech, Marsden's missionary object had been clear:

> Rev. Mr. Marsden, in a concise and appropriate speech, emblazing every object which the expediency of the measure could suggest to a benevolent and enlightened mind; and concluding by moving several Resolutions, which had for their object the protection from want or injury of such natives of the South Sea Islands as should occasionally come to this Colony; to instruct them in such simple and useful branches of professsion [sic: professions] as they should be capable of acquiring, and endeavouring to disseminate principles of Christianity among them. […]

Having spoken of the necessity, to get the business of the meeting started Marsden then moved quite simply, that such a Society be formed.

---

62 Snape, 'Pendle Forest Riots', 268. See also Spurr, 'Church, Societies'; Rack, 'Religious Societies'; Walsh, 'Religious Societies: Methodist and Evangelical'. Hylson-Smith, *Evangelicals*, 9–10: 'the religious societies, especially in London, had for many decades helped to keep alive a concern within the established church for vital personal faith and a relating of that faith to the social needs of the time'.

63 In 1846, *The Hobart Courier* published a list of 33 different Religious and Benevolent Societies existing in the United Kingdom, presumably to encourage a similar spirit in Australia; *The Hobart Courier* 15/8/1846. Some of the societies that emerged in NSW from 1813 were: New South Wales Society for Promoting Christian Knowledge and Benevolence (1813), reorganized as the Benevolent Society (1818); 'Philanthropic Society' (1813); Bible Society (1817); Society for the Education of the Young (1818); Institution of Public Schools; Religious Tract Society (1823); Australian Subscription Library (1826); Temperance Society (1834); Australian School Society (1834); General Committee of Protestants (1836). In 1819, Philanthropus bewailed it as 'very strange that no Society of Christians has yet commissioned their [the indigenous peoples of Australia] cause', *SG* 24/7/1819.

64 *SG* 11, 18/12/1813. Co-incidentally, December 11 was the second day of Walker's hearing.

65 *SG* 25/12/1813.

In formulating the regulations of the new society, Marsden drew heavily on those of the Church Missionary Society.[66] The first of fifteen introduced the name of the society. Six more resolutions dealt with the regularizing of the Society through its constitution and delegations. Alongside the Annual January meeting, special meetings could be called at any time (Resolution 5), and none of the rules could be altered except at a proper meeting (Resolution 7). Another resolution decreed who would preside over all meetings if the Patron was not present (Resolution 6). The Committee shall consist of twelve Laymen, and all the Clergymen of the Settlement (Resolution 8). The General Committee, which would meet Quarterly, could be formed of three members (Resolution 11). A Treasurer, Secretary, and Collector were to be chosen and these three would conduct the real operations of the Society, transacting business as directed by the Committee and paying all bills (Resolution 12).

Five Resolutions regulated the finances of the Society. The second deemed that 'Every Person subscribing annually One Guinea and upwards, shall be a Member of this Society during the Continuance of such Subscription'. The Third and Fourth also related to money. If a person gave a Benefaction of Ten Guineas, they were a Member for Life (Resolution 3), and an Annual Meeting will be held each January, to hear the Proceedings of the previous year, appoint new Office-Bearers, and to have the Accounts presented (Resolution 4). All payments were to be signed by two members of the General Committee and the secretary (Resolution 10). The Annual Meeting was to elect 'a Committee of Accounts; whose Duty shall be to see that the Subscriptions are duly received, and all the Accounts of the Society regulated' (Resolution 9).

After Regularizing the Society's constitution and Finances, the Final Three Resolutions described its Objects:

> *Thirteenth.* The Object of this Society shall be, to afford Protection and Relief to the *Natives of the South Sea Islands* who may be brought to PORT JACKSON, and to defend their just Claims on the Masters and Owners of the Vessels who bring them; and to see justice done to their Persons and Property; and also, to instruct them in the Principles of Christianity, and in the different Branches of

---

66 Marsden to Pratt, 15/3/1814. For the resolutions, see *NSW Philanthropic Society, Minutes*.

Agriculture; and in such other simple Arts as may best lead to their Civilization and general Improvement.

Fourteenth. No Native of the South Sea Islands shall reside with any Person in this Settlement, without the Consent of the General Committee, when once received under the Protection of this Society.

Fifteenth. A Committee of three Members, chosen annually from the General Body, shall be appointed to hear all the Complaints of the South Sea Islanders, against the Owners, Masters, or Crews of Vessels; and to bring such Owners, Masters, or Crews before a Court of Justice, whenever it may be deemed necessary so to do.

On the grand scale, the protection to be afforded by the Society served Marsden's greater missionary purposes (Resolution 13), but it reached down to the grass-roots level of the household, where people like the missing Foo Foo would henceforth be protected (Resolution 14). Its final object (Resolution 15) clearly showed the special nature of this Society: it was designed to investigate complaints from the natives of the South Seas, in order to prosecute European sea-farers before their own courts of law. This indicates that the Philanthropic Society was designed to be an antipodean 'proclamation society'.[67]

When Marsden called the meeting he would have been riding on the wave of the news of yet another parliamentary victory for William Wilberforce, Marsden's fellow-Yorkshireman and, over the years, supporter.[68] When Marsden arrived in England in November 1807, the evangelicals were rejoicing at the great victory of February, when parliament passed the bill to abolish the slave trade, promoted by Wilberforce every year since he entered Parliament in 1787.[69] In 1810, as Marsden arrived back in NSW, slave trading became a felony.[70] As he pressed towards the Philanthropic Society, news arrived of the success

---

67 Metaxis, *Amazing Grace*, Chapter 7. Yarwood, *Samuel Marsden: Survivor*, 150, notes that the Society was formed 'to supplement the governor's actions [ie his proclamation]', but does not delve into the nature of this supplementation, its precedents, or what role and effect Marsden expected from it. Sharp, *The World, the Flesh & the Devil*, explicitly refers to the English Proclamation Society as a palpable influence on Marsden generally (pp. 71–74, 674), but does not explicitly draw the connection to the Philanthropic Society—even if they slide together on the same page at one point (p. 364).
68 Cf. Gladwin, 'Marsden's Generals', 18.
69 Metaxis, *Amazing Grace*, Chapter 18. Marsden arrived 8/11/1807; see *Morning Chronicle*, 11/11/1807.
70 Metaxis, *Amazing Grace*, 217.

of what was 'next to abolition [...] the single most important issue for [Wilberforce]', namely, the June 1813 repeal of 'a long-standing law that forbade missionaries from entering India'.[71] This victory against the powerful vested interests of the East India Company was also a victory for mission more generally, for Wilberforce had argued that 'Christianity alone could open a way to help the people of India and that it could provide the philosophical underpinnings for doing so'.[72] When the bill was passed in the Commons 89–36:

> it marked a major turning point in Britain's dealings with the world, [... arguing] for the full humanity of all those in the Indian nation [... and] establishing for the first time in the history of the world that the Golden Rule was to be raised as the standard of behavior not only between individuals but between entire nations and peoples.[73]

Despite the disappointment over Walker's case, with British Parliament now behind him, Marsden could have even greater confidence in British law to reform the practices of British subjects amongst the human beings of NSW and the South Pacific.

Marsden was well aware of the means by which the Abolition of the Slave Trade had been achieved. In many ways, it was a victory *against* vested interests in Parliament, brought about by sustained grass-roots action. Although not as visible to the English nation as the sufferings of the African, the sufferings afflicted upon human beings in the South Seas arose from the same problematic mindset buried deeply within the European *modus operandi*. In order to overcome South Seas' atrocities, Marsden's grass-roots would have to overcome corrupted generations of ship owners, merchants, high society, sailors, and ordinary citizens, who saw nothing wrong with stealing people to put them to work on ship's crews, or dumping them far from home when they were no longer needed, or stealing from them, using them, brutalizing them, or even murdering them, in order to achieve the Europeans' goals. They were treated so badly, because they were regarded as less civilized—less than human.

The June 1813 parliamentary victory was another grass-roots victory

---

71 Metaxis, *Amazing Grace*, 226, and, for the political battle, Chapter 20.
72 Metaxis, *Amazing Grace*, 231.
73 Metaxis, *Amazing Grace*, 232–233.

THE FAILURE OF THE PHILANTHROPIC SOCIETY 153

over vested interests—this time those of the powerful East India Company with its 200 year-old history of bringing wealth to the nation. The Company had long refused to have missionaries due to their clear threat to some of the immoral practices the Company encouraged or tolerated.[74] Like the slave-traders, the East India Company held:

> that some human beings—were naturally and self-evidently inferior and should be treated as such by those who were naturally and self-evidently superior, and that this should be done without any hint of guilt about it. This was the "natural" way of things, in their view, and it was "God's will".[75]

Long before the British arrived in the South Seas, the East India Company had already established patterns of oppression over non-British peoples. At about the same time Marsden was stirring NSW to action, some of his brethren in England were moving towards the formation of the 'Society for the Protection and Relief of Lascar Sailors'.[76] Lascars are often listed amongst the crews calling in at Port Jackson and they were a group that the London Missionary Society were working amongst, due to 'the oppressions under which these men were found to labour'. When this Society was formed it was specifically against abuses permitted by the Company:

> It appears that these men are often kidnapped on board the Company's ships, by crimps employed for that purpose; defrauded of their full bounty-money and wages; left destitute of proper medical assistance; and are not seldom materially injured in their health, and even lose their lives, from want of proper food, clothing, and lodging, while waiting in this country the return of the Company's ships to India.[77]

When British shipping entered the South Seas—considered the territory of the East India Company—, the patterns of abuse were

---

74 See further, Metaxis, *Amazing Grace*, Chapter 20.
75 Metaxis, *Amazing Grace*, 230. Contrary to some suggestions (e.g. Harris, *One Blood*, 29; Gunson, 'Introduction', 8–9), this was not the attitude of the evangelical Anglicans in Australia, nor in England, even if similar views can be found in Congregationalists like W.P. Crook, or in some continental theology at the time. As the political face of English evangelicalism, Wilberforce is the parade example of a very different theological position.
76 After noting the LMS work amongst the lascars in the August issue (p.327), the December issue of the *Missionary Register* 1814, reported the establishment of the society; [*Missionary Register*], 'Society for the Protection', 479–480.
77 [*Missionary Register*], 'Society for Protection', 480.

already *de jour*. Wilberforce's second great victory in June 1813 would have given Marsden further confidence that grass-roots action now had the backing of the rule of law, further buoying him up to create his own Society for the Protection of those in his particular mission-field.

In the year he entered Parliament (1787), Wilberforce had revived the concept of a 'proclamation society' in association with his second great object, the 'reformation of manners'.[78] On ascending the throne and following in the tradition of previous monarchs, George III issued a 'Proclamation for the Encouragement of Piety and Virtue and for the Preventing of Vice, Profaneness and Immorality', to then almost immediately ignore it, as 'mere formalities, part of the larger hypocrisy of eighteenth-century society, which gave rouged lip service to Christianity, and simultaneously dismissed it with all of the requisite winks and mandatory nods'.[79] Wilberforce had learned, however, that the proclamation of William and Mary (1689–1702) achieved good effects because they had also formed a 'Proclamation Society', by which society at large was 'thereby deputized to put into effect what the royal proclamation had proclaimed'.[80] Finding allies in Prime Minister William Pitt, Queen Charlotte, Beilby Porteus, Bishop of London, and the Archbishop of Canterbury, in 1787 Wilberforce sought to get George III to reissue his proclamation of 1760, alongside the formation of a 'Society for the Reformation of Manners', made up of Wilberforce and his friends, which, especially in the early days, was known as 'The Proclamation Society'.[81]

Wilberforce realized that it was only the victims of a crime that pressed for prosecution, but crimes against society at large had no-one to prosecute the case and so nothing was done. The local proclamation society could now take up the case, and 'a whole host of horrors were suddenly no longer beyond the ameliorating reach of the law'.[82] It also

---

78 Wilberforce had already begun working towards the 'reformation of manners' before he wrote in his diary on 28/10/1787: 'God almighty has set before me two great objects: the suppression of the slave trade and the reformation of manners'. He did not coin the term, but drew it from an older book that had influenced him, *History of the Society for the Reformation of Manners in the Year 1692*; Metaxis, *Amazing Grace*, 85, 81.
79 Metaxis, *Amazing Grace*, 81.
80 Metaxis, *Amazing Grace*, 82.
81 Sharp, *The World, the Flesh & the Devil*, 72. About 100 people signed up in Feb 1788, see the list in [Anon.], *Characteristics of Public Spirit*, xi–xii.
82 Metaxis, *Amazing Grace*, 83.

THE FAILURE OF THE PHILANTHROPIC SOCIETY 155

gave leaders of society responsibility to be moral exemplars:

> When a local proclamation society was formed, prominent members would be invited to take part. They would give in to the social pressure to accept, and would soon find themselves in a rather interesting position, for their own moral standards would be seen in light of their participation in the society. It was a subversive and politically brilliant strategy.[83]

When Wilberforce sprang into action after George III issued the proclamation on June 1, 1787, the first proclamation society met in November 1787, and, with Wilberforce 'convinced of the need to decentralize the Society so as to harness local energies as a widespread network of voluntary associations',[84] others flourished thereafter,[85] providing grass-roots muscle for high-level laws, by recruiting interested parties as potential prosecutors. Having been elected mayor in September 1787, William Hey set one up in Leeds and began prosecuting sins and crimes. Thus, in his home territory, 'Marsden imbibed these views, and though he probably saw them first put into action by Hey in Leeds, they were widely shared by all his mentors'.[86]

Wilberforce's revival and good use of proclamation societies provides a backdrop that helps to make sense of the membership that Marsden attracted into the NSW Philanthropic Society. At the first Annual General Meeting on 12 January 1814, chaired by Deputy Commissary General Allan, the Resolutions were slightly altered before being ratified and ordered to be published and distributed to

---

83 Metaxis, *Amazing Grace*, 83. Sharp, *The World, the Flesh & the Devil*, 76–77, notes that Wilberforce was aware that the higher classes needed to be shamed into doing the right thing, which he attempted to do by getting them involved in philanthropy (pp.77–80). Marsden adopted the same strategy, as revealed just days before he called the Society together for the meeting that would prove to be its failure: 'One great object I had in view in wishing this Society to be formed was that I might in a political Sense, disarm many who are open Enemies to all true Religion, as far as respected the Establishment of the Mission at New Zealand— If they became members of a Society for the Protection and Civilization of the Natives of the South Sea Islands, they could not afterwards with any degree of Propriety oppose that Establishment, admitting that they contributed nothing to its Support. [...] It was a great object to get the Society formed, as they cannot oppose openly the Resolutions to which they have subscribed their names', Marsden to Pratt, 29/9/1814 (MS 54/52).
84 Sharp, *The World, the Flesh & the Devil*, 72.
85 Metaxis, *Amazing Grace*, 84, 86, and, for the first, 89.
86 Sharp, *The World, the Flesh & the Devil*, 72–74 and notes: Hannah More wrote on the Society in 1788 and 1790, with a new edition in 1809, as did John Scot in 1807, and it was satirized by Sydney Smith in 1809.

the Members.[87] On that occasion Allan was elected as Treasurer, Marsden as Secretary, Robert Jenkins as Collector, and Twelve laymen as a General Committee. The first eleven read like a who's who of the Colony at that time, magistrates, traders, ship owners, landholders, doctors, a ship's captain, and one LMS missionary (Garnham Blaxcell; William Redfern; William Broughton; Alexander Riley; Charles Hook; Simeon Lord; D'Arcy Wentworth; Edward S Hall; John Oxley; James Birnie; Rowland Hassall). And then— to single him out for the sake of dramatic emphasis— the twelfth man amongst this band of apostles was the Governor's personal Secretary, J.T. Campbell, Esq. Perhaps we could add, as with Christ's Judas, 'who betrayed him' (Mark 3:19).

Two special committees were formed, one 'For Protection' and the other 'For Accounts', but the same three men sat on both: Alexander Riley, William Broughton, and Rev. William Cowper.[88] For a Society with benevolent intents, money was essential and already after just one month of the Philanthropic Society coming into existence, the Accounts department was well under weigh. The *Sydney Gazette* announced that Subscriptions and Donations could be received by the Treasurer (Allan) at Sydney, the Secretary (Marsden) at Parramatta,[89] or through William Cox or Rev Robert Cartwright at Windsor; and by Resident Magistrate and prominent Christian Layman at Liverpool, Thomas Moore. The fifty-two subscribers so far and their amounts paid were then published for the *Gazette* readers' interest and, presumably, for public accountability for the new Society.[90]

---

87 *SG* 22/1/1814; and 1/1/1814.
88 The personnel on these committees remained constant across the next few years. Although too late for the Almanac of 1814, the committee was listed as part of the Civil Establishment in those of 1815 (p.22), 1816 (p.24), and 1817 (pp.27–28), disappearing (understandably) in 1818. This constant presence in the pockets of Sydneysiders must have added both to the Society's prestige, as well as to questions about its (in)activity. See the question asked by 'A Spectator', 'what has become of the Society altogether, as it is now no where to be found but in the 27th page of the present year's Almanack?'; *SG* 11/1/1817.
89 Ratcliffe, '"Pens Dipped in Gall"', 15, mistakenly says J.T. Campbell held this office.
90 *SG* 22/1/1814.

THE FAILURE OF THE PHILANTHROPIC SOCIETY

Figure 8: Subscribers to the Philanthropic Society, January 1814.[91]

	£	s	d	£	s	d
His Excellency the Governor [Macquarie]	21	0	0	1	1	0
His Honor the Lieutenant-Governor [O'Connell]	10	10	0	1	1	0
The Judge Advocate [Bent]	10	10	0	1	1	0
Reverend S. Marsden	10	10	0	1	1	0
Deputy Commissary General Allan	10	10	0	1	1	0
William Broughton, Esq.	10	10	0			
D'Arcy Wentworth, Esq.	10	10	0			
John Oxley, Esq.	10	10	0			
Simeon Lord, Esq.				1	1	0
J.T. Campbell, Esq.	10	10	0			
Garnham Blaxcell, Esq.	10	10	0			
Alexander Riley, Esq.	10	10	0			
William Walker, Esq.				1	1	0
Rev. William Cowper	5	5	0	1	1	0
Rev. Robert Cartwright	5	5	0	1	1	0
Rev. Henry Fulton	5	5	0	1	1	0
Mr John Eyre				1	1	0
Rowland Hassall				1	1	0
G.T. Palmer, Esq.				1	1	0
R.W. Loane, Esq.				1	1	0
Mr Thomas Kendal				2	2	0
Mr W.P. Crook				2	2	0
Mr Thomas Bowden				2	2	0
Mr Robert Jenkins				1	1	0
William Redfern, Esq.	10	10	0			
Mr Thomas Hassall				1	1	0
Mr W.I. Speed				1	1	0
Mr Reuben Uther				1	1	0

91 This list of names is probably not exhaustive, as indicated by the totals being incorrect, E.S. Hall not being on the list despite being on the General Committee, and reports of amounts collected varying (see n.111).

Gregory Blaxland, Esq.				1	1	0
John Blaxland, Esq.				1	1	0
Mr George Howe	10	10	0			
Mr Edward Eagar				2	2	0
Joseph James, Esq				1	1	0
Mr James Meehan				1	1	0
Mr Robert Williams				1	1	0
Mr Edward Quin				1	1	0
Mr Isaac Nichols				1	1	0
Capt. Mitchell (Earl Spencer)				1	1	0
Mr James Gordon				1	1	0
Charles Hook, Esq.				1	1	0
William Campbell, Esq.	10	10	0	1	1	0
William Gore	10	10	0	2	1	0
Brigade Major Antill	5	5	0	1	1	0
Mr Thomas Ivory				1	1	0
Mr John Yates				1	1	0
Mr Hovill				1	1	0
Mr Samuel Otoo Hassall				1	1	0
Mr Hosking				1	1	0
James Birnie, Esq.				1	1	0
Mr William Brodie				1	1	0
Hannibal McArthur, Esq.				1	1	0
William Cox, Esq.	10	10	0			
Totals [incorrect!]	**£189**	**0**	**0**	**49**	**7**	**0**

After being visited by a delegation the day after the initial meeting, the Governor, his Lieutenant, and Judge-Advocate Bent enthusiastically added their support[92]—which also practically guaranteed the presence of Secretary Campbell in the Society. Macquarie promised to endorse the Society to his superiors.[93] Seven out of ten of the magistrates in

---

92 *SG* 25/12/1813.
93 *SG* 22/1/1814; and Marsden to Pratt, 15/3/1814 (Extract: *Missionary Register 1814*, 461–462).

NSW subscribed—the other three perhaps being too far removed (T. Moore, Liverpool; J. Mileham, Castlereagh; J. Skottowe, Newcastle).[94]

Unsurprisingly, those with a personal interest in the Christian mission to the South Seas were amongst the membership: Marsden and all his clergy (Marsden, Fulton, Cowper, Cartwright); former or current LMS missionaries (Youl, Hassall and two sons, Eyre, Crook); recently arrived CMS missionary Kendall);[95] and prominent Christian laymen (Oxley, Riley, Bowden, Eagar, Antill, Hosking, Birnie, Williams).

It is worth noting, however, that although many of Marsden's friends and associates were amongst this number, so were some of his opponents—both 'secular' (J.T. Campbell, D'A. Wentworth) and 'Christian' (Bowden, Eagar, Hosking).[96] This was no factional grouping, but a genuine attempt to harness the whole community.

Recently arrived Deputy Commissary General David Allan, also proved to be a great support to Marsden and the mission,[97] and several of his Commissariat colleagues also subscribed (Broughton, Brodie, Yates). As the Government supplier of goods for the colony, the Commissariat had an indirect interest in trade, as did banker W. Walker, who had arrived in July to collect debts for his Indian firm against Robert Campbell.[98]

Those with a more direct interest in South Pacific trade made up the bulk of the membership, including ship's captains (Birnie, Mitchell, W. Campbell, J. James, W. Hovill), ship owners and traders (Birnie, Blaxcell, J. Blaxland, W. Campbell, Howe, Ivory, Loane, Lord, Nichols—owner of Walker's *Endeavour*), and merchants (Riley, Uther, Speed, Jenkins, Williams, Gordon, Hook, Hosking, Ivory)—several of whom would form during 1814 the New Zealand Trading Company

---

94 *Almanac 1813*, 28. Another explanation may be that their subscription had not yet been received. T. Moore was slated to receive subscriptions so it would be unusual for him not to also contribute.

95 Recruited by Marsden, Thomas Kendall disembarked in Sydney on 10 October 1813, and first visited New Zealand on 8 June 1814; Kendall to Pratt, 15/6/1814.

96 These three opposed Marsden because they were fearful that he might hinder their Methodist cause; Sharp, *The World, the Flesh & the Devil*, 497. Eagar, in particular, was 'a long and treacherous acquaintance of Marsden's', 'intent on disgracing' him (pp. 435, 497).

97 Allan (and Brodie) arrived on the *Fortune* on 11/6/1813 (*SG* 12 & 19/6/1813). For his support, see Marsden to Pratt, 12 and 13/7/1819. In a letter written on the day the Civil decision went against Campbell, Macquarie placed Allan on his list of malcontents, along with Marsden; Macquarie to Bathurst, 1/12/1817 (*HRA* 1.9, 499).

98 Parsons, 'Walker, William'.

(Lord, Blaxcell, Broughton, W. Campbell, Hovell, [E.S. Hall]).[99] Not only were the business interests of these men arguably at the forefront of the problem evoking the new Society, but they also stood to profit from its promised solution.

Some would know this from bitter personal experience. Simeon Lord and William Broughton were both amongst the group who summoned the initial meeting (probably as magistrates) and both elected to the General Committee. Lord was a part owner of the *Boyd*, with Thomas Moore, and when the ship was lost, so was a considerable potential profit, compounded by the fact that his portion of the cargo was uninsured.[100] Broughton's wife Elizabeth, a passenger on the *Boyd*, was amongst those killed and eaten,[101] and his daughter Betsey, a toddler, one of only four survivors, had been rescued and taken to South America and had only just found her way home on the *Atalanta* in May 1812.[102] These two men, who had each already lost an enormous amount in a 'massacre', could be forgiven for running the usual narrative of cannibalistic treachery. But they were evidently persuaded that, in order for such problems to be solved, something had to be done to curb the excesses of European shipping. It is hard to imagine the internal turmoil provoked for Broughton, as he sat in his magistrate's role on the Sydney Bench hearing depositions about further atrocities from ship's captains similar to those provoking native retaliation in the case of the *Boyd*. On 4 and 11 December, he sat with Bent, Wentworth, Riley, and Lord to hear Walker's case,[103] and all these men now joined the new society.

If the theory of Wilberforce's proclamation societies proved true

---

99 This represents more than half of those who formed the New Zealand Trading Company. In June 1814, four subscribers to the Philanthropic Society, S. Lord, G. Blaxcell, W.H. Broughton, and W. Campbell (along with R. Brooks, and John Dickson), announced the Company's formation (*SG* 18/6/1814). In October, Lord and Blaxcell were joined by fellow members W.H. Hovell and E.S. Hall (along with R. Brooks) in presenting a memorial to Macquarie, unsuccessfully requesting the East India Company-like privilege of having a monopoly of trade in New Zealand. Memorial of Merchants, Traders, and Others, to L. Macquarie, 3/10/1814; Macquarie to Bathurst, 24/6/1815 (*HRA* 1.8, 561). See also in this volume, Bolt, 'The Letter', n.19.

100 Lord claimed he had lost £12000 in the disaster; Memorial of Merchants, Traders, and Others, to L. Macquarie, 3/10/1814.

101 She is therefore the New Zealand counterpart to Ann Butcher, who qualified 'for the unenviable distinction of being the only European woman in all Polynesia to be eaten', Maude & Crocombe, 'Rarotongan Sandalwood', 44.

102 Her father commissioned a portrait of her for those who looked after her in Lima, which he would send in May 1814; Broughton to Rico, 8/4/1814.

103 See Macquarie to Bathurst, 17/1/1814, Enclosure 5, Items [3-7].

in NSW, this group of Sydney citizens, and those associated with them, should have not only modelled the good behaviour required by Macquarie's proclamation, but by their membership they themselves should have been restrained from the vices it prohibited.

Three years later and one week after Philo Free was published, one of those involved, calling himself 'A Spectator', recalled that this was 'the first (and as far as I can speak), the only Meeting of the Society that ever did take place', declaring 'there ends the short-lived history of a Society from which so much benefit was expected, and so little advantage has been derived'.[104] But he was wrong. There had been a second meeting in October 1814.

2. The External Failure of The Philanthropic Society—Philo Free

In January 1817, Philo Free attacked apparent missionary success because of the Philanthropic Society's failure.

2.1 A Society 'Obliviated'

By the time Philo Free put pen to paper, many subscribers were wondering what happened to their money.[105] Some appreciated the question at last being asked publicly, since many had thought it impolite to raise it.[106] J.T. Campbell admitted that 'in common with many other of its Members I had often lamented it should have lain so very long in a dormant state'.[107]

Subscribers had just cause for concern. 'A Spectator' asked, 'where was the necessary hurry of collecting it, unless for active purposes? and as a single shilling has never been applied that I can learn of, I can perceive no pressing reason why it should have been collected'. Those, like him, who paid the ten guineas for life membership could rightly complain about the loss of interest on their money (nearly £60). He

---

104 *SG* 11/1/1817.
105 Marsden himself complained that 'not one Shilling has ever been expended for their use and Benefit', Marsden to Pratt, 26/10/1815.
106 'A Spectator' reported conversations with others, who, 'though they did not think proper to engage in a public enquiry into the transaction, yet could not refrain from expressing a wish that somebody would do so'; *SG* 11/1/1817.
107 Campbell to Wylde, 14/1/1817.

spoke of subscribers feeling:

> indignant at the strange absurdity of an Institution that had commenced with peculiar advantages being permitted to vanish as it has done, without any cause being assigned, or the money that was collected for its uses reimbursed. [...]
>
> we pay our money for an express purpose in January 1814, and in January, 1817 are quite in the dark as to what has become of it. Surely I may say without apologizing to any man for my opinions, that the Subscribers to this Institution have not [sic] been ingenuously dealt with; and that somewhere lies a blame. [...]
>
> what has become of the Society altogether, as it is now no where to be found but in the 27th page of the present year's Almanack?[108]

Edward Eagar, who was also present at its formation, positively connected the Society with the missionary cause and, for this reason, at the October 1817 criminal trial, he expressed his regret that the Society seemed to have lapsed:

> I consider the Missionary purposes of general national importance and public general feeling. I thought the Philanthropic Society would be extremely useful. I did and do regret still that the Institution was not carried into effect.[109]

As the man behind its foundation, Marsden deeply shared in Eagar's disappointment. In the same court, he admitted that the bright hopes at its beginning had never amounted to anything:

> Some time ago a Philanthropic Society was introduced at this place, 1813. I was Secretary to it. The object was to civilize the Natives of the South Sea Islands and to relieve and protect them; a Sum of Money was subscribed. I do not know that it was collected. I was told so by the Collector; the purposes of that Society were never I believe put into effect.[110]

---

108 'A Spectator', *SG* 11/1/1817. According to the list published in *SG* 22/1/1814, those who paid ten guineas were Lieut-Gov. O'Connell, Judge-Adv. Bent, Marsden, Allan, Broughton, Wentworth, Oxley, J.T. Campbell, Blaxcell, Riley, Redfern, Howe, W. Campbell, Gore, and Cox. Paying £21, Macquarie can also be included.

109 Examination of Eagar, 23/10/1817.

110 Examination of Marsden, 21/10/1817 (*HRA* 1.10: Marsden: 451-455; his quotation: 454, under cross-examination from Garling). Ellis, *Lachlan Macquarie*, 372, followed by Ratcliffe, "'Pens Dipped in Gall'", 43–44, therefore invents a mystery as to why Jenkins did not produce a financial statement at the trial. There was no such statement. Jenkins knew how much had been collected, but everyone knew that nothing had been spent.

THE FAILURE OF THE PHILANTHROPIC SOCIETY

When the Society was formed, about £130 pounds were taken, and a further £100 or more pledged.[111] Philo Free complained that the subscription money was never utilized, to the discontent of the subscribers. In the same paper that 'A Spectator' asked his own questions, yet confident that 'there can be no doubt the sums which they have respectively advanced will at some future period be forthcoming, in some shape or other', the collector, Robert Jenkins, immediately assured the public that the funds were safe. He objected to Philo Free's 'palpable insinuation that they have been improperly employed'.[112]

There may have been rumours abroad that Marsden spent the money to purchase the *Active* from Rowland Loane,[113] for when he was re-examined at the criminal trial he was questioned about both matters in close proximity. This can be pieced together from his answers, recorded in the judge's notes:

> Loane was a merchant here, none of the monies collected by Jenkins ever came into my hands. I was nothing more than the Secretary. The Defendant [J.T. Campbell] is a Member of the Committee; he was elected so; many Vessels touch at New Zealand besides the *Active*, generally the Whalers; they are in the habit of trading with the Natives for supplies. Muskets are thought the most valuable with the Natives. The Brig was bought in 1813 or 1814, it was in 1813.[114]

Jenkins explained that he had not returned the funds because as collector he did not possess that authority,[115] presumably because the Society had never officially dissolved itself. But his comments also hint that he well-knew its fate. In the words of 'A Spectator', it had become 'this obliviated Institution'.[116]

---

111 Eagar recalled that 'some Subscriptions were raised to the amount of £130, but put down for £250'; Examination of Eagar, 23/10/1817. After the first meeting, the *Gazette* (22/1/1814) reported total moneys subscribed as £238 7s —the amount recalled by 'A Spectator', *SG* 11/1/1817. However, immediately after Philo Free appeared, collector Jenkins assured the public that he had collected £138 4s. and it was all safe, 'no part of it having ever been called for'; *SG* 11/1/1817.
112 *SG* 11/1/1817.
113 Eagar was 'privy to the purchase of the Brig *Active* of Mr Loane, December 1813, or 1814, if 1814 very early'; Examination of Eagar, 23/10/1817, 466, 467 (for £1400 paid in cash and sheep).
114 Re-Examination of S. Marsden, 21/10/1817 (*HRA* 1.10, 453).
115 As reported by 'A Spectator', *SG* 11/1/1817.
116 *SG* 11/1/1817.

Despite the committee calling a meeting for 24 March 1817 with the intention of refunding the subscriptions, this may not have occurred.[117] In October, Eagar was sure that no subscriptions had yet been returned. He also reported the occurrence of a meeting in May (not March), but not its agenda or outcome.[118] In his evidence, Eagar also noted that the Society had collapsed within its first year of existence:

> There was a Committee formed but it was never generally carried into effect; [...] as by the rule Officers were to be chosen every Year and they have not been, I presume it to have expired.

When the Society was not renewed in 1815, Eagar—no friend of Marsden—took it as due to Marsden's absence from the country—perhaps implying neglect of or disinterest in the Society which he founded:

> The first Monday in February, 1815, the Officers should have been appointed, but Mr Marsden the Secretary was at New Zealand, and no meeting ever took place; [...] I should think it was not carried into effect because of the absence of Mr Marsden.

On 19 November 1814, Marsden had sailed in the *Active*, with missionaries King, Hall, and Kendall and their families, with Ruatara and some nine other New Zealanders on board, and two Tahitians (Purnee, and Tahee —who, as we shall see, had a story to tell).[119] After the delay caused by the *Boyd* incident, the time had finally arrived when the CMS mission could be established amongst the people of the Bay of Islands, and it was launched on Christmas Day with Marsden preaching on Luke 2:10, perhaps in their own language.[120] Having witnessed his long-standing dream at last taking shape, Marsden returned to NSW on 22/3/1815— well after the due time for reappointing office bearers for the Philanthropic Society.

---

117 *SG* 15 & 22/3/ 1817. Pace Sharp, *The World, the Flesh & the Devil*, 336, who speaks as if it did.
118 Eagar recalled that 'a meeting has taken place among the Subscribers, who have paid their money, in May last [1817]'; Examination of Eagar, 23/10/1817, 468.
119 The *Active* had arrived back from its first voyage on 21/8/1814, Marsden to Pratt, 20/9/1814 (*Missionary Register 1815*, 195). For further detail about her voyages, see Falloon, 'Mission Trading', in this volume.
120 Pettett, 'Strategy', 81; 'Samuel Marsden—Christmas Day 1814'; and *Samuel Marsden*, 40–48.

But it wasn't that Marsden had simply lost interest in the Society.[121] Even before he sailed for New Zealand, he knew that the Society had already failed. Evidently unbeknown to Eagar—perhaps because not all members attended—,[122] the Committee had met in October 1814, and in the Society's first 'trial of strength'[123] it had failed.

3. The Internal Failure of the Philanthropic Society— The *Cumberland* Cover-up

Ironically, one of the late 1813 investigations into atrocities in the South Seas that provoked the Society's foundation, also provoked the series of events that led to its failure. On the same day that Marsden called his meeting, 11 December 1813, Theodore Walker, master of the *Endeavour*, appeared before Judge Advocate Bent, with magistrates William Broughton, D'Arcy Wentworth, Alexander Riley, and Simeon Lord also on the Bench, to face an inquiry into his killing of a lascar.[124] As noted above, Amile had played a leading role in the mutiny on the *Daphne*, and after the *Endeavour* had rescued her, Walker had hung and shot him. As part of the investigation, Walker submitted his log book to the magistrates, and when D'Arcy Wentworth examined it, something other than what he needed for the inquiry caught his eye.[125]

---

121 Compare the position taken by Ratcliffe, '"Pens Dipped in Gall"', that J.T. Campbell had 'observed first hand [Marsden's] lack of commitment to schemes he initiated and subsequently lost interest in' (p.15), and that when Philo Free was published, Marsden was 'clearly irritated by the revelation that Campbell felt satisfaction that the subject of the Philanthropic Society had resurfaced' (p. 31).
122 'I herewith send you a Copy of all the Proceedings I could get taken at the general meeting last October'; 'I therefore called a general meeting of the Society. Some of the members attended, and some did not', Marsden to Pratt, 26/10/1815. Elsewhere in the letter, Marsden speaks as if it was 'the Committee' who met, rather than the whole Society, which, given the numbers involved, must have been the General Committee.
123 Yarwood, *Marsden of Parramatta*, 48; *Samuel Marsden: Survivor*, 150.
124 Theodore Walker declaration of Not Guilty, 11/12/1813. For the details of the killing, see Deposition of Abraham Hendrike, 16/11/1813.
125 'In consequence of some Cruelties, which were committed in the vessel, the log book was submitted to my father's perusal'; W.C. Wentworth to T. Moore, 6/6/1815. Maude & Crocombe, 'Rarotongan Sandalwood', 35.

3.1 The Rarotongan Sandalwood Company sends the *Cumberland*

Walker's log recorded the sighting of an island not previously known to English shipping—although also sighted by Fletcher Christian and his mutineers on the *Bounty* in 1789—now known as Rarotonga, the principal island in the Cook Islands.[126] The log noted that 'the island abounded in sandalwood', an important item of trade at the time. Magistrate Wentworth couldn't help being distracted from his legal inquiry into mayhem and murder in the South Seas by the potential commercial advantage of his incidental discovery. W.C. Wentworth later reported that his father:

> questioned the Master particularly about the truth of it, which he reportedly vouched for and even gave him a specimen of the sandalwood, which he alledged [sic] the island produced in lush abundance.[127]

This conflict of interest then led to some insider trading. At the time, when competition for scarce trade items was high, a key strategy was secrecy.[128] D'Arcy told his friends and the Sandalwood Company of Rarotonga was 'hastily formed'.[129] William Charles Wentworth, D'Arcy's son and just twenty-three at the time,[130] was amongst them. He had contracted a severe cough during his famous crossing of the Blue Mountains with Gregory Blaxland and William Lawson in June. He

---

126 Credited with the European 'discovery' of Rarotonga, the island was briefly known as Walker's island. In fact it was the *Bounty* mutineers who first arrived, providing the natives who came out in their canoes with the island's first orange trees. See Maretu, *Cannibals*, 46ff. Kloosterman, 'Discoverers', 48, notes American charts appear to name it Armstrong Island, said to be discovered by Captain Reynolds in 1817—oblivious to the earlier visits of the *Bounty*, *Endeavour*, *Cumberland*, *Seringapatam*, *Campbell Macquarie*, and *Governor Macquarie*.
127 W.C. Wentworth to T. Moore, 6/6/1815.
128 Cf. Maude & Crocombe, 'Rarotongan Sandalwood', 34: 'The prizes in this intensely competitive trade went to those who could keep their plans secret, while endeavouring to learn what the others were up to'.
129 Sykes, 'Sandalwood', 77.
130 He was born in August 1790, despite later claims it was 1794; Tink, *William Charles Wentworth*, 8; Tink, 'William Charles Wentworth', 35; Persse, 'Wentworth, William Charles (1790–1872)'. *HRA* 1.9, 875, has 'October 1793'.

later claimed that this was the reason he went to Rarotonga,[131] and later authors repeat his 'medicinal voyage' scenario. With his health taken as the primary concern, his hopes of profit are played down, or even denuded, by drawing the implication that, almost incidentally, he was only looking after his father's interest in the venture.[132] However, his words and actions at the time reveal that he was always fully involved, and for his own sake:

> A speculation was entered into between Messrs Blaxcell, Riley, [D'Arcy] Wentworth, myself and Captn Wm. Campbell, for the purpose of procuring sandalwood at this Island.[133]

From the beginning the group planned to send the *Cumberland*, owned by Garnham Blaxcell, one of the four prominent sandalwood traders in the colony (see Figure 9). A second vessel would follow, once it could be procured, captained by William Campbell. The *Cumberland* was to gather as many shipments of sandalwood as possible and form a stockpile on Palmerstone Island. The second vessel would load it and young Wentworth, sailing as supercargo, would then take it 'to the China Market, or to Manilla' where it would be 'disposed of [...] to the best advantage'.[134] That was the grand plan.

---

131 The party started out from Blaxland's South Creek farm on, May 11, 1813, and returned on 6 June. Wentworth was probably the man referred to in Blaxland's *Journal* on 20 May who was 'taken dangerously ill with a cold'. By their return, 'the whole party were ill with bowel complaints' (30 May). The start of the journey was announced in *SG* 10/5/1813, and despite the various illnesses, on their return the party was said to be 'without injury', reporting 'a prodigious extent of fine level country' (*SG* 12/6/13). 'Wentworth later recalled that "In accomplishing this important object, I contracted an inflammation in my lungs, which nearly terminated in consumption, and was at last induced to quit the colony in order to try what effect a long voyage and change of climate might have in re-vigorating my constitution"'; cited from Tink, 'William Charles Wentworth', 36. Ritchie, *The Wentworths*, 148: 'To recover from a pulmonary disease, William joined the schooner as supercargo'.
132 Maude & Crocombe, 'Rarotongan Sandalwood', 36. Persse, 'Wentworth, William Charles'.
133 W.C. Wentworth to T. Moore, 6/6/1815, writing preliminary to pursuing a share in the profits from the sister ship to the *Cumberland*, which is further evidence that he was a full partner in the enterprise, not just a hapless bystander.
134 W.C. Wentworth to T. Moore, 6/6/1815. See also the *Articles of Agreement concerning the Sandalwood Company,* January —, 1814.

Figure 9: Estimate of Duties Collected by the Naval Officer 1/7 to 30/9/1813 (HRA 1.8, 196), sandalwood duties, by notes payable at 12 months:

Name	On tons	At	Total duties
Charles Hook	175 ½	£2.10	£438.15.0
Garnham Blaxcell	224 ½	£2.10	£561-5-0
Mary Reiby	37 & 84	£2.10	£92.11.10 ½
George Howe	37 & 84	£2.10	£92.11.10 ½
			£1185.3.9

Presumably to avoid tipping off another trader about this previously unexploited sandalwood bonanza, when the *Cumberland* sailed on 20 January 1814, her true destination was concealed behind the *Gazette*'s 'Otaheite and the Palmottoes'[135]—the first of her many cover-ups. She was captained by Philip Goodenough, with a crew of perhaps fourteen on board. Yarwood notes the 'grotesque coincidence' that the same *Gazette* (*SG* 11/12/1813) advertised the meeting to form the Philanthropic Society, with D'Arcy Wentworth amongst the signatories, and the need for crew for the *Cumberland*, which will take his son William to Rarotonga and into the sequence of events that would lead to the Society's first (and only) action—and its collapse.[136]

A recently emancipated convict, Ann Butcher, also sailed as an unannounced passenger.[137] As a twenty year old woman, already married and with one child, Ann had been sentenced at the Old Bailey to seven years transportation for theft of items of clothing worth 39 shillings from her master's household.[138] She arrived in Sydney on the *Sydney Cove*, on 18 June 1807, served out her time,[139] and, by the time Goodenough sailed, Ann had become the captain's consort.[140]

Despite advertising a false destination, Goodenough was instructed

---

135   *SG* 22/1/1814. A later report puts her departure on 18th (*SG* 22/10/1814).
136   Yarwood, *Samuel Marsden: Survivor*, 150.
137   'Ann Butcher, an unfortunate woman who had gone from this port in the vessel', *SG* 22/10/1814.
138   Trial of Ann Butcher, 17/9/1806. She had only worked there for about ten days, and she claimed the theft was committed while she was at Portsmouth to see her husband whose ship had come in, by the woman who testified against her at the trial.
139   Butcher, Ann, Time expired, 16/4/1813.
140   In 1811 she served a few months in Newcastle, but returned when her time expired on 16 April 1813. If she hadn't immediately joined Goodenough before he sailed for black oil at the Derwent in early May, this would have happened after his return to Port Jackson on 11th September. *SG* 1/5/1813, then 21/8/1813; *SG* 18/9/1813.

by his masters to find 'Walker's Island'.[141] Sailing directly would have brought them to Rarotonga sometime in March, but, no doubt due to their detour to Tonga and the difficulties of finding their uncharted destination, they probably arrived in the last week of May.[142] When the *Endeavour*'s report proved false (there had never been a stick of sandalwood on Rarotonga),[143] they employed sixty locals to load 60 tons of *nono* wood (*Morinda citrifolia*), used for yellow dye, in the misguided hope of still making a profit.[144]

By the time the Sandalwood Company dispatched William Campbell

---

141 For 'Walker's Island', see *SG* 11/3/1815, and *Empire* 12/4/1853 in which the co-ordinates are mistaken: 'Walker's Island in lat. 3° 55' N., long. 149° 15' W., a small Island with a Coral Reef round it'. Rarotonga is situated 21.2292° S, 159.7763° W.

142 Maude & Crocombe, 'Rarotongan Sandalwood', 37, guess 'She should have arrived at Walker's Island during March', but other indications confuse the portrait.

   Kloosterman, 'Discoverers', 48, notes in the literature a great deal of confusion even about the year in which the *Cumberland* arrived, with suggested dates out by from between 4 to 7 years: 1818; 1820; 1821. There is, however, no major confusion in the primary references, whether the white man's documentary evidence or the island's oral history. The *Cumberland* left Sydney on 18 or 20 of January 1814 (*SG* 22/1 and 22/10/1814), and Wentworth gave an account of the visit to 'Larotonga' as soon as they returned, *SG* 22/10/1814. Even if by 1856 island memory on the west of the island was vague for Gill ('about 1820')—, in 1827 it was more precise for Williams when, drawing on the reports of (at least) two eyewitnesses, Williams wrote in *SG* 22/3/1827 of 'a vessel leaving your colony 14 or 15 years ago'. Informed by the *Gazette* report, reprinted in the *Naval Chronicle for 1816*, Pitman referred to the 'skirmish about seven years before the introduction of the Gospel into this land', evidently dating the latter to the arrival on Papeiha on Aitutaki in 1821; Pitman to Ellis, 10/8/1839.

   At the other end, we know that Croker was killed on 12 August (*SG* 22/10/1814), but the ship remained on Rarotonga until the 18th, missing by a week Siddons, who arrived in the *Campbell Macquarie* on 25th; *SG* 11/3/1815. After calling at Aitutaki, the *Cumberland* arrived in Sydney on 20/10/1814.

   It seems that Gill and Maretu draw independently on oral tradition to give further rather precise chronological indications. After first unsuccessfully landing at Ngati-Tangii, she went to Avarua 'for nearly a week', before returning to Ngati-Tangii harbour for 'three months'; Gill, *Gems*, 6–7; Maretu, *Cannibals*, 42 [2].

   Kloosterman, 'Discoverers', 48, suggests she arrived in May. On May 23, 1814 the *Seringapatam* came close to Rarotonga, and the next day some natives, who came out in their canoes, came aboard, who 'seemed to have no knowledge whatever of ever seeing a Ship or any White Person'; Seringatapam, Journal. Rather than the *Cumberland* being hidden from view (so Maude & Crocombe, 'Rarotongan Sandalwood', 57, the *Seringatapam*'s lack of awareness of her indicates she had not yet arrived. This would clearly show the 3 months to be precise.

143 Maude and Crocombe, 'Rarotongan Sandalwood', 40, record that 'there was not in fact a single sandalwood tree to be found on all Rarotonga'. The bemusement of the locals (at least in the west of the island may be reflected in Gill's comment that, 'the real object the captain had in view in so long a stay, among such a people, we have never been able to discover, except that he employed his men, some portion of the time, in cutting down large quantities of "*nono*" trees', *Gems*, 7.

144 On 20/10/1814 she arrived in Sydney 'with what must surely have been the most useless cargo ever brought to New South Wales', charged merely 5/- duty; Maude & Crocombe, 'Rarotongan Sandalwood', 49, 40, drawing on *SG* 22/10/1814. The wood had no market at all.

in the *Governor Macquarie* (28/8/1814), another of Blaxcell's vessels, the *Cumberland* had already left the island (on 18 August). After discovering for himself that the sandalwood was a myth, Campbell sailed on. Deprived of hoped-for profits from the *Cumberland*, the younger Wentworth later attempted to sue for a share of Campbell's cargo, claimed to be worth some £4000—but apparently, nothing came of it.[145]

However, the *Cumberland* is not significant for her failed cargo, but for what occurred during its collection. The scattered European source material does not tell the whole story.[146] By spinning yet another version of the usual narrative about the treachery of the South Seas cannibals, the truth was covered over—and, almost certainly, deliberately so.

When the *Cumberland* returned to Sydney on 20 October 1814, the report immediately printed in the *Sydney Gazette* read like an official version issued by Goodenough, but was probably crafted by Wentworth.[147] Even the islanders had called the twenty-three year old 'the talking captain',[148] and, besides, this highly ambitious 'father of Australia's freedoms'[149] probably had most to lose if the truth came out.

As at the beginning of the voyage, 'with probably deliberate inexactitude' the account clouded the location of the island, claiming these things happened at 'Loratonga, 16 leagues E of Tongataboo'.[150] Slanted to fit with the usual genre of 'treachery and blood', it told of two initial attempts to land being prevented by natives dexterously slinging stones of up to 6 pounds [2.72 Kg] in weight. The white men

---

145 W.C. Wentworth to T. Moore, 6/6/1815. The *Governor Macquarie* left Sydney on August 28, 1814 'for Otaheite and the neighbouring islands', *SG* 3/9/1814, and returned on 23/2/1815, from the 'South Seas, laden with 52 tons 19 cwt sandalwood, duty £132.12.6' (*HRA* 1.8, 595). Despite the claimed value, falling prices meant that the cargo gained only £2200 in Canton and after expenses, the profit was closer to £1000; Hainsworth, *The Sydney Traders*, 176.

146 Maude & Crocombe, 'Rarotongan Sandalwood', 38.

147 *SG* 22/10/1814. This report was reprinted in the *Naval Chronicle for 1816*, 113. Maude & Crocombe, 'Rarotongan Sandalwood', 46, speak of it as Goodenough's report, but it is really Wentworth's story and it is difficult to imagine him not telling it. If it is true that he had navigated home (cf. Persse, 'Wentworth, William Charles'), perhaps Goodenough was too unwell to speak to the press.

148 Maude & Crocombe, 'Rarotongan Sandalwood', 37 n.18, citing Maretu's term 'rangatira paraparau', 'On Rarotongan History', 1.

149 Cf. Tink, 'William Charles Wentworth. Father of Australia's Freedoms'.

150 Maude & Crocombe, 'Rarotongan Sandalwood', 46. As another example of the *Cumberland*'s persistent subterfuge, this is a vastly underestimated distance— some 90km rather than 1603km. For comparison (although sailing westward), it took Bligh 17 days from finding Aitutaki (11/4/1789) until the mutiny near Tonga; Maretu, *Cannibals & Converts*, 46 n.51.

'nevertheless effected a landing afterwards' and 'became very friendly' with the natives, whom they employed to gather their cargo, paying them suitably, of course. This continued until 12 August when crew member John Croker was assaulted with a club and instantaneously killed (no back story given). Several high-sounding sentences tell of young Wentworth, whom the sailor had accompanied onshore, being unable to heroically rescue him due to a misfiring pistol. '[H]aving now only to provide for his own safety', Wentworth grabbed Croker's pistol to menace his way against the murderer back to the boat. Again with no explanation, the report noted that 'in another quarter' (giving the impression that a native conspiracy was at large) 'a similar assault had been made on others of the crew', namely, 'William Travis, George Strait, and an Otaheitan'. These men were (so innocently) 'on shore for provisions', but (out of the blue) they were 'all massacred'. The horror of the account was enhanced, penultimately, by the report that Ann Butcher was killed at the same time (treacherously), 'when ashore on a visit to some native women who had shewn her much kindness'. As this latest version of the usual narrative reached its fitting climax, the horror was made the worse by the sober manner of the reporting:

> Mr. Goodenough affirms it to be his opinion, that all the murdered persons were afterwards devoured, as they had seen a part of one that exhibited every appearance of its remaining a fragment of a cannibal festival.

Thus, within two days after the *Cumberland*'s return to Sydney, the innocence of the white men and the inexplicable treachery and inhuman savagery of the once friendly and well-paid natives of 'Loratonga' was made clear to a Sydney reading public already receptive to the idea that the islands were full of treacherous cannibals.

But, at least at an official level, the usual narrative was becoming unstuck. The *Boyd* was known to be an atrocious result of prior European atrocities. More atrocities had now been documented by Sydney magistrates into the British legal record. The Governor had issued a proclamation to warn ship's captains against committing further atrocities, and, if possible, to punish them if they did. And a proclamation society had been formed to enable those from a significant segment of society with vested interests in the South Seas to prosecute the Governor's ruling. All this was known by the Company sending the *Cumberland* before she had sailed. These changed circumstances evidently applied the pressure that ensured the account given to the *Gazette* showed no hint of any untoward behaviour on Rarotonga—as long as its readers asked no further questions to penetrate its opacity.

For what the *Gazette* didn't explain, is why it all happened—or, more precisely, what happened between the third landing and the 12 August killing of Croker in Wentworth's company.

3.2 What Really Happened on Rarotonga?

As we shall see below, the cover-up was more elaborate than simply an initial well-worded press-release from those ultimately responsible for the ship's behaviour. The well-orchestrated snow-job was successful both at the time, and for perpetuity.[151] But truth will out.

Although the exact details of what happened in 1814 may remain elusive, the sources are sufficient to allow a good re-construction of events.[152] For years, the people of Rarotonga were left to talk about the horrors of their first substantial encounter with the white man, the story being told and retold in conversation and song.[153] The places where events took place, and the grave-sites of the people killed backed

---

151 The pro-Wentworth spin continues into significant contemporary accounts, such as Persse, 'Wentworth, William Charles': 'At Rarotonga, an affray broke out with the islanders, and Wentworth was nearly killed as he attempted to rescue a sailor whom they clubbed to death'. Persse also claims that the 'Captain died during the troubles, and Wentworth brought the ship to Sydney', but when the ship arrived in Sydney, Goodenough was alive enough to confirm the incident for the *Gazette* (*SG* Sat 22/10/1814), and he sailed several more voyages before dying sometime in December, 1815; Deposition of Ann Goodenough, 3/6/1817. Tink, *William Charles Wentworth*, 23, basically re-writes the *Gazette* article. See also the maximal spin in Ritchie, *The Wentworths*, 148, who blames the affray on the behaviour of the crew, has William 'narrowly escape death while attempting to save a sailor', and then navigating the ship home safely with skill apparently gained on an earlier voyage from England (on 8/10/1802 he was sent for his education, aged 12, and arrived home on 24/3/1810, aged 19; Tink, *William Charles Wentworth*, 14, 18). With such heroic behaviour, one wonders why, 'D'Arcy Wentworth, Blaxcell, Riley and their fellow traders quashed [Marsden's request for an inquiry] and quietly buried the incident'.
152 For the first composite account, see Maude & Crocombe, 'Rarotongan Sandalwood'. Marjorie Crocombe also told the story of the *Cumberland*'s visit to Rarotonga in the children's book, *They Came for Sandalwood*, first published in 1964. For my own attempt, see 'What Really Happened on Rarotonga in 1814?'. For the difficulties of reconstructing the story, see my 'A Dramatic Event'.
153 'The *Cumberland*'s visit, the details of the incidents with which it was involved, and the political repercussions outlined above were recorded and preserved in the traditional manner by the island's sages, the *are korero*, and in less esoteric versions, in the historical chants or *pe'e*', Maude & Crocombe, 'Rarotongan Sandalwood', 51.

THE FAILURE OF THE PHILANTHROPIC SOCIETY 173

up the memories with vivid and constant silent testimony. Although native oral tradition has long struggled to be heard over the official Western documentary tradition,[154] it too found its way into written sources, and when it comes to the *Cumberland*:

> the sources on the Rarotongan side are much more detailed and specific, and from the fine histories of Maretu, Papehia and Terei, supplemented by more incidental material by Itio and Teariki Taraare, one can reconstruct the main events of the visit with an appreciation of their causation and significance such as Goodenough and Wentworth clearly never possessed at the time.[155]

Over the years, another version floated from the Islands into the European record. Even at the time, there were many who had their own personal memories of the event. Some Europeans, despite their silence, knew the truth, and others were in touch with the eyewitness accounts from the island itself.[156]

The story that emerges is not pretty. With his moralistic slant and clear suspicion that a cover up had taken place, William Gill, LMS Missionary on the west of Rarotonga (1839–1852), was not impressed with what he had heard:

> the whole history of their stay on the shores of Rarotonga was a continued series of rapine, cruelty, vice, and bloodshed. So disgraceful was their conduct that the captain did not, either for his own credit or safety sake, publish the latitude and longitude of this lovely island; of which but for his wickedness, he might have received the honour of being the discoverer.[157]

---

154 After the oral accounts of the story of the *Cumberland* long sat in repositories of Western documentary evidence, they were brought to scholarly attention by H. Maude, working with Rarotongan, Marjorie Crocombe, in 1961. See Maude & Crocombe, 'Rarotongan Sandalwood', 32–33.
155 Maude & Crocombe, 'Rarotongan Sandalwood', 38. Note how even Maude & Crocombe are positive in their comments about Wentworth and Goodenough.
156 Wentworth and Goodenough were certainly apprised of the facts, as would be at least some of the crew, if not all. Why were they silent? See Bolt, 'What Really Happened?'.
157 Gill, *Gems*, 7. Gill's suspicion of a cover up is hinted at in 'for [...] safety sake'. Worse than not publishing at all, when the *Cumberland* returned, she misreported the co-ordinates (see above, nn. 136 & 137); *SG* 22/10/1814.

After leaving Sydney and before sailing via the Friendly Islands [Tonga],[158] the first stop for the *Cumberland* was the Bay of Islands, where she picked up two of Ruatara's men— the giant tattooed warrior Veretini and Tupe— and also a woman, ultimately bound for Marsden's hospitality at Port Jackson.[159] Two Tahitian men (Te Are, Tomi), and two Tahitian women (Tavai and Tumai) also probably embarked at this time.[160]

Figure 10: Map of Rarotonga, 2017.

158 This is indicated by the fact that in the *Gazette* report (*SG* 22/10/1814) they orient the reader by giving a precise distance from Tongataboo to Loratonga [sic]. Even if the distance itself is (deliberately?) mistaken, the general direction probably reflects the actual voyage.
159 Marsden to Pratt, 26/10/1815; Gill, *Gems*, 7. Only Gill reports the New Zealand woman, who, I speculate, as Wentworth's consort, may have played a key role in events; see Bolt, 'What Really Happened?'.
160 'The *Cumberland* had touched on her outward bound Voyage at the Bay of Islands, where she had received two men from Duaterra [Ruatara]', Marsden to Pratt, 26/10/1815. For their names, Maretu, *Cannibals*, 42 [1]. There is no hint that the Tahitians were on board since Port Jackson, and when they spoke of Christianity in Rarotonga, as far as can be discovered, it was from what they knew of Tahiti, not Sydney; see Willliams, *Journal*, 28; Maretu , 'On Rarotongan history', 1: 'that "the servants of Jehovah, and Jesus Christ, the white man's God, had come and were still residing there [Tahiti]', cited by Maude & Crocombe, 'Rarotongan Sandalwood', 53.

THE FAILURE OF THE PHILANTHROPIC SOCIETY

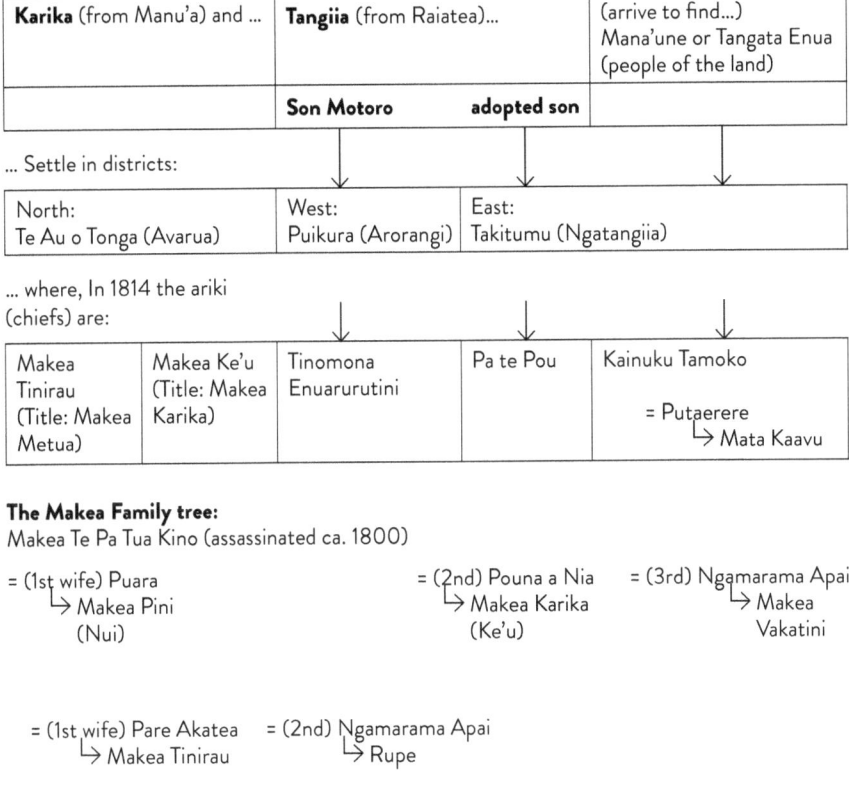

Figure 11: Rarotongan 'Royalty'—a partial genealogy
From 12th Century to 1814
Ancestry (end of 12th Century):

Karika (from Manu'a) and ...	Tangiia (from Raiatea)...		(arrive to find...) Mana'une or Tangata Enua (people of the land)
	Son Motoro	adopted son	

... Settle in districts:

North: Te Au o Tonga (Avarua)		West: Puikura (Arorangi)	East: Takitumu (Ngatangiia)	

... where, In 1814 the ariki (chiefs) are:

Makea Tinirau (Title: Makea Metua)	Makea Ke'u (Title: Makea Karika)	Tinomona Enuarurutini	Pa te Pou	Kainuku Tamoko = Putaerere ↳ Mata Kaavu

The Makea Family tree:
Makea Te Pa Tua Kino (assassinated ca. 1800)

= (1st wife) Puara   = (2nd) Pouna a Nia   = (3rd) Ngamarama Apai
  ↳ Makea Pini   ↳ Makea Karika   ↳ Makea
    (Nui)   (Ke'u)   Vakatini

= (1st wife) Pare Akatea   = (2nd) Ngamarama Apai
  ↳ Makea Tinirau   ↳ Rupe

= ?   = Ngamata a Taramai-te-Tonga
  ↳ Makea Pori   ↳ Tepaeru

After the initial attempted landing in the Ngatangiia district on the south east, the ship sailed north to the Avarua district and stayed for a week. While there, assisting in a local squabble, Veretini and Te Are killed several from the Arorangi district, simultaneously demonstrating European firepower and scaring everyone enough to make them want the foreigners to leave. Returning to Ngatangiia, the *Cumberland* stayed for three months. After soon learning there was no sandalwood on Rarotonga, they gathered *nono* wood instead, for an alternative source of profit.

When the locals had enough of the foreigners' excesses, a conspiracy formed and the New Zealander Tupe, who had come with the schooner but was living on shore, helped hatch a scheme to get rid of them.[161] This probably involved luring Ann Butcher, known to be the captain's consort, and the New Zealand woman, probably associated with Wentworth, on shore where they were kidnapped, and later killed. When the conspiracy was discovered, very early on August 12 two men from the ship were sent to kill Tupe as an example. Presumably because the captain was also making hurried preparations in case the ship had to leave and needed provisions, another party was sent north to steal the coconuts in the storehouse of the high chief of the district (Makea Tinirau Ariki). In a spree of vengeance, the warrior Rupe killed three of the crew, one of the Tahitians (probably Te Ara), and the New Zealander, Veretini. In keeping with the killings being acts of revenge, two of the victims were also later eaten.[162] In the aftermath, a deal was struck with the locals to enable the loading of the cargo to be completed. Probably as part of the deal, but staged as another kidnapping,[163] when the *Cumberland* sailed off on August 18,[164] she took with her Rupe's daughter, the chieftainess Tepaeru; Mata Kavaau, who was Tepaeru's neice and, more importantly, the daughter of Kainuku (one of the two chiefs of the Ngatangiia); and a man named Kupauta.[165] (For the relationships, see Figure 11).

---

161 What follows is my own reconstruction, which differs somewhat from that of Maude & Crocombe, 'Rarotongan Sandalwood'. For my argument, see 'What Really Happened on Rarotonga in 1814?'.
162 In 1838, knowing only the *Gazette* report and after inquiring whether the four Europeans killed had been eaten, LMS missionary Charles Pitman was told 'two of them were, Ko Tiore (George) [=George Strait] and Nati (Nancy) [=Ann Butcher], the other two were not. One was taken away by the officers of the schooner [=probably William Travis], & the other was ~~taken over~~ carried by a native in his canoe and put into the sea [=probably John Croker],' Pitman, Extract from Journal, 2/6/1838, in Pitman to Ellis, 10/8/1839.
163 Note the hint in Tepaeru, 'Grave Plaque': 'the 18 year old Tepaeru-ariki was kidnapped along with her niece Mata Kavau [...] and a seaman, Kupauta, by the mischievous crew of the "Cumberland" under the command of an atrocious Captain Philip Goodenough who wanted revenge for the killing of some of his crew by Rupe'.
164 Croker was killed on the 12 August, but the ship didn't leave then (contra Kloosterman, 'Discoverers', 48; and Tepaeru, Grave Plaque). According to Maretu, *Cannibals*, 45 [8], after six days in the mountains, the people returned and she left soon after. Relying on the usual precision of Maretu's account, this means that the last day was the 18 August.
165 Maretu, *Cannibals*, 46 [9]. According to Crocombe's annotations (n.49), Tapairu (or Tapaeru) was a sister (probably classificatory) of Makea Tinirau, the high chief of the Avarua district. Her companion, Mata Kavaau, was the daughter of the chief Kainuku Tamoko of Avana, but Kupautu's antecedents are uncertain. Tapairu died on 19 February 1881 at the age of eighty-five. See Tepaeru, 'Grave Plaque'. Her return to Rarotonga in 1823, and her long life gave her plenty of opportunity to re-tell the story of the *Cumberland*.

3.3 The Failure of the meeting (25 Oct 1814): Compromise and Cover-Up

The *Cumberland* arrived back in Sydney on Thursday 20 October 1814, with yet another dramatic story of sudden and inexplicable native treachery. With the young Australian-born hero of the Blue Mountains crossing now acting as the central heroic figure and chief witness in the account, the usual narrative no doubt gained greater credibility.[166]

But just as swiftly as that immediate written record, a different oral version was reported. It wasn't simply generalized 'ugly rumours of what had transpired in Rarotonga [… circulating] on the waterfront' that 'soon reached the ears of the Rev. Samuel Marsden',[167] still less did Marsden learn about the event from reading the *Gazette*![168] His grass-roots connections brought him the well-founded inside story.

Having returned to Sydney on the *Active* on 21/8/1814, Ruatara and ten other New Zealanders were at Parramatta with Marsden.[169] If everything had gone to plan, when the *Cumberland* came in, Ruatara would have welcomed the two men placed on her in the Bay of Islands earlier in the year, and helped them settle into Marsden's circles. But he didn't find them on board. His inquiries receive swift answers, however, because he was able to talk to several eyewitnesses.[170]

---

166 *SG* 22/10/1814.
167 Maude & Crocombe, 'Rarotongan Sandalwood', 49. Yarwood, *Samuel Marsden: Survivor*, 150, also makes the circumstances vaguer than they were through a similar tendency to generalize: 'stories soon gained currency in Sydney'.
168 So Ritchie, *The Wentworths*, 148. Sharp, *The World, the Flesh & the Devil*, 315, also has Marsden '[inferring] much' from the *Gazette* report, although acknowledging Ruatara as another source.
169 Marsden to Pratt, 20/9/1814 (*Missionary Register 1815*, 195). He names them in Marsden to Pratt, 12/10/1814: Duaterra, Shunghee, Coro-Coro, Toohe, Parow, Repreero, Warrakee, Mowhee, Pyhee, Tinana, Whycattoo.
170 Marsden to Pratt, 26/10/15, uses the plural.

Figure 12. Sketch of Tapaeru. Reproduced in Rere, *Nga Mataiti Mua o te Evangelia*, 4; and Maretu, *Cannibals*, 47.

Even though Tapairu and Mata Kavaau had been dropped off as the ship passed Aitutaki, Kupauta was kept on board—presumably to supplement the crew,[171] now severely depleted by the loss of Travis, Strait, and Croker, not to mention any assistance once provided by Te Ara, Tupe, and Veretini. Maretu reports that:

> Kupauta was taken on to Botany Bay. There he learnt about the word of God and it is said that he was sent back but was left on Tupuai where he married two wives and died there.[172]

---

171 Note the local memory that he was 'a sailor'; Tepaeru, Grave Plaque.
172 Maretu, *Cannibals*, 46 [9]. Crocombe points out that Ponapi in the original is not the Caroline Islands, as Savage had rendered it (followed by Tepaeru's grave plaque), but Botany Bay. Tupuai, or Tubuai, is in the Austral group, south of Tahiti.

The surviving Tahitian man—probably Tomi[173]—and the two Tahitian women (Tavai and Tumai) were probably also still on board. Although if some of the events on the island sat uneasily with members of the crew, the fact that Marsden did not gain any depositions shows they kept the silence of their superiors, Goodenough and Wentworth. It was through the islanders reporting to Ruatara, that Marsden learned 'that the most dreadful Murders had been committed in one of the Islands by some of the People belonging to the *Cumberland*'.[174] Tupe's murder became the clear focus, for when Ruatara learned that one of the men he put on the *Cumberland* had been killed by a European, 'he was anxious to know the Cause'. Marsden sprang into action and called a general meeting of the Philanthropic Society.

This was the Society's first opportunity to press for a prosecution under Macquarie's proclamation of 1/12/1813. Back in December 1813, even as D'Arcy Wentworth added his signature to the list of prominent men who called the meeting to form the Philanthropic Society, he was already in a flurry to get to the Rarotongan sandalwood he had discovered during Walker's inquiry.[175] When the *Cumberland* sailed (20/1/1814), she was the first vessel required to sign the bond, after Macquarie's Proclamation

---

173   There are good reasons to believe that it was Te Ara who was killed on Rarotonga; see Bolt, 'What Really Happened?'. Immediately after the fiasco following the *Cumberland*'s return, Marsden sailed to New Zealand on the *Active*. Amongst his party there were two Tahitians. The first, listed as 'Otaheitian, Sailor', was called Tahee by Marsden (Marsden to Pratt, 28/11/1814), but 'Dicka-hee, Otaheitan' by Nicholas (*Narrative* 1, 37).

   In the *Gazette*, he is called 'Dick' (*SG* 26/2/1814), and prior to joining the *Active*, sailed on the *Perseverance* (SG 28/11 & 5/12/1812, mistakenly as 'New Zealander'; 27/3 & 3/4/1813) and the *Trial* (SG 24 & 31/7, 7/8/1813). On another occasion when Nicholas lists the crew (*Narrative* 1, 371), he is called 'Tow, sailor, Bolabolan'.

   Punnee is the second 'Otaheitian' mentioned by Marsden (Marsden to Pratt, 28/11/1814), and by Nicholas as a 'Bolabolan' (*Narrative* 1, 37) and a 'Otaheitian' (1, 371). Although he had not appeared before in the shipping notices (unless —improbably— amongst the Otaheiteans sometimes listed unnamed), he appears as the *Active* is about to take her second voyage, Marsden's first (*SG* 29/10/1814 ['Punney, Otaheitan']; 5 & 12/11/1814 ('Poney, Otaheitian'). He also sailed on the *Active*'s third voyage (*SG* 8/4 [Panney], 15/4/1815 [Poney]), but does not turn up again in shipping notices by that name. However, following a suggestion made to me by Malcolm Falloon, he may be the Tahitian 'Tommy' who sailed on the *Active*'s fourth (*SG* 26/8/1815) and eighth (*SG* 25/4, 9/5/1818) voyages, but he did not use his European name when first on the *Active*, because Mowhee was also on board, who was already well known as Tommy Drummond. This would therefore mean that the 'Punney' who turned up in Sydney to sail with Marsden at the end of 1814 and who then crewed with the *Active* for two more voyages, was Tomi the Tahitian, who had been on the *Cumberland*.

174   Marsden to Pratt, 26/10/1815.

175   Walker's hearing was on 4 and 11, and advertisements for the meeting to form the Philanthropic Society on 11 and 18 December 1813.

had come into force on 1 January.[176] When W.C. Wentworth embarked as her supercargo, he knew of the formation of the Philanthropic Society in which his father had played a key role, just one week before he sailed. The *Cumberland* left Sydney in a new era in which the safety of South Seas islanders was guaranteed by Government proclamation and the Philanthropic Society primed for prosecution. But on her return, the voyage that started with one cover-up to protect the trading interests of those involved, ended with another.

The Society met on 25 October 1814, just five days after the *Cumberland*'s arrival, chaired by David Allan—at some personal cost.[177] Marsden was soon disappointed:[178]

> I was in hopes that it would have been attended with some benefit at the time it was instituted; but I had soon Cause to alter my Opinion. [...]
>
> Some of the members attended and some did not. At the meeting many objections were started against examining into any of the transactions of the *Cumberland* while she was amongst the islands. I used every Argument I could to prevail upon the Committee to hear what I had got to say, and to examine the witnesses I had to bring to prove the facts, agreeable to the resolutions entered into at the first formation of the Society: but to little purpose—one could not because he was part owner [Blaxcell], another was interested some other way [e.g. D. Wentworth, Riley], hear any evidence or examine in any way into the Business. Several Europeans as well as natives had been killed, but no notice whatever was taken of the death of the Europeans even. I have no doubt, had the Committee allowed me to have investigated this Subject, but an horrid Scene of Rapine, murder and Violence would have been laid open to the public eye. I then clearly saw from the Spirit of Opposition manifested at this meeting that no relief was to be expected from the leading men of this Colony for the injured Savages in these Seas.

The meeting ended in systematic—and effective—cover-up. Although writing one year later, Marsden was caustic:

---

176 The *Cumberland* is the first vessel reported in the January issues of the *Gazette*.
177 Marsden praises Allan for his support in the formation of the Philanthropic Society, and in the final meeting, suggesting that on both occasions Allan risked his own life, without saying how that was so; 'Mr. Allan stept forward at the Risk of his own Life at the time the Philanthropic Society was formed in this Colony to support that Institution'; Marsden to Pratt, 13/7/1819. For the final meeting, see n.174.
178 Marsden to Pratt, 26/10/1815.

Tho' Duaterra attended the meeting and wished to know the Cause of the death of the man whom he had Committed to the care of the Master; and several of the Crew belonging to the *Cumberland* had been killed and one Otaheitian, yet the matter would not bear examination. The whole was hushed up in Silence and remained so to this very day. All that Duaterra could learn was that his man had been shot by one of the Ship's Company, but for what reason he was not told.

There were too many vested interests. Three of the colony's four major traders in Sandalwood were members (Hook, Blaxcell, and Howe; see Figure 9). Blaxcell owned both vessels sent to Rarotonga. Apart from W.C. Wentworth, the other four members of the Rarotongan Sandalwood Company had subscribed as life members of the Philanthropic Society,[179] and Blaxcell, Riley, and Wentworth senior made up one quarter of the Committee 'and the remainder for the most part [were] their business associates'.[180]

But it is worth pausing to ask a question not often asked: by preventing a thorough investigation, what was it exactly that they were protecting—especially with such ferocity?[181] Wentworth's *Gazette* story had the Europeans the innocent victims, with himself as the hero, so what was there to hide? Surely there was more at stake than simply the widespread embarrassment of the Rarotongan Sandalwood Company flopping on a useless and unsaleable cargo? If Ann Butcher had left the colony illegally, surely it would be Goodenough to blame, if anyone? It is certainly clear that the *Cumberland* breached Macquarie's 1/12/1813 GGO at a vast number of points: trespass on property (food, women, robbery of Makea Ariki's coconuts); interfering in local disputes and making war (Te Are and Veretini shooting several Arorangi); stirring

---

179   Garnham Blaxcell, D'Arcy Wentworth, Alexander Riley, and Captain William Campbell; *Articles of Agreement concerning the Sandalwood Company*, January —, 1814. On the Subscription list in *SG* 22/1/1814, Sixteen men subscribed the Ten Guineas for life membership.

180   Maude & Crocombe, 'Rarotongan Sandalwood', 50; cf. Yarwood, *Samuel Marsden: Survivor*, 150, who notes Marsden was 'frustrated from the outset by a heavy representation of *Cumberland* shareholders, one of them D'Arcy Wentworth, whose son had been active in the encounter'. The others on the committee were: William Redfern; William Broughton; Charles Hook; Simeon Lord; Edward S Hall; John Oxley; James Birnie; Rowland Hassall; J.T. Campbell; *SG* 22/1/1814. Yarwood also notes that 'Macquarie appears to have taken no action'—and we might wonder why not.

181   Cf. Marsden to Pratt, 12/7/1819: 'In one instance in supporting the Cause of the natives of the Islands, he went so far as to risk his life in my Presence, when I was pleading at a public meeting for them. [...] This took Place at the meeting of the Philanthropic Society which I was compelled to relinquish altogether'.

up animosities (such that a conspiracy formed, assisted by Tupe, to get rid of them); interfere with religious practices (theft of Makea Ariki's coconuts; possible desecration of marae through digging nono); perhaps shipping native men without their free will and consent (Kupauta), certainly shipping native women without their consent (Tapaeru, Mata Kavaau, ?the New Zealand woman), or their parent's consent (Rupe), and certainly without the Governor's prior written consent; and once shipped, they did not return the women to their own island, but left them stranded on Aitutaki.[182] Any or all of these offences could have resulted in the forfeiture of the £1000 bond by the Master and Owners of the vessel—in this case, Philip Goodenough and Garnham Blaxcell. But why would others be concerned? Was it an attempt to scuttle Macquarie's order to give maximum freedom to other owners and masters? If so, why didn't Macquarie step in to rule against the *Cumberland*? Why did Marsden only press for a hearing in the Philanthropic Society, not before the Governor himself, or in one of the courts of the colony which were, at that time, still operating? There are mysteries here, and it seems that something of great significance at the core of the events simply had to be covered-up at all costs.[183] If we follow the lead of the intelligence that came to Marsden, based in the eyewitness testimony of the Islanders who had been there and reported through Ruatara, then the heart of the issue appears to be the killing of the New Zealander Tupe by one of the ship's company. The Philanthropic Society was destroyed by powerful men connected to the commercial and governmental interests of New South Wales, it seems, to prevent the name of the perpetrator seeing the light of day.

---

182 Compare GGO, 1/12/1813.
183 It seems extraordinary that this has been accepted so casually. Ritchie, *The Wentworths*, 148, notes 'D'Arcy Wentworth, Blaxcell, Riley and their fellow traders quashed [Marsden's request for an inquiry] and quietly buried the incident', even though William was, apparently, the hero. Yarwood, *Samuel Marsden: Survivor*, 150, who hints at more with Marsden being 'frustrated from the outset by a heavy representation of *Cumberland* shareholders, one of them D'Arcy Wentworth, whose son had been active in the encounter'—but asks no more questions. Tink, *William Charles Wentworth*, 24, 35, is happy to report that 'D'Arcy, Blaxcell, and Riley used their numbers to block' Marsden's attempt to have 'the Society investigate the killings'; and that William was glad Riley, 'had stood by him during the *Cumberland* affair', but as such a hero, why would William have been at all concerned? And why was the 'quashing', 'frustration', 'blocking' and 'standing by' of such a ferocity that, in opposing it, Allan acted 'at the risk of his life'? Sharp, *The World, the Flesh & the Devil*, 336, hints at the real reason, when he notes Marsden 'had called the last meeting of the Society to examine the murderous doings of the *Cumberland* in the Cook Islands'.

THE FAILURE OF THE PHILANTHROPIC SOCIETY

If someone can be named now, with the perspective of historical distance, it was almost certainly the younger Wentworth with most to lose by Marsden's evidence being heard. For when events on Rarotonga are examined carefully, he appears to be the one holding the smoking gun.[184]

3.4 The Failure of the Rule of Law

When his proclamation society unraveled before Marsden's eyes so soon after its formation, the Parramatta Magistrate viewed it as yet another failure of the rule of law:

> I am of opinion that when a vessel belonging to the Colony returns from the Islands with only part of her Crew, the others said to be killed, it is the duty of Government to inquire into the Cause of these men who are missing, losing their lives. Such an Inquiry, if it had no Regard to the Natives would tend to bring to Light many Acts of Darkness & Cruelty.[185]

In January 1817 in his 'scandalous libel upon [Marsden] and the Missionaries belonging to the Church & London Missionary Societies in the South Sea Islands',[186] Philo Free cast things exactly in reverse. Contrary to his assertions, it was those who saw the islands ripe for temporal profits who were prepared to sacrifice their fellow human beings, whether black or white, and to thumb their nose at British law to line their own pocket and protect their own skin. Despite a Government Proclamation and a Society to prosecute it, nothing had changed. When Philo Free deliberately cast victim as perpetrator, the enemy gloated as Mammon triumphed over Mission.

Marsden's prayers for the South Seas stretched back over many years, as did the frustration he felt about their apparent lack of outcome. But despite the steady spin of the white man's stories, random acts

---

184 See Bolt, 'What Really Happened on Rarotonga in 1814?'. That Marsden knew what happened on Rarotonga goes a long way towards explaining W.C. Wentworth's dislike for Marsden and his long-term and vicious campaign to discredit him. Again, Sharp, *The World, the Flesh & the Devil*, 315, hints at this underlying dark reality, when he notes that the collapse of the Philanthropic Society turned both Wentworth's even further against Marsden.
185 Marsden to Pratt, 26/10/1815.
186 Marsden to Bathurst, 28/11/1817. Yarwood, *Samuel Marsden: Survivor*, 150, recognizes that Campbell 'seized upon the inaction of the society as a convenient ground for attacking Marsden'.

of treachery and savagery amongst the cannibals were not the real problem. Disillusioned by the failure of proper means, Marsden named the deep prejudice against the people of the South Seas as one of the chief hindrances to the mission:

> I believe the work to be of God. It has as yet gone on slowly, but progressively. I have not had the means, till lately, to make the attempt; though I have wished most ardently to see the work begun. If the public prejudice had not been so strong against the Natives of this island [New Zealand], the difficulty and expense of forming the settlement would not have been so great.[187]

With the failure of the Philanthropic Society, he resigned himself to the possibility that nothing could ever be done. One year after its meteoric failure, it still hurt:

> I do not expect now that any thing will be done by that Society for the Benefit of the Natives of these Islands; and for certain Reasons. Was a Society here to act, it would be a Check upon that plundering, murdering System, which has so long disgraced the European name amongst the Inhabitants of these Islands; but this would wound the Interest & Honor of Individuals of some weight and Influence.[188]

Reading the mood in NSW, Marsden felt it was not the time to even form an auxiliary for CMS, for:

> if any public auxiliary Society was attempted to be formed as yet [, the] People here would think their Craft was in danger.[189]

On 6 November 1815, he wrote of 'not less than one hundred' natives killed near the River Thames, New Zealand. So much for Macquarie's second proclamation of November 1814.[190] When the offending parties sailed on to the Bay of Islands, they would have been killed by the natives (who had heard of the murders) if the *Active* hadn't been there to intervene. The problems just weren't going away.

But neither was Marsden's pursuit of solutions through the rule of

---

187 Marsden to Pratt, 14/6/1815 (*Missionary Register 1816*, 197).
188 Marsden to Pratt, 26/10/1815. Yarwood, *Samuel Marsden: Survivor*, 164, notes that after the failure of the Philanthropic Society, it would be years before he entrusted the mission to a local committee.
189 Marsden to Pratt, 26/10/1815. He reiterates his reasoning in Marsden to Pratt, 22/1/1817.
190 Government and General Order 9/11/1814, *SG* 12/11/1814.

law. Despite his disappointments, he could not desert Christ's mission to the nations. Neither would he concede that British law could not protect the nations under Christ's gaze.[191] Even if local means failed, perhaps those at home could tap into the higher powers. In 1815 Marsden wrote to Pratt:

> an Act of Parliament for the Protection of the natives belonging to the South Sea Islands. I have had several Conversations upon this Subject with our Judges, and they have recommended to his Majesty's Government that a Court should be established in New South Wales to try Crimes committed in these Seas and Islands. I wish that if any Act should be past [sic] and a Court of Justice instituted in New South Wales for the Trial of Europeans, who may commit any Act of Violence one upon another, that some Provision may be made at the same time for the Protection of the natives—at present there is none.[192]

Marsden could see that, without a firm footing in British law, his own exertions would continue to fail:

> it is in vain for me to attempt to bring any of these men to justice; nothing can be done, unless the British Parliament will take into consideration the unprotected state of both the missionaries and natives in all the islands in these seas. The Europeans may, and at present do, commit every crime with impunity, and there is no law either to restrain or punish them. The natives have no means but to repel by force.[193]

Cast down but not knocked out (see 2 Corinthians 4:9), a month after the failed Philanthropic Society meeting, Marsden pressed for another prosecution. On 20/12/1815 and 6/1/1816, he pressed charges 'as agent for the London and Church Missionary Societies, with various acts of cruelty and oppression' against John Martin, Captain of the brig *Queen Charlotte*, 'whose conduct towards the inhabitants of Santa Christiana [=Tahuata in the Marquesas Islands] appears to have been equally

---

191 Yarwood, *Samuel Marsden: Survivor*, 150–151: 'Although Marsden's and Macquarie's actions were conspicuous for their immediate ineffectualness, they were important as marking the beginning of a long struggle to cope with the ethical and moral problems that had been brought to the South Pacific by the penetration of white men. [...] Frustrated by the collapse of his Society, Marsden conducted for the remaining twenty four years of his life a weighty correspondence with governors, parliamentarians, missionary societies and secretaries of state, which reflected his continuing absorption in the question'.
192 Marsden to Pratt, 15/6/1815.
193 Marsden to Pratt, 6/11/1815 (Extract: *HRNZ* 1.424–425).

inconsistent with the dictates of justice and humanity'.[194] After Marsden's witnesses were heard, Martin presented his defence in writing. No doubt aware that Theodore Walker's December 1813 case was still unresolved and that Lasco Jones had already successfully evaded conviction in April, —and probably that the Philanthropic Society had just collapsed—Martin challenged both Marsden's authority and the jurisdiction of the NSW courts:[195]

> after questioning the power and competency of the Court, and protesting against Revd. Mr Marsden's authority to bring these charges, he not having exhibited his authority from the societies which he professes to represent, or proved those societies were incorporated bodies, [the accused] calls upon the Bench of magistrates to acquit him upon the evidence before them.

On 6 January the Bench of magistrates, which included D'Arcy Wentworth with all he knew about the Rarotongan cover-up, handed down the decision that they:

> Do adjudge the whole to be fully substantiated, and they feel it their duty to recommend that His Excellency the Governor will be pleased to take into his consideration the expediency of some measures being adopted that may prevent a recurrence of similar acts of fraud and violence.

But Wentworth and the others on the Bench already knew that Macquarie's first proclamation had failed within ten months of its issue—and his second was in the process of failing just as soon. Now Martin sailed away scot-free. As a memorial from CMS to Earl Bathurst in 1817 explained:

> That in a recent case proceedings have been instituted at Port Jackson against the captain of a trading vessel for acts of oppression and cruelty against the chiefs and other natives of one of the Marquesas Islands, in which after a full investigation a conviction took place on the whole of the charges; but the party convicted has escaped with impunity, on

---

194 Burder to Marsden, 5/6/1817.
195 Proceedings, John Martin, 20/12/1815 and 6/1/1816. The charges brought by Marsden: 1. Ordering on or about 28/7/1815 some war canoes to be brought off Santa Christiana and later selling them at other islands; 2. at that same time holding several chiefs hostage in the hold of the *Queen Charlotte* under armed guard; 3. For compelling at musket-point the natives who brought the war canoes to him 'to leap into the sea, and struggle for life in the best manner they were able'.

account of the inadequacy of the powers vested in the Magistrates to punish the offence.[196]

When Philo Free publicly slandered the mission and its 'worthy head', Marsden was still smarting that 'the Philanthropic Society could not be brought to answer any benevolent Purposes, tho' honoured with the names of Persons in the first Situations from the same Cause'. And yet, he wrote positively to CMS, hoping they would not be discouraged by the opposition to their views, and that:

> The wisdom of your Committee will suggest what use may be made of all the Information I have transmitted. I have laboured to put them in Possession of Facts: and leave the Cause with them.[197]

Marsden's reports home did not fall on deaf ears. The memorial from CMS documented the atrocities, and enclosed the deputations taken by Marsden in November 1813 as well as Macquarie's two proclamations.[198] After reporting Martin's flight from justice, they then added the more general comment, probably reflecting Marsden's settled opinion after the Bench, as with Walker, was powerless to convict him:

> That your memorialists are informed that there is no competent jurisdiction in New South Wales for the cognizance and punishment of such offences as have been enumerated, nor any adequate means for their prevention; and that no remedy at present exists but sending persons charged with the perpetration of such enormities to be tried at the Admiralty Sessions in England.
>
> That in the recent conviction before stated the party found guilty not only departed from Port Jackson with impunity, but was not even held to bail to appear before any Sessions in England.
>
> That even the establishment of a tribunal with adequate power of punishment in New South Wales would not in all cases be effectual to remedy the evil, since it frequently happens that the vessels whose captains and crews have committed these atrocities do not return thither, and that some further measure seems therefore requisite for the protection of the islanders, and the prevention of the crimes by which the moral character of Great Britain is degraded by the conduct of her subjects trading in those seas.

196 Memorial of CMS to Bathurst, [1817] (*HRNZ* 1.420).
197 Marsden to Pratt, 22/1/1817.
198 See Memorial of CMS to Bathurst, [1817].

> That, in consequence of the want at present of any sufficient provision by colonial tribunals or otherwise for the prevention or the punishment of crimes committed in the islands of the South Seas, your memorialists submit that not only the lives of the missionaries and settlers in those islands are exposed to the most imminent hazard, but that all endeavours to extend the blessings of Christianity and civilization among the natives must thereby be in a great measure frustrated, and the reasonable hope of advantage which might be derived therefrom even to our own country is destroyed.

As Bathurst read the CMS memorial asking him 'to devise [...] measures for remedying the evils therein stated, and for preventing the recurrence of similar enormities',[199] the representatives of the other missionary society wrote a letter to Marsden. Just before his case against Philo Free was heard, and about nine months after Marsden appeared to 'despair even of life itself' (2 Corinthians 1:8),[200] Marsden received their expression of gratitude for all he had done to bring Martin to justice, and their assurance that they were agitating Government to bring reform.[201]

In May 1819, Pratt informed Marsden that he had sent his previous letter, expressing his disturbed state of mind prior to prosecuting Campbell, to Mr Wilberforce and Mr Fowell Buxton. These two 'friends', and Mr Bennett, were now sitting on a House of Commons Committee investigating Prisons, which 'has taken up the state of New South Wales, & is instituting a close enquiry into it'. Marsden's reputation is intact and, as Pratt assured him:

> Our gracious God, My Dear friend, while He tries your faith & patience, will vindicate the character of His Servants in His good time. You have able & determined friends here.[202]

His friends at LMS were likewise delighted at the proceedings in Parliament, Burder reporting that:

> our valuable friend Mr Wilberforce is about to bring into Parliament a Bill to prevent & give power to punish acts of oppression committed in

---

199 Memorial of CMS to Bathurst, [1817] (*HRNZ* 1.421).
200 See Marsden to Pratt, 26/9/1818: 'I was not surprised at men committing Suicide, if left to themselves for a moment, under such anguish as I experienced'.
201 Burder to Marsden, 5/6/1817.
202 Pratt to Marsden, 19/5/1819.

THE FAILURE OF THE PHILANTHROPIC SOCIETY

the South Sea Islands, and we have furnished him with the information you sent us respecting Captn Martin &c &c. We heartily wish him success.[203]

In the April following, CMS reported more good news. After returning to England in July 1819,[204] David Allan had now reinforced Marsden's accounts in person, and:

> This [...] is, we believe, now so well understood in this Country, and in that quarter where a right impression is of the greatest importance, that, we apprehend, those causes which have occasioned you so much disquietude will soon cease to operate.

CMS was hopeful that this relief for Marsden might induce him:

> to remain at a Post, which opens so wide a prospect of usefulness, and where your experience and information may, with so much advantage, be brought to bear on the interests of the Gospel.[205]

But after his desperately low point in January 1817,[206] Marsden had already turned the corner. Even by mid 1819 when reporting his joy at John Butler's arrival for New Zealand: 'I hope now the Bitterness of Death is past. [...] I maintain my Post. I am not driven from the field'.[207] Despite Philo Free's slander, the mission hadn't failed, and neither had Marsden.

---

203 Burder to Marsden, 2/6/1819. Wilberforce had personal experience of a very similar case in 1792, in the acquittal of Captain Kimber for flogging a 15 year old African girl to death; See Metaxis, *Amazing Grace*, 156.
204 Allan sailed on the *Surry* in July 1819; Dowd, 'Allan, David (1780–1852)'. After returning in 1829, he lived out his days in Sydney, dying in 1852.
205 Bickersteth & Pratt to Marsden, 5/4/1820. Marsden never lost the support of either LMS or CMS, and he was something of a missionary hero amongst their ranks. See Second Report of the Leicester & Lancashire Association of CMS, January 1816; *Missionary Register 1816*, 11; G. Burder (for LMS directors) to S. Marsden, April 1818 (pp72-75); Marsden to Pratt, 26/9/1818; The Missionary Society moved a vote of thanks to Marsden at their anniversary meeting in 1819. See J.B. Marsden, *The Life of Rev. Samuel Marsden*, 101–102. His mentor, Charles Simeon, also sent words of encouragement, (p.104).
206 Recall his reflections on being near suicidal at that time; Marsden to Pratt, 26/9/1818.
207 Marsden to Pratt, 12/7/1819.

4. The Success behind the Failure

The 'openings of Providence'[208] are often difficult to discern, even by those who believe in God's constant involvement in human affairs, both good and evil—let alone by the sceptic. But just as God worked good for Israel out of the evil plans of Joseph's brothers (see Genesis 50:20), or, even more significantly, just as he worked good for the whole world out of the evil destruction of his Messiah through crucifixion (Acts 2:23), the Lord who launched the mission to the nations was still working through British evils in the South Seas to bring about his good. Despite Marsden's disappointments at the apparent impotence of British law, he knew that the gospel ultimately needed no protection. Even in the disaster that caused the Philanthropic Society to crumble on its feet of human clay, the goodness of divine Providence had found another opening. After its collapse in October, Marsden's earlier words in March sound strangely prophetic:

> I see the footsteps of Divine Providence strongly marked in many circumstances, that have happened in these parts of the world: all tending to make way for the blessing of the Gospel. The attention of those in authority would not have been awakened to the sufferings of the Natives of the South Sea Islands, unless some great crimes had been committed. Those crimes will produce the effect.[209]

When Goodenough sailed off, at least according to Gill, the islanders wished for no further contact with 'the Kookes', having concluded 'the whites were far wickeder than they'.[210] However, just one week later, on 25 August, Richard Siddons' *Campbell Macquarie* arrived and left, following the same rumour that launched the Rarotongan Sandalwood Company in the first place, but without the knowledge of its failure. Some six weeks later, they were similarly glad to see the last of William Campbell in the Sandalwood Company's second vessel, the *Governor*

---

208 Falloon, '"Openings of Providence"'. Cf. Marsden's words just prior to the launch of the New Zealand mission: 'The Divine Governor will, in his gracious providence, order all things well. Great objects are seldom obtained without great sacrifices and many difficulties', Marsden to Pratt, 20/9/1814 (*Missionary Register 1815*, 197).
209 Marsden to Pratt, 15/3/1814 (Extract: *Missionary Register 1814*, 461).
210 Gill, *Gems*, 9.

Macquarie, who also left quickly to find a profitable cargo elsewhere.[211] Even if they landed in Ngatangiia, it is unlikely that either man heard anything of the affray from the now suspicious locals—especially now the white men somewhere held hostage several of their own. And so, after the *Cumberland*, Rarotonga was 'soon forgotten by the outside world'.[212] But it was not forgotten by Providence.

When the next vessel arrived in 1823, LMS Missionary, John Williams, dropped off Tahitian convert Papeiha [Papehia], whose preaching began the rapid and prodigious conversion of Rarotonga for which he is still remembered.[213] But the story behind the story is not so often told: the seeds of this success were sown nine years earlier during the visit of the *Cumberland*.[214]

As already noted, after leaving Sydney, the *Cumberland* picked up Tupe, Veretini, and a New Zealand woman in the Bay of Islands, with Sydney as their ultimate destination. Probably at this point in the journey, Te Are and Tomi, and Tavai and Tumai, also joined the vessel—Tahitians, who knew of the gospel of Christ and the great impact it had had in their islands. After arriving on Rarotonga, while the white men cut their *nono*, these islanders sowed the seeds for a different harvest. As Maretu reported the island memory:

> The knowledge that was learned from that ship, actually from Veretini and Teara [Te Ara], was of a new god called Tiova [Jehovah] and Tititarai [Jesus Christ], who was almighty in the heavens as well as on the earth.[215]

Joined by one of the Tahitian women,[216] these islanders spoke about the gospel, probably during the first week, while staying on the *koutu* of the

---

211 She left Sydney on 28 August under the guise of proceeding 'for Otaheite and the neighbouring islands', also called at Rarotonga to find no sandalwood before sailing elsewhere for a cargo, even managing to recover some integrity by fulfilling her promise to drop off some school supplies for the Tahitian mission schools. Campbell took the *Governor Macquarie* to the Marquesas, where he obtained 50 tons of sandalwood, as well as some metal salvaged from wrecks; SG 3/9/1814; SG 25/2/1815.
212 Maude & Crocombe, 'Rarotongan Sandalwood', 50.
213 Despite being informed by the *Gazette* report of 22/10/1814, as reprinted in the *Naval Chronicle for 1816*, Charles Pitman referred to the 'skirmish about seven years before the introduction of the Gospel into this land', Pitman to Ellis, 10/8/1839. Evidently the oral memory dated the latter to the arrival of Papeiha on Aitutaki in 1821, when he met the Rarotongan exiles, who later accompanied him in his mission.
214 Maude & Crocombe, 'Rarotongan Sandalwood', 52–53.
215 Maretu, *Cannibals*, 42 [2].
216 Maude & Crocombe, 'Rarotongan Sandalwood', 53, citing Maretu , 'On Rarotongan history', 1. The same woman was mentioned by Williams, *A Narrative*, 28.

Makea Ariki Tinirau and Ke'u (Karika). Although he may be confusing these Makea with their successor (Makea Pori), who was known to the missionaries as a key player in Rarotongan Christianity, in 1838 Williams claims that the testimony of this woman:

> excited so much interest, that the king, Makea, called one of his children "Tehovah" (Jehovah), and another "Teeteetry" (Jesus Christ). An uncle of the king, whom we hope is at this time a truly good man, erected an altar to Jehovah and Jesus Christ, and to it persons afflicted with all manner of diseases were brought to be healed; and so great was the reputation which this *marae* obtained, that the power of Jehovah and Jesus Christ became great in the estimation of the people.[217]

However, the tragic events of the final day were even more helpful to the later missionary cause. As the *Cumberland* departed, Tapaeru Ariki, the daughter of the warrior Rupe, was taken by Goodenough—perhaps intended as a substituted for the murdered Ann Butcher. And—speculatively—perhaps replacing Wentworth's New Zealand consort,[218] Mata Kavaau was also taken on board.[219]

If the *Cumberland* had arrived in Sydney with two abducted Rarotongan women on board, Goodenough would be liable to prosecution under Macquarie's proclamation. The subsequent inquiry would have also flushed out the further atrocities committed on the island. This accounts for Tapairu and Mata Kavaau being dropped off as the ship passed Aitutaki (264 km to the North) two days later[220]—a further instance of the unspoken European maxim 'if they're an islander, any island will do', but now also forbidden by Macquarie's proclamation. On the island they came across two men, Tairi and Teiro, who had come from Rarotonga on a canoe.[221] This little group of exiles were still

---

217 Williams, *Journal*, 28.
218 For this speculation, see Bolt, 'What Really Happened on Rarotonga in 1814'.
219 In Maretu, *Cannibals*, 46 n.49, Crocombe notes that William Gill, William Wyatt Gill, and Itio say that the women were abducted.
220 Maretu, *Cannibals*, 46 [9]; Tepaeru, Grave Plaque; Two days later: Gill, *Gems*, 21. Island women would have attracted attention (see the case of Dillon, n.32), and the abduction would have been discovered. Perhaps it was felt that nobody would have noticed another South Seas sailor amongst the crew. The Tahitian women could be accounted for, presumably, having been voluntarily put on by Ruatara's people.
221 Maude & Crocombe, 'Rarotongan Sandalwood', 45 n.50, with Maretu, 'On Rarotongan History', 39; Tepaeru, 'Grave Plaque': 'Tepaeru on Aitutaki met up with Tairi and Te Iro from Ngatangiia and their wives and another woman, who had drifted to the island some years before, and converted to Christianity'.

there in 1821 to hear Tahitian convert Papeiha, when LMS placed him on Aitutiki to introduce Christianity to the Cook Islands.[222] By the time LMS missionary John Williams called at Aitutaki in 1823, they had been converted and wanted to share the gospel with their homeland. Determined to find their island, after doing so Williams became known as the European discoverer of the island—as he even thought himself.[223] When Williams dropped Papeiha off to begin his gospel work, Tapaeru Ariki, Mata Kavaau, Tairi and Teiro all returned to Rarotonga and without them Papeiha would not have had such success. Because of her family links to Makea Karika, Tapaeru protected him in the early days, enabling the success of his mission.[224] Tairi and Teiro also supported him in his work, preaching the gospel backed up by the accounts of conversions on Aitutaki.[225]

Such was the success that by 1827 LMS missionary John Williams—even if he ignored the indigenous missionaries—, wrote to the *Sydney Gazette*:

> Perhaps you recollect a vessel leaving your colony 14 or 15 years ago, for an Island called Rarotonga, in quest of sandal wood. There were gentlemen on board, by the names of Goodenough, Wentworth, &c. (I do not know the vessel's name, or I should not mention those of the gentlemen) some of the crew were murdered, and I believe eaten there. It is a beautiful Island, and very populous. Now will you believe us, Mr.Editor, we have had the temerity to attack this stronghold of cannibalism and idolatry, and by means of one Christian native who went on shore, at the hazard of his life, without a single particle of property, or a change of raiment, and a second whom we sent about six months after, a mighty conquest has been obtained; for, in the short space of 18 months, every idolator is brought to see the folly of his superstitious fears, and cast his paltry idols from him with contempt [...][226]

---

222 Maretu, *Cannibals*, 46, n.49. Cf. Rupe, 'The Voyages', 151: 'the time of the "Word of God" in Aitutaki, from the year 1821 [...]'.
223 Maude & Crocombe, 'Rarotongan Sandalwood', 52.
224 Williams, *Journal*, 26–27. For her genealogy, see Figure 11.
225 Maude & Crocombe, 'Rarotongan Sandalwood', 53, with Terei & Savage, *Tuatua Taito*, 50.
226 *SG* 22/3/1827. Note that Williams ignores the role of the Rarotongans. Cf the concluding paragraph of Maude & Crocombe, 'Rarotongan Sandalwood', 53, citing Gill, *Gems*, 24: 'Indeed it seems unlikely that the gospel could have been introduced into Rarotonga without bloodshed had it not been for the visit of the *Cumberland* nine years before'.

As Philo Free, J.T. Campbell attacked Marsden and the South Seas missions overtly because the Philanthropic Society had failed, misrepresenting motives and implying questionable practice, the characters of both were brought into disrepute. As a member of the Society and a close insider to events, he knew the real story, especially if he was also an insider to the cover-up. But despite external appearances, the Philanthropic Society in both its formation and its failure, played its part in bringing about better things for the peoples of the South Pacific.

CHAPTER 8

A FRIENDSHIP REVEALED

The Marsden & Stokes Family Correspondence

Jane M. Tooher

Introduction to the Letters: Personal but Cautious

Samuel Marsden often polarizes historians. One result of this is that two readers, reading two accounts of Marsden by two different authors, may be left with quite different images of the man. This is where primary documents can help, and particularly personal letters between family members and friends. Such personal correspondence often reveals a deeper picture of someone's true character as they may feel free to be more themselves. They may feel freer to be honest about the good things that are happening in their life, as well as be frank about the disappointments, struggles, and sufferings they're facing.

Although this is true to a certain extent with Marsden's letters, he was guarded to a degree as these letters were mostly not private as we would understand that term today. Although written from one individual and addressed to another, the letters may well have been read by others, e.g. family members and missionary societies. Added to this was Marsden's cautiousness about his letters falling into the wrong hands:[1]

> At this remote distance it is not always prudent for me to state by letter what I wish you to know; from the peculiar circumstances I am placed under. Letters have sometimes miscarried, and I have known mine to

---

1 Marsden was aware that his private letters were sometimes stolen (No. 13).

fall into the hand of our enemy. On this account it requires much caution to avoid danger from this quarter.²

This paper will look at the 33 extant letters from the Marsden family to the Stokes family, a correspondence that lasted thirty years (see Figure 13).³

> The [...] series of letters covers the [...] span of almost thirty years, and includes the whole of the administrations of Governors Hunter, King, Bligh, Macquarie and Brisbane. Historically, their value is twofold. First, they throw light on certain important phases of Australian history then in the making; second, they reveal, as perhaps no other extant material does, the texture of Marsden's intellectual and moral make-up, with sidelights on the character and doings of other contemporary notables.⁴

Most of the letters were written by Samuel Marsden to Mary Stokes,⁵ however, there are also letters to Mary from Samuel's wife Elizabeth (Eliza), and from the Marsden's daughter Ann (who married Thomas Hassall). There are also letters from Samuel Marsden to John Stokes, Mary's husband.⁶ Other family members from both families are mentioned at different times in the letters. What is unclear is the exact nature of their connection. As one commentator has written: 'Neither Samuel Marsden's biographer nor the compiler of the family's letters explains the nature of the relationship which existed between the two families'.⁷ But what we do know is that the Stokes associated with known evangelicals in England since the Marsden's mention some of them in their letters, e.g. Miss Amey.⁸

---

2   Marsden to Pratt, 13/7/1819.
3   The 33 extant letters between the two families are published in: Mackaness, *Some Private Correspondence of the Rev. Samuel Marsden and Family, 1794–1824*. When each letter is quoted or referenced in this paper, it will be footnoted simply as 'No. 1'. etc., and cited as per Mackaness' transcription.
4   Mackaness, 'Introduction'.
5   Little is known of Mary Stokes, but we do know that she was married (and had children) from various letters including No. 4, when Marsden writes to her, 'As you are married I may mention this to you without risk of being laughed at'.
6   Mary Stokes place of residence is initially 'No. 8 Goldsmith Street, Cheapside, and later at 39 Gutter Lane, Cheapside. Some letters are directed to Mr. John Stokes, Senior, at 33 Gutter Lane', Mackaness, 'Introduction'.
7   Bremer, 'Domestic Disclosures', 87.
8   Margaret Amey was also known to others who were 'intimately involved in the propagation of the gospel to New South Wales'. E.g. she was a witness at Richard Johnson's wedding in 1786. See Amelia Schwarze's unpublished paper 'Goff and Amey: An Evangelical Bureau in the City of London'. Sharp, *The World, the Flesh & the Devil*, 279.

The letters were not sent by regular post, but were entrusted to people they knew, who were travelling on ships, e.g. Charles Grimes[9] and Mr. Grant.[10] There seems to be no evidence that these letters revealed more personal details than any other letters, in fact No. 19, delivered by Mr. Grant, is chiefly concerned with agricultural matters.

By looking at these letters we hope to:

(i) Gain a fuller picture of Samuel Marsden's character leading up to the publication of the Philo Free letter;
(ii) Gain an insight into some of the women in his life;
(iii) Note the importance of Christian friendship; &
(iv) See if the letters shed any light on the situation of the day leading up to the Philo Free controversy.

This will be done by looking at:

1. The Letters Before Philo Free (1794–1816);
2. The Letters After Philo Free (1817–1824).

1. The Letters Before Philo Free (1794–1816)

1.1 Early signs of trouble

Samuel and Eliza Marsden sailed from London on July 1, 1793 and arrived in Port Jackson on March 10, 1794, with their baby Ann who was born onboard. Five months later Marsden wrote to Mary Stokes of Cheapside, and this first letter reveals a taste of things that were to come for him.

> You will have heard of Mr. Johnson's quarrel with the present Lieut. Govr. [Grose], and how uncomfortably we are situated in point of religion. Mr. John. informs me that things in that respect were never anything like as bad as present. There is so little attention paid even to mere morality.[11]

But this first letter also reveals much about Marsden's relationship with God, including his desire to be dependent on God and his concern for

---

9 Mr. Grimes delivered No. 14.
10 Mr. Grant delivered No. 19.
11 No.1.

evangelism.¹² We know because of what is written in the letters that Mary Stokes shared a similar worldview to Marsden.¹³

> We have much to bless the Lord for who conducted us safe through the mighty waters [...]. I wish I had a greater sense of the Divine mercies and were more humbly dependent upon the goodness of Providence and Grace. [...] I bless God my congregation is constantly increasing, and two or three have begun to enquire what they must do to be saved. [...] Things are better on the whole than I expected to find them among such abandoned people. I am not surprised to see them cast such contempt upon God and Religion knowing the human heart to be so full of enmity to Christ and his Gospel. [...] All the higher ranks are lost to God and Religion, and you may so form an idea of the characters of the lower orders.¹⁴

This first letter is in many ways optimistic and Marsden is enjoying a better relationship with Grose than Johnson is. Yet his comment about the 'higher ranks' being lost recurs again in later letters and begins to set the tone for the Philo Free controversy years later.¹⁵ By 1795, Marsden speaks frankly of his discouragement, and he wonders how the great preachers of England would feel if they preached for six months and no-one enquired about being saved. Added to this is the fact that the Government has still not given him a place in which to perform public worship.¹⁶

Given this discouragement, it is of little surprise that letters from Christian friends in England were much appreciated.

> We feel ourselves greatly indebted to you for your kind remembrance of us in this distant port. News from Old England come from whom it may is welcome and much more if it comes from a lover of Jesus. We have many things to struggle with here which have a natural tendency to deaden our affections and stupify our souls.¹⁷

Marsden's burdens were not confined to those of a spiritual nature, but God is clearly the reason why he is in NSW.

---

12 God's sovereignty and evangelism are consistent themes across the 30 year span of the letters.
13 E.g. No. 8.
14 No. 1.
15 E.g. No. 4., No. 8.
16 No. 4. Eliza also mentions this in No. 5.
17 No. 6.

> I have much to occupy my time and a great variety of duties to perform. I am a Gardener a Farmer a Magistrate & Minister so that when one duty does not call me another always does. [...] Now is our Harvest-time. Yesterday I was in the field assisting in getting my wheat. To-day I have been sitting in the civil court hearing the complaints of the People. To-morrow if well must ascend the pulpit and preach to my people. In this manner I chiefly spend my time. It may appear strange but it is necessary situated as we are. [...] It is my opinion that God will ere long visit New South Wales with his heavenly grace. Out of these stones he will raise up children unto Abraham.[18]

Marsden as gardener and farmer is seen throughout his letters,[19] and his agrarian interest seems part of his friendship particularly with John Stokes,[20] though it is also shared with other members of the Stokes family. We see Marsden's delight that in 1795 he was able to write to John that the Colony was now independent of other countries for dry provisions.[21] And in a letter to Mary he writes, 'I beg my kindest respects to Mr. Stokes. Inform him our crops are immensely great—we have the greatest abundance of wheat now. [...] Would be very thankful if you could by any means send me out a few Hop-cuttings'.[22] The friendship between the two families included seemingly ordinary things such as giving each other seeds or asking for seeds.[23] Yet this 'ordinary' thing highlights the uniqueness of Marsden's ministry and location—trialing new plants to help feed a colony, and exotic seeds from a faraway land for those back in England.

1.2 Eliza: A wife fit for Samuel

In the second letter we begin to get to know Eliza, as she writes to Mary Stokes.

> I have one companion at Parramatta the commanding officer['s] wife[24] [...] a very pleasant agreeable Lady [...] At Sydney there are several Ladies [...] Upon the whole my situation is far more comfortable than I

---

18 No. 6.
19 E.g. Nos. 12, 14, 18, 19, 20, 22, 23. He recognizes that it is God that causes the land to be so plentiful, e.g. No. 6.
20 E.g. No. 10.
21 No. 3.
22 No. 6.
23 E.g. Nos. 1, 6, 8.
24 Elizabeth Paterson, wife of Captain William Paterson.

expected to find. I experience a great loss of Religious Society. Our general conversation in company is very different from what I have been accustomed to in England. It all turns upon worldly affairs. Religion is seldom a subject of conversation excepting to ridicule its doctrines or professions, never to edify one another. There appears humanly speaking little prospect of doing good—however I do not despair for the work is not man's but the Lord's. I trust we are not forgotten at a Throne of Grace by the faithful in England. The Lord had some grand design in sending his gospel to this dark benighted part of the world and therefore this consideration should resign us to his Dispensations who worketh all things according to the Counsel of [_____]²⁵.[26]

This letter demonstrates that Marsden chose an intelligent, articulate wife who is grieving the loss of Christian conversation and fellowship she once experienced to be the norm back in England, but a woman nonetheless who has a grasp on God's sovereignty for her life and situation and for the people of the colony. Eliza also reveals that she gave birth on the ship from London. In her description there is no fuss, drama, nor self-pity, rather she just states it as fact, but more significantly, Eliza recognises God's preservation of her and her baby through it all.

> You would hear from Miss Amey that I got a daughter off the South Cape of New Holland. The Lord preserved us both in a wonderful manner and by good nursing of Mrs. Johnson, we both of us soon recovered the fatigues of a storm.[27]

Considering some of the difficulties that would later come Marsden's way, it was fortunate that he married a wife who seems so strong and resilient.[28] His happiness in her comes out in different letters, e.g. 'I have great reason to be thankful that I am happy in my own family; I believe few more so. [...] I should have been wretched and miserable

---

25 Words obscured by seal.
26 No. 2.
27 No. 2.
28 Over the course of the letters Eliza shows her resilience in a number of ways including: living for such a long time in the early days of the penal colony; enduring long absences of her children being away in England for their education; enduring long absences at times when her husband was away; having people stay in their home for long periods of time; the death of two of her children; and living with the effects of a stroke. Her physical fitness and stamina is demonstrated in the fact that Eliza was an excellent horsewoman, riding for both amusement and exercise, well able to ride from Parramatta to Sydney (about 20 miles) and back in one day. No. 14.

here without a wife, now I am happy and comfortable'.[29] Mary seems to have requested in her writings to Marsden, and also in at least one letter to Mr. Johnson, that Marsden take care of Eliza and be kind to her, for he reassures her several times that he is doing so.[30]

Eliza sees Mary as a kind friend[31] and writes openly of her longing for conversations with like-minded friends. She misses this type of friendship. Although perhaps simply noting the limitations of letter writing compared to the depths one can have in a conversation, like her husband she may well be cautious about what she writes:

> I long for an opportunity of conversing with you face to face. This would enable me to open my mind more fully than I can do now with paper and ink but whether I shall ever be indulged with that privilege or no is still in the dark womb of Providence. [...] I feel as if I had once conversed with friends, united in love by the same spirit—some faint remembrance of those pleasures still remain and I cannot but flatter myself with some distant hope that it will be again with me as in months past. Had we only a few pious friends to pass away an hour with it would render this colony more tolerable.[32]

One thing disturbing for the modern reader about Eliza is how she writes, what appears so casually and briefly, about an Aboriginal boy.

> I have also a little Native Boy who takes up part of my attention. He is about six years old, and now begins to read English and wait at table and I hope at some future period he may be an useful member of society. He has no inclination to go among the natives and has quite forgot their manners.[33]

This Aboriginal boy is not mentioned in further correspondence to the Stokes but he is mentioned in other letters.[34]

Eliza is concerned that the children (at this stage her daughter Ann and the Johnson's daughter Milbah) don't have the education and good society in NSW that they would in England. Despite her only being 5 ½ years of age, the plan was for Ann to go to England for her schooling,

---

29 No. 4.
30 E.g. Nos. 4, 6.
31 No. 7.
32 No. 5.
33 No. 5.
34 For further details, Bremer 'Domestic Disclosures'; Sharp, *The World, the Flesh & the Devil*, 140–1.

travelling with LMS missionaries, Mr. and Mrs. Cover.[35] In a later letter, Marsden revealed the difficulty of this decision: 'Her mother did not wish to part with her, but I prevailed at length'.[36]

Bremer and Heney seem to suggest Eliza is not an interesting person because of the topics she limits herself to.[37] Yet these 'topics'—religion, family, and the home, are in fact substantial. They are, and have always been, key foundations to any stable society and therefore should not be underestimated. These ordinary, feminine things Eliza writes about are not trivial or uninteresting. Added to this is the way Eliza speaks about them, and this reveals for us part of her character and what life was like in early colonial NSW. As mentioned earlier, Marsden acknowledges that he doesn't know how he would have coped in the colony if he wasn't married.[38] What Eliza gave to her husband in terms of love, support, companionship, friendship, theological like-mindedness, children, and managing a household, was indeed extremely substantial,[39] enabling a so-called (by some accounts) more interesting figure than herself to achieve what he achieved, and to be the man he was in terms of character. So much so, that whatever Samuel bequeathed to Australasian heritage should be seen, more accurately, as the fruit of this ministry partnership.

Even the more supposedly trivial topics, if noted rather than dismissed, are of historical interest. Fashion, for example, comes up occasionally in the letters. When Eliza receives a new bonnet and ribbons from England, she commented, 'We are surprised to see the alteration in the fashion'.[40] As a woman who is so isolated, in a situation with very few other women, this gift from a kind friend brought her some joy, and most likely helped remind her of her femininity, which is good and right and far from inconsequential. Eliza's interest in the bonnet and ribbons in no way downplays her over-riding concern

---

35 No. 7.
36 No. 10.
37 Bremer comments: 'Historian Helen Heney decides that of the early colony's matrons, Eliza is one of the least interesting, for her "strong religious views" confined her to "sober domestic interests". Reading Eliza's letters to Mrs. Stokes does little to undermine Heney's assessment: her epistolary self-presentation is restricted to what she regards as proper feminine topics: matters of religion, family, and the home'; Bremer, 'Domestic Disclosures', 79.
38 No. 4.
39 What Eliza gave Samuel is not limited to this list.
40 No. 7.

for more 'weighty' matters. Eliza's recent detractors would do well to heed alternative views of femininity expressed even amongst their own contemporaries, such as the comment by Sofia Coppola: 'You're considered superficial and silly if you are interested in fashion, but I think you can be substantial and still be interested in frivolity'.[41]

Although Eliza conformed to gender stereotypes in many ways, she should not be despised for being a woman of her times. But, more, this is not a negative thing and she should be applauded for her contribution. She spent her time wisely—investing in people and on good and worthwhile things. Like other women who lived in early Colonial NSW, she was in many ways a pioneer.

1.3 Fightings without and fears within

By February 1800 Marsden writes that things are worse than ever spiritually, conveying a clear sense of the isolation and hardships that those ministering in the colony endured.

> You will wish to hear how the Kingdom of our lord succeeds among us. I am sorry to say appearances are worse than ever. [...] I long to quit the Colony and retire from such scenes of ungodliness and wrong. Our friends can form little more idea of our situation in the Country than they can of the invisible regions. I have made application to Government to return. Whether I shall obtain permission or no I know not. [...] Should any material change take place so as to afford any prospect of real good to this Colony I might be induced to remain longer. [...] I think it probable Mr. Johnson will return soon it is his present determination to do so. We may say on our departure from this country we have been fairly hunted out of the settlement. Our life is one continued scene of contention and opposition where iniquity abounds so much and our civil connexion with the worst of men render our souls dry and barren.
>
> We feel so little of that real vital spiritual life which is so essential to the happiness and progress of the real Christian. To be cut off from all the society and conversation of the righteous and to hold a situation in the state that calls you forth to act continually with wicked men in power is painful and distressing. We are not situated in this country like clergymen in England who have only to attend to their studies & their flocks. Many other unpleasant duties devolve upon me. In the midst of

---

41 Fraser, 'Kirsten Dunst: Teen Queen'.

> all my only consolation is the Lord knows how I am situated and foreknew it. [...] I am busy building a Church at Parramatta. Shall be happy to see it completed. I think it would never be done if I was to leave the settlement. I can only say it is my present intent and wish to quit the colony yet my times are in the Lords hands, it will be enough if I am found faithful when my work comes to be done. The building on an Orphan House is another object which lies near my heart.[42]

The next two letters we have are written 18 months later, one by Marsden and the other by Eliza, both dated the same day, 22 August 1801. Have things changed for Marsden?

> The Orphan home been open for 30 girls and will be ready for 30 more in a short time. Mr. Marsden has sent the proceeding home and sermon [sic.] he preached the first Sunday the children attended. The governor gives it every support. Mr. King and Mr. Paterson attends every day that it may be properly managed.[43]

With the joy of the Orphan home being opened, Eliza also mentions two things that were difficult. Firstly, that she has great regret in the Johnsons leaving and that their kind attention to her will always endear them to her.[44] Secondly, after previous letters telling of plentiful physical food, it is clear from this letter they are now experiencing quite the opposite.

> The prospect before us is rather unpleasant. We are on short allowance of meat and grain from the public store and it wants three months to the harvest. Many of the inhabitants have not a grain of wheat or corn in their possession nor is it to be purchased. [...] Mr. Palmer had a great loss for himself and the Colony, he had a large stack of wheat calculated at a thousand bushels burnt.[45]

Interestingly in Eliza's comment about the Governor trying to source some pork, she notes it should be an advantage to the missionaries at Otaheite.

> The Governor has sent the "Porpoise" to Otaheite and the other Islands to see if they can get Pork for us. The Governor seems desirous for

---

42 No. 8.
43 No. 9.
44 No. 9.
45 No. 9.

A FRIENDSHIP REVEALED

establishing communication between Port Jackson and Otaheite. This might prove a great advantage to the poor Missionaries and be a great protection to them should a ship constantly visit them from this colony they would be able to keep a constant correspondence with their friends in England.[46]

In this letter there is a mix of good and bad news, and it is clear that Eliza appreciates very much receiving letters from Mary and other friends:

it gives me the greatest pleasure to hear from you or from our friends and connexions, you don't know the happiness it gives me not only for the moment, when I am alone and dull I amuse myself with reading my friends letters and find myself refreshed.[47]

In Marsden's letter, he also mentions the Johnsons and hopes that the Stokes have received a visit from them, but importantly he also says how things have changed since their departure:

From them you will learn the exact state of this Colony and what a miserable place it is in a moral and religious sense. Since my colleagues departure it is quite changed. [...] Our present Governor has almost put a total stop to the introduction of spirits into the Colony. [...] We have a good prospect at present of a plentiful harvest next Season but before then the sufferings of many will be very great. [...] The school is now opened and more than 30 girls received. I spent the last evening with them for the first time and made a beginning to instruct them in the principles of Christianity, sang a hymn and went to prayers with them.

New South Wales while I was performing this duty appeared more like a Christian Country than it had ever done since I first entered it.

[...] There are still great differences amongst our leading men which renders the situation of those would who would be quiet far from pleasant. [...] This is a very ungracious soil for the growth of Piety. The Lord knows best where to place me.[48]

The suffering that the Marsden's underwent become very personal in Eliza's next letter:

You will have no doubt heard what an affliction we have been visited

46 No. 9.
47 No. 9.
48 No. 10.

> with in the melancholy death of our dear little boy. [...] I am conscious that his was a happy transition yet hear Madam picture to yourself my feelings to have him in health and spirits and the next moment to behold him in the arms of Death. I was wonderfully supported and had one consolation which the world cannot give neither take away. He who is faithful has promised when thou passed through the waters I will be with thee and through the rivers they shall not overflow thee. God is a refuge & strength, a very present help in time of need. This is the first time I have taken up my pen to write to England since I lost him though it is now fifteen months. I am afraid I am very sinful. I often think could I know his little thoughts he would reprove me for wishing him back in this troublesome world, but his removal has stirred me up to be more earnest in Divine things, and though he cannot come to me I may meet him in that place, where sin & sorrow and sighing are fore ever [sic] done away.[49]

The next letter has the great news of the church being consecrated at Parramatta. But there is still no place for public worship in Sydney and Marsden fears there will be none for a long time. What is more shocking for Marsden is that the Government has allowed a Irish prisoner who was a Roman Catholic priest (James Dixon), to conduct Catholic services. Since there is still no replacement for Johnson, Marsden preaches at both Parramatta and Sydney every Sabbath.[50]

A later letter reveals Marsden has heard sad news from England with the deaths of Mrs. Goff and Milbah Johnson. The letter itemises difficulties Marsden continues to face, and reveals why his private letters were not always so private:

> Government seems not to pay much attention to religion here, as they send me no assistance. My duty is very hard, the Colony is become very extensive now, and a great number of people in it, with only myself as a Minister. Should any come, I hope he will be a pious man and hearty in the cause of God. [...] My private letters are sometimes stolen, and if not stolen, opened by some person unknown. The greatest rogues in the world come and go from this Colony.[51]

After expressing much longing in his letters to go back to England,

---

49 No. 11.
50 No. 12.
51 No. 13.

Governor Bligh allowed Marsden a trip in 1807.[52] The first letter Marsden writes on their arrival he tells of Eliza giving birth to a girl in Hull. The letter also shows Marsden's awareness of his own sin and his desire to have a greater esteem for the Saviour of the world.[53] One year later they are aboard the "Ann" and he writes of their time in Rio.[54] Five months later we find they are safely back in NSW.[55] Little did they realise that they were about to enter the most difficult decade of their ministry.

In 1811 Elizabeth had a stroke while giving birth and was left permanently disabled. In November 1812 Marsden grieved:

> This is a very heavy trial and loss to me. None knew the value of such a companion as she has been to me. I am thankful that she is spared and is something better. She is able to walk about a little, and can make herself understood, and manage the family to a certain extent. One hand is in measure useless and she is very lame, complains frequently of pains in her head. [...] Providence is particularly kind to us and always has been—the Lord will provide. I have no cause to complain of the Divine Goodness.[56]

Alongside the sadness of his wife's stroke, Marsden can share some good news about the colony.

> We have now cleared the Colony of all the catholic priests[,] have schools established in almost every district so that the rising generation will be brought up in the principles of the Protestant religion. We have 5 pious schoolmasters and with my two colleagues I hope something will be done.[57]

Having lost movement in her right arm, Eliza was unable to write and so she gets Ann to write to Mary instead. Ann mentions some missionaries and that sadly two of them died soon after their arrival in Otaheite, and that Mrs. Henry has since died:

---

52 See Mackaness, *Some Private Correspondence*, footnote 24.
53 No. 16.
54 No. 17.
55 No. 18.
56 No. 20.
57 No. 20. The five school teachers were: Thomas Bowden (Sydney), Isaac Nelson (Liverpool), John Eyre (Parramatta), Matthew Hughes (Windsor), I. Brown (Kissing Point). *NSW Almanac 1813*, 30. Marsden's clerical colleagues were Revs. William Cowper in Sydney and Robert Cartwright at Windsor.

> My Mama regrets her death very much and is afraid it will be severely felt as she was of a true missionary spirit. Mr. Henry came to Port Jackson for another wife, and was married last week: he brings the welcome tidings that Pomare the King of Otaheite & some of his subjects have embraced Christianity.[58]

In the postscript to this letter there is a request for Mrs. J. to send out different articles of ladies' dress. One week later another letter is written, but this time by Marsden. Again there is a request from Eliza for ribbons and sewing silk with Marsden confidently writing, 'You will know what she will want'.[59] The tone of the letter is extremely positive.

> I am happy to say Mrs. M is much recovered [...] The Governor is very attentive to the Sabbath day and is a very moral man. A very good understanding has existed between him & me for some time past, [...] I have applied for three more Clergymen and some Schoolmasters. Should you know of any that will answer me, will you communicate their names to Mr. Wilberforce. I have written to him on the subject. [...] You will hear that King Pomare has embraced Christianity. The New Zealand chief who lived with me has at lengths got to his native land. I have heard the most flattering accounts of him and trust that he will open the way for the introduction of the Gospel into that Island. God had very important designs in view when he induced the British Government to establish a colony here.[60]

The positive tone continues in the next letter to John Stokes. Marsden writes descriptions of rich agriculture, potential for trade, and that a road is being built over the Mountains. They are continuing to ensure there are good schools in all the districts, and that he is putting a roof on the Female Orphan House at Parramatta that will house about 200 girls.[61]

In June 1815 Marsden sends his condolences to Mary upon hearing of the death of her husband, John, and included some reflections from his recent trip to New Zealand. He assumes Mary will hear a fuller version as he has given an account to the Church Missionary Society. What Marsden does include is fascinating considering 6 years earlier

---

58 No. 21.
59 No. 22. Mrs. J. is probably Mrs Mary Johnson, wife of the first Chaplain to NSW, Rev. Richard Johnson.
60 No. 22.
61 No. 23.

the *Boyd* was seized and burnt by Māori who killed about 60 people, with only 4 people being spared.[62]

> I sat down and conversed with these people as a man with his friend and then laid down amongst them and slept in safety. When I viewed the men whom I knew had massacred, and afterwards eat our people particularly in the case of the *Boyd*, I cannot express what my feelings were, how dreadfully had been debased the human mind, where men were intelligent, kind, and friendly and shewed a readiness to do every thing that was proper and yet could be guilty of a crime so repugnant to the feelings of nature.
>
> Amongst heathen Nations we may see more into the dreadful nature of sin, than in civilized nations. But are we better than they—In no wise—Though we may not be Cannibals we may be Murderers, and we are unbelievers and guilty of all other crimes. I am persuaded [sic] the inhabitants of New Zealand will become a great and powerful nation when once the Light of Divine Revelation begins to dawn upon them.[63]

Although Marsden seems hopeful about the Māori people turning to Christ, his negative feelings about NSW return.

> My soul has been so vexed with the wickedness of some in this Colony that I have been strongly tempted to leave it altogether. I have wished myself in any corner of the world only let me get from this present Society. I have spoken of it several times lately to Mrs. M. and told her I wished her to be off. Her answer is 'What will New Zealand do? What will the missionaries at Olaketa do?' My burden is sometimes greater than I can bear. We have need of patience in this miserable world, and to look for our reward in the next—we are sure not to have it here.[64]

Marsden's passion for the Māori people is seen clearly in the next letter when Ann writes that her father's time is now completely occupied with the Mission. This ranged from preparing things to send on ships to New Zealand, spending time with New Zealanders in his home, or writing letters to the Church Missionary Society.[65]

In the final letter before the Philo Free controversy, Marsden writes

---

62 See Mackaness, *Some Private Correspondence*, footnote 36. For a recent account of events, see Bolt, 'The *Boyd* Set-Back'.
63 No. 24. As to why the Māori might have treated Marsden with such respect, see Prentis, 'Rangatira and Tohunga of Parramatta'.
64 No. 24.
65 No. 25.

to Mary and includes in it some reflections about friendship, and lack of it.

> I was much rejoiced to hear from you respecting your dear departed Companion and trust that your long fervent & ardent prayers were heard for him. I find that by every vessel my old friends are dropping off and that I am likely to be left alone on earth. I think little of Common acquaintance, but much where the friendship has been long and sincere. Our best friend will not die, he remains unchangeable and to him we may at all times apply for comfort in the day of trouble. [...] The Lord is good and kind and gracious, and I have obtained one object that was much upon my mind by my returning, the establishment of a Mission at New Zealand. [...] I should be happy to spend my remaining days in New Zealand could I do this with propriety but many ties secure my stay here at present, though my life is a continuous warfare, and I have fighting without and fears within.[66]
>
> We have some very profane and wicked men here in power and it is impossible either to conciliate their favor or to avoid the shafts of their hatred. I know that some of my friends in England will not always approve of my public conduct but they can neither enter into my feelings nor comprehend the reasons for my actions.
>
> I have felt aggrieved and have appealed unto Caesar again and again. Men in power like religion so far as it agrees with their political measures and tends to support their dignity and consequence but no further.[67]

Do the letters change at all after the Philo Free letter has been published in January 1817?

2. The Letters after Philo Free

Ann writes at the request of her mother in March 1817, just after the publication of the Philo Free letter. She says that her mother has proof of Mary's affection for her as she has received her letters for more than twenty years. Ann also speaks of, Thomas Hassall, who would become her future husband.[68]

---

66 Marsden uses the phrase 'I have fighting without and fears within' several times in his letters (see 2 Cor 7:5).
67 No. 26.
68 They were married on 12 August 1822.

A FRIENDSHIP REVEALED

> The bearer of this is a young friend of ours who is going home with the intention of entering College. During his stay in London how much shall we feel obliged by your sometimes allowing him to visit you. I believe he is a truly pious young man, & the hopes of his being useful to his Colony some years hence (should his life be spared) induced him to leave his friends. He is the son of Mr. Hassall, who came out in the *Duff*, as a Missionary to Otaheite, you have heard of him no doubt. I think you will be pleased to hear that a Bible Society has been formed at Sydney.[69]

Ann also writes of a school opening in Parramatta for native children, missionaries in Otaheite and in New Zealand. But there is no mention of the Philo Free letter.

Marsden's letter is written two days later. He also mentions Thomas Hassall:

> This will be delivered to you by a pious young man who is coming to England with the intention of entering into holy orders [...]. I hope he will stand in my place and preserve the holy seed in this distant land. I consider him a little like Timothy and I hope he will be an honour and a blessing to the Church of Christ.[70]

He also thanks Mary for the gifts of dolls and dresses which his young daughters delighted in so much, and he notes Mary's request for minerals. The tone quickly changes though and given the date of the letter, it seems that Marsden is alluding to the Philo Free controversy.

> As I advance in years I am involved in greater difficulties, it will be no small portion of the happiness of the Saints to be where the wicked cease from troubling. I have had harder to contend than ever lately and never passed thro' so much anxiety in a given time at any former period of my life. I must prevail in the end though the struggle is very painful.
>
> Should you see my friend Mr. Good he will explain more fully my situation. Unconverted men in power roar like lions at the sound of the Gospel. They shew their enmity in every possible way. [...] Some Ministers are bold in preaching the Gospel in the pulpit but out of it they are very careful what they say or do lest they give offence to the Ungodly—I see such men but I cannot approve of their plans.

---

69 No 27.
70 No. 28.

> I have lately in some heavy storms stood alone and the storm is not over yet. From a wicked world I expect no favor, no peace.[71]

Marsden's next letter is December 1817. Much of it is taken up with the good news that 2000 Natives in the South Sea Islands are now able to read and have embraced Christianity as their national religion. He also sees that prospects in New Zealand are fair, and he currently has five New Zealander's living with him, teaching them agriculture.[72] But amongst the description of mission work, Marsden tells of his most difficult year.

> There is great opposition to the work in this colony but I trust that God in his own good time will remove the enemy and give a little peace. I have been tried more this last year than at any former period of my life but blessed by God I still stand my ground against all the powers that be a hope I shall continue to stand. [...] I have always overcome in time though the contest has sometimes been long and severe. He that hath helped me can & will help at all times if we only depend upon his power and goodness. No doubt you will learn somewhat of our late struggles though all has turned out well for the cause of religion in the end.[73]

Once again Marsden writes of desiring to be back in England but then thinks, as his wife challenged him two years earlier to think,[74] but what will the New Zealanders do, and what would the missionaries to the Islands do?

It is eighteen months until we have another of Marsden's letters, 14 June 1819. He writes of missionaries telling him that Pomare has built an enormous chapel in Otaheite (760 feet long!). There was to be a great meeting when all the Chiefs were to assemble together for the purpose of devotion.

> I apprehend nothing like this has occurred since the Apostles days. I hope they would have a real Pentecost and that the Holy Spirit would be poured out upon all above measure [...]. I am astonished above all measure at the success of the Mission. Never perhaps were there more weak and unlikely instruments than have been employed in this work.[75]

---

71   No. 28.
72   No. 29.
73   No. 29.
74   No. 24.
75   No. 30.

He mentions that all is going well in New Zealand, but once again his struggles are in NSW, and this time he explicitly mentions the Philo Free controversy.

> The question which I often have put to myself when smarting under the scourge of Power & Injustice is am I at my post? Do I believe that God sent me here. The answer of my mind has always been Yes. I will then defend my post. I will not quit till I am relieved. I have little communication with the great men of this World and never enter Government House but twice in the Year as a matter of form on public days. The following little circumstance will show you the spirit of the times. News of the Queens death arrived last week. I looked for the general order for mourning on the occasion but instead of mourning the feast of Pentecost has been consecrated to horse racing all this week cock fighting &c by the Sanction of the Government. The annual feast has been thus observed. I have little hopes of doing much good in this colony. God is making here and there young fools wise unto salvation. [...] God is from these very stones, from the sweepings of the Jails Hulks and brothels raising up Children unto Abraham. [...].
>
> You mention the trial and that the damages were small.[76] I did not seek for damages and that the Judge and the Court were sensible of. All I wanted was to set my character right with the public and to prove the conduct of those in authority towards the cause in which I was engaged and towards me individually. I received none of the money nor ever intended. I did not turn and attack the enemy till I could flee no longer from him, and then I was moved to vindicate my cause by an appeal unto Caesar and I was saved out of the mouth of the lion. How long the warfare I know not or when a change will come. I view God governing the world, he puts down one and raises up another according to his Sovereign will. I esteem the excellent ones of the Earth and I wish to be esteemed by them as I hope to live with them ere long, when the wicked cease from troubling, but I value little the friendship of those who are enemies to the Cross of Christ. I have had my share of their hatred and yet I have no reason to believe that it has been in their power to do me any real injury.[77]

---

76 Marden was awarded 200 pounds in damages from the libel case. See Mackaness, *Some Private Correspondence*, footnote 50.
77 No. 30.

Marsden's next letter the following month, carried by his son Charles,[78] speaks of going back to New Zealand. But he soon returns to his difficulties with those in authority in the colony:

> Hard has been the struggle and painful the Contest but the issue will be for the good of the Church of Christ. Fightings without and fears within have literally attended me. I have lived as a spark in the Ocean. Wave after wave have rolled over me but not swallowed me up. I shall be very glad when a changed Government is made. Things may be better. They will not be better under the present system nor am I to expect any cordial reconciliation to take place between me and the existing authority. Had I been vanquished the enemy would have been more inclined to a reconciliation. As that is not the case the enemy will only lie like hot embers under a heap of ashes ready to be blown up into a flame by the first gust of temptation. For this reason I must not sleep as do others but watch and be sober and pray for divine wisdom that I may walk wisely towards them that are without and with well doing put to silence the ignorant & foolish man.[79]

In the second last letter the following year, Ann tells of a Bible Society being established at Parramatta with a female committee that is attached to it. She makes some brief comments about the success of the Sunday School and the education of some of the Aboriginal children. She notes that her father has now been gone for 6 months to New Zealand.[80]

The final letter is written three and a half years later by Marsden, 12 February 1824. He begins by acknowledging that it is a long time since he has written, 'though I often think of your kindness to me and mine and am grateful for your past attentions'.[81] Mr. Woodhouse is the bearer of the letter and Marsden says that Mary can hear more information from Woodhouse as to 'what we are doing'.[82] The mix of good and bad things happening that we have seen in previous letters is also throughout this final one, as is the theme of friendship:

---

78 Samuel and Eliza had 2 sons named Charles Simeon Marsden. The first was killed in a chaise accident when he was a young boy. See No. 11.
79 No. 31.
80 No. 32.
81 No. 33.
82 No. 33.

A FRIENDSHIP REVEALED   215

> I have still to contend with unreasonable and wicked men and believe I shall have to the end of life. However, much good has been done in the Colony in various ways for the furtherance of Religion. On the 11th Inst I consecrated a very fine Church in Sydney in which I trust the everlasting Gospel will be preached to the end of time. I have now consecrated five Churches in this part of the world and shall soon have the pleasure God willing of setting apart another of his immediate worship. God has overruled the wickedness of man for the advancement of his glory.[83]

Perhaps the most interesting thing in this final letter is when he writes, 'I this day marked out a building which I purpose to erect at Parramatta for a Seminary for the natives of New Zealand and have the labourers at work'.[84] He also has plans for the children of missionaries and also of some of the Chiefs to be brought to NSW for their education. But he sadly says that some of the missionaries have acted very badly and that he has had to dismiss them from the Mission, which has caused him much grief.

He further outlines some of the trials he has endured the previous year:

> The last year was a year of toil & danger and much vexation. I spent near three months in different parts of Van Diemen's land and travelled from Sea to Sea. On my return I sailed for New Zealand and was there ship wrecked and the ship was lost.[85] We had many dangers as I sailed in four different vessels during the year. I had my troubles on shore as well as on the water and was compelled to appeal unto Caesar for redress. Who can tell what he may meet with in his pilgrimage through life. Infinite wisdom cannot err. All we want is to commit our way to him and he will direct our paths. Should you be in London and see Mr. Justice Field or his lady you may know all our concerns from them. Mr. Justice Field was one of our Judges and sailed for Europe a few days ago. We were

---

83 No. 33. He alludes to the consecration of St James, Sydney. The other four churches at this stage were St Phillip's, Sydney; St John's, Parramatta; St Luke's, Liverpool; St Matthew's, Windsor. St Peter's, Campbelltown commenced building in 1822, to open in June 1823, but apparently not consecrated. Outside Sydney, Christ Church, Newcastle, was erected 1817, and St Thomas', Port Macquarie, would be constructed 1824–1827.

84 No. 33. See also Prentis, 'Rangatira and Tohunga of Parramatta', 49, who notes that the seminary operated from 1815–1827 (so it was already operating before the building Marsden writes about), and that it struggled as some students had serious health problems, including several deaths. After it closed, mission education was focused in New Zealand.

85 The *Brampton* was wrecked on 9 September 1823. Elder, *The Letters and Journals of Samuel Marsden*, 366.

very intimate and found him at all times very friendly. I esteemed him and Mrs. Field very much and regret their departure. Mr. and Mrs. Hassall are very well [Thomas and Ann]. Mr. Hassall retains his spirituality his pious feelings and promises to be an useful member of the Gospel of Christ. He has got no appointment yet. I believe it is partly owing to the very little esteem some of the ruling powers have for me that he is not provided for. Many settlements are totally without Clergy. At one settlement there are nearly 1500 Convicts and no Minister. I have written to the Bishop of London on this subject and hope some remedy will be provided. If Government will not employ Mr. Hassall I must do it myself. In short I have ever since he came to the Colony. If I could make up my mind to court the friendship of the world all would be well. But this will not do for a Christian who hopes to enter a better world than this in due time. You, my dear Madam must now be near your prize. Your race must be nearly run and your reward in full view.

Conclusion

This collection of letters provides a window into Marsden's inner world. There is a consistency both before and after the Philo Free letter, with several themes appearing regularly: (i) Marsden's discouragement and longing to be back to England; (ii) His anguish and despair at the spiritual state of those in the colony; (iii) That those in authority have no desire for things to be more Christian; (iv) Marsden's strained relationship at times with those in authority; (v) His great interest in farming & trade and the expansion of the colony; (vi) His missionary passion for New Zealand and for the Islands; (vii) His belief in the sovereignty of God; and (viii) His desire for people to hear the gospel of Jesus Christ and be saved.

The letters reveal a long enduring friendship between the Marsden and Stokes families. This friendship was based on Christian fellowship and was part of the relational support that sustained Marsden across his ministry.

Not only do the letters show Marsden's consistent character throughout this period, but they provide evidence of his deep appreciation for his wife and family. He acknowledges that he did not know how he would have coped in the colony without her or their children. Without doubt, he would have drawn strength from those he loved, as he suffered the trials caused by Philo Free.

A FRIENDSHIP REVEALED

Figure 13: The Marsden-Stokes Correspondence

Letter number	Sender & receiver & place names	Date written	Date received	Length of time it took to receive
1	SM to MS Parramatta	24/08/1794	28/02/1795	6 months
2	EM to MS Parramatta	13/12/1794	29/07/1795	7 months
3	SM to JS Sydney	16/09/1795	20/02/1797	17 months
4	SM to MS Parramatta	26/10/1795	04/08/1796	9 months
5	EM to MS Parramatta	01/05/1796	14/05/1797	12 months
6	SM to MS Parramatta	03/12/1796	19/03/1798	16 months
7	EM to MS Parramatta	06/09/1799	02/06/1800	9 months
8	SM to MS Parramatta	22/02/1800	?	
9	EM to MS Parramatta	22/08/1801	?	
10	SM to MS Sydney	22/08/1801	?	
11	EM to MS Parramatta	13/11/1802	?	
12	SM to MS Parramatta	27/04/1803	?	
13	SM to MS Parramatta	13/03/1804	?	
14	SM to MS No place given	Undated but postmark is 10/08/1804	?	
15	EM to MS Parramatta	15/01/1805	?	
16	SM to MS Hull, England	07/12/1808	?	
17	SM to JS On board the "Ann" Rio	01/12/1809	?	
18	SM to JS Parramatta	04/05/1810	?	
19	SM to JS Parramatta	26/11/1811	?	
20	SM to MS Parramatta	07/11/1812	28/02/1814	16 months
21	AM to MS Parramatta	18/06/1813	28/02/1814	8 months
22	SM to MS Parramatta	25/06/1813	?	
23	SM to JS Parramatta	08/10/1814	?	
24	SM to MS Parramatta	15/06/1815	?	
25	AM to MS Parramatta	04/03/1816	?	
26	SM to MS Parramatta	14/03/1816	?	
27	AM to MS Parramatta	25/03/1817	23/02/1818	11 months
28	SM to MS Parramatta	27/03/1817	23/02/1818	11 months
29	SM to MS Parramatta	16/12/1817	29/06/1818	6 months
30	SM to MS Parramatta	14/06/1819	04/11/1819	4-5 months
31	SM to MS Parramatta	14/07/1819	04/12/1819	4-5 months
32	AM to MS Sydney	20/08/1820	05/02/1821	5-6 months
33	SM to MS Parramatta	12/02/1824	06/08/1824	6 months

Key to table: SM = Samuel Marsden, EM= Elizabeth / Eliza Marsden, AM = Ann Marsden, MS = Mary Stokes , JS = John Stokes

CHAPTER 9

MARSDEN'S SUPPORTIVE CIRCLE—CONTROVERSY AND FRIENDS

David B. Pettett

Setting out for the colony of New South Wales for the first time in 1793, the Rev Samuel Marsden entertained pious thoughts of his labours in the antipodes. His hope was simply that he would achieve great things for the Kingdom of God. He imagined that his faithful preaching of the 'everlasting gospel' would bring the joys of salvation and eternal bliss to the ignorant natives of the South Seas. In his journal Marsden expressed the desire that, 'the end of my going may be answered in the Conversion of many poor Souls'.[1] Little could he have imagined that, 25 years on, the stresses upon him would impinge with such great force that he would express the desire to leave the colony altogether and retire to New Zealand.

Rising stress

After a two year absence, in 1810 Marsden returned to the colony, unaware of the tensions about to emerge between himself and the new governor. Marsden delayed his return by 12 months because of the January 1808 uprising against Governor Bligh. Back in England he had successfully recruited new chaplains and teachers for the colony and missionaries for New Zealand. The joy that stood before him with the prospect of the new chaplains extending the work of the gospel in the

---

1 Marsden, *Diary, 1793-1794*. Entry dated 27/7/1793.

colony and the missionaries taking the good news to the natives of New Zealand for the first time was soon met with disappointment and opposition. Marsden entertained high hopes of working with the new governor who, in the words of Marsden's daughter Anne was a 'great friend of the gospel'.[2] Little did he know, nor could he have expected, that the relationship with Lachlan Macquarie would get off to a rocky start and continue with nothing more than polite tension until it finally deteriorated to such an extent that the Governor called Marsden to a meeting where he expressed in writing his total discontent with the chaplain and that he wished therefore never to see Marsden again.[3]

The controversy brought about not only by the publication of the 'Philo Free' letter, but also by Marsden's subsequent legal actions and by the complete breakdown in relations with the Governor resulted in great stress for the Chaplain. Just a few days after his unfortunate meeting with Governor Macquarie, Marsden complained to Josiah Pratt, Secretary of the Church Missionary Society saying, 'My situation is trying in the extreme'. Reflecting on what he considered his most important work namely, the mission to New Zealand,[4] Marsden continued, 'I should consider it one of the happiest days of my life could I leave the Colony and retire to New Zealand'.[5]

The stresses on Marsden continued all through the year of 1817 from the publication in the *Sydney Gazette* dated 4 January of the letter signed 'Philo Free' into the early part of 1818 when he met with the Governor to be told he was no longer welcome. Yet the stresses did not end there. Nine years later Marsden was still defending himself against those who challenged his motives as a minister of the gospel with the publication of his *Answer to Certain Calumnies* in 1826. From the 'Philo Free' letter in January 1817 through to the Supreme Court ruling against J. T. Campbell in December the stresses on Marsden were building.

2   Ann Marsden to Mrs. Stokes, 18/6/1813 (Mackaness, 48–49).
3   On 8 January 1818, Macquarie summoned Marsden to a meeting at which the Rev. William Cowper, the Governor's Secretary J. T. Campbell and Lieutenant John Watts were present. Macquarie informed Marsden that, because he now viewed him, 'as the head of a seditious low cabal and consequently unworthy of mixing in private society or intercouse with me, I beg to inform you, that I never wish to see you except on public duty'; Macquarie's *Journal. 1816–1818*. Sharp, *The World, the Flesh & the Devil*, 476–478.
4   Marsden had written to Pratt on 20/9/1814 with regard to the New Zealand mission, 'this I consider of more importance than any other, and feel it my call to follow the openings of Providence'.
5   Marsden to Pratt, 12/2/1818.

In January immediately after the letter appeared, Marsden proceeded against Campbell for malicious libel. The case spent three days in the Criminal Court in Sydney from 21 to 23 October, 1817. The Court found Campbell 'guilty of having permitted a public letter to be printed [...] which tended to vilify the public conduct of Mr Marsden'. However, as Ron Solomon has noted, 'As this was a verdict "[S]o bad in law that judgment could not be prayed upon it" Campbell was immediately discharged without an order for costs'.[6] Marsden was not satisfied and took the matter to the Supreme Court which, on 1 December found in his favour, ordering damages of 200 pounds be paid to him.

Marsden's hopes of seeing the everlasting gospel bringing salvation to a lost world may have been dealt a hard blow by these circumstances. The breakdown of relationships, the long legal battles and the considerable effort to restore his reputation were not episodes in his life Marsden might have imagined when he first set out from England. While he may well have felt the pressure of the times and of those who opposed him, in the words of his biographer, A. T. Yarwood, Marsden was the beneficiary of, '[M]assive support from the missionary societies and parliamentarians'.[7]

Friends in England

Late in his life Marsden made his last trip to New Zealand between 7 February and 4 July, 1837. On a voyage in June that year, down the east coast to Cloudy Bay in upper South Island, he had a conversation with the Rev. Albert N. Brown.[8] Brown recorded some powerful friends Marsden listed who had gone before him into glory. They were, in Brown's account of the conversation, 'Romaine, Newton, the Milners, Scott, Atkinson, Robinson, Buchanan, Mason Good, Thomason, Rowland Hill, Legh Richmond, Simeon'.[9] Most of these were known as great evangelical preachers. None had greater influence on Marsden's preaching than the Rev Charles Simeon of Cambridge. In his own preaching Marsden used Simeon's sermon outlines extensively which

---

6   Solomon, 'Barron Field', 95; quoting Judge Field's opinion, see *HRA* 1.10, 444.
7   Yarwood, *Samuel Marsden: Survivor*, 201.
8   Hall, *A Biography of Alfred Newbit Brown*, 90–91.
9   For Brown's account of the conversation, see J.B. Marsden, *Life and Labours of Rev. Samuel Marsden*, 259.

no doubt kept his evangelical vision strong even in the face of great opposition.[10] They remained close friends and constant correspondents until Simeon's death.

Simeon's influence on and shaping of Marsden was not limited to the pulpit. Marsden's decision to take up a position as a magistrate in the colony may well have been developed by following Simeon's teachings and practice.[11] Simeon was not only actively preparing young men for evangelical ministry, but also, as a university fellow, was in a position to exercise authority over disorderly behaviour of students and townsmen. In his memoirs Simeon declared that he saw it his duty to be firm over disorderly behaviour.[12] Simeon's writings are filled with ideas of the importance of civil order. He believed that the magistrate's role was to ensure civil order. Marsden may have taken these ideas of his mentor to justify becoming a magistrate himself. He may also have taken some justification from these ideas of civil order to instigate his proceedings of libel against Campbell.

Marsden believed it was common practice in the colony to speak libellously against fellow colonists. In a sermon in the Moore Theological College Library collection, Marsden declared, 'Many of us study to slander our neighbour and injure his character and reputation in the world'.[13] Alongside his desire to see civil order Marsden may have seen Campbell's accusations in his 'Philo Free' letter as the catalyst for him to take action against this common practice in colonial New South Wales.

There are also family links in Brown's list of influential and supportive friends. Marsden's wife, Elizabeth, was the niece of the Rev. Thomas Scott, a man not only well regarded as an evangelical preacher but also the author of a series of pamphlets on evangelical Christianity

---

10 For a comprehensive look at Marsden's sermons see Pettett, *Samuel Marsden: Preacher, Pastor, Magistrate and Missionary*; and *The Sermons of Samuel Marsden* (forthcoming).

11 Gladwin, 'Marsden's Generals', 15, points out that the evangelical movement of which Marsden was a part was not simply about preaching and evangelism but included social and political activism: 'Marsden's clerical and intellectual formation coincided precisely with a dramatic expansion of evangelical activism in the social and political spheres'.

12 Carus, *Memoirs*, 89–93. Marsden also adopted the idea of being 'strict'. For Marsden it was not the quantity of punishment that deterred people (severity) but the certainty of punishment (strictness). See Sharp, *The World, the Flesh & the Devil*, 506. Also, Marsden to Coates, 17/3/1825: 'General Macquarie told the Commissioner I was sever [sic] as a Magistrate; the Commissioner asked Judge Advocate Wylde in my presence if I was... The Judge replied, he would not say I was severe, but that I was a strict Magistrate'.

13 Sermon 88, p.22.

which he finally published in one volume: *Essays on the Most Important Subjects in Religion*. What binds all these names together more than anything else is their common allegiance to evangelicalism, to the missionary societies, and to a fervent desire to see the gospel proclaimed both at home and abroad. The list includes one missionary, Dr Claudius Buchanan—a missionary to India. In an address to the May, 1810 Anniversary Meeting of the CMS, appealing for more missionaries and supplies for the mission field Buchanan mentioned Marsden as his inspiration for these ideas.[14] Marsden may also have gained his knowledge of Indian funeral and other religious rites from Buchanan.[15]

Brown's list makes one significant omission in William Hey. As with many other close friends and mentors, Marsden maintained a lifelong correspondence with Hey. Hey had become the President of Magdalene College Cambridge in 1788 where Marsden had been a student. Like Marsden, Hey was a Yorkshireman. He had been at Magdalene since he entered as a student in 1766. Hey 'was that extraordinary rarity in the Cambridge of King George III, a devout Evangelical'.[16] He gathered around him men who helped change the character of Magdalene. The College developed a reputation of 'extreme godliness' and increased scholarship before Marsden arrived in 1790.[17]

Also missing from Brown's list are the names of powerful parliamentarians who, in Yarwood's words, gave Marsden 'massive support'. The most famous of these was William Wilberforce who led the campaign in the United Kingdom and all its colonies for the abolition of the slave trade. It was probably Wilberforce on behalf of the Eclectic Society who had lobbied government, and the Prime Minister in particular, to send chaplains to the penal colony of New South Wales.[18] Marsden first wrote to Wilberforce from Parramatta in 1799 about the plight of orphaned and abandoned children in the colony with a hope of persuading government to provide accommodation for them.[19] Marsden and Wilberforce maintained a correspondence throughout Marsden's time in the colony.

---

14 See Sharp, *The World, the Flesh and the Devil*.
15 See the transcript of Marsden's sermon in the Moore College Collection. Sermon 34, p.15.
16 Cunich, Hoyle, Duffy, & Hyam, *A History of Magdalene College*, 185.
17 Cunich, Hoyle, Duffy, & Hyam, *A History of Magdalene College*, 186.
18 See Cable, 'Johnson, Richard (1753–1827)'.
19 Marsden to Wilberforce, 1799.

MARSDEN'S SUPPORTIVE CIRCLE—CONTROVERSY AND FRIENDS

At the same time Marsden had powerful parliamentary friends he did not even know. A year after expressing his desire to leave the colony, events in England took a turn which would see the chaplain gain the highest support. On 7 May 1819, parliamentarian Sir Thomas F. Buxton wrote to Marsden to inform him of an enquiry into the state of prisons.[20] This inquiry would inevitably focus attention on the penal colony in New South Wales. Buxton and Marsden did not know each other but Buxton informed Marsden that:

> your character & conduct with regard to Botany Bay & New Zealand & the hardships you have endured from persons in Authority are very familiar to me, & have excited in my mind a lively interest & desire to rescue you from the oppression of those, who hate you and the cause in which you are engaged & Providence has happily given me the opportunity of assisting in a work which will I trust relieve your mind from that deep anxiety.

Such comments from Buxton must have given Marsden a great lift in his spirits. But there was more to come. Buxton continued:

> Be assured of this—you have friends in the Committee who will guard your reputation as if it were their own. Mr Wilberforce, Mr Bennett[21] & myself all feel that it is with us a matter of sacred duty to protect you from that gross injustice to which you have hitherto been exposed.

At what was undoubtedly his hardest time, Marsden suddenly found himself the recipient of protection and friendship from the highest places and most respected people. In 1825 Buxton took up leadership of the campaign to abolish not just the slave trade but slavery itself in Britain and all its colonies.

Buxton had mentioned Wilberforce as a great supporter of Marsden. Earlier, despite being a great supporter of Marsden and his evangelical cause, Wilberforce had sided with Macquarie against Marsden in the matter of the role of emancipists. In a letter to Macquarie of March 1814 Wilberforce said, 'I am sorry Mr. Marsden differs from us on this subject. He is a very worthy man [...but] he is liable to error [...] I think

---

20 Buxton to Marsden, 7/5/1819.
21 Henry Grey Bennet, 1777–1836. Second son of Lord Tankerville. Member of Parliament for Shrewsbury 1806–7 and again in 1811–1826. Bennet chaired a committee on the State of the Police of the Metropolis (1817) and was also a member of the committee on prison reform. See Escott, 'Bennet, Hon. Henry Grey (1777–1836)'.

his opinions erroneous in this instance'.[22] Wilberforce's allegiances were quickly swayed, however. Later that same year he learned, to his horror, that Simeon Lord, an emancipist whom Macquarie continued to support, was still living in a *de facto* relationship with the mother of his children and that Lord was implicated in improper behaviour with two young women from the female factory. By 1819, when Buxton wrote to Marsden, Wilberforce, together with Buxton and Bennet, now considered it a 'matter of sacred duty'[23] to protect Marsden's reputation.

The enquiry into the state of prisons about which Buxton had written to Marsden was to commence, headed by John Thomas Bigge, an eminent lawyer who had distinguished himself in service in Trinidad. In fact, by the time Buxton wrote to Marsden Bigge had already received his commission and was on his way to New South Wales. Bigge, who was clearly biased against Macquarie, would prove to be yet another powerful friend of Marsden.

Friends in New South Wales

Bigge arrived in the colony in September 1819 and returned home in February 1821. After spending fifteen months in New South Wales and Van Diemen's Land collecting evidence for his enquiry, Bigge produced three reports which were published in 1822 and 1823. The reports clearly show Bigge's dislike for Macquarie and his favour towards Marsden. In the first report, Bigge declared he had found evidence of Macquarie's favouritism. Investigating how the distribution of labour was managed on the arrival of new convicts to the colony Bigge reported, 'the assignment of a mechanic has always been considered the greatest favour that could be bestowed by the [G]overnor, and it has been granted only to individuals whom he wished to distinguish or oblige'.[24]

Bigge also deplored Macquarie's excuses for not building a reception place for female convicts at Parramatta, whom he described as 'licentious women' engaged in 'unrestrained prostitution'. While stating that he thought Marsden could have done more to secure the building of such a place, Bigge recognised that the Chaplain had long implored

---

22   Yarwood, 'Marsden, Samuel (1765–1838)'.
23   Buxton to Marsden, 7/5/1819.
24   Bigge, *Report of the Commissioner of Inquiry into the state of the Colony*, 28.

the Governor to undertake the project. 'I cannot help regarding, therefore, the want of authority alleged by Governor Macquarrie as a feeble and unsafe justification of himself, for the delay that has taken place in undertaking the construction of a house of reception for the female convicts at Parramatta'.[25]

Bigge was more happily disposed towards Marsden. While he criticised him for 'being less sensible than he ought to have been to the impropriety of combining operations of a mercantile nature with the duties of his profession', Bigge continued, 'yet I do not find that in this instance it extended further than the purchase of a vessel with his own funds for the benefit and for the purposes of the Missionary Societies'.[26]

In May 1816, on the nomination of John Wylde, Barron Field was appointed to replace Jeffery Bent as judge of the Supreme Court of Civil Judicature in New South Wales. Field became a strident colonial supporter of Marsden. According to Ron Solomon, Field informed Marsden on 21 November 1824, 'I am writing a long review of Bigge's reports and Wentworth's book for the *Quarterly Review* but it must be temperate as that is a ministerial publication'.[27] The articulate criticisms of the colonial born William Charles Wentworth—whose mother was an emancipist and whose father, Dr. D'Arcy Wentworth, was slighted by the 'Exclusives'— have helped shape an enduring legacy of Marsden as a man out of step with the visionary developments of Macquarie and Macarthur. But at the time, Field along with Josiah Pratt and Dr William Good committed themselves to work to defend their friend against the attacks of Macquarie and Wentworth and determined to publish Marsden's pamphlet *An Answer to Certain Calumnies*, which they did in 1826.

Marsden was not only supported by powerful friends at home. Remembering his support in 'troubled times' Marsden spoke of his fellow clergyman, the Rev. Robert Cartwright, with high regard and great affection. Along with the Rev. William Cowper, Cartwright had been one of Marsden's recruits on his trip back to England in 1808–1809. While Cowper went on ahead, Cartwright accompanied Marsden

---

25 Bigge, *Report of the Commissioner of Inquiry into the state of the Colony*, 93.
26 Bigge, *Commissioner of Inquiry on the State of Agriculture and Trade*, 40 (21 February 1823).
27 Solomon, *Barron Field*, 211. The quotation is cited as CYA1992 p. 429. 'Wentworth's book' refers to W.C. Wentworth's *Statistical, Historical and Political Description of the Colony*. Solomon indicates that in his review Field is disparaging of Wentworth and his ideas of a more egalitarian society.

back to the colony, arriving in 1810 whereupon he took up the chaplaincy at the Hawkesbury settlement of Windsor. In February, 1819 Marsden wrote to Pratt outlining the support he had received from Cartwright, 'Mr Cartwright is 20 miles distant but is very ready to join with me in every thing that will promote the Cause of the mission. I have found him a constant Friend, and we have been very happy together. Troublesome times did not change his affection or conduct towards me'.[28] In July of the same year Marsden again wrote to Pratt still expressing high praise of Cartwright and adding the support he also received from the Rev. John Youl. Youl had first gone to Tahiti in 1798 with the London Missionary Society as a lay missionary. In January, 1810 he married Jane Loder who bore him nine children. Youl returned to England in 1813 and was ordained by the bishop of Chester in 1815. After the Colonial Secretary commissioned him as the first chaplain to Port Dalrymple in Van Diemen's Land, he finally arrived there in November 1819. Landing in Port Jackson on his way to Port Dalrymple, Macquarie made use of him at Liverpool (1816–1819) until a house could be made ready for him at his new appointment. This gave him opportunity to be a support to Marsden in a period his mentor needed it most. Marsden wrote, 'Messrs. Cartwright & Mr. Youl will do the best they can. I am indebted to them, because they did shew under all trying Circumstances their Kindness and Affection'.[29]

Marsden also enjoyed friendship with a variety of people, whom he used as confidential advisers to the CMS and LMS when back in London: Francis Oakes, Chief Constable at Parramatta, a member of Auxiliary Society of LMS;[30] Eber Bunker, Pioneer whaler in South Pacific, and an expert adviser for the mission ships;[31] Joseph Underwoood, merchant trader, purchased consignment of timber from the *Active*'s first voyage;[32] Captain John Brabyn, veteran company of 102nd Foot, and an old acquaintance, though Marsden describes him as not 'pious';[33] Dr Bromley, Royal Navy;[34] and David Allan, deputy

28 Marsden to Pratt, 24/2/1819.
29 Marsden to Pratt, 12/7/1819.
30 Marsden to John Stokes, 4/5/1810 (Mackaness, No. 18).
31 Marsden to Pratt, 30/9/1814.
32 Marsden to Pratt, 30/6/1815.
33 Charles Simeon Marsden married his daughter Elizabeth (Elder, *The Letters and Journals*, 25). Marsden to Mary Stokes, 14/3/1816 (Mackaness, No. 26).
34 Marsden to Pratt, 12/2/1818.

Commissary General, 'not a religious man but friendly to the Cause of Mission'.[35] This shows that Marsden was not isolated in NSW, even if he felt that way at times. Nor did he just cultivate powerful friends, but got on with a wide range of people, whom he trusted to speak to the CMS. He didn't try to restrict communication with the CMS simply to his letters, but, through his friendship circle, they had a variety of expert witnesses to keep them up-to-date with what was going on in NSW. Surrounded by so many, Marsden felt:

> most grateful to my friends who have vindicated my Character, and am truly thankful to Almighty God who has the Hearts of all men in his Hands, that he has in his superintinding Providence, raised me up Friends to advocate my cause—in which the future welfare of this Colony is involved.[36]

Also in the colony Marsden had the benefit of friendship with those at the highest level of the legal profession. Ellis Bent, the Judge Advocate, had won Macquarie's approbation by supporting his attempt to persuade Lord Bathurst that a jury system, with juries made up of freemen, including emancipists, should be introduced into New South Wales. While Bent later fell into severe disagreement with the Governor over port regulations, he remained close friends with Marsden until his untimely death in November 1815. Marsden said of Bent, 'With respect to the doctrines of the Christian religion I had many conversations with him. [...] The word of God appeared to be very precious to him'.[37]

Before his death Bent had persuaded Macquarie that his older brother Jeffery would also be a very suitable legal officer for the colony. Jeffery arrived in July 1814 to take up his position as judge of the Supreme Court.[38] Over more than two years in this role, the court sat for just two days. Bent had closed it in dispute with Macquarie over the role of emancipists as legal representatives in the court. The court was not to open again until the appointment of Barron Field as Judge Advocate on 5 April, 1817. Field also became firm friends with Marsden and

---

35 Marsden to Pratt, 12/7/1819; Marsden to Pratt, 13/7/1819.
36 Marsden to Pratt, 14/1/1820.
37 See Marsden, Sermon following the death of Ellis Bent, 29–30.
38 Jeffery Bent wrote Marsden a letter of sympathy after the Philo Free letter was published. J.H. Bent to Marsden, 3/4/1817. When he returned to England, Marsden commended him to both the CMS and LMS as an informant.

remained a regular correspondent after returning to England where he spent considerable time and energy promoting the parson's reputation.

Conclusion: Together for the Gospel

The majority of Marsden's circle of friends who defended him at every opportunity and with the judicious use of every connection of polite as well as powerful society, shared with him evangelical convictions. Those whom Marsden named in the colony as showing nothing but kindness and affection to him in these times of trial not only shared an evangelical stance but were, like Marsden, actively engaged in evangelical ministry. All of Marsden's mentors were men of evangelical conviction. The Philo Free letter had publicly questioned Marsden's motives as a minister of the gospel. As a result Marsden became embroiled in protracted legal proceedings and enquiries which examined and weighed all his words closely. He wished to be free of such political grandstanding, expressing in his letter to Pratt of February, 1818, the hope that he could just be a humble missionary in retirement in New Zealand.

The cause to which Marsden had committed himself as he set out from England in 1793, and of which he expressed the hope of seeing many converted to Christ, was not his cause alone. Marsden did not go to the ends of the earth as a lone soldier to fight the good fight. He went with the backing of men of power and influence. As he read the letter of Philo Free in January, 1817, and as he suffered the embarrassment of exclusion by the Governor in January, 1818, Marsden must have felt very much alone, as evidenced by his desire to retire to New Zealand. Yet because the cause was not his alone, he was not allowed to desert the post Providence had assigned him. His powerful friends gathered around to defend his reputation. Friends he had himself nurtured in their own spiritual growth returned the favour in their Christian care and concern for their mentor. And yet, none of this support and protection was simply for Marsden alone. Marsden's circle of friends gathered around him for a cause they saw as bigger than both Marsden and themselves. They were there to defend the gospel.

CHAPTER 10

UNMASKING A SHIELDED SECRET ENEMY

John Thomas Campbell and the Philo Free Trials

Elizabeth G. Moll

'The Enemy that I have is powerful from the manner in which he is shielded'.[1]

1. Introduction

Historians have been harsh towards Samuel Marsden for taking John Thomas Campbell to court over the Philo Free letter. Printed in the *Sydney Gazette* of 4 January 1817, this libelous letter was a sarcastic account of the Principal Chaplain's evangelistic endeavors in the South Seas. Despite his name not being mentioned, the 'Christian Mahomet' in the letter was doubtlessly referring to the Principal Chaplain in New South Wales.

Campbell and his brothers were educated by their father at home. William Campbell's influence obviously made a strong impression on his children—his youngest sons both became clergymen in the Armagh Diocese: Charles replaced him as vicar of Newry while James was Rector

---

1 Marsden to the LMS Directors, 14/3/1817.

in nearby Forkhill.[2] Naturally, being educated by a clergyman father would have instilled certain views about religion and character from an early age. It is not surprising then, that a large part of Campbell's criticism of Marsden related to how he lived out his Christianity and fulfilled the role of a Christian minister.

Rather than becoming a clergyman like his father, uncle and brothers, Campbell worked for the Bank of Ireland between 1793 and 1795. After this he was at the Cape of Good Hope. He enjoyed the patronage of the Earl of Caledon who recommended him to Lachlan Macquarie, when he stopped there en route to New South Wales in 1809. Campbell joined Macquarie, with the understanding that he would have a situation working for the Governor elect upon arrival in New South Wales. Once in Sydney, he was made Secretary to the Governor on 1 January 1810.[3] During his eleven years in the role, he was Macquarie's loyal assistant and intimate friend. It is hardly surprising that he should have been at odds with Marsden, whom Macquarie, by the end of his governorship, had placed at the top of a list of malcontents in the colony.[4]

1.1 The man himself

Apart from the Edward Close sketch of the Philo Free trial with its caricature of Campbell in court, we do not have a portrait of Campbell as we do for Marsden.[5] According to Captain Henry Colden Antill, he 'had the appearance of being a gentlemanly well-informed man'.[6]

From the content and style of his letters, it appears that Campbell had a witty and wry sense of humor. He named his estate *Mount Philo* in reference to his libellous attack on Marsden's character.[7] His sense of humor is in contrast to the serious nature of the Chaplain, whose biographer noted that 'no study of Marsden could possibly be as serious

---

2 Association for the Preservation of Memorials of the Dead in Ireland. Macquarie, most likely upon the suggestion of Campbell, recommended as further chaplains for the colony both Charles Campbell and G.P. Ker, an acquaintance of the Campbell brothers. However, neither accepted the offer. Macquarie to Liverpool, 27 & 28/10/1811. Cf. Sharp, *The World, the Flesh & the Devil*, 306.
3 Holder, 'Campbell, John Thomas (1770–1830)'.
4 Macquarie to Bathurst, 1/12/1817.
5 Close, 'Courtroom scene, Sydney: the 'Philo Free' civil libel trial, 1 December 1817', housed at the Mitchell Library, State Library of New South Wales. The sketch is reproduced on the front cover of this volume.
6 Holder, 'Campbell, John Thomas (1770–1830)'.
7 Clark, *A History of Australia*, 1.361.

as the subject himself'.[8]

In terms of relationship status, Campbell never married, while Marsden married Elizabeth Fristan of Hull not long before embarking on the voyage to New South Wales, and together they had eight children, two of whom died in infancy.[9]

As for religion, Campbell was most likely anti-evangelical. He commended to the readers of the *Sydney Gazette* an anti-Church Missionary Society protest speech. In contrast, Marsden was an evangelical Christian minister and agent for both the London and Church Missionary Societies.

Campbell was a noted horse breeder, who presumably enjoyed horseracing. Indeed we can be certain that he went to the Sydney races in August 1811, because it was due to a quarrel after these races that he severely injured a military officer in a duel.[10] In contrast, Marsden was staunch in his opposition to horseracing and gaming.[11] As an evangelical minister, Marsden commented that his primary role was concerned with 'preaching the everlasting Gospel' of Jesus Christ, yet in doing so he also used his sermons to condemn the immorality of the colony in speaking against such vices as gambling, reviling and foul language.[12]

Campbell lived in Hunter Street, Sydney and at the time of his death in 1830, he was the third senior magistrate in the Colony[13] (compare Figure 4). Being a magistrate himself, Campbell was critical of Marsden's magisterial decisions. He was scathing of Marsden's harsh treatment of William Refraine—a convict who had been tried and acquitted by the criminal court. In writing to Marsden of the incident,

---

8   Yarwood, 'The Missionary Marsden: An Australian View', 21. At this point, however, Yarwood may simply be repeating the usual caricature. Macquarie's own account is more likely, since it comes from Macquarie as a hostile witness. He noted that Marsden's 'deportment is at all times that of a person the most gay and happy: when I was honoured with his society, he was by far the most cheerful person I met in the Colony'; Macquarie, *Letter to Sidmouth*, 18.
9   Yarwood, *Samuel Marsden: Survivor*, 20.
10 According to Robert Willson, Campbell found himself 'mixed up in what has been called the first doping case in Australian turf history' at the August 1811 race meeting in Sydney. The horse Matcham, owned by Judge Advocate Ellis Bent, had been doped on green feed before the race and subsequently missed out on winning the championship cup. After this event Campbell had a heated dispute with a military officer, and the two men fought a duel. Campbell severely wounded the officer, who nearly died of his wound, but he recovered and the incident was hushed up. Willson, 'Lost diary's strange history', 4.
11 Yarwood, 'The Missionary Marsden: An Australian View', 31.
12 Yarwood, 'The Missionary Marsden: An Australian View', 22; Pettett, *Samuel Marsden*, 10, 107, 112 and 118.
13 *SG* 9/1/1830, page 3. He had been appointed magistrate in October 1815; *SG* 28/10/1815..

he quoted the Biblical narrative of Jesus' treatment of the woman caught in adultery, where rather than condemning her, Jesus showed mercy and compassion. Campbell lamented that Marsden, rather than being compassionate, behaved with 'such a spirit of intolerance and oppression towards the lower classes of Society'.[14]

1.2 Loyal Secretary to Governor Macquarie and censor of the press: 1810 to 1821

Although acquiring a variety of other appointments—including being a magistrate and sitting on various committees—[15] Campbell's role as Secretary to the Governor itself included a range of tasks, such as conducting the correspondence of the Governor throughout the colony, assisting in the preparation of dispatches to England, and preparing pardons and tickets-of-leave for convicts.[16]

Another task amongst his secretary's duties was censoring the content of the *Sydney Gazette*. It contained government and general orders as well as news and advertisements. George Howe was the printer, yet as an official government publication all the material printed in the *Gazette* required censoring. This role of censor proved to be a very useful tool in Campbell's hand for conveying his frustration at Marsden's behavior and lack of support for Macquarie's policies.

1.3. A *Free Settler* letters: 1814

The Philo Free letter was not the first time that Marsden had been libelled in the *Gazette*. That dubious honour went to a series of letters penned in 1814 concerning the Chaplain's failure to establish a lending library in the colony. While in England between 1807 and 1810, Marsden had advertised for donations of books to establish a lending

---

14 Campbell to Marsden, 24/7/1815. See also Marsden to Campbell, 22/7/1815, as cited in Yarwood, *Samuel Marsden: Survivor*, 186–7; Ellis, *Lachlan Macquarie*, 333.
15 Campbell's other appointments were: Secretary and Treasurer of the Committee of Management for the Native Institution (appointed on 10 December 1814), Registrar of the Court of Vice Admiralty (11 June 1810), Trustee and Agent for Intestate Estates (22 June 1811), Justice of the Peace and Magistrate (25 October 1815), Committees of the Male and Female Orphan Institutions (1818). State Records of New South Wales, 'CAMPBELL, John Thomas. Secretary to Governor Macquarie; Provost Marshal'.
16 Other tasks included receiving fees on registering grants of land and marriage licenses, and clearance and pilotage fees for people leaving the colony from colonial vessels. Clark, *A History of Australia*, 1.361.

library in the colony. Many books were received which Marsden brought back to Parramatta, and had a small room built in his garden to store them.[17] Yet, it appears that only a few people were aware of the books, let alone borrowed them. Marsden was shocked to read a series of letters by 'A Free Settler' and 'Another Free Settler' in the *Sydney Gazette* satirizing his failure to establish the promised lending library.[18]

After witnessing his reputation libelled in the *Sydney Gazette*, Marsden responded with a letter to the Editor. The Chaplain emphatically stated that there was no public library, nor were there funds to support one.[19] Applying in vain to the Editor to give up the author of the anonymous letters, Marsden then appealed to Macquarie for redress, from 'the Envious and Malicious' assassination of his reputation.[20] He lamented that any charge against him in the *Sydney Gazette* would carry a degree of Government sanction, which would be especially damaging to his reputation in England. To give weight to his request for redress, Marsden employed the Biblical analogy that:

> a Kingdom divided against itself cannot stand, whosoever holds up the Clergy and Magistrates to public Contempt, stabs at the very Vitals of that Government which supports and protects him.[21]

An attack against the Chaplain was construed as an attack against the Government itself.

However, Macquarie was unmoved by Marsden's impassioned plea. Writing a few days later, Macquarie noted that 'much care has been taken to prevent the *Gazette* from becoming the Medium of Slander or illiberal attacks upon any Individual', and as he did not consider the letters to be criminal, he felt it unreasonable to surrender the author's name, suggesting instead that Marsden should take the matter to court if he was still dissatisfied.[22]

---

17 The books were worth between £300 and £400. Marsden to Bigge, 9/1/1821.
18 *SG* 4/3/1814; 12/3/1814; 19/3/1814 and 2/4/1814.
19 This letter was dated 23/3/1814 and was printed in *SG* 26/3/1814.
20 Marsden to Macquarie, 9/4/1814.
21 Marsden to Macquarie, 9/4/1814.
22 Macquarie to Marsden, 13/4/1814; Marsden to Bathurst, 8/12/1817. Pursuing the matter in court appeared to be Macquarie's personal preference for such matters, as when the Governor himself was libelled by Dr William Bland he swiftly commenced legal action. Dr Bland was found guilty of 'composing, writing and publishing [...] a manuscript book, containing divers libels' and was sentenced to twelve months imprisonment and fined £50. See *R v Bland* [1818] NSWKR 5; [1818] NSWSupC 5; Cobley, 'Bland, William (1789–1868)'.

Needless to say, Marsden was unimpressed. Various unpleasant words arose and Marsden accused Campbell of being the author of the libellous anonymous letters.[23] Indeed, it is highly likely that these letters were written by Campbell. As censor, he had the ability to insist that the printer take on the risk of publication.[24] If it was Campbell, was his exposure of the Chaplain's seeming hypocrisy warranted? One wonders why Marsden advertised for and then accepted donations of books, yet failed to establish a public lending library. Yarwood accounts for this oversight due to Marsden being overcommitted as a minister, magistrate, missionary, farmer and family man.[25] He had more things to do than capability to carry them out. Perhaps Campbell had the Chaplain's failure to establish a library in mind when he later made the bequest of his large book collection to the Australian subscription library.[26]

1.4. Campbell the anti-evangelical

On a later occasion, Campbell used his position as censor of the press to permit anti-evangelical views to be circulated within the colony. In May 1818, the anti-evangelical speech of Archdeacon Josiah Thomas protesting against the establishment of a Church Missionary Society branch in Bath was printed in the *Sydney Gazette*. The lengthy letter was introduced as if needing no further elaboration:

> [t]he following remarkable, and, in our opinion, important, document (copied from the Leicester Journal), we communicate to our readers without any comment.[27]

Permitting the publication of this letter, introduced with the words 'remarkable' and 'important', suggests that as censor Campbell was sympathetic to the anti-evangelical sentiments expressed by the Archdeacon of Bath. Perhaps this was another motivation for Campbell penning the Philo Free letter to attack Marsden, who was both an evangelical minister, and agent for the Church Missionary Society.

---

23 Ellis, *Lachlan Macquarie*, 323.
24 Yarwood, *Samuel Marsden: Survivor*, 155.
25 Yarwood, 'The Missionary Marsden: An Australian View', 32. A simpler solution is to take Marsden's denial seriously: he was given the books for the clergy to lend at their discretion, so it was a misnomer to consider it a public lending library.
26 Holder, 'Campbell, John Thomas (1770–1830)'.
27 *SG* 23/5/1818.

Indeed Marsden's evangelical practices did come under the scrutiny of Campbell. In a letter to the London Mission Society Directors in May 1817, Marsden links Campbell to the ban on hymn singing in church by noting:

> [t]he author will not allow me so much as to sing a Hymn in my church, his mind is so bitter against all methodists, and only a few days ago accused me of countenancing methodists, and expressed his high displeasure at my conduct.[28]

2. The colonial legal system: criminal and civil jurisdiction

Prior to shedding light on the law of defamation and the Philo Free trials, it is first necessary to gain an understanding of the colonial legal system. A brief survey of the criminal and civil jurisdictions will be provided, including an outline of the events which brought civil law in the colony to a standstill for the two years immediately before the Philo Free trial.

2.1 The criminal and civil jurisdiction

A Court of Criminal Jurisdiction was established by the first Charter of Justice for New South Wales and the imperial *New South Wales Courts Act 1787*.[29] This court arbitrated on matters pertaining to the penal code, with English criminal law being applied where relevant to the colony. However, given the penal nature of the colony, there were variations from English criminal law including the absence of a trial by jury. Indeed the Court of Criminal Jurisdiction had more of a military appearance than the English criminal courts. It was presided over by the Judge Advocate and 'six officers of His Majesty's forces by sea or land' who served as members of the tribunal. In the absence of a jury, the members of the court were the sole triers of fact and law. Unlike the requirement for a unanimous verdict by jurors in the English Courts, a decision of the Criminal Court could be attained with a bare majority of four members including the Judge Advocate. The judgments of the

---

28 Marsden to LMS Directors, 17/5/1817.
29 Warrant for the Charter of Justice, 2/4/1787; *New South Wales Courts Act 1787* 27 Geo III c2.

court were carried out by the Provost Marshal. There was no right of appeal against convictions.[30]

The First Charter of Justice for New South Wales also created a Court of Civil Jurisdiction. It was presided over by the Judge Advocate, who was assisted by 'two fit and proper persons inhabiting' the territory appointed by the Governor.[31] The Second Charter of Justice for New South Wales established by Letters Patent on 4 February 1814 abolished the Court of Civil Jurisdiction and created a Supreme Court. This was presided over by a Judge, appointed by Royal Commission, sitting with two lay magistrates appointed by the Governor. It was a court of both Common Law and Equity.[32] The Second Charter of Justice also created a Governor's Court, which was presided over by the Judge Advocate and had jurisdiction to hear matters where the cause of action did not exceed £50.[33]

2.2 The dormant civil jurisdiction: 1815–1817

The initial Judge Advocates in the colony had been military men (see Figure 14). It was not until Ellis Bent, 'a barrister of some eminence' was appointed as Judge Advocate on 1 January 1809 that the colony had its first legally trained barrister Judge Advocate.[34] Bent sailed on the *HMS Dromedary* at the same time as Macquarie, and the two became friends.[35] However by 1814, the once cordial relations between the Governor and the Judge Advocate had become strained. The point of contention related to their differing views on the independence of the judiciary from executive interference. The arrival of Ellis' older brother, Jeffery Hart Bent, in 1814 marked the beginning of an irreconcilable breach in their dealings with each other.[36]

---

30 Warrant for the Charter of Justice, 2/4/1787; Castles, *An Australian Legal History*, 46–48.
31 Warrant for the Charter of Justice, 2/4/1787; Castles, *An Australian Legal History*, 90–94.
32 Letters Patent to Establish Courts of Civil Judicature in New South Wales, 4/2/1814; Castles, *An Australian Legal History*,104–105.
33 Letters Patent to Establish Courts of Civil Judicature in New South Wales, 4/2/1814; Castles, *An Australian Legal History*, 105; Currey, 'Bent, Ellis (1783–1815)'.
34 Bent arrived in the colony one year later, on 1 January 1810. Currey, 'Bent, Ellis (1783–1815)'.
35 Currey, 'Bent, Ellis (1783–1815)'.
36 Currey, 'Bent, Ellis (1783–1815)'.

Figure 14: Judge Advocates of New South Wales
The title was Deputy Judge Advocate, yet the role was mostly referred to as Judge Advocate.

Name	Background	Appointment	Left office
David Collins	Military	Commission dated 24 October 1786, warrant dated 1 January 1787	August 1796 upon return to England for leave
Richard Atkins	Military	Acting Deputy Judge Advocate from August 1796	1798
Richard Dore	Lawyer	Commissioned on 9 September 1797, arrived in May 1798	13 December 1800 (died)
Richard Atkins	Military	Acting Deputy Judge Advocate after 13 December 1800	1809
Ellis Bent	Barrister	Appointed 1 January 1809, arrived on 1 January 1810	10 November 1815 (died)
Frederick Garling	Lawyer	Acting Deputy Judge Advocate by commission from 12 December 1815	5 October 1816
John Wylde	Barrister	Arrived 5 October 1816	1824 when role of Deputy Judge Advocate was abolished with the creation of the Supreme Court.

The brothers Bent and Macquarie had a falling out over the matter of ex-convict (emancipist) lawyers. As there were no free solicitors in the colony, out of necessity, Judge Advocate Ellis Bent had permitted emancipist lawyers to practice as law agents in the Court of Civil Jurisdiction. Macquarie was in favour of emancipist lawyers, yet by 1815, the Bent brothers were opposed. They believed that ex-convicts were barred by statute and common law from practicing as lawyers. After the two days of its first sitting (1 May 1815), Judge Bent adjourned the Supreme Court until an expression of opinion on emancipist lawyers could be obtained from Lord Bathurst in England.[37] Thus the newly created Supreme Court was rendered impotent. In order for the Court to sit, two solicitors were required: one to represent the plaintiff and the other for the defendant. However, at the time when the Court was opened in May 1815, William H. Moore was the only free lawyer in the colony.[38]

---

37 Castles, *An Australian Legal History*, 106–108; Currey, 'Bent, Ellis (1783–1815)'.
38 William H. Moore arrived in January 1815 and Frederick Garling arrived in August 1815.

Then two weeks later, the Governor's Court presided over by Judge Advocate Ellis Bent similarly held that emancipist lawyers would not be permitted to practice before the Governor's Court.[39]

These incidents, combined with a difference of opinion over the legality of port regulations, caused Macquarie to write in frustration to Lord Bathurst. He tendered his resignation as Governor if the Bent brothers were not removed from office.[40] The Colonial Office was faced with the decision of retaining the Governor on one hand, or the Judge and Judge Advocate on the other. While endorsing the Bents' legal opinion, Lord Bathurst was critical of their actions in adjourning the courts in the colony. The 'evil consequences' of the differences between the judicial officers and the Governor 'cannot but be particularly unfavorable' to the tranquility of New South Wales.[41] So the Governor was to remain and the brothers were dismissed.

However, prior to receiving notice of his dismissal, Ellis Bent died on 10 November 1815.[42] As a friend of the late Judge Advocate, Marsden was obviously saddened by his untimely death. In turn, misunderstanding a sermon Marsden preached shortly after Bent's funeral, Macquarie censured the Chaplain for committing blasphemy by eulogizing Ellis Bent in terms too high for any man.[43] By this stage it was apparent that Macquarie's relationship was not only strained with the Bent brothers, but Marsden as well. Indeed, there were similarities in his dealings with them all. Macquarie perceived that these men were seeking to place themselves above his authority, and this tension caused him such frustration that he tendered his resignation once after the disagreement with the Bent brothers concerning closing the courts, and again on 1 December 1817, the day the verdict was delivered in the Philo Free civil trial.[44]

In April 1817, nearly two years after its closure, the Supreme Court was finally able to sit with Barron Field installed as Judge.[45]

---

39 Currey, 'Bent, Ellis (1783–1815)'.
40 Macquarie to Bathurst, 1/7/1815.
41 Bathurst to Macquarie, 18/4/1816; Currey, 'Bent, Ellis (1783–1815)'.
42 Currey, 'Bent, Ellis (1783–1815)'.
43 Yarwood, *Samuel Marsden: Survivor*, 185. See the discussion in Pettett, *Samuel Marsden*, 58–70.
44 Macquarie to Bathurst, 1/7/1815. Macquarie to Bathurst, 1/12/1817.
45 Castles, *An Australian Legal History*, 106–8; Yarwood, *Samuel Marsden: Survivor*, 185.

3. A brief history of defamation law
3.1 Defamation in English Law

The English law of defamation received in the colony was far from simple. Defamation law had derived from a variety of sources over eight centuries: including the ecclesiastical courts, the royal courts, the Star Chamber, the statutory offence of *scandalum magnatum*, and the local courts.[46]

It was through the ecclesiastical jurisdiction that defamation law came into English law. Initially it was treated as a spiritual wrong, for it was a sin to tell lies about another person, but it was not an actionable wrong until the 16th century.[47]

The royal courts took an interest in defamation matters from the 15th century onwards. Unlike the ecclesiastical jurisdiction, these courts could award monetary remedies. By the 17th century, the common law recognized three categories of defamation which were actionable without the need to prove damage: imputations of a crime, professional incompetence, and imputations of a contagious disease.[48]

The Star Chamber was another source of English defamation law. It had the role of regulating the printing press as well as dealing with cases of *scandalum magnatum* (literally the 'scandalizing of magnates'). Enacted in 1275, it was a statutory criminal offence to publish words which disparaged the upper echelons of society, namely peers, bishops and judges. The offence not only preserved social stability, but afforded protection to reputation based on status and rank.[49] The Star Chamber also regulated the printing press in addition to having a judicial function in punishing authors and printers of unauthorised publications.[50] Unlike the ecclesiastical courts which could not order the payment of damages as a remedy for the defamed party, the Star Chamber could award substantial damages. This was particularly relevant in discouraging the practice of dueling to protect personal honour.[51]

Local courts were a further avenue for defamation cases, which

---

46 Rolph, *Defamation Law*, 39–40, 52.
47 Rolph, *Defamation Law*, 40.
48 Rolph, *Defamation Law*, 43–44.
49 Rolph, *Defamation Law*, 48–49.
50 Rolph, *Defamation Law*, 46.
51 Rolph, *Defamation Law*, 46–47.

provided yet another alternative to dueling for protecting honour.[52]

These three concurrent jurisdictions: the ecclesiastical courts, the royal courts, and the Star Chamber were all responsible for defamation law until the Restoration period when the royal courts bore the main responsibility for developing the criminal and civil law of defamation, including libel and slander.[53] The distinction between libel and slander was stated in *King v Lake*, which designated libel as an actionable wrong by virtue of it being written and published:

> although such general words spoken once, without writing or publishing them, would not be actionable; yet here they being writ and published, which contains more malice, than if they had but been once spoken, they are actionable.[54]

The content of defamation law was continuing to evolve in early 19th century England. Since the 14th century it had been an established principle that truth was a complete defence to defamation, however it was not until 1812 that the distinction between libel and slander was finally settled. *Thorley v Lord Kerry*[55] held that the publication of written words which exposed one to hatred, ridicule or contempt was actionable without proof of special damage. However, if the words were spoken, then special damage needed to be proved, except in certain circumstances.[56]

3.2 Defamation in Australia before Philo Free

Criminal and civil defamation cases have been a 'persistent feature of Australian life' since the earliest years of the colony of New South Wales until the present day.[57] At the time of the Philo Free trial, libel could be both a crime and a civil wrong, and therefore matters could be brought in the criminal or civil jurisdictions. Criminal libel historically fell into four categories: defamatory, blasphemous, obscene, and seditious.[58] Another distinction between early matters were that the defamatory

---

52 Rolph, *Defamation Law*, 51.
53 Rolph, *Defamation Law*, 48.
54 (1670) Hardres 470; 145 ER 552 at 553 (ER) as cited in Rolph, *Defamation Law*, 44.
55 (1812) 4 Taunt 355. See Mitchell, 'The Foundations of Australian Defamation Law', 478.
56 Imputations of a crime, professional incompetence and imputations of a contagious disease. Mitchell, 'The Foundations of Australian Defamation Law', 478.
57 Rolph, *Defamation Law*, 52.
58 Encyclopaedic Australian Legal Dictionary, 'criminal libel'.

statements could be classified as either libel (written) or slander (spoken).

Despite the claims of the *Sydney Gazette* that the Philo Free criminal trial was 'the first trial for a libel in this country',[59] there had been other libel matters prior to 1817. However, prior libel matters in the colony could be distinguished from *R v Campbell* (1817) in that they were for seditious libel,[60] slander,[61] or were civil as opposed to criminal matters.[62] It was most likely on account of these differences that the *Sydney Gazette* article claimed *R v Campbell* was 'the first trial for a libel' in the colony.

4. The Philo Free letter

The letter signed 'Philo Free' in the *Sydney Gazette* of Saturday 4 January 1817 accused the 'Christian Mahomet' of misappropriating the Philanthropic Society's funds for personal gain, rather than the protection and civilization of the South Sea Islanders. It suggested that his missionary endeavours were centred on the material reward of 'extravagant profits' from trade with the South Sea Islanders, rather than evangelizing the 'abject Natives of New South Wales'. The author suggested that the Philanthropic Society's funds would be put to better use in establishing schools for the poor children and 'heathen natives' in the colony, directing a pointed barb at the failure to establish the lending library 'originally destined for the poor'.[63]

Angered and eager to take swift action, Marsden wrote to Judge Advocate John Wylde informing him of the letter which he believed contained a libel on his character as Principal Chaplain of the colony.[64]

---

59 *SG* 1/11/1817.
60 See *R. v. Webb* [1794] NSWKR 1; [1794] NSWSupC 1, where a settler was found guilty of seditious libel against Lieutenant Governor Francis Grose.
61 The first civil libel case was *Probart v Grose* in 1792 where the ship's mate Probart sued Major Grose for defamation, after the latter accused him of tricking 40 or 50 of his soldiers. The court found in favour of the plaintiff, yet in consideration of his conduct only awarded nominal damages of one shilling. *Probart v Grose* [1792] NSWKR 3; [1792] NSWSupC 3. Kercher, *Debt, Seduction and Other Disasters*, 24.
62 For an example see *Atkins v Harris* [1799] NSWKR4; 1799 NSWSupC 4 where the second Judge Advocate in the colony brought an action for defamation against the surgeon of the New South Wales Corps, for calling him a swindler. The verdict was in favour of the plaintiff for £50 damages and costs of the suit. See Macquarie University Law School Research Project.
63 *SG* 4/1/1817.
64 Marsden to Wylde, 7/1/1817; J. T Bigge's examination of J. Wylde, *HRA* 4.1, 797.

He requested the Judge Advocate to file a criminal information against George Howe, the Printer of the *Gazette*, before the next session of the Criminal Court.[65] In his later evidence to Commissioner Bigge, Marsden noted: 'I had been Driven by the Government into a Corner & I had now thrown away the scabbard and would never give in till I had gained redress'.[66]

Eager to resolve the matter, upon receiving Marsden's letter, John Wylde wrote to Secretary Campbell to enquire whether the letter had received Government sanction for insertion in the *Gazette*.[67] Campbell replied a few days later on 14 January, giving a lengthy account detailing how busy he was with Government orders, letters and dispatches prior to the printing of the 4 January edition of the *Gazette*.[68] The Secretary noted that, as the first and last paragraphs of the letter were concerned with the 'dormant' Philanthropic Society (of which he was an interested member), he decided to admit it for publication, even though he only had a hasty perusal of the letter. Campbell then expressed his surprise that Marsden filed a criminal information against the Printer, without first consulting him as Censor of the press for a more 'friendly explanation' of the letter. However, up until seeing Campbell's letter to the Judge Advocate, Marsden was unaware that the Secretary was also censor of the press.[69]

Possibly having second thoughts about writing the Philo Free letter, and to his credit, the Secretary remarked that neither the Printer nor the Governor were complicit in the letter's publication. Campbell was desirous that the Printer be relieved 'from any possible responsibility consequent on its publication' as he merely performed his duty in printing a document which had received official imprimatur. As for the

---

65 Marsden to Wylde, 7/1/1817.
66 Marsden's evidence to Bigge, as quoted in Yarwood, *Samuel Marsden: Survivor*, 197.
67 Wylde to Campbell, 11/1/1817.
68 Campbell to Wylde, 14/1/1817.
69 Marsden to Wylde, 16/1/1817. Ratcliffe, '"Pens Dipped in Gall"', 22, argues that Marsden was aware as early as 1814 that Campbell was censor, when the Chaplain unsuccessfully petitioned Macquarie to direct the editor to give up the name of the author of the anonymous lending library letters (see Marsden to Macquarie, 9/4/1814). The source cited by Ratcliffe is an anonymous undated 'Statement of the Case between Mr Sec. Campbell and Rev. Marsden' in J.T. Bigge, Report, Appendix, BT, Box 15, 1676. However, in his letter to the Governor, Marsden makes no mention of 'Campbell', 'Secretary' or 'censor'. He simply makes the request for redress concerning the 'Editor'. See Marsden to Macquarie, 9/4/1814. For further support that Marsden only realized Campbell was censor of the press on or after 14 January 1817, see Yarwood, *Samuel Marsden: Survivor*, 196.

Governor, he was residing at Parramatta on the day in question, and Campbell was unable to submit the letter to him for perusal prior to printing.

Could Campbell's eagerness to relieve others of responsibility suggest he was hinting at his own culpability for the Philo Free letter? Whatever message the Secretary intended to convey relieving the Printer and Governor from responsibility for the letter's publication, the Judge Advocate did not understand. Perhaps things might have turned out differently if John Wylde questioned the Secretary directly as to his responsibility for the letter.

Immediately upon receiving Campbell's explanation, the Judge Advocate replied to Marsden. He was not convinced that the letter in its 'plain, obvious and natural construction' was written with the malicious purpose of defaming Marsden in a particular manner.[70] Such were the requirements necessary to establish defamatory libel. With this belief, he declined to bring the indictment against the printer. Wylde had only been in the colony a few months[71] and it was conceivable that he was unacquainted with how the letter could be construed as libelling Marsden. He suggested Marsden exhibit the indictment himself against the printer.

Once the Judge Advocate had replied to Marsden, he then informed the Governor of the Philo Free letter and the subsequent communications between himself, Marsden and Campbell.[72] In his reply the next day, the Governor lamented that the Philo Free letter had been published and was eager for a Government and General Order to be published withdrawing sanction for it.[73] The Judge Advocate met with Macquarie to discuss the matter and then prepared a draft order for the Governor to approve.[74] On the following Saturday, 18 January, two weeks after the Philo Free letter was printed, the Government Order appeared in the *Gazette*. It stated that the Governor was eager to:

> express his Disapprobation of the Letter [...] and his Regret that it should inadvertently, from the great Pressure of Government Business

---

70 Wylde to Marsden, 14/1/1817.
71 He arrived on 5 October 1816; McKay, 'Wylde, Sir John (1781–1859)'.
72 Wylde to Macquarie, 14/1/1817.
73 Macquarie to Wylde, 15/1/1817.
74 J. T Bigge's examination of J. Wylde, *HRA* 4.1, 796–797.

in the Secretary's Office, have got Admission into the Gazette; from which His EXCELLENCY would thus publicly withdraw all of Government Sanction, Authority, or Concurrence its Insertion might perhaps otherwise be considered to have bestowed.[75]

It was usual for communications from the Government to be printed over Campbell's signature. In this instance, this standard procedure led to the bizarre turn of events, that Campbell's signature was placed on the order withdrawing Government sanction for a letter which he had both written and approved for publication. Presumably Macquarie was aware of Campbell's authorship, in which case he too would have been complicit in his Secretary's duplicitous actions.[76] However, the Judge Advocate was eager to resolve the matter—and so the Government Order drafted by him, under command of the Governor and issued from the desk of the Secretary, was printed.

5. The Philo Free criminal trial

While later commentators accuse him of vindictiveness in prosecuting Campbell, Marsden claimed he was motivated solely by the need to clear his character.[77]

5.1 Preparation

Prior to the trial, Marsden needed to secure affidavits to show that the libel in the Philo Free letter applied to him. However, he experienced significant difficulty in securing the necessary sworn statements. Judge

---

75　SG 18/1/1817.
76　Marsden considered this order to be an 'official falsehood' and a 'further laceration'. He believed Macquarie only wrote the order once he knew legal action was inevitable. Macquarie's evidence to Bigge, 1829 (Ritchie, *Evidence*, 2.113); Marsden to Bigge, 6/1/1821; Sharp, *The World, the Flesh and the Devil*, 448.
77　Marsden was accused of neglecting Scripture by showing a 'rash disregard of the warning against taking one's adversary to the law courts', Clark, *A History of Australia*, 1.311. Commissioner Bigge was of the opinion that Marsden commenced criminal proceedings to punish Campbell. See Yarwood, *Samuel Marsden: Survivor*, 197. Marsden represented to the Judge Advocate that clearing his character from the aspersions of the libel 'was his only concern'. See J. T Bigge's examination of J. Wylde, HRA 4.1, 798. In addition to his righteous anger at the *Philo Free* libel, Marsden was also in despair from the sustained attacks of 'unconverted men in power [who] roar like lions at the sound of the gospel'; Marsden to Mary Stokes, 27/3/1817. See Sharp, *The World, the Flesh and the Devil*, 428–430 for further discussion of Marsden's anguish and despair. Sharp also adds psychological strain to Marsden's perception that the struggles he faced were that of a cosmic drama, the battle of a Christian against the Devil (pp. 441–442).

Advocate Wylde had warned deponents that they 'should duly pause' before swearing an affidavit that the libel applied to Marsden.[78] This phrase was construed as intimidation. It was more than an idle threat, for some of Marsden's acquaintances had been previously dismissed from public employment and had had promised land grants withdrawn as a result of signing the Vale petition to parliament which criticized Governor Macquarie as authoritarian.[79]

Marsden had initially planned to exhibit a criminal information against George Howe, the government printer and editor of the *Sydney Gazette*. Indeed, Howe was aware of the repercussions of printing the Philo Free letter, so would not have been surprised at Marsden's course of action. His son Robert, on seeing the letter which was being composed for printing by employee George Williams at Howe's instruction, exclaimed 'Father for God's sake do not print the Letter Philo Free, it is so gross a Libel, you will get into trouble about it'.[80] Yet Howe was placed in the difficult position of being the government printer, and had no option but to print what was requested by the Secretary as censor to the press. In response to his son's warning, he stoically replied, 'I have no choice, print it let the consequence be what it may'.[81]

On 18 April 1817, Marsden retained William H. Moore as his solicitor in the criminal matter against the printer.[82] Then, three days later on 21 April, Marsden informed Wylde that he was instigating a criminal indictment for libel against Campbell.[83] The criminal information was that Campbell had written and published in the *Sydney Gazette* of the 4th of January 1817:

> a letter with the signature of *Philo Free*, and which the Reverend Prosecutor contended contained libellous matter against him, in his clerical and magisterial capacities, and as the agent and representative here of certain Religious Societies in England.[84]

---

78   Wylde to Marsden, 14/1/1817. See also Sharp, *The World, the Flesh and the Devil*, 447–448; Yarwood, *Samuel Marsden: Survivor*, 197.
79   For example George Williams was dismissed as compositor from George Howe's printing office. Clark, *A History of Australia*, 1.307–308; Yarwood, *Samuel Marsden: Survivor*, 197.
80   Deposition of Richard Jones, 13/11/1817.
81   Deposition of Richard Jones, 13/11/1817.
82   Marsden to Moore, 18/4/1817.
83   Marsden to Wylde, 21/4/1817.
84   *SG* 1/11/1817.

The Secretary pleaded not guilty to the charge. Moore was hopeful that the matter would be heard at the 27 April session of the Criminal Court, however Campbell had a right to traverse until the next session of the Court, thus delaying the trial until October—some ten months after the Philo Free letter was initially published.[85]

The trial of *R v Campbell* commenced on Tuesday 21 October 1817 in the Court of Criminal Jurisdiction in Sydney and ran for three consecutive days.[86] The Court consisted of Judge Advocate John Wylde, together with six officers of the newly arrived 48th Regiment. This was the first court in which the officers sat after their arrival in the colony.[87] Wylde himself had only been Judge Advocate in New South Wales for one year.

5.2 The Prosecution

As prosecutor, Marsden appeared with the assistance of his solicitor William H. Moore. No doubt Moore was laden with affidavits, depositions and other notes, possibly yawning and bleary eyed too. He had only found out the night before, that he was handling the 'voluminous' matter by himself, the other solicitor, T.S. Amos, having abandoned the case, fearful of the consequences of prosecuting the Governor's loyal assistant.[88] Indeed, Moore himself would later come to regret taking on this case, believing he had been disadvantaged by the Philo Free trial.[89]

The first witness called was Marsden himself. As prosecutor, he gave the majority of the evidence in the trial—being recalled by his solicitor a number of times during the three days. He conceived that the letter applied to him as the 'worthy head' of the London and Church

---

85 J. T Bigge's examination of W. H. Moore, HRA 4.1, 833. See also Bigge, *Report of the Commissioner of Inquiry on the Judicial Establishments*, 23.
86 Given the date of the Philo Free trial, there are minimal records of the court proceedings. It would have been exceedingly difficult to piece together the following details of the trials were it not for the Colonial Office's request for this information to be forwarded to England, as this resulted in the Judge's notes being replicated in the *Historical Records of Australia*. For Lord Bathurst's request, see Bathurst to Macquarie 18/9/1818, HRA 1.9, 836; Bathurst to Macquarie, 14/7/1820, HRA 1.10, 313.
87 J. T Bigge's examination of J. Wylde, HRA 4.1, 794.
88 T. S. Amos arrived as a free settler on the *Morley* on 10/4/1817. L. Macquarie, *Diary 1816–1818*, 97.
89 In a letter to Lord Bathurst written shortly after the civil trial, Moore lamented Macquarie's personal hostility towards him, who apart from having his salary withheld by the Governor, claimed that he had been disadvantaged in the Philo Free trial. Moore to Bathurst, 15/12/1817.

Missionary Societies for which he was Agent.[90] His examination-in-chief centred on the expenses and administration of funds of the missionary societies. During cross-examination, he explained his role as agent for the societies as well as for the produce of the Islands. He then explained that while there were muskets on the brig *Active*, these were for the protection of the vessel, not for trade. He believed that the writer of the Philo Free letter meant to ruin his private character, on account of his public conduct as the Agent of the missionary societies.[91]

Other witnesses were called in varying capacities—offering evidence of Marsden's role as agent for the missionary societies and owner of the *Active* or attesting to the Philo Free letter being delivered to the printing office for composing and it being in Campbell's handwriting.

A significant amount of time was spent on the issue of George William's evidence. Williams had been a compositor in Howe's printing office. However, he was dismissed from employment not long after the Philo Free letter was printed. He tendered evidence that he was present in the printing office when the Philo Free manuscript was delivered by Campbell, and that the letter was in Campbell's handwriting.[92] However, his evidence was discredited by the printer, who believed that his former compositor was seeking revenge on Campbell for the hand he played in his dismissal, and had subsequently misled the court. The printer was aware of Campbell's handwriting, and did not think that the Philo Free letter matched the Secretary's hand.[93]

In what seemed more like a school yard tit-for-tat, than a criminal trial, witnesses were then called who either discredited or affirmed the character of the printer. One witness, after initially discrediting the printer's evidence, then subsequently changed the content of his own evidence the following day.[94]

5.3 The Defence

Throughout the trial, Campbell was represented by his solicitor, Frederick Garling. Believing his client innocent, Garling had no

---

90   Wylde, 'The Report of the Judge-Advocate [Criminal Trial]', 463–466.
91   Wylde, 'The Report of the Judge-Advocate [Criminal Trial]', 452–453, 463–466.
92   Wylde, 'The Report of the Judge-Advocate [Criminal Trial]', 455–458. See also Deposition of George Williams, 18/3/1817.
93   Wylde, 'The Report of the Judge-Advocate [Criminal Trial]', 458–460.
94   Wylde, 'The Report of the Judge-Advocate [Criminal Trial]', 469.

prepared opening address.

Once the witnesses for the prosecution had given their evidence, the opportunity arose for Campbell to defend the libel charge. However, he did not call any witnesses, and neither did he speak. Rather, his solicitor mounted his case based on cross-examination of the prosecution's witness.[95] He sought to convince the court that the letter did not constitute a libel, rather, that it was a free discussion on public acts, lacking any malicious intent, and that it was based on a general observation rather than relating particularly to Marsden.

In addressing the court, Garling spoke of 'free discussion serviceable to religious and moral subjects'.[96] He implored the court to consider whether the author of the letter had exceeded the bounds of fair discussion on a public subject. Of particular note was '[n]ot the mere act of the party issuing the writing but the intention of the party issuing it'.[97] He claimed that the subjects in the libel were open to fair and free discussion. On the topic of missionaries, he stated that there was no subject of a nature more free and proper for discussion. The author of the letter merely expressed the opinion that improper means to propagate Christianity has been adopted.[98]

The solicitor commented upon the libel itself relating to 'spirituous liquor distillation', 'pigs and pine trees', and 'Muskets'. He noted that public actions and public conduct may be rightly animadverted on, with the animadversion based not upon individual persons as such, but upon the acts themselves.[99] Basically, that acts done in public were not immune from criticism or censure. Garling asserted that the substantive part of the letter relating to these public acts was proved true. However, if the court found that these were all false then malice would be inferred in the author. The defendant's actions would not be considered as criminal unless they were done with an evil and criminal intention.[100]

In an interesting turn of events, Garling went as far as to suggest that the author of the letter was actually driven by a Christian-like motive of the primary importance of the civilization of the natives. As a

---

95 Wylde, 'The Report of the Judge-Advocate [Criminal Trial]', 470.
96 Wylde, 'The Report of the Judge-Advocate [Criminal Trial]', 470.
97 Wylde, 'The Report of the Judge-Advocate [Criminal Trial]', 470.
98 Wylde, 'The Report of the Judge-Advocate [Criminal Trial]', 470.
99 Wylde, 'The Report of the Judge-Advocate [Criminal Trial]', 471.
100 Wylde, 'The Report of the Judge-Advocate [Criminal Trial]', 471.

consequence of this Christian-like motive, the object of the Philo Free letter was mainly good.[101] He believed that the libel in question was no more than an observation arising out of the subject of the civilization of the natives, rather than an attack on a particular individual. However, if the libel was particularly directed at Marsden, Garling claimed that it only attacked him as a missionary and not as a magistrate.[102] In the course of his address, Garling implied that Marsden avoided a trial in the Supreme Court out of fear that the libel could be justified. He was of the opinion that Marsden instituted criminal proceedings in an attempt to harass Campbell, rather than to vindicate his character.[103]

5.4 The Verdict

After three days of hearing evidence, the Court retired to deliberate. They were faced with the task of deciding the great question of whether Campbell was guilty or not guilty. Judge Advocate Wylde was of the opinion that the evidence presented by the prosecution did not amount to sufficient proof of publication of the libel nor of Campbell's authorship of the letter.[104] For this reason, his preferred judgment for the court would have been a not guilty verdict.[105] Two of the military members sided with the Judge Advocate, while the remaining four members believed that Campbell was guilty.[106] According to Lieutenant Leroux, part of his reasoning for preferring a guilty verdict was that:

> Mr Garling made a speech of nearly two hours in reply and that as he had called no witnesses I did not think myself bound to pay any attention to it.[107]

With remarks like this, it is little wonder that the construction of the

---

101 Wylde, 'The Report of the Judge-Advocate [Criminal Trial]', 471.
102 Wylde, 'The Report of the Judge-Advocate [Criminal Trial]', 472.
103 Wylde, 'The Report of the Judge-Advocate [Criminal Trial]', 471.
104 Wylde advised the court that because there was a mistaken substitution of the word 'let' for 'led' in the criminal information where Philo Free was quoted, no charge against Campbell as 'author' could be brought. He could only be tried as publisher (p. 474). See also Sharp, *The World, the Flesh and the Devil*, 445.
105 J. T. Bigge's examination of J. Wylde, HRA 4.1, 794.
106 The four members favouring a guilty verdict were: Lieutenant Leroux, Captain Parry, Major Morrisset and Lieutenant Cuthbertson. J. T. Bigge's examination of G. W. Leroux, 48th Regiment, HRA 4.1, 854–855. The two military members favouring a not guilty verdict were Major G. Druitt and Lt. Col. Cimitiere. J. T. Bigge's examination of Major G. Druitt, HRA 4.1, 830.
107 J. T. Bigge's examination of G. W. Leroux, 48th Regiment, HRA 4.1, 855.

Court of Criminal Jurisdiction was considered ill-suited to the needs of colony. Military members with no legal training had as much influence in deliberations on criminal cases as the Judge Advocate himself.

Wylde noted the difficult situation faced by members of the Court, that while there was insufficient evidence to prove that Campbell was the author of the letter, since Campbell was the official censor of the *Gazette*, the Court believed that the letter was published 'with his connivance and consent'.[108] To the members, the guilty verdict was less objectionable than a not guilty verdict.[109] It was thus a guilty verdict which was handed down by the Court on Thursday 23 October 1817. The elements established were that Campbell was guilty of: 'having *permitted* a public letter to be *printed* in the Sydney Gazette, which *tends* to vilify the public character of [Marsden], as the Agent of the Missionary Societies for propagating the Gospel in the South Seas'.[110]

5.5 The Judgment

The court resumed the following week for the purpose of judgment. However, Marsden's solicitor did not move the Court for judgment on the defendant, as the Chaplain was eager to bring a civil action for damages in the Supreme Court.[111] So, despite being found guilty, Campbell was permitted to depart from the courthouse without being sentenced.[112] As a result, the Court did not have to consider whether he should be punished for the libel, and if so, what degree of punishment would be appropriate.[113]

5.6 Allegations of judicial bias

A few months after writing his report on the Philo Free trial for the Colonial Office, the Judge Advocate had occasion to write again to Lord Bathurst on the topic of *R v Campbell*. This time, Wylde was defending his own actions during the trial in response to criticism levelled at him by parliamentarian Henry Grey Bennett. He was eager to refute claims that he was influenced by 'worldly' motives in handling the case and

---

108 J. T. Bigge's examination of J. Wylde, HRA 4.1, 795.
109 J. T. Bigge's examination of J. Wylde, HRA 4.1, 795.
110 SG 1/11/1817.
111 Wylde, 'The Report of the Judge-Advocate [Criminal Trial]', 472.
112 J. T. Bigge's examination of J. Wylde, HRA 4.1, 795–796.
113 Wylde, 'The Report of the Judge-Advocate [Criminal Trial]', 476.

showing favourable treatment to Campbell as Secretary to the Governor.¹¹⁴ Indeed, it was not only the Judge Advocate who was accused of showing partiality in Court, for, when examined by Commissioner Bigge, Wylde himself made reference to the perceived bias of the military members.¹¹⁵

6. A 'most false and scandalous' account of the trial

Residents in the colony were hardly oblivious to the libel trial between two persons of such prominence and would have turned to the *Sydney Gazette* for a report of the trial. However, what they got from the editorial comments on 1 November 1817 was a most biased and inaccurate account. After casting doubt on the reliability of witness evidence, which was stated to have 'failed in establishing the points at issue', the editor then doubted whether the letter written by Campbell to Judge Advocate Wylde 'on the first blush of this business' was sufficient evidence to mount the prosecution's case that Campbell 'had any part in the publication of Philo Free's letter'.¹¹⁶

As to the verdict, the editorial stated that Campbell was not declared guilty of 'writing and publishing' the letter, merely that he '*permitted* the *printing* of a letter'. The construction of the verdict was also critiqued, which seemed to contradict the established law for libel cases where the verdict of a jury should be unqualified in declaring the defendant guilty or not guilty. Emphasis was made of the fact that the verdict did not state that the letter 'did vilify' Marsden, rather that it 'tended' to vilify. The editorial inferred that from the content and shape of the verdict, the court did not consider the injury to be significant. As for judgment, the defendant's solicitor 'very earnestly prayed the Court to proceed to judgment', even though the prosecution did not call for judgment, noting that the he was anxious for the opinion of the Court's 'sense of the offence complained of' and the role the defendant played to be known.¹¹⁷ Elsewhere in the same edition, the *Gazette* contained

---

114 Wylde to Bathurst, 20/7/1821, HRA 4.1, 347. Marsden had also implied to Lord Bathurst that Wylde acted with partiality in the matter, making it difficult for him to commence a criminal indictment against Campbell: 'I met with the greatest opposition from a Quarter where I had a right to expect the greatest impartiality', Marsden to Bathurst, 28/11/1817.
115 J. T. Bigge's examination of J. Wylde, HRA 4.1, 792.
116 *SG* 1/11/1817.
117 *SG* 1/11/1817.

a lengthy letter from the printer rebutting the testimony of Marsden's witnesses.[118]

If only the *Sydney Gazette* report had survived, a very different picture of the criminal trial would emerge to that which actually unfolded in the courtroom. Yet, as a Government sanctioned paper which was censored by the defendant in the case (who most likely wrote this account of the trial), one can hardly be surprised.[119]

Judge Advocate Wylde first saw this account of *R v Campbell* when he happened to read it in the *Gazette*. He was naturally unimpressed. Considering 'its tenor so improper' he promptly called upon Garling, Campbell's solicitor for an explanation of the report. However, it appeared that Garling likewise was unaware of this account of the trial prior to reading it in the *Gazette*. At the suggestion of the Judge Advocate, Garling wrote a letter to the printer 'correcting the general account as well as the principles that were stated to have regulated the decision of the Court'. However, this was a futile effort. Rather than being printed in the following Saturday's edition, the letter was returned to Garling by the printer who stated that he had instructions not to insert it.[120] There is little doubt from whom these instructions came.

When later asked by Commissioner Bigge whether he had shared these reflections of the *Gazette's* incorrect account of the trial with Macquarie, Wylde responded that he had not informed the Governor. When pressed, he stated that mentioning this subject seemed to excite in the Governor 'disagreeable sensations'.[121] So, for fear of displeasing Macquarie, Wylde chose to overlook the biased and inaccurate account of the Philo Free trial. Yet it is this account of the criminal trial of *R v Campbell* which has been preserved in the law reports.[122] If Wylde had foreseen this disastrous outcome, surely he would have risked incurring the wrath of the Governor to set the record straight. But alas, this was not so.

---

118   George Howe, 'A Respectful Address, From the Printer to a liberal Public', *SG* 1/11/1817.
119   Ratcliffe surmises that this account of the trial was Campbell's opportunity to present his defence to the libel charge, as he was denied the right of appeal in the criminal court. On his later examination by Commissioner Bigge, Campbell gave evidence that the *R v Campbell* criminal trial report printed in the *Sydney Gazette* was in the handwriting of his clerk Michael Robinson. Bigge, *Report of the Commissioner of Inquiry on the Judicial Establishments*, 32.
120   For this paragraph, J. T. Bigge's examination of J. Wylde, *HRA* 4.1, 799.
121   J. T. Bigge's examination of J. Wylde, *HRA* 4.1, 799.
122   See the Macquarie University Law School research project 'Decisions of the Superior Courts of New South Wales, 1788-1899'. *R v Campbell* [1817] NSWKR 5; [1817] NSWSupC 5.

7. The Philo Free civil libel trial

Marsden was concerned that although the Court of Criminal Jurisdiction found in his favour, with the scandal being 'publicly wiped away' from his character, the reporting of the trial in the *Sydney Gazette* was most 'false and scandalous'.[123] There was hope that a civil trial would be more effective in vindicating his reputation. *Marsden v Campbell* was heard in the Supreme Court one month later, on 1 December 1817, before Judge Barron Field.

Whatever liberties Judge Advocate Wylde might have granted to Campbell's solicitor Garling in the criminal proceedings, Judge Barron Field in the Supreme Court was not so easily moved. At the commencement of the trial, Garling objected to the very proceeding of the civil trial on the grounds that a criminal charge for the same offence had already been heard in the Court of Criminal Jurisdiction with the defendant found guilty. In an attempt to persuade the Court, Garling stated that despite Marsden declining to press for judgement on the verdict, 'yet by the law of England, a party, who files a Criminal information, is deprived of the power of bringing an action for the same offence'.[124] While bringing both a criminal charge and a civil action for the one act of libel might seem to fall foul of the rule against double jeopardy, Judge Field was open to Marsden bringing the civil action, as the Judge Advocate had not imposed a term preventing civil action.[125]

Once this issue had been dealt with, the Judge proceeded to call the witnesses for the plaintiff to give their evidence to the Court. The first witness called to the stand was George Williams, who had observed Campbell deliver the Philo Free letter to the printer Howe in the printing office.[126]

Another witness called was Edward Eager who explained his

---

123 Marsden to Bathurst, 8/12/1817. In fact Marsden considered the account of the trial in the *Sydney Gazette* as 'worse than the publication of the Libel itself'. Marsden to Bigge, 6/1/1821.
124 Field, 'The Judge's Report [Civil Trial]', HRA 1.10, 443.
125 Field, 'The Judge's Report [Civil Trial]', 443.
126 Deposition of George Williams, 18/3/1817, reproduced in Marsden to Bathurst, 8/12/1817. George Williams had been a compositor in George Howe's printing office, until he had his employment terminated by Howe upon an order from Macquarie. This was due to his signing the 'Vale petition' which contained a list of the Governor's arbitrary actions and was given to Parliament by Mr Vale after he left NSW in 1816. See Clark, *A History of Australia*, 1.307–308.

acquaintance with Marsden and the missionary societies. When he ventured to comment that he believed both societies were alluded to in the Philo Free letter, Garling objected on the grounds that it was not appropriate for the witness to explain the libel. To strengthen his objection, Garling remarked that the Judge Advocate refused to admit such evidence in the criminal trial, holding that it was the task for the Court to judge of the applicability of the language amounting to libel, not the witness. Judge Field was not convinced, and over-ruled the objection thereby allowing 'this kind of evidence in this Case, in which the libel was obscure to all but those who knew the parties'.[127]

Once the evidence had been given, it was time for Garling to cross-examine the witnesses as to the truth of the libel. Whether out of frustration that the civil trial was proceeding against his client's wishes, or his desire for Judge Field to show Campbell leniency, Garling remarked that he had been permitted considerable latitude in his cross-examination of witnesses in the Criminal Court. Once again Judge Field showed that he was not going to be trifled with, and disallowed the solicitor's request, refusing to permit him latitude based on Campbell's plea of not guilty.

Michael Robinson, Clerk in Campbell's office was called as another witness for the plaintiff. What is remarkable about this witness was that Campbell appeared completely unaware of his clerk's evidence as a witness for Marsden.[128] The startling evidence was that he had observed the manuscript of the Philo Free letter before it was printed, being held by Campbell and in his own handwriting.[129] Campbell had been unmasked as Marsden's secret enemy by his own clerk.

As is practice in the law courts, once all the witnesses for the plaintiff have been called, the opportunity then arose for the defendant to call witnesses to defend the suit. However, as defendant, Campbell did not call any witnesses.

The court gave judgment for the plaintiff Marsden and awarded

---

127 Field, 'The Judge's Report [Civil Trial]', 446.
128 Yarwood is of the opinion that had Campbell been aware that his clerk Michael Robinson would be taking the stand as a witness for the plaintiff, he might have changed his plea of not-guilty. Yarwood, *Samuel Marsden: Survivor*, 198.
129 Field, 'The Judge's Report [Civil Trial]', 446.

damages of £200 with costs.¹³⁰ Campbell had considered appealing to the New South Wales Governor's Court, however Judge Field pronounced this move legally unavailable.¹³¹

Needless to say, Marsden was much more satisfied with the outcome in the Supreme Court. He wrote to Bathurst that he 'obtained Justice without any difficulty, to the general satisfaction of the Public, and to the honour of the Judge and Members of the Court for their impartiality and independence'.¹³² This favourable verdict marked an end to a difficult year for Marsden, who had at one point contemplated leaving the colony, so vicious was the attack of his secret enemy. Family friend Samuel Hassall wrote a few days after the civil trial that Marsden was 'scarcely the same man he used to be' and was 'much impaired' by the Philo Free libel.¹³³

Unsurprisingly, there is no mention of the civil trial or Campbell's guilty verdict in the *Sydney Gazette*. Nor do the law reports contain Judge Field's notes on the case. The entry for *Marsden v Campbell* in the law reports is a duplicate of the report for the criminal trial, which was the misleading *Gazette* account.¹³⁴ What does remain however is a sketch of the courtroom scene by Edward Close, with caricatures of Marsden, Campbell and their lawyers, Moore and Garling.¹³⁵ With the paucity of records of the event, it is hardly surprising that Campbell has successfully portrayed himself as the innocent victim of a vindictive and un-Christian chaplain, and that this is how subsequent generations

---

130 Field, 'The Judge's Report [Civil Trial]', 447; Yarwood, *Samuel Marsden: Survivor*, 198. However, the overall cost of the two cases and damages cost Campbell well over £400. In his examination by Commissioner Bigge, Frederick Garling estimated that the amount of the verdict and costs paid by Campbell for the criminal and civil trials came to £476 3s. 9d. See 'Examination of F. Garling', *HRA* 4.1, 854. In his apology, Campbell himself stated that the trials cost him 'not less than £500'. See Campbell to Macquarie, 31/3/1819, *HRA* 1.10, 141. Marsden later assured friends that the sum of £200 awarded as damages never came into his possession; nor did he have any desire for it. Marsden to Mrs Stokes, 14/6/1819.
131 Marsden to Burder, 24/12/1817. It is likely that the Supreme Court judgment would have been overturned with the Governor's Court finding in favour of Campbell, given that two of the three members of this court were magistrates appointed by Macquarie, and so may have shown partiality to his Secretary.
132 Marsden to Bathurst, 28/11/1817.
133 Samuel Hassall to Thomas Hassall, 9/12/1817, as quoted in Yarwood, *Samuel Marsden: Survivor*, 200.
134 *Marsden v Campbell* [1817] NSWKR 7; [1817] NSWSupC 7.
135 Close, 'Courtroom scene, Sydney: the 'Philo Free' civil libel trial, 1 December 1817'. This is reproduced on the cover of this volume; see also the key to the persons involved, Figure 1.

have come to view these two men.¹³⁶ Perhaps things might have been a little different if the 'secret Enemy' libelling Marsden was not the Government censor and gatekeeper of printed information in the colony, shielded by the Governor.

8. The aftermath of the Philo Free trials
8.1 Censure from the Colonial Office

Macquarie did not inform Lord Bathurst of the Philo Free trials in either the criminal or civil courts. It was obviously an embarrassing incident and one which the Governor wished to forget. The trials were only brought to the Colonial Office's attention when Marsden sought Bathurst's protection from Campbell's ongoing harassment.¹³⁷ He writes of the 'scandalous libel', a 'most deadly weapon' inflicted upon him by Campbell calculated to wound his reputation. There is a sense that the Chaplain perceived spiritual forces at play, when he writes of the 'dark and secret attempts to injure' him.¹³⁸

Then, expressing in similar terms to the statutory offence of *scandalum magnatum*, Marsden writes of the importance of upholding the respectability of persons in high official situations for the good of government and the general welfare of society. This goes to the heart of Marsden's complaint, that while a libel against an individual is serious, to leave it unchecked amounts to an even deeper wound inflicted on the honour of the Government.¹³⁹

The Chaplain's argument seemed compelling to Bathurst, who wrote to Macquarie to express his displeasure.¹⁴⁰ He instructed Macquarie to censure Campbell not only for the libel, but for abusing his official position, noting that it was only on account of Campbell's 'having so long filled his present Situation with credit' that he decided to forego 'any more severe notice of a proceeding'.¹⁴¹

Macquarie dutifully conveyed Bathurst's censure to Campbell. In

---

136 See Yarwood, *Samuel Marsden: Survivor*, 199–200.
137 Marsden to Bathurst, 28/11/1817; Marsden to Bathurst, 8/12/1817. Yarwood, *Samuel Marsden: Survivor*, 198.
138 Marsden to Bathurst, 28/11/1817.
139 Marsden to Bathurst, 28/11/1817.
140 Bathurst to Macquarie, 18/9/1818.
141 Bathurst to Macquarie, 18/9/1818.

response Campbell wrote to Macquarie acknowledging censure for his 'hasty and inconsiderate Letter'.[142] This apology was Campbell's first acknowledgement of responsibility for penning the Philo Free letter and appears to have been prompted, not by a guilty conscience, but by the censure Macquarie received on his behalf from Lord Bathurst. Indeed, his apology was written more than two years after the Philo Free letter was printed. Campbell was aware that he could not justify his writing the letter, yet he offered a 'slight extenuation' that the 'letter was written in the midst of much hurry and with little previous reflection'. The letter, he stated was dictated by '[i]ndignation at the marked disrespect shewn [sic] by Mr Marsden' in not attending the meeting of the Natives at Parramatta.[143]

Now that he had the ear of the Secretary of State, he expressed his displeasure in having the matter dragged through the criminal and civil courts at 'an expense of not less than £500'.[144] His next sentence conveys his perception of Marsden's hypocrisy and vindictiveness, once again drawing attention to behavior which he believes is inconsistent with the role of Christian minister:

> Mr Marsden, a Christian Pastor, might have well desisted from making a further Appeal with a view to my ruin in the estimation of His Majesty's Ministers and of your Excellency.[145]

This apology highlights the double standards of the Secretary. He vented his displeasure at Marsden alerting his supporters to the libel, which the Chaplain perceived was 'with a view to my ruin'. Yet if the Philo Free letter penned by Campbell was not written with a view to tarnishing Marsden's reputation, then why was it written, printed and subsequently denied in both the criminal and civil courts? It is unlikely that Campbell intended it as a mere harmless jest, with no lasting consequences for Marsden's reputation.

---

142 Campbell to Macquarie, 31/3/1819, HRA 1.10, 140.
143 Campbell to Macquarie, 31/3/1819, HRA 1.10, 140. On the other side, Marsden complains that he was completely excluded from any involvement with the Native Institution and he felt slighted that he was never invited to be involved in any way. Despite the Native Institution being in his parish of Parramatta, Marsden was not invited to join the Committee. He was on leave in New Zealand when Macquarie announced his plans for the Institution on 10 December 1814, with himself as patron and Campbell as secretary and treasurer. See Yarwood, *Samuel Marsden: Survivor*, 188.
144 Campbell to Macquarie, 31/3/ 1819, HRA 1.10, 140–141.
145 Campbell to Macquarie, 31/3/ 1819, HRA 1.10, 141.

By the time Lord Bathurst received Macquarie's letter with Campbell's token apology, the inaccurate report of the criminal trial printed in the *Gazette* had also reached the Colonial Office.[146] This report of the trial was obviously very different from the account of *R v Campbell* which Marsden and others had shared with Bathurst. He subsequently called on Macquarie to give an account of the publication of the report of the criminal trial.[147] Bathurst requested the whole of the evidence and proceedings, so that he could form his own opinion as to the correctness of the report. If the report was proven to be incorrect, then it would represent 'no immaterial aggravation' of Campbell's offence.[148]

In turn, Macquarie requested further information from Judge Advocate John Wylde and Judge Barron Field. Their detailed reports composed from minutes taken at the Philo Free trials were then forwarded to the Colonial Office.[149] However, by this stage, Campbell had been demoted from his office as Secretary to the Governor.[150]

8.2 Strained relations in the Colony: a planned piracy attack and past libel attacks

Needless to say, after the Philo Free trials the already strained relationship between Marsden and Campbell only deteriorated. Despite unmasking his secret enemy, the Chaplain still felt threatened and in need of protection. An example of this was the August 1818 rumour that runaway convicts planned to attack the Brig *Elizabeth Henrietta* while Macquarie was on board. Details of the plan having reached his ears, Campbell wrote to Marsden requesting an urgent reply as to whether the Chaplain knew of the planned piracy, and if immediate action should be taken to prevent the attack.[151]

Marsden took offence at the tone of the letter, believing that Campbell insinuated he was aware of the plan, indeed 'privy to the diabolical purpose', yet failed to raise the alarm.[152] Marsden gave voice to his indignation by writing a lengthy letter to Macquarie the following

---

146 Macquarie to Bathurst, 31/3/1819, *HRA* 1.10, 139.
147 Bathurst to Macquarie, 14/7/1820, *HRA* 1.10, 313.
148 Bathurst to Macquarie, 14/7/1820, *HRA* 1.10, 313.
149 Macquarie to Bathurst, 20/3/1821, *HRA* 1.10, 442.
150 See Section 8.3 below.
151 Campbell to Marsden, 3/8/ 1818.
152 Marsden to Macquarie, 11/8/1818.

week. He commenced with a complaint of the insult he felt upon receiving the letter which he considered an 'unfounded, malicious and impertinent attack upon my feelings and Character'.[153] He then described the history of Campbell's attack on his character as his 'secret Enemy' with the 1814 anonymous letters and the Philo Free libel.[154] He concluded with a plea for 'present redress and future protection' from Campbell, noting that if his complaint was ill-founded then he would rather leave New South Wales, as 'without your Excellency's Protection, I have no present prospect of remaining a single day in Comfort'.[155] While this response seems entirely out of proportion to Campbell's letter, it does convey Marsden's fear that his character would continue to be attacked by the Secretary.[156]

Macquarie's response two days later was brief, noting that 'the only Reply necessary' was that he found Marsden's explanation of the intention of the runaway convicts satisfactory.[157] He then expressed his astonishment that Marsden was insulted by Campbell's letter. There was no interaction with the larger part of Marsden's letter dealing with the 'past injuries' and 'continued Provocation' he endured at the hands of the Governor's secretary. Despite Macquarie remaining silent on the provision of protection, the Chaplain did not follow through on his plan to retire from the colony, but went on ministering for another 20 years until his death.

8.3 Campbell's downfall—demotion to Provost Marshal

After Campbell's apology and the Judge's reports of the trials had been sent to the Colonial Office, no doubt the Governor and his Secretary thought that at last the Philo Free incident was well and truly closed. However, there were repercussions of the letter which neither would have foreseen.

When Macquarie suspended William Gore in 1819 from the position

---

153 Marsden to Macquarie, 11/8/1818.
154 Was Marsden intentionally using the same phrase that Macquarie used of him in January 1818? See Macquarie to Marsden, 8/1/1818.
155 Marsden to Macquarie, 11/8/1818.
156 In a subsequent letter to Pratt in England, he remarked that the object of Campbell in writing 'that Letter is to mix me up with the dregs of Botany Bay pirates, murderers and Thieves'; Marsden to Pratt, 11/8/1818.
157 Macquarie to Marsden, 13/8/1818.

of Provost Marshal, he filled the vacancy by appointing his 'faithful Secretary' to the office.[158] Once this had been done, the Governor needed approval from the Colonial Office for the appointment to be effective. Macquarie commended the 'honest and upright' Campbell to Bathurst for his 'long, labourious, faithful and able services' as Secretary.[159] In further support, Macquarie mentions 'that part which I have most at Heart' in commending Campbell, who in an honorable gesture on the day he was appointed Provost Marshal, presented Mrs Gore, the wife of the suspended Provost Marshal, with the entire salary attached to the office. This was to be hers for as long as he continued to hold the two offices of Secretary and Provost Marshal.[160] No doubt Campbell viewed this as a gesture of practical Christian charity in contrast to the hypocrisy he perceived in Marsden's Christianity.

Macquarie closes his letter 'cheerfully and confidently' leaving Campbell's claims to Bathurst's judgement. However, the fact that the Governor went to great lengths to extol the virtues of his Secretary, suggests that he was at least cognizant of the Colonial Office's displeasure with Campbell over the Philo Free affair. Did Macquarie fear that the guilty verdict of the Philo Free trials would impede Campbell's continued service in the government? Why else would the Governor commend him as an 'honest' and 'upright man' to the Colonial Office, when his prior actions had been exactly the opposite?

It seems that Macquarie's fears were realized. In reply, Bathurst conveyed that His Majesty was pleased to confer upon Campbell the vacant office of Provost Marshal. However, assuming that Campbell's role of Secretary was now vacant, the Colonial Office had renamed the position as Colonial Secretary and conferred the Office on Major Frederick Goulburn.[161] It appears that this was the first time that holding double offices was seen as incompatible in the colony.[162] As a result of being demoted from the illustrious role of Governor's secretary to the more mundane Provost Marshal, Campbell's salary was reduced

---

158 Macquarie to Bathurst, 8/3/1819, HRA 1.10, 39–40, 42.
159 Macquarie to Bathurst, 22/3/1819, HRA 1.10, 66.
160 Macquarie to Bathurst, 22/3/1819, HRA 1.10, 65–67.
161 Bathurst to Macquarie, 24/3/1820, HRA 1.10, 294–295.
162 For example D'Arcy Wentworth held two paid positions together as Principal Surgeon, Metropolitan Magistrate, head of the Police and Treasurer of the Police Fund. Ellis, *Lachlan Macquarie*, 457.

from £1,200 to £700.¹⁶³ This news would have been a double sting for Campbell—not only was he demoted from a position which he had faithfully performed for the previous eleven years since his arrival in 1810, but the title of Colonial Secretary which Macquarie had earlier sought for him was now going to another.

Major Frederick Goulburn was sworn in as Colonial Secretary on 1 January 1821. In announcing his appointment in the *Sydney Gazette* a few days later, Macquarie devoted the larger part of the Government Order to praising the meritorious, zealous, and useful services rendered by Campbell, as outgoing Secretary.¹⁶⁴ The great capabilities of Campbell, as well as the intimacy and friendship he enjoyed with Macquarie, are prominent. Yet, it is with a critical eye that one reads of Campbell's 'integrity' and 'his strict impartiality', because as this chapter has uncovered, his dealings with Marsden have shown Campbell to be significantly lacking in integrity, using his official position as censor to defame the Chaplain, then pleading not guilty to writing the libellous letter in both the criminal and civil courts.¹⁶⁵

Macquarie's 'unqualified Praise and Approbation' for his friend is more akin to a eulogy than a Government Order announcing his retirement as Secretary. This highlights the double standards of the Governor—who saw no problem in his unrestrained praise of his friend, yet was scathing in his admonishment of Marsden when he thought the Chaplain spoke too highly of Ellis Bent upon his death.¹⁶⁶

Perhaps anticipating that Campbell might not fare so well in the colony without him, Macquarie was eager to recommend Campbell's 'long, important, and meritorious Services' to the Colonial Office.¹⁶⁷ One can only wonder at how much of this Government Order praising

---

163 Ellis, *Lachlan Macquarie*, 456–457.
164 *SG* 6/1/1821.
165 See Watson's introductory remarks in the *Historical Records of Australia* where he noted that Campbell 'did not consider it dishonourable to make use of his official position as censor of the *Sydney Gazette* in order to publish a libel on the Reverend Samuel Marsden, for which he was tried and mulcted in damages; even after the trial he aggravated his offence by permitting to be published, or perhaps actually by publishing, in the same paper, a garbled account of the proceedings at the trial', Watson, 'Introduction', *HRA* 1.10, vi.
166 Much has been made of Macquarie's admonishment of Marsden after his 'blasphemous' eulogy of his late friend Ellis Bent (e.g. Yarwood, *Samuel Marsden: Survivor*, 185). For a careful re-evaluation of this incident in the light of Marsden's sermons, see Pettett, *Samuel Marsden*, 58–70.
167 *SG* 6/1/1821.

Campbell's service was targeted to readers in the Colonial Office, as opposed to the colonial readership of the *Gazette*.

8.4 Campbell's later years—the able banker and administrator

Despite the censure from the Colonial Office, and his demotion to Provost Marshal, Campbell did not shrink into obscurity. He remained active in the Bank of New South Wales, after his appointment as the inaugural president of the Board in February 1817.[168] The two subsequent Governors noted his ability, both recommending him for official roles. In 1824 Governor Thomas Brisbane suggested Campbell for the Legislative Council. Then in 1826 Governor Ralph Darling made him a member of the Land Board and the Board for General Purposes, to reorganize the administrative offices of government.[169] In 1829, he was made a member of the extended Legislative Council, filling the place of Captain Phillip Parker King who was absent from the colony.[170] While on the Legislative Council he played a significant role in agitating for trial by jury.[171]

When Campbell died on 7 January 1830, aged 59, after a 'short but severe illness', his passing was noted by two short paragraphs in the *Sydney Gazette*. The first paragraph gave brief particulars of his death, while the second reminded readers that he was 'Secretary to Governor Macquarie during the greater part of His Excellency's long administration until superseded by [...] Major Goulburn'.[172]

There was no effusive praise of his meritorious zeal and capabilities in this edition. According to the *Gazette*, his funeral was attended by a considerable number of magistrates and gentry of Sydney, with William Charles Wentworth being one of the two chief mourners.[173] This is the same Wentworth who was very uncomplimentary in his treatment of Marsden in his biased account of the colony.[174] No doubt Wentworth

---

168 *SG* 8/2/1814.
169 Holder, 'Campbell, John Thomas (1770–1830)'.
170 *SG* 12/1/1830.
171 Holder, 'Campbell, John Thomas (1770–1830)'.
172 *SG* 9/1/ 1830. Yarwood, *Samuel Marsden: Survivor*, 263. NSW Parliament, 'John Thomas Campbell'.
173 *SG* 12/1/ 1830.
174 Wentworth was also at the centre of the affray on Rarotonga, into which Marsden requested the Philanthropic Society investigate, only to be met with the cover-up that led to its demise. See Bolt, 'The Failure of the Philanthropic Society', Chapter 7 in this volume. It is interesting to speculate the role this sequence of events had in souring Wentworth's attitude to Marsden.

and Campbell shared similar sentiments of the Chaplain, and it is their image of Marsden as the selfish un-Christian flogging parson which has endured to this day.[175]

9. Conclusion

John Thomas Campbell was the capable Secretary and intimate friend to Governor Macquarie. Yet for all his praiseworthy qualities, he caused significant embarrassment to his superior on two occasions—the duel after the Sydney races in 1811 and the Philo Free letter in 1817.[176] While these are different events, both are connected by the notions of character, honour, and reputation. Indeed, it was out of the very desire to protect personal honour from which the law of defamation developed. Defamation law evolved as an alternative to resorting to dueling, while the Star Chamber bore a regulatory function in controlling the press to prevent libellous material being published. Yet it seems that Campbell perceived himself above the law—he had no qualms in engaging in a duel after the races to settle a personal dispute, and instead of controlling the press as the official government censor to the *Sydney Gazette* in preventing libellous content being printed, he was the very author of defamatory material. What was particularly underhanded about his libel of Marsden in the *Sydney Gazette*, was that Campbell, Secretary to the Governor, used a channel open only to himself, hiding behind the cloak of his official position as censor to wound the character and reputation of the Chaplain.[177]

As Marsden's 'secret enemy' Campbell inflicted a deep and lasting blow to the reputation of the Chaplain. The wounds ran deep and have endured these two hundred years later. Marsden is remembered as the vindictive and un-Christian Chaplain who ignored the Scriptural warnings against taking an adversary to court in pursuing legal action over the Philo Free libel.

However, history has been more favourable to Campbell. He is remembered as the loyal Secretary to the 'Father of Australia', a capable,

---

175 Wentworth, *A Statistical, Historical and Political Description* (Third Edition), as discussed in Yarwood, 'The Missionary Marsden: An Australian View', 20. See also Sharp, *The World, the Flesh and the Devil*, 435.
176 Holder, 'Campbell, John Thomas (1770–1830)'.
177 Marsden to Bathurst, 8/12/1817.

witty, and generous man who could not bear to tolerate the hypocrisies of the evangelical Chaplain. To him, Marsden was a mere 'Christian Mahomet'—more concerned with self-aggrandizement than showing Christian charity to those who needed it most: the lower classes of society appearing before his magisterial bench, poor settlers in want of library books, and, most of all, the 'abject Natives of New South Wales'.

While Campbell succeeded in portraying himself as the innocent victim of an un-Christian chaplain, as the accounts of the trials and their aftermath have shown, it is Marsden who is more the victim. Despite the notable displeasure of the Colonial Office, Campbell's libellous attacks on Marsden's character are today seen as little more than an amusing although slightly embarrassing and expensive jest, rather than a malicious attack on a man carrying out his onerous yet sometimes conflicting roles of minister, missionary, and magistrate.

This chapter has sought to illuminate how far the chicanery of Campbell went, extending beyond penning the libels of 1814 and 1817 to the reporting of the Philo Free trials in the *Sydney Gazette*—a scandalous misrepresentation of the criminal trial and failure to report the verdict of the civil trial. Uncovering the truth of this matter has shown that in actual fact the accusation of 'Pens dipped in gall'[178] belonged not to Samuel Marsden but to John Thomas Campbell—who was indeed a secret enemy, shielded in his attacks as the loyal secretary to Governor Macquarie.[179]

---

178   To evoke the title of Lorraine Ratcliffe's thesis; Ratcliffe, '"Pen's Dipped in Gall"'.
179   The extent to which Campbell's actions against Marsden were part of a campaign against Marsden originating with Macquarie, remains an open question.

Chapter 11

THE BIGGE PICTURE: COLONIAL MANNERS, MISSION

and the Imperial Context of Australia's First Libel Case

Michael Gladwin

Introduction

In March 1816 Governor Macquarie pronounced a court-martial (illegally as it turned out) on the Rev. Benjamin Vale and had him marched unceremoniously through the dusty streets of Sydney before rebuking him sternly in a private meeting.[1] Vale had been in the colony only three years. In 1814, fresh out of Christ's College Cambridge and newly married, the scholarly twenty-six-year-old had been posted to Sydney after securing a position as assistant chaplain for the colony. Avowing patriotic impulse, Vale had helped W.H. Moore, a colonial solicitor, seize an American cargo schooner in February 1816 as a prize of war, despite Macquarie's approval of its entry.[2] In the aftermath of the court-martial, Vale, Moore and the Rev. Samuel Marsden protested to Lord Bathurst (Secretary of State for War and Colonies from 1812 to

---

1 For the incident and its larger context, see Gladwin, *Anglican Clergy*, 216–27, from which the substance of this paragraph is adapted. See also Border, *Church and State*, 34; Vale, *Proceedings*; Melbourne, *Early Constitutional Development*, 25–28, 52, 53; Ritchie, *Lachlan Macquarie*, 152–54, 161, 165, 172; Marsden to Bigge, 24/9/1821. For Vale's biographical background—including his writing accomplishments in relation to stenography, rhetoric, Odd Fellows, Druidism, theology and the early history of Egypt—see [ADB], 'Vale, Benjamin (1788–1863)', 2.550.
2 Yarwood, *Samuel Marsden: Survivor*, 209; Border, *Church and State*, 34–35.

1827) against Macquarie's autocratic intemperance, secure in the knowledge that since 1810 Australian clergy had been placed under a civil rather than a military commission.[3] The affair had far-reaching implications: Bathurst's subsequent rebuke to Macquarie was a factor in Macquarie's resignation, but it also affirmed the Church's separation from its chaplaincy status as an institution in its own right. The petition of Vale and Moore was also seized upon in Parliament by Henry Grey Bennett, a reforming Whig politician, as a means of urging reform of Tory colonial policy. One result of this was the Bigge parliamentary enquiry and an ensuing *volte-face* in imperial policy regarding Australia.[4] The Philo Free case—another clash between Macquarie and an Anglican clergyman, in this case Samuel Marsden—needs to be understood against the backdrop of such developments in the larger colonial and imperial contexts.

A crucial development in this regard was the abovementioned Bigge parliamentary enquiry (or 'Bigge Commission' as it has come to be popularly known). Although Bigge's royal commission was not established until 5 January 1819 (Bigge arrived in Sydney later that year), Bathurst had decided as early as 1817—the year in which the Philo Free controversy erupted—that there was need for an examination into both the mounting costs associated with NSW and the effectiveness of transportation as a deterrent to felons. Bigge was charged with investigating the legal system and courts, civil administration, convict management, the Church, trade, revenue and natural resources. Bathurst had been concerned about Macquarie's 'ill considered compassion for convicts' and, in three letters of additional instructions to Bigge, the imperial master disclosed the policy outcome he sought for the Australian colonies: that transportation should be made 'an object of real terror'. The equivalent term today would probably be 'deterrent'. The outcome of the commission was, therefore, a *fait accompli*, prompting the observation of one of Bigge's biographers that he was going out to Australia 'in the dual guise of public commissioner of the Crown and of private inquisitor for the government'.[5]

---

3 The change to a civil commission was a result of Marsden's lobbying efforts at the Colonial Office while in England during 1807–09.
4 Bathurst to Macquarie, 26/7/1818 (*HRA* 1.9, 824–25); Border, *Church and State*, 35–37; Yarwood, *Samuel Marsden: Survivor*, 209–10, 212–13.
5 Bennett, 'Bigge, John Thomas (1780–1843)'.

As we shall see below, the Bigge Commission provides important context for the Philo Free case: first, for showing how imperial policy favoured Marsden's vision for the Australian colonies, *contra* Macquarie's, during the years following the Philo Free case; and second, for the valuable light it sheds on the Philo Free case via Bigge's voluminous evidence, collected in bower-bird fashion over several years. Marsden wrote incessantly to Bigge—by 1821 almost daily—to vindicate both his character and his actions in relation to the affair.[6] Significant portions of this correspondence were attempts by the chaplain to justify—to Bigge, his imperial masters and his neighbouring colonists—his decision to pursue the Philo Free matter in the courts.

This chapter also considers the broader metropolitan and empire-wide contexts of the Protestant missionary movement, as well as the broader cultural and social context of the 'reformation of manners' and the cult of middle-class respectability. Neglect among historians of both of these contexts has, I shall argue, led to inadequate caricatures of Marsden's position and, in some cases, assessments of his motivations that read more like pop psychology than careful historical analysis.

That Bigge picture, its colonial, imperial and social contexts, and the various ways in which it illuminates Australia's first libel case and Marsden's role in it, are the focus of this chapter.

The metropolitan and imperial context

By way of background, is important to appreciate some of the key social, political and intellectual developments of the period. These contexts constrained and encouraged the activity of colonial players and their imperial masters at different times. Although generalisations tend towards monolithic descriptions and obscure the diverse strands that go to make up any particular period, some broader trends can be sketched in relation to the metropolitan context. These years were marked by almost continual warfare up until the end of the Napoleonic Wars (1803–1815). This was the time of the early industrial age, with the shift from rural to urban, unprecedented population growth, widespread poverty in town and country, and significant social problems

---

6 For the context of Marsden's correspondence during this period, see Sharp, *The World, the Flesh & the Devil*, 488.

—including crime—that resulted.[7] Postwar economic depression and high unemployment in agricultural districts prompted the Spa Fields rioters of 1816 and a series of other riots and revolts before 1820. Britain's maritime supremacy helped make her an imperial superpower (helping to create the so-called Second British Empire) and bolstered foreign commerce, yet this was accompanied by a sense of uncertainty produced by enormous commercial and financial crises.[8]

A constant fear of radicalism and revolution, whether in Britain or her empire, pervaded a nervous and sometimes reactionary government and élite, which was expressed most violently at a reform meeting in Manchester in 1819, when a twitchy military broke up the meeting with force, leaving 11 dead and 400 injured (causing it to be dubbed the 'Peterloo massacre', a bitterly sarcastic reference to the victory over Napoleon at Waterloo only four years previously). Popular agitation for the legislative dismantling of Anglican privileges and rowdy pleas for the extension of middle-class political franchise only accentuated élite fears. Intellectually, British thinkers wrestled with the assumptions of the Scottish and English Enlightenments, as well as Romanticism, while utilitarian political economy and Whig reformism exerted a significant political challenge to the prevailing Toryism.[9] Meanwhile, an explosion of print culture and literacy contributed to the so-called 'march of mind' and to the expansion of civil society.[10] The ecclesiastical landscape was marked by polarisation over questions about the relationship between Church and State, the rise and politicisation of Nonconformity (especially Methodism in its conservative Wesleyan and more radical Primitive complexions), expanding Evangelical missions both within and outside the control of the British Empire, and sectarian division between Catholics and Protestants.

In the colonial Australian context, the 1810s marked a turning point in the transition of NSW—now thirty years old and demonstrating economic promise in its fledgling pastoral industry—from a largely publicly-funded penal colony ruled by a military governor to a free and democratic society. The colony was deeply riven by divisions between,

---

7   Turnbull, 'The place of the seventh Earl of Shaftesbury', 15.
8   Hilton, *The Age of Atonement*, 23. The crises of 1811 and 1825 were particularly serious.
9   Turnbull, 'The place of the seventh Earl of Shaftesbury', 15.
10 For the 'march of mind' and expansion of a public sphere and civil society, see Hilton, *A Mad, Bad, and Dangerous People?*, 20.

on the one hand, Macquarie, his supporters (including Campbell) and freed convicts ('emancipists'); and, on the other hand, increasingly powerful free setters ('exclusives') such as Marsden. The Philo Free case itself was a test-run of the colony's newly formed judiciary and demonstrated the need for judicial, constitutional and political reform if the transition to free society were to be successful.[11] Aside from the maintenance of good law and order in the colony, imperial masters also faced increasing pressure from the British Treasury, the Home Office and law officers over the cost of convict transportation, colonial expenditure (especially Macquarie's liberal spending on public works) and the legality of colonial acts. These tensions, and their larger political and economic contexts, presented both the Colonial Office and colonial governors with considerable challenges, and need to be kept in mind when considering the Philo Free case and its fallout.

Competing visions

In the first place, the Bigge Commission and its evidence are crucial for understanding the aforementioned tensions. This evidence discloses fundamentally different visions for Australia that underpinned the conflict between Marsden and the Macquarie–Campbell faction. Macquarie was attempting to provide employment for ever-growing numbers of convicts by expansion of public works. However, as Beverly Kingston points out, there were many in Sydney and Westminster who had a different vision of convicts as cheap labour for 'capitalists wishing to create local enterprises such as the production of wool'.[12] Marsden was, of course, a chief exponent of the latter. The clergyman was also proving immensely successful in his pastoral endeavours (regarding the four-footed kind, at least).

This alternative vision of clergy such as Marsden, and its underpinning social theory, has received relatively attention from historians.[13] Nevertheless, it is helpful for understanding the context of the Philo Free case, particularly when situated within wider historical debates

---

11 Ratcliffe, '"Pens Dipped in Gall"', 4.
12 Kingston, 'Introduction', xv.
13 The following paragraphs are adapted from Gladwin, *Anglican Clergy*, 134–35, which is part of a detailed discussion of all pre-1850 Australian Anglican colonial clergy's social theory (pp. 129–36).

about Anglican Evangelicals' influence on contemporary social, economic and political thought in Britain. Boyd Hilton has influentially attributed to Evangelicalism a greater shaping influence on social theory than classical economists or utilitarians.[14] In Hilton's schema 'moderate Evangelicals' adhered to a view of general providence which generated 'doctrines of self-help, *laissez-faire*, and Free Trade' concerning economic relations, which at the same time fostered a concern for the moral welfare of society.[15] Accordingly, moderate Evangelicals shunned state intervention in economics and welfare.

Marsden's social thought needs to be understood against this backdrop. Given the longstanding tradition of public finance and cheap convict labour in eastern Australia, most clergymen's economic thought —like their attitude to social welfare—was unsurprisingly pragmatic, favouring a balance between government intervention and free trade, not unlike the pragmatic conservatism that Alan Atkinson discerns in James Macarthur's 'root paradigms'.[16] As a key pioneer of Australia's pastoral industry and a scion of the Claphamite Evangelical networks that epitomize Boyd Hilton's 'economists of providence', Marsden is of particular importance.

Marsden's 1810s vision of colonial society—based on the leavening influence of free settlers and a pastoral industry that could benefit from convict labour—clashed strongly with Governor Macquarie's vision of a society of reclaimed emancipists and high public-sector expenditure. In a period of fiscal crisis in the metropole during which the British Treasury was footing the bill for 90 per cent of colonial Australian expenses, Macquarie was spending lavishly on public works (often without imperial approval) and retaining for the public sector the overwhelming majority of skilled migrants. This was also an age when Adam Smith's *laissez-faire* doctrines were gaining traction, and in which efforts were being made in the post-war metropole to reduce government and public-sector expenditure through retrenchment. Bigge's reports confirmed Bathurst's decision—and, incidentally, Marsden's vision—in terms of the policy settings for land, administration and transportation. And Marsden's vision won out, of course, after Bigge's 1821 report

---

14 Hilton, *Age of Atonement*, 3, 8–16.
15 Hilton, *Age of Atonement*, 16.
16 Atkinson, 'Time, Place and Paternalism'.

rubber-stamped Bathurst's plans for a free pastoral industry and the increased severity of transportation as a deterrent for British crime.[17]

Nevertheless, lest we overstate Marsden's *laissez-faire* sympathies, it is worth noting that in 1822 Marsden and other Evangelical clergymen sought protectionist exemptions from wool export duties to protect the local industry until it could compete with European wool suppliers.[18] In any case, Marsden's support for a pastoral industry based on convict labour clearly satisfied the imperial desire for increasing privatisation in harness with convict labour and convict transportation as a form of social control.

Also in Marsden's favour were Bathurst's moderate Tory politics, his sympathy with Marsden's patron William Wilberforce and the powerful Evangelical interest in Parliament, and his genuine concern for the place of the Church of England in the colonies.[19] James Spigelman has discerned a further difference in political temperament between Bathurst and Macquarie: Bathurst had 'unwavering faith in the old order' and was 'at heart a sceptic' with 'little faith in the improvement of men or society'. Macquarie, on the other hand, was an 'improver', believing that 'individuals and social arrangements could be always be made better'. His confidence in the civic virtues was more 'a product of the Scottish Enlightenment', in contrast with Bathurst's *ancien regime* sympathies.[20]

Bigge's evidence also reveals major religious fault-lines and controversies between Marsden and Macquarie, some of which predate the Philo Free by several years. As early as 1810, Marsden was complaining to Wilberforce and the Archbishop of Canterbury about the governor's

---

17 For a revealing summary of Marsden's contrasting vision, see Marsden to Buxton, 24/9/1821. This letter has been wrongly attributed by the Mitchell library to Bigge (there is a small note to that effect on A1993, p. 76). The letter discusses Bigge in the third person. Because the letter is addressed 'Honourable Sir', it was probably written to a member of parliament, either Wilberforce or Buxton (Bennett is discounted as he is mentioned in the letter), with Buxton being the most likely given that he had written to Marsden on 7 May 1819. My thanks to Malcolm Fallon for this clarification. For a recent perceptive analysis of Marsden's broader vision, including his negative assessment of colonial rule my military or naval officers, see Sharp, *The World, the Flesh & the Devil*, 490–94.
18 'The Humble Memorial of the Undersigned Landholders', enclosed 7 Sep. 1822; Yarwood, *Samuel Marsden: Survivor*, xix. See also Wilton, 'Australian Sperm Whale Fishery', for pragmatic notions of private enterprise and government pump-priming in his proposal for the establishment of a sperm whale fishery.
19 [ADB], 'Bathurst, Henry (1762–1834)'.
20 Spigelman, 'The Macquarie Bicentennial: A Reappraisal of the Bigge Reports', 4.

elevation of emancipists to the magistracy.²¹ In relation to specifically religious matters, Macquarie's sober 'establishment Anglicanism' and concern for authorized punctilio in worship had been offended back in 1814, when, during divine service in that year, he noticed the Rev. William Cowper using William Goode's new Evangelically-inflected version of the psalms, rather than one of the four authorized versions.²² Marsden had ordered 1,000 copies from England and had distributed them to clergy for use in public worship.²³ Macquarie immediately rebuked Marsden and Cowper for introducing innovations that gave latitude to Dissent and injured 'that established Uniformity of Worship' that was so important to the 'Peace and Harmony' of the colony.²⁴ Marsden wrote to Bathurst and then to Goode. Goode, in turn, approached the Bishop of London on Marsden's behalf.²⁵ Such a high-handed act of government, argued Marsden, was 'impolitic in its principle, and cruel in its Execution'. If the psalms, he added defiantly:

> are not to be admitted into the Temple, they will meet those who are in the high ways and hedges: they will find their way into the prisoners [sic] cell; and into the public schools, and the house of the remote colonists'.²⁶

---

21 Ratcliffe, "'Pens Dipped in Gall'", 9.
22 The Bishop of London's letter to Goode reveals that there were four authorized versions of the Psalms, two in prose and two in verse; each required the sanction of royal authority before they could be authorized for use in public worship. For Hilary Carey's definition of 'establishment religion', see her *Believing in Australia*, 3–10, where she distinguishes it from Evangelicalism. The substance of this paragraph expands on the discussion in Gladwin, *Anglican Clergy*, 111–12.
23 The work in question was *An entire new version of the book of Psalms*, published in London in 1811, 1813 and 1815. The author was the Rev. William Goode (1762–1815), an Evangelical clergyman of Dissenting origins, likened to Edward Perronet and a successor of William Romaine's pulpit. Goode also helped to found the CMS and was secretary to the Society for the Relief of Poor Pious Clergymen, established in 1788 with the help of William Wilberforce and John Newton. See Newton to Wilberforce, 5/7/1788, quoted in Gareth Atkins, 'Wilberforce and his milieux', 27. See also Goode's correspondence with the Bishop of London in Lambeth Palace: Goode to Howley, 18/3/1815; Howley to Goode, 20/3/1815. Pace Bolt, *Cowper*, 126–29, the author of the Psalms is not Dr John Mason Good (a metropolitan correspondent and friend of Marsden).
24 Macquarie to Bathurst, 7/10/1814 (HRA 1.8, 336–38); Colonial Secretary to W. Cowper, 26/8/1814.
25 Bathurst to Macquarie, 2/12/1815 (HRA 1.8, 637); Marsden to W. Goode, 12/10/1814. Marsden was incensed, not least because hundreds of convicts were being sent to the colony without a single Prayer Book. Moreover, Goode's version of the psalms had been warmly received by many in the colony, including one young man who had mentioned its profound personal impact to Marsden.
26 Marsden to W. Goode, 12/10/1814.

In the event, Bathurst and the Bishop of London upheld Macquarie's course of action while absolving the clergymen of any motive of promoting 'peculiar doctrines'.[27] Goode's psalms were consequently distributed in schools only.[28] The incident bore unexpected fruit, however, in becoming the catalyst for an arrangement with the Prayer Book and Homily Society for a regular supply of Prayer Books.[29]

Marsden's correspondence with Bigge also sheds light on diverging moral visions for the colonies. One example is the rupture between Macquarie and Marsden over government policy regarding public morals and marriage. In the face of what they perceived to be Macquarie's inertia, Marsden and other clergymen lobbied Whitehall and Lambeth persistently for reforms: first, for a 'Female Factory' to protect women and orphans from prostitution and abuse; and second, for a policy that might allow wives of soldiers and convicts to be sent to the colonies, thereby redressing the gender imbalance believed to be a root cause of prostitution.[30] As it turned out, Bigge concurred with Marsden that marriage, 'even in NSW, operates as a corrective of vicious propensities' and that the best way to correct convict morals was early marriage.[31]

The Bigge reports reveal further deterioration of relations between Marsden and the Macquarie–Campbell faction in the wake of the Philo Free case. On the Parramatta bench in 1818, Marsden and John Macarthur attracted Macquarie's public censure for ignoring orders to muster convicts before constables and magistrates on Sunday mornings.[32] Marsden believed that such a measure could only be effective if convicts attended divine service, rather than constables' houses where opportunities abounded for vice or criminal plotting.[33] Marsden also refused Macquarie's order that he sit on the bench with emancipist magistrates Simeon Lord and Andrew Thompson as turnpike road trustees. Marsden cited the notorious immorality of

---

27 Marsden to W. Goode, 12/10/1814; Bathurst to Macquarie, 2/12/1815 (*HRA* 1.8, 637); Howley to W. Goode. 20/3/1815.
28 Marsden to W. Goode, 12/10/1814.
29 Bathurst to Macquarie, 15/12/1814 (*HRA* 1.8, 387), noting that the Prayer Book and Homily Society had contacted him regarding the provision of prayer books for the Australian colonies.
30 Marsden to Bigge, 18/10/1821; Yarwood, *Samuel Marsden: Survivor*, 103–5, 119–20, 188; Colonial Secretary to Keane, 25/11/1828, 14/7/1829; Colonial Secretary to Reddall, 9/7/1828.
31 Bigge & Bathurst, *Report of the Commissioner of Inquiry*, 104–6,
32 *SG* 7/2/1818.
33 Bigge, *State of the Colony*, 78; Marsden to Bigge, 1820.

Lord and Thompson's private lives: both kept mistresses, and Lord had been accused of seducing two Orphan School girls, for whom Marsden had responsibility. Marsden has been accused of 'exclusive' class snobbery, but the refusal surely reflected Marsden's high view of the clerical office and concern for the moral tone of colonial society and its leaders (a view forcefully seconded by his patron, Wilberforce, who was 'so enraged' by the affair that he threatened to raise the matter in Parliament). Marsden's actions also reflect his concern that Christian morality be exemplified and supported by those in higher stations.[34]

Finally, the Bigge evidence reveals how even a predominantly ecclesiastical duty such as baptism could become a key site of conflict between Marsden and Macquarie—and later between the doughty clergyman and the so-called 'new chum' coterie around Governor Brisbane. During 1819–23, Parramatta magistrates prevented the Female Factory's children from being christened and from attending public worship.[35] The situation deteriorated in August 1821 after Macquarie authorized an order preventing clergymen from visiting, baptizing or preaching outside their own districts. Marsden, the Rev. Thomas Hassall and their Parramatta vestry opposed these measures, outflanking colonial authorities by writing to Bigge and the Bishop of London (the latter also had the ear of Lord Bathurst at the Colonial Office). Bathurst eventually ordered the obstructions repealed and baptism was allowed.[36] The subtext of these incidents was the fallout from the deeply controversial Ann Rumsby affair, which in itself became a sordid battle in a much larger contest for political influence between the 'Parramatta party' of magistrates, of which Marsden was a prominent member, and a coterie of 'new chums' around Brisbane.[37] Yet it was also an assertion of ecclesiastical authority in the face of an obstructive government, and on behalf of some of the colonies' most

---

34 Bigge, *State of the Colony*, 79–83; Yarwood, *Samuel Marsden: Survivor*, 129–31; Wilberforce to Marsden, 21/3/1814. The substance of this paragraph is taken from Gladwin, *Anglican Clergy*, 118.
35 Marsden to Bigge, 18/10/1821.
36 Marsden to Bigge, 24/9/1821, 18/10/1821; Marsden to Colonial Secretary, 22/4/1823, 24 & 28/5/1823; T. Hassall to Colonial Secretary, 28/5/1823; Marsden to Bishop of London, 5/6/1823 (*HRA* 1.11, 388–89); Bathurst to Brisbane, 30/10/1824 (*HRA* 1.11, 619).
37 The best account of this political feud and Marsden's role in it is Yarwood, *Samuel Marsden: Survivor*, 231–50; Golder, *High and Responsible Office*, 31, notes the Parramatta magistracy as the 'cockpit' of colonial politics during this period.

vulnerable members. An important political issue was at stake between Marsden and Macquarie, namely the role of law under military rule and a growing population of free settlers who were once again unwilling to be treated as adjuncts to a military garrison under a Scottish laird.

Direct evidence for the case

The written evidence for the Bigge reports of course throw valuable light on the details of the Philo Free case itself. In conversation between Bigge and Marsden, Bigge probed Marsden in relation to the breakdown of relations between the chaplain and Macquarie, as well as why Marsden did not accept Macquarie's public disavowal of the offending Philo Free letter in a General Order. Marsden replied that he did not believe Campbell's assertion that the letter had escaped his notice due the pressure of business.[38] 'I fully believed', averred Marsden, 'as well as most others at the time that Mr. Campbell was the author. I looked upon the Order as an official falsehood & I anticipated that I shd be able to prove it so'.[39] Marsden noted a long conversation subsequently in the Judge Advocate's dining room. The Judge Advocate pointed out the difficulties Marsden would have in proving the libel. 'I got up', recalled Marsden:

> & stood up in the corner of the room, & said, I had been Driven by the Government into a Corner & I had now thrown away the scabbard & wd never give in till I had gained redress.

Marsden recalled that the Judge Advocate had initially asked why matters could not be settled out of court, but upon 'finding at last what my grievances were … said ["]I cannot blame you["].' In the event, Bigge believed that the statement justified Marsden's course of action in pursuing the suit.[40]

Marsden's voluminous correspondence with Bigge reveals a tenacious determination both to clear his name and to vindicate his decision to pursue the case in the courts. Marsden's correspondence with Bigge, along with his well-placed missives to powerful metropolitan allies

---

38 Bigge & Ritchie, *The Written Evidence*, 112.
39 Bigge & Ritchie, *The Written Evidence*, 113.
40 Bigge & Ritchie, *The Written Evidence*, 111–15.

such as William Wilberforce MP and the Archbishop of Canterbury, also made him an invaluable conduit for those in London who were intent on changing the infant colony of New South Wales according to their various visions and purposes.

Much has been written about Bigge's criticism of Macquarie and his administration, but for our purposes it is also helpful to probe what Bigge made of Marsden and the Anglican clergy generally. In sum, the Bigge reports reveal his high estimation of their work in the colonies. Bigge highlighted, for example, the clergy's crucial role in the provision of colonial welfare. Early hospitals, asylums and orphanages had clergy on their committees and began with government funding, although voluntary initiative recommenced in 1813 with the creation of a Benevolent Society in Sydney.[41] The absence of a Poor Law system of Parish Vestry and Guardians of the Poor suited colonists because a significant proportion of funds could therefore be drawn from the British Treasury. There were calls for land and endowments from the profits of grazing stock along Poor Law lines, but these were unsuccessful, forcing reliance mainly on voluntary contributions. Because most of its clientele had convict associations, however, various government subsidies accounted for about 70 per cent of Benevolent Society income in the longer term to 1850. By 1820, under what Bigge characterized as the 'vigilant control' of the Rev. William Cowper, the society had subdivided into districts, overseen by clergy, magistrates and selected landholders, promoting regionalized case work and home visiting.[42] It was also ecumenical in character. The Society's focus was the 'deserving poor', to whom it dispensed outdoor relief until the 1850s.[43]

The clergy also worked tirelessly in pastoral visiting and in government-run institutions such as the Female Factory, the Native

---

41 Dickey, *No Charity There*, 4–5.
42 Bigge, *State of Agriculture And Trade*, 77, notes the decentralization by 1820 of the NSW Benevolent Society; Dickey, *No Charity There*, 14, who draws comparisons with Thomas Chalmers' similar efforts to avoid the imposition of central administration of relief in Glasgow; Horsburgh, 'Government Policy and the Benevolent Society', 77.
43 Dickey, *No Charity There*, 15.

Institution and the Male and the Female Orphan Schools.[44] As befitted their traditional metropolitan role as local gentry, clergy sat on the committees and governing bodies of these institutions. Surveying the clergy's work in 1820, Bigge concluded that they had 'neglected no opportunities of extending the influence of their sacred duties, by frequent visits to the houses of the poorer classes and to the hospitals and gaol'. In particular, Bigge singled out the 'equally attentive performance' of the work of Marsden and Cartwright, despite the heavy burden of their magisterial duties.[45] The work of the Benevolent Society, added Bigge, was 'greatly supported by all ranks of the community and [had] served to break down class distinctions'.[46] In Tasmania before the 1820s such expenses fell fully on government, mainly due to the large proportion of government employees and the extension of welfare to lower class settlers and the military. Bigge thought it too generous and recommended more stringent means tests.[47] Accordingly, when Governor Arthur arrived in 1826 he declined government subsidies for similar public societies after the 1820s, although orphans schools, hospitals and Houses of Correction were created and subsidized by government funds until the 1860s.[48] The privatising drift of Bigge's recommendations clearly fits with the abovementioned vision of Marsden.

---

44 The Rev. Robert Cartwright was on the committee of the Orphan Institution and heavily involved with the Native Institution at Black Town. See Colonial Secretary to Cartwright, 5/10/1822; Colonial Secretary to Cartwright, 12/4/1825. The Rev. Richard Hill was Secretary of the Benevolent Society, a director of the Native Institution, founder of the NSW Society for Promoting Christian Knowledge among the Aborigines, and acting treasurer and trustee of the Male and Female Orphan Institutions. See Colonial Secretary to Hill, 18 & 23/9/1819. Henry Fulton was on the committees of the Native Institution and the Orphan Schools, and Director-General of all public (government) schools. See Colonial Secretary to Fulton, 10/12/1814; Colonial Secretary to Fulton, 1/1 & 18/8/1824. Samuel Marsden was trustee and treasurer of the Orphan Institutions and the Female Factory in Parramatta. See Yarwood, *Samuel Marsden: Survivor*, 74, 82, 87–88, 111, 135, 154, 187–88, 204, 231–32. For William Cowper, see Bolt, *Cowper*, 134–36. The Native Institution was established in 1814 with the aim of 'endeavouring to improve the condition of the natives of NSW'. Hill was secretary, with Cowper and Fulton on the founding committee. See Bigge, *State of Agriculture And Trade*, 73; Bubacz, 'The Female and Male Orphan Schools', 315.
45 Bigge, *State of Agriculture And Trade*, 70. A particularly helpful account of social welfare provision in Tasmania during our period is Brown, '"Poverty is not a crime"', 1–73.
46 Bigge, *State of Agriculture And Trade*, 76–77.
47 Bigge, *State of Agriculture And Trade*, 82.
48 Dickey, *No Charity There*, 18–20, 27; Colonial Secretary to Palmer, 28/9/1833; Colonial Secretary to Bedford, 5/4/1834. Government finances were under pressure from large convict numbers and strained resources.

Bigge's reports shed light on Marsden's much maligned role as magistrate for much of 1795–1822. This is, of course, the most well-known and controversial aspect of his legacy and has given rise to a 'flogging parson' tradition in Australian history.[49] In 1800 Marsden condoned the flogging of an Irish political prisoner to secure information about a suspected rebellion; on another occasion he imposed—with a fellow magistrate—regular floggings on a thief to elicit the surrender of stolen goods.[50] His illegal sentences and use of the magisterial office to attack political opponents resulted in his dismissal from the magistracy in 1822.[51] Several contemporary observers commented on the 'undue severity' of his sentences.[52] Bigge, a more impartial observer than most, concluded that Marsden's 'sentences are not only, in fact, more severe than those of the other magistrates, but that the general opinion of the colony is, that his character, as displayed in the administration of the penal law in NSW, is stamped with severity'. Nevertheless, only Marsden was singled out by contemporaries for severity in sentencing.[53] Even the Church's longstanding critic, the Presbyterian Rev. John Dunmore Lang, was at pains to avoid insinuating that clerical magistrates were 'more severe in their penal inflictions than laymen'. 'On the contrary', he argued, 'I should imagine they were generally the reverse'.[54]

Excepting Marsden, however, the reports of Bigge and governors relating to clergy *qua* magistrates are effusively positive. Governor King, for example, had observed in 1803 that '[t]he Rev. Marsden, chaplain and magistrate [...] conducts the public affairs at Parramatta and its neighbourhood, much to the public benefit [...] for which he receives no other reward than the labour of 12 convicts on his farm'.[55] The magisterial bench of Castlereagh, on which the Rev. Henry Fulton sat with two other magistrates, had no case where repeated punishment was inflicted to compel disclosure. Fulton was singled out by Bigge as

49 For further discussion, see Gladwin, 'The journalist in the rectory'; Gladwin, 'Marsden's Generals'.
50 Yarwood, 'The Missionary Marsden'.
51 Yarwood, *Samuel Marsden: Survivor*, ch. 16.
52 Bigge & Bathurst, *Report of the Commissioner of Inquiry*, 91; Grocott, *Convicts, Clergymen And Churches*, 233–34, marshals several contemporary complaints about Marsden.
53 Grocott, *Convicts, Clergymen and Churches*, 234.
54 Lang, *An Historical And Statistical Account of New South Wales*, 2.248.
55 See P.G. King to Hobart, 9/5/1803 (HRA 1.4, 168); Brisbane to Bathurst, 11/8/1825 (HRA 1.11, 857).

'diligent and respectable' in his magisterial duties, which reflected the 'sacred character with which he was invested' and was desirable in a relatively remote region.[56] The same verdict was returned regarding the bench of the Windsor and Wilberforce districts, where the Rev. Robert Cartwright served from 1811 to 1817. Macquarie extolled Cartwright for the able, zealous and upright manner and service which, in Macquarie's opinion, reflected credit to himself and advantage to the public service.[57]

'Polish or perish': respectability, gentility and social status

There is no doubt that Marsden was deeply concerned about his reputation and character. In an incident in 1814 that to some extent adumbrated the Philo Free case, Marsden had been publicly criticised by a 'Free Settler'. Reflecting on that incident three years afterwards, Marsden observed that the letter writer had intended to injure his 'Reputation in the Christian World, and among clergymen especially'.[58] By 1821, as we noted above, Marsden was writing daily to Bigge and still referencing the Philo Free case. In one letter Marsden complained of the 'personal' and 'low and ungentlemanly' language used by Campbell's barrister, Frederick Garling, during the cross-examination.[59] Legal scholar Graham Fricke observes that the law of defamation is expected to provide for a proper balance between two strongly competing interests: a protection of 'the individual's right to exercise his freedom of speech and his fellow citizen's right to protection against attack upon his reputation'.[60] Marsden's comments gesture towards the fundamental importance of protecting one's personal reputation, which in the early nineteenth century was linked to notions of respectability and gentility—and, in turn, social authority and public

---

56 See Bigge, *State of the Colony of New South Wales*, 84, 135; Colonial Secretary to T.H. Scott, 22/5/1827, for Scott's assurance to Reddall and Fulton that government entertained 'a very just sense of their zeal in the performance of their Duties'. See also Bigge, *State of Agriculture And Trade*, 70, and for Bigge's commendation of the clergy's pastoral labours, 76–77, 82–83.
57 See *SG* 31/1/1818; Cable, 'Cartwright, Robert (1771–1856)', 1.211–12; Grocott, *Convicts, Clergymen and Churches*, 234; Clark, *A History of Australia*, 1.314–15.
58 Marsden to Wylde, 18/1/1817.
59 Ratcliffe, '"Pens Dipped in Gall"', 46.
60 Fricke, *Libels, Lampoons And Litigants*, vii.

standing. This applied to clergymen and missionary administrators just as much as it applied to governors and free settlers, whether of genteel or humble origins. This is a crucial factor in understanding the context and outworking of the Philo Free case, as more than one scholar has pointed out.[61]

In an incisive recent reassessment of Macquarie and the Bigge commission, Spigelman points out this was an age preoccupied by status, and for those who could not rely on the respectability that was 'conferred by aristocratic birth or lesser forms of "breeding"', it was 'actual conduct alone' that:

> revealed the character entitling one to gentry status. Once a person had manifested a defect in character, only his or her exclusion from polite society could restore the proper social order. This policy of social exclusion was so widely accepted that those, like Macquarie, who took a different view could not escape censure by those whose status was thereby rendered less secure.[62]

Bathurst reflected these sentiments in a private letter to Bigge:

> I allude to the Propriety of admitting in Society Persons, who originally came to the Settlement as Convicts. The Opinion, entertained by the Governor and sanctioned by The Prince Regent, has certainly been with some few exceptions, in favour of their reception at the expiration of their several Sentences upon terms of perfect Equality with the Free Settlers. But I am aware that the Conduct of the Governor in this respect, however approved by the Government at home, has drawn down upon him the Hostility of many persons, who hold associations with Convicts under any circumstances to be a degradation. Feelings of this kind are not easily overcome.[63]

Macquarie had attempted to restore pardoned convicts to the position in society to which they had occupied before their conviction. Spigelman rightly points out just how deeply Macquarie's approach clashed with the entrenched social mores and expectations of those he

---

61 So Ratcliffe, '"Pens Dipped in Gall"'; Spigelman, 'The Macquarie Bicentennial: A Reappraisal of the Bigge Reports'; Sharp, *The World, the Flesh & the Devil*, 487–88 (for the 'politics of armour-propre').
62 Spigelman, 'The Macquarie Bicentennial: A Reappraisal of the Bigge Reports', 14. Spigelman, it should be noted, was himself a Chief Justice of NSW.
63 Bathurst to Bigge, 6/1/1819, enclosure no. 4 (*HRA* 1.10, 11); also quoted in Spigelman, 'Reappraisal of the Bigge Reports', 14.

governed—whether the military, the judiciary, many free settlers or clergy such as Marsden.⁶⁴

There is also an unmistakable emphasis during the Philo Free affair on a related—and equally important—criterion of social worth and standing for nineteenth-century Britons and clergymen: gentility. J. F. C. Harrison succinctly captures the essence of this slippery concept:

> When anyone in early Victorian times was asked to define exactly what he meant by gentleman he had as much difficulty as we do today. Anthony Trollope [...] confessed [...] that although a man might be defied to define the term gentleman, everyone knew what he meant. Essentially the term was held to include gentle birth, ownership of a landed estate, and an income sufficient to permit the enjoyment of leisure. But the concept of gentility also implied certain moral qualities—honour, courage, consideration for others—which were embodied in a fairly strict code of what was 'done' and 'not done'. What was most clearly expected of a gentleman was public service, given voluntarily if necessary at his own expense. In return he was accorded immense respect and his authority and privileges were accepted.⁶⁵

In the same period, however, gentility was being recast by a rising, self-assured financial and commercial middle class, many of whom did not feel the need to ground their social status in the traditional markers of land or birth.⁶⁶ This meant that a man of humble social origins such as Marsden could attain genteel status through his role as an Anglican clergyman and through his public character.⁶⁷ That said, land was still valuable currency on the gentility market, and Marsden's growing wealth from land ownership and pastoral interests could only serve to bolster his status in colonial society. Nevertheless, his university education (even if incomplete) and clerical profession were still enough to secure genteel status, especially in the colonies. It has been suggested that Marsden was merely grasping for wealth and social status, but it has to be remembered that for a man like him with humble beginnings in the *petit bourgeoisie* or aspirational middle class, the little social capital he possessed was his on account of his character, conduct and reputation. For the *bourgeoisie parvenu*, as Roy Porter put it pithily, it

---

64   Spigelman, 'The Macquarie Bicentennial: A Reappraisal of the Bigge Reports', 13–17.
65   Harrison, *Victorians*, 125–6, 163.
66   See Hilton, *Mad, Bad, and Dangerous People?*, 121–51.
67   For greater detail, see Gladwin, *Anglican Clergy*, chs. 2–3.

was a case of 'polish or perish'.[68]

In this respect, Macquarie's estimation of Campbell was strikingly different from his estimation of Marsden. One of Macquarie's biographers notes that Campbell was Irish-born but of Scottish descent, aged 39 when Macquarie met him, well-informed and with experience in banking. Campbell 'gave every appearance of gentility' and seemed to Macquarie a contrast to the 'troublesome gentry of NSW about whom he had heard vapourish tales'.[69] On the other hand, Macquarie had in 1814 complained to Bathurst of Marsden's 'low Rank', lack of a liberal education '*in the Usual way*', and his being 'much tinctured with Methodistical and other Sectarian Principles'.[70] It should be kept in mind, however, that Macquarie himself had humble social and material origins (albeit with some claims to Scottish gentility—his father was a cousin of the last chieftain of the clan Macquarie). He was a practical soldier, pragmatic in outlook, and a self-made Scot on a salary of £2,000. It is also worth noting that Macquarie's terse relations with Bigge were exacerbated by their disparity in social status: Bigge was 20 years Macquarie's junior, an Oxford-educated barrister from *haute bourgeoisie* stock, and on a salary of £3,000.

These notion of respectability and gentility reveal other important fault-lines between Marsden and the Macquarie-Campbell faction. A cult of respectability had taken root in the middle and upper classes by the early nineteenth century. The main function of respectability in this period, as Harrison suggests:

> was the strengthening of a common culture, based on middle class social norms, into which the working classes could be integrated. Respectability was the goal to be striven for, and self-improvement the way to attain it.[71]

In relation to colonial Australian gentry, Penny Russell adds that gentility was a means of establishing social position, defining prestige and legitimizing social leadership.[72] In the colonial context gentility ensured that clergy could influence the middle and higher echelons of

---

68 I have borrowed this quotation by Roy Porter from Russell, *Savage or Civilised?*, 119.
69 Ritchie, *Macquarie*, 117.
70 See Macquarie to Bathurst, 7/10/1814 (*HRA* 1.8, 336–38).
71 Harrison, *The Early Victorians*, 134; so Young, *Victorian England*, 25.
72 Russell, *Savage or Civilised?*, Ch. 4.

society as well as the low.⁷³

By the early nineteenth century, however, in the wake of efforts from the late 1780s by Wilberforce and other prominent Anglicans such as Hannah More to reform élite manners, the traits of gentility, respectability and social leadership were being transposed into a Christian key. In 1787 Wilberforce had famously written that God had set before him 'the reformation of manners' and slavery abolition, and advised leading Yorkshire Evangelical William Hey (also a mentor of Marsden) that Evangelical-led voluntary societies should become 'the guardian of the religion and the morals of the people'.⁷⁴ In the same year Wilberforce secured the King's proclamation of encouragement of piety and virtue, and established a society to promote its implementation. Targeted offences included profanation of the Sabbath, swearing, drunkenness and licentious publications. Also significant, in light of Marsden's later involvement as magistrate, was Wilberforce's remark that the institution of such a society would induce 'well-meaning and active men to act as magistrates or constables, who [had] now so little encouragement to discharge obnoxious duties with fidelity and strictness'.⁷⁵ Fallout from the French Revolution prompted Wilberforce in 1793 (the same year Marsden left for NSW) to begin his manifesto, the title of which is revealing: *A Practical View of the Prevailing Religious System of Professed Christians in the Higher and Middle Classes in this Country, Contrasted with Real Christianity*. In this immensely influential book he further expounded the promotion of Evangelical Christianity and virtue among the upper classes, and the enforcement, by 'men of authority and influence', of laws to protect morality. Historian Gareth Atkins notes wide scholarly acceptance of this so-called 'reformation of manners':

> [T]he late eighteenth and early nineteenth centuries, broadly speaking, formed a period in which the serious-minded middle classes came to

---

73 Le Couteur, 'Brisbane Anglicans', 118. See also Strong, 'The Reverend John Wollaston', 266–71; Atkinson, *Camden*, 98–9. Atkinson notes that varying ranks and degrees existed among Australian gentlemen. Gentility in the cities and towns consisted of the principal government officers and clergy, and at a lower level the leading professional men and merchants. In the country, however, gentility could reach down to a Clerk of Petty Sessions, the better educated medical men or even a 'superior tradesman'.
74 W. Wilberforce to Hey, n. d.
75 Ibid.

prominence in British life, as stern critics of both Frenchified aristocratic corruption and the squalid vices of the poor. It is also acknowledged that the rise of 'vital religion' [evangelicalism] was closely tied in with this development, and that, as a number of recent commentators have pointed out, politicians and public men increasingly spoke the languages of evangelicalism, even if not all shared its theological temper. 'Evangelicalism, national and provincial', reminds Boyd Hilton, 'was undoubtedly an important element in the mentality of the *haute bourgeoisie* that dominated British politics from 1784 to the 1840s'.[76]

While it was still possible to be both respectable and a gentleman without being a 'vital' or 'serious' Christian, as Evangelicals put it, by the early nineteenth century it was difficult to escape society's diffused 'Christian tint'.[77] The complexion of this tint is evident, for example, among Jane Austen's fictional clergymen, such as Edmund Bertram of *Mansfield Park*. A crucial point here is that Marsden's most powerful metropolitan patron and ally after 1790 and for most of his career in Australia, William Wilberforce, was one of the architects and driving forces of the 'reformation of manners'. Through legislation, incorrigible activism and writing, Wilberforce influenced not only Marsden but a generation of young Evangelicals. Marsden thoroughly imbibed his mentor's worldview.[78] This also helps to explain why Macquarie's abovementioned elevation to the magistracy of a figure like Simeon Lord, notorious for his immoral personal life, so enraged Wilberforce, for whom gentility and respectability were understood in moral (i.e. Christian) terms. Likewise Marsden. While Macquarie appeared to measure convict reformation in terms of worldly success, Marsden and Wilberforce clearly measured it more in moral terms.[79] Macquarie was, to Wilberforce and Marsden, breaching both social and moral norms in admitting ex-convicts and infamously immoral men to his table and to positions of power. The downside from a later vantage point, of course, was that this tended to reinforce a caste system and division in Australian society between 'exclusives' and 'emancipists' that would last

---

76 Atkins, 'Wilberforce', 4.
77 Le Couteur, 'Brisbane Anglicans: 1842–1875', 34–5. So, Atkins, 'Wilberforce', 7–8, ch. 7, amongst others.
78 See Gladwin, 'Marsden's Generals'.
79 Golder, *High and Responsible Office*, 13.

for generations. It also risked conflations of Christianity with personal morality and social status.

Men on a mission

An absence in the literature on Philo Free is recognition of the context of the Protestant missionary movement and Marsden's place within it. One of the hallmarks of early nineteenth-century Evangelicalism was activism, which flowed from conversion. This was an impulse that the great American 'father' of Evangelicalism, Jonathan Edwards, had characterized as a 'great desire for the conversion of others'. After the 1790s this activistic bent was being powerfully channelled through voluntary societies, not least missionary societies that sought the conversion of peoples worldwide.[80] After the 1790s an explosion of missionary enthusiasm among Evangelical Protestants issued in the creation of several voluntary lay missionary societies, few of which had close connections with established authorities in church and state: the Baptist Missionary Society (BMS; 1792); the London Missionary Society (LMS; 1795, initially non-denominational but eventually Congregational); and the Anglican Church Missionary Society (CMS; 1799). The Edinburgh and Glasgow societies (1796) were followed by the American Board of Commissioners for Foreign Missions (ABCFM; 1810); the Basel Missionary Society (1815); the constitution of the Wesleyan Methodist Missionary Society (WMMS; 1818); the Berlin Missionary Society (1824) and the Rhenish Missionary Society (1828), to name only a few of the most prominent. Various factors converged to launch the movement: British maritime supremacy and imperial expansion; popular awareness of overseas cultures via the exploits of explorers such as James Cook; the impact of transatlantic Evangelical 'revivals' or 'awakenings'; the expansion of Evangelical contacts and influences (transatlantic and continental) through religious, friendship, family, humanitarian and professional networks; and a shared stock of theological, philosophical and economic ideas that were subject to intense discussion and debate.[81] This was accompanied by structural shifts in Western society that included accelerating population growth

---

80 Bebbington, *Evangelicalism in Modern Britain*, 2–17.
81 Porter, *Religion Versus Empire?*, 40–1.

and the emergence of a commercial middle class, which further exposed the inability of traditional state churches to meet the people's spiritual needs and created space for a transition from old models of Christendom to new voluntarist movements and associations.[82]

The institutional Anglican Church, most political élites, and polite society initially showed little interest in a movement that smacked of 'Methodism' and 'enthusiasm' (bywords for fanaticism), propagated by men of relatively humble social and educational standing.[83] Only nine years before the Philo Free case in 1808, the Rev. Sydney Smith had lampooned Baptist missionaries in Bengal in an infamous *Edinburgh Review* article, describing them as 'little detachments of maniacs'. '[I]f a tinker is a devout man', Smith added, 'he infallibly sets off for the East'. More worrying for Smith and the imperial government was the potential of missionary meddling with indigenous cultures that might expose 'the best possessions of the country to extreme danger'.[84] Only in 1813 were Wilberforce and his supporters able to secure from Parliament and the East India Company legal permission to send missionaries to India (an outcome that they had unsuccessfully sought twenty years before).[85] Andrew Porter observes, moreover, that it was only in the 1830s—around 15 years after the Philo Free case—that Evangelical missions began to attract widespread public acceptance and even official support. By that time the LMS had established a strong missionary presence in the Western Pacific and South Africa; the CMS in Sierra Leone, India and New Zealand; the Baptists in Bengal and the West Indies, with the Methodists and Presbyterian similarly poised for further expansion.[86] Marsden, as a coordinator for the CMS and LMS missions, had of course been instrumental in shoring up the position of those missions in New Zealand and the South Pacific.

It is understandable, then, why during the 1810s and early 1820s there was such strong concern among missionary advocates, not least Marsden, to promote the missionary cause favourably and to attract public support, both politically and among the wider public. There was

---

82 Hutchinson & Wolffe, *A Short History of Global Evangelicalism*, 35. The substance of this and the next paragraph is adapted from Gladwin, 'Missions and Colonialism', 284–85.
83 Porter, *Religion Versus Empire?*, 39–41; Walls, *The Missionary Movement*, 249.
84 Smith, 'Indian Missions', 179–80.
85 Carson, *The East India Company and Religion*.
86 Porter, 'Missions and Empire', 47.

a real sense that in the Philo Free case it was the Evangelical overseas mission project (especially in the enormously promising fields of New Zealand and the South Pacific) as much as Marsden that was on trial. Campbell's description of Marsden as the 'Christian Mahomet' of the South Seas was perceived as a slight on the cause of missions, of which there was no greater supporter than Wilberforce and his well-connected Evangelical networks. This concern is evident in the response of metropolitan missionary leaders to the outcome of the case (though on this point it should be remembered that Campbell's letter was also highlighting concern for missions to Indigenous Australians). At the 1819 anniversary meeting of the Church Missionary Society (CMS) at the Freemasons' Tavern in London, a warm vote of thanks was presented to Marsden, an honour that had not previously been paid to any individual member by the Society. Dr John Mason Good, a member of the CMS committee and a correspondent of Marsden, apprised Marsden of the event:

> [T]he severe and important battle you [Marsden] have fought [by means of the Philo Free case], and the triumph you have so gloriously achieved, have induced the Society to step out of their usual routine on this occasion, and to show, not only to yourself, but to the world at large, the full sense they entertain of the honourable and upright part you have taken, and their unanimous determination to give you all their support. I agree [...] that your contest has not been a personal one, but that the important objects of the Society have been at stake, and that the victory you have obtained is of more importance to the cause of virtue, honour, and true religion, and more especially to the cause of Christian missions in Australasia, than to yourself.[87]

Scholarship on the Philo Free case is also yet to incorporate a significant body of research about the social location, education and motivation of both overseas missionaries and colonial Anglican clergy during this period, notably for India, the South Pacific and the Australian colonies.[88] Historians have stressed most missionaries' relatively humble social origins in the aspirational or lower middle class (*petit bourgeoisie*). This scholarship has also demonstrated that professionalism and genuine missionary vocation were not thought

---

87 J. M. Good to Marsden, n.d., in Marsden, *The Life and Labours*, 124.
88 Piggin, *Making Evangelical Missionaries*; Gunson, *Messengers of Grace*.

incompatible with aspirations for social status and economic security. As I have demonstrated elsewhere, the same can be said of colonial Australian clergy, challenging conventional accounts that emphasise social and economic push factors in clergy's motives and aspirations, rather than a genuine colonial missionary vocation.[89] For a figure like Marsden, then, it could be a case of 'both/and' rather than 'either/or'.

Conclusion

Some historians have viewed Marsden's strenuous efforts at vindication as vengeful politicking against Macquarie or merely self-justifying attempts to shore up his hard-won worldly success and status. The most detailed scholarly examination of the Philo Free case, apart from the chapter in Yarwood's biographical study of Marsden and Andrew Sharp's incisive recent assessment, is Ratcliffe's honours thesis.[90] Ratcliffe has no hesitation in declaiming on Marsden's motives. Disagreeing with Yarwood's more modest criticisms of Marsden (and in stark contrast with Sharp's measured conclusions), she contends that in Marsden's decision to pursue the suit there 'was no longer any concern for the reputation of the missions, for the restoration of his own reputation or of the good name of the societies in the colony'.[91] This was not an attempt to 'to rescue his own character', as Marsden's defence lawyer put it, but rather the pursuit of a personal vendetta. Marsden was vindictive, bent upon revenge against Macquarie and concerned with protecting his own position and interests.[92] Marsden's 'primary motive', contends Ratcliffe, 'loomed as the demise of the government through the Secretary'.[93] Yet, as any historian knows, a person's motivations can be multifarious and immensely difficult to assess. 'The heart has its reasons, of which reason knows nothing', as Pascal astutely noted.[94] It takes a bold historian indeed to eschew the longstanding wisdom of Elizabeth I and instead seek to make windows of men's souls.

89 Gladwin, *Anglican Clergy*, ch. 3.
90 Ratcliffe, '"Pens Dipped in Gall"'. For Sharp's far more careful assessment, see Sharp, *The World, the Flesh & the Devil*, Chs. 18–19 (pp. 431–506).
91 Ratcliffe, '"Pens Dipped in Gall"', 35.
92 Ratcliffe, '"Pens Dipped in Gall"', 45.
93 Ratcliffe, '"Pens Dipped in Gall"', 49.
94 "*Le cœur a ses raisons que la raison ne connaît point.*"

This chapter has demonstrated instead that a more historically tenable and full-orbed understanding of Marsden's actions in relation to the Philo Free case may be gained by considering his larger contexts, not least in the light of the Bigge Commission. Marsden's vision for the colony, as we have seen, was framed by his Evangelical mentors' (and his own) 'economics of providence'. Similarly, social mobility was not thought incompatible with a genuine missionary vocation by many *petit-bourgeois* men who made up a large percentage of the workforce for overseas missionary service, both as clergy in the settler colonies and as missionaries beyond the purview of the British Empire in the South Pacific. Character, manners, and patronage were still crucial for the success of most major enterprises undertaken by middle-class men in the early nineteenth-century British world. Marsden's course of action also needs to be understood within the broader context of an Evangelical quest—most notably in these decades after the French Revolution—both for a 'reformation of manners' in Britain and for the creation of a missionary movement with global reach. Such findings are in broad sympathy with the most nuanced and rigorous recent scholarly assessment of Marsden and the Philo Free case.[95]

It is interesting to note that the word 'libel' derives from the Latin word for 'a little book', having the same etymology as the word 'library'. This is mainly because most libels are written or printed. In the case of the context of the Bigge Commission and its role in the Philo Free case, it is clear that another 'little book', Bigge's report to Parliament, was an important factor in the rancour between Marsden and the Campbell–Macquarie faction.

---

95 Sharp, *The World, the Flesh & the Devil*, Chs. 18–19 (pp. 431–506).

Chapter 12

FREEDOM OF SPEECH AND FREEDOM OF THE PRESS IN COLONIAL NEW SOUTH WALES

Caitlin Hurley

'A free Press is the most legitimate, and at the same time the most powerful weapon that can be employed to annihilate such influence, frustrate the designs of tyranny and restrain the arm of oppression'.
The *Australian* 14th October 1824

The first printing press arrived in colonial New South Wales with the First Fleet in 1788. Fifteen years after the arrival of European settlers this screw press was used to print the first newspaper of the colony. In January 1817, the author of Philo Free used one of these government-controlled pages to lampoon a public figure, and subsequently had to bear the costs of exercising this freedom. This essay will explore the history of the press in New South Wales, its contribution to colonial society and the attempts by Governor Darling to restrain the licentiousness of the press in the 1820's. Through such an analysis it will be shown that while the colonial administration did attempt to restrict freedom of speech and the press in the colony, the residents of New South Wales enjoyed for the most part a freedom of speech not experienced or enjoyed by their contemporaries back in England.

The *Sydney Gazette*

The first newspaper in the colony of New South Wales was printed on the 5th of March 1803 by George Howe. The *Sydney Gazette and New*

South Wales Advertiser would remain in almost uninterrupted circulation until October 1842.

In his first editorial Howe stated that the pages of the *Gazette* would 'open no channel to political discussion or personal animadversion [...] information is our only purpose'.[1] This information would take the form of General Orders, agriculture extracts, moral and religious admonitions, law reports and general news.[2] True to its word, the first edition of the *Gazette* reported the arrival of granaries in Parramatta, the Governor's Orders for the distribution of 4000 gallon of spirits throughout the colony, the shipping news, news from Europe, local market prices as well as news of 'a wife selling at Manchester, and of several public executions'.[3]

Censorship in the colony

Governor King supported the creation of the first colonial newspaper. In a despatch back to Colonial Secretary Lord Hobart, King described Howe as an 'ingenious man' and seems to suggest that it was Howe's idea to create a newspaper that would facilitate the distribution of information throughout the colony for settlers and the inhabitants at large.[4] While the creation of a newspaper was considered beneficial to the colony, the *Gazette* was produced under the watchful eye of Governor King. Not only was the press housed at Government House, but the Governor also provided the paper and the ink. While King encouraged Howe to gather information and news that would inform the inhabitants of the colony, each edition of the paper was to be 'inspected by an officer'.[5] Howe's son Robert, who replaced his father as the publisher of the *Gazette* in 1821 noted many years later that more often than not this officer was Governor King himself.[6] King also ensured that copies of the *Gazette* were sent back to the Colonial Secretary.[7]

From its first edition, the *Gazette* was perceived as the paper of the colonial government. This is probably because of where the press

---

1 SG/3/1803
2 Walker, *The Newspaper Press in New South Wales, 1803–1920*, 3.
3 Bonwick, *Early Struggles of the Australian Press*, 4.
4 King to Hobart, 9/3/1803 (*HRA* 1.4, 85).
5 King to Hobart, 9/3/1803 (*HRA* 1.4, 85).
6 *SG* 7/3/1828, 2.
7 Watson, 'Introduction', *HRA* 1.13, vi.

was stored, Government House, and its content. For most of its print run the *Gazette* 'was chiefly preoccupied with the official orders and notifications of Government'.[8] The colonial historian Bennett noted that 'officials of all grades, when mentioned at all, were spoken of in terms of the most fulsome manner'.[9] Likewise, Robert Walker notes that through the pages of the *Gazette* ran a rule of prudence and a deference to authority.[10]

It is hard to know to what extent the residents of the colony were aware of the censorship carried out in the *Gazette* by the Governor or his designated officials. On the one hand the Philo Free incident seems to indicate that there was very little awareness of any censorship taking place. Marsden himself wrote to Sir John Wylde that he was not aware that 'Mr Secy Campbell is Censor of the press'.[11] Furthermore, it appears that he believed that there was to his knowledge 'no Law that authorizes a Censor of the Press in any British Colony, nor is there to my knowledge any such Law in the British Empire as delegates that Authority to any individual'.[12] On the other hand, Bonwick argues that the reason officials were spoken so well of in the *Gazette* was a direct result of it 'being under the strictest censorship'.[13] Even if NSW residents were not aware of its censorship, the publication of the colony's second newspaper lifted censorship from the pages of the *Gazette*.

The *Australian*

The *Gazette* remained the sole newspaper in the colony until October 1824. On Thursday the 14th of October the *Australian* was published by William Charles Wentworth and Robert Wardell. Wentworth, a son of the colony, and Wardell, born in England, were both Barristers who shared chambers in Macquarie Place. In their first editorial Wentworth and Wardell claimed that the time was ripe in the history of the colony for the emergence of a free Press. They argued that the colony was no longer an infant society preoccupied with its own survival but was

---

8   Bonwick, *Early Struggles of the Australian Press*, 4.
9   Bonwick, *Early Struggles of the Australian Press*, 4.
10 Walker, *The Newspaper Press in New South Wales, 1803–1920*, 4.
11 Marsden to Wylde, 7/1/1817.
12 Marsden to Wylde, 7/1/1817.
13 Bonwick, *Early Struggles of the Australian Press*, 4.

rather an advancing society where its territory was being expanded and land cultivated and, as a result, people were accumulating wealth. As a progressing society, the colony was becoming a place where conflicts of interests and opinions were beginning to occur. In such a society, they declared, 'a free Press is the most legitimate, and at the same time the most powerful weapon that can be employed to annihilate such influence, frustrate the designs of tyranny and restrain the arm of oppression'.[14]

From its first edition the *Australian* contained a regular section called 'Freedom of the Press'. In their editorial in January 1825, Wentworth and Wardell called for guidelines against any form of censure in the colonial press. They stated that 'the sooner the duties and privileges of Editors of Newspapers are defined and proclaimed to them the better; for as yet but few seem to have any notion either of the boundaries of discussion, or the law which regulates the principles, and admire our independence; but our best friends will censure when they fancy they are included in any reproof, or their public conduct reprehended by us'.[15]

Unlike the *Gazette* with its aversion to political comment, the *Australian* sought out this interaction with its reader by aiming that 'it should become the medium of extensive and general communication among all members of the Colony, thereby concentrating public opinion and giving a tone and a direction to public feeling'.[16] The *Australian* aimed to be a free but not licentious publication.[17] In March 1825 it declared itself to be an independent paper.[18]

Wentworth and Wardell were so committed to the notion of the utility of a free press that they did not ask Governor Brisbane for official permission to produce the paper. As a result of its publication, Howe asked Brisbane to lift the official censorship of the *Gazette*. This request was granted on the 15th of October 1824. While censorship was officially lifted, the *Gazette* continued to be printed under the subheading 'Published by Authority'. The lifting of the censorship of the *Gazette* and the publication of the *Australian*, even without his consent, appeared to

---

14   *Australian* 14/10/1824, 2.
15   *Australian* 27/1/1825.
16   *Australian* 14/10/1824.
17   *Australian* 14/10/1824.
18   *Australian* 31/3/1825.

please Brisbane. He noted to Lord Bathurst that removal of the *Gazette*'s censorship and 'the experiment of the full latitude of the freedom of the press had been beneficial'.[19]

The *Monitor*

On the 19th of December 1825 Lieutenant General Sir Ralph Darling replaced Governor Brisbane and became the seventh Governor of the Colony of New South Wales. Shortly after his arrival the colony got its third newspaper. *The Monitor* was first published on Friday the 19th of May 1826 by Edward Smith Hall. Initially, Governor Darling regarded the *Monitor* favourably. In a letter back to Under Secretary Hay he wrote that, although the *Monitor* was independent, 'it speaks of the Govern't in very favourable terms'.[20]

Newspapers as shapers of colonial society

The newspapers of the colony played a significant role in shaping the public debate of colonial society. As explored previously, the *Gazette* was for the first two decades of its circulation primarily the mouthpiece of the colonial administration. Its target demographic was the entire population of the colony. Besides 'offering news of auctions, shipping and other commercial events', the *Gazette* reported extensively on court proceedings.[21] Through this reporting it shaped debate and determine what was perceived as morally right and wrong within the colony.

As the *Gazette* aimed to be non-political, any political criticism within the colony was delivered through the use of 'pipes'. 'Pipes' were essentially poems of discontent lobbed over a fence into the homes of its subjects.[22] Instead of using the *Gazette* as a means to critique individuals and speak out against the authorities, anonymous 'pipes' were the preferred method of free speech. While the *Gazette* aimed to be non-political it did report on the use of 'pipes'. The *Gazette* reported one such pipe on the 9th of March 1816, after copies were circulated in the town of Sydney to the Lieutenant Governor, the Provost Marshall,

---

19 Brisbane to Bathurst, 12/1/1825 (*HRA* 1.11, 471).
20 Darling to Hay, 24/5/1826 (*HRA* 1.12, 327).
21 Atkinson, *The Europeans in Australia*, 1. 275.
22 Persse, 'Wentworth, William Charles (1790–1872)'.

the hospital, and lawyers. The paper reported that the pipe contained 'a false, malicious and scurrilous attack upon the character of His Honour the Lieutenant Governor'.[23] The author was later discovered to be the young W.C. Wentworth—evidently exercising the freedom of expression that he would later champion when editor of the *Australian*.

The *Australian* set itself up from the beginning as the opposition to the *Gazette*. Its editors wanted it to be an independent paper 'which may serve to point out the rising interests of the colonists, and become the organ of their grievances and rights, their wishes and wants'.[24] The *Australian* from its creation was a political newspaper. It's aim was 'to convert a prison into a colony fit for a freeman to inhabit himself and to bequeath as an inheritance to a free posterity'.[25]

The publication of the *Australian* marked a turning point in the life of the colonial press. Newspapers were no longer just a source of information and entertainment, but were a means of changing society and shaping debate. The editors of the colonial newspapers were public figures who yielded social power. Through their editorials they could pontificate on various issues. Hall at the *Monitor* used his editorials to shout 'about types of misery that for other editors were only passing colour on the local stage'.[26]

Because of their different editors, each paper had a certain flavour. The *Australian* was considered as a men's paper. Its editors Wentworth and Wardell were 'both young, unmarried, trained at the English bar, eager for notoriety, and angry with the restraints of life in New South Wales'.[27] Its main content was 'contests in the law courts, constitutional reform, fisticuffs and horse racing'.[28] In its reporting, the *Australian* often ridiculed women.[29]

The *Monitor* on the other hand appealed to female readers. Its editor recognised that women were good for circulation.[30] Atkinson notes that Hall 'made no effort to flatter the men, arguing against boxing and

---

23 *SG* 9/3/1816.
24 Bonwick, *Early Struggles of the Australian Press*, 12.
25 Bonwick, *Early Struggles of the Australian Press*, 12.
26 Atkinson, *The Europeans in* Australia, 2.69.
27 Atkinson, *The Europeans in Australia*, 2.66.
28 Atkinson, *The Europeans in Australia*, 2.66.
29 *Australian* 13/9/1825; 18/11/1824.
30 *Monitor* 29/12/1826.

betting at the races, and he dwelt on the needs of women shoppers'.[31] The *Monitor* refrained from court reporting in order to spare the women. Through his editorials and sourcing of articles Hall was a big promoter of women's equality.[32]

Anonymity in the colonial press

In the colonial press there was a lot of interaction between editors and members of the public. This interaction took place through the publication of letters to the editor or printer and the editor's editorial. Prior to the publication of the *Australian* and the *Monitor*, letters to the printer ranged from 'subjects of morality, farming, gardening, mission to the natives or such like non-political matters'.[33] With the launch of these papers, editorials and letters journeyed into the political arena with almost every edition. In some instances, letters to the editor were so voluminous they had to be issued as supplements to the regular edition of the paper.[34]

While there was much political debate in the colonial papers, from 1824 almost all the letters to the editor were published under pen names or pseudonyms. This was a practice that had existed since the publication of the *Gazette* in 1803. These pseudonyms were often linked to the subject matter of the letter, as either a play on words or a source of derision. Authors seemed to play with certain characters and names. Campbell in writing about Marsden chose the pseudonym 'Philo Free'. When writing about issues back in England or fighting for English rights in the colony it was not uncommon to read letters from 'an English Spirit', 'a British Spark', 'a true born Scotsman', or this very impassioned author: 'The cause for which Hampden bled in the field and Sydney died on the scaffold'.[35] The use of pen names was a way of maintaining anonymity while commenting on issues of the day. In such a small colony, the use of pseudonyms enabled people to speak on issues without fear of immediate retribution or litigation.

While it could be argued that the primary audience of the colonial

---

31 Atkinson, *The Europeans in Australia*, 2.68.
32 *Monitor* 21/7/1827; 11/8/1827.
33 Bonwick, *Early Struggles of the Australian Press*, 8.
34 *SG* 16/12/1824.
35 *Monitor* 29/12/1826.

newspapers was those living in New South Wales, the editors and the colonial administration were aware of a secondary audience. This secondary audience was Westminster and the Colonial Office. Governors were required to send copies of all the colonial newspapers to the colonial offices.[36] As such, newspaper editors were aware that their newspapers were a means of advertising their desires and causes to their colonial overseers and 'provided weapons for their allies in Westminster'.[37]

Restraining of the Press

Governor Darling inherited from Governor Brisbane a culture where the three newspapers of New South Wales had been allowed to operate rather freely. On the 12th of July 1825, Earl Bathurst proposed that Darling should introduce to the Executive Council some measures to restrict the freedom of the press in the Colonies of New South Wales and Van Diemen's Land. Bathurst was concerned that 'the entire exemption of the Publishers from all restraint of the local government, must be highly dangerous in a Society, of so peculiar a description'.[38] Bathurst was concerned that a free press in a penal colony could have negative effects on the civil order of the colony. But he was also wary of not violating the rights of the Free Settlers granted under British Law. Bathurst suggested to Darling that 'no Newspaper be published without a licence to be applied for to the Governor'.[39] This licence would be forfeited if a newspaper was convicted of blasphemy or seditious libel. Furthermore, Bathurst proposed the introduction of a stamp duty for licenced newspapers.

By the time of the launch of the *Monitor*, Governor Darling had not implemented Bathurst's instructions in regards to the restraining of the newspapers in New South Wales. In a rather bold move he wrote to Bathurst that he did not feel these instructions were necessary in the colony. He noted that the 'Government has experienced no attacks, having on the Contrary, been most honourably spoken of on all occasions

---

36 Hirst, *Convict Society and Its Enemies*, 173.
37 O'Malley, 'Class Formation and the "Freedom" of the Colonial Press. New South Wales 1800–1850', 431.
38 Bathurst to Darling, 12/7/1825 (*HRA* 1.12, 16–17).
39 Bathurst to Darling, 12/7/1825 (*HRA* 1.12, 17).

since my arrival (I mean even by the *Australian*)'.⁴⁰ In his mind invoking such injudicious Laws would be detrimental to the local government and not worth the reputational risk for such a 'paltry amount of an obnoxious Tax'.⁴¹ It appears that Darling felt it best to refrain from implementing Bathurst's instructions until the licentiousness of the press had reach a level that warranted the imposition of such legislation.

Darling consulted the Executive Council, including the Chief Justice of New South Wales Sir Francis Forbes, for their opinion in regards to implementing Bathurst's recommendations. Forbes felt that any licensing laws were repugnant to English Law and therefore beyond the power of the Executive Council in New South Wales to enact.

As a result of Darling's restraint, the press in New South Wales in 1826 had a greater degree of freedom than their contemporaries back in Britain. Walker notes that 'in point of law the Press in the remote gaol of exile was now freer than in the country of origin, for there was no registration, no stamp and advertisement duties'.⁴²

The role of the press in colonial life

When the *Gazette* was first published in 1803, the Colony of New South Wales had a population of approximately 7000. Of these 7000 inhabitants, roughly 1000 were free citizens with the remainder being convicts.⁴³ The state of the colony was rather exceptional as there were but two classes in the colony: 'those who ruled, and those who obeyed'.⁴⁴ In this unique society newspapers played a significant and key role in the life of the young colony. They were effectively the lifeblood of the colony as they were not only a source of information but entertainment. As colonial society grew and matured by the 1820's the newspaper of the colony operated as the voice of, and agitators for, change within the colony.

While the size, paper quality, and days of distribution varied dramatically in the early life of the press in the colony the format of the three original newspapers was fairly consistent. Page one of a publication

---

40 Darling to Hay, 24/5/1826 (*HRA* 1.12, 327).
41 Darling to Hay, 24/5/1826 (*HRA* 1.12, 328).
42 Walker, *The Newspaper Press in New South Wales, 1803–1920*, 6.
43 Walker, *The Newspaper Press in New South Wales, 1803–1920*, 3.
44 [The *Empire*], 'Australian Descovery and Colonisation. Chapter XII', 2.

was usually comprised of official government news or advertisements. The editorial was usually published on the second page. The remainder of the publication could be comprised of poems by locals, auction information, meetings minutes or gossip. From the outset the colonial papers 'encouraged precision–if not accuracy–as to who people were and when things happened'.[45] As such they paint a vivid picture of early colonial life in Sydney.

Newspapers as a source of information in the colony

The *Gazette* was originally created in part through the need for the colonial authorities to circulate orders and information throughout the colony. With the creation of the *Gazette* these orders were published as 'General Orders' and were typically published on the first page of the *Gazette*. Through these General Orders the government regulated the words, habits and conduct of the residents of the colony. In 1865, another Australian paper, the *Empire*, noted that the General Orders of the *Gazette* 'were of the most extraordinary kind'.[46] They regulated the time that people were to rise and go to bed, punishments for seditious words or actions, and the imposition of tariffs.[47]

The *Gazette* was a key tool in the colonial administration's ability to control and manage society. Between 1803 and 1833 the content of the *Gazette* was 'chiefly occupied with the official orders and notifications of the government'.[48] Through General Orders published in the *Gazette*, the inhabitants of the colony were made aware of the government's intentions. This is beautifully illustrated in the *Gazette*'s coverage of the arrival of spirits in the colony in its first issue. Readers were informed of how many gallons of spirits had landed and how the authorities would distribute the spirits. Of the 4000 gallons landed, Governor King allocated 1000 for Officers on the Civil Establishment, 1000 Gallons for Naval and Military Commissioned Officers, and 1000 gallons for licensed people. The remaining 1000 gallons would be allocated to 'such persons as the Governor may think proper'.[49]

45 Atkinson, *The Europeans in Australia*, 2.64.
46 [The *Empire*], 'Australian Descovery and Colonisation. Chapter XII', 2.
47 [The *Empire*], 'Australian Descovery and Colonisation. Chapter XII', 2.
48 Bonwick, *Early Struggles of the Australian Press*, 4.
49 *SG* 5/3/1803.

The papers also reported on the movements and priorities of the Governor. This included detail reports of trips through the colony, such as Governor Brisbane's visit to Moreton Bay in 1824.[50] During the Rum Rebellion the *Gazette* gave a significant amount of inches to the search for Governor Bligh.[51] The tradition of reporting on Vice Regal visits is still in practice today.

In addition to Government Orders and Vice Regal news, newspapers were not surprisingly the main source of information within the young colony. This news ranged from coverage of criminal cases being heard at the local police station to personal news about jilted lovers as 'mere talk, footpath gossip was stimulated by print'.[52] Newspapers regularly featured extracts from newspapers back in England and around the empire. This international news, often lifted verbatim, would detail the proceedings of parliament, the colonial office, and the health of the sovereign.[53] The *Australian* was quite partial to reprinting and commenting on articles about censorship of the press in other parts of the Empire.[54]

Newspapers were the key means for reporting on and engaging with the issues of the day. Issues discussed in the papers included the soap shortage of 1805, with calls for all members of the colony to help. Farmers were taught the best ways to plant and harvest various crops. And the weather was reported on extensively. A key issue in the early decades of the colony was the relationship between Europeans and the aboriginal community, reports highlighting 'troubles' in certain localities and any attempts made for peace. Rev. Marsden's attempt to hold a conference with natives was recorded by the *Gazette* in January 1805.[55] The *Monitor* took a great interest in the relationship with the aboriginal community and encouraged discussion of this issue through its reporting, editorials and letters to the editor.[56]

Advertisements in the colonial newspapers of meetings encouraged people to become involved in the civil and religious aspects of colonial

---

50 *Australian* 9/12/1824.
51 *SG* 26/1/1808.
52 Atkinson, *The Europeans in Australia*, 1.276.
53 *SG* 17/4/1803, 1.
54 *Australian* 2/12/1824.
55 *SG* 27/1/1805, 3.
56 *Monitor* 2/6/1826, 3; 15/12/1826, 3.

life. On the religious front, locals were notified of the opening of new churches. In April 1803 locals were invited to the opening of St Johns Parramatta by Rev. Marsden. In the same issue, members of the Roman Catholic church were summoned to a meeting at Government House on the 20th of April to register as Catholics.[57] This gathering was then reported in the following issue.[58]

As the colony grew locals were invited to participate in the creation of civil societies and organisations. Through the *Gazette* free settlers were invited to meetings in regards to the establishment of the Bank of New South Wales. This bank, the first in the colony, was established after three meetings, all duly covered by the *Gazette*.[59] The meetings of other civil societies such as the Agricultural society and the creation of schools, including Sydney Grammar School, were detailed exhaustively.[60]

Newspapers were the key source of discovering what goods and wares were available within the colony. This information was captured through traditional advertising of local business but also by the inclusion of shipping news. Traditional advertisements gave when auctions were taking place, and the going rate for particular foods and vegetables. The shipping news detailed the arrival and departure dates of ships, where they are coming from or going to, and the cargo they were carrying. The shipping news also contained warnings about hazards for mariners and news of ships being wrecked.[61]

Newspapers as a source of entertainment

The early colonial press was not only the primary means of disseminating information that was integral to the life of the colony, but also a source entertainment. Atkinson in his history of Australia states that newspapers 'gave a sparkle to daily events and to daily speech and encouraged a thirst for stories'.[62] Through its coverage of everyday instances, such as the escape of a goose in 1805, 'local stories were

57 *SG* 17/4/1803, 1.
58 *SG* 24/1/1803.
59 *SG* 5/12/1816.
60 *Australian* 24/10/1824.
61 *SG* 12/3/1803.
62 Atkinson, *The Europeans in Australia*, 2.63.

thereby fixed within the mind of every reader'.[63] They regularly published the verse and poetry of those living in the colony. These verses and poems, written by men and women, detailed their experiences in the colony and reflections upon their heritage.

For a small colony, the newspaper business was growing. By 1827 the *Gazette* was publishing three issues a week with a circulation of approximately 600. The *Australian* published two issues a week with the same circulation as the *Gazette*. The *Monitor* produced one issue a week with a circulation of 500.[64]

Attempts to restrain the press

In the 1820's, the colonial newspapers played an integral part in the life of the colony. While Darling had inherited a positive relationship with the press, this relational status was to be short lived. By the time Darling arrived in New South Wales two major political groups had begun to emerge within the colony. These groups were the exclusives and the emancipists. The exclusivists, comprised mostly of free settlers including officers of the old New South Wales Corps and colonial officials, were unified by the desire to 'exclude those with the convict taint from positions of status and power'.[65]

The emancipists, on the other hand, argued that freed convicts and their children should be able to participate in the affairs of the colony. Throughout 1826 they agitated for political and legal institutions in accordance with their English birthright, such as the right to a trial by jury and representative legislative councils.[66] Leading the charge for the emancipists were the editors of the *Australian*, Wentworth and Wardell. In their minds, Governor Darling epitomised the exclusivist cause.

Throughout 1826 the *Australian* and the *Monitor* argued passionately for the emancipist cause. Throughout the course of the year, the *Monitor* accused the exclusivist élite of receiving stolen goods, embezzling fines for personal use, and using force to extract confessions from convicts.[67] The criticism of Darling and the ruling exclusivists reached boiling

---

63 *SG* 29/3/1805; Atkinson, *The Europeans in Australia*, 1.276.
64 Walker, *The Newspaper Press in New South Wales, 1803–1920*, 56.
65 Neal, *The Rule of Law in a Penal Colony*, 18.
66 *Australian* 3/2/1825.
67 *Monitor* 30/6/1826; 11/8/1826; 22/9/1826.

point in November 1826 with an incident now known as the *Sudds Affair*.

In September 1826, Joseph Sudds and Patrick Thompson, privates in the 57th Regiment, stole a bale of cloth from a store on York Street. In stealing the cloth, Sudds and Thompson had hoped they would be caught and after a brief time of imprisonment be dismissed from the regiment and allowed to begin a new life as free settlers in the colony. At around this time, a culture had developed within the Army where soldiers were keen to be discharged from the Army instead of living by the harsh realities and regimen of military life. Darling was concerned that 'transportation to Australia had lost its deterrent effect and its role as punishment'.[68] In order to deter others from acting similarly, in a General Order of the 22nd of November, Darling had the sentence of Sudds and Thompson commuted 'to one of working in chains on the public roads of the colony'.[69] Sudds and Thompson were stripped of their clothes, dressed as prisoners, and put in a set of chains weighing fourteen pounds in total.[70] Unbeknown to Darling, Sudds was at this stage critically ill. He died five days later, on the 27th of November 1826.[71]

Initially the press expressed support for Darling's attempt to deter officers and convicts from committing crimes to remain in the settlement, but after Sudd's death the *Australian* and the *Monitor* were harshly critical of Darling's actions. The *Australian* accused Darling of overreacting and acting illegally by changing Sudds and Thompson's sentence.[72] By 1827, the *Monitor* and the *Australian* 'attacked the alleged cruelty of Darling with increasing vehemence', citing it as proof of the defectiveness of the autocratic government'.[73] They argued that only the enactment of trial by jury and a representative legislative council could overcome such tyranny. The war of words continued to escalate with the conflict ending up, either in legal action, or challenges to a duel. In late 1826 and early 1827, Darling twice attempted to have Hall prosecuted for publishing alleged inflammatory and seditious material.

---

68 Spigelman, 'Foundations of the Freedom of the Press in Australia', 89.
69 Walker, *The Newspaper Press in New South Wales, 1803–1920*, 9.
70 Spigelman, 'Foundations of the Freedom of the Press in Australia', 89.
71 Walker, *The Newspaper Press in New South Wales, 1803–1920*, 9–10.
72 *Australian* 29/11/1826.
73 Walker, *The Newspaper Press in New South Wales, 1803–1920*, 10.

Darling eventually withdrew both suits. In March 1827 Colonel Dumaresq, Darling's private secretary, challenged Wardell to a duel. After three shots were fired, neither man was injured and both parties' honour satisfied.[74]

With cases of libel potentially being brought to the courts, Chief Justice Forbes began to consider the role and liberty of the press in the colony. In February 1827, Forbes wrote to a his friend Under Secretary Horton that the purpose of the press is to 'equalise mankind'.[75] Such a press is 'excellent, indispensable, in a free state, because of its tendency to counteract that eternal propensity of our social natures to makes slaves or dupes of one another'.[76] Therefore 'a free press is not quite fitted to a servile population' such as New South Wales 'where one half of the community are worked in chains by the other'.[77] To his mind a free press is not suitable or desirable in a penal colony. But Forbes was concerned for a free press for the free settlers of the colony. For those who fell into this category not to have a free press was to have one of their legal rights taken away.

Forbes was also concerned that press in the colony was revelling in licentiousness. While the press was licentious, he believed that within English law there were sufficient means to curtail and prosecute this licentiousness. He passed blame on the Attorney General Saxe Bannister for failing to initiate prosecutions for libel.[78] In light of his concerns and the present state of the colony, Forbes concluded that he was 'a friend to a defined limitation upon the press'.[79]

After a failed trial of Wardell for libel, Darling wrote to Forbes on the 2nd of April stating that he believed 'that measures for restraining the Press cannot with safety to the colony be any longer delayed'.[80] He asked Forbes to consider how to enact the measure proposed by Bathurst back in July 1825. Forbes replied that he would be 'quite ready to certify an Ordinance which you may desire to be prepared, and to have laid before me, so as far as I am authorised by law'.[81]

74 Currey, *Sir Francis Forbes: The First Chief Justice of the Supreme Court of New South Wales*, 212.
75 Forbes to Horton, 6/2/1827 (*HRA* 4.1, 681–682).
76 Forbes to Horton, 6/2/1827 (*HRA* 4.1, 681).
77 Forbes to Horton, 6/2/1827 (*HRA* 4.1, 681).
78 Forbes to Horton, 6/2/1827 (*HRA* 4.1, 682).
79 Forbes to Horton, 6/2/1827 (*HRA* 4.1, 684).
80 Darling to Forbes, 2/4/1827.
81 Forbes to Darling 2/4/1827.

Darling began his endeavour to restrain his perceived licentiousness of the press by implementing legislation. On the 11th of April 1827, he brought two bills to the New South Wales Executive Council. These bills, known collectively as *The Newspaper Acts (1827)*, were the *Newspaper Regulation Bill* and the *Newspaper Duty Bill*. Forbes gave his apology for the meeting, as he was exhausted from continuous sessions of the Supreme Court.[82]

The *Newspaper Regulation Bill* was a bill with two principle measures: the licensing and regulation of newspapers.[83] Resumable licensing measures were prescribed in the first six clauses of the Bill. The remainder of the clauses imposed regulations on the newspapers and required that newspapers have to 'pay any fines that might be imposed for blasphemous or seditious libel'.[84] Furthermore, these clauses 'invested the Supreme Court with a discretionary power to banish from the Colony persons convicted, for the second time of having [...] composed, printed or published any seditious libel tending to bring into hatred and contempt the Government of the Colony'.[85] As he felt the first six clauses of the Bill were repugnant to English law, Forbes did not certify these clauses.[86] Forbes believed these clauses were repugnant to English Law as English law ensured that 'the freedom of the press is a constitutional right'.[87] He felt that to certify these clauses would 'destroy the freedom of the press and to place it at the discretion of the government'.[88] Through such a measure, the Governor would have the sole right to license newspapers in the colony. The remainder of the *Newspaper Regulation Bill* was passed into law on the 25th of April 1827.

The *Newspaper Duty Bill* was passed into law on the 3rd of May 1827. It was to come into effect on the 1st of June 1827, but was rescinded before it came into effect for several reasons. First, there were some questions regarding its authenticity as a certified Bill. Forbes certified the Bill with the space for the amount of the duty to be imposed blank.

---

82 Currey, *Sir Francis Forbes: The First Chief Justice of the Supreme Court of New South Wales*, 213.
83 O'Malley, 'Class Formation and the "Freedom" of the Colonial Press. New South Wales 1800–1850', 434.
84 Walker, *The Newspaper Press in New South Wales, 1803–1920*, 12.
85 Currey, *Sir Francis Forbes: The First Chief Justice of the Supreme Court of New South Wales*, 215–216.
86 Forbes, 'Newspaper Act Opinion 1827, NSWKR 3; [1827] NSW SupC 23'.
87 Forbes, 'Newspaper Act Opinion 1827, NSWKR 3; [1827] NSW SupC 23'.
88 Currey, *Sir Francis Forbes: The First Chief Justice of the Supreme Court of New South Wales*, 216.

Forbes believed that his certificate of the Bill applied only to the principle of the Bill and he would need to certify the final Bill once the amount of duty was agreed upon.[89] There was discussion at the Executive Council as to whether the duty was to be four pence as per English practice or sixpence. The Executive Council decided to follow the English precedent and carried a duty of four pence. The Bill was then passed into law without Forbes certifying it in its final form.

Second, Forbes began to believe that the purpose of the Bill wasn't to defray the cost of printing official publications, but to suppress the power and circulation of the colonial papers. Forbes argued that the imposition of a duty at four pence on every newspaper in the colony would send the newspaper broke. As such he believed he could not certify such a Bill as the proposed duty was 'oppressive and contrary to the provisions of the Law and every admitted principle of taxation'.[90] Forbes was effectively accusing Darling of using the Bill to silence the colonial newspapers that disagreed with him and his government.

Third, the colonial press, not surprisingly, was livid that such a law had come to pass. The *Australian* and the *Monitor* raised questions about the legality of the law and whether it was aligned with English law, and accused the Bill of being a means of crushing newspaper publishers and suffocating the liberty of writing.[91] Hall frequently referred to the Bills as the 'gagging acts'.[92] Darling complained to Forbes that 'the papers persevered in their mischievous endeavours to bring the Government into hatred and contempt, and in fact succeeded in exciting a strong spirit of discontent among the prisoners'.[93] Despite his frustrations, in the face of such criticism from Forbes and the press and questions of its legality, Darling had the Bill rescinded by the Executive Council on the 31st of May 1827.

The *Newspaper Acts* plagued the rest of Darling's tenure as Governor. His attempt to restrain the press through legislation had failed. He continued to be lampooned in the press and his relationship with the Chief Justice was severely damaged.[94] In late 1827, the *Australian* was

---

89 Forbes to R. Darling, 31/5/1827 (*HRA* 1.13, 392–394).
90 Forbes to R. Darling, 31/5/1827 (*HRA* 1.13, 395).
91 *Australian* 9/5/1827; 18/5/1827; *Monitor* 8/6/1827.
92 *Monitor* 4/5/1827; 11/5/1827.
93 Darling to Forbes, 14/4/1827.
94 Hirst, *Convict Society and Its Enemies*, 117.

still critical of Darling for his role in the Sudds affair. The colonial press was to his mind still licentious. Edgeworth notes that Darling 'had no option but to return to the courts in view of continuing hostility from the press'.[95]

Initially his attempts to restrain the press in the court room were unsuccessful. In both September and December of 1827, Wardell was charged and tried for printing scandal and libel concerning Darling. In both cases, he was acquitted after the jury was unable to reach of verdict. Furthermore, the Attorney General and the Solicitor General informed the Governor they would not try any further libel cases, unless they were 'extraordinarily flagrant' in nature.[96]

In September 1828, the tide began to turn against the press. Newly arrived Justice James Dowling found Hall guilty of libel against Archdeacon T.H. Scott. Dowling's delivery on the case 'signalled a distinct change of attitude on the part of the judiciary to press practices'.[97] He noted that 'the public press has on frequent occasions in latter times, exceeded those bounds which fairly and justly belong to its province'.[98] Furthermore he warned the press that unless it changes its tone and started to 'represent the people of this Colony in their true colours' they will bear the consequences.[99] In April 1829, Hall was convicted of libel against Darling and sentenced to six months imprisonment. A few days later, Edwin Hayes, who had become the part owner and editor of the *Australian* in 1828, was convicted of seditious libel against Darling for further comments about his role in the Sudds Affair.[100] By year's end Hall had been convicted of six charges of libel.[101] What had begun in 1817 with the Philo Free case had apparently now reached its apogee. Spigelman notes that 1829 cemented 'Sydney's position as a world capital of defamation litigation'.[102]

While Dowling was successfully prosecuting the press for libel in the courts, the Crown delivered its opinions on the *Newspaper Acts (1827)*. In 1828, the *Newspaper Regulation Bill* was deemed to be

95 Edgeworth, 'Defamation Law', 70.
96 Edgeworth, 'Defamation Law', 72.
97 Edgeworth, 'Defamation Law', 73.
98 Dowling, 'The Notebooks of Justice Dowling', 14.98.
99 Dowling, 'The Notebooks of Justice Dowling', 14.99–100.
100 Edgeworth, 'Defamation Law', 75.
101 Spigelman, 'Foundations of the Freedom of the Press in Australia', 99.
102 Spigelman, 'Foundations of the Freedom of the Press in Australia', 100.

repugnant to English law by the Crown.[103] In 1829, the King disallowed the *Newspaper Duty Bill* because 'a tax amounting to four pence on each Newspaper, has appeared to Him too high a duty to be levied for the purposes of mere Revenue under existing circumstances in New South Wales, and because, in the original enactment of the Law, very serious informalities appear to have occurred'.[104] Darling was further criticised by the colonial office for the cost of prosecution of the press in the courts in 1829. The Colonial Secretary, Sir George Murray, suggested a commission be set up to explore how these costs could be reduced.[105]

In January 1830, Darling made another attempt to restrain the licentiousness of the colonial press through legislation. The *Newspaper Regulation Bill* had allowed the Supreme Court to banish an individual who had been found guilty of seditious libel a second time from the colony for such a time as they saw fit. In January 1830, Darling successfully had this act amended so that the Supreme Court lost this discretionary power. Instead those successfully convicted would be banished for 'not less nor more than seven years'.[106] Writing from his prison cell, Hall 'seized upon the statute to pillory His Excellency as the enemy *par excellence* of the freedom of the press'.[107] The *Monitor* on the 20th of February 1830 contained an illustration of a coffin lid with an inscription in Latin which, when translated, stated:

> Under the Government of Sir Thomas Brisbane, Knight, liberty (of the press) was born. Under the Government of Ralph Darling, Esquire, it was strangled on the 29th day of January 1830. I shall rise again.[108]

The *Australian* condemned the amended act and referred to it as the 'GAGGING-STRANGLING-PRESS EXTINCTION'.[109]

The *Monitor* and the *Australian* shouldn't have worried, for the amended Act was doomed from its adoption. Due to changes in government and the political temperament in England at this time, the amended Act was deemed repugnant to English law and repealed. Darling also received criticism for allowing the situation with the press

---

103 Murray to Darling, 31/7/1828 (HRA 1.14, 276).
104 Murray to R. Darling, 1/1/1829 (HRA 1.14, 576–577).
105 Edgeworth, 'Defamation Law', 78.
106 Currey, *Sir Francis Forbes: The First Chief Justice of the Supreme Court of New South Wales*, 371.
107 Currey, *Sir Francis Forbes: The First Chief Justice of the Supreme Court of New South Wales*, 371.
108 *Monitor* 20/2/1830.
109 *Australian* 20/2/1830.

in the colony to get so out of control. Colonial Secretary Goderich agreed that the 'Colonial Press is an evil of a very serious nature', who 'without regard to truth or decency have been engaged in a systematic and preserving endeavour to bring into contempt those to whom the Administration of the Colony has been entrusted'.[110] But he was opposed to any permanent system for controlling the press. Furthermore, any proceedings against the press should be 'confined, under the pressure of extreme necessity, to the occasional exigency of some particular cause'.[111]

The change of government in England, the rebuke from the Colonial Secretary, and the failure to pass the amended *Newspaper Regulation Bill* marked the end of Darling's campaign to restrain the colonial press.

On 26 October 1831, the day that Darling left New South Wales, the front page of the *Monitor* declared: 'HE'S OFF! THE REIGN OF TERROR ENDED'.[112] The *Australian* encouraged all Australians to 'Rejoice Australia! Darling's reign has passed!'.[113] The *Sydney Gazette* reported that Wentworth hosted a party for 4000 Sydney-siders as they sang 'over the hills and far away' while drinking Wright's strong beer and eating tables loaded with 'comestibles, roast beef and mutton'.[114]

Freedom of press in colonial New South Wales

Darling was replaced by Governor Bourke. Bourke appears to have been more sympathetic to the politics of the emancipists and 'favoured trial by jury, a representative government and full civil rights for emancipists'.[115] Bourke also supported the notion of a free press. He believed that 'without free institutions where the Press is wholly unrestricted no Government can go on'.[116] Walker notes that under Bourke's tenure there were limited restrictions on the press, few libel suits, and a lack of enforcement of newspaper registrations.[117]

From Bourke onwards the colonial press was predominantly a free

---

110 Goderich to Darling, 6/1/1831 (*HRA* 1.16, 11).
111 Goderich to Darling, 6/1/1831 (*HRA* 1.16, 11).
112 *Monitor* 26/10/1831.
113 *Australian* 21/10/1831.
114 *SG* 22/10/1831.
115 Walker, *The Newspaper Press in New South Wales, 1803–1920*, 20.
116 Walker, *The Newspaper Press in New South Wales, 1803–1920*, 20.
117 Walker, *The Newspaper Press in New South Wales, 1803–1920*, 20.

press. The number of papers grew significantly in the 1830's. There were the general interest papers, which included the *Sydney Gazette*, the *Australian*, the *Monitor*, and the newly formed *Sydney Herald*. More specialist papers also began to emerge. These included the likes of the *Colonist*, the *Sydney Times*, and the *Commercial Journal*. In 1836 newspapers paid a stamp duty of one penny per newspaper. By 1840 the *Sydney Herald* was a daily newspaper.

In the contemporary era, where claims of fake news reign and a significant lack of trust in the media prevails, Australia can nevertheless be thankful for being a nation that has inherited a press not restrained by government. Ironically, even though the man behind Philo Free was a censor of the press, he used it to express his opinion with the freedom a later age will assume as a right. But along with such freedom comes responsibility. When Marsden prosecuted Campbell, he utilised the natural counter-balance. Unrestrained by government, the press is an organ through which a citizen is free to speak their mind of another person. But if they go too far, as Campbell was forced to learn, the courts exist to protect against a libel the reputation of the one wrongfully maligned.

CHAPTER 13

NORMATIVE ETHICS IN EARLY COLONIAL AUSTRALIA

and the Country's first Libel Case

*Alexander C. Bolt, Paul R. Cerotti
& Konrad Peszynski*

1.0 Introduction.

Context is everything.[1]
How can we even begin to imagine life in New South Wales in 1817 and interpret both the ethics and events of that era? A British penal colony, established just twenty-nine years earlier with the arrival of the First Fleet of eleven ships and its' cargo of 759 convicts, in January 1788.[2] By 1850 England had transported 162,000 convicts to Australia.[3] In a harsh, unfamiliar climate, with little cleared farmland and frequent crop failures, the settlement was often on the brink of starvation.[4] The fragile lifeline to England was a seventeen thousand kilometer, treacherous ocean journey of seven months. This was a brutal, frontier society forged in misery, isolation and hardship.

Viewing this society objectively is a daunting challenge for

---

1 'Context', here, embraces Quentin Skinner's notion of the interaction between both religious and intellectual history; see, Chapman et al, *Seeing Things Their Way*, 1–23.
2 Dunn, *The Founders of a Nation*.
3 Dunn, *The Founders of a Nation*.
4 J.B. Marsden, *The Life and Work of Samuel Marsden*, 25.

twenty-first century western capitalists. Our post-modern, politically correct, egalitarian and secular world-views inhibit our comprehension of early colonial Australian society—a place and time broadly at odds with these ideological positions. Max Weber's (1904) widely read methodological essay, 'The "Objectivity" of Knowledge in Social Science and Social Policy',[5] articulates the absurdity of believing 'facts' that have not been filtered (and tainted) by prior ideas. Separating statements of fact from statements of value, Weber believed 'the knowledge of the cultural significance of concrete historical events and patterns is exclusively and solely the final end'.[6] Beyond making 'sociological sense', through understanding the meaning for the actors involved, one must also embrace the prior ideas from which *they* derive meaning.

2017 marks the two hundredth anniversary of the first case of libel in colonial Australia R. v. Campbell,[7] heard in the Superior Court of New South Wales (Court of Criminal Jurisdiction) on the 21st October 1817, and of the succeeding Civil action heard in the Supreme Court on 1 December. The trials centered on the contents of a letter published in the *Sydney Gazette* on 4 January 1817, pseudonymously authored under the nom-de-plume 'Philo Free'. Aptly described as an 'elaborately sarcastic review' of the Reverend Samuel Marsden's missionary work in Australasia and the South Pacific, the Philo Free author was subsequently revealed to be Governor Lachlan Macquarie's secretary, Mr. John Thomas Campbell.[8]

The verdict of guilty against Campbell in the Criminal Court was reported in a confused and cloaked account in the government-controlled *Sydney Gazette*, compelling Marsden to seek restitution in a Civil Court to clear his name. Here, he was awarded £200 damages (with Campbell also paying a further £500 in costs[9]) in a Supreme Court civil action—a sum equating to over AUD $30,000, in today's value.[10]

---

5   Weber, 'The "Objectivity" of Knowledge in Social Science and Social Policy'.
6   Moody, *Weber*.
7   The Criminal Trial: *R v Campbell* [1817] NSWKR 5; [1817] NSWSupC 5; The Civil Trial: Marsden v Campbell. [1817]. NSWKR 7; [1817]. NSW Sup C 7.
8   SG 4/1/1817; see also the 'Philo Free' Trial, 21–23 October 1817 (reported in SG 1/11/1817; HRA 1.9, 891–893).
9   J.B. Marsden, *The Life and Work of Samuel Marsden*, 90.
10 Conversion to modern day GBP equivalence using Morley, *Historical UK inflation rates and calculator*.

While the libel case demonstrates palpable tensions between Macquarie and Marsden, it can be viewed as merely an eddy cloaking much larger social and political undercurrents. Beneath the surface of this case are the swirling, murky waters of: the subjection of the church to the state; complicated twin loyalties to Australia and the British Crown; identity, power and authority issues; and, implications for broader notions of 'freedom'.[11]

The *Australian Dictionary of Biography*'s[12] description of the Reverend Samuel Marsden as 'chaplain, missionary and farmer' errs toward oversimplifying the fuller dimensions of his many roles and status in the colony. As a civil magistrate, he was accused by his adversaries as being 'extraordinarily severe' in his sentencing. Straddling the dual roles of chaplain and magistrate, Marsden became (unfavorably) labeled as 'the flogging parson'.[13] He was remembered more positively, however, for both his entrepreneurial endeavours and his substantial political influence at home, in England. These further dimensions of Marsden (*magistrate, entrepreneur, political influencer*) will be shown to also be significant factors in events leading to the libellous statements being made about him. Why did Marsden proceed with libel charges? What does his decision to prosecute mean, and what were the wider implications of these events?

Foremost in this discussion, therefore, are multiple social identity constructs (in an 1817 context) and the poignancy of the Philo Free libellous article, which publicly discredited Marsden's reputation. 'Who we are, or who we are *seen* to be can matter enormously'.[14] Denigrating Marsden's social identity in the colony was an attack on his honor/reputation, his status in society (in both the colony and England), and his Christian values. It also potentially threatened his ecclesiastical tenure, if disparaging reports of his character reached his employers in England. Effectively, this was an attack on Marsden's entire sense of 'self'.

11 Gascoigne, *The Enlightenment*, 20–26.
12 Yarwood, 'Marsden, Samuel (1765–1838)'.
13 Allen's examination of the data of Marsden's cases actually shows him to be 'typical if not lenient'; 'The Myth of the Flogging Parson', 487. Allen traces the myth of his severity back to 1817, when 'in the context of his growing feud with Governor Macquarie' (p.489), the governor told his superiors that when compared to other magistrates, Marsden was 'extraordinarily severe'; Macquarie to Bathurst, 4/12/1817 (*HRA* 1.9, 509).
14 Jenkins, *Social Identity*, 4.

'Identities are the traits and characteristics, social relations, roles, and social group memberships that define who one is',[15] and which enable a person to achieve certain objects. It is, therefore, insufficient to merely place Samuel Marsden in an 1817 colonial Australia historical setting without considering the complexities of: the (then) evolving social constructs of the colony; Marsden's background and belief system; the social hierarchy of his country of origin; the complexities of Marsden's relationship with Governor Macquarie; and, the tumultuous global psychosocial revolution framing the times.

In order to comprehend the ethical implications of this libel case, therefore, the aim of this chapter is to contextualize the philosophical, historical, and cultural factors of New South Wales in 1817. Beyond simply, 'wearing an 1817 hat', this re-contextualization process seeks to comprehend the narratives, motivations, and belief-systems of both the society and individuals within it at that time, *and* the influences shaping belief systems over preceding millennia. We are reminded, 'the historian's task is never to simplify the past but rather to see multiple causes and complex interactions'.[16]

Others in this volume will consider the details of the Philo Free case. This chapter will attempt, instead, to view the interactions between the major players in the broader perspective of the history of ideas—especially those related to normative ethics. It highlights, therefore, the complex interactions between historical events, Philosophical/Enlightenment thinking, English social hierarchy, and Western Christianity as significant factors impacting the interwoven and perpetually evolving ethical values of early colonial Australia.

2.0 Background

The penal colony in New South Wales owes its' origins to the industrial (and agricultural) revolution, rising crime, and overcrowding of jails in Britain, and, perhaps ironically, to the individual freedoms won in the American War of Independence.

Cathy Dunn[17] describes an eighteenth century 'agrarian revolution'

---

15 Oyserman et al, *Self, Self-Concept and Identity*, 69.
16 Boles, 'Turner, the Frontier, and the Study of Religion in America', 216.
17 Dunn, *The Founders of a Nation*.

in Britain, a population explosion in their cities, and a consequential increase in crime. 'The Old Bailey Proceedings of 1763 recorded 433 trials of people for murder, burglary, robbery and theft'.[18] Just five years later the 1768 Proceedings record a staggering increase to 613,246 trials.

The industrial revolution (1760–1860) progressively transformed England into 'the workshop of the world',[19] amid enduring ideological debate between the defenders and critics (especially Marxists) of free markets. Early in the industrialization transformation (throughout the 1700's), however, urban England was yet to escape the squalor, overcrowding, and unemployment that typified the 'grinding poverty that had characterized most of human history'.[20] At an earlier period, Thomas Hobbes (1651) lamented, 'the life of man [is], solitary, poore, nasty, brutish and short'.[21] From Hobbes' Whig perspective, the poor were philosophically resigned to their 'lot in life', having endured centuries of insufficient food and the mandatory servitude ascribed to their social class.

These 'revolutions' (agrarian and industrial), however, broke the Malthusian (agricultural-deficiency resulting in population-culling) cycle[22] by increasing (improved) agricultural production, enabling 'Britain and its' colonies to support hitherto undreamed-of levels of population'.[23] Moreover, John Gascoigne notes that this 'importation of "improved" agriculture was seen as giving the establishment of a penal settlement some sense of moral purpose', quoting the *St James Chronicle* of the time:

> The expedition to Botany Bay comprehends in it more than the mere Banishment of our Felons; it is an Undertaking of Humanity [...] [B]y the number of Cattle now sending over of various sorts, and all the different Seeds for Vegetation, a capital Improvement will be made in the Southernmost part of the New World.[24]

18　McLynn, *Crime and Punishment in Eighteenth Century England*, 300.
19　Nardinelli, 'Industrial Revolution'.
20　Nardinelli, 'Industrial Revolution'.
21　Hobbes, T. *Leviathan*, p. 186 (pt. 1, Ch. 13).
22　Malthus, *An Essay on the Principle of Population*.
23　Gascoigne, *The Enlightenment*, 69.
24　*St James Chronicle* 16–18/1/1787, 271.

The American Revolution (US War of Independence) (1775–83)[25] culminated in Britain's surrender at Yorktown, Virginia in 1781. Fighting did not formally finish, however, until the 1783 signing of the *Treaty of Paris*, in which Britain recognized America's independence. As a consequence, Britain was no longer able to transport her prisoners to America. Thus, within four years of American independence, the first fleet departed Portsmouth, England (1787), under the command of Captain Arthur Phillip and bound for Botany Bay.

2.1 The Enlightenment

Broadly spanning one hundred years from the mid seventeenth century, *The Enlightenment* was a tumultuous historical period, also shaped by 'multiple causes and complex interactions'.[26] The comprehensive alteration of western society's structure and belief systems cannot be understated. This was a turning point in civilization's history:

> Characterized by dramatic revolutions in science, philosophy, society and politics; these revolutions swept away the medieval world-view and ushered in our modern western world. Enlightenment thought *culminates* historically in the political upheaval of the French Revolution, in which the traditional hierarchical political and social orders (the French monarchy, the privileges of the French nobility, the political power and authority of the Catholic Church) were violently destroyed and replaced by a political and social order informed by the Enlightenment ideals of freedom and equality for all, founded, ostensibly, upon principles of human reason.[27]

The *scientific revolution* of the sixteenth and seventeenth centuries marks the origins of Enlightenment thinking. The success of new science in explaining a wide array of phenomena and the natural world both undermined conceptions of the cosmos and challenged belief systems.

The *Stanford Encyclopedia of Philosophy* highlights the shifting relationship between religion and philosophy during the Enlightenment. If Philosophy was characterized as 'the handmaiden of theology'

---

25 [History.com], 'American Revolution History'.
26 Boles, 'Turner, the Frontier, and the Study of Religion in America', 216.
27 [SEP], 'Enlightenment'.

prior to this time, the writings of Enlightenment philosophers, such as Francis Bacon (1561–1626), Thomas Hobbes (1588–1679), René Descartes (1596–1650), John Locke (1632–1704), Isaac Newton (1643–1727), Voltaire (1694–1778), David Hume (1711–1776), Jean-Jacques Rousseau (1712–1778), Adam Smith (1723–1790), and Immanuel Kant (1724–1804) promoted the independence of philosophical thought.[28] Philosophy repositioned itself through this process as, 'an independent force with the power and authority to challenge the old and construct the new',[29] bringing the dawn of rationalism, individualism, and an increasingly secular society.

The central tenet of Enlightenment thinking was the idea that progress and prosperity were possible for all, through human reason. Further, prominent seventeenth century Enlightenment philosopher Francis Bacon espoused a holistic concept of 'progress', encompassing material, mental, and moral worlds: 'the improvement of man's lot and the improvement of man's mind are one and the same thing'.[30]

There are differing views of the influence of The Enlightenment in shaping early Australian society. Gaining scant attention in Manning Clark's epic, *A History of Australia,* he views the Enlightenment as antithetical to religion (Protestant and Catholic).[31] In contrast, John Gascoigne portrays a harmonious co-existence between the two, and Henry May proffers the concept of the *Enlightenment as religion.*[32] Given the mutually aligned 'self-improvement' themes of both Christianity and Enlightenment doctrines, over time churches likely synthesized both views at the pulpit, a position broadly supported by government. Gascoigne aptly describes a 'mind-set associated with the Enlightenment',[33] which permeated early colonial Australia.

The Enlightenment and its' principles of reason (inalienable rights of individuals) had explosive implications for a social order ruled by absolutist monarchies (ruling by Divine Right) and aristocratic privilege, as had been graphically demonstrated by the (very recent) French Revolution (1787–1799). The determination of good and bad,

---

28 [IEP], 'Philosophy of History'.
29 [SEP], 'Enlightenment'.
30 Bacon, *Redargutio Philosophiarum,* 92.
31 Clark, *A history of Australia,* 1.109.
32 May, *The Enlightenment in America.*
33 Gascoigne, *The Enlightenment,* 15.

right and wrong, informed solely by reason, had disruptive ramifications for both Christian theology and ethics. These societal dimensions, therefore, require review.

2.2 Social Hierarchy

Eighteenth century England was a society ordered by broad social classes (The Gentry, Middle and Lower Classes).[34] Thomas Heyck, in his book, *The Peoples of the British Isles*, more accurately defines the structure, however, as a *status hierarchy*, not a class society:

> The basic sets of relationships should be envisioned as vertical, not horizontal. Each person was thought to have been ascribed at birth a position in the natural—indeed, divinely established—pecking order, and each felt that his or her loyalty was to social superiors, not to fellow workers. Hence the social structure was like a status ladder, or rather a number of parallel ladders, each rung being a status gradation with its own generally accepted duties and privileges. If a person moved up or down the ladder, it was off one rung and onto another, the ladder itself remaining unchanged [...] Thus, when the English talked about social position, they spoke in terms of 'degrees', 'order', and 'ranks'—gradations of status, not of class.[35]

Heyck's work outlines these social group memberships. In an eighteenth century total British Isles population of around six million people, the top of the hierarchy were titled nobility (fewer then two hundred families)—great landlords earning an average £8000 per year, living in palatial country homes. Immediately below the nobility, earning around £1000 per year, were large landlords (baronets, knights, esquires, and gentlemen), an estimated fifteen thousand families. The nobles and the gentry, comprising 3% of the population, earned 15% of the country's wealth. In addition, they

> also enjoyed the vitally important status of 'gentleman'—a position of honour, to be fought for if necessary, assigned to the lucky few born into 'good' families, and displayed by badges of status like genteel education, graceful deportment, and conspicuous consumption.[36]

---

34 [W.E.], *English Social Structure in the Early 18th Century*.
35 Heyck, *The Peoples of the British Isles*, 48.
36 Heyck, *The Peoples of the British Isles*, 49.

Atop the middle class were the merchants and professional people (clergymen, lawyers, and doctors), with artisans, shopkeepers and tradespeople at the lower end. By the end of the eighteenth century these professional men (women were not permitted to enter professions until the late nineteenth century) had increasingly gained respectability and were 'thought of as satellites of the landed orders'[37] and thus considered *genteel*—a position of great honour.

Central to the social hierarchy was the notion that property (land) determined status, a reversal from medieval society where property *followed* status. Wealth could be acquired, land could be purchased, and one could rise to the appropriate rung on the social ladder. Therefore, *honour* and *reputation* were ubiquitous and of great significance in eighteenth century English society. In this status hierarchy these notions were fundamentally, 'how individuals in this society conceived of the relationship between the personal and the public, and between the projection and the perception of one's character'.[38] In addition to acceptance into élite social circles, a genteel reputation was used to establish credit worthiness.[39] 'Only those with substantial property or wealth were entitled to vote'[40] and prestigious social roles (such as magistrates) were offered to the genteel.

Given these prevailing social patterns, it is the contention of this chapter, that the central tensions between Macquarie and Marsden were threats to honour, reputation, and (most importantly) status hierarchy. Macquarie's view of Marsden as insubordinate and subversive, simmering for many years, finally culminated in the events triggered by the Philo Free publication of 1817. A social hierarchy, already threatened by the tumultuous social/philosophical upheaval of enlightenment thinking and global historical events, was further distressed by disruptions and threats to society's (imported from England) *status quo* particular to the fledgling penal colony.

A 'gentleman's' reputation in the 1800's was sacrosanct. With duels fought until the 1840's,[41] men *were prepared to die* in defense of injury to their character and reputation. Further, strongly embedded in the

---

37   Heyck, *The Peoples of the British Isles*, 49.
38   Dabhoiwala, 'The Construction of Honour, Reputation and Status', 202.
39   Post, *The Social Foundations of Defamation Law*, 695.
40   White, *Popular Politics in the 18th Century*.
41   McCord, 'Politics and Honor', 103.

military culture was *an expectation* that officers (deemed gentlemen by rank) would demand satisfaction when insulted. This culture was further reinforced by the 'view, widely held in the army, that an officer who *failed to issue a challenge after being insulted* was a coward'.[42] The Governor, Major-General Lachlan Macquarie, a career army officer, would have been acutely aware of this culture. Knowing that his Secretary, John Thomas Campbell, had wounded a military officer in a duel as recently as 1811,[43] one can only speculate whether Marsden was being goaded into a more direct action by the provocative Philo Free affair (if indeed Macquarie had been complicit). Perhaps in this context, a veiled cowardice insult may also have been implied.

At this point in history the credentials for the title of 'gentleman' were in mid-transition. No longer a social status reserved by birthright exclusively for the aristocracy, wealthy landowners and certain professions such as clergy, medical practitioners, army officers, members of parliament and magistrates 'were [now] recognised as gentlemen by virtue of their occupations'. Further, 'there was also a moral component inherent in the concept'.[44] Seen as social leaders, in addition to their deportment, clothing and language, the gentleman's code included 'civility, religious principles and moral virtue'.[45] In Morgan's comprehensive study of mid-Victorian behavioural literature (cultural and etiquette guides), *Manners, Morals and Class in England 1774–1858*, she asserts that prior to the mid 1800's, 'the prevailing view [was] that manners and morals were inextricably linked'.[46]

As 'gentlemen' themselves, this social hierarchy construct was inextricably embedded in both Marsden and Macquarie's DNA, evidenced in their language. In 1808 Marsden was invited (by the Colonial minister, Lord Castlereagh) to provide a review of the Colony of NSW to Parliament in England[47]—a rare honour for any civilian. In his prescription of character attributes desired in prospective missionaries, Marsden advised they 'should not (be) taken from the

---

42 McCord, 'Politics and Honor', 103 [Italics added].
43 Holder, 'Campbell, John Thomas (1770–1830)'.
44 Cody, 'The Gentleman', 1. See Morgan's commentary on Richard Edgeworth's *Essays on Professional Education* (1809); *Manners, Morals and Class*, 133.
45 Morgan, *Manners, Morals and* Class, 10.
46 Morgan, *Manners, Morals and* Class, 11.
47 J.B. Marsden, *The Life and Work of Samuel Marsden*, 36.

dregs of the common people, but possessed of some education, and liberal sentiments.'[48] In correspondence to Mary Stokes (in England), dated 22 February 1800, he refers to the 'wickedness, poverty and ruin of the *lower ranks* of the inhabitants of NSW'.[49] Likewise, when Macquarie insulted Marsden he struck at his social standing, that the Reverend was 'of low birth' and 'unworthy of mixing in Private society',[50] and, in an 1814 letter to Lord Bathurst, Secretary for the Colonies, he described the Reverend as, 'originally of low Rank and not qualified by liberal Educations in *the Usual Way*'.[51] The social hierarchy construct was both evident and perpetuated in the everyday language, literature, and attitudes of society. In his 1798, *Essay on the Principle of Population*, Thomas Malthus refers to the 'lower classes, and, the lowest orders of society',[52] further demonstrating élitist attitudes in the everyday language of the times.

This broader perspective suggests that, central to the Philo Free affair is the denigration of Marsden's reputation, honour, and social standing—and why Campbell felt so threatened by them. In his own words, penned to Mary Stokes in 1819, so well after the trials, Marsden asserts, 'I did not seek for damages [...] All I wanted was to set my character right with the public'.[53] It would be a grave error to oversimplify Marsden's motivation to file for libel merely as 'defence of his reputation' without considering the complexity of that 'reputation'. The complexity that was Marsden's multi-dimensional character, *gentleman, Chaplain, missionary, farmer, entrepreneur and magistrate*, irritated Campbell and served to magnify the insults of Philo Free. Not only did he accused Marsden of being of a 'more humble cast' (lower class) than the greatly despised Jesuits; of commercially profiteering as a missionary; but also, declared him a 'Christian Mahomet'—a fraudster or charlatan.[54] Widely recognized, from his own time until today, as having a 'profound conviction that he was an instrument in God's hand,

---

48 J.B. Marsden, *The Life and Work of Samuel Marsden*, 32.
49 Marsden to Mary Stokes, 22/2/1800. (Italics added).
50 Yarwood, 'Marsden, Samuel (1765–1838)'.
51 Gascoigne, *The Enlightenment*, 25.
52 Malthus, *An Essay on the Principle of Population*, 23.
53 Marsden to Mary Stokes, 14/6/1819.
54 See Professor Jeremy Gregory's review of David Hempton's *The Church in the long Eighteenth Century*, in which he observes, 'Islam [...] was frequently seen as a primitive heresy'; Gregory, 'Review of Hempton'.

that he worked under His divine guidance',[55] 'an unambiguous servant of the Gospel',[56] and 'a sincere and devoted Christian evangelist',[57] Marsden's fundamental evangelical Christian beliefs to which he had devoted his life were viciously maligned by Philo Free.

2.3 Religion and Eighteenth Century English Society

Comprehending the centrality of religion in eighteenth century English society presents, perhaps, one of the more difficult conceptual challenges for twenty-first century people. Progressing from the Enlightenment, the profoundly psychosocial influences of nineteenth and twentieth century writers such as Charles Darwin, Karl Marx, Sigmund Freud and Friedrich Nietzsche,[58] further shaped the thinking of western societies, contributing to rising individualism, secularism and rationalist beliefs. Thus when viewed through a modern lens, conceptualising a complex 1800's triumvirate of monarchy, church, and state is an alien construct, mired with parochial bias.

W.M. Jacob's, *Lay People and Religion in the Early Eighteenth Century*, deals, however, with the eighteenth century period in its own right. Jacob draws on J.C.D. Clark and Stephen Taylor's view[59] of the largely symbiotic and co-dependent relationship between politics and theology, that 'Anglicanism and society remained virtually coterminous' and in this relationship the Church was not subservient to the State; there was 'a deep attachment to Christian faith among a broad cross-section of people'; and 'Christianity was in the social air which everyone alike breathed'.[60]

Jacob draws his data from extensive Parish records of the era, 'the Parish was the basic unit of local Government',[61] the centre of the community. Elected lay officials (Churchwardens) were responsible for, and monitored, the moral life of their neighbours, conduct of the clergy, maintenance and beautification of the parish churches, management of schools and significant philanthropic activities (England's welfare

---

55 J.B. Marsden, *The Life and Work of Samuel Marsden*, 7.
56 Jensen, 'Samuel Marsden'.
57 Yarwood, 'The Missionary Marsden', 29.
58 Ryan, *Moral Education*.
59 Jacob, *Lay People and Religion*, 3–4 and notes for academic sources in his argument.
60 Peter Laslett in Jacob, Jacob, *Lay People and Religion*, 3.
61 Jacob, *Lay People and Religion*, 11.

budget in 1798 was around £3 Million).[62] Local community affairs were addressed by a meeting of the vestry—Ratepayers of the Parish. These Ratepayers were landowners and lessees in the district, responsible for maintaining communal facilities. They could levy rates for infrastructure construction/maintenance and elected not only churchwardens, but also local officials such as surveyors and police.

The *potpourri* of commercial, state, and religious interests which gave society its complex flavour, illuminates therein many mixed motives at play. For example, the Church provided most social services (funded by Ratepayers), including orphanages. The Church's anti-promiscuity position was grounded in Biblical teaching, and also served to reduce the financial burden on orphanage patrons (Ratepayers and the Church itself). Macquarie, Marsden, and Campbell (as all in the new colony) were products of this English heritage and were each conflicted, to some extent, by their own commercial, state and religious interests in the new land.

Eighteenth century English politics, society and Christianity were inextricably interwoven, as they had been for well over a thousand years prior. Clive Field's research into the period[63] shows 88.2% of the population in 1800 were 'nominally Anglican'. However, for readers today to fully appreciate the significance of this society's religious beliefs, when including all categories, such as 'dissenters (e.g. Methodists)' and followers of Jewish faith only 0.1% had no religious affiliation. Max Weber's notion of the 'protestant work ethic'[64] contributing to the growth of Capitalism provides *prima facie* support for how religious beliefs were widely held at this time. Weber's construct rests on the predictability of *whole-of-society* behavioral traits, in turn resting on the (almost) *whole-of-society* religious belief system, shown by Field to be 99.9% of the English population in 1800 (albeit at widely varying levels of personal commitment—from 'nominal' to 'evangelical zealots').

From a government perspective, there is little doubt the Church was viewed as providing a social utility dimension. Accordingly, in Australia, Governor Phillip was instructed to, 'enforce a due observance of religion

---

62 Jacob, *Lay People and Religion*, 9.
63 Field, 'Counting Religion in England and Wales', 693–720.
64 Weber, *The Protestant Ethic and the Spirit of Capitalism*.

and good order among the inhabitants of the new settlement'.[65] The State looked to the Church as its exclusive source of moral instruction, explicitly acknowledging the connection between Christian teaching and a cohesive, virtuous society. Religious beliefs themselves, however, were not immune to ideological upheaval.

Although England was nominally Anglican since 1701, there has never been a unified church. The Civil War (1642–49), while framed by European Catholic and Protestant tensions, was politically motivated in England—a struggle for power between the King and Parliament. Support for each of these factions, however, was largely based on religious convictions. Royalists favored a more conservative 'High Church' form of worship, not too dissimilar to Roman Catholicism, a heavily hierarchical construct of pomp, rituals and ceremony. Parliamentarians 'preferred a congregational form [...] that allowed individuals to worship according to their own consciences'.[66] Within these two broad religious positions, individuals held varied ideological perspectives drawn from the myriad of theological and philosophical prevailing influences.

'Humanism can be described as the cultural and philosophical life based on the classical world'.[67] Middle Ages Italian poet Francis Petrarch (1304–1374), believed to be 'the greatest scholar of his age', was the first to use the expression 'Dark Ages' and is credited as the founder of Humanism.[68] Rejecting the sterile, dialectical scholarly arguments of his day, Petrarch sought illumination, values, and moral guidance from the Ancients. At its core, Humanism placed greater emphasis on the dignity of human beings than the sovereignty of God. Humanism was an assertion of one's independence and individual expression. Humanism rests on the notion that human nature is intrinsically good.

Where medieval Christianity had explained phenomena in a prescribed, uniform point of view Renaissance man was beginning an experiential, *this-world* (less concerned with the *after-life*) journey— from witchcraft to scientific discovery. Petrarch's work sparked

---

65 Gascoigne, *The Enlightenment*, 23, drawing on, 'Instructions for our trusty and well-beloved Arthur Phillip', 25/4/1787, *HRNSW* 1.2, 90.
66 Hager, A. 'Introduction', ix.
67 Hager, A. 'Introduction', ix.
68 Whitfield, 'Petrarch'.

renewed interest in secular (non-religious) learning. He was followed by notable 'conservative' humanists, including, Desiderius Erasmus (1466–1536) and Sir Thomas More (1478–1535). Neither anti-Christian nor non-Christian (Petrarch, Erasmus and Moore all held deep religious convictions—Thomas More was executed for refusing to denounce his Catholic faith), 'progressive thinkers saw themselves as Christian humanists'.[69] Humanism began to take a more agnostic and skeptical leaning in the works of later philosophers, such as Francis Bacon (1561–1626) and Michel Montaigne (1533–1592).

The catalyst for the rapid spread of Renaissance culture throughout Europe (and the western world) after 1450 was Johannes Gutenberg's (c.1398–1468) invention of the movable-type printing press. 'By 1500 over nine million books were in print throughout Europe',[70] co-relationally increasing both literacy and therein demand. Italian educator, Vittorino da Feltra's (1378–1446) curriculum, built on the study of history, moral philosophy, Greek and Latin, was widely adopted throughout Europe. One should note, however, that scholars at this time were predominantly the sons of the aristocracy—thus only about 2% of the population received a formal education.[71]

Similarly, the spread of Reformation thinking—King Henry VIII's sixteenth century challenge to the authority of the Catholic Church and the Protestant teachings of reformers, such as Martin Luther and John Calvin—were enabled, and propagated by the printing press. Martin Luther has been credited with publishing more works 'than the 17 other major Evangelical publicists combined' (between 1518 and 1525).[72] King Henry VIII commissioned the translation of The Bible (from Latin to English) and had it widely distributed.

In 1517, when Martin Luther (1483–1546) published his *Ninety-Five Theses*, it became a major activator of what is now known as the Protestant Reformation. To him the prevailing Catholic commercial enterprise of selling 'tickets to Heaven', epitomized all that was wrong with the Church. It 'placed salvation in the hands of traveling salesmen hocking indulgences', while, in his view, 'we do not have to achieve

---

69 Hager, 'Introduction', ix.
70 Hager, 'Introduction', x.
71 Hager, 'Introduction', x.
72 Siedlecki, *Luther*.

salvation; rather, it is a gift to be received'[73]—a view that underpinned his progression to a *theologia crucis* (Theology of the Cross).

A fundamental dialectic in Luther's thinking was the distinction between the Law and the Gospel. He saw God's law as *the only valid law*, articulated in the Bible and the Ten Commandments. Here was an unwavering definition of Sin; a check for the excesses of human nature; a sacred, external 'code of conduct' by which a 'bad' person or act could be recognized; and, a defined 'conscience' for its Christian members. Prior to this time, Catholic canon law had underpinned society, now the Lutheran Reformation led to a reconstruction of civil laws. Luther saw the purpose of civil laws 'to restrain people from sinful conduct by threat of punishment'[74]—a civil reinforcement of Biblical law.

John Calvin (1509–1564) was a Biblical theologian, Renaissance humanist, and Protestant Reformer, who 'sought to appeal rhetorically to the human heart. [...] The Calvinist form of Protestantism is widely thought to have had a major impact on the formation of the modern world'.[75] Calvin's theological position was broadly aligned with Luther's, with his enduring legacy said to be the doctrine of Predestination (the complex notion for whom, and by what process God has 'pre-determined' each individual's salvation or otherwise).

The Protestant Reformation brought about by Luther and Calvin dismissed outright the Catholic Church's pay-as-you-go salvation, the notion of purgatory and any doctrine of 'good works'. However, while Protestant salvation rested on faith in Christ's atonement alone, there were ramifications for how that faith would be manifest in the believer's daily life, 'the idea of the necessity of *proving one's faith* in worldly activity'.[76] Protestantism, combined with Calvin's doctrine of predestination, therefore, gave rise to a worldly asceticism (with Puritans the staunchest champions). In Max Weber's view Calvinism was, 'a systematic rational ordering of the moral life as a whole'.[77]

Weber viewed Protestant religion (Calvinism), as a pro-individualist yet socially unifying doctrine. In sweeping away the hierarchy and institutions of the Catholic Church, Calvinism preached a message of

---

73 Whitford, ' Martin Luther', section (2b), Theology of the Cross.
74 Witte, *Between Sanctity and Depravity*, 746.
75 Bouwsma, 'John Calvin'.
76 Bouwsma, 'John Calvin'. (Italics added).
77 Weber, *The Protestant Ethic and the Spirit of Capitalism*, 79.

individual faith-based, egalitarian salvation. It (through the gospel) reinforced the virtue ethics of the ancients, promoted order and moral values in society, and provided a 'work ethic' in the populace, which Weber credits as a strong contributor to the growth of Capitalism. Although his thesis has attracted criticism, Weber considered the Calvinist values of hard-work, thrift and avoidance of ostentatious displays of wealth as strong contributors for capitalism's growth. Further, Weber sees support for the character, conduct and deportment of gentlemen in the Calvinistic 'respect for quiet self-control which still distinguishes the best type of English or American gentleman today'.[78] Christianity, therefore, satisfied the existential dimensions of the individual, provided a strong work ethic, provided social cohesion, and defined the moral conduct of 'gentlemen' within it.

Alongside the broad ideological divisions within the Protestant church, a proliferation of sects and alternative belief systems adds to the complexity of the Enlightenment and Reformation thinking. Along with the development of mainstream Protestant faiths, such as Lutheran, Puritan, Presbyterian, Baptist, and Methodist, there was a parallel development of organizations, such as the Sydney Odd Fellows, the Temperance Association, and the Freemason movement. 'Christianity and the Enlightenment endorsed the nineteenth century's preoccupation with the notion that human nature was capable of being reshaped into what were considered better forms'[79] – the moral and intellectual improvement of humankind.

3.0 Marsden and Macquarie

Against the complex psychosocial forces that have been considered, the idiosyncrasies of both Marsden and Macquarie can be better understood. While multiple factors and lofty ideals may frame much of each man's motivation, the inescapable human orientation toward self-interest— Rousseau's (1712–1788) *amour propre*[80]—must be considered in relation to each man's actions. In order to strike a balance in interpreting motivations of these men accurately, and to avoid 'leading the reader' to

---

78   Weber, *The Protestant Ethic and the Spirit of Capitalism*, 73.
79   Gascoigne, *The Enlightenment*, 115.
80   Rousseau, *Basic Political Writings*, xxx.iii. Sharp, *The World, the Flesh & the Devil*, 300–301, 506.

forgone conclusions (bias), what follows is an attempt to refer to a few issues particularly pertinent Philo Free.

On social status, Macquarie regularly insulted Marsden, referring to him as 'low birth' and 'low rank' yet Macquarie's own father was a poor tenant farmer. His family 'had fallen on hard times requiring them to sell the island [Isle of Ulva in the Hebrides] which had been in the family's possession for 900 years'.[81] Macquarie was born and raised in poverty. His father died when Lachlan was fourteen and his admission to (and promotion in) the army was due to his maternal uncle (Murdoch Maclaine, Baron of Moy). Macquarie biographers depict an 'ambitious and vain' man,[82] who sought promotion as a means to acquire land (and therefore status), but remained in debt until his early thirties. A devastatingly bittersweet £6,000 inheritance from the death of his wife of just three years (Jane Jarvis) in 1796, combined with promotion and 'prize money' for military successes enabled him to acquire a part of the Lochbuy estate in Scotland (10,000 acres) 'which his uncle was being forced by his creditors to sell',[83] for £10,060. Not a prudent investment, this estate would prove over time to be poor pastureland of dubious commercial value. Perhaps Macquarie's impoverished beginnings and the personal difficulties he experienced in his life contributed to his intolerance of any challenge to his control and authority in the colony.

Having arrived in NSW in 1794,[84] Marsden's social status in the Colony was already firmly established before Macquarie's arrival in 1810, sixteen years later. Marsden was appointed a magistrate (against his wishes) and superintendent of government affairs (in Parramatta) in 1795, he was involved with evangelizing and commenced trading with Pacific Islands (Tahiti) in 1798, had opened a new church (St. John's, Parramatta) and schools, was an administrator of an orphanage, and the local superintendent of the London Missionary Society, being involved as well, in time, in both the Church Missionary Society and the British and Foreign Bible Society. Described by Governor King as 'the best practical farmer in the colony',[85] by 1805 Marsden had also acquired (by both government grant and purchase) 1730 acres of land

---

81 Bashir, 'Lachlan Macquarie', 98.
82 McLachlan, 'Macquarie, Lachlan (1762–1864)'. [Encyclopedia.com], 'Lachlan Macquarie'.
83 McLachlan, 'Macquarie, Lachlan (1762–1864)'.
84 Yarwood, 'Marsden, Samuel (1765–1838)'.
85 Yarwood, 'Marsden, Samuel (1765–1838)'.

and over 1000 sheep. By the 1820's his land holding increased to over 3,500 acres. Acquiring such assets, Marsden was perhaps jealously viewed by Campbell as merely pursuing material wealth.

Consistent with Weber's thesis, but probably requiring better documentary support, Yarwood holds the view that Marsden 'believed that material advance was a proof of the genuineness of his personal sense of salvation; and, that he was spurred by the temper of the colony on his arrival'.[86] The combination of government salaries, land grants, and an abundance of convict (free) labor had lured the military officers in the Colony into a 'single-minded pursuit of wealth'[87]—notably John Macarthur (1767–1834), who amassed 60,000 acres of farmland! As an evangelical Calvinist, however, Marsden saw the cultivation of crops and livestock, and the development of the Colony's economy, as his personal responsibility. Further, while Marsden's pastoral and entrepreneurial endeavors brought him significant wealth, that wealth was used for his extensive philanthropic activities. There are many accounts of Marsden's generosity, including paying £900 to erect new schools,[88] an £800 advance to erect a female orphanage in Parramatta (which Governor Macquarie refused to reimburse),[89] the gift of valuable land in Windsor to the Wesleyan Methodists to erect a church,[90] and his practice of regularly opening his private residence as a private seminary to large numbers of Maori nationals for months at a time—although his expenses for this were retrospectively reimbursed by CMS.

Given Macquarie's personal aspirations, his background and the prevailing view that the established aristocracy held of colonial pastoralists, the dimension of Marsden-the-pastoralist may have also fed Macquarie's resentment. Referred to as a 'Bunyip Arisocracy', 'Harlequin aristocrats', and 'Botany Bay magnificos'[91] by the English parliament and established aristocracy, the colonial pastoralists and 'self-made' wealthy citizens were openly ridiculed. Contrary to an element of Turner's (American-based) 'frontier thesis', where the fertility of the soil supported small farms, hence self-sufficiency/

---

86 Yarwood, 'Marsden, Samuel (1765–1838)'.
87 Yarwood, 'Marsden, Samuel (1765–1838)'.
88 J.B. Marsden, *The Life and Work of Samuel Marsden*, 60.
89 J.B. Marsden, *The Life and Work of Samuel Marsden*, 117.
90 J.B. Marsden, *The Life and Work of Samuel Marsden*, 192.
91 Gascoigne, *The Enlightenment*, 57.

reliance and the birth of democracy, Gascoigne argues Australia's 'poorly-watered soils did not favour the smallholder',[92] a view supported by both Commissioner Bigge in his 1822–23 report and by Fitzpatrick's 'big man's frontier'.[93] In political terms, a natural environment that favored large grazing properties and the societal links between land and power contributed to a developing landowning oligarchy. Powerful pastoralists with influence in England, such as Macarthur and (to a lesser extent) Marsden, were increasingly influencing colonial policy. Given Macquarie's immediate purpose—to restore order after the 'Rum Rebellion' (and Macarthur's direct role in that)—, he was naturally nervous about any erosion of his own authority.

Although Marsden exhibited internal conflict in some areas, the notion of Marsden actively pursuing personal wealth is not consistent with a holistic view of his life. Here was an evangelical Christian whose unshakable faith produced a lifelong commitment (over 40 years) to missionary service, amid extraordinary personal and social adversity. Sandy Yarwood describes Marsden's pastoralist activities as a 'drift into worldly activities',[94] seemingly to imply some avarice in the Reverend's actions. However, on Marsden's arrival in 1794, 'one cask of meat was all the King's stores contained',[95] and in Marsden's own words, 'I entered a country which was in a state of Nature, and was obliged to plant and sow or starve'.[96] He considered his diligence in rapidly establishing a productive farm, soon recognized for its 'superior management', as his Christian duty in assisting Governor Hunter in providing for the colony.

Further, while visiting England in 1808, Marsden made a commitment to Parliament to feed and clothe all the convicts from Australian production within a given period,[97] if they would waive the existing manufacturing prohibition of the day and agree for the Crown to employ four tradesmen in the colony. His request was approved. He had an audience with King George III and requested two Merino sheep to improve the Australian breed. The King provided five. Marsden requested three additional clergy and three schoolteachers and

---

92 Gascoigne, *The Enlightenment*, 36.
93 Fitzpatrick, 'The big man's frontier and Australian farming'.
94 Yarwood, 'Marsden, Samuel (1765–1838)'.
95 J.B. Marsden, *The Life and Work of Samuel Marsden*, 26.
96 J.B. Marsden, *The Life and Work of Samuel Marsden*, 26.
97 J.B. Marsden, *The Life and Work of Samuel Marsden*, 38.

'happily the selection [of these people] was intrusted (sic) to his own judgment'.[98] Marsden personally recruited people for all these positions while in England, at his own expense. All of these benevolent actions are contrary to a man accused of self-centered motivation.

It was Macquarie's propensity for the social elevation of immoral emancipated convicts, however, that contributed to the greatest tension between himself and Marsden, the judiciary, officers in the military, and ultimately the English government, leading to the 1822 colonial report by Commissioner Bigge. Despite his proven military, administrative, and nation-building skills, Governor Macquarie was politically naïve.[99] His emancipatory vision for convicts who had served their sentence would have met with little resistance if more prudent vocations were assigned than judiciary roles. Given the status hierarchy already discussed, appointing persons (who had not only been convicted of crimes but were also in continuing immoral personal relationships) to the position of magistrate was foolhardy on many levels—insulting the integrity of the judiciary and the social status of those 'gentlemen' within it, and re-opening wounds in the battle for the independence of the judiciary from the state. Marsden's 1810 refusal to accept an appointment to the board of trustees for the Parramatta Turnpike, where two such emancipists would be his fellow board members, shows his refusal to even *associate with these men*, which further inflamed Macquarie. Yet, as both Senior Chaplain and magistrate, Marsden's views 'were less about human status than a belief in how God has ordered the world'.[100] Macquarie demonstrates his political naivety in viewing Marsden as insubordinate on this issue.[101] Yet, would such immoral men as these two emancipists be even accepted into public office today?

This chapter attempts to comprehend the complexity of individual belief systems in an early colonial Australian context. Power and authority, social hierarchy, the concept of a 'gentlemen', the privilege and entitlement of aristocracy, and Christian doctrine were richly interwoven in this society.

---

98   J.B. Marsden, *The Life and Work of Samuel Marsden*, 39. (bracketed comments added).
99   See both Gascoigne, *The Enlightenment*, 20–26, and Yarwood, 'Marsden, Samuel (1765–1838)'.
100 Pettett, 'Samuel Marsden, Blinkered Visionary', 262.
101 See both Gascoigne, *The Enlightenment*, 20–26, and Yarwood, 'Marsden, Samuel (1765–1838)'.

Macquarie's ideological separation of the emancipists from moral virtue, his autocratic authority, a censured press and the government control of society, military, judiciary and church, were the seeds of his demise in the colony. As a direct result of James II's autocratic rule, after his abdication a Bill of Rights had been introduced by parliament (1689) severely restricting the power of the Crown. The bill restricted the Crown's right to suspend or dispense laws without parliamentary consent, decreed that parliament would control the nation's finances, and limited the executive power of the monarch over the individual (by disbanding standing armies in peacetime, since such armies ultimately enslave the individual). 'In fact, eighteenth century English politics were heavily influenced by a political outlook that was habitually suspicious of any increases in the executive power of the government.'[102] Yet, in a colony under military rule, with no local parliament, Macquarie's rule was ostensibly absolute.

Further, all these belief systems were subject to ever-increasing corrosion by Enlightenment thinking, questioning society's ethical foundation.

4.0 Normative Ethics and Eighteenth Century Colonial Society

This chapter has highlighted the tumultuous scale and scope of religious, social and philosophical upheaval at the end of the 18th century—both for English society itself and for Britain's fledgling Australian colony.

Humans have a curious propensity to broadly categorise individuals, professions, belief systems, societies, and eras. However, change is a process—it *occurs over time*. Actors are both influenced and influencers of societal values. Therefore both individual and societal values are viewed as multifactorial and through a continuum lens.

On this continuum, in 18th century English society, we see the changing influences of Greek, Christian, and contemporary secular virtue ethics. The Reformation embraced Renaissance culture (the 'flourishing', 'well being' of ancient eudaemonists—Plato, Aristotle,

---

102 Willis, 'Transportation versus Imprisonment', 194.

the Stoics), virtue ethics and Christianity. Christianity augments the cardinal virtues (prudence, justice, temperance and courage) with theological virtues (faith, hope and love) as Divine Command Theory, articulated in the teachings of Thomas Aquinas (1225–1274), and continued in contemporary authors, such as John Milbank and Robert Merrihew Adams. The Ten Commandments reinforce these virtues, and rich biblical narrative, including parables and didactic examples, demonstrate virtuous action.

While Calvin echoes the eudaemonist sense of 'purpose' in an individual's life, John Milbank makes the distinction between a self-giving (*agapē*) Christian virtue in contrast to the ancient's Greek *arête*, 'superiority' and agonistic orientation. Thus, Christian virtue 'is a relational, rather than self-contained, internal matter', and it's relevance is gained in the context of community.[103] Both, however, stress the primacy of the virtue of character.

Proponents of narrative theology, including Stanley Hauerwas, David Burrell, and Hans Frei 'advance an ethic of virtue that is rooted in a narrative conception of human agency',[104] that the relationship between stories, action and consciousness develops our sense of personal identity. As opposed to the view-from-nowhere 'reality' of Rationalism, they posit that interaction with the community provides meaning and value. A familiar storyline, for example, is the rags-to-riches narrative of self-made millionaires. A person shaped by this narrative values hard work, self-discipline and frugality. These virtues, in turn, shape one's character.

This narrative is a component feature of Calvinism, the Enlightenment's promise of improvement, and the social construct of the 'gentleman', and is encapsulated in Weber's Protestant work ethic. For Marsden, this narrative is particularly poignant. The rags-to-riches narrative is reinforced in every aspect of his life—Christian, temporal and 'gentleman' (by both vocation and ownership of land). Further, eighteenth century English society reinforced the belief that moral values came from both the church and gentlemen in society. 'Civilization' itself was a notion synonymous with morality—a 'civilized' (Christian) society.

---

103   Millbank, *Difference of Virtue, Virtue of Difference*, 363.
104   Pettigrove, 'Virtue ethics, virtue theory and moral theology', 92.

Thus, we see an eclectic mix of 'doctrine' played out in Marsden's life. He saw a providential link in 'civilizing before salvation', that, 'commerce and the arts having a natural tendency to inculcate industrious and moral habits, open a way for the introduction of the Gospel'.[105] Marsden personally subscribed to an ethic of hard work and prescribed it for others, 'four qualifications are absolutely necessary for a missionary—piety, industry, prudence, and patience'.[106] In his view, agriculture and commerce were also hallmarks of a 'civilized' society, and an individual's diligent application to these pursuits, punctuated by keeping a regular Sabbath, was an outward sign of their Christian faith.

Marsden also incorporates, quite strongly, a 'social hierarchy' narrative in his sense of self, an area where he is most criticized. Flowing from his 'work ethic' are Marsden's pastoral pursuits and commercial endeavors. His 'self-made man' and 'hard work' narratives construct this ethic as virtuous, inseparable and embedded in his Christian faith. Seeing himself as a 'self made' aristocrat, having the social status of a 'gentleman', however, may have clouded his vision of an egalitarian society. We may understand his motivation in, 'protesting, as he never ceased to do, against the monstrous impropriety of placing men, however wealthy, who had themselves been convicts, on the Magisterial Bench'.[107] His prejudices, however, demonstrated in his language against those deemed 'lower class' ('dregs'[108]) in society and his refusal to serve with immoral emancipists on the Turnpike board, 'considering this association derogatory to his sacred functions',[109] have been taken to belie a social arrogance, cloaked in piety.

Governor Macquarie was a highly ambitious career military officer. He wrote to his superiors requesting promotions and when the man originally selected to replace the deposed William Bligh in the colony, Major-General Miles Nightingall, changed his mind and declined the

---

105 J.B. Marsden, *The Life and Work of Samuel Marsden*, 42.
106 J.B. Marsden, *The Life and Work of Samuel Marsden*, 32.
107 J.B. Marsden, *The Life and Work of Samuel Marsden*, 37. The issue is more complex, however, for Marsden's colleague and magistrate, Rev. Henry Fulton, had been a convict. Marsden was probably more concerned with perceptions of a magistrate's morality, than their emancipist status.
108 J.B. Marsden, *The Life and Work of Samuel Marsden*, 32.
109 Yarwood, 'Marsden, Samuel (1765–1838)'. However, see Yarwood's further explanation in *Samuel Marsden: Survivor*, 129–130, and Sharp, *The World, the Flesh & the Devil*, 301–305, where it is clearly recognized that morality was the issue, not emancipation *per se*.

appointment, Macquarie (initially due to 'accompany' the Regiment), 'boldly wrote to Castlereagh [...] offering his services as governor'.[110] Lord Castlereagh (Secretary of State for the colonies) provided confidential instructions prior to Macquarie's departure, that:

> the Great Objects of attention are to improve the Morals of the Colonists, to encourage Marriage, to provide for Education, to prohibit the Use of Spirituous Liquors, to increase the Agriculture and Stock, so as to ensure the Certainty of a full supply to the Inhabitants under all Circumstances.[111]

With Governor Macquarie's appointment, the Colony was under military rule: Macquarie's authority was absolute. Unrestrained by a parliament, he was more powerful in Australia than the King was in England. Reminiscent of King James I's (reigned 1603–25) absolutism (the Sovereign deriving his authority from God), Macquarie could dictate to ecclesiastical rulers. As if dealing with junior clergy he 'wished to prescribe the hymns they should sing, as well as the doctrines they should teach' and, after demanding Marsden produce a copy of a sermon he had preached a year earlier, returned it with the comment, 'almost downright blasphemy' written on it.[112] His 'absolutism was compounded by gullibility, irritability and vanity [... and he] was cordial only to those who agreed with him'.[113] Fortunately, he 'had the good of the colony much at heart',[114] and Macquarie, 'employed his power to achieve enormous improvements'.[115]

Macquarie's belief system was also complex. His Christian beliefs were grounded in the Church of England, primarily valuing the social utility of religion 'as a source of public decorum and order, [however], in the manner of many of the British landed classes, he thought overt displays of religious emotion were in bad taste and liable to lead to division and discord'.[116] He viewed Evangelical religion as undermining the stately ritual, pomp and ceremony he admired in the Established Church. In a letter to Lord Bathurst, he stated that Marsden's Methodist

---

110 Yarwood, 'Marsden, Samuel (1765–1838)'.
111 Yarwood, 'Marsden, Samuel (1765–1838)'.
112 J.B. Marsden, *The Life and Work of Samuel Marsden*, 56.
113 Brendon, *The Decline And Fall of The British Empire*, 70.
114 J.B. Marsden, *The Life and Work of Samuel Marsden*, 55.
115 Brendon, *The Decline And Fall of The British Empire*, 70.
116 Gascoigne, *The Enlightenment*, 25.

(synonymous with Evangelical in these times) principles led to 'a hasty Adoption of new Systems [...] to the Exclusion of the Old Establishment of the Church of England'.[117]

'Those who joined the officers corps in the eighteenth century became members of an exclusive club with its own distinctive values'.[118] The predominant virtues of the military are courage, discipline, loyalty and obedience,[119] hence Macquarie's fury over Marsden's refusal to serve on the Turnpike board, seen by him as insubordination.[120] The 'loyalty' and 'obedience' themes are clearly demonstrated (in the Governor's own words), when rebuking Marsden in 1818. Macquarie writes that Marsden, as a magistrate and clergyman, 'ought to be the first to set an example of loyalty, obedience, and proper subordination',[121] revealing his autocratic perspective of the social hierarchy.

John Gascoigne argues that the irreconcilable tensions between the values, traditions and rituals of the military and clergy accounts for the popularity of the Masonic cult within military circles, in which some anti-clericalism sentiment existed. Macquarie had been a Freemason since the 1790's, and when the Sydney lodge was formed in 1814 it, ironically, did not permit emancipists joining as, 'a former convict would impugn our respectability both Military and Masonic'.[122]

5.0 Change and Society

The impact of Enlightenment thinking broadly moved western society from the virtue ethics position of Divine Command Theory (DCT) towards Rationalism; variants of God-down (God-the-creator) to human-up (Science/reason can create a God we are comfortable with) to ideological positions with no God at all. The shift from DCT and its external, 'sacred' and pro-community values toward a more secular, individualistic, every-one-for-themselves, consequentialist value base brought about change on a monumental scale.

---

117 Gascoigne, *The Enlightenment*, 25.
118 Gilbert, 'Law and Honor', 1.
119 Olsthoorn, 'Virtue ethics in the military', 365.
120 Yarwood, 'Marsden, Samuel (1765–1838)'.
121 Macquarie to Marsden, 8/1/1818.
122 Gascoigne, *The Enlightenment*, 26.

The explosion of literature and literacy facilitated by Gutenberg's printing press (the internet of the 1500's), in parallel with scientific and agricultural revolutions, enabled the Enlightenment; reformed the church; overturned absolutism; fractured social classes; empowered the individual; and ushered in the dawn of modernity. The printing of books, pamphlets and newspapers developed both a literary explosion and thirst. 'By the late eighteenth century the newspapers were almost certainly the most widely read source of printed information about crime and justice'.[123] Readers formed and published opinions in a world suspicious of those who ruled, and were highly critical of the power of governments, the church and the privileged class. With the explosion of printed material, the world got smaller, as ideas crossed continents, spreading the enthusiasm for change.

The rapidly changing philosophical, spiritual, political, legal, economic and social changes spawned the law of libel. 'The eruption of religious and constitutional controversy in the sixteenth and seventeenth centuries increased official concern over sedition, political dissent, and particularly the influential role of the press in promoting these ideas'.[124] As society shifted from the 'sacred' (unquestioned) Christian laws toward rationalism (where everything is now 'scientifically' questioned), western society began the arduous task of redefining itself, as did individuals within it. From a Biblical, Ninth Commandment perspective (Thou shalt not bear false witness), libel laws were superfluous to Christian ethics, in turn reinforced by both aristocratic and military 'honor-codes' (based on Christian virtues). As Christians, Officers, and Gentlemen one would not 'bear false witness', as the perjurer would *damage their own honor* in so doing.

This chapter has highlighted individual change on a continuum, neither placing any significance on any 'optimum' point on it, nor defining outer boundaries. Utilizing a narrative framework from which individuals construct their sense of 'self' it has sought to understand the Philo Free actors in their historical/societal context.

What, then, of the 'mysterious' J.T. Campbell? Deserving more study in his own right, John Thomas Campbell offers the historian much intrigue. Knowing his family origins in Ulster, Ireland, why and when

---

123 King, 'Newspaper reporting and attitudes to crime and justice', 74.
124 [CFAS], 'Libel, Slander & Freedom of Speech'.

did he travel to Cape Town? Was he fleeing or seeking his fortune? He was forty-one when Macquarie found him in Cape Town. His past is, at best, vague, and most accounts indicate a lack of support for claims he was involved in Cape Town's banking origins (Macquarie seems complicit in this fable).[125] Given John Bardwell Ebden is credited with the beginnings of the Cape of Good Hope Bank in 1831,[126] any involvement by Campbell seems improbable.

Campbell's association with 'an old friend from Cape Town',[127] fellow Irishman Laurence Hynes Halloran, is also curious. Halloran has the profile of a career criminal: acquitted of murder after stabbing a midshipman in 1783; serving as Chaplain to the Navy and Rector to a school in 1807, in Cape Town, before discovery that his letters of ordination were forged; convicted of defamatory libel (against the Cape Town Governor) he was expelled from the colony in 1811; and, eventually transported to Australia for defrauding the Post Office in England. A petition for clemency for Halloran was signed by his Cape Town parishioners in 1808—both J.T. Campbell and J.B. Ebden were signatories. Halloran's colorful history, often on the boundaries of the law, continued in Australia from when he arrived in 1819. J.T. Campbell often supported him in his various endeavors.

Therefore, it is apparent that in what little we know of J.T. Campbell that he had, philosophically, moved beyond an ethic of virtue (if, indeed he was ever bound by such) as he was unconcerned with the damage to his own honor/character 'bearing false witness' was likely to cause. Even if excusing Philo Free within the genre of 'lampooning' (popular in the day), lampoonists rarely published libellous content.

Conversely, Macquarie as Governor, Christian, 'officer and gentleman' was bound by embedded honor-codes, on many levels. 'Bearing false witness', for him, would impugn his honor as a Christian, a gentleman, and would be seen also as 'conduct unbecoming an officer'. Given his autocratic, 'micromanaging' style and his absolute authority one can only speculate if he was complicit, behind-the-scenes, in the Philo Free events. Was Campbell merely his mouthpiece?

---

125   Holder, 'Campbell, John Thomas (1770–1830)'.
126   Nedbank Group, 'Our History'.
127   [ASA], 'Rev. Dr. Laurence Hynes Halloran'.

6.0 Epilogue

Society's moral parameters in the 18th century were co-reinforced by both external and internal value systems based on Christian virtue ethics. For the convicts, it was compulsory to attend church, although it was seen as yet another 'rule' imposed by the privileged class. Right and wrong, good and bad, and biblical teaching was preached from the pulpit each Sunday, regularly reinforcing the moral standards. Although most convicts had been sentenced for offences judged today to be trivial, justifying anger against both the state and a God who appeared to have abandoned them, there was little active protest against the church. Gascoigne[128] believes, at worst, religion was largely treated with indifference. Even though Enlightenment thinkers were contemplating the reach of God and the relationship between themselves and Him, few contemporary philosophers were proposing atheism at this point in history.

One exception is Baruch Spinoza (1632–1677), whose radical views resulted in him being excommunicated from his Jewish community in 1656. His ideas would become 'a systematic and unforgiving critique of the traditional philosophical conceptions of God'.[129] He pursued a notion of happiness and wellbeing removed from our passions, worldly goods and superstitions, based in a life of reason. Scholarly literature (arguably) also places Spinoza's views on a continuum between *pantheist* and *atheist*.

The inescapable propensity for humans to act out of 'self-interest' is central to: the *theological* notion of humankind's natural state since 'The Fall'; the *sociological* concept of Max Weber's Protestant work ethic; the *philosophical* thinking of theorist's such as Rand, Hume, Rousseau and Locke; and, the *economical* basis of Adam Smith's capitalism.

In the eighteenth century the human propensity for self-interest was moderated by 'sacred', external value systems based on DCT's virtue ethics and reinforced by notions that Christian morals were synonymous with both 'civilization' and 'gentleman'. Further, the state openly reinforced this value-base both for the social utility benefits and as the foundation of the legal system, and because The Crown was the

---

128 Gascoigne, *The Enlightenment*.
129 [SEP], 'Baruch Spinoza'.

head of the Church of England.

Campbell lied about Marsden. Until then, libel laws (seditious libel) had predominantly been used as a political tool by the government to suppress freedom of the press. The corrosive effect of Enlightenment thinking had progressively decayed the honor of a Christian and a 'gentleman' for Campbell to think so little of the perjury.

As society increasingly moved towards a more secular, individualist, and Rationalist orientation, the community-centered virtue ethics of DCT became an ends-justifies-the-means (consequentialist), every-person-for-themselves orientation. From the environmental degradation, fraud, and abusive labor practices of our corporations to the deception and ethical scandals of both politicians and individuals, lying is now commonplace. In the absence of an adequate external belief system the only check to dishonesty, today, is getting caught.

In our postmodern, *social anthropogenic* (if we may) *era*, human purpose and wellbeing has been 'polluted', along with our planet, and requires revision. The relentless separation of Church and State under Rationalism ushered in the new 'church' of capitalism—and its greatest fraudulent doctrine, consumerism. Today, seventy-two percent of adults in America believe the moral values of society are declining,[130] money is our God, from it we now derive our social status and sense of self. Acquiring it has become our life's purpose.

---

130   Pew Research, 'Religion & Public Life' (2015).

CHAPTER 14

THE BREAKING OF THE STORM: MARSDEN AND THE MISSIONARY CAUSE

Malcolm Falloon

The breaking of the Storm

Samuel Marsden greeted the arrival of the *Baring* in June 1819 with feelings of inexpressible joy: 'I hope now the Storm is broken', he wrote in reply to the CMS.[1] The reason for his elation was two-fold. Firstly, the presence on board of five new missionaries for the New Zealand mission: John and Hannah Butler, James and Charlotte Kemp, and Francis Hall. Secondly, his joy was sparked by receiving a letter from the clerical secretaries of the CMS, Josiah Pratt and Edward Bickersteth.[2] In their letter, not only did Marsden receive confirmation that a new governor had been appointed for New South Wales, but more importantly from Marsden's perspective, he received the full approval of the CMS Committee for his prosecution of John T. Campbell for the Philo Free libel. Until now, although Marsden knew that the CMS had given their full support to his cause, he also knew that they had done so while being unaware of his subsequent legal proceedings, and he feared that they would consider his 'appeal unto Caesar' a mark of imprudence on his part and a step too far.[3]

---

1 S. Marsden to J. Pratt, 12/7/19.
2 E. Bickersteth & J. Pratt to S. Marsden, 14/12/1818.
3 The quotation comes from S. Marsden to Mary Stokes, 14/6/1819. Marsden had expressed this anxiety to Pratt the previous year: 'How far my friends may approve or condemn my conduct in the whole affair I cannot say'; S. Marsden to J. Pratt, 26/9/1818.

Receiving this letter, Marsden's concerns were allayed, for it was a ringing endorsement from the CMS Committee: 'They feel', wrote Bickersteth and Pratt, 'that, under the blessing of God, the New Zealand Mission owes every thing to you'. And far from countenancing Marsden's withdrawal from the colony (as he had been seriously contemplating), the secretaries informed him that, 'the Committee would most deeply regret your removal'.[4] It had been over two years since he had informed the CMS of his legal proceedings, and 18 months since the successful conclusion to the libel trials—but such were the realities of communication between London and this remote outpost of the British empire.[5] Though the storm seemed to have broken, however, Marsden's hopes for a final end to the 'long and difficult warfare' were not to be realised for many years to come.[6]

Throughout the decade-long conflict, Marsden had found himself at the centre of a maelstrom where his public conduct and personal character had been closely questioned. These questions, surprisingly, persist even into our modern era. For there are many today who consider the vilification of Marsden as a mark of cultural identity. For many, Samuel Marsden's name is inextricably linked with the myth of the 'Flogging Parson' and the brutality of the convict system. Matthew Allen, however, in a recent study has challenged the veracity of that myth by concluding, '[Marsden's] reputation for severity, at least as it is commonly understood, is undeserved'.[7] Instead, the evidence indicates

---

4   E. Bickersteth & J. Pratt to S. Marsden, 14/12/1818.
5   Marsden began formal proceedings against Campbell 23 April 1817; S. Marsden to J. Wylde, 23/4/1817. Marsden forwarded the letter to London via the *Sir William Bensley* departing 17 May 1817, but it was not received in London until 3 June 1818. The bearer of the letter was Justice Jeffery Bent, brother of the late Judge Advocate, Ellis Bent, who was retiring from the colony along with his brother's widow. The letter was considered by the CMS Committee at its June meeting, but not formally acknowledged until 14 December 1818. Such was the lag in communication, that when Marsden finally received this letter by the *Baring*, another two from London were already in transit via the *David Shaw* and the *Regalia*.
6   The quotation is from S. Marsden to J. Pratt, 12/7/1819. The conflict had three more phases to go: Commissioner Bigge arrived in the colony in November of that year (1819) to begin his inquiry; Governor Macquarie wrote his public *Letter to the Rt. Hon. Viscount Sidmouth* in January 1820 in which he openly criticised Marsden (published in England, 1821, but not seen by Marsden until the September of that year); William Wentworth continued the conflict after Macquarie's death in 1824 with the publication of his third edition of *Statistical, Historical and Physical Description*. Marsden replied to both Macquarie and Wentworth with his own publication (*An Answer to Certain Calumnies*), written in July 1825, but not published in England until 1826.
7   Allen, 'The Myth of the Flogging Parson', 487.

that Marsden resorted to flogging less often than other magistrates, and when he did so, ordered only a typical number of lashes. Given the social conditions faced by the bench of magistrates in Parramatta, Allen's conclusions undermine the myth that Marsden's work as a magistrate was at all unusual for the time.[8] In an earlier study, Janice White also concluded that convicts assigned to Marsden experienced better-than-average living conditions and were more successful in their future lives.[9]

Yet, for a complex range of reasons, Marsden's character continues to be a symbol for the perceived wrongs of religion in general and Christianity in particular—at least within Australian and New Zealand. Why this should be the case is worthy of further study, but the essays in this book have sought to challenge the colonial caricature that has been handed down to us by a post-war generation of historians and have sought instead to understand Marsden within his own colonial milieu and upon his own terms.[10]

Consequently, this concluding chapter will first suggest that the colonial caricature of Marsden is no longer tenable and needs to be revised in favour of a more coherent and believable historical portrayal. Secondly, it will maintain that if we are to see things as Marsden saw them, we must seek to understand his central concerns, particularly his commitment to Christian missions. Finally, it will consider the important role played by the London CMS leadership in support of

---

8   In defending himself against Macquarie's charge of 'extraordinary severity', Marsden pointed out to Commissioner Bigge that Parramatta contained 'the sweepings of the public Gaols in every district in the Colony'; see S. Marsden to J. Bigge, 10/1/1821; see also Marsden, *An Answer to Certain Calumnies*, 38–39. Marsden had previously indicated to Macquarie that the guilty were often discharged without conviction on compassionate grounds due to the lack of accommodation for convicts in Parramatta; see Marsden, *An Answer to Certain Calumnies*, 17–18. Marsden, while rejecting the accusation that he was severe, was prepared to concede, in line with Judge Advocate Wylde's opinion expressed to Bigge, that he was nevertheless a strict magistrate: 'I conceive there is a very material difference between severity and strictness in a magistrate. I ever considered that the certainty of punishment operated more powerfully upon the mind of the delinquent than the severity of punishment; and upon this principle I acted. Long experience in this Colony has taught me that this opinion is correct, and founded upon a sound, wise, and, I may add, a humane policy'; Marsden, *An Answer to Certain Calumnies*, 38.
9   White, 'A Master and his Men', 104–107.
10 Skinner writes: 'I am only pleading for the historical task to be conceived as that of trying so far as possible to think as our ancestors thought and to see things their way. What this requires is that we should recover the concepts they possessed, the distinctions they drew and the chains of reasoning they followed in their attempts to make sense of their world'; Skinner, 'Introduction: Seeing Things Their Way', 47. For a discussion of the relationship between intellectual and religious history see Chapman, Coffey, & Gregory, *Seeing Things Their Way*.

Marsden in order to show that the conflict was no mere parochial dispute limited in scope to New South Wales. This allows a reconsideration of the opposition that Marsden faced from Governor Macquarie and his Secretary, John Campbell, before making some concluding comments as to the overall significance of the Philo Free controversy.

Colonial caricatures

It is the failure to take account of Marsden's missionary motivations that has led many to form outlandish caricatures—'assessments of his motivations that read', as Michael Gladwin tells us in chapter eleven, 'more like pop psychology than careful historical analysis'.[11] For Gladwin, the problem stems from neglecting the broader cultural and social contexts of the Philo Free case, particularly the context of the Protestant missionary movement and Marsden's place within it. This neglect of Marsden's missionary perspective is also highlighted by David Pettett in chapter two. Pettett is concerned that many writers continue to accept an uncritically negative assessment of Marsden and thereby perpetuate erroneous stereotypes. Pettett gives two examples: Robert Hughes characterising Marsden as, 'a grasping Evangelical missionary with heavy shoulders and the face of a petulant ox'; and David Hunt (not to be out-done in physiognomic abuse) describing him as a man 'with a ruddy face, piggy snout, melon-shaped head and the strength of an ox on steroids'.[12] It appears that these abusive descriptions of Marsden's appearance are based on little more than their own subjective responses to Richard Read Jr.'s 1833 portrait of the Principal Chaplain. Yet, as Pettett perceptively observes, 'Marsden's critics, almost without exception, fall into the camp of those who do not understand, or who oppose, the evangelical agenda of Christian mission'.[13]

These colonial caricatures of Marsden bear all the hallmarks of an analytical framework gone awry. For the darker the tones with which they render Marsden's portrait, the less believable he becomes as an actual historical figure. In contrast to these dark portrayals, several

---

11   Gladwin, 'The Bigge Picture', 267.
12   Pettett, 'Marsden in the Hands of Australasian Historians', 36, 45.
13   Pettett, 'Marsden in the Hands of Australasian Historians', 37. The ignorance becomes almost willful—particularly when, as Pettett points out, claims are made concerning Marsden's preaching that bear no relation to the archival sources.

chapters in this volume have demonstrated that Marsden in reality maintained a wide variety of healthy relationships—evidence that decisively counters claims of his sociopathy.[14] For instance, in chapter eight Jane Tooher describes a deeply humane Marsden who cared about the colony and enjoyed the support of significant women, particularly Eliza his wife.[15] Similarly, in chapter nine David Pettett illuminates the social context in which Marsden was embedded, showing that he maintained a wide network of friends and associates through the colony both 'pious' and otherwise.[16]

To these more realistic hues can be added Marsden's personal influence in sustaining the missionary enterprise in the south seas. Joel Atwood, in chapter three, has usefully highlighted the important role that Marden played as the LMS agent. This required him to inspire, encourage, and fortify the often-dejected missionaries who were in danger of giving up the cause.[17] Never was Marsden's personal influence more vital in this regard than when he encouraged the missionaries to return to the Society Islands in 1810.[18] Even more telling, was Marsden's friendship with Māori rangatira (chiefs). This is particularly evident with Ruatara, who had invited Marsden to establish the first mission station in New Zealand. Yet the mission almost floundered before it left the Sydney heads, when Marsden discovered that Ruatara's mind had been poisoned by some unknown European.[19] Only the personal reassurances of Marsden and the strength of his friendship with Ruatara ensured that the mission was able to continue. Even so, Marsden realised that incalculable damage had been done by this anonymous and deliberately malicious source.

Given that Māori rangatira were careful observers of a person's character and conduct—traits essential for the protection and well-being of their people—their esteem for Marsden over many years was no small matter. Though both Kendall and Butler at times wished they could dispense with Marsden's oversight, the reality was that his

---

14 A case in point is Quinn's bizarre claim that Marsden was a psychopath; Quinn, *Samuel Marsden*, 171–174.
15 Tooher, 'A Friendship Revealed', 199–203.
16 Pettett, 'Marsden's Supportive Circle', 225–227.
17 Atwood, '"So important in its nature"', 68.
18 Sharp, *The World, the Flesh & the Devil*, 348–350.
19 Marsden was unable to discover the European's identity but it may well have been Campbell.

personal influence with Māori was a vital ingredient to the eventual success of the New Zealand mission.

The missionary cause

For Marsden, it is clear that the central issue at stake was the cause of Christian missions. Indeed, it was Campbell's continued obstruction of the missionary brig *Active* that finally convinced Marsden to take him to court.[20] Up until that point, Marsden had been reluctant to initiate formal proceedings. In fact, in March 1817 he had written to the LMS all but ruling out that option:

> I have little chance of success by appealing to Cesar [sic], by an application to the laws of my Country in this Colony. I might at present as well leap into the Sea to save myself from drounding as to seek Redress in this way.[21]

Marsden, instead, looked to rely on prayer alone: 'The Cause is God's and he will defend it', he told them.

Consequently, when Marsden sent the Philo Free correspondence to the CMS in April 1817 there was no suggestion that he would be seeking a legal remedy. The dispatches were carried by Thomas Hassall, returning to England for theological training and ordination on the *Kangaroo*, departing 9 April 1817. Later the same month, however, Marsden had a change of heart. As he later explained, he had had no peace and was alarmed to find himself experiencing the same physical symptoms that had led to the death of his friend, Ellis Bent.[22] Then, when Campbell again hindered the sailing of the *Active*, Marsden resolved to take a stand, whatever the cost.

> It was not my Intention to have brought Mr Campbell to the Bar of Justice, if I could possibly have avoided it. I felt myself totally unequal (under existing Circumstances) to the danger and difficulty of such a

---

20 Falloon, 'Mission Trading', 119.
21 S. Marsden to G. Burder, 14/3/1817.
22 S. Marsden to J. Pratt, 26/9/1818. Marsden wrote, 'When I retired to my Bed weary in Body, and mind, I found my Sleep, was departed from me, and I could truly say "wearisome nights were appointed unto me." I had no pain of Body, but the Vital Strings of the mind were ready to break'. Before his death in November 1815, Bent was the Judge Advocate and had become embroiled in conflict with Governor Macquarie over the legal governance of the colony; see Sharp, *The World, the Flesh & the Devil*, 320–326.

measure, on political Grounds, and on Christian Principles I was more unwilling to take such a Step. But as Solomon justly observes "Oppression maketh a man mad", so it was with me. I did not feel for myself, so much as I did for the important Cause of the mission. I was fearful from opposition, it might be crushed in its Infancy.[23]

In proceeding to prosecute Campbell, Marsden was reacting to what he considered a seven-year pattern of opposition: 'I have at last been compelled to open war', he told a friend (probably John Mason Good) in the May. 'I had no alternative; but either to give up the Cause of the missions, and conform my conduct to the Laws of others; or to defend myself and the interests of Religion'.[24]

The missionary cause not only precipitated Marsden's libel action, but it was also the reason that held him in New South Wales, even though he considered leaving the colony on a number of occasions. He had first talked of leaving in 1815 after returning from his first trip to New Zealand. He told Mary Stokes that he had discussed the possibility with Eliza, his wife, but she had responded, 'What will New Zealand do? What will the missionaries at Olaketa do?'.[25] It was a gentle reminder that stayed with him, for in the aftermath of the Philo Free trials in December 1817, he again told Mary Stokes: 'I often wish to return to the bosom of my country and frequently resolve to do this but then I am immediately checked with the thought, What will the New Zealanders do. What will the missionaries in all the Islands do if there is none to care for them & administer to their wants and to console them under difficulties'.[26]

In 1818, when communication with Governor Macquarie had completely broken down, Marsden again sought to return to England. This time, it was Macquarie who barred the way. He told Pratt, 'I do not murmur at this Disappointment, well knowing that if it had been right for me to come to England, it would not have been in the Power of the Governor— he could have no Power against me except it was given him from above'.[27] Later events would vindicate Marsden's confidence

---

23 S. Marsden to J. Pratt, 26/9/1818.
24 S. Marsden to [John Mason Good], 17/5/1817.
25 S. Marsden to Mary Stokes, 15/6/1815.
26 S. Marsden to Mary Stokes, 16/12/1817.
27 S. Marsden to J. Pratt, 20/5/1818.

in the 'kind hand of Providence'.²⁸ In hindsight Marsden realised that, had he not been present when Commissioner Bigge was conducting his inquiry, his opponents would have taken every advantage of his absence to malign him. Instead, Marsden could look back on Macquarie's refusal with a sense of gratitude: 'Governor Macquarie preventing my return to England, when I so much wished it, was one of the most providential Events that ever happened to me at any time'.²⁹

Perhaps Marsden's clearest statement of his commitment to the missionary cause came not in his public letters to the CMS, but in a private letter to Mary Stokes just before the arrival of the *Baring* and the second wave of New Zealand missionaries:

> N. S. Wales would not have detained me had it not been the post which the Great Captain of Salvation assigned me for the good of the Heathen. I would not have lived under the rod of oppression for any human authority unless I had been chained hand and foot. The question which I often put to myself when smarting under the scourge of Power and Injustice is am I at my post? Do I believe God sent me here. The answer of my mind has always been Yes. I will then defend my post. I will not quit till I am relieved.³⁰

It is clear that Marsden saw the cause of missions as the overriding priority of his life and he considered himself a 'Missionary in body and soul', as his colleague John Youl had testified.³¹ Marsden's most recent biographer, Andrew Sharp, comments, 'If Marsden's anger at this juncture [the Philo Free libel] is to be understood, the missions must be seen from the points of view of the missionaries and the man himself as he worked for their success'.³²

Consequently, it is important to give Christian mission its full weight in evaluating Marsden's motives and conduct throughout the Philo Free controversy. For Marsden's religious commitments are not able to be adequately explained as a function of other motives, such as political self-interest, social ambition, or some inner psychological need. Yet, if Marsden's central concern was the cause of missions, then it raises

---

28 S. Marsden to J. Pratt, 19/3/1821.
29 S. Marsden to J. Pratt, 9/2/1821.
30 S. Marsden to Mary Stokes, 14/6/1819.
31 J. Youl to J. Pratt, 29/3/1817.
32 Sharp, *The World, the Flesh & the Devil*, 335.

important questions over his apparent neglect of an aboriginal mission. Greg Anderson, in chapter four, gives a helpful overview of the early colonial engagement with the indigenous populations of New Holland: 'There are few happy stories in that history', Anderson says, 'but providing some context around the particularities of the Philo Free matter can give further depth to our understanding of some of the dynamics in play'.[33] It is clear that at the time of the Philo Free controversy, Marsden faced two major obstacles in pursuing an aboriginal mission project. Firstly, as Anderson rightly observes, Marsden was greatly perplexed by the cultural divide that existed between British society and the aboriginal peoples of New Holland, rendering ineffective strategies that had been successfully deployed with New Zealand Māori.[34] Secondly, as Anderson again points out, Marsden was stung by the injustice of Macquarie's accusation that he had neglected aboriginal Australians—particularly when he had been deliberately excluded from any involvement with the government institution in Parramatta.[35]

When the CMS committee in London had first received the Philo Free letter, they had immediately responded by proposing to fund a joint seminary for aboriginal youth as well as with Māori, as Marsden had proposed. The CMS committee, having read the accusations of Philo Free and knowing that Marsden had been excluded from the Native Institution, passed the following resolution: 'That Mr Marsden and his Colleagues be requested to take the most effective measures in their power for extending the benefits of Christian Education and instruction in the arts, in the Seminary at Parramatta, to the most promising young Natives both of New South Wales and New Zealand'.[36] The CMS were in effect authorising Marsden to work independently of the government in conducting a mission to the Aboriginal population of New South Wales.

The CMS resolution had the effect of forcing Marsden to explain why he did not consider their proposal to be feasible. He gave three reasons: firstly, that the present government institution had largely failed to produce any positive outcomes, with the implication that he

---

33 Anderson, 'The early colonial mission context', 79.
34 Anderson, 'The early colonial mission context', 88–92. See also S. Marsden to J. Pratt, 24/2/1819 [No. 1].
35 Anderson, 'The early colonial mission context', 80–81. See also S. Marsden to J. Pratt, 22/1/1817.
36 Minutes of the CMS Committee, 9/3/1818.

was at a loss as to how a CMS-run seminary could remedy the situation; secondly, that Māori were in fact reluctant to co-habit with New Hollanders thus making a joint institution problematic to establish even if desirable; and thirdly, it was generally considered by his colleagues that it would be most unwise to even raise the subject with the Governor, who would view the seminary as undermining his own initiatives. Given these reasons, Marsden considered it to be out of his power to put the CMS committee's resolution into effect. Rightly or wrongly, he consoled himself with a broader view of God's providence: 'Time may alter the present circumstances and something then may be done; but if we may be allowed to judge from what we see and know of the natives of N. S. Wales, the time is not yet arrived for them to receive the great blessings of civilization and the knowledge of Christianity'.[37]

The metropolitan counter

Along with Marsden's commitment to the missionary cause, it is also important to understand the role played by the CMS in countering the effects of the Philo Free libel in London. Marsden had sent the first batch of correspondence concerning the Philo Free letter to the CMS via the *Kangaroo*, departing 9 April 1817 and arriving in London, 23 Feb 1818.[38] A special meeting of the CMS committee was immediately called to consider the correspondence in detail. The committee met 3 March 1818, with Lord Gambier, the CMS President, in the chair.[39] Also present were two members of Parliament, Thomas Babington and William Wilberforce (both of whom served as vice-presidents of the society), the Treasurer, John Thornton, and eleven clergy and seventeen laymen. Pratt described the meeting as one of the longest committee meetings yet held and informed Marsden that most of the active CMS members had been present.[40]

Realising that the well-being of their mission was at stake, the

---

37 S. Marsden to J. Pratt, 24/2/1819 [No. 1].
38 Marsden had first informed Pratt about Campbell's libel in a letter dated 22 January 1817 which was received in London, 29 October 1817. Pratt had replied via the *Tottenham*, 24 November 1817, expressing his full confidence in Marsden's conduct, though the ship did not arrive in Sydney until one month after the *Isabella*, which had delivered the CMS responses to the *Kangaroo* dispatches. S. Marsden to J. Pratt, 22/1/1817; J. Pratt to S. Marsden, 24/11/1817.
39 Minutes of the CMS Committee, 3/3/1818.
40 J. Pratt to S. Marsden, 12/3/1818.

committee called upon their vice-presidents to meet as a separate subcommittee to consider how best to respond. The vice-presidents settled on a two-pronged strategy. Firstly, William Wilberforce and Fowell Buxton, together with their fellow MP, Henry Bennett, were asked to take up Marsden's cause in the newly established House of Commons select committee on the state of gaols.[41] Pratt assured Marsden that all three members were committed to defending his reputation and ensuring that the Parliament had full access to the evidence Marsden had submitted to the CMS.[42] In fact, Buxton wrote to Marsden assuring him that they considered it their 'sacred duty' to protect him from that 'gross injustice to which you have hitherto been exposed'.[43] As a result of their work, the final parliamentary report was able to clearly state Campbell's guilt and completely exonerate Marsden. For Pratt, this was particularly important in order to counter the 'garbled & false representation' of the first Philo Free trial that appeared in the *Sydney Gazette*.[44] In addition, in order to give wider publicity to the work of the select committee, Bennett published two letters summarising the evidence presented and the final findings.[45] The second part of the plan adopted by the CMS vice-presidents was for John Thornton, the CMS treasurer and a director of the Bank of England, to make an approach to his friend, Henry Goulburn, who served as the under-secretary in the Colonial Office, to see if anything could be done on Marsden's behalf.[46] Thornton did manage to persuade Goulburn to become a vice-president of the society, though the official response from the Colonial Office remained one of non-inference. The implementation of these two strategies illustrates the tight connections that existed at the time between the British Parliament, the Colonial Office, and the CMS—connections (as Bolt suggests in chapter seven) that Campbell may well have underestimated.[47]

---

41 Sharp, *The World, the Flesh & the Devil*, 432–434.
42 J. Pratt to S. Marsden, 19/5/1819.
43 T.F. Buxton to S. Marsden, 7/5/1819.
44 J. Pratt to S. Marsden, 12/5/1819; *Sydney Gazette*, 1/11/1817. See Moll's discussion of the *Sydney Gazette's* trial report; Moll, 'Unmasking A Shielded Secret Enemy', 251–252.
45 H. G. Bennett, *Letter to Viscount Sidmouth*. The former letter arrived in the colony in early January 1820 and prompted Macquarie to defend himself with his own letter; Macquarie, *A Letter to the Rt. Hon. Viscount Sidmouth*.
46 J. Pratt to S. Marsden, 14/12/1818. Henry's younger brother, Frederick Goulburn, would become John T. Campbell's replacement as Colonial Secretary in New South Wales from 1 February 1821.
47 Bolt, 'The Failure of the Philanthropic Society', 185–189.

The CMS then cemented their public support for Marsden by thanking him in the Society's annual reports for 1818 and 1819.[48] In the Annual Report for 1819, for instance, Marsden was singled out for special mention: 'Before the Committee proceed to report the actual state of the Settlement at the Bay of Islands, they beg to renew the acknowledgements of the Society to its able and unwearied friend Mr. Marsden, not only for his measures at Parramatta in reference to New Zealand, but for the watchful eye which he keeps on the interests of the Mission, and the judicious steps taken by him in its favour'.[49]

The reason why the CMS were so committed was because, like Marsden, they considered the issues at stake to involve more than one man's reputation. Marsden's friend and CMS Committee member, John Mason Good, expressed the general view when writing to Marsden, 'I agree with you most fully that your contest has not been a personal one, but that the important objects of the Society have been at stake, and that the victory you have obtained is of more importance to the cause of virtue, honour, and true religion, and more especially to the cause of Christian missions in Australasia, than to yourself'.[50] As Gladwin observes in chapter eleven, 'There was a real sense that in the Philo Free case it was the Evangelical overseas mission project [...] as much as Marsden that was on trial'.[51]

Secret enemies

This metropolitan perspective becomes important for making sense of Marsden's continued determination to defend himself from attack. For having rallied the CMS to his defence, Marsden needed to protect the reputation of those who had lent their support. Marsden reassured one unnamed supporter (probably Buxton) of his care: 'I should be much concerned if upon any grounds my friends should be charged with supporting a cause unworthy of their attention: and that I had deceived them'.[52] Lorraine Ratcliffe, however, in her study of the Philo Free case,

---

48 *Proceedings of the Church Missionary Society for Africa and the East*, 1818, 128; *Proceedings of the Church Missionary Society for Africa and the East*, 1819, 13, 197.
49 *Proceedings*, 1819, 197.
50 J.M. Good to S. Marsden, n.d.
51 Gladwin, 'The Bigge Picture', 286–287.
52 S. Marsden to [T.F. Buxton], 24/9/1821.

is exasperated by the sheer volume of correspondence between Marsden and Commissioner Bigge. For her, this could only be a function of Marsden's peculiar pathology: 'Marsden's resentment of the administration's executive power, underpinned by his territorial approach to his long-standing office, provoked an intensely personal conflict which was finally acted out in a very public way through the courts'.[53]

Ratcliffe goes further in claiming that Marsden's libel action against Campbell was in reality only a proxy battle in a larger campaign against the Macquarie administration: 'For all the reasons he gave as smoke-screens for snaring Campbell, his serious intent was to fell the governor'.[54] While it can be agreed that Marsden's tenacity was generated by larger ambitions than merely personal status, to make Macquarie the primary target of Marsden's libel action remains unconvincing. As argued here, the missionary cause provided a sufficient motivation to explain Marsden's actions without having to accept uncritically Macquarie's accusation that Marsden was his 'secret enemy'![55]

In chapter five, Craig Schwarze helpfully documents the deteriorating relationship between Marsden and Macquarie. While it is clear, as Schwarze writes, 'that Macquarie was no neutral arbiter in the conflict between his secretary and the colonial chaplain', the exact nature of the enmity between the pair is less clear.[56] Schwarze rightly avoids an easy polarisation between Emancipists and Exclusivists, or between Church and State, and in the end opts for it being 'simply a clash of wills, a dispute between two powerful men who were both proud and even egotistical, and unwilling to overlook a slight'.[57] This might well be the case—at least for Macquarie—though as Moll suggests, the extent of Macquarie's complicity in the Philo Free libel still remains an open question.[58]

Strangely, however, it appears that Marsden was just as baffled as we are by Macquarie's antagonism towards him. He had admitted their

---

53 Ratcliffe, '"Pens Dipped in Gall"', 66.
54 Ratcliffe, '"Pens Dipped in Gall"', 67.
55 Macquarie used the phrase in his admonishment of Marsden; L. Macquarie to S. Marsden, 8/1/1818.
56 Schwarze, 'A Secret Enemy', 101.
57 Schwarze, 'A Secret Enemy', 105.
58 Moll, 'Unmasking A Shielded Secret Enemy', 264 n. 179. For further discussion of the social context of their dispute see Bolt et al., 'Normative Ethics In Early Colonial Australia', 326–332.

political disagreements to Commissioner Bigge, but did not see these as providing sufficient warrant to incur his resentment.[59] Marsden even got Bigge to put the question directly to the Governor, yet Bigge returned with only an admission of Marsden's exemplary conduct: 'It is singular', wrote Marsden to Pratt, '[that] the Govr should say so much in my favour, and still be so anxious to injure me if it was in his Power'.[60] Marsden's only conclusion was that Macquarie had had his mind 'wrought upon by secret Enemies'.

Among those secret enemies was John T. Campbell.[61] For, although Macquarie had concluded that Marsden was his secret enemy, Marsden's suspicions were directed more towards the Governor's Secretary than the Governor himself.[62] Certainly, there is no consistent body of evidence that warrants the conclusion that Marsden had mounted a concerted campaign against Macquarie's administration, as Ratcliffe claims.[63] It is a better reading of the sources to take Marsden's claim seriously that Campbell was the primary—and not the proxy—target of his litigation. Furthermore, we should not underestimate Marsden's claim that Campbell was also religiously motivated in his attacks. He told Pratt on a number of occasions that he believed there never existed a greater enemy to the Gospel, and that 'as far as can be ascertained from the opposition to the measures of the Church M[issionary] Society the object was to annihilate the mission altogether'.[64] Elizabeth Moll in chapter ten suggests that Campbell in fact harboured anti-evangelical sentiments.[65] And in publishing his pseudonymous letter in the *Gazette*, Campbell would have, in all probability, anticipated a readership far beyond the shores of New South Wales. This would account for the relatively sophisticated genre of satire that Campbell employed in writing his letter, as Peter Bolt details in chapter one.[66] Campbell was clearly attempting to damage Marsden's reputation with the people that mattered back in London, and with it the cause of evangelical mission.

59 S. Marsden to J. Bigge, 10/1/1821.
60 S. Marsden to J. Pratt, 19/3/1821.
61 For a discussion of Campbell in this present volume see Moll, 'Unmasking A Shielded Secret Enemy', 230–235 and Bolt et al., 'Normative Ethics In Early Colonial Australia', 337–338.
62 As Marsden had forlornly tried to tell Macquarie; S. Marsden to L. Macquarie, 11/8/1818.
63 Ratcliffe, '"Pens Dipped in Gall"', 49–50.
64 S. Marsden to J. Pratt, 11/8/1818; S. Marsden to J. Pratt, 13/7/1819.
65 Moll, 'Unmasking A Shielded Secret Enemy', 234; also Schwarze, 'A Secret Enemy', 99.
66 Bolt, 'The Letter', 13–24.

As Peter Bolt explains in chapter seven, Campbell may have had further reasons to make Marsden his enemy as a result of the demise of the Philanthropic Society.[67] Campbell's knowledge of the 1814 *Cumberland* murders in Rarotonga and its subsequent cover-up, may have aligned Campbell with darker interests within the colony. In this regard, the connection between Campbell and William Wentworth, and the reasons for their relentless attacks on the Principal Chaplain, is worthy of further study. As it was, Marsden was fully aware that 'Interested Individuals had no wish that any thing should be done for the poor Heathens in the South Sea islands, lest their Crimes should be exposed, and they should not be able to plunder as they were wont to do'.[68] He was also aware that Campbell continued to use the *Sydney Gazette* to undermine the CMS mission by portraying Māori as an inhuman race of treacherous cannibals.[69] Campbell's opposition to Marsden is a reminder that not everyone within the British empire was in sympathy with the humanitarian campaigns and missionary agendas of the evangelical party within British politics.

Concluding comments

This concluding chapter seeks to demonstrate that Marsden's commitment to the missionary cause explains much of the passion with which he engaged in the Philo Free controversy. It also suggests that religion forms the central issue for Campbell just as much as it did for Marsden. Consequently, the Philo Free controversy provides a valuable vantage point for viewing the contested nature of the missionary agenda during the early period of the Protestant missionary movement. Other chapters in this volume give a similar vantage point on colonial life. Elizabeth Moll's essay helpfully sheds light on the emerging colonial legal system and the law of defamation,[70] while Caitlin Hurley traces the way in which the press in New South Wales emerged as an independent voice, unrestrained by government control.[71] Achieving the right balance between the rule of law and the

---

67 Bolt, 'The failure of the Philanthropic Society', 194.
68 S. Marsden to J. Pratt, 19/3/1821.
69 For an example of this campaign, see Falloon, 'Mission Trading', 125 n. 71.
70 Moll, 'Unmasking A Shielded Secret Enemy', 235–241.
71 Hurley, 'Freedom of Speech', 302–310.

freedom of speech remain relevant issues within our media-saturated society. Increasingly today, the power of social media to destroy a person's reputation with false accusations is bringing us closer to the past world inhabited by Marsden and Campbell.

There is always the danger, of course, that in considering the Philo Free trial that we simply reflect our present concerns onto the past, rather than allowing the concerns of the past to illuminate our present. Part of the difficulty is that the historical past is such a foreign landscape that it is hard for us to discern its features. Rather ambitiously, Alexander Bolt, Paul Cerotti and Konrad Peszynski in chapter thirteen, have attempted to sketch the contours of that past while drawing connections with the present, that we might better understand both territories. Their discussion of the role played by honour, reputation, and status in maintaining the patterns of social hierarchy helpfully informs our understanding of the conflict between Macquarie, Campbell and Marsden.[72]

So, what is the significance of the Philo Free controversy for our understanding of Samuel Marsden and this period of Australia's colonial history? As can be seen by the diverse range of essays contained in this volume, there is not a straight-forward answer to this question. The controversy affected almost every aspect of colony life (and beyond): political, judicial, ecclesiastical, commercial, and social—to list but a few. Yet through being so well documented, the Philo Free controversy shines an intense and, at times, uncomfortable light on the emerging nation state of Australia. It also functions as a bellwether for many future trends and developments that affected the colonies of New Holland, and indeed the wider Pacific, in the years ahead.

---

72 Bolt et al., 'Normative Ethics In Early Colonial Australia', 318–332.

BIBLIOGRAPHY

Abbreviations

[ ]	Square brackets indicate material not present in the original
ATL	Alexander Turnbull Library, Wellington
BFBS	British and Foreign Bible Society
BT	Bonwick Transcripts. Mitchell Library, Sydney.
CMS	Church Missionary Society
CRL	Cadbury Research Library. University of Birmingham.
HL	Hocken Library, University of Otago.
HRA	*Historical Records of Australia*
HRNSW	*Historical Records of NSW*
HRNZ	*Historical Records of New Zealand* (R. McNab, ed.; 2 vols; Wellington: John Mackay, 1908 & 1914).
KJV	King James Version
LMS	London Missionary Society
LPA	Lambeth Palace Archives. London.
Mfm	Microfilm
Mitchell	Mitchell Library, State Library of NSW. Sydney.
NLA	National Library of Australia. Canberra.
SG	*Sydney Gazette*
SLTAS	State Library of Tasmania. Hobart.
SLNSW	State Library of NSW. Sydney.
SOAS	School of Oriental and African Studies Library, University of London.
SRNSW	State Records of New South Wales. Kingswood, NSW.
WAMS	Wesleyan Auxiliary Missionary Society

Primary Sources
Collections of Sources

Britton, A. (ed.)   *Historical Records of New South Wales*, Vol. 1, part 2—*Phillip 1783–1792* (Sydney: Charles Potter, 1892). www.archive.org

Britton, A. & F.M. Bladen (ed.)
Historical Records of New South Wales, Vol 2—*Phillip and Grose* (Sydney: Charles Potter, 1894).

Broughton Papers.   Moore College, Sydney.

Colonial Secretary Papers.
Index: http://colsec.records.nsw.gov.au.

Elder, J.R.   *The Letters and Journals of Samuel Marsden, 1765-1838* (Dunedin: Coulls, Somerville, Wilkie, and A. H. Reed for the Otago University Council, 1932). http://www.enzb.auckland.ac.nz/.

Mackaness, G. (ed.)   *Some Letters of Rev. Richard Johnson, B.A., First Chaplain of New South Wales: Collected and Edited, with Introduction, Notes and Commentary* (2 vols.; Australian Historical Monographs, 21; Sydney: D. S. Ford, 1954). http://www.chr.org.au/ documents.html.

Mackaness, G. (ed.)   *Some Private Correspondence of the Rev. Samuel Marsden and Family, 1794–1824* (Australian Historical Monographs; Sydney: G. Mackanass, Feb 28, 1942; Reprinted: Dubbo: Review Publications, 1976). http://www.chr.org.au/documents.html.

McNab, R.   *Historical Records of New Zealand* (Wellington: John Mackay, 1908), vol. 1. http://nzetc.victoria.ac.nz/tm/scholarly/tei-McN01Hist.html OR https://archive.org/details/historicalrecord01mcnauoft.

McNab, R.   *Historical Records of New Zealand* (Wellington: John Mackay, 1914), vol. 2. http://nzetc.victoria.ac.nz/tm/scholarly/tei-McN02Hist.html OR https://archive.org/details/historicalrecord02mcnauoft.

Marsden Sermon Collection
Moore College, Sydney

Marsden Online Archive   Hocken Library, University of Otago. http://marsdenarchive.otago.ac.nz.

Watson, F. (ed.)   *Historical Records of Australia. Series 1: Despatches to and from England*. Vol. 4: *1803 to June 1804* (F. Watson, ed.; Australia: The Library Committee of the Commonwealth

BIBLIOGRAPHY

Parliament, 1915). https://archive.org/details/historicalrecord00v4aust.

Watson, F. (ed.)   *Historical Records of Australia. Series 1: Despatches to and from England.* Vol. 7: *January 1809 to June 1813* (F. Watson, ed.; Australia: The Library Committee of the Commonwealth Parliament, 1916). https://archive.org/details/historicalrecord00v7aust.

Watson, F. (ed.)   *Historical Records of Australia. Series 1: Despatches to and from England.* Vol. 8: *January 1813 to December 1815* (F. Watson, ed.; Australia: The Library Committee of the Commonwealth Parliament, 1916). https://archive.org/details/historicalrecord00v8aust.

Watson, F. (ed.)   *Historical Records of Australia. Series 1: Despatches to and from England.* Vol. 9: *January 1816 to December 1818* (F. Watson, ed.; Australia: The Library Committee of the Commonwealth Parliament, 1917). https://archive.org/details/historicalrecord00v9aust.

Watson, F. (ed.)   *Historical Records of Australia. Series 1: Despatches to and from England.* Vol. 10: *January 1819 to December 1822* (F. Watson, ed.; Australia: The Library Committee of the Commonwealth Parliament, 1917). https://archive.org/details/historicalrecord00v10aust.

Watson, F. (ed.)   *Historical Records of Australia. Series 1: Despatches to and from Sir Thomas Brisbane.* Vol. 11: *January 1823 to November 1825* (F. Watson, ed.; Australia: The Library Committee of the Commonwealth Parliament, 1917). https://archive.org/details/historicalrecord00v11aust.

Watson, F. (ed.)   *Historical Records of Australia. Series 1: Governors' Despatches to and from England.* Vol. 12: *June 1825 to December 1826* (F. Watson, ed.; Australia: The Library Committee of the Commonwealth Parliament, 1919). https://archive.org/details/historicalrecord00v12aust.

Watson, F. (ed.)   *Historical Records of Australia. Series 1: Governors' Despatches to and from England.* Vol. 13: *January 1827 to February 1828* (F. Watson, ed.; Australia: The Library Committee of the Commonwealth Parliament, 1920). https://archive.org/details/historicalrecord00v13aust.

Watson, F. (ed.)   *Historical Records of Australia. Series 1: Governors' Despatches to and from England.* Vol. 14: *March 1828 to May 1829* (F. Watson, ed.; Australia: The Library Committee of the Commonwealth Parliament, 1922). https://archive.org/details/historicalrecord00v14aust.

Watson, F. (ed.)	*Historical Records of Australia. Series 1*: Governors' Despatches to and from England. Vol. 16: *1831–1832* (F. Watson, ed.; Australia: The Library Committee of the Commonwealth Parliament, 1923). https://archive.org/details/historicalrecord00v16aust.
Watson, F. (ed.)	*Historical Records of Australia, Series IV: Legal Papers. Section A. Vol 1. 1786–1827* (F. Watson, ed.; Australia: Library Committee of the Commonwealth Parliament, 1922). http://arrow.latrobe.edu.au:8080/vital/access/manager/Repository/latrobe:34607.

Accounts, Returns, & Other Financial Statements

[Brooks, Richard]	*Certificates Concerning the Active*, 22/9/1814 (http://www.marsdenarchive.otago.ac.nz/MS_0054_049)
CMS	*CMS's Account with Marsden on Account of the brig Active*, 4/10/1814 (http://www.marsdenarchive.otago.ac.nz/MS_0054_050).
Marsden, S.	Account of Expenses, 25 Feb – 1 Nov 1814 = see next item.
Marsden, S.	An Account of Expenses of the Active and the Different Necessities for the Settlement of New Zealand, 21/6/1815 (http://www.marsdenarchive.otago.ac.nz/MS_0055_010).
Marsden, S.	Account to Church Missionary Society, 7/3/1816 (http://www.marsdenarchive.otago.ac.nz/MS_0056_001).
Marsden, S.	Account with the CMS, in S. Marsden to CMS, 8/3/1816 (http://www.marsdenarchive.otago.ac.nz/MS_0056_002).
[Naval Officer]	Estimate of Duties Collected by the Naval Officer 1/7 to 30/9/1813 (*HRA* 1.8, 196–197).
Hall, Walter	Walter Hall's Return, 6/7/1815; enclosure in S. Marsden to J. Pratt, 26/10/1815 (http://www.marsdenarchive.otago.ac.nz/MS_0055_033).
Hall, Walter	Walter Hall's Return, 2/10/1815, in An Account of Trading from B. Smiths Shop, 10 July to October 1815 (http://www.marsdenarchive.otago.ac.nz/MS_0055_029).

'Schedule of Duties', *SG* 26/6/1813 (http://trove.nla.gov.au/newspaper/page/7054).

Valuation of the Brig *Active*, 8/12/1819 (CRL: CMS/B/OMS/C N M1: 59).

Addresses, Orations, and Sermons

Cuvier, Baron Georges	Funeral oration [for Sir Joseph Banks] at the Academy of Sciences, Paris (2 Apr 1821). Quoted in Cameron, *Sir Joseph Banks, K.B., P.R.S.: the Autocrat of the Philosophers* (Sydney: Angus & Robertson, 1952), 209.
Howe, G.	'A Respectful Address, From the Printer to a liberal Public', SG 1/11/1817.
Marsden, S.	Sermons 18, 34, 81, 88 (Moore College). Transcriptions (by D.B. Pettett) of the sermons in the Moore College collection can be found at https://www.moore.edu.au/Media/Default/Library/PDFs/Marsden%20Sermons%20Transcription.pdf
Marsden, S.	Sermon following the death of Ellis Bent. (Mitchell: Marsden Papers. C244, 17–40).
Scott, T.	'An Address to the Rev. John Godfrey Wilhelm, and the Rev. Jonathan Solomon Klein, about to Proceed as Missionaries to the Western Coast of Africa, Delivered at an Open Committee Meeting of the Church Missionary Society, August 28, 1811', in John Scott (ed.), *The Works of the Late Rev. T. Scott, Rector of Aston Sanford, Bucks.* (London: Seeley and Son, 1824), 6:120–163.
Thomas, J.	Protest against the CMS, 1/12/1817, re-published in SG 23/5/1818.

Almanacs

Howe, G. (printer)	*New South Wales Pocket Almanack, for the Year of our Lord and Saviour 1813* (Sydney: G. Howe, 1813).
Howe, G. (printer)	*New South Wales Pocket Almanack, for the Year of our Lord 1814* (Sydney: G. Howe, 1814).
Howe, G. (printer)	*New South Wales Pocket Almanack, for the Year of our Lord 1817* (Sydney: G. Howe, 1817).

Articles & Reviews

[Analytical Review],	'Art. I: The Voyage of Governor Philip to Botany Bay, compiled from the several journals of various persons who made the journey', *Analytical Review, or History of Literature, Domestic and Foreign* Vol. 6 (Jan–April, 1790), 1–10.

[Analytical Review], 'Art. XIII. A Benevolent Epistle to Sylvanus Urban, alias Master John Nichols, Printer, Common-Councilman of Farringdon Ward, and Censor General of Literature: not forgetting Master William Hayley. To which is added an Elegy to Apollo; also Sir Joseph Banks and the boiled fleas, an Ode. By Peter Pindar, Esq.', *The Analytical Review, or History of Literature, Domestic and Foreign* Vol. 6 (Jan–April, 1790), 437–440.

[Critical Review], 'Review of *A Benevolent Epistle to Sylvanus Urban &c*', *The Critical Review: Or, Annals of Literature*, Volume 69 (London: A. Hamilton, 1790), 426–429.

[Eclectic Review], 'Art. I. *Voyage de Découvertes aux Terres Australes. A Voyage of Discovery to the Southern Hemisphere*, compiled by M. Péron *Eclectic Review* (Nov. 1809), 977–996.

[Eclectic Review], 'Despotism, or the Fall of the Jesuits', *Eclectic Review* 8. Jan to June 1812, 584–589.

[Eclectic Review], 'A Concise Account of the Present State of the Missions established by the Protestant Church of the Unitas Fratrum, or United Brethren [Moravians], among the Heathen', *Eclectic Review* 8. Jan to June 1812, 621–625.

[Edinburgh Magazine], 'Review of *Sylvanus Urban*', in *The Edinburgh Magazine, or Literary Miscellany* vol. 11 (Edinburgh: John Murray, 1790), 349.

[Edinburgh Magazine], 'Sir Joseph's Breakfast, by Peter Pindar', in *The Edinburgh Magazine, or Literary Miscellany* vol. 11 (Edinburgh: John Murray, 1790), 360.

[Empire] 'Australian Descovery and Colonisation Chapter XII', *Empire* 29/9/1865.

[Evangelical Magazine] 'New South Wales', *The Evangelical Magazine 1809*. vol 17 (London: Williams & Smith, 1809), 343.

[Evangelical Magazine], 'Account of the Rev. Samuel Marsden's Exertions for the Benefit of New South Wales', *The Evangelical Magazine* 1809, vol. 17 (London: Williams & Smith, 1809), 498–503 and 537–539.

[Evangelical Magazine], 'A Concise View of The Present State of Evangelical Religion Throughout The World. No. XIII: The Islands of the Pacific Ocean', *Evangelical Magazine 1811*, vol. 19, 498–501.

Haweis, T. 'The Very Probable Success of a Proper Mission to the South Sea Islands', *The Evangelical Magazine*, 1795, 261–270.

BIBLIOGRAPHY   363

Howe, G.   'A Respectful Address, From the Printer to a liberal Public',
                                  SG 1/11/1817.

Itio, 1870:   'E akatara, no te tamaine a Rupe i te riroanga ki te pai o
                                  Kurunaki', 'Extracts from the papers of the late Rev W.
                                  Wyatt Gill, LL.D — No 13 [Addendum]'. *J. of the Polynesian
                                  Society* 20.4 (80) (1911), text: 195-196. (Addendum to
                                  Gill's extract no.13). S. Savage did not think it worthwhile
                                  to translate this song, 'for it only embodies what has
                                  already been translated in [Maretu's] story' (p.196).

[Literary Gazette],   'Dr John Wolcott (Peter Pindar)', *Literary Gazette*
                                  (13, 20, 27 February 1819), 107–09, 122–25, 140.
                                  http://spenserians.cath.vt.edu/BiographyRecord.
                                  php?action=GET&bioid=36265.

[Missionary Register],   'Origin, History, and Manner of Conducting the
                                  Intercourse of the United Brethren with their Settlements,
                                  by a Vessel of their own', *Missionary Register 1815*, 229–242
                                  (https://archive.org/details/1815CMSMissionaryRegister).

[Missionary Register],   'New South Wales Society for affording Protection to the
                                  Natives of the South Sea Islands, and Promoting their
                                  Civilization', *The Missionary Register for the Year 1814* vol. 2
                                  (London: Seeley, 1814), 459–462.

[Missionary Register],   'Society for the Protection and Relief of Lascar Sailors',
                                  Missionary Register 1814, 479–480.

[Missionary Register],   'British & Foreign Bible Society', *Missionary Register 1816*,
                                  92–95.

[Missionary Register],   'British & Foreign School Society', *Missionary Register 1816*,
                                  99–100.

[Missionary Register],   'Church Missionary Society. 15th Anniversary', *Missionary
                                  Register* (1815), 224–251. (https://archive.org/
                                  details/1815CMSMissionaryRegister).

[Missionary Register],   'Vessel for NSW', *Missionary Register* (1815), 227–242.
                                  (https://archive.org/details/1815CMSMissionaryRegister).

[Missionary Register],   'Mr Marsden's Second Visit to New Zealand', *The
                                  Missionary Register for 1820: Containing the Principal
                                  Transactions of the Various Institutions for Propagating
                                  the Gospel with the Proceedings, at Large, of the Church
                                  Missionary Society* (London: L. B. Seeley, 1820), 305–311.

[Missionary Register],   'Polynesia. Mr Marsden's View of the Mission', *The
                                  Missionary Register for 1820: Containing the Principal
                                  Transactions of the Various Institutions for Propagating*

	the Gospel with the Proceedings, at Large, of the Church Missionary Society (London: L. B. Seeley, 1820), 127–128.
Smith, S.	'Indian Missions', in The Edinburgh Review, 12 (1808), 151–81.
[Southey, R.]	'Transactions of the Missionary Society in the South Sea Islands', The Quarterly Review 2.3 (1809), 22–57.
[Sydney Gazette]	[Obituary of James Bath], SG 2/12/1804.
[Westminster Review]	'Art. XIII: [Review of] Crotchet Castle. By the Author of "Headlong Hall" (London, 1831)', The Westminster Review, Volumes 15 (July-October 1831), 208–218. https://books.google.com.au/books?id=t0dDAQAAMAAJ&pg

Books and Pamphlets

[Anon.]	Characteristics of Public Spirit and National Virtue; occasioned by the Honourable Union of Nobility, Clergy, and Gentry, in support of a late Royal Proclamation (London: R. Faulder, 1788).
Bennett, H.G.	A Letter to Earl Bathurst, Secretary of State for the Colonial Department on the Condition of the Colonies in New South Wales and Vandieman's Land, as set forth in the evidence taken before the Prison Committee in 1819 (London: James Ridgway, 1820). Google Books.
Butler, S.	A Letter to the Rev. C.J. Blomfield, A.B., One of the Junior Fellows of Trinity Coll. Cambridge: containing Remarks on the Edinburgh Review of the Cambridge Aeschylus, and Incidental Observations on that of the Oxford Strabo (Shrewsbury: W. Eddowes, 1810).
Davies, J.	The History of the Tahitian Mission 1799–1830 (C.W. Newbury, ed.; Works Issued by the Hakluyt Society, Second Series, No. 116; New York & Cambridge; Ibadan & Cambridge University Press, 1961).
Ellis, W.	The History of the London Missionary Society: Comprised of an Account of the Origin of the Society; Biographical Notices of Some of Its Founders and Missionaries; with a Record of Its Progress at Home and Its Operations Abroad. Vol. 1. (London: John Snow, 1844).
Fox, J.	An Appeal to the Members of the London Missionary Society (London: J. Fox, 1810). Google Books.
Good, J.M.	'Dr Good's Summary of the Character and Labours of Rev Samuel Marsden', in O. Gregory, Memoirs of the Life, Writings, and Character of the late John Mason Good

	(London: Fisher, Fisher, & Jackson, 1833), Appendix to Section 3, 387–395. Google Books.
Goode, W.	*An entire new version of the book of Psalms* (London: W. Wilson, 1811, 1813 & 1815).
Gregory, O.	*Memoirs of the Life, Writings, and Character of the late John Mason Good* (London: Fisher, Fisher, & Jackson, 1833). Google Books.
Haweis, T.	*An Impartial and Succinct History of the Rise, Declension, and Revival of the Church of Christ.* Vol. 3. (Worcester: Daniel Greenleaf, 1803).
Lang, J.D.	*An Historical And Statistical Account Of New South Wales, Both As A Penal Settlement And As A British Colony* (London: Cochrane & McCrone, 1834; A.J. Valpy, ²1837). Archive.org.
La Trobe, B.	*A Succinct View of the Missions Established Among the Heathen by the Church of the Brethren: Or Unitas Fratrum. In a Letter to a Friend.* (London: M. Lewis, 1771).
Macquarie, L.	A letter to the Rt. Hon. Viscount Sidmouth, in refutation of statements made by the Hon. Henry Grey Bennet, M.P. in a pamphlet "On the transportation laws, the state of the hulks, and of the colonies in New-South Wales" (London: Richard Rees, 1821).
Maretu,	Ko te Taeanga mai o te pai o Kurunaki ki Rarotonga nei, i ta mataiti 1820. The Coming of Goodenough's Ship to Rarotonga in 1820, in: JPS 20(1911) 189–191, 191–196 (Gill's Extracts, no.13). Now translated in Maretu, *Cannibals and Converts*.
Maretu,	*Cannibals and Converts: Radical Change in the Cook Islands* (Marjorie Tuainekore Crocombe, transl., ed., annot.; Suva, Fiji: Institute of Pacific Studies University of South Pacific, 1983; repr. 1987, 1993, 2001). https://books.google.com/books?isbn=9820201667.
Maretu,	MS. On Rarotongan History, 1871. Polynesian Society, Wellington.
Marsden, S.	*An Answer to Certain Calumnies in the Late Governor Macquarie's Pamphlet, and the Third Edition of Mr. Wentworth's Account of Australasia* (London: Hatchard & Son, 1826). http://nla.gov.au/nla.obj-52774134/view?partId=nla.obj-89396355.
Murray, H.	*Enquiries Historical and Moral respecting the Character of Nations and the Progress of Society* (Edinburgh: Longman, Hurst, Rees & Orme, 1808).

Pratt, J. H.	*Eclectic Notes: Or, Notes of Discussions on Religious Topics at the Meetings of the Eclectic Society, London. During the Years 1798–1814* (London: J. Nisbet and Company, 1865).
Pratt, J. & J.H. Pratt,	*Memoir of the Rev. Josiah Pratt, B.D.: Late Vicar of St. Stephen's, Coleman Street, and for Twenty-One Years Secretary of the Church Missionary Society* (London: Seeleys, 1849).
Rere, T. (ed.)	*Nga Mataiti Mua o te Evangelia. Tataia e Papehia Orometus* (Rarotonga: T. Rere, 1976).
Spangenberg, A. G.	*Instructions for the Members of the Unitas Fratrum Who Minister in the Gospel among the Heathen* (London: Brethren's Society, 1784).
Spangenberg, A. G., & B. La Trobe,	
	A Concise Historical Account of the Present Constitution of the Unitas Fratrum Or, Unity of the Evangelical Brethren, Who Adhere to the Augustan Confession (London: M. Lewis, 1775).
Terei, T. & S. Savage,	*Tuatua Taito* (Tai Tekeu, trans.; Avarua: Rarotonga Government Printer, 1908).
Wentworth, W.C.	*A Statistical, Historical and Political Description, of the Colony of New South Wales, and its dependent Settlements in Van Diemen's Land, with a particular enumeration of the Advantages which these Colonies offer for Emigration, and their superiority in many respects over those possessed by the United States of America* (London: G. & W.B. Whittaker, 1819, 21820; G.B. Whittaker, 31824). 1st and 2nd: Archive.org; 3rd: Google Books.
Woodward, J.	*An account of the societies for reformation of manners, in London and Westminster, and all other parts of the kingdom. With a persuasive to persons of all ranks, to be zealous and diligent in promoting the execution of the laws against prophaneness and debauchery, for the effecting a national reformation* (London: B. Aylmer, 1699). Usually referred to as: *History of the Society for the Reformation of Manners in the Year 1692*. Hathitrust.org.

BIBLIOGRAPHY   367

Journals

Banks, J. The Endeavour Journal of Sir Joseph Banks, http://gutenberg.net.au/ebooks05/0501141h.html. The text file of this work was prepared in 1962 from the manuscript 'The Endeavour Journal of Sir Joseph Banks, 1768—1771' held at the State Library of NSW. Cf. SLNSW: Collation of Endeavour Journal, 1768–1771 of Sir Joseph Banks (Feb, 1977), MLDOC 2728.

Blaxland, G. Journal of a tour of discovery across the Blue Mountains, New South Wales, in the year 1813 https://ebooks.adelaide.edu.au/b/blaxland/gregory/b64j/complete.html.

Butler, J. Journal (CRL: CMS/B/OMS/C N M2: 86-89).

Clark, R. 'Journal Kept on the *Friendship* during a Voyage to Botany Bay and Norfolk Island; and on the *Gorgon* Returning to England'. n.d. (Mitchell: http://acmssearch.sl.nsw.gov.au/search/itemDetailPaged.cgi?itemID=412905).

Cook, J. *Voyage to the Pacific Ocean*. Vol. 2 (London: H. Hughs, 1785).

Hall, W. *Son of Carlisle—Māori Missionary: the Diary of C.M.S. Missionary William Hall 1816-1838* (M. McLennan, ed.; Kellyville, NSW: Privately published, 2012).

Hall, W. Journal (CRL: CMS/B/OMS/C N M1:14–15).

Kendall, T. Journal (Mitchell: DLMSQ 300: 27).

LMS *A Missionary Voyage to the Southern Pacific Ocean, Performed in the Years 1796, 1797, 1798, in the Ship Duff, commanded by James Wilson, Compiled from the Journals of the Officers and the Missionaries, and Illustrated with Maps, Charts and Views.* (London: T. Chapman, 1799).

Macquarie, L. *Journal 1816–1818* (Mitchell: Macquarie Papers, A773; Mfm CYA 773, 97). https://www.mq.edu.au/macquarie-archive/lema/1816/1816april.html [starting entry].

Macquarie, L. 'Journal of a Tour of Governor Macquarie's first Inspection of the Interior of the Colony', 6 November 1810 - 15 January 1811 (Mitchell: A778 pp.1-45; Mfm CY302 Frames #434–4790). https://www.mq.edu.au/macquarie-archive/lema/1810/ [starting entry].

Macquarie, L. *Memoranda & Related Papers. 22 December 1808-14 July 1823.* (Mitchell: A772 29f. [CY301]). http://www.mq.edu.au/macquarie-archive/lema/

Marsden, S. *Diary—1793–1794* (Mitchell: C245). Portions published in Elder, *Letters and Journals*.

Marsden, S.	Account of First Visit to New Zealand, 18/11/1814 (*HRNZ* 1.331–399).
Nicholas, J.L.	*Narrative of a Voyage to New Zealand* (2 Vols.; London: James Black & Son, 1817). http://www.enzb.auckland.ac.nz/document/?wid=521. http://www.enzb.auckland.ac.nz/document/?wid=538.
Péron, F.	*A Voyage of Discovery to the Southern Hemisphere Performed by Order of the Emperor Napoleon during the years 1801, 1802, 1803 and 1804* (London: Richard Phillips, 1809). Google Books.
Péron, F.	*Voyage de Découvertes aux Terres Australes*. French edition: https://fr.wikisource.org/wiki/Livre:Péron_-_Voyage_de_découvertes_aux_terres_australes,_1807,_volume_1.djvu
Quiros, P. F. de	*The Voyages of Pedro Fernandez de Quiros: 1595–1606*. Vol. 1 (C. Markham, transl.; London: The Hakluyt Society, 1904). http://www.gutenberg.org/files/41200/41200-h/41200-h.htm.
Seringapatam	*Journal of the ship Seringapatam from the island Nooevah towards Port Jackson, 6 May to June 22, 1814*. Anonymous MS. Written on the back of two charts, Nos. 8 and 9 of Arrowsmith's Chart of the Pacific Ocean in 9 sheets (Mitchell: MS X980/7).
Smith, W.	*Journal of a Voyage in the Missionary Ship Duff, to the Pacific Ocean in the Years 1796, 7, 8, 9, 1800, 1, 2, &c.: Comprehending Authentic and Circumstantial Narratives of the Disasters which Attended the First Effort of the "London Missionary Society"* (New York: Collins and Co., 1813). https://archive.org/details/cihm_17670.
Williams, J.	*A Narrative of Missionary Enterprises in the South Sea Islands with remarks upon the natural history of the islands, origin, languages, traditions and usages of the inhabitants* (London: J. Snow, 1837). https://babel.hathitrust.org. OR https://archive.org/stream/narrativeofmissi00willuoft.
Wilson, J.	*The Life and Dreadful Sufferings of Captain James Wilson, In various Parts of the Globe, including a Faithful Narrative of Every Circumstance during the Voyage, to the South Sea Islands, In the Missionary Ship Duff, for the Propagation of the Gospel; with an Authentic and Interesting Account of the Sufferings and Calamities of the Missionaries; from the Year 1797, to the Present Period* (Portsea: G.A. Stephens, 1810). Google Books.

Legal Papers

Articles of Agreement concerning the Sandalwood Company, January —, 1814 (Mitchell: Wentworth Papers A752, pp. 97-100).

Case Law

English cases:

King v Lake (1670) Hardres 470; 145 ER 552.

Thorley v Lord Kerry (1812) 4 Taunt 355; 128 ER 367.

Trial of Ann Butcher, 17 September 1806, *The Proceedings of the Old Bailey*. https://www.oldbaileyonline.org/browse.jsp?id=t18060917-70-punish383&div=t18060917-70#highlight

NSW cases:

All NSW cases below can be found through Macquarie Law site: http://www.law.mq.edu.au/research/colonial_case_law/nsw/cases/case_index/

Atkins v Harris [1799] NSWKR4; [1799] NSWSupC 4

Marsden v. Mason [1806] NSWKR 1; [1806] NSWSupC 1

Marsden vs. Campbell [1817]. NSWKR 7; [1817]. NSW Sup C 7 [libel].

Probart v Grose [1792] NSWKR 3; [1792] NSWSupC 3.

R v Bland [1818] NSWKR 5; [1818] NSWSupC 5.

R. v. Campbell [1817] NSWKR 5; [1817] NSWSupC 5.

R v Webb [1794] NSWKR 1; [1794] NSWSupC 1.

Court Examinations and Depositions

Besent, J. [*Boyd*]   S. Marsden and John Besent, Deposition of John Besent Relating to the Loss of the *Boyd*, 10/11/1813. *HRNZ* 1.421–422. (http://www.marsdenarchive.otago.ac.nz/MS_0054_016).

Besent, J. [*Parramatta*]   Marsden, Reverend Samuel, and John Besent. Deposition of John Besent Relating to the Loss of the *Parramatta* Schooner, 10/11/1813. *HRNZ* 1. 423–424. (http://www.marsdenarchive.otago.ac.nz/MS_0054_017).

Bigge, J.T.   Examination of:

    Major G. Druitt, 48th Regiment, 6/1/1821 (*HRA* 4.1, 830–831).

    F. Garling, 23/1/1821 (*HRA* 4.1, 849–854).

    John Hunter [mate, *Active*], 4/1/1821 (*HRNZ* 1.503–506).

    Lt. G. W. Leroux, 48th Regiment, February 1821 (*HRA* 4.1, 854–855).

    L. Macquarie, 1829. Ritchie, ed. *Evidence to the Bigge Reports*, Vol. 2, 113.

    S. Marsden, 27/12/1820. (Mitchell: BT, Bigge Appendix, Box 8, 3448–9).

    Mr W.H. Moore, 9/7/1820 (*HRA* 4.1, 831–838).

    Joseph Thompson, 8/12/1820 (*HRNZ* 1.499–502).

    J. Wylde, 1820 (*HRA* 4.1, 779–829).

Blaxland, G.	Testimony before J. Wylde [January 1817], included in S. Marsden to J. Wylde, 28/1/1817, now filed with J. Wylde to S. Marsden. 23 January 1817. http://www.marsdenarchive.otago.ac.nz/MS_0056_038.
Blaxland, G.	Examination, 1/12/1817, from Field, The Judge's Report [Civil Trial] (*HRA* 1.10, 446–447).
Dillon, P.	Deposition sworn before D'Arcy Wentworth, 6/11/1813. Enclosure No.1, in L. Macquarie to H. Bathurst, 17/1/1814, Encl. 4: Depositions and Papers Relating to Transactions in the South Sea Islands (*HRA* 1.8, 103–107).
Dillon, P., to Capt. Glenholme, 6/11/1813, explaining he had deposed that morning before D'Arcy Wentworth.	Enclosure No. 2, in L. Macquarie to H. Bathurst, 17/1/1814, Encl. No. 5: Depositions and papers relating to an affray on the Feejees and the Daphne (*HRA* 1.8, 111–112).
Eagar, E.	Examination, 23/10/1817, from Minutes of J. Wylde [Criminal Trial] (*HRA* 1.10, 466–468).
Eagar, E.	Examination, 1/12/1817, from Field, The Judge's Report [Civil Trial] (*HRA* 1.10, 446).
Elder, James	Deposition before Marsden Re *General Wellesley*, 12/11/181, Enclosure 2 in Memorial of the Committee of the Church of England Missionary Society to Earl Bathurst, [1817] (*HRNZ* 1.422–423; http://www.marsdenarchive.otago.ac.nz/MS_0054_018).
French, Thomas	Deposition of Thomas French sworn before Samuel Marsden, 16/11/1813. Enclosure No.4, in L. Macquarie to H. Bathurst, 17/1/1814, Encl. No. 4: Depositions and Papers Relating to Transactions in the South Sea Islands

	(*HRA* 1.8, 110–11). [Marsden Online Archive mistakenly has 14/11/1813]. http://www.marsdenarchive.otago.ac.nz/MS_0054_019
French, Thomas	Deposition before Judge Advocate Bent, W. Broughton, D'A. Wentworth, A. Riley, S. Lord, 4/12/1813 [re the *Daphne*]. Encl. No. 3, in L. Macquarie to H. Bathurst, 17/1/1814, Encl. No. 5: Depositions and papers relating to an affray on the Feejees and the *Daphne* (*HRA* 1.8, 112–113).
Garling, F.	for the Defendant, 23/10/1817, from Minutes of J. Wylde [Criminal Trial] (*HRA* 1.10, 470–472).
Glenholme, Capt., to P. Dillon, 5/11/1813.	
	Enclosure No. 1, in L. Macquarie to H. Bathurst, 17/1/1814, Encl. No. 5: Depositions and papers relating to an affray on the Feejees and the *Daphne* (*HRA* 1.8, 111).
Goodenough, Ann	Deposition, 3/6/1817, Philip Goodenough Probate Pack (SRNSW: 14/3175, Series 1–6), Date of death December 1815 [date in month not known], Probate granted on [not known; circa 3 June 1817].
Hendrike, Abraham	Deposition sworn before Samuel Marsden at Sydney, 16/11/1813. Enclosure No. 4, in L. Macquarie to H. Bathurst, 17/1/1814, Encl. No. 4: Depositions and Papers Relating to Transactions in the South Sea Islands (*HRA* 1.8, 107–110). [Marsden Online Archive wrongly has 14/11/1813]. http://www.marsdenarchive.otago.ac.nz/MS_0054_019.
Hendrike, Abraham	Deposition before Ellis Bent, W. Broughton, D'A Wentworth, A. Riley, S. Lord, 4/12/1813, Enclosure No. 6, in L. Macquarie to H. Bathurst, 17/1/1814, Encl. No. 5: Depositions and papers relating to an affray on the Feejees and the *Daphne* (*HRA* 1.8, 115-116).
Howe, G.	Examination, 21/10/1817, from Minutes of J. Wylde [Criminal Trial] (*HRA* 1.10, 458–460).
Jones, John	Deposition sworn before Samuel Marsden at Sydney, 16/11/1813. Enclosure No. 3, in L. Macquarie to H. Bathurst, 17/1/1814, Encl. No 4: Depositions and Papers Relating to Transactions in the South Sea Islands (*HRA* 1.8, 110).
Jones, John	Deposition before Ellis Bent, W. Broughton, D'A Wentworth, A. Riley, S. Lord, 4/12/1813, in L. Macquarie to H. Bathurst, 17/1/1814, Encl. No. 5: Depositions and papers relating to an affray on the Feejees and the *Daphne* (*HRA* 1.8, 114–115).

Jones, R.	Sworn Testimony of Richard Jones, 13/11/1817, Enclosure No. 7, in S. Marsden to H. Bathurst, 28/11/1817 (https://marsdenarchive.otago.ac.nz/MS_0056_069).
Jones, R.	Examination, 22/10/1817, from Minutes of J. Wylde [Criminal Trial] (*HRA* 1.10, 461–463, 469).
Jones, R.	Examination, 1/12/1817, from Field, The Judge's Report [Civil Trial] (*HRA* 1.10, 447).
Macquarie, L.	[Responsibility of J.T. Campbell in comparing depositions], L. Macquarie to H. Bathurst, 17/1/1814, Encl. No. 4: Depositions and Papers Relating to Transactions in the South Sea Islands (*HRA* 1.8, 111).
Marsden, S.	Examination, 21 & 22/10/1817, from Minutes of J. Wylde [Criminal Trial] (*HRA* 1.10, 452–455, 463–466).
New Zealanders	Testimony of New Zealanders to Marsden, Extract from journal of S. Marsden Re the *Jefferson* and *King George*; Enclosure 6 in Memorial of the Committee of the Church of England Missionary Society to Earl Bathurst, [1817] (*HRNZ* 1. 425–426).
Randall, John	Deposition sworn before Samuel Marsden at Sydney, 16/11/1813. Enclosure 5 in L. Macquarie to H. Bathurst, 17/1/1814, Encl. No. 4: Depositions and Papers Relating to Transactions in the South Sea Islands (*HRA* 1.8, 111).
Randall, John	Deposition before Ellis Bent, W. Broughton, D'A Wentworth, A. Riley, S. Lord, 4/12/1813, Enclosure No. 7, in L. Macquarie to H. Bathurst, 17/1/1814, Encl. No. 5: Depositions and papers relating to an affray on the Feejees and the *Daphne* (*HRA* 1.8, 116–118).
Robinson, M.	Examination, 1/12/1817, from Field, The Judge's Report [Civil Trial] (*HRA* 1.10, 446).
Walker, Theodore	Declaration of Not Guilty, at the examination before Judge Advocate Bent, W. Broughton, D'A. Wentworth, A. Riley, S. Lord on 11/12/1813. Enclosure No. 4, in L. Macquarie to H. Bathurst, 17/1/1814, Encl. No. 5: Depositions and papers relating to an affray on the Feejees and the *Daphne* (*HRA* 1.8, 113).
Williams, G.	Deposition of George Williams, 18/3/1817, Enclosure No. 6 in Marsden to Bathurst, 28/11/1817 (https://marsdenarchive.otago.ac.nz/MS_0056_069).
Williams, G.	Examination, 21/10/1817, from Minutes of J. Wylde [Criminal Trial] (*HRA* 1.10, 455–458).

BIBLIOGRAPHY

Williams, G.   Examination, 1/12/1817, from Field, The Judge's Report [Civil Trial] (HRA 1.10, 444–445).

Williams, Jacob   Marsden, Reverend Samuel, and Jacob Williams. Deposition of Jacob Williams before Marsden, 19 November 1813. http://www.marsdenarchive.otago.ac.nz/ MS_0054_020

Court Minutes & Proceedings

[Anonymous]   'Statement of the Case between Mr Sec. Campbell and Rev. Marsden', undated (Mitchell: J.T. Bigge, Report, Appendix, BT, Box 15, 1676).

Field, B.   The Judge's Report [Civil Trial], Enclosure 1 in Macquarie to Bathurst, 20/3/1821 (HRA 1.10, 443–447).

[Magistrates]   Proceedings of the Magistrates Court [Lasco Jones], Sydney, 12/4/1815, http://www.marsdenarchive.otago.ac.nz/MS_0055_028.

[Magistrates]   Proceedings before Bench of Magistrates in regard to John Martin, Master of the *Queen Charlotte*, held 20/12/1815 and 6/1/1816; in Memorial of CMS to Bathurst [1817], Enclosure 9 (HRNZ 1, 426–427; commentary by CMS committee, p. 420).

Wylde, J.   [Minutes of Criminal Trial], The Report of the Judge-Advocate as to the Criminal Trial, 21–23 Oct 1817. Enclosure No. 2 in Macquarie to Bathurst, 20/3/1821 (HRA 1.10, 447–477).

Wylde, J.   Decision of Criminal Trial, 23/10/1817, Minutes of J. Wylde [Criminal Trial] (HRA 1.10, 472).

Government and General Orders, and other Proclamations

Butcher, Ann,   Time expired, 16/4/1813 (Col.Sec.: Reel 6066; 4/1805 p.125).

George III   'Instructions for our trusty and well-beloved Arthur Phillip', 25/4/1787 (HRNSW 1.2, 84–91).

Henry, William   Commission from Governor to act as magistrate for Otaheite and the adjacent islands, 18/11/1811 (Col.Sec.: Reel 6043; 4/1726 pp.166–166c).

Henry, William   Appointed Magistrate and Justice of the Peace in Otaheite, 28/9/1811 (Col.Sec.: Reel 6038; SZ758 p.237).

Korra Korra,	Authorised by Lachlan Macquarie to grant permission for Commanders or crew of vessels to take Māoris with them, 15/8/1811 (Col.Sec.: Reel 6044; 4/1730 p.329).
Korra Korra,	By General order invested with power re removal of natives from New Zealand, 9/11/1814 (Col.Sec.: Reel 6038; SZ759 p.2).
Macquarie, L.	Government and General Order 1/12/1813, *SG* 4/12/1813 (*HRNZ* 1.316–318, 429).
Macquarie, L.	Government and General Order 9/11/1814, *SG* 12, 19, 26/11/1814 (*HRNZ* 1.328–329, 427–428).
Macquarie, L.	Government and General Order, 12/11/1814 (*HRNZ* 1.330).
Macquarie, L.	Proclamation 1/1/1814, Enclosure No 1, in L. Macquarie to H. Bathurst, 17/1/1814 (*HRA* 1.8, 98–100).
Marsden, S.	Notice to Natives of the South Sea Islands, 1/12/1813 (https://marsdenarchive.otago.ac.nz/MS_0054_022).
Philanthropic Society	Formation of a Society for the Protection and Civilization of the Natives of the South Sea Islands who may come to Sydney, 20/12/ 1813 (https://marsdenarchive.otago.ac.nz/MS_0054_059).
[Ruatara] Dewaterra,	Authorised by Lachlan Macquarie to grant permission for Commanders or crew of vessels to take Māoris with them, 15/8/1811 (Col.Sec.: Reel 6044; 4/1730 p.329).
[Ruatara] Dewaterra,	By General order invested with power re removal of natives from New Zealand, 9/11/1814 (Col.Sec.: Reel 6038; SZ759 p.2).
Shungie,	Authorised by Lachlan Macquarie to grant permission for Commanders or crew of vessels to take Māoris with them, 15/8/1811 (Col.Sec.: Reel 6044; 4/1730 pp.327–329; Reel 6039, SZ756 pp.41–42).
Shungie,	By General order invested with power re removal of natives from New Zealand, 9/11/1814 (Col.Sec.: Reel 6038; SZ759 p.2)

Legislation & Legal Opinion

Dowling, J.	'The Notebooks of Justice Dowling'. Vol 14, NSW State Archives & Records, 98–100. http://www.law.mq.edu.au/research/colonial_case_law/nsw/cases/case_index/

BIBLIOGRAPHY

Forbes, F. 'Newspaper Act Opinion 1827, NSWKR 3; [1827] NSW SupC 23', 16 April 1827 (Mitchell: A 748, Reel CY 1226, pp 24–28, 63–66).

Letters Patent to Establish Courts of Civil Judicature in New South Wales, 4/2/1814 (*HRA* 4.1, 77–94).

New South Wales Courts Act 1787 (UK), 27 Geo. III C 2. http://www.foundingdocs.gov.au/resources/transcripts/nsw3i_doc_1787.pdf.

Warrant for the Charter of Justice, 2/4/1787 (*HRA* 4.1, 6–12).

Letters

E. Abbott to J. Piper, 18/9/1809 (Mitchell: Piper Papers Vol 1, 151. A254).

H. Bathurst to J.T. Bigge, 6/1/1819, Enclosure no. 4, in H. Bathurst to L. Macquarie, 30/1/1819 (*HRA* 1.10, 9–11).

H. Bathurst to T. Brisbane, 30/10/1824 (*HRA* 1.11, 388–89).

H. Bathurst to L. Macquarie, 28/4/1814 (*HRA* 1.7, 704–705).

H. Bathurst to L. Macquarie, 15/12/1814 (*HRA* 1.8, 387).

H. Bathurst to L. Macquarie, 12/7/1815 (*HRA* 1.8, 622–623).

H. Bathurst to L. Macquarie, 2/12/1815 (*HRA* 1.8, 637).

H. Bathurst to L. Macquarie, 18/4/1816 (*HRA* 1.9, 107–110).

H. Bathurst to L. Macquarie, 4/4/1817 (*HRA* 1.8, 646–647).

H. Bathurst to L. Macquarie, 26/7/1818 (*HRA* 1.9, 824–825).

H. Bathurst to L. Macquarie, 18/9/1818 (*HRA* 1.9, 836).

H. Bathurst to L. Macquarie, 18/10/1818 (*HRA* 1.9, 838–840).

H. Bathurst to L. Macquarie, 24/3/1820 (*HRA* 1.10, 295–296).

H. Bathurst to L. Macquarie, 14/7/1820 (*HRA* 1.10, 313).

H. Bathurst to R. Darling, 12/7/1825 (*HRA* 1.12, 16–17).

J.H. Bent to S. Marsden, 3/4/1817 (https://marsdenarchive.otago.ac.nz/MS_0056_054).

E. Bickersteth & J. Pratt to S. Marsden, 14/12/1818, (https://marsdenarchive.otago.ac.nz/MS_0056_105)

E. Bickersteth & J. Pratt to S. Marsden, 5/4/1820 (http://www.marsdenarchive.otago.ac.nz/MS_0056_201).

T. Brisbane to Bathurst, 12/1/1825 (*HRA* 1.11, 470–471).

T. Brisbane to Bathurst, 11/8/1825, Enclosure No. 1, Report of Enquiry by the Council on Alleged Illegal Punishments, 27/9/1825 (*HRA* 1.11, 854–858).

T. Brisbane, F. Forbes & T.H. Scott to H. Bathurst, 11/8/1825 (*HRA* 1.11, 782–807).

W. Broughton to Don Gasperde Rico, 8/4/1814 (NLA: MS 4256).

W.G. Broughton to E. Coleridge, 14/2/1842 (Moore College: B. Kaye Transcription).

G. Burder (for LMS directors) to S. Marsden, 21/12/1813 (Mitchell: CY 229, Samuel Marsden Papers 1794-1838, Letters from LMS 1802-1836, pp. 43-44; Vol 4, A1995).

G. Burder (for LMS directors) to S. Marsden, 5/6/1817 (Mitchell: CY 229, Samuel Marsden Papers 1794-1838, Letters from LMS 1802-1836, Vol 4, A1995, pp. 66–69).

G. Burder (for LMS directors) to S. Marsden, 2/6/1819 (Mitchell: CY 229, Samuel Marsden Papers 1794-1838, Letters from LMS 1802-1836, Vol 4, A1995, pp. 89–91).

J. Butler to S. Marsden, 8/1/1822 (CRL: CMS/B/OMS/C N M2: 177–180).

T.F. Buxton to S. Marsden, 7/5/1819. (https://marsdenarchive.otago.ac.nz/MS_0056_152).

J.T. Campbell to Marsden, 24/7/1815 (Mitchell: BT [Bigge Appendix], Box 14, 1103–1105).

J.T. Campbell to J. Wylde, 14/1/1817, enclosed in S. Marsden to J. Wylde, 7/1/1817 (http://www.marsdenarchive.otago.ac.nz/MS_0056_036).

J.T. Campbell to S. Marsden, 3/8/1818 (http://www.marsdenarchive.otago.ac.nz/MS_0056_088).

J.T. Campbell to L. Macquarie, 31/3/1819. Enclosure to Macquarie to Bathurst, 31/3/1819 (*HRA* 1.10, 139–141; Enclosure: 140–141).

Robert Campbell to the CMS, 10 Aug 1820 (CRL: CMS/B/OMS/C N M1: 213–214).

Robert Campbell to the CMS, 2 Sep 1820 (CRL: CMS/B/OMS/C N M1: 214–215).

Robert Campbell to William Kermode, 11 Feb 1820 (CRL: CMS/B/OMS/C N M1: 60–61).

Colonial Secretary to W. Bedford, 5/4/1834 (SLTAS: Colonial Secretary's Department Letterbooks on clerical and educational matters, 1830–1837, CSO 44/1/1).

Colonial Secretary to R. Cartwright, 5/10/1822 (SRNSW: 4/1762, Mfm 6055).

Colonial Secretary to R. Cartwright, 12/4/1825 (SRNSW: SZ1044, Mfm 6038).

Colonial Secretary to W. Cowper, 26/8/1814 (SRNSW: 4/3493).

Colonial Secretary to H. Fulton, 1/1/ & 18/8/1824 (SRNSW: 4/424, Mfm 6039).

Colonial Secretary to H. Fulton, 10/2/1814 (SRNSW: 4/1730, Mfm 6044).

Colonial Secretary to R. Hill, 18 & 23/9/1819 (SRNSW: SZ1044, Mfm 6038).

Colonial Secretary to J. Keane, 25/11/1828, 14/7/1829 (SRNSW: CSOL, 4/3613–15, Mfm 2981).

Colonial Secretary to P. Palmer, 28/9/1833 (SLTAS: Colonial Secretary's Department Letterbooks on clerical and educational matters, 1830–1837, CSO 44/1/1).

Colonial Secretary to T. Reddall, 9/7/1828 (SRNSW: CSOL, 4/3613–15, Mfm 2981).

BIBLIOGRAPHY

Colonial Secretary to T.H. Scott, 22/5/1827 (SRNSW: CSOL, 4/3615, Mfm 2981).

R. Darling to F. Forbes, 2/4/1827, 'Letter from Governor Darling to Chief Justice Forbes, 2 April 1827, and Reply, 2 April 1827 Manuscript, A748'. State Library of New South Wales Archive. http://www2.sl.nsw.gov.au/archive/discover_collections/history_nation/justice/freedom_press/restrain/licensing.html.

R. Darling to F. Forbes, 14/4/1827, 'Letter from Governor Darling to Chief Justice Forbes, 14 April 1827, and Reply, 16 April 1827 Manuscript, A748'. State Library of New South Wales Archive. http://www2.sl.nsw.gov.au/archive/discover_collections/history_nation/justice/freedom_press/restrain/disagree.html.

R. Darling to R. Hay, 24/5/1826 (*HRA* 1.12, 326–328).

J. Davies to LMS Directors, 24/2/1810 (Extract: *Evangelical Magazine*, 1810, vol. 18, 407-408).

J. Davies to L. Macquarie, 11/9/1813. Enclosure No 3, in L. Macquarie to H. Bathurst, 17/1/1814 (*HRA* 1.8, 102–103).

J. Davies to S. Marsden, 13/8/1816 (Mitchell: A 1996, 51).

F. Forbes to R. Darling, 31/5/1827 (*HRA* 1.13, 392–397).

F. Forbes to R.W. Horton, 6/2/1827 (*HRA* 4.1, 679–687).

Baron James Gambier to L. Macquarie, 22/3/1813 (http://www.marsdenarchive.otago.ac.nz/MS_0054_004).

V. Goderich to R. Darling, 6/1/1831 (*HRA* 1.16, 11–13).

J.M. Good to S. Marsden, n.d., in J.B. Marsden, *The Life and Labours of the Rev. Samuel Marsden* (London: Religious Tract Society, 1858), 123–124.

W. Goode to W. Howley, 18/3/1815 (LPA: Fulham Papers, Howley Letter Book, vol. 17, fol. 149).

F. Grose to H. Dundas, 4/9/1793 (*HRNSW* 2.64; *HRA* 1.1, 451).

W. Hall to the Secretary, 6/4/1822 (CRL: CMS/B/OMS/C N M2: 322–324).

T. Hassall to Colonial Secretary, 28/5/1823 (SRNSW: 4/1764, Mfm 6056).

T. Hassall, (undated), Account of Tristan's disappearance (Mitchell: Hassall family correspondence, 1793–ca.1900, A1677-2, p.84).

S. Hassall to T. Hassall, 9/12/1817 (Mitchell: Hassall Correspondence, A1677-4, 682).

T. Haweis to J. Hardcastle, 24/3/1802 (SOAS: CWM/LMS/01/06/01, box 2, item 1).

W. Henry to Macquarie, 16/11/1813, Enclosure No 2. in Gov. Macquarie to Earl Bathurst, 17/1/1814 (*HRA* 1.8, 100–102).

W. Henry to Marsden, 12 Aug 1816, (Mitchell: A 1996, 47).

W. Henry to Wilks, Port Jackson Sept 1811 (*Evangelical Magazine 1812*, 280–281).

W. Howley to W. Goode, 20/3/1815 (LPA: Fulham Papers, Howley Papers, vol. 5, ff. 11–12).

Captain Irvine to the Assistant Secretary, 20/3/1821 (CRL: CMS/B/OMS/C N M1: 308–315).

R. Johnson to H. Fricker, 30/5/1787 (Mackaness, *Richard Johnson* 1, No. 1).

R. Johnson to H. Fricker, 9/4/1790 (Mackaness, *Richard Johnson* 1, No. 8).

R. Johnson to H. Fricker, 18/3/1791 (Mackaness, *Richard Johnson* 1, No. 11).

R. Johnson to H. Fricker, 4/10/1791 (Mackaness, *Richard Johnson* 1, No. 12).

T. Kendall to B. Woodd, 13/2/1815 (http://www.marsdenarchive.otago.ac.nz/MS_0054_081).

T. Kendall to S. Marsden, 6/3/1818 (http://www.marsdenarchive.otago.ac.nz/MS_0056_073).

T. Kendall to [CMS] the Chairman of the Missionary Committee, 28/9/1822 (CRL: CMS/B/OMS/C N M2: 249–251).

T. Kendall to S. Marsden, 3/3/1818 (https://marsdenarchive.otago.ac.nz/MS_0056_072).

T. Kendall to S. Marsden, 20/4/1818 (http://www.marsdenarchive.otago.ac.nz/MS_0056_082).

T. Kendall to S. Marsden, 21/4/1819 [No.1] (http://www.marsdenarchive.otago.ac.nz/MS_0056_150).

T. Kendall to S. Marsden, 21/4/1819 [No. 2] (https://marsdenarchive.otago.ac.nz/MS_0056_151).

T. Kendall to S. Marsden, 6/7/1815 [Marsden Online Archive labels 27/5/1815] (http://www.marsdenarchive.otago.ac.nz/MS_0055_012).

T. Kendall to S. Marsden, 27/9/1821 (CRL: CMS/B/OMS/C N M1: 570-582.

T. Kendall to S. Marsden, 26/2/1822 (http://www.marsdenarchive.otago.ac.nz/MS_0057_074).

T. Kendall to J. Pratt, 15/6/1814. (http://www.marsdenarchive.otago.ac.nz/MS_0054_043).

T. Kendall to J. Pratt, 19/10/1815 (http://www.marsdenarchive.otago.ac.nz/MS_0055_021).

P.G. King to Hobart, 9/3/1803 (*HRA* 1.4, 73–86).

P.G. King to Lord Hobart, 9/5/1803, Enclosure No.2, Seditious Anonymous Papers, with Remarks Thereon (*HRA* 1.4, 168–169).

S. Leigh to A. Clark, 14/10/1817, cited by Woolmington, *Early*, p. 104.

LMS Missionaries to Directors, 21/10/1812 (*Evangelical Magazine* 1813, 473–476).

LMS to S. Marsden, 15/9/1802 (Mitchell: Marsden papers, 1794-1838. Letters from the London Missionary Society, 1802–36, A1995).

LMS to S. Marsden, 19/3/1810 (Mitchell: Marsden Papers, MS A1955, 4/9).

BIBLIOGRAPHY

LMS to S. Marsden, 28/4/1818 (Mitchell: A 1995, 72).

L. Macquarie to H. Bathurst, 17/1/1814 (*HRA* 1.8, 96–98).

L. Macquarie to H. Bathurst, 7/10/1814 (*HRA* 1.8, 336–337).

L. Macquarie to H. Bathurst 24/6/1815 (*HRA* 1.8, 553–566).

L. Macquarie to H. Bathurst, 1/7/1815 (*HRA* 1.8, 620–622).

L. Macquarie to H. Bathurst, 18/3/1816 (*HRA* 1.9, 52–73; Re T. Walker: 66–67).

L. Macquarie to H. Bathurst, 31/3/1817 (*HRA* 1.9, 236–243; on Monetization: 241–242).

L. Macquarie to H. Bathurst, 1/12/1817 (*HRA* 1.9, 495–501).

L. Macquarie to H. Bathurst, 4/12/1817 (*HRA* 1.9, 502–509).

L. Macquarie to H. Bathurst, 8/3/1819 (*HRA* 1.10, 39–40, 42).

L. Macquarie to H. Bathurst, 22/3/1819, *HRA* 1.10, 65–67.

L. Macquarie to H. Bathurst, 31/3/1819 (*HRA* 1.10, 139).

L. Macquarie to H. Bathurst, 20/3/1821 (*HRA* 1.10, 442–477).

L. Macquarie to Liverpool, 27/10/1810 (*HRA* 1.7, 341–348).

L. Macquarie to Liverpool, 28/10/1811 (*HRA* 1.7, 448–9).

L. Macquarie to S. Marsden, 13/4/1814 (http://www.marsdenarchive.otago.ac.nz/MS_0056_021).

L. Macquarie to S. Marsden, 8/1/1818 (Mitchell: Letter book, 1809-1822. A797 pp.141–144. [CY Reel 306]; http://www.mq.edu.au/macquarie-archive/lema/1818/marsdenjan1818.html).

L. Macquarie to S. Marsden, 13/8/1818 (http://www.marsdenarchive.otago.ac.nz/MS_0056_095).

L. Macquarie to J. Wylde, 15/1/1817, enclosed in S. Marsden to J. Wylde, 7/1/1817 (http://www.marsdenarchive.otago.ac.nz/MS_0056_036).

Ann Marsden to Mrs. Stokes, 18/6/1813 (Mackaness, *Samuel Marsden*, No.21).

Eliza Marsden to Mary Stokes, 1/5/1796 (Mackaness, *Samuel Marsden*, No. 5).

S. Marsden to H. Bathurst, 28/11/1817, is found as part of J. Wylde, S. Lord, J.T. Campbell, and S. Marsden to H. Bathurst, 28/11/1817 (https://marsdenarchive.otago.ac.nz/MS_0056_069).

S. Marsden to J.T. Bigge, 28/12/1819 (*HRNZ* 452–453).

S. Marsden to J.T. Bigge, c. 1820 (Mitchell: BT 20:3498–9).

S. Marsden to J.T. Bigge, 1820 (NLA: CO 201/118, AJCP/PRO, fos 387–92).

S. Marsden to J.T. Bigge, 6/1/1821 (Mitchell: BT, Bigge Appendix, 20, 5561–9)

S. Marsden to J.T. Bigge, 6/1/1821 (Mitchell: J.T. Bigge, Report, Appendix BT, Box 25, 556).

S. Marsden to J.T. Bigge, 9/1/1821 (Mitchell: BT [Bigge Appendix] Box 25, 5629–30).

S. Marsden to J.T. Bigge, 10/1/1821 (HL: MS-0177/040; Mitchell: BT [Bigge Appendix] Box 25, 5634-45)

S. Marsden to J. T. Bigge, 18/10/1821 (Mitchell: Marsden Papers, A1993, vol. 2, CY Mfm 228, ff. 748–49).

S. Marsden to Bishop of London, 5/6/1823, cited in Earl Bathurst to Sir Thomas Brisbane, 30/10/1824 (*HRA* 1.11, 388–389).

S. Marsden to W.G. Broughton, 3/11/1832 (Mitchell: BT, Box 54).

S. Marsden to G. Burder, 7/10/1814 (SOAS: CWM/LMS/03/02, box 1b, item 12).

S. Marsden to G. Burder, 14/3/1817 (SOAS: CWM/LMS/03/02, box 1b, item 41).

S. Marsden to G. Burder, 24/12/1817 (SOAS: CWM/LMS/03/02, box 1b, item 47).

S. Marsden to J. Butler, 22/1/1822 (CRL: CMS/B/OMS/C N M2: 181–188).

S. Marsden to [T.F. Buxton], 24/9/1821. This letter has been wrongly attributed by the Mitchell library to Bigge (there is a small note to that effect on A1993, p. 76). The letter discusses Bigge in the third person. Because the letter is addressed 'Honourable Sir', it was probably written to a member of parliament, either Wilberforce or Buxton (Bennett is discounted as he is mentioned in the letter), with Buxton being the most likely given that he had written to Marsden on 7 May 1819.

S. Marsden to the Church Missionary Society, 8/3/1816 (http://www.marsdenarchive.otago.ac.nz/MS_0056_002).

S. Marsden to J.T. Campbell, 22/7/1815 (Mitchell: BT [Bigge Appendix], Box 14, 1095).

S. Marsden to D. Coates, 17/3/1825 (CRL: CNM3 488; HL, MS-0057/133).

S. Marsden to D. Coates 21/11/1825 (CRL: CNM4 56; HL, MS-0057/142).

S. Marsden to Colonial Secretary, 22/4/1823, 24 & 28/5/1823 (SRNSW: 4/1764, Mfm 6056).

S. Marsden's Instructions to Mr Dillon, 9/3/1814 (*Missionary Register 1815*, 104–105).

S. Marsden to [John Mason Good], 17/5/1817 (ATL: *Marsden family*. Papers. Outward correspondence. MS-Papers-0453-01, Item 3).

S. Marsden to W. Goode, 12/10/1814 (LPA: Fulham Papers, Howley Papers, vol. 17, ff. 153–54).

S. Marsden to W.A. Hankey & G. Burder, 12/9/1826, cited by Bollen, 'English Missionary Societies', 284.

S. Marsden to J. Hardcastle, 25/10/1810 (SOAS: Box 1a, item 76).

S. Marsden to T. Kendall, 17/1/1822 (CRL: CMS/B/OMS/C N M2: 161–167).

S. Marsden to T. Kendall, 11/6/1822 (CRL: CMS/B/OMS/C N M2: 212–213).

S. Marsden to T. Kendall, 17/1/1822 (CRL: CMS/B/OMS/C N M2:165).

BIBLIOGRAPHY

S. Marsden to [LMS] the Assistant Secretary, 30/6/1825 (CRL: CMS/B/OMS/C N M3: 492-493).

S. Marsden to LMS, 30/1/1801 (SOAS: CWM/LMS/03/02, box 1a, item 15).

S. Marsden to LMS, 15/8/1801 (SOAS: CWM/LMS/03/02, box 1a, item 20).

S. Marsden to LMS, 5/11/1801 (SOAS: CWM/LMS/03/02, box 1a, item 22).

S. Marsden to the LMS, 5/3/1817 (SOAS: CWM/LMS/03/02, box 1b, item 40).

S. Marsden to LMS Directors, 14/3/1817 (SOAS: CWM/LMS/03/02, box 1b, item 41).

S. Marsden to LMS Directors, 17/5/1817 (SOAS: CWM/LMS/03/02, box 1b, item 46).

S. Marsden to L. Macquarie, 1/11/1813 (https://marsdenarchive.otago.ac.nz/MS_0054_014; *Missionary Register 1814*, 465–69).

S. Marsden to L. Macquarie, 9/4/1814. (http://www.marsdenarchive.otago.ac.nz/MS_0054_037).

S. Marsden to L. Macquarie, 30/5/1815 (*Missionary Register 1816*, 115–118).

S. Marsden to L. Macquarie, 11/8/1818. (http://www.marsdenarchive.otago.ac.nz/MS_0056_090).

S. Marsden to W.H. Moore, 18/4/1817 (Mitchell: J.T. Bigge, *Report*, Appendix, BT, Box 16, 1870).

S. Marsden to the NSW Auxiliary Committee of the LMS, 8/2/1817 (SOAS: CWM/LMS/03/02, box 1b, item 37).

S. Marsden to J. Pratt, 24/3/1808 (https://marsdenarchive.otago.ac.nz/MS_0498_001).

S. Marsden to J. Pratt, 9/5/1809 (http://www.marsdenarchive.otago.ac.nz/MS_0498_020).

S. Marsden to J. Pratt, 25/10/1810 (HL: MS-0498/008, item 237).

S. Marsden to J. Pratt, 15/3/1814 [No. 1] (http://www.marsdenarchive.otago.ac.nz/MS_0054_027; Extract: *Missionary Register 1814*, 460–462; *HRNZ* 1.321–322).

S. Marsden to J. Pratt, 15/3/1814 [No. 2] (http://www.marsdenarchive.otago.ac.nz/MS_0054_030).

S. Marsden to J. Pratt, 15/3/1814 (For extract: [Missionary Register], 'New South Wales Society for affording Protection', 460–62).

S. Marsden to J. Pratt, 20/9/1814 (http://www.marsdenarchive.otago.ac.nz/MS_0054_047; *Missionary Register 1815*, 195–197).

S. Marsden to J. Pratt, 22/9/1814 (http://www.marsdenarchive.otago.ac.nz/MS_0054_048; *Missionary Register 1815*, 265–268).

S. Marsden to J. Pratt, 29/9/1814 (https://marsdenarchive.otago.ac.nz/MS_0054_052).

S. Marsden to Pratt, 30/9/1814 (https://marsdenarchive.otago.ac.nz/MS_0054_055).

S. Marsden to J. Pratt, 30/9/1814 (http://www.marsdenarchive.otago.ac.nz/MS_0054_057)

S. Marsden to J. Pratt, 12/10/1814 (http://www.marsdenarchive.otago.ac.nz/MS_0054_061).

S. Marsden to J. Pratt, 18/11/1814 (http://www.marsdenarchive.otago.ac.nz/MS_0054_076).

S. Marsden to J. Pratt, 28/11/1814 (https://marsdenarchive.otago.ac.nz/MS_0054_077).

S. Marsden to J. Pratt, 10/6/1815 (http://www.marsdenarchive.otago.ac.nz/MS_0054_086).

S. Marsden to J. Pratt, 14/6/1815 (http://www.marsdenarchive.otago.ac.nz/MS_0055_001. *Missionary Register 1816*, 197–198 [dated 12/6/1815])

S. Marsden to J. Pratt, 15/6/1815 [No. 1] (http://www.marsdenarchive.otago.ac.nz/MS_0055_002).

S. Marsden to J. Pratt, 15/6/1815 [No. 2] (http://www.marsdenarchive.otago.ac.nz/MS_0055_003).

S. Marsden to J. Pratt, 30/6/1815 (http://www.marsdenarchive.otago.ac.nz/MS_0055_007).

S. Marsden et al. to J. Pratt, 25/10/1815 (http://www.marsdenarchive.otago.ac.nz/MS_0055_031).

S. Marsden to J. Pratt, 26/10/1815 [Marsden Online Archive labels 28/10/1815] (http://www.marsdenarchive.otago.ac.nz/MS_0055_032).

S. Marsden to J. Pratt, 26/10/1815 (http://www.marsdenarchive.otago.ac.nz/MS_0055_035).

S. Marsden to J. Pratt, 28 Oct 1815 (http://www.marsdenarchive.otago.ac.nz/MS_0055_039).

S. Marsden to J. Pratt, 6/11/1815 (http://www.marsdenarchive.otago.ac.nz/MS_0055_040; Extract: *HRNZ* 1.424–425).

S. Marsden to J. Pratt, 10/3/1816 (http://www.marsdenarchive.otago.ac.nz/MS_0056_003).

S. Marsden to J. Pratt, 22/1/1817 (http://www.marsdenarchive.otago.ac.nz/MS_0056_037).

S. Marsden to J. Pratt, 3/3/1817 (http://www.marsdenarchive.otago.ac.nz/MS_0056_042).

S. Marsden to J. Pratt, 27/3/1817 (http://www.marsdenarchive.otago.ac.nz/MS_0056_048).

S. Marsden to J. Pratt, 3/4/1817 (http://www.marsdenarchive.otago.ac.nz/MS_0056_053).

BIBLIOGRAPHY

S. Marsden to J. Pratt, 4/2/1818. [Marsden Online Archive labels 5/2/1818] (https://marsdenarchive.otago.ac.nz/MS_0056_070).

S. Marsden to J. Pratt, 12/2/1818 (https://marsdenarchive.otago.ac.nz/MS_0056_071).

S. Marsden to J. Pratt, 20/5/1818 (https://marsdenarchive.otago.ac.nz/MS_0056_087).

S. Marsden to J. Pratt, 11/8/1818 (HL: MS 69/91).

S. Marsden to J. Pratt, 13/8/1818 (http://www.marsdenarchive.otago.ac.nz/MS_0056_093).

S. Marsden to J. Pratt, 26/9/1818 (http://www.marsdenarchive.otago.ac.nz/MS_0056_098).

S. Marsden to J. Pratt, 24/2/1819 [No. 1] (http://www.marsdenarchive.otago.ac.nz/MS_0056_136).

S. Marsden to J. Pratt, 24/2/1819 [No. 2] (http://www.marsdenarchive.otago.ac.nz/MS_0056_137).

S. Marsden to J. Pratt, 22/3/1819 (https://marsdenarchive.otago.ac.nz/MS_0056_177and178).

S. Marsden to J. Pratt, 8/6/1819 (https://marsdenarchive.otago.ac.nz/MS_0056_164).

S. Marsden to J. Pratt, 9/6/1819 (http://www.marsdenarchive.otago.ac.nz/MS_0056_167).

S. Marsden to J. Pratt, 12/7/1819 (http://www.marsdenarchive.otago.ac.nz/MS_0057_002).

S. Marsden to J. Pratt, 13/7/1819 (http://www.marsdenarchive.otago.ac.nz/MS_0056_180).

S. Marsden to J. Pratt, 14/7/1819 [Marsden Online Archive labels 15/7/1819] (http://www.marsdenarchive.otago.ac.nz/MS_0057_004).

S. Marsden to J. Pratt, 14/1/1820 [Marsden Online Archive labels 12/1/1820] (https://marsdenarchive.otago.ac.nz/MS_0057_013).

S. Marsden to J. Pratt, 7/2/1820 [No1] (http://www.marsdenarchive.otago.ac.nz/MS_0057_012).

S. Marsden to J. Pratt, 7/2/1820 [No2] (http://www.marsdenarchive.otago.ac.nz/MS_0057_014).

S. Marsden to J. Pratt, 10/2/1820 (http://www.marsdenarchive.otago.ac.nz/MS_0057_016).

S. Marsden to J. Pratt, 22/9/1820 (http://www.marsdenarchive.otago.ac.nz/MS_0057_026).

S. Marsden to J. Pratt, 9/2/1821 (HL: MS-0057/028)

S. Marsden to J. Pratt, 19/3/1821 (HL: MS-0057/041).

S. Marsden to J. Pratt, 10/6/1821 (http://www.marsdenarchive.otago.ac.nz/MS_0057_044).

S. Marsden to J. Pratt, 19/9/1821 [Marsden Online Archive labels 18/9/1821] (https://marsdenarchive.otago.ac.nz/MS_0057_052).

S. Marsden to J. Pratt, 11/3/1822 (http://www.marsdenarchive.otago.ac.nz/MS_0057_067).

S. Marsden to J. Pratt, 7/9/1822 [No1] (http://www.marsdenarchive.otago.ac.nz/MS_0057_082).

S. Marsden to J. Pratt, 7/9/1822 [No2] (https://marsdenarchive.otago.ac.nz/MS_0057_083).

S. Marsden to J. Pratt, [25/9/1822] [The letter is undated, but as it was conveyed to England by Captain King of the HM surveying-brig Bathurst, which departed NSW 25/9/1822, SG 27/9/1822, the letter must have been written shortly before that date] (http://www.marsdenarchive.otago.ac.nz/MS_0057_086).

S. Marsden to J. Pratt, 7/2/1825 (CRL: CNM3 330; HL: MS-0057/131).

S. Marsden to J. Pratt, 8/2/1825 (CRL: CNM3 332; HL: MS-0057/132).

S. Marsden to Alexander Riley, 19/5/1818, printed in H.G. Bennett, *A Letter to Earl Bathurst, Secretary of State for the Colonial Department*, 124–126.

S. Marsden to the Settlers, 24/2/ 1819 (http://www.marsdenarchive.otago.ac.nz/MS_0056_134).

S. Marsden to T.H. Scott 1826, cited in John Harris, *One Blood*, 43.

S. Marsden to John Stokes, 4/5/1810 (Mackaness, *Samuel Marsden*, No. 18).

S. Marsden to Mary Stokes, 22/2/1800 (Mackaness, *Samuel Marsden*, No. 8).

S. Marsden, to Mary Stokes, 22/8/ 1801 (Mackaness, *Samuel Marsden*, No. 10).

S. Marsden to Mary Stokes, 15/6/1815 (Mackaness, *Samuel Marsden*, No. 24).

S. Marsden to Mary Stokes, 14/3/1816 (Mackaness, *Samuel Marsden*, No. 26).

S. Marsden to Mary Stokes, 27/3/1817 (Mackaness, *Samuel Marsden*, No. 28).

S. Marsden to Mary Stokes, 16/12/1817 (Mackaness, *Samuel Marsden*, No. 29).

S. Marsden to Mary Stokes, 14/6/1819 (Mackaness, *Samuel Marsden*, No. 30).

S. Marsden to W. Wilberforce, 1799 (Mitchell: BT, Missionary Box 49, p. 77).

S. Marsden to J Wylde, 7/1/1817 (http://www.marsdenarchive.otago.ac.nz/MS_0056_036).

S. Marsden to J. Wylde, 16/1/1817, enclosed in S. Marsden to J. Wylde, 7/1/1817 (http://www.marsdenarchive.otago.ac.nz/MS_0056_036).

S. Marsden to J. Wylde, 18/1/1817 (Mitchell: JT Bigge Report, Appendix, BT, Box 15, 1648).

S. Marsden notes on J. Wylde's letter of 23/1/1817, 28/1/1817 [unsent], now filed with J. Wylde to Samuel Marsden, 23/1/1817. http://www.marsdenarchive.otago.ac.nz/MS_0056_038.

BIBLIOGRAPHY

S. Marsden to J. Wylde, 28/1/1817, now filed with J. Wylde to S. Marsden, 23/1/1817 (http://www.marsdenarchive.otago.ac.nz/MS_0056_038)

S. Marsden to J. Wylde, 21/4/1817 (Mitchell: J.T. Bigge, *Report*, Appendix, BT, Box 16, 1871).

S. Marsden to Wylde, 23/4/1817 (https://marsdenarchive.otago.ac.nz/MS_0056_055).

J.J. Moore to S. Marsden, 21/7/1819 (http://www.marsdenarchive.otago.ac.nz/MS_0057_006).

W.H. Moore to Bathurst, 15/12/1817 (*HRA* 4.1, 261–263).

G. Murray to R. Darling, 31/7/1828 (*HRA* 1.14, 275–276).

G. Murray to R. Darling, 1/1/1829 (*HRA* 1.14, 576–577).

J. Newton to W. Wilberforce, 5/7/1788, quoted in Gareth Atkins, 'Wilberforce', 27.

T.F. Palmer to R. Lindsay, 15/9/1797 (*HRNSW* 2.881).

C. Pitman to W. Ellis, 10/8/1839 (SOAS: London Missionary Society Correspondence: South Seas, Box 12).

J. Pratt to S. Marsden, 18/3/1814 (HL: MS-0175/001, item 3).

J. Pratt to S. Marsden, 18/8/1814 (HL: MS-0175/001, item 4).

J. Pratt to S. Marsden, 16/12/1814 (HL: MS-0175/001, item 5).

J. Pratt to S. Marsden, 5/9/1816 (HL: MS-0175/001, item 9).

J. Pratt to S. Marsden, 24/11/1817 (HL: MS-0175/001, item 14).

J. Pratt to S. Marsden, 12/3/1818 (http://www.marsdenarchive.otago.ac.nz/MS_0056_074).

J. Pratt to S. Marsden, 14/12/1818 (http://www.marsdenarchive.otago.ac.nz/MS_0056_105).

J. Pratt to S. Marsden, 12/5/1819 (http://www.marsdenarchive.otago.ac.nz/MS_0056_154).

J. Pratt to S. Marsden, 19/5/1819 (http://www.marsdenarchive.otago.ac.nz/MS_0056_160).

J. Pratt to S. Marsden, 13/3/1821 (CRL: CMS/B/OMS/C N L1: 47–51).

J. Pratt to S. Marsden, 15/6/1821 (CRL: CMS/B/OMS/C N L1: 54–55).

J. Pratt to S. Marsden, 16/4/1822 (CRL: CMS/B/OMS/C N L1: 96–99).

J. Pratt to S. Marsden, 7/9/1822 (http://www.marsdenarchive.otago.ac.nz/MS_0057_083).

J. Pratt to Missionaries and Settlers, 6/9/1822 (CRL: CMS/B/OMS/C N L1: 129–132).

W. Shelley to L. Macquarie, 8/4/1814 (*HRA* 1.8, 370–371).

C. Simeon to S. Marsden, [1819], J.B. Marsden, *The Life and Labours of Rev. Samuel Marsden*, 104.

L. Threlkeld to S. Bannister, 27/9/1825. (Mitchell: BT Box 53).

J. Thompson to S. Marsden, 22/3/1817 (http://www.marsdenarchive.otago.ac.nz/MS_0056_046).

J. Thompson to the CMS, 8/8/1820 (CRL: CMS/B/OMS/C N M1: 241–242).

B. Vale, H. Fulton, R. Cartwright, W. Cowper and S. Marsden to J. Pratt, 25/10/1815 [Marsden Online Archive labels 26/10/1815] (http://www.marsdenarchive.otago.ac.nz/MS_0055_031).

W. Walker to WAMS, n.d. (Mitchell: Bonwick Transcripts, Box 53).

W.C. Wentworth to T. Moore, 6/6/1815 (Mitchell: Wentworth family papers, 1783–1827; A 756 [CY 700]).

W. Wilberforce to W. Hey, n.d., in R.I. & S. Wilberforce, *The Life of William Wilberforce*, 1.71.

W. Wilberforce to W. Hey, 29/5/1787, in R.I. & S. Wilberforce, *The Life of William Wilberforce*, 1.131.

W. Wilberforce to S. Marsden, 21/3/1814 (Mitchell: Marsden Papers, C244).

W. Wilberforce to J. Pratt, 23/1/1812 (HL: MS-0498/001, item 26);

J. Wylde to H. Bathurst, 20/7/1821 (*HRA* 4.1, 344–347).

J. Wylde to J.T. Campbell, 11/1/1817, enclosed in S. Marsden to J. Wylde, 7/1/1817 (http://www.marsdenarchive.otago.ac.nz/MS_0056_036).

J. Wylde to L. Macquarie, 14/1/1817, enclosed in S. Marsden to J. Wylde, 7/1/1817 (http://www.marsdenarchive.otago.ac.nz/MS_0056_036).

J. Wylde, S. Lord, J.T. Campbell, and S. Marsden to H. Bathurst, 28/11/1817 (http://www.marsdenarchive.otago.ac.nz/MS_0056_069).

J. Youl, R. Cartwright, and S. Marsden to J. Pratt, 27/3/1817 [Marsden Online Archive labels this letter 2/3/1817] (http://www.marsdenarchive.otago.ac.nz/MS_0056_047).

J. Youl to J. Pratt, 29/3/1817 (http://www.marsdenarchive.otago.ac.nz/MS_0056_049).

Memorials, Memoranda, Minutes

[AgSocNSW]	'The Humble Memorial of the Undersigned Landholders and Proprietors of Live Stock, Being Members of the Agricultural Society of the Colony of NSW', encl. in T.Brisbane to H. Bathurst, 7/9/1822 (*HRA* 1.10, 782–83).
[CMS CorCom]	Minutes of the Corresponding Committee, 2 Mar 1821 (CRL: CMS/B/OMS/C N M1: 315-317).
[CMS, London]	Minutes of the CMS Committee, 3/3/1818 (HL: micro 121/2)

[CMS, London]	Minutes of the CMS Committee, 9/3/1818 (HL: micro 121/2)
[CMS, London]	*Proceedings of the Church Missionary Society for Africa and the East, Nineteenth Year. 1818–1819* (London: B. Bensley, 1819). Archive.org
[CMS, London]	*Proceedings of the Church Missionary Society for Africa and the East, Twentieth Year. 1819–1820* (London: R. Watts, 1820). Archive.org
[CMS Missionaries, NZ]	Minutes of Special Committee, Rangihoua, 12/4/1820 (CRL: CMS/B/OMS/C N M1: 232–233).
[CMS Missionaries, NZ]	Minutes of Quarterly Meeting of Missionaries and Settlers, 2 Oct 1821 (CRL: CMS/B/OMS/C N M2: 45-51).
[CMS UK]	Memorial of the Committee of the Church of England Missionary Society to Earl Bathurst, [1817] (*HRNZ* 1.417–421; Enclosure 5: Marsden to Pratt, 6/11/1815, *HRNZ* 1.424–425).
Irvine, Capt. F.	Minute relative to the "Active", 22/3/1821 (CRL: CMS/B/OMS/C N M1: 506-513).
London Missionary Society	'Board Minutes, 28 September 1795', in *L.M.S. Board Minutes*, 1 (London: London Missionary Society, 1795).
[LMS NSW-Aux]	Rules for the New South Wales Auxiliary Missionary Society, 10/2/1817 (SOAS: CWM/LMS/03/02: box 1b, item 38).
LMS	Memorandum concerning the New South Wales Auxiliary Missionary Society, 3/2/1817 (SOAS: CWM/LMS/03/02, box 1b, item 36).

Memorial of Merchants, Traders, and Others, to L. Macquarie, 3/10/1814; L. Macquarie to H. Bathurst 24/6/1815, Enclosure 6 (*HRA* 1.8, 583–586).

NSW Philanthropic Society Minutes, 20 Dec 1813, SLNSW PAM Q81/45 http://acms.sl.nsw.gov.au/album/albumView.aspx?itemID=1290511&acmsid=0

Newspapers and Periodicals

Analytical Review, or History of Literature, Domestic and Foreign
Hathitrust.org. AND Google Books.

Asiatic Mirror & Commercial Advertiser
http://www.18thcjournals.amdigital.co.uk/Documents/Details/AsiaticMirrorandCommercialAdvertiser

Asiatic Journal and Monthly Miscellany, Volume 6, July 1818, (London: Black, Kingsbury, Parbury, & Allen, 1818). Google Books.

Australian	http://trove.nla.gov.au/newspaper.
Colonial Times & Tasmanian Advertiser	http://trove.nla.gov.au/newspaper.
Courier [Hobart]	see *Hobart Courier* http://trove.nla.gov.au/newspaper.
Critical Review, or Annals of Literature	Hathitrust.org. AND Google Books.
Eclectic Review	Hathitrust.org. AND Google Books.
Edinburgh Review	Hathitrust.org.
Edinburgh Magazine	Hathitrust.org. AND Google Books.
Empire [Sydney]	http://trove.nla.gov.au/newspaper.
Evangelical Magazine	Hathitrust.org.
Gazette	see *Sydney Gazette*. http://trove.nla.gov.au/newspaper.
Gentleman's Magazine	Hathitrust.org.
Hobart Courier	*Courier [Hobart]*. http://trove.nla.gov.au/newspaper.
Literary Gazette. A weekly journal of literature, science, and the fine arts.	Hathitrust.org.
Missionary Register	Hathitrust.org.; Archive.org. AND Google Books.
Monitor	http://trove.nla.gov.au/newspaper.
Morning Chronicle (London)	https://www.britishnewspaperarchive.co.uk/titles/morning-chronicle.
Naval Chronicle	https://archive.org.
Quarterly Review	hathitrust.org.
Oakleigh Leader	http://trove.nla.gov.au/newspaper.
St James Chronicle [London]	https://newspaperarchive.com/uk/middlesex/london/st-james-chronicle-or-british-evening-post/.
Sydney Gazette and New South Wales Advertiser	http://trove.nla.gov.au/newspaper.
Sydney [Morning] Herald	http://trove.nla.gov.au/newspaper.
Sydney Mail	http://trove.nla.gov.au/newspaper.
Truth [Sydney]	http://trove.nla.gov.au/newspaper.
World's News Sydney	http://trove.nla.gov.au/newspaper.

BIBLIOGRAPHY   389

Portraiture and Realia

Allen, George,   portrait of (SLNSW: ML 1241).

Close, E.   'Courtroom scene, Sydney: the 'Philo Free' civil libel trial,
                         1 December 1817'. Edward Charles Close, New South
                         Wales Sketchbook (Mitchell: SAFE/PXA 1187).

Garling, Frederick,   portrait of (SLNSW: GPO 1 - 12061).

Marsden, Samuel,   portrait of, from R. Jones' collection (SLNSW: PXA 972_5).

Tapaeru   'Grave Plaque'. Plaque marking the grave of Tepaeru Ariki.
                         Cook Islands Christian Church, Avarua, Raratonga.

Tapaeru   Sketch of Tapaeru. From Maretu, *Cannibals & Converts*, 47.

Reports

Bigge, J.T. & H. Bathurst, *Report of the commissioner of inquiry into the state of the colony of New South Wales (Commons paper 448)* (London: House of Commons, 1822; Facsimile Edition: Adelaide: Libraries Board of South Australia, 1966).

Bigge, J.T.   *Report of the commissioner of inquiry on the state of agriculture and trade in the colony of New South Wales (Commons paper 136)* (London: Govt. Printer, 1823; Adelaide: Libraries Board of South Australia, 1966).

Bigge, J.T.   *Report of the Commissioner of Inquiry on the Judicial Establishments of New South Wales and Van Diemen's Land 1823* (London: The House of Commons, 1823; Adelaide: Libraries Board of South Australia, 1966).

Bigge, J.T.   *The Evidence To The Bigge Reports. New South Wales Under Governor Macquarie.* Volume 1 *The Oral Evidence.* Volume 2 *The Written Evidence* (J. Ritchie, select. & ed.; Melbourne: Heinemann, 1971).

[CMS Leicester]   Report of the Leicester and Leicestershire association, *Missionary Register 1815* [Jan], 7–11.

[Macquarie, L.]   Entries of Colonial Vessels at the Naval Office, Sydney, from 1st July to 30th September, 1815. Enclosure No. 9 in L. Macquarie to H. Bathurst, 18/3/1816 (*HRA* 1.9, 84).

[Macquarie, L.]   Entries of Colonial Vessels at Port Jackson for the Quarter ending 31st December, 1815. Enclosure No. 9 in L. Macquarie to H. Bathurst, 18/3/1816 (*HRA* 1.9, 88).

[Macquarie, L.]   List of Persons holding Civil and Military Appointments in NSW on 31/3/1817, Enclosure in L. Macquarie to H. Bathurst, 31/3/1817 (*HRA* 1.9, 244–247).

Vale, B.   *Proceedings of a general court martial, ordered by Governor Macquarie, to try the Rev. Benjamin Vale, for seizing an American vessel trading in Sydney Cove* (London: J. Asperne, 1817).

Secondary Sources

[ADB]   'Bathurst, Henry (1762–1834)', *Australian Dictionary of Biography*, http://adb.anu.edu.au/biography/bathurst-henry-1751/text1945, published first in hardcopy 1966.

[ADB]   'Vale, Benjamin (1788–1863)', *Australian Dictionary of Biography* (Melbourne, 1967), II, 550.

Aitken, G.A.   'Nichols, John (1745–1826), *Dictionary of National Biography* Vol. 41, 2–5. https://en.wikisource.org/wiki/Nichols,_John_(1745-1826)_(DNB00).

Allen, M.   'The Myth of the Flogging Parson: Samuel Marsden and Severity of Punishment in the Age of Reform', *Australian Historical Studies* 48 (2017), 486–501.

Anderson, G.D.   'Culture and Mission: How Māori Culture Affected Marsden's Mission Practice', in P.G. Bolt & D.B. Pettett (eds.), *Launching Marsden's Mission. The Beginnings of the Church Missionary Society in New Zealand, viewed from New South Wales* (London: The Latimer Trust, 2014), 89–100.

[ASA]   'Rev. Dr. Laurence Hynes Halloran—the Fake Minister', Ancestors South Africa. http://www.ancestors.co.za/articles/famous-people/rev-laurence-hynes-halloran-minister/.

Atkins, G.   'Wilberforce and his milieux: the worlds of Anglican Evangelicalism, c.1780–1830' (unpublished PhD dissertation, University of Cambridge, 2009).

Atkinson, A.   *The Europeans in Australia: A History. Vol. 2: Democracy*, (Melbourne: Oxford University Press, 2016).

Atkinson, A.   *The Europeans in Australia: A History. Vol. 1: The Beginning* (Melbourne: Oxford University Press, 1997).

Atkinson, A.   'Time, Place and Paternalism: Early Conservative Thinking in New South Wales', *Australian Historical Studies* 23 90 (1988), 1–18.

Atkinson, A.   *Camden. Farm and Village Life in Early New South Wales* (Melbourne: Australian Scholarly Publishing, ²2008 [1988]).

Bacon, F.   *Redargutio Philosophiarum* (1608), in B. Farrington (ed.), *The Philosophy of Francis Bacon* (Liverpool: Liverpool University Press, 1964).

Barton, R. J.	*Earliest New Zealand: The Journals and Correspondence of the Rev. John Butler* (Masterton, N.Z.: 1927). http://www.enzb.auckland.ac.nz/document?wid=1455.
Bashir, M.	'Lachlan Macquarie, 5th Governor of New South Wales: His Life and Legacy to Australia'. Speech to the Royal Society of New South Wales annual dinner. *JRAHS* 148.457–458 (2015), 96–108. https://royalsoc.org.au/images/pdf/journal/RSNSW_148-2_Bashir.pdf
Bebbington, D.W.	*Evangelicalism In Modern Britain: A History From The 1730s To The 1980s* (London: Unwin Hyman, 1989).
Belich, J.	*Making Peoples: A History of the New Zealanders from Polynesian Settlement to the End of the Nineteenth Century* (Auckland: Penguin, 1996).
Bennett, J.M.	'Bigge, John Thomas (1780–1843)', *Australian Dictionary of Biography*, http://adb.anu.edu.au/biography/bigge-john-thomas-1779/text1999, published first in hardcopy 1966.
Binney, J.	*The Legacy of Guilt: A Life of Thomas Kendall* (Wellington, NZ: Bridget Williams Books, 2005).
Black, D. W.	*Bad Boys, Bad Men: Confronting Antisocial Personality Disorder (Sociopathy)* (London: Oxford University Press, 2013).
Boase, G.C.	'Josiah Conder (1789–1855)', *Dictionary of National Biography*, Vol. 12, 2–3. https://en.wikisource.org/wiki/Conder,_Josiah_(DNB00).
Boles, J.B.	'Turner, the Frontier, and the Study of Religion in America', *Journal of the Early Republic* 13.2 (1993), 205-216. http://www.jstor.org/stable/3124087
Bollen, J.D.	'English Missionary Societies and the Australian Aborigine', *Journal of Religious History* 9.3 (1977), 263–291.
Bolt, P.G.	'What Really Happened on Rarotonga in 1814?' (Forthcoming).
Bolt, P.G.	'A Dramatic Event in the South Pacific: Lessons for Synoptic Comparison in Gospels Research', in J.R. Harrison & P.G. Bolt (eds.), *The Impact of Jesus* (Macquarie Park, NSW: SCD Press, Forthcoming, 2019).
Bolt, P.G.	'The Boyd Set-Back to Marsden's Mission: The View from New South Wales', in P.G. Bolt & D.P. (eds.), *Launching Marsden's Mission: The Beginning of the Church Missionary Society in New Zealand, Viewed from New South Wales* (Oxford: The Latimer Trust, 2014), 61–78.

Bolt, P.G.	*A Portrait in his Actions. Thomas Moore (1762–1840). Part 1: From Lesbury to Liverpool* (Studies in Australian Colonial History 3; Camperdown, NSW: Bolt Publishing, 2010).
Bolt, P.G.	*William Cowper (1778–1858): The Indispensable Parson. The Life & Influence of Australia's First Parish Clergyman* (Studies in Australian Colonial History 2; Camperdown, NSW: Bolt Publishing, 2009).
Bolt, P.G. & D.B. Pettett (eds.)	*Launching Marsden's Mission. The Beginnings of the Church Missionary Society in New Zealand, viewed from New South Wales* (London: The Latimer Trust, 2014).
Bonwick, J.	*Australia's First Preacher, the Rev. Richard Johnson, First Chaplain of New South Wales* (London: Sampson Low, Marston & Co., 1898).
Bonwick, J.	*Early Struggles of the Australian Press* (Sydney: Gordon & Gotch, 1890).
Bonwick, J.	*First Twenty Years of Australia: A History Founded on Official Documents* (Melbourne; Sydney: Sampson Low, Marston, Searle, & Rivington, 1882).
Booth, W.C.	*A Rhetoric of Irony* (Chicago: University of Chicago Press, 1974).
Border, R.	*Church and State in Australia, 1788–1872: A Constitutional Study of the Church of England in Australia* (London: SPCK, 1962).
Bouwsma, W. J.	'John Calvin: French Theologian'. *Encyclopaedia Britannica*. (2013).
Bremer, A.	'Domestic Disclosures: Letters and the representation of cross-cultural relations in early Colonial New South Wales', *Frontiers: A Journal of Women Studies*. Vol. 28, No. 1/2, Domestic Frontiers: The Home and Colonization (2007), 77–95.
Brendon, P.	*The Decline And Fall of The British Empire 1781–1997* (London: Vintage Books, 2008).
Breward, I.	*A History of the Churches in Australasia* (The Oxford History of the Christian Church; Oxford; New York: Oxford University Press, 2001).
Bridges, B.	'The Church of England and the Aborigines of New South Wales, 1788–1855' (Unpublished PhD thesis, University of New South Wales, 1978).

Brockway, L.	'Plant Imperialism', http://www.britishempire.co.uk/science/agriculture/plantimperialism.htm.
Bromhead, H.	*The Reign of Truth and Faith: Epistemic expressions in 16th and 17th century English* (Berlin: Mouton de Gruyter, 2009).
Brown, A.J.	*Ill-Starred Captains: Flinders and Baudin* (Fremantle, W.A.: Fremantle Press, 2008 revised edition [Original: 2000]).
Brown, J.C.	*'Poverty is not a crime': The Development Of Social Services In Tasmania, 1803–1900* (Hobart: Tasmanian Historical Research Association, 1972), 1–73.
Bubacz, B.M.	'The Female and Male Orphan Schools in New South Wales 1801–1850' (Unpublished PhD thesis, University of Sydney, 2007).
Buse, J., & R. Taringa	*Cook Islands Māori Dictionary* (B. Biggs & R. Moeka'a, eds.; Canberra: Ministry of Education, Government of the Cook Islands, 1995). See the updated dictionary at: http://cookislandsdictionary.com.
Cable, K. J.	'Cartwright, Robert (1771–1856)', *Australian Dictionary of Biography*, http://adb.anu.edu.au/biography/cartwright-robert-1882/text2211, published first in hardcopy 1966.
Cable, K.J.	'Johnson, Richard (1753–1827)', *Australian Dictionary of Biography*, http://adb.anu.edu.au/biography/johnson-richard-2275/text2921, published first in hardcopy 1967.
Cameron, H.C.	*Sir Joseph Banks, K.B., P.R.S.: the Autocrat of the Philosophers* (Sydney: Angus & Robertson, 1952).
Campbell, M.	'History in Prehistory. The Oral Traditions of the Rarotongan Land Court Records', *JPH* 37.2 (2002), 221–238.
Carey, H.	*Believing In Australia: A Cultural History Of Religions* (Sydney: Allen & Unwin, 1996).
Carmody, J.	'Chicken Pox or Small Pox in the Colony at Sydney', *Ockham's Razor*, ABC Radio National, September 19, 2010. http://www.abc.net.au/radionational/programs/ockhamsrazor/chicken-pox-or-smallpox-in-the-colony-at-sydney/2972652.
Carr, W.	'Wolcot, J. (1738-1790)', *Dictionary of National Biography* Vol. 62, 290–293. https://en.wikisource.org/wiki/Wolcot,_John_(DNB00).
Carson, P.	*The East India Company and Religion, 1698-1858* (Cambridge: Cambridge University Press, 2013).

Carus, W. (Ed.)	*Memoirs of the Life of the Rev. Charles Simeon* (London: Hatchard & Son, 1847). Archive.org.
Castles, A.C.	*An Australian Legal History* (Sydney: The Law Book Company Limited, 1982).
[CFAS]	'Libel, Slander & Freedom of Speech'. California State University, The Centre for First Amendment Studies. (2013). http://www.firstamendmentstudies.org/wp/libel.html.
Champion, B.W.	'Lancelot Edward Threlkeld: His Life and Work 1788–1859', *JRAHS* 25 (1939), 341–411. https://downloads.newcastle.edu.au/library/cultural%20collections/pdf/champion1939b.pdf.
Chapman, A., J. Coffee, & B.S. Gregory (eds.)	
	Seeing Things Their Way: Intellectual History and the Return of Religion (Notre Dame, Indiana: University of Notre Dame Press, 2009).
Church Missionary Society	
	The Church Missionary Society: A Manual Outlining Its History, Organization and Commitments (London: The Highway Press, 1961).
Clark, C.M.H.	*A History Of Australia*. Vol. 1: *From The Earliest Times To The Age Of Macquarie* (Melbourne: Melbourne University Press, 1962).
Clark, J.C.D.	*English Society 1688–1832: Ideology, Social Structure, and Political Practice During the Ancien Regime* (Cambridge: Cambridge University Press, 1985).
Clayton, J.M.	*An Alphabetical List of Ships Employed in the South Sea Whale Fishery from Britain: 1775–1815* (Chania, Greece: Jane M. Clayton, 2014).
Cobley, J.	'Bland, William (1789–1868)', *Australian Dictionary of Biography*, http://adb.anu.edu.au/biography/bland-william-1793/text2027, published first in hardcopy 1966.
Cody, D.	'The Gentleman'. The Victorian Web: Literature, History and Culture in the age of Victoria. (2011). http://www.victorianweb.org/history/gentleman.html
Cole, K.	*A History of the Church Missionary Society of Australia* (Melbourne: Church Missionary Historical Publications Trust, 1971).
Courtney, W.P.	'Woide, Charles Godfrey (1725–1790)', *Dictionary of National Biography* Vol. 62, 289–290. https://

	en.wikisource.org/wiki/Woide,_Charles_Godfrey_(DNB00).
Cox, J.	*The British Missionary Enterprise Since 1700* (London: Routledge, 2007).
Crocombe, M.	*They Came for Sandalwood* (Wellington, N.Z.: Islands Education Division, Dept. of Education for Dept. of Island Territories, 1964, repr. 1981, 1975, 1978, 1981, 1992 and 1993). Google Books. https://books.google.com.au/books?id=b0UH9uY6ieAC&pg=PA39&lpg=PA39&dq
Crocombe, M.T.	'Maretu's Life, Work, and Context', *Cannibals and Converts: Radical Change in the Cook Islands* (Marjorie Tuainekore Crocombe, transl., ed., annot.; Suva, Fiji: Institute of Pacific Studies University of South Pacific, 1983; repr. 1987, 1993, 2001), 1–30. https://books.google.com.au/books?id=NjCFqMMu5YwC&pg=PA45&lpg=PA45&dq. Numbers in [square brackets] indicate the pagination of Maretu's manuscript.
Cumpston, J.S.	*Shipping Arrivals and Departures: Sydney, 1788-1825* (Canberra: J. S. Cumpston, 1963).
Cunich, P., D. Hoyle, E. Duffy, & R. Hyam	
	A History of Magdalene College Cambridge 1428–1988 (Cambridge: Magdalene College, 1994).
Currey, C.H.	'Bent, Ellis (1783–1815)', *Australian Dictionary of Biography*, http://adb.anu.edu.au/biography/bent-ellis-1772/text1985, published first in hardcopy 1966.
Currey, C.H.	*Sir Francis Forbes: The First Chief Justice of the Supreme Court of New South Wales* (Sydney: Angus & Robertson, 1968).
Dabhoiwala, F.	'The Construction of Honour, Reputation and Status in Late Seventeenth and Early Eighteenth-Century England', *Transactions of the Royal Historical Society*, 6 (Cambridge: Cambridge University Press, 1996), 202. http://www.jstor.org.ezproxy.lib.rmit.edu.au/stable/pdf/3679236.pdf
Davidson, A. K.	'Culture and Ecclesiology: The Church Missionary Society and New Zealand', in K. Ward & B. Stanley (eds.), *The Church Missionary Society and World Christianity, 1799-1999* (Studies in the History of Christian Missions; Grand Rapids & Cambridge: Eerdmans, 2000), 198–227.
Davey, C.J.	*Chief of Chiefs. Samuel Marsden of Australasia* (London: Edinburgh House Press, 1961).
Dickey, B.	*No Charity There: A Short History of Social Welfare in Australia* (North Sydney: Allen & Unwin, 1989).

Dowd, B.T.	'Allan, David (1780–1852)', *Australian Dictionary of Biography*, http://adb.anu.edu.au/biography/allan-david-1695/text1829, published first in hardcopy 1966.
Dudgeon, R.E.	'Chapter 13: Lectures and Societies', *Colymbia* (London: Trübner & co, 1873). https://en.wikisource.org/wiki/Colymbia/Chapter_13.
Dunn, C.	'The Founders of a Nation: Australia's First Fleet'. (January 17, 2013). http://www.australianhistoryresearch.info/the-first-fleet/
Edgeworth, B.	'Defamation Law and the Emergence of the Critical Press in Colonial New South Wales (1824– 1831)', *Australian Journal of Law and Society* 6.4 (1990), 50–82.
Ellis, M.H.	*Lachlan Macquarie: His Life, Adventures and Times* (Pymble, NSW: Angus & Robertson, 2010 [1947]).
[Encyclopedia.com]	'Lachlan Macquarie'. *Encyclopedia of World Biography*. The Gale Group. (2004). http://www.encyclopedia.com/people/history/australian-new-zealand-and-pacific-islands-history-biographies/lachlan-macquarie
Encyclopaedic Australian Legal Dictionary, 'criminal libel' (LexisNexis Australia, January 2011).	
Escott, M.	'Bennet, Hon. Henry Grey (1777–1836), of Walton-on-Thames, Surr. and Camelford House, Oxford Street, Mdx', in D.R. Fisher (ed.), *The History of Parliament: the House of Commons 1820–1832* (Cambridge: Cambridge University Press, 2009). http://www.historyofparliamentonline.org/volume/1820-1832/member/bennet-hon-henry-1777-1836.
Falloon, M.	'Research Note: Incomplete Marsden Letter Misleads Modern Critics', *New Zealand Religious History Newsletter*, no. 29 (December 2016), 9–10.
Falloon, M.	'"Openings of Providence": The Shaping of Marsden's Missionary Vision for New Zealand', in P.G. Bolt & D.B. Pettett (eds.), *Launching Marsden's Mission. The Beginnings of the Church Missionary Society in New Zealand, viewed from New South Wales* (London: The Latimer Trust, 2014), 129–138.
Falloon, M.	*To Plough or to Preach: Mission Strategies in New Zealand During the 1820s* (London: Latimer Trust, 2010).
Field, C.	'Counting Religion in England and Wales: the Long Eighteenth Century, c. 1680-c. 1840', *Journal of Ecclesiastical History* 63.4 (2012), 693–720.

Fitzpatrick, B.   'The big man's frontier and Australian farming', *Agricultural History* 21 (1947), 8–12.

Fletcher, J.J.   *Clean, Clad and Courteous: A History of Education in New South Wales* (Carlton: J.J. Fletcher, 1989).

Fraser, K.   'Kirsten Dunst: Teen Queen', *Vogue* (September 1, 2006). http://www/vogue.com/865326/Kirsten-dunst-teen-queen/.

Fricke, G.L.   *Libels, Lampoons And Litigants: Famous Australian Libel Cases* (Melbourne: Hutchinson of Australia, 1984).

Garrett, J.   *A Way in the Sea. Aspects of Pacific Christian History with Reference to Australia* (J.D. Northey Memorial Lectures, 1980; Melbourne: Spectrum, 1982).

Garrett, J.   *To Live Among the Stars: Christian Origins in Oceania* (Geneva & Suva: WCC & USP, ²1985 [1982]).

Gascoigne, J.   'The Scientist as Patron and Patriotic Symbol: the Changing Reputation of Sir Joseph Banks', in M. Shortland & R. Yeo (eds.), *Telling Lives in Science: Essays on Scientific Biography* (Cambridge: Cambridge University Press, 1996), 243–266.

Gascoigne, J.   *The Enlightenment and the Origins of European Australia* (Cambridge: Cambridge University Press, 2002).

Gilbert, A.N.   'Law and Honor Among Eighteenth-Century British Army Officers', *The Historical Journal* 19.1 (1976), 75–87. http://www.reenactor.ru/ARH/PDF/Gilbert_00.pdf

Gilbert, L. A.   'Banks, Sir Joseph (1743–1820)', *Australian Dictionary of Biography*, http://adb.anu.edu.au/biography/banks-sir-joseph-1737/text1917, published first in hardcopy 1966.

Gill, W.   *Gems of the Coral Islands, or, Incidents of contrast between Savage and Christian Life of the South Sea Islanders* (London: Ward & Co, 1856).

Gill, William Wyatt   *The Genealogy of the Kings of Rarotonga and Mangaia as illustrating the colonisation of that island and the Hervey Group*. Extract from Proceedings of Section G Australasian Association for the Advancement of Science (1889).

Girola, S. & R. Pizzini (eds.)
    Nagoyo: The Life of Don Angelo Confalonieri Among the Aborigines of Australia 1846–1848 (Trento, Italy: Fondazione Museo Storico del Trentino, 2013).

Gladwin, M.   'Missions and colonialism', in J. Rasmussen, J. Wolfe & J. Zachhuber (eds.), *The Oxford Handbook of Nineteenth-*

	Century Christian Thought (Oxford: Oxford University Press, 2017), 282–304.
Gladwin, M.	*Anglican clergy in Australia, 1788–1850* (Suffolk: Royal History Society and Boydell Press, 2015).
Gladwin, M.	'Marsden's generals: the metropolitan roots of Marsden's mission', in P.G. Bolt & D.B. Pettett (eds.), *Launching Marsden's Mission: The Beginnings of the Church Missionary Society in New Zealand, viewed from New South Wales* (Oxford: Latimer Trust, 2014), 13–29.
Gladwin, M.	'The journalist in the rectory: Anglican clergymen and Australian intellectual life, 1788–1850', *History Australia* 7 (2010), 56.1–28.
Golder, H.	*High and responsible office: a history of the NSW magistracy* (Melbourne: Sydney University Press, 1991).
Gossett, R.W.G.	'Notes on the Discovery of Rarotonga', *The Australian Geographer* 3 (1940), 4–15.
Gregory, J.	Review of D. Hepton, *The Church in the Long Eighteenth Century*. Review No. 1357. (December, 2012). http://www.history.ac.uk/reviews/review/1357.
Grocott, A.	*Convicts, Clergymen And Churches: Attitudes Of Convicts And Ex-Convicts Towards The Churches And Clergy In NSW From 1788 To 1851* (Sydney: Sydney University Press, 1980).
Gunson, N.	*Messengers Of Grace: Evangelical Missionaries In The South Seas, 1797–1860* (Melbourne: Oxford University Press, 1978).
Gunson, N.	'Gill, William Wyatt (1828–1896)', *Australian Dictionary of Biography*, http://adb.anu.edu.au/biography/gill-william-wyatt-3615/text5615, published first in hardcopy 1972.
Gunson, N.	'Elder, James (1772–1836)', *Australian Dictionary of Biography*, http://adb.anu.edu.au/biography/elder-james-2021/text2485, published first in hardcopy 1966.
Gunson, N.	'Evangelical Missionaries in the South Seas, 1797–1860' (PhD Thesis, Australian National University, 1959).
Hager, A.	'Introduction', in A. Hager (ed.), *Encyclopedia of British Writers, 16th, 17th and 18th Centuries* (New York: Book Builders LLC, 2005), vii–xii.
Hainsworth, D.R.	*The Sydney Traders. Simeon Lord and his Contemporaries 1788–1821* (Melbourne: Melbourne University Press, 1981).
Hall, N.	*"I Have Planted...": A Biography of Alfred Newbit Brown* (Palmerston North, NZ: Dunmore Press, 1981).

Harris, J.	*One Blood. 200 Years of Aboriginal Encounter with Christianity: A Story of Hope* (Sutherland, NSW: Albatross, ²1994 [1990]).
Harrison, J.F.C.	*The Early Victorians, 1832–1851* (London: Fontana, 1988 [1971]).
Harvard Business School	'South Seas Bubble Collection: History'. http://www.library.hbs.edu/hc/ssb/history.html.
Harvard Business School	'South Seas Bubble Collection: Humour'. http://www.library.hbs.edu/hc/ssb/recreationandarts/humor.html
Heyck, T.W.	*The Peoples of the British Isles: A New history*. Vol. 2: *From 1688–1870* (Lyceum Series; Oxford: Oxford University Press, ³2009 [original: 1992]).
Heydon, J. D.	'Brisbane, Sir Thomas Makdougall (1773-1860)', *Australian Dictionary of Biography*, http://adb.anu.edu.au/biography/brisbane-sir-thomas-makdougall-1827/text2097.
Hilliard, D.	*God's Gentlemen: A History of the Melanesian Mission, 1849–1942* (Brisbane: University of Queensland Press, 2013 [1978]).
Hilton, B.	*A Mad, Bad, and Dangerous People?: England, 1783–1846* (Oxford: Clarendon Press, 2008).
Hilton, B.	*The Age Of Atonement: The Influence Of Evangelicalism On Social And Economic Thought, 1795–1865* (Oxford: Oxford University Press, 1988).
Hirst, J.B.	*Convict Society and Its Enemies: A History of Early New South Wales* (Sydney: Allen & Unwin, 1983).
[History.com]	'American Revolution History'. (2016). http://www.history.com/topics/american-revolution/american-revolution-history
Hobbes, T.	*Leviathan: Or the Matter, Forme, and Power of a Commonwealth Ecclesiasticall and Civil* (Michael Oakeshott, ed.; New York: Simon & Schuster, 2009 [1651]).
Hodgkinson, R.	*Eber Bunker of Liverpool: 'The Father of Australian Whaling'* (Roebuck Society Publication No. 15; Canberra: Roebuck Society, 1975).
Holder, R.F.	'Campbell, John Thomas (1770–1830)', *Australian Dictionary of Biography*, http://adb.anu.edu.au/biography/campbell-john-thomas-1873/text2191, published first in hardcopy 1966.

Hole, C.	*The Early History of the Church Missionary Society for Africa and the East to the End of A.D. 1814* (London: Church Missionary Society, 1896).
Horne, C. S.	*The Story of the L.M.S.: 1795–1895*. New ed. with appendix up to 1904 (London: London Missionary Society, 1908).
Horsburgh, M.	'Government Policy and the Benevolent Society', *Journal of the Royal Australian Historical Society*, 63.2 (1977), 77–93.
Hughes, R.	*The Fatal Shore: A History of Transportation of Convicts to Australia, 1787-1868* (London: The Havill Press, 1987).
Hunt, D.	*Girt: The Unauthorised History of Australia* (Melbourne: Black Inc., 2013).
Hutchinson, M., & J. Wolffe	*A Short History of Global Evangelicalism* (Cambridge: Cambridge University Press, 2012).
Hylson–Smith, K.	*Evangelicals in the Church of England, 1734–1984* (Edinburgh: T. & T. Clark, 1989).
[IEP]	'Philosophy of History', Internet Encyclopedia of Philosophy. (2016). http://www.iep.utm.edu
Jacob, W.M.	*Lay People and Religion in the Early Eighteenth Century*. (Cambridge: Cambridge University Press, 1996).
Jenkins, R.	*Social Identity* (London & New York: Routledge, ⁴2014 [original: 1996]).
Jensen, P.D.	'Samuel Marsden'. http://www.phillipjensen.com/articles/samuel-marsden/ (2016).
Jensz, F.	*German Moravian Missionaries in the British Colony of Victoria, Australia, 1848-1908: Influential Strangers* (Studies in Christian Mission 38; Leiden; Boston: Brill, 2010).
Jensz, F.	'Three Peculiarities of the Southern Australian Moravian Mission Field', *Journal of Moravian History* 7 (2009), 7–30.
Jensz, F.	'Imperial Critics: Moravian Missionaries in the British Colonial World', in A. Barry, J. Cruickshank, A. Brown-May, and P. Grimshaw, in *Evangelists of Empire?: Missionaries in Colonial History* (Melbourne: University of Melbourne eScholarship Research Centre, 2008), 187–197.
Johnstone, S. M.	*Samuel Marsden: A Pioneer of Civilization in the South Seas* (Sydney: Angus & Robertson, 1932).
Jones, A., & K. Jenkins	*Words between Us—He Korero First Māori—Pakeha Conversations on Paper* (Wellington: Huia Publishers, 2011).

Karskens, G.	*The Colony: A History of Early Sydney* (Sydney: Allen & Unwin, 2009).
Kent, G.	*Company of Heaven: Early Missionaries in the South Seas* (Wellington: A. H. & A. W. Reed, 1972).
Kercher, B.	*Debt, Seduction and Other Disasters: The birth of civil law in convict New South Wales* (Sydney: Federation Press, 1996).
Kercher, B.	*An unruly child: A history of law in Australia* (St Leonards, NSW: Allen & Unwin, 1995).
Kerr, J. & H. Falkus	*From Sydney Cove to Duntroon. A Family Album of Early Life in Australia* (Richmond, Vic.; Hutchinson, 1982).
King, P.	'Newspaper reporting and attitudes to crime and justice in late-eighteenth and early-nineteenth-century London', *Continuity and Change* 22.1 (2007), 73–112.
Kingston, B.	'Introduction', in M.H. Ellis, *Lachlan Macquarie: His Life, Adventures and Times* (Pymble, NSW: Angus & Robertson, 2010 [1947]), xi–vii.
Kloosterman, A.M.J.	'Discoverers Of The Cook Islands And The Names They Gave', *Cook Islands Library And Museum Bulletin* 1 (Second Revised And Augmented Edition, 1976) Http://Nzetc.Victoria.Ac.Nz/Tm/Scholarly/Tei-Klodisc-T1-Body-D13.Html.
Kulikoff, A.	*From British Peasants to Colonial American Farmers* (Chapel Hill: University of South Carolina, 2000).
Lake, M.	'"Promoting the welfare of these poor heathens": Contextualising Marsden's Attitudes to Indigenous Peoples', in P.G. Bolt & D.B. Pettett (eds.). *Launching Marsden's Mission. The Beginnings of the Church Missionary Society in New Zealand, viewed from New South Wales* (London: Latimer Trust, 2014), 101–128.
Lake, M.	'Samuel Marsden, Work and the Limits of Evangelical Humanitarianism', *History Australia* Vol 7, no. 3 (2010), 57.1 - 57.23.
Lake, M.	'Salvation and Conciliation: First Missionary Encounters at Sydney Cove', in A. Barry, J. Cruickshank, A. Brown-May and P. Grimshaw (eds.), *Evangelists of Empire?: Missionaries in Colonial History* (Melbourne: University of Melbourne eScholarship Research Centre, 2008). Available at: http://msp.esrc.unimelb.edu.au/shs/missions.

Lake, M.	'Such Spiritual Acres: Protestantism, the Land and the Colonisation of Australia, 1788-1850' (Unpublished PhD dissertation, University of Sydney, 2008).
Lange, S.	'Admiring, Disdainful, or Somewhere in the Middle: Interpretations of Missionaries and Christian Beginnings among Māori', in G. Troughton & S. Lange (eds.), *Sacred Histories in Secular New Zealand* (Wellington: Victoria University Press, 2016), 24–39.
Le Couteur, H.	'Brisbane Anglicans: 1842–1875' (unpublished PhD dissertation, Macquarie University, 2006).
Lovett, R.	*The History of the London Missionary Society, 1795–1895*. Vol. 1, (London: Oxford University Press, 1899).
MacClancy, J.	*To Kill A Bird with Two Stones: A Short History of Vanuatu* (Vanuatu Cultural Centre Publications 1; Port Vila, Vanuatu: Vanuatu Cultural Centre, 1981).
MacColl, N.	'Campbell, Thomas (1733-1795)', *Dictionary of National Biography, 1885-1900*, Volume 08. https://en.wikisource.org/wiki/Campbell,_Thomas_(1733-1795)_(DNB00).
McCord, Jr., J.N.	'Politics and Honor in Early-Nineteenth-Century England: The Dukes' Duel', *Huntington Library Quarterly* 62.1/2 (1999), 88–114.
McDonald, R.	*The Ballard of Desmond Kale* (Sydney: Random House, 2005).
Mackaness, G.	'Introduction', *Some Private Correspondence of the Rev. Samuel Marsden and Family, 1794–1824* (Australian Historical Monographs; Sydney: G. Mackanass, Feb 28, 1942). www.chr.org.au/documents.
McKay, R.J.	'Wylde, Sir John (1781–1859)', *Australian Dictionary of Biography*, http://adb.anu.edu.au/biography/wylde-sir-john-2822/text4045, published first in hardcopy 1967.
McLachlan, N.D.	'Eagar, Edward (1787–1866)', *Australian Dictionary of Biography*, http://adb.anu.edu.au/biography/eagar-edward-2013/text2467, published first in hardcopy 1966.
McLachlan, N.D.	'Macquarie, Lachlan (1762–1824)', *Australian Dictionary of Biography*, http://adb.anu.edu.au/biography/macquarie-lachlan-2419/text3211, published first in hardcopy 1967.
McLynne, F.	*Crime and Punishment in Eighteenth Century England* (London: Routledge, 2002).
McNabb, Robert	*From Tasman to Marsden: a history of northern New Zealand from 1642 to 1818* (Dunedin, N.Z.: J. Wilkie, 1914).

BIBLIOGRAPHY

Maiden, J. H. — *Sir Joseph Banks: the 'Father of Australia'* (Sydney: William Applegate Gullick; London: Kegan Paul, Trench, Trubner & Co., 1909).

Malthus, T.R. — *An Essay on the Principle of Population, as it Affects the Future Improvement of Society with Remarks on the Speculations of Mr. Godwin, M. Condorcet, and Other Writers* (London: St. Paul's Church-Yard, 1798). http://www.esp.org/books/malthus/population/malthus.pdf

Marchant, L.R., & J. H. Reynolds,
'Péron, François (1775–1810)', *Australian Dictionary of Biography*, http://adb.anu.edu.au/biography/peron-francois-2545/text3463, published first in hardcopy 1967.

Marchant, L.R., & J. H. Reynolds,
'Baudin, Nicolas Thomas (1754–1803)', *Australian Dictionary of Biography*, http://adb.anu.edu.au/biography/baudin-nicolas-thomas-1753/text1949, published first in hardcopy 1966.

Marsden, J.B. — *Memoirs of the Life and Labours of the Rev. Samuel Marsden, of Paramatta, senior chaplain of New South Wales: and of his early connexion with the missions to New Zealand and Tahiti* (London: Religious Tract Society, 1858). Hathitrust.org. AND archive.org.

Marsden, J. B. & J. Drummond,
Life and Work of Samuel Marsden (London: Whitcombe & Tombs, 1913).

Mason, J. C. S. — *The Moravian Church and the Missionary Awakening in England, 1760-1800* (Woodbridge: Boydell & Brewer, 2001).

Matthews, L.H. — 'Lobster-Krill. Anomuran Crustacea That Are The Food Of Whales', *Discovery Reports, VoL V*, pp 467–484, *Plate IV, text-fig. 1, November, 1932*. https://decapoda.nhm.org/pdfs/29855/29855.pdf.

Maude, H.E. — 'The Tahitian Pork Trade: 1800–1830', *Journal de la Société des Océanistes* 15 (1959), 57–91.

Maude, H., & M. Crocombe
'Rarotongan Sandalwood. The Visit of Goodenough to Rarotonga in 1814', *J. of the Polynesian Society* 71.1 (1962), 32–56. http://www.jstor.org/stable/20703963. Originally presented as a paper at the Tenth Pacific Science Congress of the Pacific Science Association, University of Hawaii, 21 Aug to 6 Sept 1961. Also found at http://hercolano2.blogspot.com.au/2010/08/rarotongan-sandalwood-visit-of.html?m=1.

May, H.F.	*The Enlightenment in America* (New York: Oxford University Press, 1976).
Maylon, Julie	'Peter Pindar and his World', *Paragon Review* 7 (1998). http://www.hull.ac.uk/oldlib/archives/paragon/1998/pindar.html.
Melbourne, A.C.V.	*Early Constitutional Development in Australia: New South Wales 1788–1856* (London: Oxford University Press, 1934).
Metaxis, E.	*Amazing Grace. William Wilberforce and the Heroic Campaign to End Slavery* (New York: HarperCollins, 2008).
Middleton, A.	'Missionization in New Zealand and Australia: A Comparison', *International Journal of Historical Archaeology*, Special Issue: Aboriginal Missions in Australasia, 14.1 (2010), 170–187.
Millbank, J.	'Difference of Virtue, Virtue of Difference', in *Theology and Social Theory: Beyond Secular Reason* (Oxford: Blackwell, ^{2}2006 [1990]), 327–381.
Mitchell, P.	'The Foundations of Australian Defamation Law', *Sydney Law Review* 28 (2006), 477–504.
Moody, J.	'Weber: Objectivity in Social Science, Theory Notes'. Duke University. (1977). http://www.soc.duke.edu/~jmoody77/TheoryNotes/weber_OSS_BasicTerms.htm
Morgan, M.	*Manners, Morals and Class in England 1774–1858* (Studies in Modern History; J.C.D. Clark, ed.; London: Macmillan, 1994).
Morley, S.	*Historical U.K. inflation rates and calculator.* (2016). http://inflation.stephenmorley.org/
Morrell, W. P.	'The Transition to Christianity in the South Pacific', *Transactions of the Royal Historical Society* 28 (1946), 101–120.
Murray, K.	'In the Shadow of the Missionary Captain: Captain James Wilson and the LMS Mission to the Pacific', *International Bulletin of Missionary Research* 31.2 (2007): 73–77.
Nardinelli, C.	'Industrial Revolution and the Standard of Living', *The Concise Encyclopedia of Economics* (2008). Library of Economics and Liberty. http://www.econlib.org/library/Enc/IndustrialRevolutionandtheStandardofLiving.html
Neal, D.	*The Rule of Law in a Penal Colony: Law and Power in Early New South Wales* (Studies in Australian History; Cambridge: Cambridge University Press, 1991).

BIBLIOGRAPHY

Nedbank Group	'Our History'. https://www.nedbank.co.za/content/nedbank/desktop/gt/en/aboutus/about-nedbank-group/who-we-are/Our-history.html
NSW Parliament	'Mr John Thomas Campbell (1770–1830)', Members, https://www.parliament.nsw.gov.au/members/Pages/profiles/campbell_john-thomas.aspx.
O'Malley, P.	'Class Formation and the "Freedom" of the Colonial Press. New South Wales 1800–1850', *Media, Culture and Society* 7 (1985), 427–444.
O'Malley, V.	*The Meeting Place: Māori and Pakeha Encounters, 1642-1840* (Auckland: Auckland University Press, 2013).
Olsthoorn, P.	'Virtue ethics in the military', in S. Van Hooft (ed.), *The Handbook of Virtue Ethics* (Durham: Acumen Publishing, 2014), 365-374.
Oyserman, D., K. Elmore, & G. Smith,	'Self, Self-Concept and Identity', in M.R. Leary & J.P. Tangney (eds.), *Handbook of Self and Identity* (New York: The Guilford Press, ²2012 [original: 2003]), 69–104. https://dornsife.usc.edu/assets/sites/782/docs/handbook_of_self_and_identity_-_second_edition_-_ch._4_pp._69-104_38_pages.pdf
Parkinson, P.	*Tradition and Change in Australian Law* (Sydney: Lawbook Co, 2013).
Parsons, V.	'Suttor, George (1774–1859)', *Australian Dictionary of Biography*, http://adb.anu.edu.au/biography/suttor-george-1270/text3813, published first in hardcopy 1967.
Parsons,V.	'Walker, William (1787–1854)', *Australian Dictionary of Biography*, http://adb.anu.edu.au/biography/walker-william-2767/text3931, published first in hardcopy 1967.
Parsonson, G. S.	'Marsden, Samuel', in *Dictionary of New Zealand Biography* (1990). http://www.TeAra.govt.nz/en/biographies/1m16/marsden-samuel.
Persse, M.	'Wentworth, William Charles (1790–1872)', *Australian Dictionary of Biography*, http://adb.anu.edu.au/biography/wentworth-william-charles-2782/text3961, published first in hardcopy 1967.
Pettett, D.B.	*The Sermons of Samuel Marsden* (Sydney: Bolt Publishing, forthcoming).
Pettett, D.B.	*Samuel Marsden: Preacher, Pastor, Magistrate & Missionary* (Sydney: Bolt Publishing, 2016).

Pettett, D.B.	'Samuel Marsden, Blinkered Visionary: A re-examination of his character and circumstances through the study of his sermons' (Unpublished PhD; Macquarie University, 2016). https://www.researchonline.mq.edu.au/vital/access/services/Download/mq:57146/SOURCE1?view=true
Pettett, D.B.	'Samuel Marsden's Strategy for Mission', in Peter G. Bolt & David B. Pettett (eds.), *Launching Marsden's Mission. The Beginnings of the Church Missionary Society in New Zealand, viewed from New South Wales* (London: The Latimer Trust, 2014), 79–88.
Pettett, D.B.	'Samuel Marsden—Christmas Day 1814. What did he say? The Content of New Zealand's first Christian Sermon', in A. Davidson, S. Lange, P. Lineham, & A. Puckey (ed.), *Te Rongopai 1814 'Takoto te pai!'. Bicentenary reflections on Christian beginnings and developments in Aotearoa New Zealand* (Auckland: General Synod Office, 2014), 72–85.
Pettigrove, G.	'Virtue ethics, virtue theory and moral theology', in S. Van Hooft (ed.), *The Handbook of Virtue Ethics* (Durham: Acumen Publishing, 2014), 88–104.
Pew Research	Religion & Public Life: America's changing religious landscape, May.2015. http://www.pewforum.org/2015/05/12/americas-changing-religious-landscape/.
Piggin, S.	*Spirit of a Nation: The Story of Australia's Christian Heritage* (Sydney: Strand, ²2004 [1996]).
Piggin, S.	*Making Evangelical Missionaries 1789–1858: The Social Background, Motives And Training Of British Protestant Missionaries To India* (Oxford: Sutton Courtney, 1984).
Pindar, Peter	See John Wolcot
Podmore, C.	*The Moravian Church in England, 1728–1760* (Oxford: Clarendon Press, 1998).
Porter, A.	'Missions and Empire, c.1873–1914', in S. Gilley & B. Stanley (eds.), *World Christianities c.1815–c.1914* (The Cambridge History of Christianity 8; Cambridge: Cambridge University Press, 2006), 560–75.
Porter, A.	*Religion Versus Empire?: British Protestant Missionaries and Overseas Expansion, 1700–1914* (Manchester: Manchester University Press, 2005).
Post, R.C.	'The Social Foundations of Defamation Law: Reputation and the Constitution'. Yale Law School, Legal Scholarship Repository. Faculty Scholarship Series. 1st January 1986,

BIBLIOGRAPHY

	695. http://digitalcommons.law.yale.edu/cgi/viewcontent.cgi?article=1216&context=fss_papers.
Poynder, J.	*A History of the Jesuits; to Which Is Prefixed a Reply to Mr. Dallas's Devence of That Order* (2 vols; London: Baldwin, Cradock, and Joy, 1816).
Poynder, J. [attrib.]	*A Brief Account of the Jesuits with historical proofs in support of it, tending to establish the danger of the revival of that order to the world at large, and to the United Kingdom in particular* (London: F.C. & J. Rivington, Hatchard, L.B. Seeley, and J. White, 1815).
Prentis, M.	'Rangatira and Tohunga of Parramatta: Samuel Marsden and the Māori Seminary', in P.G. Bolt & D.B. Pettett (eds.), *Launching Marsden's Mission: The Beginning of the Church Missionary Society in New Zealand, viewed from New South Wales* (London: Latimer, 2014), 43–60.
Quinn, R.	*Samuel Marsden: Altar Ego* (Wellington: Dunmore, 2008).
Rack, H.D.	'Religious Societies and the Origins of Methodism', *JEH* 38.4 (1987), 582–595.
Ratcliffe, L.	'"Pens Dipped in Gall": An Examination of the Conflict Between Rev. Samuel Marsden and Governor Lachlan Macquarie in the Context of the Philo Free Case of 1817' (Unpublished Master of Arts thesis, Macquarie University, 1996).
Reece, R.H.W.	*Aborigines and Colonists: Aborigines and Colonial Society in New South Wales in the 1830s and 1840s* (Sydney: Sydney University Press, 1974).
Reed, A.H.	*Samuel Marsden: Greatheart of Māoriland* (London: Pickering & Inglis, 1947).
Reed, A.H.	*Samuel Marsden, Pioneer and Peacemaker* (Dunedin: A.H. & A.W. Reed, 1936).
Reed, A. H.	*First New Zealand Christmases: Tasman 1642, Cook 1769, Marsden 1814* (Dunedin: A. H. Reed, 1933).
Ridley, W.	*The Aborigines of Australia: A Lecture* (Sydney, 1864). http://nla.gov.au/nla.obj-475652209/view?partId=nla.obj-475907487#page/n9/mode/1up.
Ritchie, J.	*The Wentworths Father and Son* (Melbourne: Melbourne University Press, 1999).
Ritchie, J.	*Lachlan Macquarie: A Biography* (Melbourne: Melbourne University Press, ²1986 [1983]).

Robb, W.M.	'The Reverend Samuel Marsden, pioneer, a man fitted for his day and generation: an estimate of his work for Australia during the years 1794–1838' (Unpublished M.A. thesis. University of Sydney, 1939).
Roberts, D.A.	'Language to Save the Innocent: L. Threlkeld's Linguistic Mission', *JRAHS* 94.2 (2008), 107–125. https://www.thefreelibrary.com/'Language+to+save+the+innocent'%3A+Reverend+L.+Threlkeld's+linguistic...-a0190941413.
Rolph, D.	*Defamation Law* (Sydney: Thomson Reuters [Professional] Australia Limited, 2016).
Rousseau, J.J.	*Basic Political Writings* (D.A. Cress, transl. & ed.; Indianapolis: Hackett Publishing, ^{2}2011).
Russell, P.	*Savage or Civilised? Manners in Colonial Australia* (Sydney: New South Press, 2014).
Rutledge, M.	'Patteson, John Coleridge (1827–1871)', in *Australian Dictionary of Biography* (Melbourne: Melbourne University Press, 1974). http://adb.anu.edu.au/biography/patteson-john-coleridge-4376.
Ryan, K.	'Moral Education—A Brief History of Moral Education, The Return of Character Education, Current Approaches to Moral Education'. (2011). http://education/stateuniversity.com/pages/2246/Moral-Education.html
Salmond, A.	*Between Worlds: Early Exchanges between Māori and Europeans, 1773–1815* (Auckland: Viking, 1997).
Salt, A.	*These Outcast Women: The Parramatta Female Factory 1821-1848* (Sydney: Hale & Iremonger, 1984).
Schwarze, A.	'Goff and Amey: An Evangelical Bureau in the City of London' (Unpublished paper).
Schwarze, C.	'Richard Johnson and Samuel Marsden: Missionaries to the South Seas', in P.G. Bolt & D.B. Pettett (eds.), *Launching Marsden's Mission. The Beginnings Of The Church Missionary Society In New Zealand, Viewed From New South Wales* (London: Latimer, 2014), 3–12.
Scifleet, P.	*Guide to the Records of the Benevolent Society of New South Wales 1813–1995 in the Mitchell Library, State Library of NSW* (Sydney: Benevolent Society of NSW, 1996).
Seddon, T.R.	*Saints and Heroes of Our Own Days* (London: Society for Promoting Christian Knowledge, 1899).

[SEP]	'Baruch Spinoza', *Stanford Encyclopedia of Philosophy.* (2016). https://plato.stanford.edu/entries/spinoza/.
[SEP]	'Enlightenment'. *The Stanford Encyclopedia of Philosophy.* (2010). http://plato.stanford.edu/entries/enlightenment/.
[SEP]	'Rationalism Vs. Empiricism'. *The Stanford Encyclopedia of Philosophy* (2004). https://plato.stanford.edu/entries/rationalism-empiricism/.
Sharp, A.	*The World, the Flesh & the Devil. The life and opinions of Samuel Marsden in England and the Antipodes, 1765–1838* (Auckland: Auckland University Press, 2016).
Shaw, A.G.L.	'Bligh, William (1754–1817)', in *Australian Dictionary of Biography*, http://adb.anu.edu.au/biography/bligh-william-1797, published first in hard copy 1966.
Siedlecki, A.	*Luther—The First Best-Selling German Author* (Atlanta, GA: Emory University, 2006). http://pitts.emory.edu/collections/rnweb/FRN29.pdf
Sivasundaram, S.	*Nature and the Godly Empire: Science and Evangelical Mission in the Pacific 1795–1850* (Cambridge Social and Cultural Histories 7; Cambridge: Cambridge University Press, 2005).
Skinner, Q.	'Introduction: Seeing Things Their Way', in *Visions of Politics.* Vol. 1: *Regarding Method* (Cambridge: Cambridge University Press, 2002).
SLNSW Catalogue	'Edward Close Sketchbook'. Edward Charles Close - New South Wales Sketchbook: Sea Voyage, Sydney, Illawarra, Newcastle, Morpeth, c. 1817-1840.
Smith, B.	*Australia's Birthstain: The Startling Legacy of the Convict Era* (Crows Nest, N.S.W.: Allen & Unwin, 2008).
Smith, E.	*The Life of Sir Joseph Banks, President of the Royal Society, with some notices of his friends and contemporaries &c* London: John Lane, 1911). https://archive.org/details/lifeofsirjosephb00smitrich.
Snape, M.F.	'Anti–Methodism in Eighteenth–Century England: The Pendle Forest Riots of 1748', *JEH* 49 (1998), 257–281.
Solomon, R.C.	'Barron Field and the Court of Civil Judicature/Supreme Court NSW' (Unpublished PhD Thesis; Kensington: UNSW, 2013).

Spigelman, J.J.	'The Macquarie Bicentennial: A Reappraisal of the Bigge Reports', Annual History Lecture, History Council of NSW, 4 September 2009. http://historycouncilnsw.org.au/wp-content/uploads/2013/01/2009-AHL-Spigelman.pdf.
Spigelman, J.J.	'Foundations of the Freedom of the Press in Australia', *Australian Bar Review* 23.2 (2003), 89–109.
Spurr, J.	'The Church, the Societies and the Moral Revolution of 1688', in J. Walsh, C. Haydon, S. Taylor (eds.), *The Church of England c1689–c1833. From Toleration to Tractarianism* (Cambridge: Cambridge University Press, 1993), 127–142.
Standfield, R.	*Race and Identity in the Tasman World, 1769–1840* (Empires in Perspective 18; London & NY: Routledge, 2016).
Standfield, R.	'The Parramatta Māori Seminary and the Education of Indigenous Peoples in Early Colonial New South Wales', *History of Education Review* 41.2 (2012), 119–28.
Stanley, B.	*The History of the Baptist Missionary Society, 1792-1992* (London: T&T Clark, 1992).
State Records of New South Wales,	'CAMPBELL, John Thomas. Secretary to Governor Macquarie; Provost Marshal' *Colonial Secretary Index, 1788-1825*, http://colsec.records.nsw.gov.au/c/F09c_cab-car-05.htm#P2371_68520.
Steven, M.	*Merchant Campbell 1769–1846. A Study in Colonial Trade* (Melbourne: Oxford University Press, 1965).
Stock, E.S.	*One Hundred Years: Being the Short History of the Church Missionary Society* (London: Church Missionary Society, ³1899).
Strong, R.	'The Reverend John Wollaston and Colonial Christianity in Western Australia, 1840–1863', *Journal of Religious History* 25 (2001), 261–285.
Suttor, G.	*Memoirs Historical and Scientific of the Right Honourable Sir Joseph Banks* (Parramatta: E. Mason, 1855). Google Books.
Sykes, W.R.	'Sandalwood in the Cook Islands', *Pacific Science* 34.1 (1980), 77–82. https://scholarspace.manoa.hawaii.edu/bitstream/10125/1543/1/v34n1-77-82.pdf.
Thompson, A. C.	*Moravian Missions: Twelve Lectures* (New York: Charles Scribner's Sons, 1882).
Tink, A.	*William Charles Wentworth Australia's Greatest Native Son* (Allen & Unwin, 2009).
Tink, A.	'William Charles Wentworth. Father of Australia's Freedoms', *Australian Heritage* (December, 2009), 35–41.

BIBLIOGRAPHY

	http://www.heritageaustralia.com.au/downloads/pdfs/Heritage1209_Noteworthy%20Wentworth.pdf
Townley, K. A.	'Darwin, Charles Robert (1809–1882)', http://adb.anu.edu.au/biography/darwin-charles-robert-1957/text2355, published first in hardcopy 1966.
Turnbull, R.D.	'The place of the seventh Earl of Shaftesbury within the Evangelical tradition, with particular reference to his understanding of the relationship of evangelistic mission to social reform' (Unpublished PhD dissertation, University of Durham, 1996).
UoNCC	'Edward Charles Close Sketchbook on Sothebys', Hunter Living Histories. https://hunterlivinghistories.com/2009/04/24/edward-charles-close-sketchbook-on-sothebys/. (posted 24/4/2009).
Walker, R.B.	*The Newspaper Press in New South Wales, 1803–1920* (Sydney: Sydney University Press, 1976).
Walls, A.F.	*The Missionary Movement in Christian History Studies in the Transmission of Faith* (Maryknoll, NY: Orbis Books, 2009).
Walsh, J.	'Religious societies: Methodist and Evangelical 1738–1800', in W.J. Sheils & D. Wood (eds.), *Voluntary religion: Papers Read at the 1985 Summer Meeting and the 1986 Winter Meeting of the Ecclesiastical History Society* (Oxford: Blackwell, 1986), 279–302.
Walsh. W.P.	*Modern Heroes of the Mission Field* (New York: Fleming H. Revell, 1884).
Wannan. B.	*Very strange tales: the turbulent times of Samuel Marsden* (Melbourne: Lansdowne Press, 1962); republished as *Early colonial scandals: the turbulent times of Samuel Marsden* (Melbourne: Lansdowne Press, 1972).
Warren, C.	'Smallpox at Sydney Cove—who, when, why?', *Journal of Australian Studies* 38.1 (2014), 68–86.
Watson, F.	'Introduction', *HRA* 1.10, v–xvii.
Watson, F.	'Introduction', *HRA* 1.13, v–xviii.
[W.E.],	'English Social Structure in the Early 18th Century', Wittenberg Education. http://www4.wittenberg.edu/academics/hist/crom/brit/socstruc.html
Weber, M.	*The Protestant Ethic and the Spirit of Capitalism* (Routledge Classics; T. Parsons, trans.; London: Routledge, 2001, e-library 2005 [original: 1905]).

Weber, M.	'The "Objectivity" of Knowledge in Social Science and Social Policy (1904)', in E. Schils & H. Finch (Transls. & Eds.), *The Methodology of the Social Sciences* (Glencoe, Illinois: Free Press, 1949), 49–112. Available at: http://anthropos-lab.net/wp/wp-content/uploads/2011/12/Weber-objectivity-in-the-social-sciences.pdf.
Wheeler, D.	*Effects of the Introduction of Ardent Spirits and Implements of War amongst the Natives of some of the South Sea Islands and New South Wales* (London: Harvey & Darton, 1839).
White, J.	'A Master and his Men. A Different Perspective on the Reverend Samuel Marsden in NSW from 1794 to 1851' (Unpublished M.Litt. dissertation, University of New England, 1993).
White, M.	'Popular Politics in the 18th Century'. British Library: Georgian Britain. https://www.bl.uk/georgian-britain/articles/popular-politics-in-the-18th-century
Whitfield, J.H.	'Petrarch, Italian Poet'. *Encyclopaedia Britannica*. (29th July update, 2009). https://www.britannica.com/biography/Petrarch.
Whitford, D.M.	'Martin Luther. Section (2b), Theology of the Cross'. *Internet Encyclopedia of Philosophy*. http://www.iep.utm.edu/luther/
Willetts, J.	'Convict Ship *Anne* 1810', http://www.jenwilletts.com/convict_ship_ann_1810.htm
Williams, J.V.	'Reparations and the Waitangi Tribunal. Paper to "Moving Forward" Conference, 15–16 August 2001', https://www.humanrights.gov.au/reparations-and-waitangi-tribunal.
Williamson, A.	*Samuel Marsden, the Apostle of New Zealand* (Edinburgh: Crawford & McCabe, 1884).
Willis, J.J.	'Transportation versus Imprisonment in Eighteenth- and Nineteenth-Century Britain: Penal Power, Liberty and the State', *Law & Society Review* 39 (2005), 171–210.
Willson, R.	'Lost diary's strange history', *Canberra Times Magazine*, 5/9/1992, 4.
Wilton, C.P.N.	'Australian Sperm Whale Fishery', *The Australian Quarterly Journal of Theology, Literature & Science*, 1 (Sydney: A. Hill, 1828), 86–94. http://acms.sl.nsw.gov.au/album/albumView.aspx?itemID=910146&acmsid=0.
Witte, J.	'Between Sanctity and Depravity: Law and Human Nature in Martin Luther's Two Kingdoms', 48 *Villanova*

BIBLIOGRAPHY

	University Law Review 727 (2003). Available at: http://digitalcommons.law.villanova.edu/vlr/vol48/iss3/1.
Wolcot, J.	*The Lousiad: an Heroi-comic Poem* (London: G. Kearsley, ⁷1787).
Wolcot, J.	*The Works of Peter Pindar Esq., in 3 Volumes* (London: John Walker, 1794), 1.273. Google Books.
Wolcot, J.	*A benevolent epistle to Sylvanus Urban, alias Master John Nichols, printer ... not forgetting Master William Hayley. To which is added, An elegy to Apollo : also Sir Joseph Banks and the boiled fleas, an ode / by Peter Pindar* (Dublin : Printed by William Porter, for P. Wogan, P. Byrne, P. Hoey, J. Moore, J. Jones, Grueber & M'Allister, W. Jones, and R. White, 1790; New Edition: London: Printed for J. Walker, No. 44, Paternoster-Row, 1794).
Wolcot, J.	*Odes, Epistles &c by Wolcott, Called Peter Pindar ; With a Sketch of His Life* (Paris: Parsons & Galignani, 1804).
Woolmington, J.	'"Writing on the Sand": The First Missions to Aborigines in Eastern Australia', in T. Swain & D.B. Rose (eds.), *Aboriginal Australians and Christian Missions* (Bedford Park, SA: Australian Association for the Study of Religions, 1988), 77–92.
Woolmington, J.	'The Civilisation/Christianisation Debate and the Australian Aborigines', *Aboriginal History* 10.2 (1986), 90–98. http://press-files.anu.edu.au/downloads/press/p71821/pdf/article084.pdf.
Woolmington, J.	'Early Christian Missions to the Australian Aborigines—A Study in Failure' (Unpublished PhD thesis, University of New England, 1979).
Wright, H.	*New Zealand, 1769–1840: Early Years of Western Contact* (Cambridge, MA: Harvard University Press, 1967).
Yarwood, A.T.	*Marsden of Parramatta* (Sydney: Kangaroo Press, 1986).
Yarwood, A.T.	*Samuel Marsden. The Great Survivor* (Melbourne: Melbourne University Press, ²1996 [1977]).
Yarwood, A.T.	'The Missionary Marsden: An Australian View', *New Zealand Journal of History* 4.1 (1970), 20–33. http://www.nzjh.auckland.ac.nz/docs/1970/NZJH_04_1_03.pdf
Yarwood, A.T.	'Marsden, Samuel (1765–1838)', *Australian Dictionary of Biography*, http://adb.anu.edu.au/biography/marsden-samuel-2433/text3237, published first in hardcopy 1967.
Young, G.M.	*Victorian England: Portrait of an Age* (London: Oxford University Press, 1953).

Websites

Archive.Com

Association for the Preservation of Memorials of the Dead in Ireland, *Journal for the Year...* Vol 3, part 2 (Dublin: Association for the Preservation of Memorials of the Dead in Ireland, 1896)   **https://archive.org/stream/journalforyear32asso_0/journalforyear32asso_0_djvu.txt**.

Google Books	**https://books.google.com.au**
Hathi Trust	**Hathitrust.org**

Macquarie University Governor Macquarie Collection
    http://www.mq.edu.au/macquarie-archive/lema.

Macquarie University Law School research project 'Decisions of the Superior Courts of New South Wales, 1788-1899'
    http://www.law.mq.edu.au/research/colonial_case_law/nsw/site/scnsw_home/

Marsden Online Archive **http://marsdenarchive.otago.ac.nz**

Moore College Sermon Collection
    https://myrrh.library.moore.edu.au:443/handle/10248/5508

New Zealand Electronic Text Collection (*Te Pūhikotuhi o Aotearoa*)
    http://nzetc.victoria.ac.nz

Trove Digitised Newspapers
    http://trove.nla.gov.au

Waitangi Tribunal **https://www.waitangitribunal.govt.nz**

World of Royalty Makea Karika. **http://members.iinet.net.au/~royalty/states/cookislands/makeakarika.html**.

www.ingramcontent.com/pod-product-compliance
Lightning Source LLC
Chambersburg PA
CBHW050525300426
44113CB00012B/1958